Hallesche Forschungen

Im Auftrag der Franckeschen Stiftungen zu Halle
herausgegeben von
Veronika Albrecht-Birkner, Thomas Müller-Bahlke
und Udo Sträter

Band 72

Daniel Jeyaraj

Christian Friedrich Schwartz
(1726–1798)

Ambassador for Faith and His Impact on South India and Beyond

Verlag der Franckeschen Stiftungen Halle
Harrassowitz Verlag in Kommission

Abbildung auf Seite III: Christian Friedrich Schwartz, Oil on canvas.
Halle, Franckesche Stiftungen: KNK R.-Nr. 3004

Bibliografische Information der Deutschen Nationalbibliothek
Die Deutsche Nationalbibliothek verzeichnet diese Publikation in der Deutschen Nationalbibliografie; detaillierte bibliografische Daten sind im Internet über https://dnb.dnb.de abrufbar.

Bibliographic information published by the Deutsche Nationalbibliothek
The Deutsche Nationalbibliothek lists this publication in the Deutsche Nationalbibliografie; detailed bibliographic data are available on the Internet at https://dnb.dnb.de.

ISSN 0949-0086
ISBN 978-3-447-12407-2
eISBN 978-3-447-39699-8

Franckeplatz 1, Haus 37, 06114 Halle, produktsicherheit@francke-halle.de

https://www.francke-halle.de und https://www.harrassowitz-verlag.de

Gedruckt auf alterungsbeständigem Papier.
Printed in Germany.

Satz: Klaus E. Göltz, Halle
Druck: MUNDSCHENK Druck + Medien GmbH & Co. KG, Lutherstadt Wittenberg

To the women who have enabled me to study,
research and serve

Contents

Abbreviations XIII

Preface XV

Introduction 1

1 Schwartz as Cāṉṟōṉ 2
2 Biography as History 7
3 The Company Raj as British-Indian Partnership 10
4 Limitations of this Biography 12
5 Structure of this Biography 14

Chapter 1: Socio-Political Contexts 17

1.1 The Kingdom of Tanjore 17
1.2 Partnership between the Company and Tanjore Elites 20
1.2.1 The Company Raj 20
1.2.2 The Regulating Act of India (1773) 24
1.2.3 Pitt's India Act of 1784 25
1.2.4 The East India Company Act of 1793 28

Chapter 2: Schwartz as an Ambassador for Faith 29

2.1 Schwartz Before Becoming an Ambassador for Faith 29
2.2 Schwartz's Call to Be an Ambassador for Faith 33
2.3 Schwartz's Job Descriptions as an Ambassador for Faith 34
2.3.1 Job Description Given by the King of Denmark 34
2.3.2 Job Description Given by the Director of the Glaucha Institutions 36
2.3.3 Job Description Given by the SPCK 37
2.4 Schwartz's Familiarity with the History of Tamil Lutheran Christianity 39

Chapter 3: Schwartz in Tranquebar (1750–1762) 41

3.1 Acclimatisation 41
3.2 Disliking Nominal Christianity 42
3.3 Overcoming Self-Doubt 42
3.4 Delight in Service 45
3.5 Visiting Ceylon 46
3.6 Embracing Celibacy 48

Chapter 4: Schwartz in Tiruccirāppaḷḷi (1762–1777) 51

4.1 Reasons for Leaving Tranquebar 51
4.2 First Contacts in Tiruccirāppaḷḷi 52
4.3 Interaction with the Roman Catholics 54
4.4 Wallajah after the Treaty of Paris (1762/63) 54
4.5 Schwartz and the British in Tiruccirāppaḷḷi 56
4.6 Decision to Stay in Tiruccirāppaḷḷi 60
4.7 Schwartz as Garrison Chaplain 62
4.8 Tulāji's First Fall (1771) 64
4.9 Tulāji's Imprisonment (16 September 1773 – 11 April 1776) 68
4.10 Tulāji's Restoration and Surrender to the Company (1776) 70

Chapter 5: Schwartz in Tanjore (1778–1798) 79

5.1 Schwartz's Move to Tanjore (October 1778) 79
5.2 Christ Church in Tanjore (March 1779) 80
5.3 Tulāji's Mismanagement of Tanjore 85
5.4 Committee of Inspection (21 June 1786 – 5 May 1787) 88
5.5 Serfoji's Adoption and Ameer Singh as the Interim Ruler 93
5.6 Tulāji's Death (31 January 1787) 98
5.7 Interim Rule by the Committee of Inspection 102
5.8 Ameer Singh as an Interim Ruler 110
5.8.1 Ameer Singh's Background 110
5.8.2 Twelve Pandits Endorsing Ameer Singh 113
5.8.3 Schwartz's Failure to Consult Sanskrit Law Books and Lawyers 114
5.8.4 Ameer Singh's Enthronement (7 April 1787) 115
5.8.5 Ameer Singh's First Treaty with the Company (1787) 117
5.8.6 Ameer Singh's Extravagance 121
5.8.7 Āyarpāṭi Village for Schwartz 124
5.8.8 Decreasing Tanjore Revenues for the Company 125
5.9 The Company's Treaty of 1787 with Wallajah 126
5.10 Agricultural Practices in Tanjore (1790) 128
5.11 The Company Seeks to Occupy Tanjore (1790) 130
5.12 Ameer Singh's Second Treaty with the Company (1792) 134
5.13 Schwartz's Death 137
5.14 Schwartz's Estate 142
5.15 Schwartz's Character 144
5.16 Schwartz's Holistic Ministry 156

Chapter 6: Schwartz's Written Documents 161

6.1 Schwartz's Linguistic Skills 161
6.2 Schwartz's Tamil Writings 161

6.2.1 Tamil Catechism 162
6.2.2 Eighteen Dialogues (1777 and 1790) 165
6.3 Schwartz's Writings for Europeans 168
6.3.1 Schwartz's Addressees 168
6.3.2 Extracts of Schwartz's Texts in German (a selection) 171
6.3.3 Extracts of Schwartz's Texts in English (a selection) 175
6.3.4 Schwartz's English Sermons 180
6.4 Biographies of Schwartz 182
6.4.1 Biographies of Schwartz: Failed Attempts 182
6.4.2 Schwartz's Biographies in English 185
6.4.3 Schwartz's Biographies in German 190
6.4.4 Schwartz's Biographies in Other Languages 194

Chapter 7: Schwartz as an Ambassador for Peace and Justice 195

7.1 Schwartz as the Company's Moral Conscience 195
7.2 Mediation with Hyder Ali 199
7.2.1 Schwartz's Embassy to Hyder Ali (5 June – 24 August 1779) 203
7.2.2 Gray's Embassy to Hyder Ali (1780) 207
7.2.3 Hyder Ali's Invasion of the Carnatic (1780) 208
7.2.4 Hyder Ali's Invasion of Tranquebar (1781) 210
7.3 Mediation for the Wadiyars of Mysore (1782) 212
7.4 Mediation Attempt with Tipu Sultan (15 December 1783 – 26 January 1784) 213
7.5 Mediation with Tanjore Farmers (1783) 219
7.6 Mediation with Tanjore Emigrants (1786) 221
7.7 Mediation with Tranquebar 223
7.7.1 Regarding Tranquebar Emigrants in Tanjore 223
7.7.2 Regarding Tranquebar Loans to Tanjore 227
7.8 Mediation with the Poligars 233
7.9 Mediation as Executor of Estates 234
7.9.1 Dealing with Money Matters 234
7.9.2 Dealing as a Guardian 236
7.10 Mediation with Fellow Missionaries 238
7.10.1 Johann Philipp Fabricius 238
7.10.2 Christian Pohle 240
7.10.3 Christoph Samuel John 242
7.10.4 Georg Heinrich Conrad Hüttemann 247
7.10.5 Johann Wilhelm Gerlach 250

Chapter 8: Schwartz as a King Maker 253

8.1 Ameer Singh's Enmity Towards Serfoji and Schwartz 253
8.2 Serfoji and Tulāji's Widows Rescued 262

8.2.1 Serfoji's Move from Tanjore to Madras . . . 262
8.2.2 Serfoji's Stay in Madras . . . 264
8.3 Serfoji's Education in Madras . . . 268
8.3.1 The Military Male Orphan Asylum . . . 269
8.3.2 Learning English . . . 271
8.3.3 The Art of Writing and Networking . . . 275
8.3.4 Mathematical Skills . . . 275
8.3.5 Spending Money Prudently . . . 276
8.3.6 Geography . . . 278
8.3.7 Astronomy . . . 279
8.3.8 Good Governance – Schwartz's Advice . . . 280
8.3.9 Good Governance – John's Advice . . . 282
8.3.10 Religious Faith and Public Life . . . 283
8.4 Serfoji as Heir to the Throne of Tanjore . . . 285
8.4.1 Schwartz's Additional Contributions . . . 285
8.4.2 Serfoji Declared as Heir and Ameer Singh's Opposition . . . 286
8.4.3 Ameer Singh's Bribery of the Pandits – Perspectives of Tulāji's Widows . . . 287
8.4.4 Ameer Singh's Bribery of the Pandits – Perspectives of Schwartz . . . 290
8.4.5 Serfoji's Return to Tanjore . . . 292
8.4.6 Schwartz's Scriptural Evidence Supporting Serfoji's Adoption . . . 293
8.4.7 Schwartz Acquainting Serfoji with Tanjore . . . 295
8.5 Serfoji's Enthronement . . . 297
8.6 Serfoji's Unreconciled Relationship with Ameer Singh . . . 303
8.7 Serfoji Surrendering Tanjore to the Company (1799) . . . 307
8.8 Serfoji's Indebtedness to Christians . . . 309
8.9 Serfoji's Indebtedness to Ancestral Habits . . . 313

Chapter 9: Schwartz as a Social Reformer . . . 317

9.1 Empowering Justice in Tanjore . . . 317
9.1.1 Tanjore's Agriculture-based Economy . . . 318
9.1.2 British Laws in the Company Territories . . . 318
9.1.3 Reforming the Court System of Tanjore . . . 319
9.1.4 Ameer Singh's Failure . . . 321
9.1.5 Schwartz's Interventions . . . 322
9.1.6 Schwartz's Sensitivity to Local Etiquette . . . 325
9.1.7 Schwartz's Opposition to Company's Extortion . . . 326
9.2 Upholding the King's Dignity . . . 327
9.2.1 By Securing the King's Consent and Ensuring Justice for Farmers . . . 329
9.2.2 By Trying to Remove the Rapacious Dubashes . . . 331

9.3 Managing Caste Distinctions 335
9.3.1 Caste as Varṇa and Jāti 335
9.3.2 Jāti during Schwartz's Times 337
9.3.3 Schwartz's Approaches to caste in Urban and Rural Settings 338
9.3.4 Schwartz's Two Chalices 339
9.3.5 Schwartz's Two Settlements 340
9.3.6 Schwartz's Two Schools 341
9.4 Transforming the Kaḷḷar-Community 341
9.5 Creating Work Opportunities 346
9.6 Promoting Health Care 348
9.6.1 Seeking a Cure for Snakebites 349
9.6.2 Seeking a Cure for Rabies 354
9.6.3 Seeking a Cure for Smallpox 355
9.7 Mitigating Poverty 358

Chapter 10: Schwartz as an Educator 361

10.1 Pietist Education 361
10.2 Schools in Tiruccirāppaḷḷi and Tanjore 362
10.3 English-Medium Provincial Schools 364
10.4 Female Asylum in Madras 371
10.5 Schwartz's School Teachers and Catechists 373
10.6 Schwartz's Students and Friends 381
10.6.1 Johann Caspar Kohlhoff 381
10.6.2 Clarinda 387
10.6.3 Vēdanāyagam Sāstiriyār 395
10.6.4 Johann Christian Obeck 396
10.6.5 Christian David 399
10.6.6 Christian Elphinstone 400
10.6.7 William Wheatley 401
10.6.8 European soldiers and others 403
10.7 Schwartz's Training of Younger Missionaries 404
10.7.1 Examples of Failures 404
10.7.2 Examples of Successes 405

Chapter 11: Schwartz and Debates about the Pious Clause in 1793 409

11.1 The Company and Failed Mission Attempts from 1698 to 1793 409
11.2 Montgomery Campbell's Opposition to Schwartz in 1793 414
11.3 No Pious Clause in 1793 416
11.4 Schwartz's Defence of Missions in 1794 417
11.5 Montgomery Campbell's Apology to Schwartz in 1796 420

Chapter 12: Schwartz and the Pious Clause of 1813 423

12.1 Growing Impact of Schwartz's 'Defence of Mission' 423
12.2 Growing Missionary Consciousness in Britain 426
12.3 Growing Challenges Posed by the Vellore Mutiny 431
12.4 Growing Missionary Consciousness in New England 433
12.5 Growing Parliamentary Scrutiny of Mission 433
12.5.1 Warren Hastings about Schwartz 434
12.5.2 John Shore about Schwartz 435
12.5.3 William Cowper about Schwartz 437
12.5.4 Thomas Graham about Schwartz 438
12.6 Contents of the Pious Clause of 1813 438
12.7 Consequences of the Pious Clause of 1813 442

Chapter 13: Conclusion 447

Appendix 457

Appendix 1: The Company's Governors and Presidents in Council in Madras 457
Appendix 2: Answers of the twelve Pandits 458
a) Longer Version 458
b) Shorter Version 461
Appendix 3: Summary of Schwartz's eighteen Tamil dialogues 462
Appendix 4: Montgomery Campbell's Letter of 10 January 1796 466
Appendix 5: Schwartz's Christmas Reflection 468
Appendix 6: Schwartz's Monuments 470
a) In St. Mary's Church, Fort St. George in Chennai 470
b) In Christ Church, Tanjore 471
c) In St. Peter's Church, Tanjore 472

Glossary 473

Bibliography 481
1 Primary Sources: Archival Manuscripts 481
1.1 The Danish-Halle Mission Archives (AFSt/M) 481
1.2 Manuscripts in the British Library in London (BL) 485
1.3 Manuscripts in the Lambeth Palace Library in London 487
1.4 Manuscripts in the Tamil Nadu Archives in Chennai (T) 488
1.5 Manuscripts in the Bodleian Library, Oxford 488
2 Primary Sources: Printed Materials 490
3 Secondary Sources 497

Index of Names 511
Index of Places 523

Abbreviations

72290ind-box1	Bodleian Library, Oxford: India General Papers: ID 2166: Description: C/IND/GEN/Box 1/3, i.e. Schwartz study notes (1749)
72290ind-box2	Bodleian Library, Oxford: India General Papers 1773–1797: ID 2168: Description: C/IND/GEN/Box 2. Chiefly Correspondence Relating to the Danish Mission in Pre-Diocesan Southeast India.
ABCFM	American Board of Commissioners for Foreign Missions (1812)
AFSt/M	Danish-Halle Mission Archives in the August Herrmann Francke Study Centre of the Francke Foundations in Halle (Saale), Germany
BL	British Library in London, England
CMS	Church Missionary Society (1799)
Company	The English East India Company
Gk	Greek
HR	Halle Reports: Der Königl. Dänischen Missionarien aus Ost-Indien eingesandter Ausführlichen Berichten. Each volume contains twelve continuations.
IOR	India Office Records and Private Papers are in the British Library, London, England. They are kept in the Asian and African Studies section.
LELM	Leipzig Evangelical Lutheran Mission (1836)
lit.	Literally
LMS	London Missionary Society (1795)
MSS	Manuscript(s)
n.p.	No place of publication or no name of the publisher
n.d.	No date of publication
NHR	New Halle Reports = Neuere Geschichte der evangelischen Missionsanstalten zu Bekehrung der Heiden in Ost-Indien. Each volume has twelve issues.
NRSV	New Revised Standard Version of the Bible
r	recto, the front page of a manuscript sheet

Skt	Sanskrit
SPCK	Society for Promoting Christian Knowledge (1698)
SPCK D 36	Microfilm Roll D 36 of the SPCK (microfilmed on 22 March 1965). This roll contains 'Letters from Schwartz' towards the end. Some pages are dark and unreadable.
SPG	Society for the Propagation of the Gospel in Foreign Parts (1701)
T	Tanjore Records in Tamil Nadu Archives, Chennai
v	verso, the back side of a manuscript sheet

Preface

In 1992, I unearthed unpublished and partially published manuscripts by and about Christian Friedrich Schwartz (1726–1798) in the Danish-Halle Mission Archives at the August Hermann Francke Study Centre of the Francke Foundations in Halle (Saale), Germany. These manuscripts ignited my passion for gathering documents about him from various archives and libraries in India, Germany, Denmark, and the United Kingdom. The more I delved into the life and work of Schwartz, the more I was captivated by his enduring impact on eighteenth-century South India and beyond. His social contributions continue to shape the lives of Protestant Christians in southern India and the institutions that owe their existence to him.

As the Dean of the Lutheran Heritage Archives at the Gurukul Lutheran Theological College in Chennai, Tamil Nadu, India, I had the privilege of organising a significant academic conference in Tanjore in 1998. This conference, which marked the 200th anniversary of Schwartz's death, was a pivotal moment in my research journey. It brought together historians and literary scholars from Germany and India to explore Schwartz's life and work from various angles. The conference highlighted the urgent need to examine the enduring legacy of Schwartz among the Tamils, underscoring the importance of primary sources. This event significantly shaped my understanding of Schwartz's contributions and set the course for my future research.

Throughout my comprehensive study of the primary and secondary source materials by and about Schwartz, I was fortunate to receive invaluable assistance from numerous individuals. While I am deeply grateful to all of them, I would like to acknowledge a few who went above and beyond to support me. Since 1991, the Francke Foundations in Halle (Saale) have become my intellectual home. They house the valuable archives of the Royal Daniel-Halle Mission (1705–1772) and its successors such as the Lutheran Mission Institute for the Conversion of Non-Christians in East India (Evangelische Missions-Anstalt zur Bekehrung der Heiden in Ostindien, Halle 1772–1848), the East India Mission Institute (Ostindische Missionsanstalt zu Halle, 1849–1880). Since 2006, the Mission Archives at the Francke Foundations have also housed the valuable archival materials of the Leipzig Evangelical Lutheran Mission, which was established in Dresden in 1836 and relocated to Leipzig in 1848. This mission inherited the major churches and mission centres of the Royal Danish-Halle Mission. Its missionaries, such as Wilhelm Germann (1840–1902), the renowned biographer of Schwartz, developed Lutheran Christianity among the Tamils from the mid-nineteenth century until the present date.

The memories of the Francke Foundations and their Mission Archives are deeply ingrained in my academic journey. Past and present colleagues at the Francke Foundations, as well as my mentors at the Faculty of Theology, Martin

Luther University Halle–Wittenberg, have been instrumental in helping me uncover vital aspects of the earliest history of Tamil Christianity in eighteenth-century southern India. I am particularly indebted to the late Professor Arno Sames (1937–2019), who accepted me as his doctoral student in 1991 and supervised my research. I also fondly remember the help I received from the eminent Professor Helmut Obst (born 1940), who, as Dean of the Faculty of Theology at Martin Luther University Halle–Wittenberg, facilitated my admission in 1991 and supervised my Habilitation thesis in 2000.

In 1991, I had the privilege of meeting Professor Thomas Müller-Bahlke, the current Director of the Francke Foundations. His dedication to preserving the manuscripts, buildings, institutions, and material culture of the Francke Foundation deeply impressed me. From the beginning, he supported my research. I am thrilled that he continues the splendid work of Professor Paul Raabe, who rejuvenated the Francke Foundations as a centre for cultural performances and academic studies. Professor Müller-Bahlke has helped preserve and popularise the spirit of August Hermann Francke in and beyond Halle (Saale), shaping the current functions of the Francke Foundations. Today, this international, academic, and cultural spirit radiates from the Francke Foundations in Halle (Saale). It influences the Ziegenbalg House Museum in Tranquebar and other institutions in Europe and North America. I am particularly grateful for the long friendship, collegiality, and generosity that enabled me to maximise my research and its output. Professor Müller-Bahlke played a significant role in completing this biography by providing a work contract that financed my travels and brief accommodations in Halle (Saale), Copenhagen, and London, allowing me to cross-check vital manuscripts and deepen my insights. He also introduced me to Metta Scholz, the Head of Publications at the Francke Foundations. Meeting Ms. Scholz and explaining the importance of this biography and its specific aspects was a pleasure. She and her team members, like Ms. Luise Müller, read the draft chapters of this manuscript and helped me to make the text more coherent. I extend my gratitude to Professor Müller-Bahlke and Ms. Scholz for publishing this biography in the esteemed *Halle Research* (*Hallesche Forschungen*) series, which focuses on the histories and impacts of Pietism and the Francke Foundations in and outside of Europe.

This biography marks a significant chapter in my life, closely intertwined with the Francke Foundations. I am deeply grateful for the warm hospitality and timely support from numerous colleagues there. I extend special thanks to Dr. Britta Klosterberg, the former Head of the Francke Study Centre; Ms. Anke Mies; Dr. Jürgen Gröschl; Mr. Dirk Glettner; Professor Holger Zaunstöck, the Head of the Research Centre at the Francke Foundations; and others, for making my research visits and stays fruitful and enjoyable. Their indispensable help in procuring primary sources, guiding me to secondary source materials, and making my work in the reading rooms memorable is something I will always cherish. One notable outcome of my research at the Francke Foundations was my case study about *Recovering Cultural Memories and Rejuvenating Tamil Christian Minorities*. The UK's *Research Excellence Framework* (2021) accepted it as an internationally leading example. I remain deeply grateful to my colleagues at the Francke Foundations for their unwavering support in this regard.

My academic career owes immense gratitude to the Faculty of Theology at Martin Luther University Halle-Wittenberg. The intellectual stimulation I received during my doctoral and Habilitation research, as well as my two subsequent guest professorships, has been invaluable. My friend, Professor Daniel Cyranka, currently the Dean of the Faculty of Theology at Martin Luther University Halle–Wittenberg, arranged these guest professorships. I also fondly remember the spiritual and practical support from the Landeskirchliche Gemeinschaft in Halle (Saale) from 1992 to 1995. Their warm and familial support, which continued the spiritual legacy of Pietists like Philip Jacob Spener and August Hermann Francke, made me feel a part of a community. I am incredibly grateful to Brigitte, Armin Dittrich, Ursula, and Gerhard Laganski for their support during my numerous stays in Halle (Saale).

Beyond Halle (Saale), I am indebted to senior academics and colleagues who encouraged me to complete this biography. Professor Emeritus Robert E. Frykenberg in Madison, Wisconsin, deserves a special mention. He reached out to me in Chennai in 1996 and has been a constant source of encouragement ever since. His unique interpretation of the British Raj as a consciously negotiated cooperation between the merchants and officers of the British East India Company, on the one hand, and the leaders of Indian communities, especially local princes, kings, interpreters, and merchant bankers, on the other, deeply impressed me. His writings illustrate how Indian elites actively cooperated with the British to safeguard their interests rather than portraying the Raj as an imposition. His perspective highlighted the active role Indian elites, their dependents and supporters played in the British Raj's success.[1] I greatly regret that Professor Freykenberg passed away suddenly in April 2025. He eagerly waited to see the publication of this volume. His acute memory and his love for historical details were admirable. He closely supervised my work on this manuscript and gave me valuable advice. I cherished his fatherly guidance.

I sincerely thank Professor Emeritus Richard Fox Young of the Princeton Theological Seminary, New Jersey, USA, for the constructive role that he has played in my academic life. He persuaded the Search Committee of Princeton Theological Seminary to appoint me as their John A. Macay Professor for World Christianity for the academic year 2001–2002. Following that year, I served as their Research Professor for a second year (2002–2003). This extraordinary opportunity transformed my scholarly focus from the general History of Christianity to the captivating new field of World Christianity. Professor Young's mastery of American English, Sanskrit, Japanese, and Chinese, along with his ability to engage with Tamil and Sinhalese texts, has been profoundly inspiring.

---

1 Robert Eric Frykenberg: The myth of English as a 'colonist' imposition upon India: a reappraisal with special reference to South India. In: Journal of the Royal Asiatic Society 120, 2011, issue 2, 305–315. Professor Frykenberg investigated how Indian participants negotiated, supported and determined the affairs of the EIC.

His brotherly counsel has been invaluable to me. With great interest and meticulous expertise, he reviewed the chapters of this biography at their final draft stage. His incisive reading and well-considered suggestions saved me from stylistic pitfalls, eliminated ambiguities, and clarified nuanced expressions. I remain profoundly thankful to him.

I am deeply grateful to Professor Emeritus Gerald Pillay, who served as Vice-Chancellor and Rector of Liverpool Hope University. It was a pleasure to work under his leadership from 2008 to 2022. I also sincerely thank Professor Atulya Nagar, the Pro-Vice-Chancellor for Research, for providing me with a travel grant to examine a rich body of Schwartz materials in Halle (Saale) and London. During these research stays, I identified numerous previously unknown manuscripts that provided new insights into the socio-economic and military contexts that influenced Schwartz's life and work. I am thankful to Reverend Dr Philip Prasad, the Deputy Executive Director of the Oxford Centre for Religion and Public Life, his wife, Dr Premila, and their son Arpith for hosting me in their house in Basingstoke, near London, for a few days during my research at the British Library in August 2024. Additionally, whenever I visited Liverpool for focused writing, the renowned dentist, Dr. Dix Premsingh Prasad, his wife, Jain, and their children, Rachel, Raphael, and Pricilla (fondly called Teddy), welcomed me into their home and looked after me well. I appreciate their love, hospitality and kindness.

I dedicate this biography of Schwartz in gratitude to all women who have played a formative role in my life. Foremost among them is my mother, Esther Rani Ponniah († 27 May 2003). Despite lacking formal education, she taught herself to read and write. She was determined to see me formally well-educated, despite opposition from her paternal family. When my father died on 27 May 1975, her parents and siblings urged her to send me to tend the village cows and to earn money for a livelihood. She discarded their advice and earned their wrath until her death. Her steadfast support enabled me to pursue my Pre-University Certificate (equivalent to the modern 12th year in high school in Tamil Nadu), join the Christian Mission Service in 1977, and study at the School for Deacons in Coonoor, the Nilgiris. Three widows in Germany, namely Mrs. Sigrid Thomas, Mrs. Ursula Aenis, and Mrs. Heidi Seiferth, funded my undergraduate studies (1984–1987) and postgraduate studies (1988–1991) in theology at the Union Biblical Seminary in Pune, India. Moreover, these women helped me to learn the German language, which, in an unforeseen way, facilitated my research based on German manuscripts. Like my mother, they took great pleasure in seeing me earn my first doctorate in Historical Theology (Dr. theol., 1995), a Habilitation degree (Dr. theol. habil., 2000), and another doctorate in German Studies (Dr. phil., 2002).

I am profoundly grateful to my wife, Reverend Dr Sheela Jeyaraj, for her steadfast support since our marriage in December 1986. Her sacrifices allowed me to delve into distant archives and write about my findings. She has been supporting me on every step of my academic journey. I also thank my daughters, Rebecca, Elisabeth, and Ruth, whose joy, laughter, intellectual acumen, and light-hearted perspectives on historical matters have been a constant source of strength and encouragement. My special thanks to Elisabeth for her meticulous proofreading of the initial stages of various chapters in this biography. The youngest women in my family are my granddaughters, Evie and Esther Leona, who bring me a smile every day. The birth of Esther Leona in December 2024 was a miracle for which I am grateful to God.

This biography provides a compelling example of the transformative potential of informed, cross-cultural service and societal change. As an ambassador of faith, peace, justice and social harmony in southern India, Schwartz demonstrated remarkable social and spiritual courage. He transcended barriers of nationality, language, culture and tradition. He fostered an environment of integrity and honesty where people could overcome their prejudices and connect with their neighbours and strangers. The communities in which he lived and worked have since become more humane, just, and harmonious. He taught his listeners and followers to take responsibility for positively engaging with others and create a better world for all.

As I studied Schwartz's life, work, and legacy, I found no written account questioning his moral integrity. His reputation was one of awe. However, in 2008, a senior civil servant in Chennai alleged that Schwartz, as an agent of the English East India Company, had manipulated the rulers of Tanjore to surrender their country to the Company. This claim prompted me to re-read and critically examine the extensive body of Schwartz-related documents I have meticulously collected since 1992. This biography is the result of that comprehensive investigation.

Introduction

In the second half of the eighteenth century, the English East India Company,[1] often referred to as "the Company," and the inhabitants of southern India experienced immense turmoil.[2] The Company had transitioned from an international commercial enterprise to a regional semi-government institution, asserting political, military, economic, and judicial dominance over the protesting Carnatic, including the Kingdom of Tanjore.[3] The uncontrollable and rampant corruption and extortion practiced by the Company's civil and military servants in India, coupled with the unrelenting greed of their Indian allies, such as the Nawab of Arcot, agents, bankers, and merchants, who demanded exorbitant sums for themselves, sparked widespread conflict and financial exhaustion. The Anglo-Indian trading company, the Madras Association, served as a bridge between buyers and sellers of goods and services, favouring the Company's servants. Continuous threats and repeated wars with neighbouring princely states, such as Mysore, further depleted the resources of the Company, Tanjore, and the Nawab. Ordinary people of these regions faced extreme impoverishment and humiliation, struggling for daily survival. In 1772, the bankrupt Company asked the British Government in London for a loan to maintain and further its Indian operations. The British Government seized that opportunity to impose its will. Gradually, it passed laws to control and claim the Company as British. These laws included the *Regulating Act of India* (1773), *Pitt's India Act* (1784),[4] and the *Charter Acts* of 1793 and 1813. From 1773, the Company functioned in India as an arm of the

---

1 Roget Jeffery and Duncan Money: India in Edinburgh: 1750s to the Present. In: India in Edinburgh—1750s to the Present. Ed. by Roger Jeffery. London 2019, 1–21, here 2: After the Governor and Company of Merchants of London Trading into the East Indies had become the United Company of Merchants of England Trading to the East Indies in 1708, the Company had proportionately more Scots as senior civil and military officers, medical doctors, and scientists.

2 J. Albert Rorabacher: Property, Land, Revenue, and Policy: The East India Company, c. 1757–1825. London 2016, here 230: The period between the Battle of Plassey in 1757 and the *Regulating Act of 1773* was monumental. The Company had no parliamentary supervision and expanded its territories in India. The company's trade and the private trades of Company servants "imposed great hardship on the people and the economy of India."

3 William Dalrymple and Anita Anand: Koh-I-Noor—The History of the World's Most Infamous Diamond. London 2017, here 7: At its inception, the Company had thirty-five permanent staff in an office in London. Over a century, it became "the most powerful and heavily militarised [multinational] corporation in history: its army by 1800 was twice the size" of Britain's army.

4 Rorabacher: Property, Land, Revenue, and Policy, 233: The Company's excess reserve declined in the 1760s. When it could not administer its territories in India, the British Government intervened in 1773. After 1784, the British Government legally determined the Company's Indian policy, "frequently resulting in indecision. Policies were formulated, hesitatingly implemented, then, discarded."

British Government for British benefits[5], and not for Indian welfare. It called itself the Government.

Amidst this "most monumental period" of complexity, corruption, violence, existential threats, and overwhelming political transitions, Christian Friedrich Schwartz (1726–1798) emerged as a beacon of peace, justice and social harmony for the benefit of Indians among whom he lived, worked for forty-eight years, and died.[6] The impact of his life and work made an indelible impact on the inhabitants of southern India, particularly in Tanjore, Tiruccirāppaḷḷi, Ramanathapuram, Kumbakonam, Pāḷaiyamkōṭṭai, Tranquebar and Chennai. Besides, it shaped the beliefs and practices of mission-minded Christians in Sri Lanka, Germany, Denmark, the United Kingdom, and the United States of America. It even influenced the British parliamentary debates about the place of the Pious Clause in the Company's Charter Acts of 1793 and 1813. Schwartz's unwavering commitment to and corresponding actions for peace, justice, and social harmony continue to resonate with the people of southern India to this day, primarily through the institutions he founded or influenced. He lives among them as the "Apostle to India,"[7] The "Apostle to the East,"[8] and the "irreproachable Missionary."[9]

1 Schwartz as Cāṉṟōṉ

Christian Friedrich Schwartz (1726–1798) was a multifaceted individual whom the Tamils respected and trusted. They seemed to have perceived him as someone who embodied the five virtues of a Tamil nobleman (the *cāṉṟōṉ*),[10] namely, love (*aṉpu*), shying away from evil (*nāṇ*), reasonably reconciled relationships (*oppuravu*), compassionate actions to better the lives of others (*kaṇṇōṭṭam*), and upholding truth (*vāymai*). These virtues were the five-pillared foundation for his

5 Rorabacher: Property, Land, Revenue, and Policy, 193: By 1773, British policymakers feared that the loss of Indian revenue, which had previously poured into British banks, markets, and leading households, could cause "a national bankruptcy." They knew how Indian goods, markets and money exchange determined the "price trends in Britain. India had become part of the economic fabric of Britain." The British Parliament took a century to effectively govern the Company's territories in India and benefit the British people in Britain.

6 In a telephone conversation on 13.01.2025, Professor Robert E. Frykenberg clarified that Schwartz served the people of Tanjore during the most corrupt and oppressive period of the Company Raj. The rulers of Tanjore were not Tamils but Marathis. They did not speak Tamil. Probably, they did not fully understand the life of ordinary inhabitants. They ruled their kingdom through greedy *diwan*s, *sirkeel*s and *dubash*es, mostly from Madras and other places. On the other hand, the Company's servants, both civil and military, had no interest in improving the quality of life for the inhabitants of Tanjore. They did not even care for the Company's economic welfare, and its near bankruptcy did not worry them greatly. Instead, they focused on enriching themselves by looting Tanjore and returning to England as *Nabobs* with great fortunes.

7 C.B. Gohdes: Schwartz—The Apostle to India. Columbus/Ohio 1923, the title page.

8 Life of the Eminent Missionary Swartz. In: The Methodist Magazine 37, 1814, 241–250, here 241. This essay's unnamed author considered Schwartz the "Apostle of the East in these latter times."

9 William Fullarton: A View of the English Interests in India and an Account of the military operations in the Southern Parts of the Peninsula during the Campaigns of 1782, 1783 and

transparent life and beneficial ministry. His commitment to upholding the "non-lying lamp of truthfulness" (*poyyā viḷakku*)[11] reinforced his reputation (*pukaḻ*) that was otherwise reserved for a Tamil nobleman.[12] The inscription on his monument in St. Mary's Church, within Fort St. George (the contemporary headquarters of the Government of Tamil Nadu), states that the native inhabitants of India, of every religious conviction, held him in the highest reverence and placed their limitless confidence in his "integrity and Truth."[13] Thus, he was a *cāṉṟōṉ*.

This biography examines different facets of Schwartz that convinced his contemporaries to perceive him as *cāṉṟōṉ*. Firstly, it examines his firm dedication to his divine mission as an envoy of the Lord Jesus Christ, a calling he believed was divinely entrusted to him. Inspired by the teachings of the leading Pietists like August Hermann Francke (1663–1727),[14] Schwartz aimed to redeem people from their sins and lead them to a fuller life, both theologically, "in Christ," and practically, within the Tamil Lutheran Pietist congregations. The Pietists, like Schwartz, were not merely theorists; they translated their theological convictions into tangible actions that profoundly impacted society. They viewed their role as a divine calling to serve their congregations and the broader public. As German Lutheran Pietists, they taught at high schools and universities, established libraries, scientific laboratories, and curiosity cabinets for virtual education, developed the pharmaceutical and printing industries, and created a network of friends in every major European city. Their theological convictions transformed the Glaucha Institutions (nowadays known as the Francke Foundations in Halle (Saale), Germany) into a hub of educational, social, and spiritual upliftment, as well as a centre for research output.

1784 in two letters addressed to the Right Honourable the Earl of ***** and to Lord Macartney and the Select Committee of Fort St. George. London: T. Cadell, 1787, 183.

10 aṉpunāṇ oppuravu kaṇṇōṭṭam vāymaiyoṭu
aintucāl ūṉṟiya tūṇ. – The 983rd couplet in Tirukkuṟaḷ

11 T Vol. 4448, 96–97: On 31.05.1795, Schwartz asked his adopted son Serfoji to follow this principle: While politicians, administrators, and other officers in Tanjore lied, the "word of every good man should be equal to an oath. This is one of the fundamental rules which ought to be strictly observed [by you, Serfoji]." James Hough: The History of Christianity in India from the Commencement of the Christian Era. Vol. 4. London, 1845, here 14: Henry Vansittart, who resided in Madras before being appointed Governor of Bengal (1759–1764), knew Schwartz and other German Lutheran missionaries. He spoke about Schwartz "in the highest terms, commending his piety, integrity, and disinterestedness. He also bore testimony to the great reverence paid him by the Natives and to the influence which he had over them by his high character."

12 ellā viḷakkum viḷakkalla cāṉṟōrkkup
poyyā viḷakkē viḷakku. – The 299th couplet in Tirukkuṟaḷ teaches that not all lamps are lamps for the noble ones, but only the lamp of truthfulness.

13 Appendix 6a.

14 For Francke's Great Essay of 1704, see Wilhelm Fries: August Hermann Franckes Grosser Aufsatz. Halle (Saale) 1894. Otto Podczeck: August Hermann Franckes Schrift über eine Reform des Erziehungs- und Bildungswesens als Ausgangspunkt einer geistlichen und sozialen Neuordnung der Evangelischen Kirche des 18. Jahrhunderts: Der Grosse Aufsatz mit einer quellenkundlichen Einführung. Berlin 1962, 10: This Great Essay revealed Francke's intentions to reform the Ruling Class, the Teaching Class and the Household Class. The marks of reform included a deep knowledge of the biblical texts, improved moral lives, and equipping the economically poor to escape suffering and enter mainstream society.

Secondly, this biography illustrates how five interrelated authorities shaped Schwartz's role as an envoy for peace, justice and social harmony. His first authority was the Danish King Frederick V (reigned 1746–1766), who sent Schwartz as his envoy to the inhabitants of Tranquebar. Bishop Peder Hersleb (1689–1757) of the Danish Lutheran Church in Copenhagen was the second authority. He ordained Schwartz on September 6, 1749, as a missionary and required him to uphold the contents of the Book of Concord. The third authority was the values of the Glaucha Institutions in Halle (Saale), Germany. Schwartz familiarised himself with how its leaders, Gotthilf August Francke and others, imparted education to underprivileged children, established and maintained diverse money-generating institutions (including kindergartens, schools, libraries, clinics, pharmacies, medicine production, and a printing press), and interacted with political authorities. The fourth authority came from additional instructions that he had received from the Society for Promoting Christian Knowledge (SPCK) in London. As their chaplain for the Company soldiers in Tiruccirāppaḷḷi and Tanjore (1762–1798), Schwartz developed a sympathetic attitude towards Anglican worship practices. The fifth authority was brief when he served as the Company's envoy to Hyder Ali in Seringapatam in 1779.[15]

Thirdly, this biography highlights Schwartz's incarnational life and service among the Tamil people from his arrival in Tranquebar in 1750 till his death in 1798. With their help, he learned to speak, read, and write at least five languages: Tamil, English, Persian, Marathi and Modi. He familiarised himself with their social customs, religious beliefs and rituals, showing a deep respect for their culture. He knew that his hearers would receive, understand, and interpret his teachings through their inherited socio-cultural filters. To facilitate a better understanding, he adapted himself to the cognitive levels of the Tamils. He believed that God, as revealed in the Bible, created every person in God's image, making every person eternally valuable and possessing innate dignity. Moreover, their life was sacred. As the envoy of God, Schwartz invited the people with whom he interacted to embrace the Lordship of Jesus Christ.

Fourthly, this biography focuses on the Indians with whom Schwartz worked. Unlike other biographies that emphasised his relevance to English- and German-speaking countries, this one concentrates on Schwartz's life and work among various Indians in southern India. He interacted with members of his congregations and schools. He met with leaders of the Tamil people, especially farmers and emigrants of Tanjore and Tranquebar. He persuaded them to return to their native villages peacefully and encouraged them to cultivate their lands. Under his

---

15 AFSt/M 1 B 74 : 31. Hugh Pearson: Memoirs of the Life and Correspondence of the Reverend Christian Frederick Swartz. Vol. 1, London 1834, 362: Schwartz informed Hyder Ali that he wanted to cement a friendly relationship between him and the Company, thus securing the blessings of peace for this devoted country and its inhabitants. This purpose did not contradict his missionary vocation. Hyder Ali agreed with Schwartz's opinion and wanted to live peacefully with the Company. He told Schwartz: If the English "offer me the hand of peace and concord, I shall not withdraw mine, provided —. But of these mysterious provisions, 'nothing,' observes Colonel Wilks, can now be ascertained." Here, Pearson cites Mark Wilkes' note in the British Library bearing the signature ADD 57313 ff 37r–42v.

guidance, their agricultural yield prevented famine in Tanjore. All inhabitants benefited from the abundance of food. Schwartz trained, employed, and supervised Tamil school teachers and catechists. His interactions and collaborations with Kings Tulāji, Ameer Singh, and Tulāji's adopted son Serfoji demonstrated his contributions to peace, justice and harmony. He attempted to negotiate a peace treaty with Hyder Ali on behalf of the Company. However, Thomas Rumbold (1736–1791),[16] appointed by King George III as Governor and President of Madras (1777–1780), thwarted his efforts, and Hyder Ali invaded the Carnatic in June 1780. Schwartz facilitated conversations between the kings of Tanjore and the governors of Tranquebar, as well as between Indian rulers and the Company officers. In these high-level discussions, he advocated for the welfare of ordinary people and created job opportunities for those in need. He introduced vaccination against smallpox, which ravaged various parts of Tanjore. Those who interacted with Schwartz – both Indians and Europeans – learned alternative ways to promote a more peaceful, just, and harmonious society.

Fifthly, Schwartz understood the meanings and practical implications of justice.[17] His twelfth Tamil dialogue teaches that God's justice (*parāparaṉuṭaiya nīti*)[18] rewards (*palaṉ*) human intentions and actions. Hence, God's worshippers should not be careless (*acati*) and commit mistakes (*kuṟṟam*). To discern God's glorious will (*cittam*), God has endowed humans with clear intellect (*teḷinta aṟivu*), spiritual wisdom (*ñāṉam*), holiness (*paricuttam*), and justice (*nīti*). Practically, if the readers or hearers of these dialogues wanted to embrace Schwartz's Lutheranism in Tanjore, fellow Tamils might not treat them justly and reasonably (*nīti niyāyam*). Even in such harsh conditions, God's justice would require them not to retaliate. Instead, they should treat others justly.[19] At the same time, he demonstrated that one should not be complacent in the face of injustice. Therefore, he opposed the injustices committed by the Company's officers, traders, creditors, and landlords, as well as the Nawab of Arcot and the kings of Tanjore. These people relentlessly exploited the inhabitants of Tanjore economically and morally.[20] As discussed below in Section 9.1.6, Schwartz urged the Company not

---

16 BL ADD 38400 ff., folio 106r: "This Indenture made the twenty-seventh Day of June in the seventeenth year of the Reign of our Sovereign Lord George the Third by the grace of God of Great Britain, France and Ireland, King, Defender of the Faith, &c., and in the year of our Lord seventeen hundred and seventy seven Between the United Company of Merchants of England trading to the East Indies of the one part and Thomas Rumbold of London Esq. of the other part witnesseth, that for and in consideration of the said Thomas Rumbold being appointed President & Governor of the said United Company's Presidency of Fort St. George on the Coast of Coromandel in the East Indies, and for and in consideration of the salary of Forty thousand Pagodas by the year agreed to be allowed."

17 Schwartz must have been familiar with the Hebrew concepts of *tzedek* and *misphat*, the Greek idea of *dikaiosunē*, and the Tamil notion of *nīti*, all related to justice.

18 Christian Friedrich Schwartz: vikkiraka pattik kāraṉukkum kiṟisatavaṉukkum uṇaṭāṉa camapāṣaṇai ('Dialogue between an image worshipper and a Christian'). Tranquebar: Mission Press, [2]1790 ([1]1777), here 30–31: According to the Satya Veda (the 'true Veda,' i.e. the Christian Bible), God judges each person's deeds fairly and impartially.

19 Schwartz: vikkiraka pattik kāraṉukkum, 139–140.

20 Elizabeth Kolsky: Colonial Justice in British India—White Violence and the Rule of Law. New Delhi 2009. Kolsky explains how British soldiers, traders, and tea garden planters, for

to exploit the people of Tanjore. On 23 November 1797, he asked Serfoji to practise justice for the true happiness of his subjects.[21]

Sixthly, Schwartz's approach to promoting social harmony was as unique as the Greek concept of harmony (*harmonia*), which endorsed the pleasing combinations of sounds and music in a symphony. He fostered social harmony among diverse groups, including his church congregation, schoolteachers, catechists, Tamil Lutheran pastors, young trainee missionaries, and government representatives. His interactions with the Vaiṣṇavite kings of Tanjore, the Muslim rulers of Seringapatam,[22] the Tamil farmers of Tanjore,[23] and the immigrants in Tanjore and Tranquebar were all marked by the same degree of enthusiasm. Over time, he guided certain Company officers, the rulers of Tanjore and Mysore, immigrants in Tanjore and Tranquebar, Tamil catechists and pastors, as well as younger German Lutheran Pietist missionaries in practicing justice, peace, and harmony. The following chapters delve into Schwartz's unique role as an envoy for social harmony.[24]

Seventhly, existing biographies on Schwartz do not cite the sources of their information. They provide details that might please their readers. By contrast, this biography is based on archival research conducted in India, Germany, Denmark, and the United Kingdom. The Danish-Halle Mission Archives, located in the August Herrmann Francke Study Centre of the Francke Foundations in Halle (Saale), Germany, preserve Schwartz's handwritten letters, reports, and diaries. It also preserves the extracts of Schwartz's letters that he sent to his friends and mission authorities in England, Denmark, and Germany. The India Office Records at the British Library in London preserve the Company records of Madras and Tanjore, some of which contain valuable information about Schwartz and his role in the public sphere. They complement the contents of Schwartz's letters in German. The Royal Library and National Archives in Copenhagen, Denmark, contain Schwartz's earliest letters from Tranquebar (1751) and Tiruccirāppaḷḷi (1766–1768). These letters are addressed to the Mission College in Copenhagen[25] and express Schwartz's inner struggles about formally leaving the Lutheran

---

example, in Assam, exploited Indians and misused British legal provisions that favoured Europeans more than Indians.

21 Pearson: Memoirs, Vol. 2, 368: "As the administration of justice is indispensably necessary to the prosperity and happiness of every state, I request you will establish regular courts and be careful that impartial justice be administered. I heartily wish you would renounce your idolatry and serve and honour the only true God. May He be merciful and enable you to do it!"

22 Pearson: Memoirs, Vol. 1, 362.

23 Pearson: Memoirs, Vol. 2, 116.

24 Ce. Irācu: palturaip paṇipurinta svārṭs pātiriyār (Tamil: 'Reverend Schwartz, who served in different fields'). In: Christian Friedrich Schwartz: His Contributions to South India. N.p. 1999, 215–221, here 215: Pandit Irācu, who worked at the Tamil University in Tanjore and assessed Schwartz's multifaceted impact on Tanjore's contemporary life, expressed his opinion as follows: Schwartz was indeed an envoy for peace (*camātāṉa tūtar*). His work on the government of Tanjore influenced how Tanjore has become a flourishing place for art and education (*kalai, kalvi*).

25 Missionskollegiet Rigsarviet 9c, Indkome Sager den Ostindiske Mission vedk. 1751–1756. This collection contains Schwartz's letters to the President of the Mission College dated 27.10.1751, 17.12.1766, 31.03.1768, 10.07.1768 and 26.10.1768.

Mission in Tranquebar, joining the Society for Promoting Christian Knowledge (an Anglican institution) as their chaplain, and assisting the Company soldiers in Tiruccirāppaḷḷi. The Tamil Nadu State Archives in Chennai, India, keeps copies of Schwartz's correspondence with various personalities about Serfoji (from 1788 to 1798). With the help of Santha Praburaj, I was able to collect the necessary details for a conference on Schwartz in 1998. His essay contains primary sources that have enriched this biography.[26]

None of the institutions related to Schwartz in Tranquebar, Tanjore, Tiruccirāppaḷḷi, Pālaiyamkōṭṭai, and Ramanathapuram preserve original manuscripts by or about Schwartz.[27] However, Babu Rao's Marathi text about Serfoji's genealogy, inscribed on a wall of the Big Temple in Tanjore, acknowledges Schwartz's adoption of Serfoji.[28] Additionally, Danish archives preserve letters in the *Moḍī* language, which the administrators at the royal palace of Tanjore used and in which they referred to Schwartz.[29] Likewise, Schwartz's stone monuments in St. Mary's Church, Fort St. George, Chennai, Christ's Church, and St. Peter's Church, Tanjore, contain significant details about Schwartz.[30]

2 Biography as History

A biography transcends a mere narrative recount of an individual's life and work. As a profound literary genre, it explores how individuals construct and convey their experiences. It situates their circumstances and activities within their unique socio-historical and political contexts, capturing the defining spirit, mood, and aspirations of their time and space. By exploring their life journey, from identity formation and self-perception to relationships with those in their sphere of influence, a biography seeks to unravel how individuals respond to the historical memories of their contexts expressed through customs and mores, attitudes and choices, actions and habits. It highlights their lived experiences, whether recorded by themselves or their contemporaries. It sheds new light on societal norms, cultural shifts, political developments and historical events that shaped their lives. Thus, a biography offers readers a deeper understanding of a society's past

---

26 S. Santha Praburaj: An Analysis of Schwartz materials in the Tamil Nadu Archives. In: Christian Friedrich Schwartz: His Contributions to South India. Ed. by Daniel Jeyaraj. Chennai 1999, 105–116.

27 These institutions include the Christ Church, Bishop Heber College and the St. John's Vestry Anglo Indian Higher Secondary School in Tiruccirāppaḷḷi, the Christ Church, St. Peter's Church and Thanjavur Maharaja Serfoji's Saraswathi Mahal Library in Tanjore, Clarinda's Church in Pāḷaiyamkōṭṭai and Schwartz Higher Secondary School in Ramanathapuram.

28 Bapu Rao: Bhonsle Vamsa Charitra Being the Marathi Historical Inscription in the Big Temple Tanjore on The History of the Maratta Rajas of Tanjore (dated 13 December 1803). Thanjavur 2009. This book contains texts in three languages. S. Gopalan's English summary of the Marathi inscription, i–xx, Babu Rao's Marathi text, 1–110 and V. Srinivachari's Tamil translation of this Marathi text, 1–139.

29 Elisabeth Strandberg: A Tanjore Marāṭhī letter in Moḍī script to Chr. F. Schwartz. In: Acta Orientalis, Vol. 41, 1980, 17–25; The Moḍī Documents from Tanjore in Danish Collections, Edited, Translated and Analysed. Wiesbaden 1983, here 319–322.

30 Appendix 6 contains a transcript of these inscriptions.

circumstances through a detailed examination. It reveals how individuals made and acted upon informed choices, navigating their lives amidst varying convictions and priorities. Moreover, it shows the underlying attitudes and forces that shape their thoughts and actions, which can be examined under specific themes. Thus, a biography serves as a window into the life of individuals and a lens through which we can better understand broader societal dynamics and historical influences.

Biographical research is inherently multidisciplinary and involves the intricate interdependence of various theories and approaches for studying texts, histories, sociologies, religions, anthropology, politics, colonialism, and subaltern studies.[31] It examines the structural settings of societies and the evolving processes of human attitudes and behaviours. When it comes to the biography of a Christian missionary, this research takes on an additional dimension. It encompasses an in-depth study of the missionary's theology, motifs, teachings, and works. Such a biography draws inspiration from the Bible, perceived as a collection of divinely inspired biographies and autobiographies of individuals who endeavoured, with various degrees of success, to translate their theological views into their immediate life contexts. In this sense, the Bible presents narratives of individuals and their relationships with God, interpreted through the lens of their experiences and specific theological convictions. Therefore, a biography of a Christian missionary weaves together theology and missiology. It illustrates how the missionaries recognised God in their lives and allowed their recognition to guide them through their life circumstances. Typically, missionaries understand God primarily through Jesus Christ, whom the New Testament reveals as Saviour and Lord. Consequently, their theological perspectives set priorities and guide their actions. Hence, a biography of a Christian missionary provides valuable insights into the theological convictions[32] that underpin their missional activities.[33] By examining the personal journeys of missionaries, a Christian missionary biography offers a deeper understanding of the broader societal and historical contexts in which they operated.

Considering this discussion about a Christian biography as a narrative account of their theology and mission, this biography of Schwartz incorporates additional research and writing principles. It contextualises Schwartz's life and work within the prevailing historical, social, and political contexts of the German Lutheran Pietists in Halle (Saale) and the Tamil people during the second half of the eighteenth century. This chronological and thematic biography demonstrates how specific events and their contexts impacted Schwartz's life and work. Its holistic

---

31 For further biographical research, see Brian Roberts: Biographical research. Buckingham 2002.

32 James William McClendon: Biography as Theology: How Life Stories Can Remake Today's Theology. Nashville 1974, 92: Biography as theology illustrates "the nature of God, man's own nature, the modes of our intercourse with him and with one another, the nature of religion, etc."

33 Ruth A. Tucker: Biography as Missiology: Mining the Lives of Missionaries for Cross-Cultural Effectiveness. In: Missiology: An International Review 27, 1999, issue 4, 429–439, here 430: "Biography as missiology, by its very nature, has a more practical bent than does biography as theology in that missiology is primarily concerned with how one does mission, while theology has traditionally focused on an understanding of the nature of God and God's relationship with humanity."

view highlights his significant contributions to the Tamil people. His personal life as a German Lutheran Pietist and his professional life as an ordained Lutheran missionary pastor enabled him to overcome personal struggles and psychological self-doubt. Remarkably, he developed a life of integrity and trustworthiness that appealed to people across diverse social strata and religious backgrounds.

Besides these aspects of a biological study, this biography recognises Schwartz's subjective reporting on people, events, and circumstances as he documented them through his perceptions. To gain a more balanced view, this biography incorporates insights from contemporary documents written by various Company officers and members of the royal household of Tanjore, as well as Schwartz's students. It also considers archived letters, diaries, and critical reports by Schwartz and others. Schwartz's writings interwove his theological and missiological convictions into his life experiences, observations, documentation, and assessments of people and events.

The author of this biography endeavoured to let the archival documents narrate Schwartz's story and strive for an objective presentation. Nonetheless, this biography may reflect the author's subjectivity. In addition to his self-disclosure in the preceding Preface, he is a trained Christian theologian, historian, and lover of the Tamil language. An ordained presbyter of the Diocese of Tirunelveli in the Church of South India, he has examined how the lives and works of German Lutheran Pietists, such as Bartholomäus Ziegenbalg and Christian Friedrich Schwartz, enriched Tamil, its language, literature, and culture. Fluent in Tamil, German and English, the author reads old Tamil manuscripts on palm leaves, hand-written German manuscripts using *Sütterlinschrift*, and German texts in *Fraktur* typefaces. With over three decades of experience as a professor of the History of Christianity and World Christianity, he has supervised research candidates and written extensively on South Indian religions.

Equipped with these personal backgrounds, academic skills, and professional experiences, the author has provided a more balanced view of Schwartz's life and work than all other biographies to date. He meticulously cross-checked various primary sources with proofs and secondary sources with their interpretations and other viewpoints. Engaging deliberately with primary sources, such as Schwartz's personal letters, diaries, and reports from the Company officers, the author resisted unsupported interpretations. He consciously mitigated unconscious biases by quoting verbatim or summarising relevant texts from Schwartz and his contemporaries. Hence, the resulting biography is verifiable, fair, and well-rounded.

This biography did not involve ethical issues about individuals' or communities' privacy, safety, or integrity, as it is a historical account. Nevertheless, it respectfully portrays individuals who interacted with Schwartz and remains sensitive to their faith communities. By carefully citing verifiable sources and demonstrating how Schwartz's life and work impacted people's lives in diverse geographical locations in southern India, it honours the legacy still cherished by these communities. Furthermore, it aims to assist them in discovering more aspects of Schwartz and his contemporaries that are hidden in various archives and libraries, while maintaining the utmost respect for historical accuracy and ethical considerations.

3 The Company Raj as a British-Indian Partnership

This biography views the establishment and growth of the British East India Company, henceforth referred to as the Company, as a mutually beneficial partnership between the British in India and Britain, as well as a select group of Indian elites. These Indian elites were not a homogeneous group. They included local rulers, merchants, bankers, *duhashes* (agents, interpreters), mercenary soldiers, and other influential figures. Rather than being a unilateral British imposition on helpless Indians, the Company's formative stages included negotiated interdependent arrangements between the Company servants and Indian elites.

Despite their interdependence, the Company servants and the Indian elites pursued different economic and political goals. The Indian elites, who often engaged in armed conflicts among themselves or with their neighbours, aimed to safeguard their preeminent roles in protecting their families, lands, temples, priests, roads and sources of perennial economic income, thus securing political stability for their benefit. Initially, the Company was primarily interested in trade with Indians. However, they soon enlisted financial and human support from within India: Indian princes, landholders, bankers, interpreters, mediators, traders, accountants, bookkeepers, soldiers, spies, police personnel, medical professionals, and other providers of essential services (e.g. cooks, guards, those who tailored and washed clothes, caretakers of army animals, etc.) enabled and supported the Company to evolve into a parallel Raj, i.e., a state with its government, military, banks and regional and international networks.

Over time, the Indian elites, who had hired Company armies and personnel, found themselves in a precarious financial situation due to the rising expenses for ammunition and weapons, salaries, accommodation, and the transportation of soldiers, as well as war reparations and high interest on borrowed money from Company creditors. In response, they began mortgaging their lands to the Company for revenue collection and eventual administration. This was not a one-sided imposition by the Company. The participating Indian elites strategically moved to secure their influence and power, at least temporarily and superficially. Like dance partners continuously responding and adjusting to each other's movements, needs, and aspirations, the Company and the Indian elites influenced each other, grew together, and became inseparably interdependent. Throughout this process of cementing interdependence, the Company considered the cultural values, religious etiquettes, social identities, and existential needs of Indian elites. Consequently, Indian elites in Tanjore and Mysore surrendered their lands to the Company. Thus, without the active will and cooperation of the Indian elites, the Company could not have become a *Raj* (government) exercising semi-sovereign control over the Kingdom of Tanjore, collecting revenues, maintaining armies at the expense of the Indian elites, and making political decisions.

Professor Robert Eric Frykenberg's methodological approach to interpreting the Company as the partnership between the British and Indian elites is insightful. He found existing theories of British ascendence in India unsatisfactory. These included theoretical assumptions about the disintegration of the highly centralised Mughal Empire, the military prowess of the British armies, and international factors related to maritime trade, travel, and communication. Likewise, the top-down Euro-centric approaches of the Imperial historians' views about the Company's coming, conquering and ruling helpless and incompetent Indians amidst chaotic, self-destructive maladministration of people, lands and resources, and the bottom-up approaches of the nationalist historians of imagining a glorious past impoverished and destroyed by the Company do not fully explain the intricate interdependence between specific groups of Indian elites (e.g. rulers, landed gentry, *dubashes*) and the Company and the resultant Company's dominance. As no single-sided theory is sufficient for the Company's success in India, Frykenberg proposes his theory of deliberate cooperation between the British and Indians. Together, they harnessed Indian resources and human capital to underpin the Company's growth and rule.[34]

For instance, Frykenberg has demonstrated how the Company in Madras, from its beginning in 1639, relied on the goodwill and support of the local Tamil and Telugu elites for its growth and dominance. The Vaiṣṇative elites validated the sale of Madras to the Company in the temple city of Tirupati, and, in turn, the Company agreed to mint coins featuring Vaiṣṇavite deities.[35] Frykenberg asserted that the local elites believed the Company brought "peace, protection and prosperity to local gods and notables alike."[36] By then, the Company's fate relied on the "cultural, economic, ritual, and socio-political support" of its Indian partners. Its roots sank deeply into the fabric of Indian society.[37]

Indian elites, including princes, bankers, agents, soldiers, spies, social service providers, and civil servants recruited from Brahmins, Kṣatriyas, and Vaiśyas, as well as influential Sudras, controlled and regulated the "vital flows of information and revenue," determining the fate of the Company.[38] To maintain favourable relations with these Indian partners, the Company's Court of Directors in London

---

34 Robert Frykenberg: India to 1858. The Oxford History of British Empire. Vol. V: Historiography. Oxford 2007, 194–213, here 198–200.

35 Frykenberg: The myth of English as a 'colonist' imposition upon India, 306: Indians helped the officers of the Company from its inception. For example, when Francis Day purchased Madras in 1639, "Velugoti Nayakas of Kalahasti and Chandragiri" (e.g. Damarla Vengadappa) negotiated terms and conditions with him. They sent him a gold *shananam* ('deed') that recognised the East India Company as their vassal. Soon, "artisans and goldsmiths of the Great Temple at Tirupati had minted Company's coins "stamped with the image of Sri Venkateswara which lent further legitimacy to the new principality." Additionally, the Indian inhabitants of Madras conducted elaborate rituals and ceremonies to welcome and support the Company.

36 Frykenberg: The myth of English as a 'colonist' imposition upon India, 306.

37 Frykenberg: The myth of English as a 'colonist' imposition upon India, 307. V. Raghavan: The Sarva-Deva-Vilāsa edited with Critical Introduction and Notes. rpt. Madras, 1958, here 68–69: Initially, Sanskrit-knowing Indians viewed the Company officers as foreigners (*hūṇa*), outcast men (*mleccha*), devouring whales (*timiṅgila*), the white-faced ones (*śvetamukha*), those with evil pride (*nīca uddhati*), and *Rāvanna*. As some elites benefited from the Company, they changed their minds favourably towards the Company as benefactors. Those Indian elites, who had experienced their mental transformation, maintained the Company in India.

38 Robert Eric Frykenberg: Christian Missions and the Raj. In: Missions and Empire. Ed. by Norman Etherington. Oxford 2005, 107–131, here 107–108.

opposed the spread of Christianity in India. This was not due to a lack of interest in religious matters but a strategic decision to avoid potential conflicts with the local elites, who were often deeply rooted in their spiritual and cultural traditions. For example, in 1793, the Pious Clause was not included in the renewed Company's Charter (Chapter 11), and as a result, Christians in Madras were prohibited from building a church for their private use.[39]

During Schwartz's era, the Company strategically aligned itself with the rulers of Tanjore and the Nawab of Arcot, Wallajah, underscoring the complexity and strategic nature of the Company's relationships in India.[40] These elites enlisted the Company's military prowess to safeguard their families, religious priests and domains. Remarkably, without apparent conflicts of interest or remorse, the Company supported Wallajah, Tanjore's archenemy, while extracting as much wealth as possible from Tanjore's elites, a stark illustration of the imbalance and exploitation in the Company's relationships in India.

4 Limitations of this Biography

This biography does not provide a comprehensive history of the Kingdom of Tanjore or the East India Company in Tanjore, nor does it survey all available literature on these subjects. Instead, it only considers the histories of key individuals and places related to Schwartz's contributions to peace, justice, and harmony ministry. Representative archival materials critically assess Schwartz's role as an envoy for peace, justice and social harmony. Therefore, it does not enumerate the vast array of archival materials by and about Schwartz in Chennai, Halle (Saale), London, Oxford and Copenhagen.

This biography does not provide biographical details of the Company's traders, civil servants, military officers, and others with whom Schwartz interacted. Readers can easily find them in printed materials[41] and online resources.[42] Biographical details of the German Lutheran pietist missionaries, Tamil catechists,

---

39 Arthur Mayhew: Christianity and the Government of India. London 1929, 49. During the time of Cornwallis, the Company officers talked of holding no horse races on Sundays and closing all Company's offices. However, in consideration of their interactions with and dependence on non-Christian Indians, they conducted their business as usual. After the British Parliament rejected including a Pious Clause into the renewed charter of the Company in 1793, Company's directors in London "agitated regarding the condition of a church-building in Madras" and charged their representatives there to preserve 'the ascendancy which our national character has acquired over the minds of the natives of India neither by disregard of the external observances of religion nor by any assimilation to Eastern manners or opinions, but rather by retaining the distinctions of our national principles, character, and usages' Wise council, indeed, on which Lord Wellesley was shortly to take vigorous action." Consequently, Indians wondered whether the Company had any religious background at all.

40 K. Rajayyan: British Annexation of the Carnatic, 1801. In: Proceedings of the Indian History Congress. Part 2 of Vol. 32, 1970, 54–62, here 55: The Company's army assisted Nawab Wallajah during the Second Carnatic War (1749–1754) in repelling the French, Hyder Ali, the Nizam, the Marathas, and the Poligars from the Carnatic area. At that time, the rice harvest was a failure. However, Schwartz persuaded the local farmers to work smarter and cultivate enough crops to feed themselves, fellow civilians and the army.

pastors, and others associated with Schwartz are available in the printed and online materials: J. F. Fenger's *List of Evangelical Lutheran Missionaries in India* contains brief biographies of fifty-four missionaries.[43] His list of Evangelical Lutheran Native Ministers has biographical details of sixteen Tamil Lutheran pastors.[44] A more up-to-date version of biographies of women and men associated with Schwartz is available in the excellent online resources of the August Hermann Francke Study Centre–Archive and Library.[45]

This biography does not focus on Schwartz's life and work in Tranquebar and Tiruccirāppaḷḷi but on his stay and work in Tanjore. During his tenure in Tiruccirāppaḷḷi, he began engaging with people outside the institutional church, specifically with Company military officers and their soldiers. However, his public ministries blossomed in Tanjore. Therefore, the fifth chapter of this biography, which is more extensive than all other chapters, is of utmost importance as it provides the context in which Schwartz's contributions as an ambassador for faith, kingmaker, social reformer, educator, and influencer of mission-related policies took place.

This biography does not discuss Schwartz's posthumous influence on the expanded version of the Pious Clause in the renewed Company Charter of 1833 (3&4 Will. IV, c. 95). The British Parliament terminated the Company's trading functions in India and permitted its political and administrative tasks on territories to be held in trust for the British monarch and the Company's Government of India.[46]

This biography does not provide verbatim translations of the German and Tamil texts but paraphrases them to highlight their main points. It retains the Anglicized names of places still in use (e.g., Tranquebar, Tanjore, and Dindigul). It replaces the archaic Anglicized place names (e.g., Trichinopoly, Tinnevelly, and Palaiyamkotta) with their modern forms (Tiruccirāppaḷḷi, Tirunelveli, and Pāḷaiyamkōṭṭai). Names of Tamil persons and places found in the German source materials follow a modified system of transliteration, as outlined in the Tamil Lexicon, to ensure easy recognisability.[47] For example, the names of Tamil

---

41 Charles C. Prinsep: Record of Services of the Honourable East India Company's Civil Servants in the Madras Presidency from 1741 to 1858. London 1885.

42 The History of Parliament: British Political, Social & Local History. URL: https://www.historyofparliamentonline.org/ (accessed on 06.01.2025).

43 Johannes Ferdinand Fenger: History of the Tranquebar Mission. Transl. Emil Francke. Tranquebar 1863, 312–320.

44 Fenger: History of the Tranquebar Mission, 323–324.

45 August Hermann Francke Study Centre–Archive and Library. URLs: https://www.francke-halle.de/en/science/archives-and-library and https://archiv.francke-halle.de/start.fau?prj=ifaust8_afst (accessed on 06.01.2025).

46 The Government of India Act of 28 August 1833 declared the Company's Governor-General in Calcutta to be the representative of the British monarch and the British Government. It centralised administrative control under the Governor General in Council. It permitted British, European, North American, and other Christian missionaries, as well as benevolent individuals, to work towards improving the moral and religious lives of Indians. All individuals should respect Britain's administrative and political principles, including the free exercise of religion.

47 Tamil Lexicon. Vols. I–VI and a Supplementary Volume. Madras 1982.

catechists such as "Ignacimuthu," "Södinaiken," "Saruweien," and "Sattianadan" appear as Iṉṉācimuttu, Jōtināyakkaṉ, Saruvaiyaṉ, and Sattiyanātaṉ.

In addition to the archival manuscripts, this biography frequently refers to unpublished and published versions of Schwartz's letters, diaries and reports, the *Memoirs of Rev. Daniel Joseph Jænicke* (1833), Hugh Pearson's *Memoirs of the Life and Correspondence of the Reverend Christian Frederick Swartz* (1834) and Wilhelm Germann's *Missionar Christian Friedrich Schwartz* (1870).

5 Structure of this Biography

This biography comprises twelve chapters divided into three broad categories. The first five chapters delve into Schwartz's life and work within diverse socio-political contexts. The second category is the sixth chapter, which analyses the characteristics of Schwartz's writings, their published versions, and their impact on select individuals across India, Germany and the United Kingdom. The third category encompasses the remaining six chapters, which are both thematic and chronological.

The first chapter immerses readers in the socio-political contexts of the Kingdom of Tanjore and the Company in Madras and Tanjore. The second chapter vividly portrays Schwartz's upbringing, his calling to missionary work, and his ministry in Tranquebar, Tiruccirāppaḷḷi and Tanjore. The third chapter highlights Schwartz's resilience, focusing on his life and ministry in Tranquebar from 1750 to 1762, a period marked by significant adjustment and learning. The fourth chapter highlights the reasons for his move to Tiruccirāppaḷḷi and his ministry there from 1762 to 1778. The fifth chapter is extensive, chronicling his ministries in public places from 1778 until he died in 1798, during which he tirelessly worked as an envoy for peace, justice, and social harmony.

The following seven chapters are thematic. The sixth chapter compiles primary and secondary materials about Schwartz in Tamil, German, and English. It examines how he acquired diverse linguistic skills and worked without the aid of interpreters. It also examines his two Tamil texts, the Catechism and Dialogues, revealing Schwartz's profound theological thoughts through his vocabulary. This chapter identifies the recipients of Schwartz's letters and reports, concluding with an analysis of significant past biographical attempts in English, German, and other languages.

The seventh chapter, the crux of his biography, explores Schwartz's diplomatic endeavours to establish peace, justice, and social harmony. His interactions ranged from meetings with Hyder Ali, the king of Tanjore, and representatives of the Wadiyars of Mysore, to Company officers, as well as engagements with Tanjore emigrants and missionaries in Tranquebar, Cuddalore, Tiruccirāppaḷḷi, and Madras. This chapter situates Schwartz's choices and actions within the dynamically changing socio-political and economic contexts of his era.

The eighth chapter corrects the current common perception of Schwartz solely as Serfoji's kingmaker. It expands his role to include Ameer Singh, Tanjore's interim ruler from 1787 to 1798, whose name Schwartz proposed to the Company. For the first time, this chapter quotes the answers of the twelve Brahmin pandits, who had denounced Serfoji's adoption after receiving bribes from Ameer Singh.[48] It also discusses Schwartz's efforts to prove Serfoji's legitimate adoption through the collection of scripture passages. Additionally, this chapter describes the tension between Ameer Singh and Serfoji. It briefly discusses Serfoji's administration and contributions to art, literature, and science. It highlights Schwartz's wise approach in introducing Serfoji to Christian teachings while respecting his religious freedom.

The ninth chapter investigates Schwartz's significant contributions to social transformation. Disturbed by the atrocities in Tanjore, Schwartz worked tirelessly to establish a fair and transparent justice system. His efforts to reform the lifestyle of the Kaḷḷar community and create job opportunities for the poor are particularly commendable.

The tenth chapter examines Schwartz's significant contributions to the field of education. Modelled after the Halle Pietists' institutions, he established Tamil-medium schools for poor and orphaned children, as well as English-medium schools for upper *varṇa* and *jāti* children, in Tanjore, Ramanathapuram, and Sivaganga. His foresight in training, employing, and supervising various professionals is noteworthy.

The eleventh and twelfth chapters reveal unknown details about Schwartz's relationship with the Pious Clause of the Company in 1793 and 813. It uncovers Montgomery Campbell's opposition to the Pious Clause in 1793 and Schwartz's powerful *Defence of Mission* (1794), which argues that Christian missionary work could offer an alternative framework for organising lives and thoughts positively. The British Parliament's inclusion of the Pious Clause in the renewed Company Charter of 1813 marked a significant milestone in the formal establishment of the first Anglican bishopric in Calcutta in 1814.

Following a brief conclusion, this biography includes six appendices with vital information about Schwartz, a glossary of non-English words, and a bibliography. The appendices include a list of Company governors and presidents in Madras, Schwartz's English translation of the answers by the twelve Marathi pandits, a summary of his eighteen Tamil dialogues, Montgomery Campbell's reply to Schwartz, Schwartz's Christmas reflection, and a verbatim transcript from Schwartz's monuments in Tanjore and Madras. A glossary of vital non-English words helps readers comprehend Schwartz's ministry within its time's socio-cultural, political, and conceptual environment.

---

48 I, the author of this biography, am grateful to Professor Richard Young for bringing to my attention the following essay on Marathi Brahmin pandits in Banaras and their association with fellow Marathi Brahmin pandits in other regions, such as Tanjore. He pointed out that the Marathi Brahmin pandits, too, accepted diverse inducements and pronounced their opinions. For further details, see Rosalind O'Hanlon: Letters Home–Banaras pandits and the Maratha regions in early modern India. In: Modern Asian Studies 44, 2010, issue 2, 201–240.

Map of South India, 1801, copper engraving [= Die Halbinsel Indiens vom Kistnah-Flusse bis Cap Comorin: mit den Theilungen von Tippoo Sahebs Ländern nach den im Jahre 1792 durch Marquis Cornwallis und 1799 durch Marquis Wellesley abgeschlossenen Tractaten / entworfen von I. Rennell. Weimar: Verlag des Industrie-Comptoirs, 1801]. Halle, Francke Foundations: BFSt: S/KEF: X 41-5

Chapter 1

Socio-Political Contexts

1.1 The Kingdom of Tanjore

Schwartz arrived in Tranquebar in 1750. At that time, Pratāpasimha (reigned 1739–1763) ruled the Kingdom of Tanjore, of which Tranquebar had been a port town rented out to the Danes since 1620. Pratāpasimha prepared his kingdom for better administration and revenue collection. He divided it into five *subas* (districts) and appointed a *subedar* to oversee each *suba*, assigning specific tasks to meet its civil and military needs. *Amildars* assisted the *subedar* and administered the day-to-day activities. The subedar and amildar collected taxes, protected the forts, fed the soldiers, maintained various temples, and provided for the priests. During the war, their armies destroyed fields, fruit trees, roads, paths, water channels, reservoirs, and wells of their enemies.[1] Despite challenges, the people of Tanjore, particularly the farmers, demonstrated remarkable resilience. They continued to pay taxes, even as the revenue officers extracted this from artisans, traders, palm wine (toddy) sellers, and visitors. The sixteen port cities belonging to the Kingdom of Tanjore, such as Tranquebar, Tirumullaivācal, and Nagari, paid higher taxes. Pratāpasimha asked his customs officers at toll booths to collect special taxes (*tīrvai*) from non-Indians entering Tanjore: a foreigner who walked paid five Pagodas; if they rode a horse, they spent more Pagodas.[2]

Pratāpasimha used the revenues to fund wars, build new temples, endow prominent temples and religious festivals,[3] and establish residential quarters for Brahmins (*agrahāras*).[4] He paid substantial amounts of war reparations to the Nawab of Carnatic, the Company's government, and the French East India Company for their support in the previous years.[5] If he delayed or did not pay these amounts, Nawab Mohammad Ali Wallajah of Arcot (1717–1795) and the

---

1 P. Suresh Kumar: The Carnatic Wars and Tanjore Politics 1736–1764. Diss. phil. Tirunelveli 2012. URL: http://hdl.handle.net/10603/133782 (accessed on 20.11.2024), here 170–174.

2 Suresh Kumar: The Carnatic Wars, 180.

3 S. Chinnaiyan: Social History of Thanjavur 1532–1799. Diss. Phil. Trichy 1999, here 163: Pratāpasimha "established *Abiseka kattalai* for pooja and other purposes at Kottur Kolunthiswarar" temple.

4 R. Krishnamurthi: The Hindu Religious Institutions: State and Society in the Thanjavur Region, AD 1532–1855. Diss. Phil. Trichy 2000, here 70: Pratāpasimha established the Dabir *Agrahara* in Kumbakonam in honour of his minister Dabir and the Sakvaramba *Agrahara* at Thirupuvanam.

5 Suresh Kumar: The Carnatic Wars, 189–191: In 1749, the French and Dost Ali, the Nawab of the Carnatic, asked Pratāpasimha to reimburse the military expenses incurred in defending Tiruchirappalli. Simultaneously, Dost Ali demanded that Pratāpasimha pay him three crore

Company fought against him. For example, on January 9, 1751, Pratāpasimha received a *farman* (order) from the Mughal Emperor in Delhi, which required him to pay tribute only to the Emperor himself.[6] After Pratāpasimha informed Governor Floyer in Madras of this order, the Governor and Nawab Muhammad Ali refused to accept it and required Pratāpasimha to pay off all arrears immediately. Pratāpasimha imposed higher taxes on agricultural produce, houses, shops and cattle to meet this demand.[7] Most people "groaned under the weight of heavy taxation" and left Tanjore. When Pratāpasimha died in 1763, he was a tributary to the Nawab's extractions. He left large debts. Severe problems with neighbouring rulers and the Company remained unresolved.

Tulāji, a son of Pratāpasimha, ascended the throne and inherited his father's debts and problems. Instead of solving these pressing problems immediately, he continued his father's example in repairing or building Vaiṣṇavite temples.[8] Therefore, local people called him a "Servant of the Vaiṣṇavite Temples" (*Viṣṇu ālayattoṇṭaṉ*). Like his father, he also established Brahmin settlements and assigned the income of certain villages to support them. To perform these duties, he taxed his subjects heavily. After two years of his rule, by 1765, he could pay off his father's debts to the Company and the Nawab.[9] The Nawab was not satisfied with the revenues from Tulāji. In 1770, he decided to conquer Tulāji[10] and waited for an opportunity to arise. When Tulāji attacked the ruler of Ramanathapuram in 1771 to reclaim Hanumantagudi, which his father had lost, the Nawab enlisted the military support of the Company and defeated Tulāji. He then forced Tulāji to pay thirty-two lakhs of Rupees as a war indemnity and to surrender the localities of Ārani and Hanumantagudi. The Nawab, with the help of the Company, imprisoned Tulāji for three years (1773–1776), looted the wealth

---

Rupees and hand Karaikal over to the French. As he delayed the payment, Chanda Sahib attacked Tanjore. After three months, Pratāpasimha agreed to pay him seven lakhs of Rupees. He donated six crore and sixty lakhs of Rupees to the French army under the command of Louis XV during the Seven Years' War (1756–1763).

6 BL MSS Eur D 1208, 15: according to Pratāpasimha this *farman* from the Mughal Emperor read as follows: "Four days ago I received a Phirmaund [*farman*] from the Great Mogul, together with a Letter from the Vakeel of Pandany Punt, as also from my own Vakeel; the purport of the Phirmaund was as follows: 'Your bravery and firmness have been represented to me by the Gazedy Cawn Phearoaz Jung; I hear that the enemy were insulting you, though my orders were to the contrary. I have, therefore, ordered an army to chastise them. Balazee Bajers Perdany has also detached his troops; those will soon arrive in your province. Do not pay the tribute money to any. About this and other affairs, you are to apply to my Court. Be perfectly easy in your own place.' I went out and received the said Phirmaund with great honour and respect. As you are my best friend and protector, I thought it necessary to communicate this to you, which I hope will give you joy. Also for further matters, I refer you to Manojee's letter, written to my order. Continue to write to me of your health and welfare."

7 Krishnamurthi: The Hindu Religious Institutions, 101–105.

8 Chinnaiyan: Social History of Thanjavur, 159–160 and 173: Tulāji built Namaskar Perumāḷ Temple, Manikanda Perumal Temple, Mēla Ciṅka Perumāḷ Temple and the like. He had appointed Brahmin priests to officiate even in the temples of protective deities. Krishnamurthi: The Hindu Religious Institutions, 59–65 and 73: Tulāji repaired Māyūranātacāmi Temple in Mayiladuthurai and Veḷḷai Piḷḷaiyār Temple in Tanjore. He donated substantial amounts of money to various temples and charitable institutions and fed Brahmins. He brought the golden

of Tanjore, and impoverished the region. Tulāji did not recover from this humiliation. In 1776, Governor George Pigot (1719–1777)[11] reinstated him as the King of Tanjore.[12] Tulāji's revenue collectors extorted the people more severely. The sudden death of his two sons increased his agony. In January 1787, he adopted the nine-year-old boy Serfoji and entrusted him to Schwartz for education and protection. Tulāji died on 31 January 1787.

Upon Schwartz's request, the Company appointed Tulāji's half-brother, Ameer Singh, also known as Ramasamy, as an interim caretaker of the Kingdom of Tanjore to prevent rebellion and bloodshed. During his rule (1787–1798), Ameer Singh attempted to kill Serfoji and usurp the throne. He even resorted to bribing religious scholars to nullify Serfoji's adoption. The officers of the Company, noticing Ameer Singh's incompetence in governance, extorted Tanjore harshly, further perpetuating his injustice.

After three years of education in Madras, Serfoji returned to Tanjore in March 1796. Schwartz played a pivotal role in confirming Serfoji's adoption, utilising documentary evidence and submitting it to the officers of the Company, who then forwarded it to their superiors in Calcutta. This led the Company to depose Ameer

---

statue of Bangaru Kamakshi Amman from Kanchipuram to Tanjore and installed it in the temple that his father had built. He gratefully remembered how his father had invited the religious leader of Kanchipuram to settle in Kumbakonam. He built settlements for Brahmins in Rameswaram and Velānkulam.

9 BL MSS Eur D 1208, 16: On 14.10.1765, the Company noted that Tulāji had "fully performed all the engagements entered into by his father and the whole sum stipulated to be paid by him, hath been received into your treasury; he has likewise punctually paid his annual tribute to the Nabob, and we have the further satisfaction of assuring you, that we are on the best terms with him."

10 BL MSS Eur D 1208, 17: On 31.01.1770, the Company chastised Tulāji for supplying "money and provisions" to the French and for not paying the July instalment of his annual tribute to Wallajah.

11 SPCK D 36, Microfilm Frame 181: In 1755, George Pigot became the Governor and Commander-in-Chief at Madras. On 07.02.1756. the SPCK congratulated him and requested his assistance to their 'English' missionaries in Madras, namely the German Lutheran Pietist missionaries Johann Christian Breithaupt and Johann Philipp Fabricius. SPCK D 36, Microfilm Frame 244: Likewise, when Robert Palk became the Governor of Madras in 1763 following Pigot's resignation, the SPCK sent him the following message: "The Society for Promoting Christian Knowledge take the liberty of addressing you in like manner, they have formerly done your worthy predecessors, the government of Fort St. George, with their humble request that you will be pleased to take the Reverend Messers Fabricius & Breithaupt, their missionaries at Madras under your protection and give them such countenance as their own personal merit and the excellent cause they are engaged in shall deserve. And as the Governor of Fort St. George have all along permitted the Society to consign whatever has been sent for the service of the Mission to the care of the Governor, so they humbly hope that you will be so good as to grant them the same indulgence."

12 BL MSS Eur D 1208, 39: On 04.10.1776, Pigot wrote from St. Thomas Mount near Madras to Tulāji: "I have done myself the pleasure of writing two letters to you from this place. I hope this will find you and your family in perfect health and that everything is conducted to your satisfaction, for I please myself with the hopes that the Dubash and all your old servants are very dutiful and affectionate to you. The troublesome visitors you have with you will probably attempt to sow discord between you and your servants. But I dare say you will guard against anything of that kind. I am Pigot."

Singh and install Serfoji as the ruler of Tanjore in June 1798. In the absence of Schwartz, who had died in February 1798, the Company treated Serfoji as their puppet. He, too, signed a treaty with the Company that was prepared beforehand without his consultation. Accordingly, he was henceforth only ceremonially king, his sway extending no further than the walled city of Tanjore. The Kingdom of Tanjore came fully under the Company's sway. The Company's civil servants collected revenues from Tanjore and gave Serfoji a stipend. By 1801, they annexed the Kingdom of Tanjore and declared it their territory. However, Serfoji remained the king of Tanjore until he died in 1832.

1.2 Partnership between the Company and Tanjore Elites

1.2.1 The Company Raj

In this biography, the word "Company" refers to the English East India Company and its various mutations in the eighteenth century. The Sanskrit noun *rājya* refers to a sovereign country, characterised by its distinct bureaucracy and politics. As an adjective, this word implies kingship. When the Company began to fortify its settlements to safeguard its immovable and movable assets, administrative and business structures, and personnel, it began to evolve as a Raj. At its formation in 1600, the Company was treated as a legal entity with the rights and obligations of a private British person, including the ability to enter into contracts, lend and borrow money, "sue and be sued," hire employees, own assets, and pay taxes.[13] As such, Indians would eventually view the Company as *Bahadur*.[14] In their mind, the Company represented a legitimate government, namely a *Raj*, with all its legal and moral privileges and obligations.

In 1639, the Company purchased the territory where the current Fort St. George stands as its headquarters. Soon, it became an independent *paṭṭanam* (city, i.e., White Town) with its administrative and military apparatuses. By 1684, it had become a Presidency with expanded administrative and judicial machinery. After the *Regulating Act of India* (1773) and *Pitt's India Act* (1784), discussed below in Sections 1.2.2 and 1.2.3, the Company's Madras became a Raj with political and judicial claims over tributary states of Nawab Muhammad Ali Wallajah and King Tulāji of Tanjore. Courtenay Ilbert (1841–1924) explained the gradual but significant transformation of the Company from a trading corporation into a powerful regional government resting on a two-fold source:

---

13 Rorabacher: Property, Land, Revenue, and Policy, 242.

14 Pramod K. Nayar: The British Raj–Keywords. London 2017, here 23–24. This honorific Mughal word *bahadur* meant "brave warrior." Since the mid-eighteenth century, Indian elites referred to the English East India Company as "Company Bahadur" and acknowledged the Company's political and cultural authority. They conceded their rights and powers to it. They also demonstrated their loyalty towards it.

15 Courtenay Ilbert: The Government of India Being a Digest of the Statue Law relating thereto with Historical Introduction and Illustrative Documents. Oxford 1898, here 1.

> British authority in India may be traced, historically, to a twofold source. It is derived partly from the British Crown and Parliament, partly from the Great Mogul and other native rulers of India. In England, the powers and privileges granted by royal charter to the East India Company were confirmed, supplemented, regulated, and curtailed by successive Acts of Parliament, and were finally transferred to the Crown.[15]

When King Pratāpasimha ascended the throne of Tanjore in 1739, the Company raised sufficient funds to cover the expenses of its armies, British bureaucrats, and Indian employees, including interpreters, mediators, sepoys, spies, police personnel, and other providers of essential services.[16] King Pratāpasimha could not ignore the Company's technological, economic, and territorial power. In a defensive move, he negotiated a treaty with them.[17] By the mid-1760s, Nawab Wallajah had a precarious financial situation, owing the Company more than £1,000,000. Unable to raise such a large sum, he was forced to borrow privately at high interest from the Company's European servants, effectively allowing them to dictate his governance.[18] Consequently, this period marked extreme corruption among the Company's servants, resulting in a situation in which the Company itself went bankrupt. In contrast, its servants became fabulously wealthy and were contemptuously known as *Nabobs* in English society.

In this context, particularly in 1761, the Company's Court of Directors in London decided not to send any further funds to help the Company recover from its mounting debts. Instead, they encouraged the Company to be content with subsidies from Bengal or to borrow money from Indian bankers. Hence, the Company doubled the cost of providing military protection to Nawab Wallajah, his family, and his territories. They increased the price of weapons and ammunition by 30%. They were not bothered about Wallajah's economic stability and ignored his complaint about this rise. This "chronic acrimony between Madras and the Nawab" lasted over twenty years, and the servants of the Company, both European and Indian, privately tried to squeeze more money from the Nawab than he could

---

16 Some of these battles include the Battle of Ambur (1749), the Battle of Āraṇi (1751), the Battle of Chengalpattu (1752), the Battle of Sri Rangam and Golden Rock (1753), the Battle of Plassey (1757) in Bengal and the Battle of Vandavasi (1760). These battles ultimately defeated the French East India Company and resulted in the capture of Pondicherry (1761). George Pigot administered Pondicherry from 1761 to 1763. Allen, 1898, 268: The SPCK missionaries returned to Cuddalore and Madras following this victory. They built a "school for the children of Christian natives" at Madras in 1761. At Cuddalore, "the Governor granted a tract of land for the use of the mission."

17 As peace prevailed, Schwartz and Johann Balthasar Kohlhoff undertook a missionary journey from Tranquebar to Madras. They met refugees from Pondicherry in Tranquebar and along their way to Madras. For details of this journey from January to June 1760, see AFSt/M 2 D 38 : 1a printed in HR, 95, 1764, 1108–1559.

18 Andrew Mackillop: Fashioning a 'British' Empire: Sir Archibald Campbell of Inverell & Madras, 1785–91. In: Military Governors and Imperial Frontiers c. 1600–1800: A study of Scotland and Empires. Ed. by Andrew MacKillop and Steve Murdoch. Leiden 2003, 205–231, here 210: Muhammad Ali "borrowed from company servants, private traders and officers at interest rates" from 12–30%. Alternatively, he employed "associates of such creditors at his court" or in his army.

afford.[19] Nawab Wallajah, in turn, extorted money from the Kingdom of Tanjore with even greater ferocity than before. The *Treaty of Paris* (1763), which recognised Wallajah as the lawful sovereign over the entire Carnatic, including the Kingdom of Tanjore, emboldened him, and he extorted more violently from Tanjore.

At the same time, the Company expanded its presence in Tanjore and the surrounding areas. In April 1764, they appointed James Rennell (1742–1830) as the Surveyor-General to map their territories and identify significant places, forts, waterways and travel routes. Four years later, in 1768, they recruited about 25,000 more sepoys. These sepoys enabled the Company, which was increasingly becoming greedy, to extort and oppress the people more harshly, thereby increasing the misery of the ordinary people of Tanjore. Coupled with crop failures, the situation was a disaster for the people of Tanjore.[20]

Influential civil and military servants promoted their private trade without paying serious attention to the loss-making Company. By that time, the Company servants could rise in rank, according to seniority, from writers to factors, senior factors, and full-fledged merchants. They compensated their small salary with enormous profits from their private trade and "by money drawn from extortions and bribes."[21] This became known as "shaking the Pagoda Tree."

Without paying serious attention to the loss-making Company, influential civil servants maintained their trade and undermined the Company's trade. The Company's shareholders in London were not satisfied with the money they got from India. They assumed that the Company, with its characteristic treasury, military, political strategy and administrative capacities, would benefit from a loan from the British Government. Hence, in 1772, they requested a loan of £ 1,000,000 from the British Government. This request disappointed the British Government, which suspected the Company's style of governing its territories and its failure to generate the expected money for Britain.

When the Company's servants were unable to remit the required funds to their directors, shareholders, and family members, the British economy began to feel its impact. The Company's Court of Directors hailed from monied and influential families in or near London. They had experience in shipping and trade. They maintained connections to London's banks, markets, politics, and influential persons. Most of the Company's shareholders had family members working in or for the Company in India. Their livelihood depended on the money that they received from these family members. The Company employed over 4,000 workers

---

19 G. J. Bryant: The Emergence of British Power in India, 1600–1784: A Grand Strategic Interpretation, Woodbridge 2013, 189.

20 Henry Pattullo: An Essay upon the Cultivation of the Lands and Improvements of the Revenues of Bengal in London. London 1772, here 28: This 33-page report by Patullo, a servant of company's government in Bengal, urgently proposed that the Company could make Bengal "the most industrious, prosperous and happy nation that perhaps ever has existed," and this success would earn "the applause of the world, the grateful feelings of their happy subjects and an immense revenue." He wrote it amidst the Great Bengal Famine (1769–1773) that killed more than ten million Indians. This was when the Company attempted to conquer Tanjore and extract its resources more brutally.

21 Ilbert: The Government of India, 88.

in its warehouses in London and elsewhere. Approximately 2,500 crew members, 20,000–25,000 sailors, numerous shipbuilders, transporters, salespersons, accountants, and others worked for the Company.

As time passed, the British Government became dissatisfied with the parallel nature of the Company's governance in India and established a committee to investigate the Company's situation.[22] This committee proved that the avarice of the Company's officers in Bengal had caused the Bengal Famine (1769–1773), resulting in the deaths of one-fifth of the entire population of Bengal.[23] Vaughan considered these officers' unquenchable greed and violence to be worse than the disgusting cruelties of the ancient Romans.[24] They depleted the Company's treasury and competed to extort more money from Indians and transfer it privately (and corruptly) to Britain. In this process, they failed to address the pressing needs of Indians and overlooked the growing threat from Hyder Ali, who had defeated the Company in 1769.

In 1772 and 1773, the Company was so bankrupt that it could not pay the Bank of England more than £1.4 million and the King his annual due of £40,000. The British Government could not make the Company's employees jobless. It was unwilling to lose the Company that shaped almost every aspect of British life. At the same time, it did not want the Company to develop its governance freely, as its home government did, with the authority to collect taxes, land revenues, manage banks, maintain armies and navies, administer civil and military affairs, formulate foreign policy, and oversee law courts. Hence, the British Parliament intervened and offered a temporary loan to bail out the Company. In return, they imposed the government's sovereign authority on the Company's operations and possessions in Britain and India. They asked the Company to repay its debt with its profits and pay better dividends to its shareholders in Britain.[25]

---

22 Penelope Carson: The East India Company and Religion, 1698–1858. Woodbridge 2012, 19: By 1772, the trading company had become a sovereign power in India and required additional funds to support its civil and military administration. A loan from the Bank of England saved it from its utter collapse in 1772. The parliament established two committees to examine the Company's government affairs: the Select Committee investigated civil matters, and the Secret Committee prepared nine extensive reports on the company's government operations. IOR/E/4/871, 717–718: On 11 April 1785, the Court of Directors instructed their governors in India to "obey the orders of the Secret Committee as stipulated in the 15th and 16th clauses of the last Session of Parliament." This committee comprised Chairman Nathaneal Smith, Deputy Chairman William Devaynes and Laurence Sullivan. The Council of Directors informed the governors in India about the *Act for the better Regulation and Management of the Affairs of the East India Company and British Possessions in India and for Establishing a Court of Judicature for the more speedy and effective trial of persons accused of offences committed in the East Indies.*

23 Christina Smylitopoulos: Portrait of a Nabob: Graphic Satire, Portraiture and the Anglo-Indian in the Late Eighteenth Century. In: Canadian Art Review, 37, 2012, issue 1, 10–25.

24 James M. Vaughan: The Politics of Empire at the Accession of George III: The East India Company and the Crisis and Transformation of Britain's Imperial State. New Haven 2019, 226.

25 Rorabacher: Property, Land, Revenue, and Policy, 239.

1.2.2 The Regulating Act of India (1773)

The British Government, under the leadership of Frederick North (1732–1792), the Prime Minister of Britain (1770–1782), intervened to regulate (and not yet to take over) the Company's activities in India and passed the *Regulating Act of India* (13 Geo. III, c. 63) in June 1773.[26] It established the office of a Governor-General with a four-member council in Calcutta to oversee all civil and military affairs in the Company's territories in Bengal, Madras, and Bombay. The Governor-General and his council could

> issue such rules, ordinances, and regulations for the good order and civil government of the Company's settlement at Fort William, and the subordinate factories and places, as should be deemed just and reasonable, and should not be repugnant to the laws of the realm, and to set, impose, inflict, and levy reasonable fines and forfeitures for their breach.[27]

This Act also established the Supreme Court in Calcutta to adjudicate civil, criminal, military, and ecclesiastical matters in accordance with English law. It was a sign that the British King claimed and exercised his power over the Company and its possessions in India. The Company's Bengal Government became the Supreme Government with powers over the Company's Presidencies of Madras and Bombay. The Company's Governor-General should carry out the orders of the Company's Court of Directors, who were answerable to the Treasury of the British Government in London.[28]

This Act made the Governors of Madras and Bombay, along with their councils, answerable to the Governor-General and required prior approval before initiating any war. Nevertheless, its ninth clause stipulated that, except in emergencies to secure revenue from regions, the Governors of Madras and Bombay should not take independent decisions to wage war against any Indian rulers. Strangely, the same clause allowed them to obey the direct orders from the Court of Directors in London. For example, the Governor of Madras and his council were unable to decisively counter the threats posed by Hyder Ali and his son, Tipu Sultan. Consequently, ordinary people, especially farmers, suffered in the Kingdom of Tanjore. The maladministration of the Bengal Government created the Chalisa Famine (1783–1784) that killed more than eleven million Indians in the Bengal Presidency. It alarmed the British parliamentarians.

---

26 In other respects, 1773 was a crucial year for Britain: the Boston Tea Party shook the British monopoly in the tea trade, and the Bengal and Bombay Presidencies suffered grave financial setbacks.

27 Ilbert: The Government of India, 50–51.

28 For additional information about this Act, see B.B. Misra.: The Central Administration of the East India Company, 1773–1834. Bombay 1959.

29 M. Ruthnaswamy: Some Influences that made the British Administrative System in India. London 1939, 17: Ruthnaswamy assessed that the main purpose of *Pitt's India Act of 1784* was to end the division among the British parliamentarians. They had a personal stake in either defending or offending Wallajah against Tulāji and vice versa. For additional details, see Section 4.11 of this biography.

1.2.3 Pitt's India Act of 1784

Warren Hastings (1731–1818), the first Governor General (until 1785), identified the loopholes in the *Regulating Act of India of 1773* and attempted to reform the Company's functions. In the meantime, both Wallajah and Tulāji sent their representatives to England to seek support from King George III, British parliamentarians, the Court of Directors, and other influential individuals.[29] These agents in London bribed influential individuals, resulting in the emergence of two opposing groups of members of parliament in London. Those parliamentarians who supported Wallajah tried to execute policies that would suppress Tulāji. Simultaneously, those parliamentarians who supported Tulāji[30] opposed Wallajah's rule. Both groups shared falsified details about others.[31] For example, supporters of Wallajah published a pamphlet entitled *Considerations on the Conquest of Tanjore* to persuade King George III to order the Company to overthrow Tulāji and hand over the Kingdom of Tanjore to Wallajah. The controversies between the supporters of Wallajah and Tulāji garnered the most significant share of public attention in Britain.[32] The British people followed these controversies closely because they directly or indirectly affected their lives. Many of them had family members working either for Wallajah or Tulāji. Some British readers wondered why the Company protected Wallajah in wars and helped him amass wealth and territories. They also wanted to know why the Company humiliated Tulāji and forced him to obey Wallajah.[33]

William Pitt the Younger (1759–1806), the Prime Minister of the United Kingdom from 1783 to 1801, disliked the division among his MPs and how it hindered the steady flow of income from India into Britain.[34] He persuaded the British Parliament to enact an Act known as the *Pitt's India Act of 1784* (24 Geo. III, c. 25). Accordingly, the British Parliament created a Board of Control consisting of six honorary but influential Commissioners for the Affairs of India: the king appointed four of his privy counsellors to this board. The remaining two members were the Secretary of State and the Chancellor of the Exchequer. They

---

30 Ruthnaswamy: Some Influences, 17: Pitt did not like the MPs, who supported either the king of Tanjore or Nawab Wallajah. Most of the MPs had family members (e.g. sons, nephews and cousins), who worked either for the king of Tanjore or Wallajah. For example, Paul Benfield, in his capacity as an MP, supported Wallajah. John Sulivan, Hector Munro and J.C. Hippisley as MPs supported Tulāji. All of them knew Schwartz.

31 An Enquiry into the Policy of Making Conquests for the Mahometans in India by the British Arms, in Answer to a Pamphlet intituled "Considerations on the Conquest of Tanjore." London: J. Dodsley, [2]1779, 2: In 1769, Wallajah sent his gifted and passionate emissaries to England to publish informative booklets extolling him as the ideal ruler for the benefit of Britain and to obtain British favours for his rule in southern India.

32 An Enquiry into the Policy, 1.

33 An Enquiry into the Policy, 16.

34 Carson: The East India Company and Religion, 18: Pitt the Elder believed that the company's governments in India brought not only Asian wealth to Britain but also the principles of despotic government. By enacting this law, Pitt did not aim at the welfare of the people of India, but at maintaining "*status quo* in Britain. [...] Despotic rule did not sit easily with Britain's self-perception as a free and incorrupt people."

controlled the civil, military, and economic aspects of the Company Raj in southern India.[35]

This Act created the office of the King's Army Commander-in-Chief to oversee the Company's military affairs. It made him one of the four members of the Council to advise the Governor-General. In the face of conflicting interests, the Governor-General could overrule the decision of this Council because he represented King George III and the British Parliament. Thus, he possessed two votes. The remaining Council members had one vote each. According to this Act, the Governor-General established a permanent settlement, allowing *zamindars* (large landowners) to retain their lands in perpetuity and exercise all rights to sell, mortgage, or transfer them to others. In return, they should pay the Company a fixed amount as tax. If they failed to pay their annual tax, the Company could auction their land.[36]

This Act viewed the Company's territories in India as British. Consequently, the Court of Directors astonishingly equated the Company with Britain. For example, on 8 April 1789, they confirmed receipt of Ameer Singh's letter of 1 June 1787 and congratulated him on his accession to the Throne of Tanjore. They further stated that King Tulāji "felt and acknowledged the friendship and protection of the British Nation." Likewise, Ameer Singh could depend on the Company for protection and guidance. They pointed out that their "Government in Madras" would remind Ameer Singh of the revenues due to them. They urged him to administer justice for the prosperity of all people under his rule and not to grant lands to anyone. They suggested establishing warehouses for British merchants to temporarily store their goods and organise periodical fairs for ordinary people. They praised the friendship between King Ameer Singh and "the British Nation, which neither time nor chance can ever lessen or dissolve." The Court of Directors welcomed Schwartz's idea of running English-medium schools in Tanjore and gladly set aside specific sums for this school. They concluded the letter:

> There is nothing we have more at heart than the prosperity of the Kingdom of Tanjore and the maintaining Your Excellency in the Government of the Country. These are the foundation of all our orders to the Government at Madras. Your Excellency may, therefore, rest perfectly assured of the inviolable friendship of the East India Company.[37]

Pitt's India Act of 1784 domesticated the Company's government in Bengal, Madras and Bombay. On 9 December 1784, the Company's Court of Directors in London instructed their Governor in Madras to promote "British interests" in their territories, as they believed this would foster "peace in India."[38] When they appointed George Macartney Governor of Madras on 10 March 1785, the Court of Directors expected him to ensure the Company's new self-understanding as an

---

35 Ilbert: The Government of India, 65.

36 *Pitt's India Act of 1784* remained in power until 1858 and paved the way for the British Government to gradually take complete control of the company's governments and their operations in India.

37 IOR/E/A/875, 699–715,

38 IOR/E/4/871, 421.

extension of the British Government in India.[39] On 21 September 1785, they asked Macartney to report the Company's day-to-day activities to four boards: (1) The Board of Council, which resembled the council "lately established by the Act of Parliament for regulating the affairs of India." It was the Superior Council to which the following three councils were accountable. 2) The Military Board, comprising the chief commanding officer and other senior members of the Company, should maintain peace in all British settlements and care for the welfare of their soldiers. 3) The Board of Revenue should regulate and oversee the income and expenses of the Madras Presidency. Moreover, 4) the Board of Trade was responsible for all "commercial concerns" of the Madras Presidency. This Board was responsible for sending only the best quality goods for sale in Great Britain.[40]

On 17 July 1786, the Secret Committee within the British Parliament directed the Governor of Madras and his officers to transact with King Tulāji and "other powers under our protection" by preserving the "respect due to their situations." Simultaneously, their "language and conduct" should remind the Indian rulers of their continuous dependence on "the Power and Prosperity of the British Nation in India." The only way the Indian rulers acknowledged their reliance on the Company's Raj was to pay the dues regularly without accumulating any arrears.[41]

The Company's self-understanding as the "British Nation" in India gained significance over time. *Pitt's India Act of 1784* had far-reaching consequences. It changed the Company's self-understanding from that of a trading Company to that of a ruling British nation. The territories controlled by the Company's government in India became British, where British laws and practices applied. Governor-General Charles Cornwallis, who arrived in Calcutta in 1786, promoted it.[42] On 19 May 1790, the Commerce Department of the Company's Court of Directors in London requested that the Governor of Madras implement their regulation to curb foreign and illicit trade, which was adversely affecting the "interests of the Company as those of the British Nation."[43]

---

39 IOR/E/4/871, 669: As soon as Macartney delivered the letter from the Court of Directors, the person in charge of Fort St. George should resign. Macartney would be the governor of Fort St. George until he took over the office of the Governor General "upon the death, removal or resignation of Warren Hastings." IOR/E/4/872, 255–256, 258: On 08.03.1786, the Court of Directors recommended Macartney, "the faithful servant of the Company," as the "true Friend" of King Tulāji of Tanjore. They praised King Tulāji for being willing to pay his tribute to the company's Madras government as new proof of his "friendship and attachment to the British nation." They congratulated themselves on supporting and protecting King Tulāji in so many instances, restoring the Kingdom of Tanjore to him as the inestimable blessing of peace, and maintaining Tulāji's family in the safe possession of his hereditary Dominion.

40 IOR/E/4/872, 41–102.

41 IOR/E/4/872, 233–234, 242–244.

42 AFSt/M 1 C 30c : 7 partly quoted in NHR 4, 1790, issue 37, 95–96: On 29 September 1788, the missionaries in Tranquebar expressed their happiness about Cornwallis' arrival in Calcutta and his reforms to benefit India. "He halted the extraordinary luxury" company employees and prevented them from amassing wealth disproportionate to their income. Many company employees were unhappy with Cornwallis's reforms. However, the missionaries thanked God for the peace that the country could enjoy. They also stated that the Company had dispatched their army to recover Guntur from Tipu Sultan.

43 IOR/E/4/876, 722.

1.2.4 The East India Company Act of 1793

The British Parliament waited for opportunities to manage the Company's governmental affairs in India more effectively for Britain's benefit. On 11 June 1793, they passed the *East India Company Act of 1793*, technically known as 33 GEO. 3. c. 52. This Act renewed the Company's trading privileges for the next twenty years.[44] At that time, they expanded the executive powers of the Governor-General and subordinated the Presidencies of Madras and Bombay to his authority. If the Governor-General visited either Madras or Bombay, he would supersede the powers of the Governors in those regions. It enabled the Company's Bengal, Madras, and Bombay governments to represent Great Britain and claim its territories for Britain legally. The new territories, which the Bengal, Madras, and Bombay governments would acquire in India, would automatically become British, thereby paving the way for the establishment of the British Raj.

This Act permitted the governments of Bengal, Madras, and Bombay to grant trading privileges to individual British traders. Strangely, as discussed in Section 11, this Act did not make any provision for establishing the Church of England, which was an integral part of any British society then, because the prospects of the governments in Bengal, Madras, and Bombay depended on the goodwill and cooperation of non-Christian Indians, who opposed any provision for the spread of Christianity in India.

As illustrated in Appendix 1, the Company had fifteen Governors and presidents in the Council during Schwartz's ministry. None of them worked for the betterment of ordinary Indian inhabitants. Unlike them, Schwartz provided stability and reliability. He lived among them, spoke their language, understood their mindset, fears, and aspirations, and assisted them as much as possible in coping with the rapidly changing situations. Reciprocally, they trusted him more than their rulers and the Company officers.

---

[44] A Collection of Charters and Statutes, relating to The East India Company with an Appendix. London 1817, 288–333.

Chapter 2

Schwartz as an Ambassador for Faith

Schwartz, a Pietist Lutheran, diligently followed the theological teachings and practices of August Hermann Francke (1663–1727) and his successors until 1785. Gotthilf August Francke (1696–1769) observed Schwartz's earnest dedication to his studies at the school in Glaucha and his learning of the Tamil language under the guidance of Benjamin Schultze. Schwartz's commitment and passion for his studies were evident to all who knew him.[1] Francke, a key figure in Schwartz's life, played a significant role in persuading Schwartz to embark on a missionary journey to the Tamils in Tranquebar. Despite initial hesitation, Schwartz accepted this invitation, marking the beginning of his missionary journey, a decision influenced by Francke's persuasion.[2] Schwartz distanced himself from the humanistic teachings of August Hermann Niemeyer (1754–1828), the great-grandson of August Hermann Francke.[3] These teachings did not consider the Lord Jesus Christ an indispensable source for Christian beliefs, virtues, and life. These teachings were dry, empty, and bombastic.[4] The life-transforming power of the Gospel of the Lord Jesus Christ profoundly influenced Schwartz's missionary approach and interactions with Indians and Europeans he knew.

2.1 Schwartz Before Becoming an Ambassador for Faith

Schwartz's autobiography of December 1749 refers to Ezekiel 18 as the motto of his missionary service: God does not want anyone to die; instead, God desires their repentance from sin and their entire life. Following this motto, this

---

1 Schultze was a native of Sonnenburg, where Schwartz was also born. After serving as a missionary in Tranquebar and Madras, Schultze returned to Halle and desired to have his Tamil version of the Bible printed. He sought to train Schwartz to proofread his prints.

2 Halle's leading German Enlightenment philosophers were Christian Thomasius (1655–1728) and Christian Wolff (1679–1754). The document AFSt/M 2 B 9 : 14 contains a 1792 poem that narrates the negative impacts of the German Enlightenment on Christians. It states that followers of the Enlightenment rejected Christian beliefs and practices. They viewed the Bible as a book of fairy tales; their religion had no devil that tempted people to sin. They rejected the concepts of Trinity and Jesus as the Son of God.

3 Niemeyer was the son of Johann Konrad Philipp Niemeyer (1711–1767) and Auguste Sophie Freylinghausen (1717–1763), the granddaughter of August Hermann Francke through his daughter Johanna Sophia Anastasia Francke (1697–1771) married to Johann Anastasius Freylinghausen (1670–1739). Schwartz might have received a copy of Niemeyer's five-volume work, *Charakteristik der Bibel* ('Characteristics of the Bible'), published in 1775. Niemeyer later befriended the most famous German poet, Johann Wolfgang von Goethe. He became the Director of the Glaucha Institutions and the Chancellor of the University of Halle.

4 Germann: Missionar Christian Friedrich Schwartz, 329–330.

autobiography describes Schwartz's life in three stages. Firstly, it narrates his life at his parents' home: he was born on 26 October 1726; at baptism, he received his name Christian Friedrich; his parents were Georg Schwartz and Maria Grunerin (née Margarethe). He recalled how his mother, on her deathbed, had requested his father to help him get a theological education because she had dedicated him to God's service in a church.[5] At eight, his father sent him to the local school in Sonnenburg, where Rector Helm explained the importance of penitential prayers and self-reflection. This training helped him overcome inner conflicts in his later life.[6]

William Germann (1840–1902), Schwartz's German biographer, gives additional information about Schwartz's family: Maria Sophia was the family's first child. She was three years older than Schwartz. On 11 October 1736, his father married the twenty-year-old Ms. Sträußler, whose father oversaw the beautiful gardens of Duke Karl of Sonnenburg. Sträußler had five children: Dorothea Louisa (1739–1805) was the first daughter. She enjoyed a long life.[7] Carl Ludwig (1743–1811) was the family's fourth child.[8] Later, Schwartz would arrange for his education in Halle (Saale) and hoped to persuade him to join him as a missionary.[9] Schwartz's other three children died young.[10] He also had relatives with whom he was not in regular touch.[11]

At eight, Schwartz joined the primary school in the nearby village of Küstrin, where Rector Helm influenced and encouraged him to spend time in prayer and repentance. Schwartz also joined the school choir, which sang songs for all worship services, weddings, and funerals in Küstrin. He particularly liked

---

5 Germann: Missionar Christian Friedrich Schwartz, 1–8: Wilhelm Germann compared Schwartz's autobiography with his baptismal record and other documents in various places, and he provided the following complementary details: Schwartz was born on 08.10.1726 in Sonnenburg (then in Prussia, but now known as Słońsk in Poland). His father, Georg Schwartz, a baker by profession, was an immigrant to Sonnenburg. His mother was Margarethe, the widow of Michael Grundt. Schwartz was baptised on 17 October as Christoph Friedrich, yet he later preferred to call himself Christian Friedrich. On her deathbed in 1731, Margarethe asked her husband to send Schwartz to study theology and prepare him for church ministry.

6 AFSt/M 1 K 10 : 71.

7 AFSt/M 1 H 9 :12 and Germann: Missionar Christian Friedrich Schwartz, 284: Dorothea Louisa married Gottlieb Friedrich Ludwig Martini, and her married life was miserable. Schwartz supported her family financially. For example, on 28.02.1785, Schwartz sent money to her via his brother-in-law Christian Friedrich Knospe, the husband of his elder sister Maria Sophia. Just before his death, Schwartz arranged for a house and a piece of land for his sister. However, he got them registered in the name of her children.

8 Germann: Missionar Christian Friedrich Schwartz, 90 and 384: six months after he arrived in Tranquebar, Schwartz wrote to G. A. Francke on 09.01.1751 that he wanted to help his parents financially with his salary. He also requested Francke to admit Carl Ludwig to the Glaucha Institutions. Francke sent Inspector Campe 20 Dollars to Schwartz's parents and admitted Karl Ludwig to the Latin School. On 29.10.1765, Carl Ludwig joined the university in Halle and became an assistant to Johann Georg Knapp. Carl Ludwig worked at the school in Weinberg in Halle and the Latin school of the Glaucha Institutions for two years (1766–1768). His behaviour was so bad that the authorities dismissed him from the school in 1768. In 1772, he became the preacher at Magdeburg School for the Poor. However, on 05.12.1775, he received his ordination in Magdeburg and worked as a pastor at Hohenziatz near Magdeburg until he died in 1811.

harmonious singing in four parts. Although Schwartz had poor health, he took pleasure in sharing food with those in need.

The second part of Schwartz's autobiography explains his experiences at the Lutheran High School in Küstrin. There, he learned to appreciate the significance of the Ten Commandments in real-life situations. Deacon Stegmann assisted him in growing his spiritual life. After some time, he met a man named Kern, who acquainted him with the works of the great pietist August Hermann Francke (1663–1727) and his educational institutions in Halle (Saale). Schwartz read A. H. Francke's *Blessed Footsteps*.[12] This book impressed him deeply. His recurring foot pain, his emotional response to his early education, and his first job teaching the daughter of a local officer all reveal his remarkable resilience and determination. His ability to overcome these challenges at such a young age was genuinely inspiring.

Knowing Schwartz's desire to study at the university in Halle (Saale), a woman allowed him to accompany her and her son up to Berlin. Her son wanted to study at the Glaucha Institution. After arriving in Berlin, Schwartz borrowed a gun from his host and went hunting. He loaded ammunition powder into the gun barrel, yet it failed to shoot. Upon returning, his host exclaimed that it was a wonder the gun had not gone off. Schwartz felt a profound sense of divine protection.

Schwartz's third stage was his academic life in Halle. In 1746, at the age of twenty, he joined the Latin School and stayed in a hostel of the Glaucha Institutions, marking the beginning of his impressive academic journey.[13] Fortunately, we have 369 pages of his handwritten lecture notes, written in both

---

9 AFSt/M 1 C 27 : 10: On 14.10.1786, Schwartz stated that Carl Ludwig did not enjoy his pastoral ministry. He had borrowed 50 Dollars from Inspector Fabricius. He did not repay it. AFSt/M 1 C 26 : 9: On 14.02.1787, Schwartz wrote to his friend Sorge about his deep disappointment with Carl Ludwig, who had not responded to his letters. Yet, Schwartz arranged for the payment of Carl Ludwig's debts. Only after Schwartz's death did Carl Ludwig appreciate him, and he wanted to have his portrait.

10 Germann: Missionar Christian Friedrich Schwartz, 3, 9 and 22: The second child, Anna Katharina Elisabeth, was born in September 1740 and died in 1742. The third child, Johann Gottlieb, was born in 1747 and died soon thereafter. The fifth child, Georg Wilhelm, was born in January 1749 and died on 15.05.1749.

11 AFSt/M 1 C 50 : 5 dated 17.06.1815 and M 1 C 51 : 8 dated 29.11.1816: One such relative was Karl Georg von Raumer (1753–1833), a lawyer in Berlin, who requested Georg Christian Knapp about getting a donation from King Serfoji II. AFSt/M 1 C 52: 18. On 05.11.1817, Schwartz's brother-in-law, Knospe, wrote to Knapp requesting gift money from Serfoji II. It is unknown how either Knapp or Serfoji II responded to these requests.

12 Blessed Footsteps of the still living and reigning, loving and faithful God discovered through a truthful and extensive description of the Orphanage and other Institutions at Glaucha near Halle, 1701.

13 AFSt/M 1 K 5 : 18: Schwartz's roommate, Johann Friedrich Backe, added the following information (ca. 1800): Soon after he arrived at the Glaucha Institutions during Easter 1746, Abraham Johann Rüdel introduced Backe to Schwartz. At that time, two Greek students wanted to stay together; Schwartz gave up his room to them and moved into Backe's room; both became soul friends. Backe also narrated how Schwartz escaped from a party of drunk friends who tried to lure him into a duel. Schwartz decided that he would never attend such frolicking parties.

German and Latin, dating back to 1749.[14] Astonishingly, he kept these lecture notes throughout his career in India and passed them on to his adopted son, Johann Caspar Kohlhoff. These handwritten notes use difficult-to-decipher shorthand forms and abbreviations.[15] He repeatedly attended lectures on Systematic Theology and Moral Theology.

During his studies at Halle, Schwartz met Benjamin Schultze (1689–1760), who had worked as a missionary both in Tranquebar (1719–1725) and in Madras (1726–1743).[16] Schultze and Schwartz came from the same town of Sonnenburg. Therefore, Schultze had a particular affinity with Schwartz and persuaded him to study theology and the humanities. This advice disturbed him deeply, but he heeded it. He studied Moral Theology, Systematic Theology, Ethics, and Polemics with Siegmund Jakob Baumgarten, as well as Church History, the New Testament, Homiletics, and the Hermeneutics of the Pauline Epistles with Johann Georg Knapp, and the Hermeneutics of the Old Testament with Johann Anastasius Freylinghausen. Additionally, he pursued Mathematics, Physics, and Philosophy under the guidance of Professor Krüger. Schwartz fondly remembered his roommate Johann Friedrich Backe (1730–1805) and his constant spiritual encouragement. Both read the Bible together and prayed together. Shortly after, another fellow student, Johann Heinrich Bernhardt Hindenburg, joined them. Backe and Hindenburg enabled Schwartz to overcome his shyness and confidently engage with people.

Schwartz assumed that learning the Tamil language with Schultze would persuade him to become a missionary to India. Therefore, he hesitated to engage with it. However, Schultze taught Tamil to him and Friedrich Joachim Turow and trained them to proofread the Tamil Bible that he wanted to print in Halle. Schwartz and Turow spent six months learning Tamil. At that time, the authorities in Halle decided not to print the Tamil Bible in Halle. This decision disappointed Schwartz. However, he comforted himself by assuring that God had allowed him to learn this language for a specific purpose. During that time, Gotthilf August Francke (1696–1769), the director of the Glaucha Institutions, asked Schwartz to preach a sermon to the teachers at the Girls' School. Schwartz expounded on Matthew 12:33, emphasising the importance of seeking God's kingdom among his hearers. Francke liked Schwartz's message.

---

14 Bodleian Library: 72290ind-box1: Swartz's notes on divinity lectures at Halle. Its front page reads: "A Manuscript of the late Rev. C. F. Swartz, being the substance of the Divinity Lectures on which he attended while at the University of Halle—presented to the Lord Bishop of Madras [George John Trever Spencer] by Thos. [… unreadable words on] July 18, 1839. Presented to the Society for the Propagation of the Gospel in F[oreign] P[arts] by Mrs. Spencer, December 1877."

15 A careful study of these lecture notes would reveal the sources of Schwartz's theological convictions and their impact on his moral life.

16 AFSt/M 1 K 5 : 18: Backe added these details about Schwartz's meeting with Schultze: Benjamin Schultze behaved as if he were Schwartz's father. He taught Tamil to Schwartz and his friend Turow for two hours a day so that they could proofread the printed copies of the Tamil Bible. After a year, they were sad to learn that the Glaucha Institutions would not print Schultze's Tamil Bible.

2.2 Schwartz's Call to Be an Ambassador for Faith

Six months later, Francke invited him to go as a missionary to the Tamil people.[17] Immediately, Schwartz excused himself. At that time, Pastor Adam Struensee (1708–1791) encouraged him to become a pastor to the miners of Rottenburg. Schwartz and his friend Johann Friedrich Backe prayed for clarity. Soon, Deacon Johann Konrad Philipp Niemeyer encouraged him to go as a missionary to the Tamil people.[18] Schwartz accepted this call gratefully and hoped that his ministry would be fruitful.[19] He understood God as Ebenezer, who had helped him that far. He also believed that God would care for him throughout his life. He closed his autobiography with a resounding *Hallelujah*.

On receiving his calling to become a missionary to the Tamil, Schwartz hurried to his father. On 11 May 1749, his elder sister Maria Sophia married Christian Friedrich Knospe, the expert baker of Sonnenburg. Four days later, on May 15, 1749, his youngest brother, Georg Wilhelm, died. The joy of his sister's marriage and the sorrow of his brother's death lingered in his mind and would become a life lesson. He requested his father's permission to travel to India as a missionary. Astonishingly, his father blessed and admonished him to forget his father's house[20] and sent him back to Halle. G. A. Francke rejoiced, and, on 20 May 1749, he informed all missionaries in Tranquebar about Schwartz's willingness to become a missionary and described his character. Schwartz's father gave him full consent and blessed him. Schwartz was renowned for his exceptional teaching skills and amiable character, which enabled him to work effectively with a diverse range of people.[21]

Schwartz and his two companions, David Poltzenhagen (1726–1756) and Georg Heinrich Conrad Hüttemann (1728–1781), departed Halle on 7 August 1749, carrying letters of introduction from G. A. Francke to his friends in Magdeburg, Hamburg, and Copenhagen.[22] They reported to Francke on their stay in each place.[23] They reached Copenhagen on 23 August 1749. Senior members of the Mission College, namely Duke Johann Ludwig von Holstein (1694–1763) and Secretary Johann Finckenhagen (1694–1778), welcomed and housed them.

---

17 AFSt/M 1 K 5 : 18: Backe added these details about Schwartz's call as a missionary to the Tamils: Schwartz received his missionary call, but his father was unhappy and did not want his son to go far away. To convince his father of the significance of his missionary vocation, Schwartz wanted to travel to his father, but he had no money to pay for the journey. At this crucial moment, Backe and his father, recognising the importance of Schwartz's mission, came forward to assist him with all necessities. Their unwavering support reassured Schwartz and strengthened his resolve. After Schwartz had met his father, his father blessed him and sent him off. On returning to Halle, Schwartz met the other missionary candidates, David Poltzenhagen and Georg Heinrich Conrad Hüttemann and travelled to Copenhagen for ordination. Backe's remarks end at this point.

18 Germann: Missionar Christian Friedrich Schwartz, 20.

19 Germann: Missionar Christian Friedrich Schwartz, 21.

20 Germann: Missionar Christian Friedrich Schwartz, 23.

21 AFSt/M 1 B 38 : 24.

22 AFSt/M 1 K 10 : 2–9.

23 AFSt/M 1 K 10 : 10–14.

On 6 September 1749, Bishop Peter Hersleb (1689–1757) of the Danish Lutheran Church in Copenhagen seated each missionary candidate in a separate room and asked him to answer questions about Jesus Christ, sin, free will, divine enlightenment, rebirth, justification, the Bible, the office of a preacher, the Eucharist, predestination and the angels. Then, he listened to each of them orally, exegeting specific biblical passages and speaking on certain themes, such as *tempore*. Hüttemann provided a copy of these questions.[24]

The missionary candidates' answers satisfied Bishop Hersleb, who ordained them on 17 September 1749, according to the rites of the Danish Lutheran Church. In his sermon on Acts of the Apostles 26:17–18,[25] he stated how the Christians in Antioch had sent Apostle Paul to the non-Jews. Likewise, with a spirit of resilience, the newly ordained missionaries headed to the non-Christians in India, inviting them to embrace the Lordship of Jesus Christ despite the challenges they knew they would face. Two days later, on September 19, 1749, the missionaries departed from Copenhagen. After six days of travel, they reached Hamburg on 26 September 1749.[26] Hüttemann travelled straight from Hamburg to Halle. Schwartz and Poltzenhagen visited their parents and received blessings for their journey to and ministry in India. Along the way, they met the friends and supporters of the mission in Tranquebar, Madras and other places. These supporters were the relatives and friends of the missionaries in Tranquebar. Schwartz spent two days (October 15–17, 1749) with his parents in Sonnenburg and returned to Halle on October 20. By the time they started their journey to London, they had received two job descriptions that would influence their ministry.

2.3 Schwartz's Job Descriptions as an Ambassador for Faith

2.3.1 The Job Description Given by the King of Denmark

Anders Nørgaard, the famous historian of the Royal Danish-Halle Mission, opined that all German Lutheran missionaries who received their ordination in Copenhagen until 1796 received a copy of the same job description, which the Court Preacher, Franz Julius Lütkens (1650–1712), had drafted for Bartholomäus Ziegenbalg and Heinrich Plütschau in November 1705.[27] Accordingly, King Friedrich IV asked the pioneer missionaries to perform the following duties: 1) They should learn from those who had already been to India during their voyage.

---

24 AFSt/M 1 K 10 : 15, partially quoted in Germann: Missionar Christian Friedrich Schwartz, 31–32.

25 "I will rescue you from your people and from the Gentiles—to whom I am sending you to open their eyes so that they may turn from darkness to light and from the power of Satan to God, so that they may receive forgiveness of sins and a place among those who are sanctified by faith in me." (NRSV)

26 Germann: Missionar Christian Friedrich Schwartz, 33.

27 Anders Nørgaard: The Mission Instruction. In: Halle and the Beginning of Protestant Christianity in India. Vol. III: Communication between India and Europe. Ed. by Andreas

They should strive to understand the local language. 2) After their arrival, according to the circumstances, they should reach out to non-Christians and preach the Gospel of the Lord Jesus Christ. 3) They should ascertain the residual knowledge of God among non-Christians and utilise it as a stepping stone for introducing the proper understanding of God, as revealed in the Bible. 4) They should uphold the beliefs and practices of the Danish Lutheran Church and the doctrines outlined in the *Book of Concord*, mainly as expressed in the *Augsburg Confession*. Just like the teaching ministry of the Lord Jesus Christ, they should highlight the essential doctrines of repentance and forgiveness of sins. 5) They should introduce the primary articles of the Lutheran faith to non-Christians in simple terms, thereby laying a firm foundation for their future growth. 6) They should demonstrate in their life what they understood as Lutherans and preached. 7) They should depend on God's grace to perform their ministry. They should remember King Friedrich IV and his royal household in prayer and request that God bless them eternally. 8) The missionaries should maintain friendly relationships with the Danish Pastors at the Zion Church in Tranquebar. 9) They should be content with the salary which the king had assigned to them. They should not seek financial support from any other source. 10) Whenever Danish ships depart from Tranquebar, they should submit a detailed report on their activities to the king and propose practical methods for improvement. 11) They should sign this instruction with a good conscience and abide by it hereafter.[28] Schwartz and his two companions would have received a copy of this job description from King Friedrich V of Denmark (reigned 1746–1766) and met other members of the royal household in Copenhagen.

This was probably the reason that Schwartz and his companions regularly wrote letters to the members of the Danish royal household in Copenhagen, thanking them for their support for missionary work in Tranquebar. Their letters of 5 October to King Friedrich V,[29] Queen Juliane Marie,[30] the widowed Queen Mother Sophie Magdalene, Princess Charlotte Amalia, and Crown Prince Christian VII explain how the missionaries performed their duties. They expressed their gratitude to the royal donors for their support. They also described the

Gross et al. Halle (Saale) 2006, 1277–1280, here 1280. Royal Appointments and Instructions to the First Missionaries [Ziegenbalg and Plütschau]. In: Halle and the Beginning of Protestant Christianity in India. Vol. III: Communication between India and Europe. Ed. by Andreas Gross et al. Halle (Saale) 2006, 1337–1339, here 1337: Ziegenbalg's appointment letter reads as follows: "We, Friedrich IV, hereby announce that We have most graciously accepted and decreed, as we accordingly accept and decree, Mr Bartholomäus Ziegenbalg from here [i.e. Copenhagen] to go as a missionary to the East Indies and there, with best diligence, to make it his goal to help the non-Christians, who live in our territory and along its borders, to know the holy teachings of the Word of God as repeated in the Symbolic Books of this country [i.e. Denmark] according to Augsburg Confession, according to Our instruction, which We will give him for this purpose. Royal Palace, 17 November 1705."

28 Royal Appointments and Instructions, 1338–1339.

29 AFSt/M 2 D 30 : 5 (1753), AFSt/M 2 D 33 : 3 (1756); AFSt/M 2 D 37 : 6 (1760), AFSt/M 2 D 39 : 4 (on 11.01.1761).

30 AFSt/M 2 D 30 : 6 (1753), AFSt/M 2 D 33 : 4 (1756) and AFSt/M 2 D 37 : 1.

devastating outcomes of various wars between the English and the French in southern India. They requested that their royal donors provide further support with prayer and financial assistance.

2.3.2 The Job Description Given by the Director of the Glaucha Institutions

In addition to the job descriptions by the Danish King, Gotthilf August Francke, the director of the Glaucha Institutions in Halle, provided Schwartz and his companions with twenty-six instructions, divided into three sections. The first nine instructions describe the activities of missionaries during their journey from Halle to London. They should keep a diary to document their experiences, studies, and other events. On reaching London, they should share their diary with the Court Preacher, Friedrich Michael Ziegenhagen (1694–1776), who also worked with the Society for Promoting Christian Knowledge (SPCK) in London.

Secondly, the next set of nine instructions addresses their attitudes and behaviours towards the senior missionaries, Tamil pastors, and catechists in Tranquebar, on the one hand, and towards non-Christians on the other. For example, they should genuinely love and respect the older missionaries, the Tamil pastors Diago and Ambrose, and the catechist Rājanāyakkaṉ. They should learn Tamil and Portuguese from them, showing their respect for the local languages. They should familiarise themselves with the contents of the Tamil Bible and be able to quote from it accurately and quickly. They should cultivate love for the Tamil people and follow the missionary principles of the Apostles. Their preaching and lives should demonstrate the Gospel that is "correct, clear, simple, and full." They should undertake long preaching tours and visit fellow missionaries in Madras and Cuddalore. Once they were among the non-Christians, they would remind themselves of their ambassadorial roles, i.e. they represented the Lord Jesus Christ among them. They should record noteworthy aspects of their conversations with the non-Christians, include them in their periodic reports and send them to Halle. These reports should edify their readers in Europe and move them to praise God for the blessings of the Tamil people.

Thirdly, the last eight instructions guide the missionaries to develop healthy interpersonal relationships and remain optimistic in the face of unexpected events, disappointments, and rivalries. For example, they should reach out to more Tamils. If they refuse to embrace the Lordship of Jesus Christ, the missionaries should not give up hope. They should rejoice over every Tamil who has come to embrace the Lordship of Jesus Christ. The new missionaries should also aspire for unity of mind and purpose with other missionaries and Tamil colleagues. Hence, they should not harbour jealousies, hostilities, or competition among themselves. They should not bring minor private grievances or misunderstandings to the joint forum of all missionaries; instead, they could learn to solve the problems privately. Their main goal was to share the Good News of the Lord Jesus Christ with the Tamils. They could study the Bible together and maintain prayer fellowship. If they neglect these two activities, their interpersonal relationships might not work well. They should postpone harsh actions to the future (because time might heal the wounds). They should prioritise their physical health to work more effectively and efficiently. They could jointly read and meditate on A. H. Francke's *Monita Pastoralia,* which was specially meant for missionaries outside of Europe. Finally, G. A. Francke admonished the missionaries, whom he affectionately called "dear Timothys," to remain steadfast in their calling, for their work in the name of the Lord Jesus Christ would not be in vain. Then, he committed them to God's grace and protection. Thus, G. A. Francke's instructions to Schwartz and his two companions are intensely personal, compassionate and positive. Schwartz took these instructions seriously and followed them not only in his ministry within the church but also in his ambassadorial ministry of mediation with diverse groups of people and reconciliation.

2.3.3 The Job Description Given by the SPCK

Schwartz, Poltzenhagen and Hüttemann left Halle on 4 November 1749 and travelled towards London. Deacon Niemeyer and Sebastian Fabricius, the brother of the missionary Johann Philip Fabricius in Madras, accompanied them to Könnern, a small town in Thuringia.[31] On their onward journey to London, they visited Poltzenhagen's family in Minden (20 Nov 1749)[32] and other mission friends in cities such as Wernigerode, Hannover, Amsterdam and Rotterdam.[33] On 8 December 1749, they arrived in London; Pastor Pittins received them and escorted them to Ziegenhagen in Kensington, a suburb of the city. During their stay with him, they diligently began learning the English language, a testament to their dedication despite the challenges of being non-English missionaries. The SPCK committee members did not meet with them because they believed that the SPCK had neither called nor appointed them as missionaries. Additionally, they appeared to be uninterested in missionary work in India.[34]

It is possible that during their stay in London, the missionaries may have received a copy of the Instruction for the English Missionaries from Ziegenhagen. Henry Newman (1670–1743), the secretary of the SPCK, prepared this Instruction

31 Germann: Missionar Christian Friedrich Schwartz, 39–40.

32 AFSt/M 1 K 10 : 30.

33 AFSt/M 1 K 10 : 55: On 29.12.1749, Schwartz summarized every place they visited, every important person they met and every significant event.

34 Germann: Missionar Christian Friedrich Schwartz, 40: Germann quotes the following passage from a letter from Albinus, who was Ziegenhagen's colleague: "We have nothing to do with the Society [i.e. SPCK]. Most of their members are [spiritually] dead; spreading the knowledge of Christ among the non-Christians is not their heart's desire. Few of them know little about it. Most of them do not wish to know it. There is no need to present the new missionaries to them because they would not understand these men. Even though they were aware of their travel to India, they assigned nothing more than their usual annual contribution of £ 50 towards the salaries of the existing missionaries.

in 1735.[35] It contains ten sections. The first section states that the pious missionary should serve as a light to the people. The second section outlines how the missionaries should organise and conduct business meetings. The third section outlines how the missionaries should treat one another with respect. The senior missionary should assist the younger ones in learning the local language, dispel their fears and clarify doubts. The fourth section emphasises the primary purpose of the missionaries: to preach the Gospel of Jesus Christ to non-Christians and invite them to become members of the local church. For example, Instruction § IV:3 reads, "A Missionary is, properly speaking, a Minister of the Gentiles." Therefore, he should dedicate himself "entirely to the service of the Gentiles and the new converts." They should not allure converts with improper means, such as "worldly promises, Gifts of money, the power of the Civil Magistrate, or conniving at some heathenish Ceremonies and superstitions, etc."[36]

The fifth section requires missionaries to visit villages and invite people to embrace the Lordship of Jesus Christ. The sixth section outlines the attitudes and methods of selecting helpful Tamil co-workers for the church and school. The seventh section emphasises the urgent need to establish schools as an effective means of growing the church. At an appropriate time, missionaries should consider building seminaries to train clergy for the church. The eighth section discusses financial stewardship. The ninth section explains the necessity of gathering opinions and consensus to print appropriate books for pastors, catechists, and schoolchildren.

Schwartz sincerely appreciated Ziegenhagen and reported to Francke on 16 December 1749: The longer he interacted with him, the more precious he became to him and radiated God's mind to him. This profound appreciation and respect for Ziegenhagen reflected the gratitude of the missionaries for his guidance and support.[37] In the same letter, Schwartz admired Ziegenhagen's genuine humility and way of exegeting biblical texts. From then on, Schwartz considered the Bible a more precious treasure. Just before leaving London by coach for Deal on 10 January 1750, Schwartz reported that Ziegenhagen had paid £150 towards the travel costs of the three missionaries on the ship *Lynn* from Deal to Cuddalore. The captain of this ship was Egerton, a son of an Anglican bishop.[38] Their boat left Deal on January 29, 1750 and reached Cuddalore on July 17, 1750. Johann Zacharias Kiernander (1711–1799), a Swedish Lutheran missionary, welcomed and housed them. Johann Christian Wiedebrock, a senior missionary in Tranquebar, travelled to Cuddalore and accompanied them to Tranquebar, where they arrived on July 30, 1750.

---

35 Instruction for the English Missionaries. In: Halle and the Beginning of Protestant Christianity in India. Vol. III: Communication between India and Europe. Ed. by Andreas Gross et al. Halle (Saale) 2006, 1391–1400. After Schwartz began working with the English in 1762, this *Instruction* might have been more meaningful to him.

36 Instruction for the English Missionaries, 1394.

37 AFSt/M 1 K 10 : 48.

38 AFSt/M 1 K 10 : 59.

2.4 Schwartz's Familiarity with the History of Tamil Lutheran Christianity

Earnestly desiring to become a more helpful missionary to the Tamil people, Schwartz devoted himself to mastering the Tamil language, immersing himself in it from dawn to dusk.[39] He thoroughly familiarised himself with the comprehensive summary of the *Halle Reports* prepared by Johann Lucas Niekamp (1708–1742),[40] a student of law at the University of Halle and accountant for the missionaries at the Glaucha Institutions. Niekamp's summary has two sections: the fifteen chapters of the first section deal with select socio-cultural themes, and the forty-two chapters in the second section trace the chronological establishment and development of the Tamil Lutheran congregations in and around Tranquebar and Madras until 1736.

Schwartz would have found the first section particularly illuminating as it introduced him to the socio-cultural, religious, and historical contexts that had shaped the thoughts, behaviours and customs of the Tamils living in the regions between Tranquebar and Madras. The first four chapters discuss these regions' geography, topography, climate, villages, towns, trade and travel routes, flora and fauna. Chapter five highlights the characteristics of the inhabitants on the Coast of Coromandel, including Tamils, Muslims, Jews, St. Thomas Christians, Portuguese-speaking Roman Catholics and Europeans from diverse countries. The sixth chapter enumerates the languages, namely Tamil, Sanskrit, Granta (i.e. Sanskrit written in Tamil scripts, known as *maṇipavaḷam*), Telugu, Marathi, Malai, and the like.

The seventh chapter provides details of various kings, their political history, relative independence and lack of beneficial governance for the ordinary people. This chapter also describes Tamil ways of administering justice, policing and other public institutions. The eighth chapter uncovers the physical, intellectual, psychological and social characteristics of the Tamil people as observed and documented by German Lutheran Pietist missionaries. These Germans admired the Tamils' rational capabilities and achievements.

The ninth chapter explores Tamil arts and sciences, beginning with the education in Tamil schools. Students learned Tamil orthography, poetry, music, ethics, physics, medicine, surgery, alchemy, mathematics, optical sciences, astronomy, cosmology, geography, chronology, history, and written literature.

Chapter ten, the longest and consisting of twenty-three subsections, discusses religion. It starts explaining the concept of One God with and without attributes. This God reveals Itself in three male forms (*mummūrtti*) as Brahma, Viṣṇu and Śiva, their genealogies, guardian deities of villages, shining heavenly beings

---

39 AFSt/M 1 B 40 : 20.

40 AFSt/M 1 B 40 : 21. Schwartz referred to this book: Johann Lucas Niekamp: Kurzgefaßte Missions=Geschichte oder Historischer Auszug der Evangelischen Missions=Berichte aus Ost=Indien. Halle: Verlegung des Wäysen=Hauses, 1740.

(*devas*), inspired sages (*ṛṣi*) and their servants. This chapter also narrates Tamil perceptions of creation and the origin of sin, transmigration of souls, evil spirits, heaven and hell. It enumerates Tamil ways to attain salvation and lead a holy life. It wonders why the Tamils have prescribed severe austerities like self-mortification. It describes polytheism, worship of images, feast and fast days and diverse sacrifices. Its description includes Tamils' purification rituals (e.g. ritual bathing), a narrative of Tamil priests and the female servants of God (*devadasī*s), various religious Orders and temples.

Niekamp's eleventh chapter is special. It presents Tamil customs, which readers in early eighteenth-century Germany could understand caste as the *varṇa*-system. It analyses the *varṇa*s of Brahmins and Sudras. Strangely, it places Pariahs, who were in classical Sanskrit thinking and practice outside of the *varṇa*-system, on par with Brahmins and Sudras. It does not refer to the Kṣatriyas and Vaisyas at all because they were at that time unimportant in Tranquebar and Madras. Moreover, this chapter describes Tamil rites of passage customs related to marriage and burial.

Niekamp's twelfth chapter summarises the Tamil lifestyle and habits regarding food, drink, dress, houses, and other necessities. The thirteenth chapter outlines the major socio-cultural, economic and political hindrances that prevented most Tamil from embracing Lutheranism. These include Tamil ways of rejecting something that they did not like. They remained polite to the missionaries and chose not to embrace Lutheranism. The missionaries wondered why the Tamils stressed the antiquity of Tamil religions and the more recent historical origin of Christianity about 1700 years ago. The Tamils deduced this date from the missionary dating of various letters and tracts: "in the year of the LORD." Tamil prejudices and hatred towards Europeans and their Christianity were another reason. The Tamil could not bear the evil life of European Christians. The Tamil rejection of Lutheranism also stemmed from its contradiction of caste-related practices, the dire poverty of most Tamils, and resistance from the Tamil Lutheran Church because it contradicted Tamil notions of caste and caste-related customary practices that arranged people's socio-religious relationships vertically and horizontally based on imaged degrees and intensities of ritual purity and pollution. Other reasons for rejecting Lutheranism included the dire poverty of most Tamils, resistance from Tamil Roman Catholics and lack of sufficient Lutheran Pietist missionaries. These socio-cultural details familiarised Schwartz with the living contexts of the Tamil people, particularly of Tamil Lutherans.

Chapter 3

Schwartz in Tranquebar (1750–1762)

3.1 Acclimatisation

When Schwartz arrived in Tranquebar, the mission work had been established there for forty-four years. The Lutherans had two church buildings for their meetings: their catechists met in the old Jerusalem Church, built in 1707, near the seashore. All Tamil Lutherans worshipped in the New Jerusalem Church, built in 1718, which was situated in a secure location within the town. The Lutherans maintained three schools: one for Tamil Christian boys, another for Tamil Christian girls, and the third for the children of Portuguese-speaking Indians and Eurasians. Tamil Lutheran pastors catered to the needs of the Christians in the countryside. The small town of Poṟaiyār, three kilometres away from Tranquebar, had a Lutheran school and the Bethlehem Church.

Eight weeks after Schwartz arrived in Tranquebar, he fell ill with fever and psychological issues. His initial attempts to learn Tamil were met with frustration, as he found it both challenging and seemingly pointless. However, he did not give up. Despite the initial difficulties, he persevered and finally succeeded in learning it. The more he read Tamil literature and interacted with Tamil children, the more he noticed a profound transformation in his attitude towards the Tamil people. After nine months, he spoke Tamil with more confidence. On 26 May 1751, he instructed a group of Tamil people and prepared them for baptism, a clear sign of his personal growth and evolving perspective.[1]

On his twenty-sixth birthday, on 26 October 1751, Schwartz stated that he had adjusted to the hot climate of Tranquebar and had made considerable progress in learning and using Tamil. He and Hüttemann visited the villages that belonged to Tranquebar. Sometimes, they also ventured to other villages. At that time, Hüttemann harboured negative views about those Tamil people whom he met. He advised Schwartz not to trust the Tamil Lutheran leaders. This was a significant struggle for Schwartz, as he found it challenging to undertake missionary tasks in and around Tranquebar.[2] He wrote about these difficulties to Gotthilf August Francke, who later provided crucial encouragement. Francke pointed out to Schwartz that the Apostles of the New Testament, too, faced and overcame problems. This support from Francke was a significant source of strength for Schwartz, reinforcing the sense of empathy and fellowship in his missionary journey.[3]

1 AFSt/M 1 B 41 : 6.
2 AFSt/M 1 B 41 : 19.
3 AFSt/M 1 B 41 : 30.

3.2 Disliking Nominal Christianity

Schwartz observed the lives of European and Indian Lutherans in Tranquebar. Their cold, nominal Christianity, without burning zeal for Christian ministry and witness, disappointed him profoundly. For instance, on October 24, 1752, he noted Lutherans who did not show repentance or remorse for their past mistakes. Yet, they partook in the Holy Communion. He was disappointed that the Holy Communion did not have a positive impact on their lives. He informed G. A. Francke about his observations. He stated that he could efficiently deal with godless people, drunkards, dancers and prostitutes and advise them not to partake in the Holy Communion. However, it was difficult for him to persuade fellow Lutherans to consider the Holy Communion seriously and to sanctify their lives accordingly.[4] On 23 March 1753, Francke responded to Schwartz, offering valuable advice. He encouraged Schwartz to be patient with fellow Lutherans, not to prevent anyone from partaking in Holy Communion, and to instruct them about true conversion and its implications. Francke's advice was clear and insightful. He further advised that if individuals showed improvement, Schwartz should encourage their progress. However, if someone did not show repentance, Schwartz could persuade them to postpone their participation in the Holy Communion to a later date rather than excluding them from it completely.[5]

3.3 Overcoming Self-Doubt

Outwardly, Schwartz performed his duties to the best of his ability. For example, on 8 October 1753, he taught the schoolchildren in the morning. In the afternoon, he visited the Tamil Lutherans in their huts and discussed spiritual matters with them. He even reported on violent interactions between the non-Christians and the Roman Catholic Christians in Tanjore over certain ritual matters. When the king of Tanjore learned of these troubles, he severely punished the Roman Catholic Christians. He did not distinguish the Roman Catholic Christians from the Lutherans, who also experienced the consequences of these punishments.[6]

Inwardly, Schwartz faced spiritual and psychological problems over certain transgressions during his childhood and youth. On August 28, 1753, he confessed to stealing money and a few items while playing with other children. He knew that the money was insignificant, and the things were trivial. However, the act of theft tormented him in the mission field. He had sent money to a local Consistory Counsellor named Beier, requesting that he hand over the money to his friends. However, Beier had died before Schwartz's letter reached him. Similarly, when he was in school, he lied and claimed he did not have money to pay the fees; hence,

---

4 AFSt/M 1 B 42 : 15.
5 AFSt/M 1 B 42 : 34.
6 AFSt/M 1 B 43 : 19.

he received free tuition. Realising that he had stolen and lied bothered him profoundly, and he lost his peace with himself. Therefore, he requested Francke's advice on repayment.[7] Two months later, on October 8, 1753, Schwartz expressed his feelings of self-doubt and incompetence. These psychological problems had deep roots in his spiritual and moral past. He confessed to Francke that during his youth, he had engaged in certain unspecified activities that he now regretted. Though he had asked for forgiveness, the memories of those activities caused him spiritual anxiety and psychological pain. He deeply desired to be a valuable tool in God's work, yet his realisation of his past actions weighed heavily on him. Amid this inner turmoil, he held onto the hope that God could anoint him with His Spirit and thus equip him for a greater purpose.[8]

Schwartz's inner turmoil lasted longer than expected. On 4 January 1754, he revealed his inner mind to Francke: he could not sleep peacefully and even dreamt that he had returned to Europe. His psychological troubles were so intense that he handed over to Zeglin the responsibilities of his domestic administration.[9] In the meantime, in November 1754, Francke responded to Schwartz's requests and explained that God rejoiced over an honest person like Schwartz. The fact that he had recognised and repented of the sins of his youth was a sign of his honesty and sincerity before God. His desire to repay those whom he had wronged earlier was noble. However, these people had gone elsewhere. None in Francke's circle knew of their whereabouts. Francke reminded Schwartz of God's repeated restoration of Israel. Likewise, he assured him of God's faithfulness: God had called him and would help him to fulfil all tasks.[10]

Despite these valuable suggestions, Schwarz's persistent feelings of guilt remained. He gradually overcame them. Notably, Francke's letter of October 4, 1756, helped him overcome his disbelief. Schwartz's continued ministry in the Portuguese church during Poltzenhagen's absence was significant. Poltzenhagen's sudden death on 28 November 1756 in Sombrero, one of the Nicobar Islands, reignited Schwarz's fearful feelings of uncertainty, plunging him back into emotional struggle.[11] On 29 December 1757, Schwartz bravely acknowledged that the sins of his past, which he had confided to Francke, still haunted him. However, he did not allow his guilt to paralyse his ministry, claiming God's forgiveness. He continued to visit local places and preach to local people, his commitment to his

7 AFSt/M 1 B 43 : 31.

8 AFSt/M 1 B 43 : 16.

9 AFSt/M 1 B 43 : 17 and AFSt/M 1 B 45 : 11: According to his letter to G. A. Francke on 10.10.1755, Schwartz often despaired the non-responsiveness of non-Christians to God's Word.

10 AFSt/M 1 B 43 : 32 and AFSt/M 1 B 48 : 19: On 10.01.1760, Schwartz reminded himself of his calling to missionary service and his father's words: if he had prevented Schwartz from going to India as a missionary, he would feel sorry on his deathbed. At that time, Schwartz recalled the 26th verse of the beautiful hymn "Oh, Lamb of God" (lit. "O Lamm Gottes"). This hymn speaks about God's overflowing blessing for those who deny themselves and suffer for believing in the Gospel of the Lord Jesus Christ.

11 AFSt/M 1 B 47 : 15.

ministry unwavering. The fervent worship of non-Christians in the town of Sīrkāḻi astonished him, but it did not deter him.[12]

In March 1759, Francke encouraged Schwartz: “You have described the condition of your soul. It is incorrect to believe that God forgives select sins; He forgives all sins, and the sin has lost its power.”[13] Schwartz, too, was aware of these things. Yet, he could not fully overcome the memories and feelings of guilt about his transgressions during his childhood days and youth years. They troubled him constantly. When the non-Christian Tamils did not respond to his preaching with enthusiasm and remained indifferent, his disappointment grew. He was unaware that they were afraid of social ostracisation.[14] Simultaneously, most European Christians, too, remained uninterested in spiritual matters. Tamil Lutherans also were not enthusiastic about their faith. All these natural and imagined troubles affected his nerves, and he complained of a nervous condition; his hands trembled. For example, on 2 September 1761, he informed Francke that his hands were weak and shaking; he considered this condition a sign of God’s chastisement for his past transgressions.[15] On January 14, 1761, he described experiencing contracted nerves that made his movements difficult. His whole body was shaking. Samuel Cnoll (1705–1767),[16] the first medical missionary in Tranquebar, was unable to help Schwartz.[17] Even after a year, Schwartz continued to suffer from nervous problems: On 8 February 1762, he informed Francke that he had visited Pondicherry and Madras. He hoped to revisit Madras, but nerve contractions in his body made travel difficult. His hands shook so much that he could barely write.[18]

12 AFSt/M 1 B 47 : 21.

13 AFSt/M 1 B 47 : 56.

14 AFSt/M 1 B 66 : 55: On 23.09.1775, Schwartz reported to Ziegenhagen the following two instances of social ostracisation: a few months ago, a family from a village in the western parts of Tiruccirāppaḷḷi accepted baptism. Later, another family came from the same town and were baptised. Upon their return, the villagers refused to let them enter their village. When they entered, non-Christian neighbours agitated and did not permit them to live among them. Schwartz sent his catechist Sattiyanātaṉ to make peace. A few days later, a new riot broke out. Again, Sattiyanātaṉ went to the same village. The rioters informed him that the Christians sang and prayed sometimes until midnight. These activities “burned them like fire.” Sattiyanātaṉ asked both Christians and non-Christians to live in amicability. Secondly, last Easter, a mother and father left their children in a village about twenty miles away from Tiruccirāppaḷḷi and came to Schwartz, where they underwent preparations for baptism. Their former priest instigated trouble against them. Their village elders sent a letter to them, warning that if they embraced Christianity, they should not return to their town and share “the fire from others” (i.e., sharing warmth, fellowship, and food). However, the parents accepted baptism. Schwartz asked one of his catechists to accompany them back to their village. Initially, they faced many problems. Gradually, they could live in their town.

15 AFSt/M 1 B 51 : 14.

16 Anantanarayanan Raman: Samuel Cnoll in Tranquebar and establishment of the first pharmacy – Laboratorium Chymicum in India in 1732. In: Current Science 11, 2017, issue 3, 368–369.

17 AFSt/M 1 B 51 : 15.

18 AFSt/M 1 B 52 : 13. Schwartz mentioned how Cnoll had become bitter towards his patients in this letter. By contrast, the medical doctor of the Moravians in nearby Poṟaiyār treated the local people with kindness and goodwill. Many people thronged to them. Their medical service opened new ways for their evangelistic work.

3.4 Delight in Service

On 12 October 1754, Schwartz informed Francke that he enjoyed teaching the school children, whom he considered his "little lambs." He thanked Francke for allowing him to gain teaching experience in the Glaucha Institutions.[19] Two years later, in 1756, he explained how he rejoiced in teaching in the Portuguese School: from 6 a.m. to 7 a.m., he read a chapter from the New Testament. He described its theological content to the children. From 9 a.m. to 10 a.m. on Mondays and Thursdays, he taught the children the Order of Salvation. In the same letter, he explained how Pratāpasimha's wars with rivals prevented him and his missionary colleagues from conducting evangelist tours to the villages and towns of Tanjore.[20] Notably, on June 30, 1756, Pratāpasimha's army destroyed the walls of Tranquebar and the town of Sirkāli. Most people suffered greatly.[21] Amidst these raging problems, on 9 July 1756, the Tamil Lutherans and their missionaries in Tranquebar celebrated the fiftieth anniversary of Ziegenbalg's arrival.[22]

It was a momentous occasion when Schwartz, accompanied by Missionary Zeglin, set foot in Tanjore for the first time from April 3 to 20, 1759. Their observations of the strong adherence to ancestral religions and social customs left a profound impact on them. Captain Wilhelm Berg, a German from Hamburg, played a significant role in their journey.[23] He informed Schwarz and Zeglin that King Pratāpasimha was not interested in worshipping images. Berg wanted to impress the missionaries with this inaccurate and exaggerated statement. He supported temples within the traditions of his ancestral heritage.[24] In the meantime, Schwartz noted that during the wars between the French and the British in southern India, the French had thrown bombs into certain temples. He wondered how a

19 AFSt/M 1 B 44 : 11.

20 AFSt/M 1 B 46 : 3.

21 AFSt/M 1 B 47 : 27: On 11.10.1756, Pastor Diago informed Francke that the Tanjore armies had plundered Sīrkāḻi, sparing neither his house. He was happy that they let him escape alive. Again, on 30.06.1757, the armies of Tanjore devastated significant parts of Tranquebar.

22 AFSt/M 1 B 47 : 7,

23 Henry Dodwell: The Nabobs of Madras. London 1926, 74–77: Typically, Company agents recruited soldiers for India among those who were the cheapest. When British soldiers were unavailable, they also chose others. For example, in 1752, the company's agents in Britain sent 60 Protestant German soldiers for their artillery unit in Madras. Later, the company's agents recruited among those German men who lived in the neighbourhood of Hamburg, Lübeck, and Bremen. Their contract was for five years; their annual salary was 25 Pagodas or £10. This money was insufficient to support their living expenses in India and help their families in Europe. They did not hesitate to acquire more wealth by exploiting others. Robert Clive, with the assistance of German soldiers, defeated the French at the Battle of Plassey (1757) on 23 June 1757 in Plassey. Muhammad Ali Wallajah became the Nawab of Arcot. On 26.06.1753, Stringer Lawrence of the Company's army defeated the French at the Golden Rock in Tiruccirāppaḷḷi.

24 Chinnaiyan: Social History of Thanjavur, 163–164: Pratāpasimha tolerated the adherents of other religions; consequently, the silk traders, including some Muslims, contributed money to the liturgical offerings and festivals of the Konganeswarer Temple on West Main Street in Tanjore. At the same time, he firmly established the *apiṣēka kaṭṭaḷai* ('Ordinance for Anointing') for regular worship services at Kōṭṭūr Koḻuntīsvarar Temple at Tiruvārūr.

group of Brahmins, who otherwise avoided coming near Europeans, fearing ritual pollution, came so close to the missionaries that they nearly touched them. Schwartz hastily concluded that these Brahmins were losing their sense of ritual impurity. He prayed for God's guidance in sowing the seeds of God's Word and its growth in its own way.[25]

Whenever Schwartz could not travel due to the hot climate, he joined fellow missionaries like Dame and read the Hebrew Bible or the Greek New Testament. For example, on 15 June 1759, he informed Francke that he and Dame had read the Hebrew Bible twice. Excessive heat prevented them from travelling to villages. However, they used their study of the Hebrew Bible to prepare for more effective evangelistic work.[26] Schwartz often became sick in Tranquebar. For example, on January 12, 1760, he informed Francke of his illness and that Zeglin's wife was caring for him. At the same time, he rejoiced in baptising people from non-Christian backgrounds. They demonstrated the impact of God's immeasurable grace on their hearts; he encouraged them to keep their bond of covenant with the Lord Jesus Christ.[27] He also reported to Francke that the German Captain Wilhelm Berg had invited them to Tanjore to preach to non-Christians freely. He and his missionary colleagues waited for an opportunity to travel to Tanjore to preach the gospel.[28]

3.5 Visiting Ceylon

German Lutherans, such as Captain von Bohren in Jaffna and Colombo in Ceylon (modern Sri Lanka), invited a missionary from Tranquebar to teach and administer the sacraments to them. Schwartz offered to travel there, believing the sea air would strengthen his breathing and heal his persistent cough.[29] On 25 April 1760, he and two of his fellow missionaries[30] walked to Karaikal and stayed there

---

25 AFSt/M 1 B 49 : 16.

26 AFSt/M 1 B 49 : 18.

27 AFSt/M 1 B 49 : 20.

28 AFSt/M 1 B 50 : 25 and AFSt/M 1 B 50 : 25: The missionaries in Tranquebar were happy that Kiernander taught over 100 children in Calcutta and preached in the church there. They also stated that Kiernander often visited Friedrichsnagar (i.e. modern Serampore) and preached to Bengali, French and Portuguese families there. In 1752, Bartholomäus Leberecht Ziegenbalg, the son of Bartholomäus Ziegenbalg, who was born in Tranquebar on July 26, 1719, became the senior administrator of the Danish East India Company in Serampore. By 1757, he had risen to become the director of the company in Serampore. Later, he became a merchant (ca. 1762) and married a French Catholic woman. He invited Kiernander to preach in Serampore. Kiernander's three letters (AFSt/M 1 B 48 : 23–25, respectively, dated 29.12.1758, 19.01.1759 and 04.11.1759) contain information about his pastoral ministry there. In 1766, Ziegenbalg returned to Denmark.

29 AFSt/M 2 D 37 :7. The published version of this diary in HR, 93 Cont., 1762, 955–1022 is an edited text. It incorporates Schwartz's details into the diaries of other missionaries and reports on the activities of the missionaries on a particular day. Germann published parts of this diary in Germann: Missionar Christian Friedrich Schwartz, 110–114.

30 AFSt/M 1 B 50 : 28: One of Schwartz's companions was Hüttemann, who had returned to Cuddalore because the English had recaptured it from the French.

overnight with the Company's commanding officer. Then, Schwartz took leave from his companions the following day and travelled to Nagapattinam. He spoke with the Tamils on the way about God's glorious deeds of saving humans. In the afternoon, he met Governor Baron van Eck of Nagapattinam, who had already readied a cabin with a table on a boat to Jaffna. On arrival in Jaffna, Schwartz realised the need to obtain prior permission to administer the Eucharist to the Lutherans. As the governor was in Colombo, he travelled on land for fourteen days, met the governor there, obtained permission and administered the Eucharist to a group of four hundred Lutherans. Although Dutch Reformed Christians had objected, Schwartz persisted and ministered to the Lutherans in Colombo for three months. Then, he returned to Jaffna and administered the Eucharist to fifty Lutherans.

During his stay in Ceylon, Schwartz observed five things: firstly, the Lutherans desperately needed a pastor and catechists. They knew the Dutch East India Company would not permit Lutheran pastors to work in their territories. Secondly, he noticed the inadequate spiritual teachings and pastoral support from a Tamil pastor in Jaffna and a Sinhalese pastor in Colombo: each visited their congregation once a year, baptised all children, solemnised marriages and administered the Lord's Supper. Schwartz met these two pastors and suggested they train more catechists. They responded that they needed money for that purpose. They could not follow his suggestion. Thirdly, the Roman Catholics did not have official permission to assemble in large groups. However, they celebrated their annual festivals in Kandy, Colombo and Mannār. The Dutch authorities did not trouble them.

Fourthly, Schwartz critiqued the cruelty and avarice of the Dutch authorities, who had impoverished the local people (lit. blut-arm, 'extremely poor'). They exploited the poor coffee growers. They sent all taxes and other income to the governor and his assistants. One governor left Sri Lanka (earlier: Ceylon) for Indonesia (lit. Batavia) with forty to fifty tons of gold. Schwartz assumed that the cruelty of the Dutch authorities would eventually force them out of the island.[31] Additionally, the Dutch and other Europeans had employed enslaved people in their homes; consequently, extramarital problems abounded. Europeans sought to send their servants for Christian education, but the scarcity of pastors and catechists made it impossible for them to obtain pastoral assistance.

Fifthly, Schwartz observed that the Dutch authorities disliked his dress. One said, "The man is good, but his dress is not suitable." Hence, an unnamed

---

31 AFSt/M 1 B 50 : 12: On 16.10.1760, Schwartz reminisced about his observations of Ceylon, noting that a persistent cough had plagued him. He was astonished to find out the abundance of fruits, vegetables, and trees. He admired the countless, beautiful Palmyra trees that people used for their buildings. They tapped the juice of these trees and made sugar from it. They stood on both sides of the roads and protected the speedy travellers. Besides, there was an abundance of coffee, pepper and cardamom. There was no shortage of wood for building. Most people were impoverished (lit. blut-arm, 'blood-poor'). The Company's officers in Madras abused them and did not pay them well. They sucked blood out of these poor people. The governor took away the money from the people.

Dutchman gave him an expensive cassock. Schwartz could not refuse it publicly, but he hesitated to wear it because he assumed the man had bought it with illegal money. Schwartz knew that he was not the first Protestant missionary to visit Ceylon. He went to Point Pedro (formerly Porto Pedro) near Jaffna and visited the large tree under which the famous Predikant Philip Baldaeus (1632–1672) had preached. When Christian Wilhelm Gericke (1743–1803) visited Ceylon seven years later, in 1767, he met people who had interacted with Schwartz. They spoke of him with respect and admiration.[32] Throughout his stay in Ceylon, he had a fever and coughed. His hosts nursed him back to tolerable health, allowing him to return to Nagapattinam on 7 September 1760. After staying with Lieutenant Freytag for a short while, he reached Tranquebar on 19 September 1760.

3.6 Embracing Celibacy

Schwartz embraced celibacy and did not reveal the reason for this choice. He might have been aware of the heated debates about the Apostolic Ideal in Germany. This Ideal, held by its proponents, suggested that all of the apostles, except for Peter and even the Lord Jesus Christ, remained unmarried. The news of the marriages of Ziegenbalg and his colleague, Johann Ernst Gründler (1677–1720), sparked controversy.[33] They believed that the missionaries had strayed from the Apostolic Ideal by marrying and settling down, a path that led to caring for their families, educating their children, and marrying them off. For instance, in 1751, Hüttemann married Elisabeth Evans in Cuddalore. She bore him sixteen children and died in 1773. Schwartz, witnessing how Hüttemann's family life had shifted his priorities, made a significant sacrifice. He chose not to marry, dedicating his time, energy, and resources to missionary service among the Tamil people.[34]

Upon his arrival in Nagapattinam on 7 September 1760, he was met with a surprise: a fiancée waited to marry him in Tranquebar.[35] Pastor Böhme, a figure who had a significant influence in the Zion Church in Tranquebar, requested that

---

32 Germann: Missionar Christian Friedrich Schwartz, 114.

33 On 24.11.1715, Bartholomäus Ziegenbalg married Maria Dorothea Salzmann, one of his former students, in Halle (Saale). She bore him three sons, one after the other. Ziegenbalg died in 1719. In the following year, Benjamin Schultze attempted to marry her, but the attempt failed. Still, she married Oluf Lygaard, a member of the Danish Administrative Council in Tranquebar, in 1720, returned to Copenhagen and became a widow two years later. On 04.02.1716, Johann Ernest Gründler married the widow Atilia Elisabeth Krahe in Tranquebar. On 21.12.1728, Christoph Theodosius Walther married Anna Christiana, the eldest daughter of Johann Burchard Brochmann, the treasurer and privy council member of the Danish Administration in Tranquebar (HR, 50th Con., 373). In 1733, Andreas Worm married Johanna Catherina Halle. She died two years later, on 01.03.1747. Daniel Zeglin then married Anna Obuch.

34 AFSt/M 1 C 25 : 33: Twenty-five years later, on 08.10.1785, Schwartz revealed his opinion for rejecting the marriage of missionaries: a married missionary should care for his family, the education of his children and other arising needs. Married missionaries could not devote undivided attention to their missionary work; consequently, their missionary work suffered.

35 Germann: Missionar Christian Friedrich Schwartz, 116.

Johann Finckenhagen, the secretary of the Mission College in Copenhagen (1737–1772), find and send two spinsters to Tranquebar. Accordingly, on 15 June 1760, they arrived in Tranquebar: Pernille Thors married Kohlhoff. As Schwartz chose to remain celibate, Anna Sophie Pap married the Governor of Tranquebar.[36] On 1 December 1761, Francke informed Schwartz that he could not endorse Pastor Böhme's unilateral decision to select and send a fiancée to Schwartz. It was indeed strange that he did not obtain Schwartz's consent. Francke felt that if God had revealed God's will for marriage to Pastor Böhme, God would have also disclosed the same will to Schwartz.[37]

36 AFSt/M 1 B 50 : 12; Germann: Missionar Christian Friedrich Schwartz, 114–116; Pearson: Memoirs, Vol. 1, 133–142: On 21.07.1760, Pernille Thors (1727–1807) married Johann Balthasar Kohlhoff, the widower, whose wife Margaretha Wilhelmina Wiger had died on 18.11.1751. He needed a woman to care for his daughter, Anna Regina, born on 01.11.1745. Kohlhoff requested that Pastor Böhme persuade Klein's wife's sister to come to Tranquebar and marry him. The other woman was Anna Sophie Pap. Besides his determination not to marry, Schwartz's friends in Copenhagen did not give a good report about Ms Pap. They questioned her reputation. Schwartz was happy that she soon married the governor of Tranquebar.

37 AFSt/M 1 B 50 : 35, Germann: Missionar Christian Friedrich Schwartz, 116–117.

Chapter 4

Schwartz in Tiruccirāppaḷḷi (1762–1777)

4.1 Reasons for Leaving Tranquebar

Schwartz remained resilient in the face of personal and professional challenges. The unexpected arrival of Anna Sophie Pap as his fiancée, a situation he was unprepared for, exacerbated Schwartz's persistent cough and chest pain. However, he persevered.[1] His heavy schedule in Jaffna and Colombo exhausted him so much that he became pale due to poor blood circulation. Although Ms. Pap's marriage to the governor of Tranquebar relieved him, he found it difficult to continue living in Tranquebar. Another factor in his discomfort at Tranquebar was Kohlhoff and his colleagues, who were unhappy about Schwartz's extended stay in Ceylon. They shouldered his responsibilities (e.g. teaching in the schools and going on evangelistic tours) during his absence and wished him to stay in Tranquebar. When he intended to travel to Madras and receive medical treatment to get rid of his cough and chest pain, they expressed their discontent with him. In the meantime, Schwartz's nervous system became weaker, and he needed appropriate medical care.

Philip Fabricius extended his invitation to Madras for better medical treatment. On 18 January 1762, Schwartz left Tranquebar and stayed with Hüttemann in Cuddalore until his dysentery subsided in February of that year. During his journey to Madras, he fell ill in Pondicherry. His companions, demonstrating the power of camaraderie, fashioned a wooden cradle tied to a pole and carried him back to Cuddalore. After spending time with Hüttemann, Schwartz continued his journey to Madras via Sadras. At Sadras, he injured his shinbone, necessitating a more extended stay. Finally, he arrived in Madras on 10 March 1761. There, his cough subsided, and the shaking of his hand reappeared. It was a painful time, during which he was unable to write for a while, but the support he received was a source of strength.[2]

The senior missionary Johann Balthasar Kohlhoff (1711–1790) assumed that Schwartz deliberately avoided his responsibilities and intended to return to Europe.[3] He convened a committee to settle Schwartz-related administrative issues, discussed the reasons and implications of Schwartz's journey to Madras, and

---

1 Germann: Missionar Christian Friedrich Schwartz, 117.

2 Germann: Missionar Christian Friedrich Schwartz, 116–118.

3 On 05.03.1761, Jacob Klein (1721–1790), who arrived in Tranquebar as a missionary in 1746, married Anna Dorothea Obuch, the stepdaughter of the missionary Daniel Zeglin (1716–1780). The married missionaries and the unmarried missionaries formed two separate groups. Schwartz joined Peter Dame (1731–1766), the other unmarried missionary.

assumed that he would return to Europe.[4] Therefore, he terminated Schwartz's appointment as a missionary and informed Francke of this on December 31, 1761.[5] In the meantime, G. A. Francke wrote to Kohlhoff about Schwartz's determination to continue working in Tranquebar. Schwartz returned from Madras to Tranquebar and attempted to seek medical help from the local doctor, Cnoll, who was unable to assist him.[6] These painful experiences led Schwartz to lead a simple, transparent, and humble life. Hence, his biographer, Wilhelm Germann, referred to Schwartz's stay in Tranquebar as a time of learning.[7] It was time for him to look for a new field where he could thrive.

4.2 First Contacts in Tiruccirāppaḷḷi

According to Ainslie Thomas Embree (1921–2017), the soldiers of the French East India Company served as a model for the Company in two significant ways.[8] Firstly, the French East India Company employed and trained Indian mercenaries for a lower wage. After evaluating their loyalty, they entrusted them with their modern weapons. These Indian mercenaries fought for the French more efficiently than European soldiers. They did not hesitate to attack and kill fellow Indians. Upon observing the success of this strategy, the Company adopted these two principles and appointed Indian soldiers as sepoys. Indian princes hired the Company's military to maintain peace in their territories.

Additionally, the Company recruited European mercenaries to serve in the courts of the local rulers. For example, Captain Johann Wilhelm Berg, a German citizen from Hamburg, served in the army of King Pratāpasimha of Tanjore (1739–1763). He and his European soldiers sought pastoral and spiritual care from ordained European clergypersons. These clergypersons would conduct worship services, administer the sacraments of baptism and Eucharist, solemnise marriages, help them maintain the knowledge of Christianity and bury their dead.[9] When the English soldiers in Tiruccirāppaḷḷi heard about Schwartz, they invited him to come to them. In October 1762, Schwartz took his fellow missionary, Klein, and travelled to Tiruccirāppalli. On their way, they stayed in Tanjore for eight days and interacted with Berg and his European soldiers. Then, they proceeded to

---

4 It was a coincidence that Major Strobel, one of Schwartz's close friends, left Tranquebar and moved to Germany. Kohlhoff assumed that Schwartz would also return to Europe.

5 Germann: Missionar Christian Friedrich Schwartz, 122.

6 AFSt/M 1 B 60 : 23 quoted in Germann: Missionar Christian Friedrich Schwartz, 116–118. This letter, dated October 1770, features Schwartz's smooth handwriting, indicating that his hand had stopped shaking by then.

7 Germann: Missionar Christian Friedrich Schwartz, 123–124.

8 Ainslie Thomas Embree: British East India Company Raj. In: Encyclopedia of India. Vol. 1. Detroit 2006, 176–183, here 179: Indian soldiers in the Company's army played a decisive role in defeating the French (1740–1748) and prolonging the Seven Years' War (1756–1763).

9 Dodwell: The Nabobs, 93: The principal activities of the Lutheran missionaries "were centred at Trichinopoly and Tanjore, where English troops were regularly in garrison; and for them, missionaries performed marriages, baptisms and funerals, which otherwise would have been conducted by an officer or dispensed with altogether."

Tiruccirāppaḷḷi, where the English soldiers welcomed and hosted them. On 12 October 1762, Schwartz explained to Francke about his journey and how he and Klein had stayed in Tiruccirāppaḷḷi in February and March 1762. He described how Captain Achilles Preston had promised to secure a place to erect a church building and to release a salaried European soldier to teach the children of Europeans, provided that the missionaries would establish a school for them.[10]

On 22 March 1762, an ammunition store exploded, killing eighteen artillerymen, wounding six soldiers and orphaning their children; Schwartz, showing his deep empathy, decided to take care of these orphans and educate them. Immediately, Preston raised three hundred Pagodas (i.e. equal to 1,000 Gulden) and requested Schwartz to identify a soldier who could teach these children.[11] The consequences of the ammunition explosion required Schwartz and Klein to stay in Tiruccirāppaḷḷi for three more months and return to Tanjore on 17 July 1762. By then, Captain Wilhelm Berg had obtained King Pratāpasimha's permission for Schwartz to stay permanently in Tanjore. Berg enabled Schwartz to visit a sick English soldier in the Fort. After a while, one of Pratāpasimha's ministers invited Schwartz to the palace. Schwartz gave him a copy of an English booklet that contained Ziegenbalg's letters and a map of India.[12] The minister requested that Schwartz explain the map. Schwartz described the various aspects of the map to him, and then he shared the Gospel of the Lord Jesus Christ with the minister and his people.

On another occasion, the minister expressed interest in learning more about Europe. Schwartz explained to him how public institutions with Christian values, such as churches, schools, and law courts, functioned for the common good of all people and enhanced the quality of their lives. During his discussion with the minister, a prince named Tulāji arrived and departed quickly. Later, Schwartz learned that King Pratāpasimha hid behind a curtain and listened to his conversation with the minister. Schwartz observed the prevalence of fear and lack of trust among the palace employees. Each employee tried to find fault with another employee. Schwartz left Tanjore on September 20, 1762 and reached Tiruccirāppaḷḷi two days later. Preston welcomed him joyfully. Schwartz conducted German worship services from 8 to 10 a.m., a Tamil worship service from 10 a.m. to 12 noon, and a Portuguese worship service in the afternoon. Preston wanted Schwartz to hold a worship service in English as well. Schwartz hesitated to accept this invitation because he felt that his limited knowledge of the English language would not be sufficient to conduct worship services.[13]

---

10 AFSt/M 1 B 52 : 14.

11 Copenhagen: Missionskollegiet Rigsarkivet 9 c, Indkomne Sager den Ostindiske Mission vedk: O.M. No 10. 1766: Schwartz's letter of 10.07.1768.

12 The English booklet might have been one of the following two works. In 1709, Anton Wilhelm Böhme (1673–1722), the German Lutheran court preacher for Prince George, the husband of Queen Anne, translated Ziegenbalg's German letters from 1706 to 1708 into English and entitled it as *Propagation of the Gospel in the East*. He published the third part in 1718. In 1715, Ziegenbalg's *Letter to the Reverend Mr Geo[rge] Lewis [... about] Method of Instruction used in the Charity-Schools of the Church Call'd Jerusalem in Tranquebar*, was published in London. Neither of these books has a map.

13 AFSt/M 2 D 39 : 3 = HR, 98th Cont., 1765, 226–263: Schwartz's diary from 26.05.1762 to

4.3 Interaction with the Roman Catholics

During his time in Tiruccirāppaḷḷi, Schwartz encountered significant challenges in his interactions with the Roman Catholic Christians. As a Danish Lutheran missionary, he struggled to accept the Jesuit missionaries of Roberto De Nobili's Madurai Mission, who had assimilated into the customs of local non-Christian Tamil priests in temples. These Jesuits, known as the *Paṇḍāraswāmi*s ('mendicants'), worked along the Kaveri River and in interior places, tending to their non-Brahmin Tamil Christian followers. When a *Paṇḍāraswāmi* came to meet Preston, Schwartz was immediately requested to speak with him. This *Paṇḍāraswāmi,* who appeared so Tamil that Schwartz could hardly recognise him as a European, wore a saffron cassock, tunic, turban, and earrings. Schwartz's aversion to this external identification of the Jesuits with the Tamil religious leaders indicates the intricate nature of religious interactions in 18th-century India.[14]

Schwartz's relationship with Roman Catholic Christians reflected Lutheran attitudes in Germany. He earnestly waited for them to embrace Lutheran Pietism, which he represented. At the same time, he welcomed Christians and catechists (e.g., Ñāṉapirakācam, Jōtināyakkaṉ, and others) who had left the Roman Catholic Church and joined the Tamil Lutheran congregations under his care. Following the papal suppression of the Madurai Mission in 1773 and the scarcity of Jesuit missionaries among the Tamils, a significant number of Roman Catholics converted to Lutheranism.

4.4 Wallajah after the Treaty of Paris (1762/63)

Meanwhile, the *Treaty of Paris* (Section 1.2.1) solidified Nawab Wallajah's position as the rightful Nawab of Carnatic, marking a significant shift in the political landscape.[15] Since his enthronement on August 3, 1749, he sought to be free from his subjection to the Mughal Emperor in Delhi and the Nizam of Hyderabad.[16] As the sovereign of Carnatic, the Nawab considered the rulers of Tanjore, Madurai and other places in southern India his tribute-paying vassals. He also viewed the

20.12.1762 contains information about his stay in Tanjore and Tiruccirāppaḷḷi, Schwartz's pastoral care to the Tamil Lutherans, his dialogues with diverse people, a camel sacrifice, meeting King Pratāpasimha and several of his officers.

14 AFSt/M 1 B 54 : 53: On 19.01.1765, Schwartz worried that living far away from his like-minded colleagues might lead him to accommodate himself more to the socio-cultural identities of the people. After he had met the *Padāraswami*, his worries about cultural adaptation increased.

15 The Nawab of Carnatic ruled over the vast area that modern Tirunelvēli, Ramanathapuram, Madurai, Tiruccirāppaḷḷi, Tanjore, South Arcot, North Arcot, Chengalpattu, Chittoor and Nellore cover.

16 This *Treaty of Paris* confirmed the privileges bestowed on Wallajah by Deccan's most senior Mughal administrators. On 26 August 1765, Shah Alam II, the Mughal Emperor in Delhi, recognised Wallajah as the Nawab of Carnatic.

Company as his servants, who executed his bidding.[17] The *Treaty of Paris* limited the French trading privileges to five places, which was advantageous to the Nawab.[18] These places were Pondicherry, Chandra Nagar near Calcutta, Karaikal near Tranquebar, Mahé in Travancore, and Yānam on the river Gōdāvari.

After the *Treaty of Paris*, King George III of the United Kingdom declared Wallajah the lawful Nawab of Carnatic and sent his representative, John Lindsay,[19] to his court. Wallajah viewed himself as equal to King George III and Queen Charlotte.[20] He began oppressing the people of Carnatic more harshly than before. He attacked anyone who did not fulfil his wish. For example, he discarded the previous help that his father, Anwaruddin Khan (1672–1749), the first Nawab of Carnatic, had received from Pratāpasimha of Tanjore. Wallajah, too, forgot Pratāpasimha's assistance to him.

The Company's army decisively defeated the French at Pondicherry in 1761. On 18 October 1762, Wallajah reminded Pratāpasimha about his agreement with his father, Anwaruddin Khan, for an annual tribute of twenty-two lakhs of Rupees. As Pratāpasimha did not pay it, Wallajah asked him to pay the arrears and the yearly tribute into the Company's accounts.[21] Endless quarrels ensued between Wallajah and Pratāpasimha.

Wallajah sought to distance himself from any French threat, and in 1766, he relocated his residence from Arcot to a location within Fort St. George in Madras.[22]

---

17 The History and Management of the East-India Company, from its Origin in 1600 to the Present Times. Volume the first containing the Affairs of the Carnatic, in which the Rights of the Nabob are explained, and the Injustice of the Company proved. The whole [is] compiled from authentic records. London: T. Cadell, 1782, here 112: Originally, the Company's government was supposed to obey the Mughal Emperor. Then, they became servants of Wallajah, the Mughal Governor of Arcot. As servants, the officers of the Company should obey Wallajah and receive rewards from him.

18 After the *Treaty of Paris*, the French power in India declined. Catholic missionaries, who depended on French support and their Indian followers, suffered. Catholics living outside the named five places could not obtain pastoral services. Some of them joined the Tamil Lutheran congregations.

19 C. S. Srinivasachari: Vignettes from the History of Wallajah Dynasty of the Carnatic, 1744–1855 – Part I & II – Lectures delivered under the auspices of the Osmania University, Hyderabad 1947, here 162–163: Lindsay, King George III's nominee to Wallajah's court, was the Admiral of the Royal Navy, Naval Commander-in-Chief in India and as Plenipotentiary. He tried to control the Company. He could not work with General Eyre Coote, the Commander-in-Chief for India. Each of them claimed to have the right to issue orders. The Company decided against Coote, and Coote returned to England. Lindsay stayed on and enjoyed Wallajah's favours. IOR/H/104, 383–85: For example, on 13.03.1771, Lindsay expressed his joy to Viscount Weymouth over his royal appointment and how pompously Wallajah had received and treated him.

20 IOR/H/104, 649: On 07.10.1771, Wallajah informed Queen Charlotte of the death of his wife, "Nabob Begum," who had written to the queen on 26.03.1771. She died hoping that King George III would protect not only Carnatic but also Wallajah and his family. Therefore, Wallajah sent pieces of ornate jewels studded with diamonds and emeralds to the queen.

21 IOR/H/104, 437–444: "Translation of A Treaty and Agreement made and concluded between Omdat ul Melek Serajah Domlah, Annawerdeen Bahauder, Mupssor Jaha, Nabob of the Carnatick [Umdat-ul-Mulk, Siraj-ud-Daula Bahadur Dilawar Jang] Payen Gall and Pratapasingh, Rajah of Tanjore."

22 C. A. Bayly: Indian Society and the Making of the British Empire, 6th rpt. (1988). Cambridge

He tried to control the power of the Company from within their fort. Contrary to his expectations, he became indebted to the Company, paying the Company seven lakh Pagodas annually to maintain its armies and three and a half lakh Pagodas as rent for the districts of Chengalpattu and Poonamallee (i.e., Pūviruntavalli). Gradually, as Wallajah could not pay the increasing expenses, existing debts and interest,[23] The Company occupied more of its territories. This expansion opened new avenues for the officers and merchants of the Company to engage in private trade; they, too, lent money to local rulers, such as the kings of Tanjore, at high interest rates. They possessed the lands of those who could not pay off their debts promptly.[24]

4.5 Schwartz and the British in Tiruccirāppaḷḷi

After Klein's departure to Tranquebar, Schwartz remained in Tiruccirappalli, where he established a school and held prayer meetings in his house. Despite fierce opposition from local non-Christians, Schwartz persevered, demonstrating his unwavering commitment to his mission and inspiring those around him with his determination.[25] His prolonged stay in Tiruccirāppaḷḷi anxious the missionaries in Tranquebar and Madras. Mission authorities in Germany suspected his motives. Schwartz became aware of these apprehensions. On 13 October 1763, he expressed his desire to return to Tranquebar.

Unexpected events and circumstances prolonged his stay in Tiruccirāppaḷḷi. He served the poor people who wandered about for food and shelter. With Preston's support, he could help them financially, and they could start their lives anew. After Preston's transfer to another place, Schwartz got no financial help from others. Famine, created by the Company, was grinding. Hungry people collapsed on the streets and died. Schwartz stated that the story of these dying

2006, here 69: "After 1763, the Nawab of Arcot settled in Triplicane, adding a community of about 20,000 northern Muslims to the old population of Tamil-speaking Muslim merchants of the coast, the Marakayyars."

23 Henry Davidson Love: Vestiges of Old Madras 1640–1800 traced from the East India Company's records preserved at Fort St. George and the India Office and from other sources with maps and illustrations. Vol. 1. London 1913, here 188–189: Wallajah's debt had three parts: "the consolidated debt of 1767, for which John Pybus, John Call and James Bourchier were trustees, stood originally at 22 lakhs of Pagodas, but it had in part been paid off; the cavalry loan of 1769 consisted of 4 lakhs advanced by James Taylor, Andrew Majendie and James Call for the satisfaction of arrears of pay of Nawab's troops; and the consolidated debt of 1777, which Rumbold placed at 63 lakhs, though it was afterwards stated to be only 35 lakhs of pagodas."

24 Love: Vestiges of Old Madras, Vol. 1, 189: Wallajah constantly needed money. He borrowed it from financiers like Paul Benfield and allowed them to collect revenues from specified regions until they could collect their capital and interest.

25 AFSt/M 1 B 52 : 33: On 01.12.1762, Francke acknowledged receiving Schwartz's recent letters and wanted to know further developments in Tanjore and Tiruccirāppaḷḷi. He perceived Schwartz as an instrument in God's hands and was eager to read about God's activities in and through Schwartz in Tanjore and Tiruccirāppaḷḷi. At the same time, he expressed his sadness over Schwartz's shaking hands and inability to write more detailed letters and reports.

people would melt the hearts of his readers. Parents who were desperate for money sold their children into slavery. Schwartz blamed the greedy officers of the Company who deepened the cruel famine. He called these officers "money leeches." In a letter to Francke, Schwartz stated that since the Nawab could not speak Tamil, he was unaware of the dire situation of the Tamil people. He also informed Francke that the English requested him to accompany their army and provide chaplaincy services to their soldiers. He stated that those English officers he had known had donated money to Schwartz to educate their children born outside of wedlock.[26]

In January 1764, the English military officers in Tiruccirāppaḷḷi needed Schwartz more urgently. An ammunition depot had exploded again, killing or maiming soldiers and leaving more orphans. Schwartz tended to the wounded and the sick. He raised money for an "English orphan school" and obtained the necessary books from Madras and Calcutta. Despite the tragedy, Schwartz's actions provided a beacon of hope for the orphans, demonstrating the resilience of the human spirit and uplifting those around him with his compassion.

In February 1764, Preston urged Schwartz to stay longer in Tiruccirāppaḷḷi and minister among the Company soldiers. Schwartz consulted his colleagues in Tranquebar, Cuddalore and Madras. Astonishingly, they encouraged him to accept the invitation because Preston, who had previously helped the poor, could also promote his missionary work.[27] John Wood, a Company military officer, helped Schwartz establish a school for the children of European fathers and Tamil or Portuguese mothers. On 3 March 1764, this school had twelve children.[28] An invalid soldier, whom Preston had assigned, taught these children. When Wallajah learned of this English school, he wanted to support it monthly with a small amount of money.[29]

In the meantime, Wallajah hired the army of the Company to defeat the Tamil General Muhammad Yusuf Khan (1725–1764)[30] in Madurai, who was the "bravest and ablest of all the native soldiers that ever served the English in India."[31]

---

26 AFSt/M 1 B 53 : 17.

27 HR, 101st Cont., 581.

28 Germann: Missionar Christian Friedrich Schwartz, 142–143.

29 AFSt/M 1 B 53 : 18 and AFSt/M 1 B 53 : 19: On the same day (03.03.1764), Schwartz informed his close friend Johann Friedrich Sorge that people in Tiruccirāppaḷḷi suffered greatly; the Tamil Lutheran church was weak in all respects. The condition of the school children remained worrisome. The twelve students in an English school were born to English soldiers; their mothers were either Tamil or Portuguese women. With immense pride, he stated that Hüttemann had baptised a Śaivite *Pandāram* called "Tondaman Mudaly." For a detailed account of this mendicant, see AFSt/M 1 B 53 : 30: On 12.01.1764, Hüttemann translated the 28-page testimony. Later, he, Schwartz and others discovered how this man faked his conversion. Published accounts about this man embarrassed the missionaries, their friends and readers.

30 Love: Vestiges of Old Madras. Vol. 1, 577: Yusuf Khan was "said to have been a Hindu of the Vellala caste." After embracing Islam, he was called "Nellore Subahdar."

31 Hill: Yusuf Khan, here the title page. Hill quoted this statement on this title page. For additional details about Yusuf Khan, see Aram Bakshian: "A Patriot for whom? Yusuf Khan – Conflicts of Loyalty in Eighteenth-Century India," History Today 37, 1987, issue 4, 40–44: Yusuf Khan was a Tamil convert to Islam. His birth name was Muthunāyagam Pillai, and he

Wallajah requested Preston's army to defeat Yusuf Khan. Preston asked Schwartz to accompany him, and he reached Madurai on 13 June 1764. He showed Schwartz a hospital where hundreds of wounded soldiers received treatment. Schwartz comforted them. He also visited the wounded military officers and other injured persons in Sikandar Malai, near modern Tirupparaṅkuṉṟam. He counselled the wounded and advised them to repent and trust in Jesus. He urged them to amend their lives before they could return to their parental home in Britain. On Sundays, he conducted a German worship service for German soldiers and an English service for the English.[32]

Schwartz's journal entry for June 26, 1764, graphically describes his last encounter with Preston in Madurai, as they stayed in the same room. Wallajah met Schwartz in his room and requested, "Pray for my people." Preston, too, asked for Schwartz's prayer and went to the battlefield before 4 am. As he climbed onto a wall to see the soldiers who had fallen into a deep ditch at 6 am, a bullet tore through his abdomen. Soldiers carried Preston into his room. As he died, he stretched out his arms to Schwartz and confessed, "My friend!" I have been punished for my sins." Wallajah came and felt sorry for Preston. Preston responded clearly: "My brave soldiers were killed without achieving anything." Schwartz comforted Preston and then visited the wounded in the hospital. He exclaimed, "What a tragic sight! I have never seen such a tragedy in my life. The war was God's terrible punishment."

Schwartz stated that he could not speak but stood still and listened to the wounded soldiers in both hospitals. As Preston lay dying, Schwartz urged him to seek Christ's grace and forgiveness humbly. Preston could not bear the pain. He took opium and slept for four hours. When he woke up, he confided to Schwartz that he wanted to become a different and better person. Schwartz took leave at midnight and revisited him on 12 July. Just before his death, he confessed: "Help me, O Lord Jesus! Before I die and come to you soon, I repent straightaway." Then he died.[33]

Charles Campbell, the commanding officer of the Company's army in Madurai, requested that Schwartz speak with the wounded soldiers. Showing great empathy, Schwartz ministered to more than 500 soldiers, including those who had fallen ill. After the soldiers had returned from Madurai to Tiruccirāppaḷḷi, Wallajah gave

grew up in Ramanathapuram. Later, he served the Company with utmost loyalty. In 1755, the Company recognised his contributions, appointed him the Commandant of all the Company's sepoys, awarded him a gold medal, and made him the governor of Madurai. Due to the Company's later treaty with Nawab Wallajah, Yusuf Khan became a subordinate to Wallajah. Yusuf Khan joined the French and supported Chanda Sahib as the Nawab of Arcot. By contrast, the Company made Wallajah the Nawab of Arcot and used him as their puppet. As soon as Yusuf Khan became a subordinate, Wallajah decided to eliminate him by accusing him of disloyalty and rebellion. The Company called and warned Yusuf Khan in 1759. Then, Captain Preston informed the Company that Yusuf Khan had gathered 6,000 sepoys and a hundred cavalrymen, cooperated with the French and might endanger the Company's interests. As a result, the Company army persuaded a friend of Yusuf Khan to betray him; they imprisoned him on 14 October 1764 and hanged him the following day.

32 HR, 101st Cont., 582.

33 HR, 101st Cont., 583–585.

Schwartz a gift of six hundred Pagodas; Schwartz spent this money on the school for European orphans and the Tamil Lutheran congregation in Tiruccirāppaḷḷi. Knowing this noble deed, Wallajah sent him an additional sum of three hundred Pagodas. Robert Palk, the president of the Company (1763–1767), attempted to raise further funds for the school to support European orphans.[34] Hill, who had studied Schwartz's ministries in Tiruccirāppaḷḷi and Madurai, concluded that there was "no more saintly character in the annals of Madras than that of the Danish missionary, Christian Frederick Schwartz."[35]

On 2 September 1764, Schwartz baptised eight persons.[36] On 17 January 1765, he reported to Francke that in October 1764, he rushed from Tiruccirāppaḷḷi to Tanjore and persuaded Captain Berg not to invite the Moravians from Poṟaiyār to Tanjore. After returning to Tiruccirāppaḷḷi, he planned to build a church where Europeans and Tamil Lutherans could worship on Sundays and weekdays; this building would also serve as a school. His European friends promised to help him. He raised 2,000 Royal Dollars within two days. Then, Schwartz requested the Nawab to provide him with a suitable location for a church within the fort. The Nawab was unwilling to assign a place. Hence, he asserted that fellow Muslims would not appreciate it. Nevertheless, he wanted to write a letter to the Company about the church and request their opinion. Though unwilling to grant any space for a church, he tried to soothe Schwartz. Schwartz waited patiently for permission from the Company. In the meantime, he started teaching five children in his Tamil school.[37]

On 6 March 1765, Schwartz related that the Company, recognising the importance of education, permitted him to build a school hall. This support from the Company Board was a significant step in the mission, highlighting the collaborative efforts in establishing the school and authorising Colonel John Wood to supervise its building.[38] Despite Wallajah's opposition, Schwartz and the

---

34 Samuel Charles Hill: Yusuf Khan—The Rebel Commandant. London 1914, here 24.

35 Hill: Yusuf Khan, 206–207. Hill arrived at this conclusion after examining records about Schwartz's meetings with Preston and Yusuf Khan, his arrival in Madurai on 18.6.1764, his two-month stay, and his ministry among five hundred wounded soldiers. He visited and prayed with the soldiers in the hospital. He thought of war as a "terrible punishment from God!" because people forgot to live in peace and deal with each other fairly and justly. Consequently, innocent people suffered greatly.

36 AFSt/M 1 B 54 : 22.

37 AFSt/M 1 B 54 : 23 and HR, 103rd Cont., 826–827: On 21.01.1765, he added more details: he continued his missionary work among Christians and non-Christians; since October 1764, he ministered to the Company soldiers in Madurai for a month. He wanted a proper church building; their temporary straw hut and the barracks room had enough space for all the soldiers who came to him. These soldiers and their officers raised 2,000 Pagodas. When they asked Wallajah for a place, he replied that Muslims would not welcome any church building. Consequently, Schwartz and the English officers sent their request to the Company and patiently waited for their reply. Schwartz reported further that the small Tamil school functioned well. The English school flourished under the leadership of Wheatley.

38 AFSt/M 1 B 56 : 21: On 10.07.1766, Schwartz recorded that on 13 March, they began building the church. After three months, this building was ready. It was dedicated on the Day of Pentecost. All school children learned from 7 to 8 a.m. God's World. After 8 a.m., they acquired professional reading, writing and record-keeping skills. After 8 am, they acquired professional reading, writing and record-keeping skills.

Company officers remained steadfast in their commitment to the project. They appointed Iṉṉācimuttu (the 'Pearl of Ignatius'), a Pariah, as a Tamil teacher and paid his salary. Schwartz established a school for British children and appointed William Wheatley as their teacher. Quickly, Wheatley's European school had sixteen children, and the growth of the Tamil school was slow.[39]

4.6 Decision to Stay in Tiruccirāppaḷḷi

On 15 January 1766, Schwartz informed Francke that he had decided to leave Tiruccirāppaḷḷi, transfer his children to Madras and then move to Tanjore or Tranquebar. However, "honest Englishmen" persuaded him to stay in Tiruccirāppalli; in December 1765, these army officers promised to find a place for a church building and sponsor its construction. For example, Major John Wood marked a spot for the construction of a new church building. On 13 March 1765, Schwartz laid the foundation for a church; the building was ready within a year. On 18 May 1766, he dedicated this church and named it *Christ Church.*[40]

In that year (1766), the Nawab paid the Company 130,000 Pagodas, from which the Company compensated Schwartz with five hundred Pagodas for his service to the soldiers until that time. Additionally, the Company gave him 200 Pagodas as a present, 100 Pagodas for the Tamil school, 40 Pagodas to build a school hall (i.e., a church building), 40 Pagodas for the English school, and 20 Pagodas as Schwartz's salary. The Nawab presented the English school with 1,000 Gulden (equivalent to three hundred Pagodas), from which Schwartz could pay a monthly salary of five Royal Dollars to the schoolteacher, Wheatley, maintain four needy children free of cost, and support all sixteen students in the school.[41]

Schwartz reported further that by September 1766, the church building had reached door level. They were about to install the roof. In the meantime, Schwartz started learning Persian.[42] As soon as he could speak Persian, Wallajah invited

---

39 AFSt/M 1 B 54 : 24.

40 Hermann Gundert: Arbeiter in der Tamil-Mission: 6. Chr. F. Schwartz. In: Evangelisches Missions-Magazin 12, 1868, 225–242, here 231: When this church was being built, a dreadful thing happened, astonishingly increasing Schwartz's sacred vocation. Gundert noted that a drunkard who mocked Schwartz fell from the roof of a building and died. Ever since, people have been careful when critiquing Schwartz directly. This church, Christ's Church, exists; nowadays, it belongs to the Church of South India.

41 AFSt/M 1 B 56 : 16.

42 AFSt/M 1 B 56: Schwartz requested that Francke send him a copy of the New Testament in Persian. He stated that Persian was the court language and was highly respected. All letters and accounts were written and exchanged in Persian. Muslims esteemed Arabic, but only a few of them understood it. Many read the Quran in Arabic but spoke and wrote in Persian or Hindustani. Hindustani did not have its own script. The Company in Tiruccirāppaḷḷi had a Persian interpreter. Around 1739, his father accompanied Nadir Shah (1688–1747), who came to Delhi. AFSt/M 1 B 58 : 40: On 06.10.1768, Schwarz expressed happiness in reading his Persian New Testament with a Muslim language teacher, who began to prefer Christianity to Islam. As soon as Wallajah knew about this matter, he placed the Muslim language teacher under house arrest. Schwartz persisted in learning the Persian language. Eventually, he could speak it with Hyder Ali and others.

Schwartz to a meeting. At that time, Schwartz explained to him the sins of our ancestors Adam and Eve, the three sources of human temptations (i.e., the material world, carnal desires, and the devil), the deplorable consequences of the Fall, and the promise of the "Seed of the woman" (Genesis 3:15). Wallajah listened to these things silently and went away. Schwartz wondered what Wallajah thought about these teachings.[43]

On 14 March 1766, Schwartz reported to Francke that most officers of the Company were dangerously greedy for money. He also confessed to his declining health and its adverse impact on his ministry.[44] On 10 July 1766, he disclosed a more profound dilemma about his stay in Tiruccirāppaḷḷi to Francke. He regretted not having requested that Mission College in Copenhagen permit him to continue serving in Tiruccirāppaḷḷi. For this purpose, he hesitated to accept any salary from an English organisation and become an English missionary. However, he was also aware of the practical advantages of remaining in Tiruccirāppaḷḷi. The inhabitants of Tiruccirāppaḷḷi could travel freely anywhere, and they did not need to answer to customs officers. By contrast, a missionary in Tanjore could not leave the boundary walls of Tanjore and travel to Tirupālāduthurai without undergoing any customs check, as Tanjore was a tributary of Tiruccirāppaḷḷi.[45] For example, a Tamil man of a "higher caste" in Tanjore was afraid to become a Christian because his relatives and friends would ostracise him. By contrast, no intense fear of social ostracisation existed in Tiruccirāppaḷḷi because more Hindus and Muslims lived there. Unlike in Tanjore, no one would require the members of the lower *jāti* groups to pull the temple cars (*tēr*) along the streets, because even the members of these lower *jāti* groups had a degree of social standing there. These and other more favorable factors persuaded Schwartz to continue his ministry in Tiruccirappalli. However, he made it clear to Francke that if Mission College in Copenhagen asked him to return to Tranquebar, he would gladly move there out of obligation, demonstrating his commitment to his duty.[46]

On 17 December 1766, Schwartz described the difficulties during his missionary travels in Tanjore. Whenever he left the town to visit the congregations in the villages, he was required to obtain prior permission from the king to leave and return to the city. Additionally, the inhabitants of Tanjore were afraid of becoming Christians and living as Christians because they could not refuse to participate in the rituals of the Śaivite or Vaiṣṇavite temples. Catechumens from upper *varṇa* backgrounds demanded a treatment that kept them separate from catechumens from lower *varṇa* and *jāti* backgrounds. By contrast, a missionary staying in Tiruccirāppaḷḷi could easily send catechists up to Madurai, and they did not need to obtain permission from anyone. They could share God's word with

---

43 AFSt/M 1 B 56 : 16.

44 AFSt/M 1 B 56 : 17.

45 AFSt/M 1 B 56 : 20: On 17.07.1766, Schwartz reiterated the same conditions: a missionary living in Tanjore could visit only the suburb (within the city limits). Along the borders of Tanjore, a customs office was established every half mile, where one had to pay a toll. By contrast, an inhabitant of Tiruccirāppaḷḷi was not answerable to any customs officer.

46 AFSt/M 1 B 56 : 18.

people along the way. For example, Sri Rangam, a Vaiṣṇavite citadel, was only a quarter of a mile away. Any Christian or any catechist could freely speak about the Lord Jesus Christ. No one would force them to participate in non-Christian festivals or rituals because all inhabitants knew that the prince of the place was a Muslim. These practical advantages, such as the freedom to share God's word with people along the way, the proximity to Sri Rangam, and the absence of religious coercion, persuaded Schwartz to stay in Tiruccirāppaḷḷi.[47]

4.7 Schwartz as Garrison Chaplain

On 24 October 1767, Schwartz reported to Francke that his health remained stable.[48] He found great joy in working alongside the catechists Iṉṉācimuttu and Jōtināyakkaṉ, who both spoke Persian, enabling them to engage with Persian-speaking Muslims. The Company extended a formal invitation to Schwartz to serve as their Garrison Chaplain, offering an annual salary of one hundred Royal Dollars. Schwartz, in turn, shared this news with his colleagues in Tranquebar, who unanimously encouraged him to accept the offer, provided that his salary would benefit the Tranquebar Mission. This arrangement, coupled with the establishment of a new worshipping congregation, two schools, and a home for the catechists and Schwartz, solidified his decision to remain in Tiruccirāppaḷḷi.[49]

At the end of their conversation, when Tulāji offered Schwartz sweets, Schwartz explained that it was his custom to pray and thank God for the food, and he did so. The king listened to the prayer and requested Schwartz to sing a Tamil song. Immediately, Schwartz sang three stanzas of the hymn „Upattiravaṅkaḷ Varātē Nīr Māttiram" ('Hardships will not come if only you are there').[50] The king was so delighted that he said he had never heard such a thing from a European. Schwartz wished Tulāji well and returned to Tiruccirāppaḷḷi.

After a while, Berg wrote to Schwartz and informed him that Tulāji desired Schwartz to come to Tanjore, build a house and live there permanently. Shortly

47 AFSt/M 1 B 56 : 20; AFSt/M 1 B 58 : 40: Schwartz was sad about Ziegenhagen's demand for Schwartz to move to Tranquebar. AFSt/M 1 B 59 : 31: On 17.01.1770, Schwartz informed Ziegenhagen that leaving Tiruccirāppaḷḷi as a garrison chaplain would have disastrous consequences for the budding ministry there. AFSt/M 1 B 60: 41: On 12.12.1771, Knapp informed Schwartz about Ziegenhagen's displeasure with receiving a salary from the SPCK and serving as a garrison chaplain. Finally, Ziegenhagen left it to Schwartz's discernment and decision.

48 AFSt/M 1 B 57: 17. On 24.10.1767, Schwartz confessed to his trusted friend Pasche that he loved meditating on God's Word and noted that more people worshipped images of deities to satisfy their carnal desires. They chose to worship images, not out of a lack of proper knowledge. A *Pandāram*, with whom Schwartz spoke, wanted to see God's work more than what he heard about God's nature.

49 AFSt/M 1 B 57 : 14 and AFSt/M 1 B 58 : 57: On 06.10.1768, Francke informed Schwartz about his happiness over Schwartz's new salaried position as the Garrison Pastor. He encouraged him to accept this position because God had given him a new ministerial opportunity.

50 Fabricius translated this Tamil text from the German hymn "Mein Gott, das Herz ich bring dir" ('My God, I bring my heart to you').

after that, Tulāji wrote to Schwartz: "Padre! I place my entire trust in you because you are not swayed by money."[51] Immediately, Schwartz asked his fellow missionaries in Tranquebar, Madras and Cuddalore for their thoughts on his moving to Tanjore. On 20 May 1769, Breithaupt and Fabricius, who worked in Madras, requested that Schwartz accept this opportunity as God's invitation. They supposed that God might shape Tulāji as God transformed King Solomon.[52]

On 13 January 1770, Schwartz told Francke about his renewed meeting with Tulāji in Tanjore. In June 1769, Tulāji asked Schwartz to accompany Colonel John Wood from Tiruccirāppaḷḷi to Tanjore and received them in a friendly manner. A Brahmin informed Schwartz that Tulāji had heard his sermon from hiding and noted his interpretations of the polytheistic deities as devils. However, Tulāji wanted to keep him in the palace so that he could teach his (ignorant) people higher ideals. On another day, Tulāji noticed Schwartz speaking with a person in the palace and sent his servant to ask him not to leave the fort. Tulāji wanted to meet Schwartz. At that time, more Brahmins came there. Captain Berg was also there. Only the chief Brahmin, who controlled the kingdom's finances, did not come. This chief Brahmin sent a servant to Schwartz to tell him that Tulāji wanted to meet him that afternoon. Schwartz waited, but Tulāji did not come.[53]

Schwartz observed that Tulāji's chief servants did not permit him to go out and treated him as a "prisoner" in his palace. They cheated him and his entire country, and they did not like Schwartz for his honesty. By then, however, most people in the palace knew Tulāji wanted Schwartz to be around him. In the meantime, Schwartz requested that Captain Berg find out why Tulāji had summoned him to the palace. That officer asked Schwartz to return to Tiruccirāppaḷḷi, at least for a while, because Tulāji had desired him to be his Padre, i.e., his *guru*, to whom he could confide anything. Captain Berg proved helpful in these interactions. Schwartz was happy that he and his Tamil catechists could diligently sow the seeds of God's Word among all peoples in Tanjore.[54]

In the meantime, Tulāji permitted Captain Berg to hold his daughter's marriage in the palace. When Schwartz solemnised the marriage after two weeks,[55] his friends placed a table in the middle of an open room and spread a white cloth.

---

51 Germann: Missionar Christian Friedrich Schwartz, 227.

52 AFSt/M 1 B 58 : 39.

53 AFSt/M 1 B 59 : 31: On 16.01.1770, Schwartz informed Pasche in London that the king wanted Schwartz to stay longer in the Fort. However, the chief Brahmin thwarted that plan. Schwartz returned to Tiruccirāppaḷḷi to care for the Tamil Lutherans there. In 1769, he had baptised twenty Tamils and admitted seven Roman Catholic Christians into the Tamil Lutheran congregation in Tiruccirāppaḷḷi.

54 AFSt/M 1 B 59 : 28.

55 AFSt/M 1 B 62 : 33: On 12.10.1772, Schwartz wrote to Freylinghausen in Halle that he had solemnised the marriage of Berg's daughter with another captain who had just arrived at the palace in March. He felt that the whole situation was strange and out of place, mainly because the king had a different purpose. He wanted to use him as a mediator between him and the Company. Schwartz realised that such political mediation was not inherently sinful, but both parties often lied and remained proud. They seemed interested in embracing Lutheranism. However, they had other motives. The Nawab considered himself the sovereign ruler of Carnatic and oppressed the people harshly.

Tulāji and his chief servants stood near Schwartz. Tulāji's wives watched the rituals from a darkened neighbouring room. Three catechists of higher *jāti* stood near Schwartz. Schwartz sang Fabricius's Tamil version of the German song "Jesu Gottes Sohn vor des Himmels Thron" ('Jesus, God's Son, before the heavenly throne'). Then Schwartz preached a sermon about God creating the first humans in God's image and the institution of marriage. He explained that the purpose of marriage was to help each other in all ways of life, to be co-creators in God's created world, to accept God's salvation and to attain eternal bliss. He enumerated the unhelpful purposes of marriage, sang another song and blessed the couple. The three catechists knelt beside him as he prayed and sang beautifully.[56]

Consequently, Tulāji permitted Schwartz to build a church in Tanjore. He warned him not to convert any of his subjects but to strengthen only those who had already embraced Lutheranism and had been following him. Schwartz responded that God wanted all people to attain forgiveness of sins and salvation. Immediately, a Brahmin intervened and asked: "What is this? On every street, we hear about the true religion?" The Brahmins and Tulāji tolerated Schwartz's presence because they wanted him to be their trusted envoy to the Company and the Nawab. When Schwartz understood their intention, he exclaimed that he could not fully trust Tulāji, the Company, or Wallajah because they were untrustworthy. He would communicate only the truth according to his conscience if they desired him to be their envoy.

4.8 Tulāji's First Fall (1771)

In this context, Pratāpasimha died on 16 December 1763; his son Tulāji succeeded him. Tulāji believed that the agreement between his father and Wallajah did not bind him. Therefore, he had no obligation to pay off the arrears or any tribute to Wallajah. He also felt that his friendship with Hyder Ali would deter Wallajah from attacking him.[57] By contrast, both Wallajah and the Company viewed Tulāji as their enemy. They accused him of murdering his people, instigating uprisings in Madurai and assisting Hyder Ali to fight against them in 1769 "up to the doors of Madras." When the Company made a peace treaty with Hyder Ali in April 1769, he required the Company to recognise Tulāji as his and their friend fully. Emboldened by Hyder Ali's support, in July 1769, Tulāji stopped paying tribute to Wallajah.[58]

By January 1770, the Company and Wallajah sought an opportunity to attack Tulāji, as they believed Tanjore could serve as a buffer zone between the French in Pondicherry and Karaikal, and the Company. On 31 January 1770, they alleged that Tulāji had assisted the French with soldiers, provisions, and money. Wallajah

---

56 Pearson: Memoirs, Vol. 1, 288–290: On 20.05.1772, Schwartz referred to the catechists Ñāṉapirakācam and Rāyappaṉ. The third catechist might have been Dēvanēsaṉ.

57 The History and Management of the East-India Company, 176.

58 The History and Management of the East-India Company, 243–245 and 249.

wanted to humiliate Tulāji and urged the Company to attack him.[59] On 23 March 1770, the commissioners of the Company, who dealt with war matters, praised Brigadier General Smith for his earlier war against Hyder Ali and judged him the right person to attack Tulāji.[60]

Not knowing this scheming between Wallajah and the Company, Tulāji wished to settle the border problems with Mutturāmaliṅgam of Ramanathapuram and Udaiyāt Tēvar of Sivaganga. He encouraged his general Māppillai Tevar to replace Mutturāmaliṅkam, who, on 11 February 1771, sent Narasiṅga Row and Raghunatha Row to fight against Mutturāmaliṅgam. His general did not know that Udaiyāt Tēvar had already sent "an army of 1,200 horses, 2,000 sepoys & 4,000 peons with eight guns, large & small, gun power & stores of war" to assist Mutturāmaliṅkam.[61] This development alarmed the Company, and on 11 September 1771, they informed the Court of Directors in London about Tulāji's war and his failure to tell them or Wallajah.[62] In September 1771, Mutturāmaliṅkam renewed his subordination to Wallajah and requested his intervention against Tulāji. Wallajah got the support of Captain Joseph Smith of the Company. Smith was already serving Wallajah on behalf of the Company. Smith led 247 artillery men, 1,236 European infantry soldiers, 5,945 Indian sepoys, 1,345 lascars, 159 smiths, 79 carpenters, 1,047 *coolie*s, 63 fascine makers, 1,110 bullock drivers, 1,755 drought bullocks and 4549 drought bullocks and defeated Tulāji.[63]

On 14 October 1771, Schwartz recounted when Tulāji attacked the Maṟavar rulers, particularly one of their widows. The Maṟavar of Ramanathapuram and Nawab's armies besieged Tanjore and closed all entry points along the border. Wallajah's army removed the Tanjore queen and her chief servants as prisoners of war to Tiruccirāppaḷḷi. Schwartz found the Nawab's greedy ambitions horrible and stated that the Nawab did not allow the neighbours to live in peace.[64] On 9 October 1771, the Company army reached Fort Wallam,[65] and soon, the Nawab's army joined them. Together, they besieged Tanjore. Tulāji knew he could not defeat them. Therefore, he negotiated with Umdat ul-Umara, a son of Wallajah, and agreed on 20 October 1771 to settle the arrears of eight lakh Rupees, relinquish his claims to lands belonging to Ramanathapuram, Sivaganga, and Pudukkottai, and cede Fort Wallam to Umdat-ul-Umara. Five days later, the unsatisfiable Umdat-ul-Umara demanded more money from Tulāji. Hence, on 25 October 1771, Tulāji leased the Māyāvaram District and a part of the Kumbakonam District to Umdat-ul-Umara, so that he could collect Rs. 16¼ lakhs (i.e., a total of 32½ lakh Rupees) annually as war indemnity. On the following day, Umdat-ul-Umara compelled Tulāji to agree to pay an annual tribute and to immediately renounce

59 BL MSS Eur D 1208, 17.
60 BL MSS Eur Orms 33, 139–140.
61 BL MSS Eur Orms 33, 155 and 167.
62 IOR/H/105, 459.
63 IOR/H/106, 69–76.
64 AFSt/M 1 B 60 : 40.

all military operations against the Nawab. Tulāji renounced his claims on Ārani and Hanumantagudi. Consequently, on 27 October 1771, Umdat-ul-Umara requested that General Smith cease his attacks on Tanjore, as Tulāji had agreed to and sworn "by his religion" to do so. As soon as Smith saw the white flag hoisted in the fort, he should have stopped the firing. Umdat-ul-Umara praised Smith by stating that the victory "has proceeded from the bravery and valour of yourself and the army."[66]

Elangovan, who studied these negotiations, concluded that Tulāji's defeat enabled the Company to gain "more commercial and military influence" in Tanjore.[67] The Company rejected this treaty because no party consulted them and stationed their army at Fort Wallam. Knowing this weakness, Hyder Ali's army invaded Tanjore towards the end of 1771. Tulāji tried vainly to get military support from the Marathi leader Trimbuck Rao.[68] Consequently, Tulāji felt exploited, humiliated and abandoned. Therefore, he did not rush to fulfil the stipulations of his treaty with Umdat-ul-Umara.

In 1772, Tulāji persuaded Schwartz to settle in Tanjore, a challenging situation he hoped would help him escape the political and economic hardships he faced. On 18 February 1772, Schwartz informed Knapp that Tulāji wanted to use him as his writer, i.e., as a go-between for Wallajah and the Company. He hesitated to assume this role because both parties discarded the truth. Finally, he agreed to assist Tulāji; otherwise, he would lose his relationship.[69] In the meantime, on 7 April 1772, the ill-informed King George III recognised Wallajah as the sovereign of the Carnatic, promised him his support and authorised him to subdue the king of Tanjore:

> George, the Third, &c. &c. &c. To Nabob Wallajah, &c. Nabob of Arcot and the Carnatic. We received with pleasure your letter, in which you express to us your gratitude for the additional naval force which we have sent for your security, as well as that of our East India Company and your CONFIDENCE, that we shall tread in the steps of our royal grandfather, by granting PROTECTION to you and your family. We have given our Commander-in-Chief and Plenipotentiary, Sir Robert Harland, our instructions for that purpose, and we flatter ourselves that he will reconcile the differences that have arisen between you and the Company's servants, to the mutual benefit of both parties. It gave us satisfaction to hear that the Governor and Council of Madras had sent the Company's troops with yours to reduce your TRIBUTARY, the Rajah of Tanjore, to obedience, in which, we hope, by the blessing of God, they will be successful; and so, we bid you farewell, wishing health and prosperity to you and your family. Given at our Court at St. James's, the 7th day of April 1772, in the 12th year of our reign. Your affectionate friend GEORGE, R.[70]

---

65 IOR/H/106, 69–76.

66 BL MSS Eur D 1208, 19.

67 I. Elangovan: Colonial Acquisitions and Socio-Economic Trends in Madras, 1765–1827. Diss. phil. Madurai, 2012, here 69–70.

68 The History and Management of the East-India Company, 210: Hyder Ali planned to invade Tanjore and advised Wallajah, the Marathi army and the Company not to interfere. Wallajah wanted to protect his country and bribed Hyder Ali's army with money, jewels, "firearms and elephants." K. R. Subramanian: The Maratha Rajas of Tanjore. Madras 1928, here 60–61: Wallajah bribed Trimbuck Rao with 400,000 Rupees so that he would not help Tulāji.

69 AFSt/M 1 B 61 : 41.

70 The History and Management of the East-India Company, 229.

Wallajah, upon receiving this recognition, felt an overwhelming sense of power. He saw himself as the undisputed sovereign ruler of the Carnatic. This acknowledgement meant that Tulāji was his vassal; the Company was his servant. He could exploit the people of the Carnatic as he saw fit, a power that he wielded with a sense of authority.

On 12 October 1772, Schwartz reported to Ziegenhagen that in March 1772, he spent five weeks in Tanjore and met Tulāji three times, of which the following encounter seemed important to Schwartz. Once, Tulāji came with an umbrella bearer, a symbol of his royal status, and asked Schwartz to sit under a tree. He had lost weight, become thin and looked emaciated. He addressed Schwartz as *Padre* and wanted to speak with him privately. At that time, the chief Brahmin came to meet him. Immediately, as a mark of respect, Tulāji prostrated before him. The chief Brahmin sat on the elevated place that was meant for Tulāji. Tulāji got up and stood before him with folded hands as his servant. Then, he requested Schwartz to speak with the Chief Brahmin. Schwartz explained to him how God had created the world and all its contents. He then described the meaning and implication of God's glory, power, wisdom and goodness. Finally, he pointed out the inappropriateness of image worship. The chief Brahmin listened to all that was said but did not respond to Schwartz in any manner. Then, the king invited Schwartz for a meal. Instead of sitting at a table, he followed local etiquette, sitting on the floor, placing a fig-leaf plate before him, and eating rice from it. Tulāji came closer and asked Schwartz about the meaning of repentance. After explaining repentance, Schwartz encouraged him to believe in Jesus Christ as Saviour and Lord. Tulāji replied that such repentance was difficult for him.[71]

During this period, Nawab Wallajah borrowed large sums from the Company officers and bankers like Paul Benfield[72] to pay off the increasing expenses for the Company army, which he had hired to protect himself, his vast family and the Carnatic. By September 1773, Wallajah had borrowed approximately seventy lakhs of pagodas from the officers and bankers of the Company. To receive these large loans, he paid a bribe of ten lakh Pagodas to the officers and traders of the Company.[73] Facing dire financial circumstances, Wallajah was compelled to act swiftly. His decision to subdue Tanjore and collect revenues from its people was a move born out of sheer desperation and the urgent need for financial relief.

---

71 AFSt/M 1 B 62 : 32.

72 Jim Phillips: A Successor to the Moguls: The Nawab of the Carnatic and the East India Company, 1763–1785. In: The International History Review 7, 1985, issue 3, 364–389, here 379: Paul Benfield, a "civil servant, architect and building contractor" in Madras, lent money to Wallajah and Tulāji. As a loan broker for Indians and Europeans, he earned commissions. After 1773, he loaned two million Pagodas to Wallajah to "meet the costs of the Tanjore campaigns and other expenses. In effect, he became the nawab's banker from 1773 to 1775, paying all expenses and securing his investment by *tankhah*s ['pay, salary'] on Tanjore and other districts." He ruined Wallajah's wealth and controlled President Alexander Wynch so much that the latter accepted "only Benfield's bills for the company's costs (payment)."

73 J. D. Gurney: The Debts of the Nawab of Arcot 1763–1776. Diss. phil. Oxford 1968, here 170 and 217.

4.9 Tulāji's Imprisonment (16 September 1773 – 11 April 1776)

The Presidents of the Company, Du Pré (January 31, 1770, to January 31, 1773) and Alexander Wynch (January 31, 1773, to December 11, 1775), were aware of the limitations of the *Regulating Act of India of 1773* (Section 1.2.2).[74] Its ninth clause permitted them to make wage emergency wars against any Indian ruler. Accordingly, Du Pré and Wynch utilised the Company's army to assist Wallajah in defeating Tulāji and plundering Tanjore. They accused Tulāji of soliciting military support from Raghunatha Rao of Satara, Hyder Ali of Mysore, the Dutch in Nagapattinam and the Danes in Tranquebar. They blamed him for plotting to rebel against the Company. Wynch charged General George Smith in Tiruccirāppaḷḷi to fight against Tulāji. Smith led the combined armies of Wallajah and the Company, besieging Tanjore on 6 August 1773. By 20 August 1773, they imprisoned Tulāji, his family and principal officers and plundered his palace.[75] They placed Tulāji in a dark room without windows.[76] They did not permit anyone to visit him. Wallajah allowed the Company to station 8,000 soldiers in the city of Tanjore, with explicit instructions to collect revenues from the inhabitants of Tanjore and distribute them to his creditors, such as Paul Benfield, who exacted the last penny from the hungry, dumb, and helpless cultivators.[77]

Wallajah's additional burden on the farmers of Tanjore, demanding 80% of their annual produce as tax, was a clear act of exploitation. Until he could pay off his debts to the Company, he allowed his British creditors, also known as renters, to collect taxes from significant parts of Tanjore. This exploitation, which led to the impoverishment of Tanjore and forced farmers to leave their lands and settle in nearby territories, was not solely the responsibility of Wallajah but also a consequence of the Company's involvement in Tanjore's politics. This emphasis on the Company's accountability in exploiting Tanjore is crucial in understanding the historical events surrounding Tulāji's imprisonment and restoration.[78]

---

74 A. P. Dasgupta: The Central Authority in British India 1774–1784. A Study of the Relations of the Supreme Council with the Company under the *Regulating Act of 1773*. Calcutta 1931, here 13–14: President Alexander Wynch was the interim head and tried to avoid trouble. He knew how many council members supported "the questionable transactions of Benfield with the Nawab of Arcot."

75 IOR//H/115, p 2: On 20.09.1773, Wynch and his council reported these details: Nawab's second son, who had accompanied the Company's army, imprisoned Tulāji and his senior officers.

76 AFSt/M 1 B 63 : 28: When Schwartz managed to visit Tulāji in the widow-less dark room, he could not console him. The Nawab and his officers did not understand the worship of non-Muslims, including Christians. The pride of non-Muslims in Tanjore faded away. Schwartz estimated that the time was ripe for Christians to preach the good news about the Lord Jesus Christ, but the Lutheran missionaries in Tranquebar were few. None of them could come and work in Tanjore.

77 Subramanian: The Maratha Rajas of Tanjore, 61–62: "In 1775, 81 lakhs of Rupees were collected, whereas the highest amount collected up to then had been 57½ lakhs in 1761." According to Lord Pigot, between 1774 and 1776, 97½ lakhs of *chakrams* were extorted by the Nawab."

78 Elangovan: Colonial Acquisitions, 71–72: During his three years of occupation of Tanjore (1773–1776), Wallajah collected approximately 120 lakhs of Rupees. In 1775, he earned eighty-one lakhs of Rupees.

On January 11, 1774, Schwartz reported to Frelinghuysen that Wallajah had conquered Tanjore on September 17, 1773. Schwartz understood this conquest theologically as God's judgment on Tulāji, who had lived a careless and impious life. This theological interpretation not only reflected the prevalent religious beliefs but also significantly influenced the political narrative of the time.[79] In the meantime, Schwartz's European friends, such as Pasche in London, assumed that the imprisonment of Tulāji would persuade him to embrace Christianity, but Schwartz had a distinctly different experience. On September 22, 1774, he met Tulāji with the assistance of an interpreter. He knew that Tulāji had recently had no opportunity to hear either the Word of God or the Lord Jesus Christ. Wallajah's Muslim employees guarded Tulāji's prison and did not permit anyone to visit him. They closed the window of his room so that he could not watch the people passing along the street. By that time, all the senior servants of Tulāji had deserted him and run away with whatever they could steal. Wallajah and the Company imprisoned some swindlers. Wealthy inhabitants of Tanjore absconded with their wealth but left their houses behind. The employees of Wallajah and the Company occupied these houses. Those inhabitants who remained in Tanjore were poor. These poor people included soldiers, vendors, manual workers and beggars.

The first year of Nawab's rule in Tanjore exacerbated the people's misery and impoverished them. The harvest in the well-watered lowlands was good. By contrast, the harvest in the higher and drier regions was poor. The Nawab confiscated all the grains and stored them in the forts for his army. He left nothing for the inhabitants. As a result, a terrible famine ensued, and it killed many people. Those who were alive did not hesitate to beg for mercy. If a kind donor distributed goods, crowds rushed to get at least something; the donor could hardly escape them. No one could imagine the hardness of the Nawab's heart. He filled the depots of his army with grain and allowed his subjects to starve and endure unspeakable misery. Schwartz mentioned that the Company elevated Wallajah for their peril and tolerated his countless unjust acts. After his elevation, Wallajah mocked the Company as mere recipients of his payments or bribes. According to Schwartz, the prevailing situation in the Madras Presidency was bleak; it was difficult for people to hold onto hope for a better future.[80]

On 20 February 1775, Schwartz informed Pasche again that he could not adequately describe the dire situation in Tanjore. The Company helped Wallajah to take over all surrounding villages. As lord of Tanjore, he bought all paddy and grains for the low price he had fixed, forcing the impoverished farmers to sell him the grains for half price. After he purchased the paddy, he sold it back to the people at a higher price than he had bought it. This exploitative practice led to thousands of inhabitants fleeing from Tanjore. Those who remained suffered great misery. In Schwartz's opinion, Hyder Ali fared better than Wallajah because, under Hyder Ali, people lived better than in other places. Hence, many inhabitants of Tanjore took refuge in Hyder Ali's land. According to Schwartz, the Nawab had forgotten

---

79 AFSt/M 1 B 63 : 28.

80 AFSt/M 1 B 65 : 42.

the meaning of righteousness, justice, and gentleness. During his travels through Tanjore in 1775, he observed the melancholic conditions of the king and his subjects.[81]

Seven months later, on 8 September 1775, Schwartz could not report anything better to Pasche: more people joined the Tamil Lutheran congregation in Tiruccirāppaḷḷi, but soon left it mainly because they could not find any jobs to earn their sustenance. The severe famine persisted for three years. Particularly, Christians suffered more than anyone else because they could hardly find a job. Schwartz travelled three times from Tiruccirappalli to Tanjore and baptised a few persons in Vallam.[82]

In the same letter of 8 September 1775, Schwartz described Tulāji's imprisonment, stating that he found it impossible to visit him. Not even his chief officers could meet him. Schwarz met a Brahmin in Sri Rangam who narrated an unbelievable story about Tulāji considering embracing Christianity and consulting his senior servants about it. By contrast, the Brahmins reminded him how his ancestors worshipped their deities and remained happy. They (supposedly) advised him to stick with his traditional faith. Some of his senior employees were imprisoned. Some wandered as fugitives. Some tilled the ground; some became farmers. In Schwartz's assessment, the sight of Tanjore broke his heart. He felt that the glory of that country was gone. The Nawab oppressed the people so harshly that they could not cultivate their lands. He leased some regions to renters for a high price; these renters oppressed the farmers harshly. In 1775, they took away 95% of the harvest, leaving just 5% for the farmers. As a result, the inhabitants had no choice but to steal edible items for survival. Conscientious people who did not steal suffered the most. Thus, during Tulāji's imprisonment (September 1773 to his restoration on 11 April 1776) and Wallajah's misrule, the entire infrastructure of Tanjore collapsed; influential people exploited the less fortunate. Misery abounded everywhere.[83]

4.10 Tulāji's Restoration and Surrender to the Company (1776)

When the Company's Court of Directors in London realised this atrocity against Tulāji, they authorised Governor George Pigot to reinstate Tulāji as the rightful ruler of Tanjore. Earlier, Wallajah had bribed Pigot heavily to give Tanjore to his second son. Additionally, he wanted to collect the revenues directly from the farmers himself. On 12 April 1775, the Company's Court of Directors in London directed the governor of Madras to uphold the stipulations of the *Treaty of 1762*, a significant agreement that had established the rights and obligations of the Company and the local rulers and reinstate King Tulāji "on the throne of his ancestors." Accordingly, Tulāji should immediately pay the Company two lakhs

---

81 AFSt/M 1 B 65 : 44.

82 AFSt/M 1 B 66 : 54.

83 AFSt/M 1 B 66 : 54.

of Rupees. He should not infringe on the rights of the Nawab and allow the Company to garrison the Big Fort in Tanjore.[84]

To execute their will, the Court of Directors sent Pigot, in his capacity as the new Governor of Fort St. George, to Tanjore in 1776. His arrival there shattered Wallajah's hopes of further exploiting Tanjore. Pigot was determined to uphold the rights of Tulāji, the local ruler, and to prevent further exploitation of the Kingdom of Tanjore at least temporarily.[85] Pigot asked Schwartz to accompany him as his interpreter. At that time, Tulāji observed Schwartz's skill and began trusting him even more. Tulāji praised the Company's Court of Directors in London for restoring his rule with these extraordinary words:

> If I had one thousand tongues, they could not express my gratitude. I shall ever consider myself as nourished and protected by the Company and shall therefore never assist or succour their enemies. [...] The country of Tanjore belongs to the Company. I have only to beg that they will preserve my honor. *Sunnud* ['Decree'] was granted to the East India Company by the Raja of Tanjore on 17 June 1776.[86]

After Tulāji became a king again, Wallajah's army left Tanjore, and the Company stationed their soldiers in the city and the forts of Tanjore. Wallajah's creditors, including Robert Fletcher, George Stratton, and Paul Benfield, became furious because they could no longer collect revenue from Tanjore. They arrested Pigot on August 24, 1776 and imprisoned him at St. Thomas Mount.[87]

On 2 September 1776, Pigot informed the Court of Directors in London about the eleven-point agreement he had secured from Tulāji.[88] 1) Tulāji should permit the Company to station its army in the fort of Tanjore.[89] He should pay the company 400,000 pagodas annually to maintain this army. He could pay this money in six instalments from November to April. 2) Tulāji should allow the Company engineers to repair and guard the fortifications. 3) Tulāji should not seek help from anyone else. 4) Should a problem arise, Tulāji could ask the Company soldiers and Wallajah for assistance. He should defray all costs. 5) Tulāji should

---

84 IOR/E/4/871, 462.

85 Dodwell: The Nabobs, 26–27: The Nawab's increasing dependence on the Company led to his unethical actions. At his request, the Company defeated Tulāji in 1773 and did not appoint his second son as the ruler of Tanjore. Wallajah bribed the Governors to achieve his goal. Governor Pigot is said to have received from him "no less than 30 lakhs of pagodas" (= £1,200,000 in 1926). Wynch got "over five lakhs" of Pagodas. Rumbold received from him "5½ lakhs" of Pagodas.

86 The Hibernian Magazine, or Compendium of Entertaining Knowledge, January 1771 – April 1785, October 1777, here 665. In his letter on 21.10.1776, Tulāji praised the Company's Court of Directors in London, which the Hibernian Magazine contains: "For Thousands of tongues would not be sufficient to express your goodness or my feelings; it is instances like this, both of justice and of honour that has spread the fame of the English company all over Hindostan and which now serve to enlighten them like the rays of the sun. I pray to God that your power and influence may increase daily and that your colours may always be spread in this country to preserve those who, like myself, look up to you for redress or protection."

87 Pigot died there on 11 May 1777.

88 An Enquiry into the Policy, 136–139.

89 An Enquiry into the Policy, 136.

not allow any other army to stay in Tanjore. 6) In times of war, if the armies of the Company and Wallajah requested his assistance, he should provide it. 7) The Company would not interfere in Tulāji's governance. 8) The military leaders of the Company in Tanjore should give Tulāji detailed accounts of their actual expenses. If the cost exceeds the agreed-upon amount, he should settle it. 9) The representatives of the Company and Tulāji should settle all disputes over expenses amicably. 10) Tulāji could keep his army at his own expense for his self-defence. 11) Tulāji should not pay the Company more tribute than the agreed amount. However, if he could not raise the necessary revenue due to unforeseen circumstances, he should pay it "from his other resources."[90]

Tulāji knew that the Company would be the sole beneficiary of this treaty, and he would become an irrecoverable debtor in his own country. The fact that he agreed to meet the increasing cost of the Company's army and to pay tribute irrespective of his income would plunge him into deeper debt. He was ready to pay whatever it took to keep his restored dignity as king of Tanjore. Therefore, he signed the agreement in desperation.[91] Moreover, he voluntarily became a puppet in the hands of the Company.

Tulāji's praise of and surrender to the Company persuaded his agents in London to praise the British government to the utmost. In 1777, they published a twenty-two-page *Memorial on behalf of the King of Tanjore presented to Lord North.*[92] Its opening paragraph states that Tulāji opened a direct communication with Great Britain to avoid "misrepresentations of all sorts." It mentions that he "venerated" King George III and requested his favour. He asserted that the "territory of Tanjore is an ancient kingdom, and the king of Tanjore is a hereditary prince. This he is bound to claim in favour of his nation, his cast[e], his family and himself. However, he claims nothing more."[93] It states that earlier, Tulāji paid tribute to the Mughal Emperor in Delhi. After the Mughal Empire disintegrated, Tulāji chose King George III as his protector. He voluntarily became a "subject to his Majesty" and held "his territories as dependent on the crown of Great Britain." He was also willing, "according to his ability to contribute, in whatever manner it shall be agreed on, to support the strength and stability of the British power in India."[94] He addressed King George III as his "father." He viewed himself as his "son," urgently needing his protection. He also confessed that he was a "Hindoo," as he is of the Brahmin caste. [As a Brahmin], his persuasion, disposition, and manners are solely

90 An Enquiry into the Policy, 139.

91 Subramanian: The Maratha Rajas of Tanjore, 62–63. Quoting the Remains of the Rev. C. F. Schwartz, 77, and adding other information, Subramanian emphasised Tulāji's powerlessness. The Company did not permit him to maintain an army in the countryside. Instead, they required him to hire the Company army to protect himself, his family, possessions and land. They appointed their officers to oversee his tribute payments to Wallajah and the Company. They did not permit him to enter into any trade agreements with other European trading companies in southern India. Thus, they made him their puppet.

92 Memorial on behalf of the King of Tanjore presented to Lord North. This booklet does not mention its author, publisher, place of publication or date.

93 Memorial on behalf of the King of Tanjore presented to Lord North, 3.

94 Memorial on behalf of the King of Tanjore presented to Lord North, 4.

confined to peace. He wanted "to possess his natural country, to exist [with] his people, to pay his debts and fulfil his engagements." He reminded King George III that Nawab Wallajah had discarded his *Treaty of 1762* with his father, King Pratāpasimha.[95] Wallajah took away "several million Sterling" from Tanjore and forced him to pay additional tribute.[96]

Tulāji confirmed further that he would pay 400,000 Pagodas annually to maintain the Company army in his territories. He wrongly believed that this payment was a token of his gratitude to "the justice and generosity of the English for taking him out of the hands of his enemy and restoring him to his kingdom."[97] Tulāji then requested that King George III no longer support Wallajah with either English money or the English army. Tulāji wanted the British power to continue and flourish in India.[98] He did not like Wallajah to have any part in Tanjore, which remained "the most fertile spot in Hindustan, perhaps in the world" and "the principal granary of all the extensive coast of Coromandel."[99] The Company should not allow Wallajah to turn the "delightful country of Tanjore" into a "frightful desert."[100] Tulāji voluntarily subjected himself, his people, and his kingdom to King George III and requested that he receive his "humble offer of allegiance." Thus, Tanjore's "distant people" would "become his" subjects.[101] Tulāji urged King George III to prevent the Company officers from lending money to Wallajah, as Wallajah, in turn, had assigned large territories of Tanjore to his English creditors, such as Paul Benfield.[102] This petition failed to attract the attention of either King George III or Prime Minister Frederick North (1732–1782).

Meanwhile, Wallajah and his associate Paul Benfield sought to extract more money from Tulāji, whom they had already exploited, to further their financial gains. On 10 September 1776, Tulāji, feeling the weight of their economic demands, expressed his distress to his *vakeel* in Madras. He lamented that Wallajah had already exploited the country so much that he "left hardly a blade of grass in my fort. He robbed my treasury, my warehouses and my stables and enjoyed the revenues of my country for three years." Tulāji could not understand why and how the Company could support Wallajah to extract more money from Tanjore. At that time, Tulāji was even considering borrowing one lakh Pagodas from the Company

95 Hill: Yusuf Khan, 137: According to this treaty, Pratāpasimha sent away some Indian sepoys, dubāshes and "the French in his service." Some people joined Yusuf Khan of Madurai, whom the Company and Wallajah killed in 1764.
96 Memorial on behalf of the King of Tanjore presented to Lord North, 6.
97 Memorial on behalf of the King of Tanjore presented to Lord North, 8.
98 Memorial on behalf of the King of Tanjore presented to Lord North, 12.
99 Memorial on behalf of the King of Tanjore presented to Lord North, 16.
100 Memorial on behalf of the King of Tanjore presented to Lord North, 16.
101 Memorial on behalf of the King of Tanjore presented to Lord North, 17.
102 Memorial on behalf of the King of Tanjore presented to Lord North, 18–19. IOR/E/4/873, 319: On 16.01.1787, the Court of Directors in London reiterated their order of 09.12.1784, which prohibited all British citizens in Madras Presidency from visiting Nawab Wallajah, his family or his court. They expressed their dismay that the British citizens in Madras discarded their prohibition. They were disappointed to learn about Paul Benfield's visits to Nawab, and he remained unpunished.

to repair the banks of the Cauvery River. He urged his vakeel to prevent Benfield and his dubash from travelling to Tanjore, fearing that Benfield would 'molest' him.[103]

However, Wallajah continued to view Tulāji as his enemy. In 1777, he urged the Court of Directors in London to consider how he had assisted their administrators in Madras to gain new territories in India. He declared himself "the first friend to the English nation and the Company" and stood with them at "all times of prosperity and adversity." He repeated that he had offered his "life and fortune" and sacrificed his "sons and friends, in their service." He was deeply committed to promoting the "honour, prosperity and advantage of the Company." He considered the Company's enemies to be his enemies. He asserted that his and the company's interests "have been so closely united that what prejudiced one must prejudice the other." He reminded the Company of their promise to assist him in preserving tranquillity in Carnatic. He implored them as his "assistants and friendly protectors" who would promote the "government, honour, and tranquility" of the Carnatic, including Tanjore.[104]

On 25 December 1777, Rajah Sri Ram Pratab, possibly another name for Tulāji, requested that Whitehill in Madras consider his petition to cancel Wallajah's claims on Tanjore, but Whitehill demanded a substantial bribe. Sri Ram Pratab assured that as soon as the Company ordered Wallajah not to claim any money from Tanjore, he would arrange for the bribe money to be deposited directly into Whitehill's account.[105] In an undated letter, probably at the end of 1777 or the beginning of 1778, Rumbold requested that Tulāji provide him with a bribe of three lakhs of Pagodas, which he intended to divide equally among himself, his son Captain Rumbold, a military general, and Mr. Redhead. On 24 April 1778, Tulāji promised to give Rumbold the revenue of the town of Nagore,

> which produces 50,000 Rupees per annum, and a Jaghire worth two lakhs of Rupees more, and this sum I cannot exceed. I will give the Governor one lakh on his own private account, and the General 30,000 Pagodas. What do I have to do with any other people, and what service can they be of to me? If I give anything to such people, the rest of the Council will not remain quiet. [...] I may give the Governor and the General 20,000 Pagodas more and let them dispose of this sum in what manner they think proper. If the Governor does not insist upon the payment of more than half the sum to be deposited, I can pay a part of his private demand this year, but not otherwise.[106]

---

103 BL MSS Eur D 1208, 23–29: By 12.09.1776, Benfield and his agent reached Tanjore. Tulāji welcomed them with fruits. Benfield was angry at Tulāji for not condemning Pigot and tried to occupy the entire Tanjore "in mortgage" and punish the *amuldars*. Tulāji felt that if Benfield stayed there any longer, farmers would leave Tanjore and expressed his anguish to his *vakkīl* in Madras: "I am in great distress as the Company have not lent money to advance the farmers; if after the Company have been so good as to restore my kingdom, if they do not determine to protect me, what can I do? My honour or dishonour remains with them. They are my only friends. You must make the Governor, Narain Pillay and every proper person acquainted with these circumstances and use all means in your power to get Mr. Benfield and [his agent] Colitapa Moodally recalled."

104 Letter from Mahommed Ali Chan, Nabob of Arcot, to the Court of Directors, to which is annexed a State of Facts relative to Tanjore with an Appendix of Original Papers. London: T. Cadell, 1777, here 2–3.

In early 1779, Tulāji and Colonel Fitzgerald (b. 1735) of the Company drafted a memorandum for Rumbold's consideration. Accordingly, 1) Wallajah should return the regions of Ārani and Hanumantagudi to Tanjore. 2) Due to the low selling price of paddy, Tulāji was unable to pay the promised dues to the Company on time. 3) The Company should hand over Kanagasabai Pillai to be prosecuted in Tanjore. He squandered vast sums of Tanjore as an amildar, and the Company should not protect him. 4) Recently, Wallajah's army destroyed Tulāji's *darbar* (official meeting with people) on an embankment (*aṇaikkaṭṭu*). The Company should instruct Wallajah not to engage in such destructive activities. 5) The Company should station two battalions of soldiers to guard Tanjore. 6) The farmers of Wallajah, who lived along the borders of Tanjore, prevented Tanjore farmers from selling paddy and agricultural produce in Nagapattinam. The Company should instruct Wallajah to ask his people not to trouble the Tanjore farmers. 7) The Governor of Madras should not send him letters in English and Persian translations, which no one at the Tanjore Court understood well. Instead, he should send his English letters with "Hindoo translations," i.e., Tamil or Marathi. 8) The cost of each sheep for the Company soldiers in Tanjore, fixed at two Pagodas, was too low. Farmers incurred heavy losses. Hence, the Company should pay the prevailing market price for each sheep. Finally, 9) as the grain was sold cheaply, the Company should allow Tulāji to pay the four lakhs of Pagodas in instalments.[107] Rumbold did not seem to have considered the memorandum favourably, and he kept the enmity between Tulāji and Wallajah alive. He let them hate each other because he knew that, in doing so, he could garner their support simultaneously.

As Rumbold, Benfield, and others attempted to extract more money from Tulāji, Major George Burghall, an army engineer, encouraged Tulāji to stand boldly and confidently, rather than bribing the Company officers, such as Rumbold. In March 1779, he expressed his joy that General Hector Munro treated him, i.e., Tulāji, respectfully, and that he had employed Padre Swartz, an honest man, as his interpreter. Like Schwartz, Burghall advised him to recognise how the Company officers in Madras and Tanjore misled him from one trouble into another and misinformed their superiors. He warned him: "If you expect to make them your friends through bribery, you are mistaken; they will receive your money and deceive you, just as they have already done, and they will do so again." Burghall insisted that if Tulāji wanted to ensure his happiness and the happiness of his subjects and to pass on his kingdom to his children, he should reduce his expenses from five lakhs of Pagodas to three lakhs, reclaim the regions that he had freely given to various persons, and reduce his allowances to Brahmins and their charities. He should not entertain the Company officers who expected more bribes from him. He should stop borrowing money from anyone because if he cannot pay off the principal amount, he will never repay both the principal and the interest.

---

105 BL MSS Eur D 1208, 141.
106 BL MSS Eur D 1208, 187.
107 BL MSS Eur D 1208, 271–272.

The accumulated debt would enable the "European saucers" to "feed upon the vitals of your country, and they will at last plunge it in misery and sink you under a load of debt, from which you never will be able to rise. Take warning from the Nabob. Mr Benfield ruined him. Colonel MacLean, Mr. Petrie, and others would have ruined you." Burghall reminded Tulāji to forcefully explain to the Company officers how they and their servants had depleted his resources, stripped his country and mismanaged its affairs. In this context, Burghall offered excellent advice on how to get out of trouble.[108]

Like Burghall, Schwartz opposed the Company's plunder of Tanjore. They demanded vast sums from Tulāji, and Wallajah dismayed Schwartz. When the Company asked Schwartz for help, he refused and replied that his missionary office would not permit him to engage in such unjust matters.[109] After that, the Company's creditors rushed from Madras to Tanjore, intimidated Tulāji and his farmers and extracted money from them. As a result, major farming communities abandoned their fields and relocated to other areas. Another famine was on the brink of occurring. Tulāji requested Schwartz to persuade the farmers to return to Tanjore and cultivate their fields to avert this tragedy. Schwartz intervened and assured the farmers of his help. Consequently, they returned and cultivated their lands. Thus, Schwartz and the farmers averted a famine. Schwartz's benevolent actions contributed to peace, justice and social harmony among farmers and other inhabitants.

On 11 October 1776, Schwartz informed Pasche about his connection with Governor Pigot, as Schwartz had translated Pigot's letter restoring Tulāji's kingship into Marathi. After completing this job, Schwartz reminded Tulāji to be mindful of the living God. Contrary to Schwartz's expectations, Tulāji replied that he chose to follow the religious faith of his ancestors.[110] At that time, Schwartz requested Tulāji to grant him a place in Tanjore. Consequently, Tulāji gave him a

---

108 BL MSS Eur D 1208, 273–275. On page 276 Burghall urged Tulāji to follow his advice: "I am afraid you are not sufficiently acquainted with your own rights and that your fears will keep you from speaking thus boldly; believe me when I tell you again and again, that as long as you perform your engagements to the Company, the Governor and Council can have no power over you. As representatives of the Company, you should treat them with respect; however, you must remember that they do not represent the Company when they disobey their orders. Pray consider your own present situation; you are not only subject to the insults of the Governor and Council but of every European when they send upon a message to you; you are in debt though that debt is but small and are consequently subject to your creditors; your necessities have obliged you to bribe your enemies to no purpose and to neglect those friends on whom you principally depend; you are in a manner confined within your capital, and in short you are poor and a prisoner though at the head of a Kingdom, and all this because you did not know how to assist your own cause. It is in your power to rise above this situation, and I hope in God you will do so. I shew you how it may be done by a little exertion. The inconvenience attending it lasts only for one year, the good consequences may be without end."

109 Germann: Missionar Christian Friedrich Schwartz, 246–247.

110 AFSt/M 1 B 68 : 42: On 14.10.1776, Schwartz applied his theological and pietist convictions to interpret Tulāji's restoration. The fact that the Company army still controlled his fort troubled him at the deepest levels. Schwartz expected Tulāji's recent humiliation would enable him to seek God's help. By contrast, Tulāji committed more sins and led a miserable life.

house that a European had built. Before Schwartz moved into this house, the news about Pigot's arrest saddened him and Tulāji. In the same letter, Schwartz narrated how a wall near a road had broken away and fallen. The falling wall terrified his horse so much that he could no longer control it. He fell to the ground, and the horse fell on him and injured his right knee.[111] Severe pain prevented him from travelling for a month.[112]

In the meantime, according to the Marathi Historian Babu Rao, Tulāji still rejoiced in the justice of the English Government (*nītiyōṭu kūṭiya āṅkila carkār*), which restored him to the throne of Tanjore. Immediately, he dismissed those of his employees who hailed from *vaṇīṣkara jāti* (the *vaṉṉiyar*, who primarily lived along the banks of the River Cauvery in Tanjore) and *īṉa jāti* ('despised birth-groups, castes'). Some of them were ministers. Tulāji was convinced that these employees caused not only *piramahatti tōṣam* ('the curse of *brahmahatyā*,' murdering a Brahmin) but also the *rājyam naṣṭam* (the 'ruin of the country, governance'). In their place, he appointed Brahmins because he believed that they belonged to the uttama jāti ('noble, excellent birth group, caste') and would not commit any cruel acts. Therefore, he staffed his palace with Brahmins only.[113]

Despite entrusting the administration of Tanjore to select Brahmin employees, the economic conditions of Tanjore did not improve. The Company demanded more money. Nawab Wallajah wanted to reoccupy Tanjore. Ordinary people suffered. Moreover, Tulāji was deeply worried about his successor. All these worries worsened his health. On 24 February 1779, Schwartz stated that Tulāji had been sick for the past three months, and there was no sign of full recovery. Whenever Schwartz met the king, the king complained about how cruelly the Company and the Nawab had treated him. Hence, the king viewed his oppressors as evil people. He complained that the Company officers, driven by insatiable greed, took as much wealth as possible from him and his people. Like Tulāji, Schwartz, too, judged the external situation as dismal. He expected God to intervene and help the people.[114]

AFSt/M 1 B 68 : 45: On 21.01.1777, Schwartz informed Pasche that Tulāji had increasingly become unfit to govern Tanjore effectively; he drank alcohol, and a few months earlier, he had married two more women in addition to his three wives. Thus, he attempted to beget a male heir to the throne of Tanjore. AFSt/M 1 B 68 : 46 and Germann: Missionar Christian Friedrich Schwartz, 407: On 03.02.1777, Schwartz reported to Freylinghausen that Tulāji remained addicted to his carnal lust. He could no longer think rationally and clearly. However, he was exceedingly kind towards Schwartz. Whenever he was alone, Schwartz spoke with him about spiritual matters.

111 AFSt/M 1 B 68 : 43.

112 AFSt/M 1 B 72 : 58 and Germann: Missionar Christian Friedrich Schwartz, 403: On 20.01.1782, Schwartz wrote to Freylinghausen that his health began declining and he became fragile. His ears and feet were in pain.

113 Bapu Rao: Bhonsle Vamsa Charitra, Tamil Section, 124.

114 AFSt/M 1 B 69 : 46.

Chapter 5

Schwartz in Tanjore (1778–1798)

5.1 Schwartz's Move to Tanjore (October 1778)

On 3 February 1777, Schwartz expressed his intention to relocate from Tirucirāppaḷḷi to Tanjore. At that time, the Company had a significant garrison there. The Christian soldiers of the garrison invited Schwartz to conduct regular worship services, a proposal that the Company did not oppose. Schwartz believed he could establish a church in Tanjore. Still, before deciding, he sought advice from his colleagues in Tranquebar and requested that they temporarily release Christoph Samuel John (1747–1813) to work in Tiruchirappalli.[1]

As John could not come to Tirucirāppaḷḷi, Christian Pohle came to Tirucirāppaḷḷi in February 1778 to learn Tamil and English from Schwartz, as a preparatory step to relieve Schwartz. It was a tumultuous time for the missionaries. The socio-political upheavals that happened between 1776 and 1778 were overwhelming. In this context, Schwartz maintained letter correspondence with fellow missionaries in Tranquebar, Cuddalore, and Madras, as well as with various Company officers. One of them was his friend, Alexander Davidson, a senior merchant and the second member of the Company's government at Cuddalore and Masulipatnam. On 26 March 1778, Davidson responded to Schwartz's letters and thanked him for appraising Tanjore's changed political situation. Davidson believed that those "transitions" and "revolutions" would form a "remarkable era" in India's history. Then, he thanked Schwartz "for being so good as to sit" for a portrait, which turned out to be with "a very striking likeness." Davidson gave that portrait to Mr William for framing. This reference indicates the personal and professional relationship between Schwartz and Davidson. Thus far, no copy of this portrait has emerged. Davidson also informed Schwartz about Major Stevens, who was Schwartz's good friend and remained "a friend to the Church." He appreciated Schwartz for promoting "morality and Christian Knowledge" and wished him good health. He stated that his two daughters, Elizabeth and Margaret, had reached England, and his two younger daughters, Lydia and Mary, were with him. He explained that he had settled the money he had borrowed from a few friends and requested that Schwartz pray for his wife, whose health was declining.[2]

---

1 AFSt/M 1 B 68 : 46. Schwartz considered the two newly arrived missionaries, Johann Peter Rottler (1749–1836) and Johann Wilhelm Gerlach (1738–1791), unsuitable for missionary work. They were unwilling to learn from senior missionaries. Gerlach did not want to learn Tamil.

2 Bodleian Library: 72290ind-box2, Document 5 dated 26.03.1778: Alexander Davidson's letter to Schwartz.

Schwartz understood the art of maintaining creative fellowship with senior Company officers and their families. His letters, which elicited detailed responses, seamlessly intertwined personal, professional, political, and religious elements.

By October 1778, Pohle could preach and catechise in these languages, and Schwartz was assured that he could travel and expand the scope of his ministry. On 9 October 1778, he reported to Freylinghausen that he planned to spend at least a month in Tanjore.[3] In the same month, he moved to Tanjore.[4] Pohle and the young Johann Caspar Kohlhoff, who spoke Tamil fluently, oversaw the missionary work in Tiruccirāppaḷḷi. Pohle preached in Tamil, catechised school children and accompanied the catechists during their evangelistic tours. Kohlhoff looked after the English school, taught the art of reading and catechised the children. The schoolchildren found his honesty and lifestyle uplifting. Forty adults and twenty children joined the Tamil Lutheran Church in Tiruccirāppaḷḷi, a testament to the impact of Schwartz's work. Schwartz adjusted his life in Tanjore and prepared three groups of inquirers for baptism.[5]

5.2 Christ Church in Tanjore (March 1779)

On 22 September 1774, Schwartz reported a significant setback. In 1773, the armies of Wallajah and the Company destroyed the hut where the Tamil Lutherans worshipped, along with the adjacent house. When Schwartz requested a place to build a church, Wallajah's eldest son promised to assign a place if his father approved. Following advice from his colleagues in Tranquebar, Schwartz journeyed to Madras to meet Wallajah in April 1774. After a prolonged wait, Wallajah denied permission, leaving Schwartz disheartened. However, a Tamil engineer named Stevens, who was repairing the fort, generously offered Schwartz a place for prayer and worship services. This significant offer, a testament to the local support for Schwartz's missionary work, demonstrated the community's involvement in his mission. Schwartz conducted services from 8 to 10 a.m. for the Tamil Lutherans and from 10 a.m. to 12 p.m. for Europeans.

At the same time, the commanding officer of the Company's army in Tanjore was Portuguese. He desired to strengthen Roman Catholicism in Tanjore and helped the Jesuits of the Madurai Mission. These Jesuits accommodated themselves to the

---

3 AFSt/M 1 B 69 : 45.

4 NHR 2, 1782, issue 24, 1424: Pohle did not like Schwartz moving to Tanjore. On 27.09.1779, he expressed his inability to speak English well and to conduct English worship services according to the rites of the Church of England. NHR 5, 1804, issue 60, 1062, dated 15.07.1802: About twenty-two years later, missionary John disclosed another reason for Pohle's frustration: when Schwartz moved from Tiruccirāppaḷḷi to Tanjore, a sizable number of Tamil Christians also accompanied him in the hope of better treatment and living conditions. As a result, the Tamil congregation in Tiruccirāppaḷḷi became smaller and weaker. John also mentioned that European soldiers who had married Indian women had permission from their superiors to stay with their families in the same place. They could even seek employment with the Royal Battalions, the Company army or others. Consequently, fewer soldiers attended Pohle's worship services.

5 AFSt/M 1 B 70 : 40.

socio-cultural and religious practices of the Śaivites and Vaiṣṇavites. One of their powerful practices was the Festival of Temple Car (*tēr tiruviḻā*), in which the Tamil Roman Catholics pulled a decorated church car with the image of Mother Mary and other saints along the streets. This practice, along with other missionary activities of the Jesuits, had a profound impact on the local population, drawing crowds and cultivating a loyal following. The Jesuits maintained a medical mission. Before distributing medicine to the sick, they prayed to Mother Mary and called on St. Xavier and St. Anthony. Those who became well remained loyal to the Jesuits and considered them their protectors. Schwartz could not comprehend how the Jesuits could have made such a powerful and lasting impression on the hearts and minds of their followers. The Jesuits received tithes from their adherents, as well as fees for marriage, infant baptism, and confession. This contrast between the Jesuits' approach, which focused on integrating with local practices and providing tangible material benefits, and Schwartz's more straightforward evangelistic goal offers a clearer picture of the religious dynamics prevalent in Tanjore.[6]

In his report dated January 21, 1775, Schwartz noted the challenges he faced. Some inhabitants requested his material support before joining the Tamil Lutheran Church in Tanjore. His two catechists, Rāyappaṉ and Sattiyanātaṉ, preached God's Word in different adjacent places, leading to an increase in the number of Lutherans. However, Muslims and Roman Catholic Christians opposed their evangelistic efforts. Schwartz reported further that hunger and misery caused many Tamils to join the Tamil Lutheran Church in Tiruccirāppaḷḷi.[7] He wondered whether he should accept them, even though their purpose for joining the church was questionable. Out of compassion, he received them. An old woman confessed to Schwartz, "When we were fat, we ignored your teaching. The Lord Jesus has made us thin so we can hear and accept your teaching." Schwartz, who had to make personal sacrifices for his mission, accepted these suffering people with compassion, demonstrating his unwavering commitment to his work as a missionary. He hoped that accepting these suffering people would not be in vain, and he faithfully taught them God's Word. Whenever Schwartz was away from Tanjore on business, problems arose, and he had to solve them later.[8]

---

6 AFSt/M 1 B 65 : 42.

7 AFSt/M 1 B 65 : 42 and AFSt/M 1 B 65 : 43: On 21.01.1775, Schwartz reported increasing church membership in Tiruccirāppaḷḷi; most members joined this church to escape hunger and starvation. When Schwartz expressed joy and apprehension over their material motives, a woman replied: "Aye! God sent this misery for hearing God's Word. Earlier, we ignored it. We were fat." After reflecting on God's calm ways and Christ's example, Schwartz confessed that he gave up his doubts about people's material motives in joining the church. On the second Sunday after Trinity, many people wanted to join the church. Again, Schwartz doubted. At that time, a catechist reminded him, "Yesterday, you admonished us to go to the edge of the settlements and invite the lame, the blind, and the poor. Now you have them." Encouraged by this reminder, Schwartz accepted those people and preached God's Word to them. He calmed his heart and worked on the newcomers patiently. AFSt/M 1 B 65: 43: In this 1776 report, Schwartz stated that more people joined the Tamil Lutheran Church in Tiruccirāppaḷḷi, and it required proper institutional administration.

8 At the end of this report, Schwartz requested Pasche to send him green spectacles because his eyesight had declined over the past three years. He could no longer read in the evening.

Schwartz's persistence proved helpful. On 21 January 1777, he hoped to receive Wallajah's permission to build a church and school in Tanjore. He even asked for a new missionary colleague to assist him.[9] However, he had to wait two more years to receive Wallajah's permission to erect a church building in Tanjore on 23 February 1779. Schwartz believed that more Tamils would become Christians because Wallajah's Islamic rule had shattered their hopes. He expected the prevailing adverse socio-political hardship might bring more Tamils into the church. However, most Tamils did not embrace Schwartz's Lutheranism. They feared social ostracism that would sever all relationships with their families, friends, employers, and social service providers. Besides, they could no longer access public places, wells, ponds, or grazing grounds for their cattle. Others, such as Muslims and Roman Catholics, were aware of Schwartz and chose to remain loyal to their socio-religious affiliations. They did not respond to his invitation to voluntarily embrace Lutheranism as their way of life. The prevailing socio-political hardship made life uncertain and complex, and many inhabitants were unable to assess the merits and demerits of different religious alternatives. Schwartz discussed his church plans with General Hector Munro,[10] the new commanding officer of the Company in Tanjore, who arrived in February 1779. Munro promised to help Schwartz and requested Schwartz to accompany him as his translator. Whenever he met Tulāji, Schwartz was with him. On 23 February 1779, Schwartz reported to Pasche that Tulāji had made an oral confession to Munro, stating that Christianity was 100,000 times better than worshipping images.[11] Schwartz did not take this confession seriously because he was familiar with Tulāji's beliefs and practices.

On 13 October 1779, Schwartz narrated his interactions with Munro:[12] Schwartz informed Munro that he and Major William Stevens lived like brothers and missed the Major.[13] Munro offered himself as a friend to Schwartz. At that time, Schwartz tried to raise enough money to erect a substantial building for worship service, but he could not mobilise enough money and materials for its

---

AFSt/M 1 B 66 : 59: On 18.01.1776, Schwartz asked Pasche to send him two green magnifying spectacles because his eyesight had become weak.

9 AFSt/M 1 B 68 : 45 and Germann: Missionar Christian Friedrich Schwartz, 405.

10 General Munro defined the Company's victory in the Battle of Buxar in Bihar (22.10.1764) and became famous. After spending a few years in Britain, Munro returned to Pondicherry in August 1778 and fought against the French. From there, he moved to Tanjore, where he met Schwartz, of whom Stevens had already given him a good report.

11 AFSt/M 1 B 70 : 40 and AFSt/M 1 B 70 : 43: On 13.10.1779, Schwartz gave a different account: Tulāji meant Christianity was 1,000 times better than image worship. Schwartz felt that Tulāji's oral confession was not meaningless and would have no practical outcome.

12 AFSt/M 1 B70 : 43, AFSt/M 1 B 71 : 30: At the beginning of 1780, Schwartz communicated additional information about Stevens to his friend Pastor Sorge in Brandenburg: Major Stevens had built a straw-thatched church for 200 Royal Dollars. He paid this money out of his own pocket. This church was cool and pleasant during the hot season, but it could not accommodate half the congregation. Besides, the straw got rotten during the rainy season, and fresh straw had to be replaced. Likewise, the church members dismantled the straw roof in early 1779. Schwartz and Stevens requested their friends to sponsor the renovation of this church building.

construction. He expected that the Company, consisting of European Christians, would assist him. When he could not obtain their support, he lamented that the Company willingly spent 20,000 Dollars on "comedy houses," but they had no money to build churches. In this dire situation, Munro donated two hundred Royal Dollars to erect a church building in Tanjore. On 10 March 1779, Schwartz invited Munro to lay the foundation stone for this church, which would be ninety feet long and fifty feet wide, accommodating five hundred worshippers. Schwartz preached a sermon on Psalm 67. Later, he reported that he had rendered General Munro "some little service." He translated the English of the Company's Court of Directors in London into Marathi for King Tulāji. Additionally, he served the Company as their army chaplain.

Munro appreciated Schwartz's help translating the Company's letter into Marathi for Tulāji. Upon returning to Madras, Munro wanted the Company to reward Schwartz with a monetary award. Schwartz refused this idea of personal gain. Instead, he requested Munro to intercede with the Company for two things: just as he received a monthly salary of 20 Pagodas for his chaplaincy services in Tanjore, he recommended a monthly salary of 20 Pagodas for Pohle for his chaplaincy services to the English in Tiruccirāppaḷḷi. Schwartz informed Munro that he had given 10 Pagodas to Kohlhoff for his services in Tanjore. Secondly, Munro should persuade the Company to donate bricks and lime for the church building in Tanjore. The Company granted both requests: They gave the recommended salary to Pohle and sent bricks and lime for the new church building in Tanjore.

In the meantime, Schwartz sought an opportunity to build a separate church for the Tamil Lutherans in Tanjore who did not want to attend the English worship services for the European soldiers in the fort. Knowing this need, Tulāji donated a square place to Schwartz, measuring 1,000 feet on each side. It was a mile away from the fort. Schwartz financed this building by selling the golden cloth he received from Tulāji as a reward for his work as an interpreter to Governor Pigot. On 25 December 1779, he dedicated this church to the Tamil congregation.[14] Four

---

13 For a slightly different version, see ADD 57313 ff 37r-42v: When Wallajah conquered Tanjore in 1773, he destroyed the church within the Fort. At that time, Schwartz's friend, Major Stevens, built a beautiful "mud wall Church" at his expense, costing more 100 Star Pagodas. As more Tamils joined this congregation, they needed more space. In January 1779, they began raising funds for a larger church building. While the Company in Madras readily sponsored playhouses, they refused to support any church building. Stevens's sudden death on 14.10.1778 near Pondicherry troubled Schwartz and hindered fundraising. "General Munro, who knew as well as everybody that Major Stevens and I lived together as Brethren, condoled me in the kindest manner, saying: 'You will not so soon get Stevens again; however, I request you'll consider me as your friend'." When Munro visited Tulāji, Schwartz served them as their translator. Once, Tulāji confessed to Munro that "the Christian Religion is a hundred thousand times better than Idolatry." He hated Europeans. On 10 March 1779, Munro entered a nine-foot-deep pit and laid the foundation stone for a church building that measured 90 feet in length and 50 feet in width. Schwartz preached on Psalm 67.

14 Pearson: Memoirs, Vol. 1, 341; Germann: Missionar Christian Friedrich Schwartz, 316 and Penny: The Church in Madras, 615: The Danish missionary Lawrence Peter Haubroe, who worked from 1819 as an assistant to Rottler in Vepery, moved to Tanjore in 1827. He wanted to renovate Schwartz's church. In 1830, he designed the renovation but died in the same year.

months later, on 16 April 1780, he dedicated the church building in the fort and named it *Christ Church*.[15]

On 31 May 1799, Governor Thomas Rumbold, Major-General Hector Munro, John Whitehill, and Colonel Charles Smith planned the preparatory steps to wage war against Hyder Ali. Their decisions included repairing the damaged parts of Tanjore's walls and drawing plans to build accommodations for British army officers, soldiers, and Indian sepoys in Tanjore's Little Fort. They also designed bomb-proof storehouses to be built in the Little Fort.[16] Interestingly, this record omits any reference to the church's foundation laid by Munro on 10 March 1779. It is also silent about Schwartz and his relationship to the Company at that point. The Company's officers and their record keepers appear to have omitted any reference to the church or Schwartz because they knew their senior officers in Bengal and London would welcome their open support of Christianity. Their assistance to a Christian cause was not in line with the Company's administrative principle of maintaining religious neutrality, and they could face disciplinary action. This omission symbolised the Company's exclusion of Christianity from its business and of Indian Christians within its structures. Although individual officers, such as General Munro, assisted Schwartz, they did not want their names to be mentioned in official records, fearing reprimand and punishment from the Company's Court of Directors in London.

King Tulāji was aware of this church building within the fort and tolerated it for Schwartz's sake, even though he otherwise despised the Christianity of the Company officers. These officers, in cooperation with Wallajah, had imprisoned him, looted his palace and extorted his subjects. In an unpublished letter of 14 March 1780, addressed to Director Freylinghausen of the Glaucha Institutions, Schwartz mentioned, without any elaboration, how bitter Tulāji was towards the English. Simultaneously, he stated that the king remained kind towards him and other (Tamil) Christians in his service.[17]

On 17 January 1786, Schwartz informed his friend Sorge that the church building in the fort could no longer serve as a church and a school because it could not accommodate his Tamil followers. He conducted worship services and prayer meetings for the English soldiers. It became difficult to conduct the Tamil school in that building. Besides, his house needed to be more spacious to accommodate his increasing civil activities. Therefore, he decided to construct a structure for

---

The renovators moved the tombs of Schwartz and his co-workers to the eastern side of the church. At that time, the SPCK gave £2,000/- for this renovation. On 31.01.1845, Bishop George Spencer of Madras dedicated this church and named it St. Peter's Church. Later, in 1900, missionary William Herbert Blake (1849–1923) of the SPG renovated this church building again. Nowadays, the area around this church is known as Makarnōmpu Cāvaṭi, and the church belongs to the Church of South India.

15 Until 1787, Schwartz lived near this church and served the soldiers of the English garrison. The Company records do not refer to this church. For example, on 20 April 1779, the Company discussed building soldiers' accommodation facilities and an ammunition store so that the Company's army could effectively face and repel its enemies.

16 BL ADD 38403, folios 261r–284v.

17 AFSt/M 1 B 70 : 45.

the Tamil school and his home in the middle of a garden, approximately 1,000 yards (or 1,000 cubits) away from the fort, where it was quieter.[18] Schwartz believed that this serene place would improve his health. His friends volunteered to support orphan children and implored him to extend the scope of his ministry. Johann Kohlhoff taught catechism to these children. His twenty-year-old brother, Elias Eobanus Kohlhoff, taught the children the art of reading and writing. Joseph, Schwartz's servant, taught the children the Tamil alphabet. Another unnamed teacher supervised all educational activities at the school.[19]

5.3 Tulāji's Mismanagement of Tanjore

Tulāji made a concerted effort to raise sufficient funds to settle all outstanding arrears and tributes to Wallajah and the Company, pay his employees' salaries, and support the needy in his kingdom. According to the letter of 1 February 1782 by John Sulivan, the Company's Resident in Tanjore, Tulāji paid two lakhs of Pagodas to the Company and loaned 10,072¾ Pagodas to General Hector Munro. Sulivan paid all outstanding wages to the Company soldiers in Tanjore with that money. On 23 February 1782, he reported to Governor Macartney that the four battalions of sepoys had enough money and provisions.[20]

On 5 July 1784, the British Parliament empowered the Governor of Madras to adhere to the stipulations of the *Treaty of 1762* in resolving the issues between Wallajah and Tulāji promptly.[21] Accordingly, Pigot concluded this treaty with King Pratāpasimha of Tanjore. Following this treaty, Tulāji should pay twenty-two lakhs of Rupees to Wallajah "in place of all arrears and the annual tribute of four lakhs in time to come."[22] This was too large an amount. Consequently, Tulāji had to raise money from his subjects, whom the Company and Wallajah had extorted on various fronts.

On 11 October 1784, Schwartz informed Pasche of the newly arrived Company officers in Tanjore and how they had exacerbated the soldiers' misery by

---

18 AFSt/M 1 C 27 : 8: On 02.10.1786, Schwartz reported to Pasche that, at his request, the Company provided not only bricks and lime but also workers to repair and modernise the church and school buildings, which the Second Anglo-Mysore War had damaged. By October 1786, Schwartz had completed all works on these church and school buildings.

19 AFSt/M 1 C 27 : 5.

20 BL ADD 29153, 434–435 and 438.

21 24 Georgii III. Cap. XXV: An Act for the better Regulation and Management of the Affairs of the East-India Company and of the British Possessions in India; and for establishing a Court of Judicature for the more speedy and effectual Trial of Persons accused of Offence committed in the East Indies, in: Collection of Charters and Statutes, relating to the East India Company, London 1817, here 228: Paragraph 38: The Court of Directors weighed the rights of Wallajah and Tulāji and decided to settle the differences between them according to the "Principles and the Terms and Stipulations contained in the Treaty" of 1762 made by Wallajah and Pratāpasimha.

22 An Impartial View of the Origin and Progress of the Present Disputes in the East-India Company, Relative to Mahomed-Ally-Khan, Nabob of Arcot and Tulja-gee, Raja of Tanjore to which are annexed Observations on Mahomed-Ally-Khan's Letter to the Court of Directors, London: T. Cadell, 1778, here 77.

withholding their salaries and proper food for an extended period. Some Indian soldiers, for example, did not receive their salary for sixteen or more months. Every day, they received insufficient quantities of rice to quell their hunger. The disappointed soldiers imprisoned their officers. The soldiers had no ammunition in reserve to counter Hyder's invasion. Grain was available with the farmers in the countryside, but they could not get oxen to transport it to the fort safely. The farmers and the oxen owners did not trust Tulāji or the Company officers. The lack of provisions heightened the suffering of the sepoys.

At the behest of Tulāji and the Company officers in Tanjore, Schwartz intervened and appointed his catechists to persuade the farmers to provide oxen and sell paddy. One thousand two hundred oxen transported 70,000 to 89,000 *kalam* of paddy into the fort. Schwartz ensured that each person received the sale price promptly and fairly. His efficient payment method astonished an officer of the Company, and he praised Schwartz for it. This officer explained that the government officer would have given at least 4,000 Pagodas more than the amount Schwartz spent. Due to the deceptive practices of the Company officers, the grain seller and the oxen owners would not have received half of their money.

An accountant responsible for keeping books stated that if the Company officers were honest, they could save at least three to four million Pagodas annually. Schwartz believed these thievish leaders, who had forsaken their spiritual values, exploited the Company and others remorselessly. They stole anything belonging to the Company, even amidst the war with Hyder Ali. The governor, the general, and the admiral of the army in Madras fought among themselves over who would send more money to England.[23] Hyder's forces looted the country as they pleased. The aged General Eyre Coote (1726–1783) struggled hard to obtain provisions for his soldiers from the Company in Madras. The Company officers had sufficient funds but did not want to spend them on the military. Due to their inaction, Hyder Ali captured 300 Company soldiers, circumcised them and forcefully converted them to Islam.[24]

Like the prophets of the Hebrew Bible, Schwartz believed that since the Company officers in Madras had rejected the true God, God also made them small and detestable. Hyder's son, Tipu, recruited new soldiers from the Company's armies because some had not received their salaries for more than fourteen months. The new Governor, George Macartney, refused to pay his officers the usual allowance (*batta*). This refusal caused great pain and unrest. Macartney and his deputy duelled, and Macartney received a bullet near his chest, but he survived. Schwartz requested Pasche to intervene with the relevant Company officers in London and persuade them to improve the behaviour of their Company's officers

---

23 Carson: The East India Company and Religion, 18: As the Company acquired enormous wealth and power, its officers became corrupt. Their returning officers were sarcastically referred to as *nabobs* due to their vast, often ill-gotten, wealth. They bought country estates and parliamentary seats. Their competition to purchase these items increased corruption among politicians. Therefore, more British people thought that the "nabobs and their wealth were harmful to political life both in Britain and India."

24 AFSt/M 1 B 75 : 24.

in Tanjore: "I have written this letter with sorrow and fear in my heart." You could use it in appropriate ways. I have written it for this purpose."[25] Schwartz wanted Pasche to contact his friends at the SPCK, who would, in turn, update the Company's Court of Directors in London about the misdeeds of the Company officers in Tanjore. Many bishops of the Church of England were members of the SPCK. They also sat in the House of Lords. They would know at least a few members of the Company's Court of Directors and shareholders. They could inform the relevant officers in London about the extortions by the Company officers in Tanjore. Schwartz knew the Company would not easily give up its oppressive practices. However, he hoped for more humane treatment of Indians.[26]

On 14 October 1784, Schwartz wrote to Freylinghausen about the Company's unbearable exploitation, which deliberately disregarded humanity, justice, and fairness. The Company officers focused solely on amassing economic wealth for themselves and neglected the well-being of Indians. Schwartz opined that just before their ruin, the ancient Greeks and Romans oppressed the poor and endangered their lives. Similarly, the oppressive behaviour of the Company could herald their ruin in Tanjore. Schwartz inferred that the misbehaviour of the Company officers, who were Anglican and thus were meant to be familiar with the teachings of the Gospel, originated from their disregard for God. As they did not fear God, they remained cruel and insensitive to the plight of the ordinary Indians. They dared to withhold the salaries of their soldiers, leaving them needy and hungry. In 1784, some disappointed and unpaid soldiers rebelled against the Company officers.[27] Despite the bleak situation, Schwartz remained a beacon of hope, unwavering in his advocacy for an impartial administration of justice in all aspects of life in Tanjore. His steadfast belief in this principle, even in the face of the Company's exploitation, inspired those witnessing these events.

As time passed, the relationship between Tulāji and the Company became more complex. All agreements between them favoured the Company and disadvantaged Tulāji and his subjects. For example, on January 14, 1785, Schwartz shared his concerns with Freylinghausen regarding the worsening condition of the farmers: the economic disaster, marked by widespread poverty and famine, had intensified. According to the prevailing *jumma system*, Tulāji asked his tax collectors to estimate the unharvested paddy. The tax collectors proposed a high tax that the farmers could not pay. If the harvest were poor or failed, the farmers would get

25 AFSt/M 1 B 75 : 24.

26 IOR/E/4/871, 673–677: Astonishingly, Schwartz's narrative of the problem in Madras, along with "late advices [sic] from Fort St. George," seems to have influenced the Court of Directors in London to note Macartney's atrocities, and they chose not to go against him. For example, on 23 March 1785, they expressed their deep sorrow about the "heights of disputes" between the Governor General of Bengal and Macartney. The latter refused to negotiate afresh with Tipu Sultan. Nevertheless, the Court of Directors ordered the Governor General not to suspend Macartney.

27 AFSt/M 1 B 75 : 23; Pearson: Memoirs, Vol. 2, 191: In 1784, Governor Macartney refused to pay the additional allowances (*batta*) to the soldiers and withheld their regular wages for many months. European soldiers were unable to send money to their families in Europe. Some of them rebelled against their superiors.

nothing in return; instead, they had to borrow money to pay the estimated taxes. Usually, the farmers bribed the tax collectors to levy a lower tax on their unharvested paddy. As a result, the king received smaller tax amounts. Manual workers, artisans, merchants and many other groups did not pay tax. Tulāji could not punctually pay the stipulated amount to the Company and became indebted to them. Schwartz interpreted these miseries because people refused to accept the teachings of God's Word, which he and his catechists were preaching to them.[28]

On 24 September 1785, Schwartz wrote to Pasche about the injustices committed by the Company officers in Tanjore.[29] After a two-and-a-half-month journey to Tuticorin, Pāḷaiyamkōṭṭai, and Ramanathapuram, Schwartz returned to Tanjore on 23 September 1785. Immediately, he noticed that the Company's attitude towards Wallajah had changed. Most inhabitants were terrified because Wallajah wanted to reconquer Tanjore and install his own man to rule it. The Company was to send its army to help Tulāji and to extort more money from him for its own benefit.

On 17 January 1786, Schwartz blamed the Company for violating peace treaties with Hyder Ali, which led to the Second Anglo-Mysore War from 1780 to 1784. Even two years after the end of the war, the people of Tanjore had not recovered from its devastation. Many people suffered indescribably as the Company soldiers collected revenues from Tanjore. Schwartz could not understand how the Company could be simultaneously a friend and defender of both Wallajah and Tulāji. During these times of betrayal and confusion, Schwartz introduced the Lord Jesus Christ to many people. He acknowledged that the number of people who responded to his invitation to embrace Lutheranism was small, but he was confident that the divine seed of God's Word would accomplish its work in time.[30]

5.4 Committee of Inspection (21 June 1786 – 5 May 1787)

The Company's mismanagement of Tanjore and its resources provided an excellent opportunity for its greedy officers to interfere in its administration. Their avarice knew no bounds, and their inhuman treatment of the local people, along with their insistence on collecting more revenues, led to the collapse of the standard administrative systems. The devastating impact of the Company's oppression and exploitation forced many inhabitants of Tanjore to move away from their ancestral places and settle elsewhere.

The last months of Tulāji's life witnessed growing problems threatening Tanjore's existence. Wallajah's servants destroyed the irrigation channels of the

---

28 AFSt/M 1 B 75 : 25: Schwartz quoted a theological statement from an old man: "Before you came, we lived in our spiritual ignorance. We cared for our material life. Nowadays, we hear you preach God's will to us. As we have failed to respond positively to your invitations, we are now facing famine, war, various illnesses, and one trouble after another. Our true knowledge is also our ruin."

29 AFSt/M 1 C 25 : 23.

30 AFSt/M 1 C 26 : 8.

rivers Cauvery and Veṇṇāṟu, as well as countless paddy fields. Tulāji asked the Company to lower his annual tribute by one lakh of Pagodas, and the Company refused to grant his request. At that time, his diwan, Baba, enriched himself through acts of injustice, cruelty, and oppression. Ordinary people, especially farmers, suffered. Consequently, many inhabitants fled to Karaikal, Nagore, Tiruchirappalli and Madras. On 8 June 1786, Campbell requested that Tulāji dismiss Baba. Still, Tulāji refused and informed the Company that Baba could sell paddy for a price higher than its market value, thereby generating revenue. However, he was unaware that Baba had enriched himself, not Tulāji's treasury. At the same time, farmers in Tanjore's southern and western districts resolved not to cultivate their lands until the rulers would treat them more favourably.[31] In this context, without consulting Tulāji, the Company in Madras unilaterally requested that Resident John Hudleston, Commander James Stuart, and Paymaster John Coxe Hippisley "take the administration of Tanjore temporarily into their own hands."[32] These men should constitute the Committee of Inspection for the Affairs of this Country.[33] and promised "to watch over Tanjore's affairs and interests."[34] They did not want to believe that their interference in Tanjore's local administration breached the treaties between the Company and Tulāji.

These members did not include Schwartz in their committee. Governor Archibald Campbell recommended an honorary seat for Schwartz and supported his recommendation with these arguments:

> There are abundant proofs on record of the zeal, ability and services of the Rev Mr Swartz, whose accurate local knowledge and facility in the country languages and whose high estimation with the rajah, from an intercourse of thirty years, must render his assistance of essential consequence on such occasions. His presence, if possible, should always be requested in the committee, in which he should have an honorary seat, and he should also be desired to interpret and translate whatever may be necessary and to subjoin his signature to all such examinations and translations.[35]

On 1 August 1786, Hudleston indicated that he was unhappy with an honorary position for Schwartz because the inhabitants of Tanjore would not welcome the Committee if Schwartz were not a full member. He confessed that until then, he had "consulted with Mr. Swartz on every occasion." He took no step of the least importance without his previous concurrence and approbation, nor has there been a difference of sentiments between us in any instance. Hudleston desired Schwartz's "advice and effectual support" and considered Schwartz's involvement

31 IOR/H/285A, 620–621.
32 IOR/H/285A, 622.
33 IOR/H/571, 184: Campbell believed the Company would govern Tanjore better than Ameer Singh. After seeing this rule, the emigrants would return and cultivate their lands. He ordered the Company in Tanjore to guard the palace, to secure the seal of Tulāji and not to declare anyone as a successor to Tulāji. He kept Baba, the diwan of Tulāji, in his office because he fully understood the "present state of the country." At this order, the Committee of Inspection began administering Tanjore.
34 Pearson: Memoirs, Vol. 2, 113.
35 Pearson: Memoirs, Vol. 2, 113.

a significant source of happiness for the Country of Tanjore, the Company and the King. Thus, Schwartz assisted Hudleston in his dealings with Tulāji and his subjects.[36]

Campbell responded that he esteemed Schwartz's "abilities and integrity" and permitted him to be a "full member of the committee, without any reservation whatever."[37] Schwartz's role in the committee was crucial, as his knowledge and influence would benefit all parties involved.[38] Schwartz consented to be a committee member, provided that the Company would not resort to violence against Tulāji or his people, as they and Wallajah had during the siege of Tanjore in 1773.[39] He also wanted to speak with Tulāji beforehand. Campbell was pleased with Schwartz's proposition.

On 3 August 1786, Schwartz met Tulāji personally and explained that the committee would "inspect the affairs of the Country" and send "to the Board a faithful account" of it. Most inhabitants of Tanjore had gone to other places. The Committee and the King should invite them back with a joint *cowle* and provide them with necessary assurances and protections. Tulāji replied to Schwartz that he had ordered his subjects to return. Most farmers returned and went to their former homes. Tulāji reiterated that he had given these returnees substantial amounts of money and paddy seeds for cultivation. Schwartz wanted to know how the inhabitants responded. Tulāji explained that returnees had repopulated five southern districts, and other returnees would soon repopulate the remaining four districts within two to three days. Tulāji informed Schwartz that he had permitted the inhabitants to keep their total share of produce, and no one else should interfere. He had also relieved them from the heavy penal tax (*teṇṭam*). Tulāji promised Schwartz that he would listen to people's complaints and arrange redress. Schwartz wanted to know whether the emigrants had returned to their ancestral village called "*Tlangadu*." Tulāji was aware of the suffering of the village inhabitants and endeavoured to safeguard them. Then, he requested that Schwartz intercede with the Committee of Inspection in Tanjore and Governor Campbell in Madras.[40] He

36 IOR/P/252/10, 1580–91 and IOR/H/285A, 923 quoted in Pearson: Memoirs, Vol. 2, 114.

37 Pearson: Memoirs, Vol. 2, 115.

38 IOR/P/252/10, 1802: On 05.09.1786, John Chamier of the Military Department conveyed to Schwartz "the high sense" of the Company Council in Madras and hoped "that his zealous exertions in promoting the prosperity of the Rajah and his country will be crowned with success."

39 Pearson: Memoirs, Vol. 2, 118.

40 IOR/H/285A, 623: The Committee of Inspection asked Tulāji to remove Baba, who had long been the pest and scourge of the Country. This Committee also informed him about Resident Hudleston, who would transact all business in Durbar Hall of the palace. Tulāji opposed this move and considered this Committee a breach of his treaty with the Company. In the meantime, all influential individuals who had benefited from Babs's cruelty had fled. The Committee required Tulāji to show them his treasury and release funds for the farmers so that they could cultivate their fields. Tulāji abolished several oppressive taxes. Consequently, farmers returned to their fields and cultivated them. By September 1786, Tulāji was so sick that people expected his imminent death. When he was conscious, he arrested Baba and his acquaintances, who abused the Tanjore revenue. The inhabitants of Tanjore rejoiced over this change.

promised to pay the subsidies promptly, just as he had in the previous year. He asked Schwartz, "to beseech them to save me the mortification of being deprived of my authority." Schwartz concluded his letter by stating that these "are the true contents of my conversation with the Rajah."[41]

On 14 August 1786, the Committee of Inspection resolved to accept Schwartz as a full member with a seat, voice and vote.[42] They decided on the following five matters.[43] Firstly, they would not permit any Indian *dubashi* to interfere in Tanjore matters, except that if Tulāji wanted to meet Hudleston on a Sunday or when Schwartz was unavailable, they would hire an Indian interpreter just for that time. Secondly, they should persuade the emigrants to return to Tanjore, cultivate their fields and pay taxes to the Company and Tulāji. Thirdly, Schwartz asked the Committee in unmistakable terms not to meet frequently, as each meeting would be a "heart-burning" to Tulāji.[44] Fourthly, Schwartz wanted the Committee not to harm the person or the dignity of Tulāji.[45] Fifthly, the Committee should not resort to violence against Tulāji, as was done in 1773, when the Company and Wallajah inflicted great injustice upon him. At his restoration, the Company acknowledged his sufferings, made "solemn promises" to safeguard his interests, and published them in Tamil, Marathi, and English. Therefore, Tulāji had the "full right to be treated with sanity" and dignity. Schwartz also reminded the committee to pay the "most sacred regard" to their promises to Tulāji. This regard should be of greater importance than "the consideration of utility."

Schwartz confessed that his friendly interactions with Tulāji would never bias him to disregard "the injustice he has done to his oppressed people."[46] He repeatedly petitioned Tulāji "to have mercy on his subjects," and Tulāji began to show some kindness to them. Now, Schwartz recalled a custom of the English legal tradition: while the law threatened the disobedient, it showed compassion to those who earnestly began to follow its dictates. Then, he pointed out how Tulāji started to exhibit positive changes, whether driven by good motives or mere fear. The people of Tanjore never had such a positive approach from their rulers. He removed his father's taxes.[47] He has charged his subaidars to publish them. The inhabitants confessed they would be happy if he kept those promises "religiously."[48] Schwartz felt that Tulāji would soon relieve his people from the cost of "Betel and Salt." He also stated his knowledge of the thousands of uncultivated fields called *veḷis*. To ascertain the extent of the uncultivated land, the Company appointed surveyors, and Schwartz accompanied them.[49] The few people who lived in these regions were unable to cultivate the available land. Thus,

41 IOR/P/252/10, 1612–5.
42 IOR/P/252/10, 1813–1815.
43 IOR/P/252/10, 1816–1845.
44 IOR/P/252/10, 1827.
45 IOR/P/252/10, 1826–1827.
46 Pearson: Memoirs, Vol. 2, 118.
47 IOR/P/285A, 620–628 and Pearson: Memoirs, Vol. 2, 119.
48 Pearson: Memoirs, Vol. 2, 119.
49 IOR/P/252/10, 1842 and Pearson: Memoirs, Vol. 2, 119; Colonel Ross, Major Stevens, Captain D. Good, and Captain Alexander Read surveyed the lands. Schwartz stated that he

Schwartz interceded for a fairer opinion about Tulāji and a better, more dignified treatment.

As a result of Schwartz's intercession on behalf of the farmers, 7,000 of them returned. Though the time of sowing was long past, the farmers worked hard. They told Schwartz: "You have shown kindness to us.". Therefore, "we intend to work night and day" and thus "manifest our regard for you."[50] Their demanding work yielded a better harvest. Schwartz's relationship with the farmers and other ordinary inhabitants of Tanjore impressed not only the Company Residents in Tanjore, but also Governor Archibald Campbell in Madras. At the recommendation of the Company Residents in Tanjore, Campbell appointed him as the Company's interpreter for an annual salary of £100 and provided £20 for his palanquin travel expenses.[51]

On January 8, 1787, Schwartz informed Pasche about the harsh conditions people suffered in Tanjore.[52] The Company formed a Committee of Inspection to oversee Tanjore's administration and taxes. Tulāji was extremely unhappy about this proposed Committee and asked Schwartz to intercede on his behalf with them. Schwartz accepted this request with one condition: namely, he would write an open letter to the inhabitants of Tanjore in the name of the king and a friend of the people, not in the name of the Committee of Inspection. He would inform the people that on 31 December 1786, the king had abolished three oppressive taxes and committed himself to justice. Even if Diwan Baba treated people unjustly, he would sack him. If any inhabitant had grievances, they could speak with Schwartz and seek redress. Consequently, people visited Schwartz daily for four months, complaining about Baba's cruelty. At Schwartz's recommendation, Tulāji imprisoned the chief minister; in his place, he appointed a separate four-member committee to oversee the country's welfare. Schwartz was happy about this development. If someone came to him with complaints, he directed them to this committee. In this context, Tulāji wanted to reward Schwartz with a considerable amount of money; Schwartz politely declined it because he did not want anyone to spread rumours.

Amidst these hectic activities, Schwartz maintained his missionary vocation. He discussed their everlasting welfare with the first inhabitants as conscientiously as possible, and they disliked image worship. As they had a prospect of seeing this country better managed —that is, with more justice — he hoped that all efforts of the Committee of Inspection would have a beneficial effect on the people.[53]

---

did not know whether these surveyors had just begun their survey or had already completed it. He confessed that he was present "on the spot" with them, when they were actually surveying.

50 Pearson: Memoirs, Vol. 2, 120.

51 Pearson: Memoirs, Vol. 2, 120.

52 AFSt/M 1 C 27 : 26.

53 Pearson: Memoirs, Vol. 2, 121.

5.5 Serfoji's Adoption and Ameer Singh as the Interim Ruler

Tulāji's two sons died prematurely.[54] As a result, he tried to ensure the continuation of his family on the throne of Tanjore. To have sons, he performed numerous religious ceremonies and married additional wives. Nevertheless, he could not have a son who would succeed him. He became addicted to alcohol and developed other habits that impaired his health. Since his attack on the Maṟavar Land in 1771 and his imprisonment (16 Sept 1773 – 11 April 1776), the death of Pigot in 1777 and subsequent attempts by the Company officers, British traders, creditors and renters, Tulāji continuously experienced severe setbacks and existential threats that affected his mental and physical wellbeing. He was anxious to preserve his house and kingdom from opponents such as Wallajah, Tipu Sultan, the Company and their creditors and rival claimants in the palace of Tanjore. After careful consideration over two to three years, Tulāji adopted a ten-year-old boy on January 22, 1787. On 26 January 1787, Tulāji informed Governor Campbell about this adopted son and acquainted him with his genealogical background: this boy belonged to his close relatives. His father was Sahaji, the son of "Soubajee rajah, my near cousin by lineal descent." This ten-year-old boy was "proper in all respects." He adopted him on the 2nd *Rubbisanni* (22nd January) [... and named him Serfoji Rajah, with all the forms of our religion; this has afforded great relief to my mind.] Then, Tulāji requested that Campbell accord his adopted son the same "favour and protection" he had received from the Company. Then he expressed his dependence on the Company: "I and my country have no resources but in your excellency. I rely on you with the greatest confidence."[55] An English reporter in Fort St. George summarised Tulāji's letter as follows: The adopted boy "was the son of Sahajee, the son of Soobajee, his near Cousin, with all the forms of his religion," and Tulāji named him Serfoji.[56]

---

54 NHR 3, 1785, issue 29, 591: On 19.03.1784, Schwartz stated he had returned from his failed attempt to meet Tipu Sultan. Tulāji summoned him and told him that his last son, the only heir, had died; his *fistula* became more painful. Schwartz advised him to turn to God and to care for his subjects.

55 Pearson: Memoirs, Vol. 2, 133.

56 IOR/H/285A, 124–125. This report aligns with Bapu Rao's Marathi text, which explains Serfoji's genealogy and adoption. Bapu Rao: Bhonsle Vamsa Charitra, Tamil section, 127–129: Tulāji respected his father Pratāpasimha and his "glorious rule." He believed his successor should not suffer the social stigma of being an illegitimate son. Due to his birth outside marriage, his half-brother, Ameer Singh Ramaswamy, was deemed unsuitable as his successor. Therefore, Tulāji adopted the ten-year-old Serfoji, befitting his royal genealogy and family (*gotra* and *kula*). Serfoji belonged to the family of King Venkoji Bhonsle (1630–1683). Tulāji, in his commitment to legality and order, meticulously followed the laws of adoption outlined in the legal treatises (*śāstras*). He had Serfoji's horoscope (*jātaka*) examined and found it acceptable. Then, he arranged for Serfoji's parade along the streets of Tanjore. At that time, Serfoji sat on an elephant. Musicians played their instruments and accompanied him. Tulāji also arranged to distribute sweets to the city's inhabitants and organised a feast for his relatives. Finally, in the presence of Resident John Hudleston, Paymaster John Coxe Hippisley, and Commander Ushdod, he handed over Serfoji to Padre Schwartz and requested that he be his guardian. After that, Tulāji convened his court (*durbar*) in the *Piratāpa Rāmaswāmi Mahāl*, honoured Serfoji as his legitimate heir and requested the Company officers to inform their superiors in Madras about Serfoji as his legal successor.

On 23 January 1787, John Hudleston informed his superiors in Madras about Tulāji's adopted son.[57] Hudleston, Hippisley, and James Stuart visited Tulāji around noon on the same day. Hudleston recorded his observations as follows:

> The child the Rajah has adopted was first shown to us, sitting on the state. We were then conducted to another wing of the same room or Veranda, where His Excellency was lying on the floor with nothing under him but a carpet and sheet. The child was brought & placed on the left hand. The Rajah was extremely ill and too weak to move his head from the pillow. After receiving our salutations, he spoke a few words which Shevaroo [i.e. Shiva Rao] interpreted. Namely, 'that he had chosen that child to be his son and successor and that he now in the presence of these gentlemen desired me to consider him as such and to write to the governor to inform him of the same.'[58]

Upon Hudleston's promise to fulfil Tulāji's request, Shiva Rao guided them out of the room, signalling that the end was near for Tulāji. Mindful of his earlier letter to Governor Campbell, Hudleston recommended confirming Serfoji as Tulāji's successor. He urged maintaining the status quo until the government's order arrived. With their influence and power, the Company officers played a significant role in the adoption process. They ensured that the new occupant would serve their interests.

> Mahalgee and Edegee were Brothers. Their Father's Name [is] unknown. Mahaljee had three sons, viz., Sivagee Rajah, Sambojee Rajah and Eckogee Rajah, of whom the eldest Sevagee Rajah founded the Mahratta Empire and transmitted it to his immediate Descendants. When Sevagee Rajah invaded the Carnatic, he carried his Brother Eckogee Rajah along with him and settled upon him the Kingdom of Tanjore, which is still governed by his lineal Descendants. Tulja Maharaje, the present Raja, being descended in the direct Line from Eckogee. Eckogee had six sons, from one of whom called Bhoangee Gungagee, the ancestor of Sherpogee, was lineally descended. Gungagee had a son called Babajee, a son called Gungagee, who had a son called Sabangee, who left two sons, Apurnna and Baba. Apurnna has a son called Sherpogee, who has been adopted by the Rajah and declared his Successor.[59]

Shiva Rao did not reveal the source of this genealogical information about Serfoji. The orthography of the Marathi names in English and their accuracy poses challenges. The identities of the Maratha progenitors, "Mahalgee and Edegee," are difficult to verify. Shivaji (1630–1680), who invaded the Carnatic and conquered Tanjore, Gingee and Vellore in 1676–1677, was the son of the military general Sahaji Bhonsle.[60] His half-brother Venkoji, also known as Ekoji, occupied these territories and established the Maratha Dynasty of Tanjore. Serfoji's genealogy linked him directly to Ekoji and claimed royal blood. However, rival claimants to the throne of Tanjore disagreed with this statement.

Tulāji's unexpected severe illness and the prospect of imminent death worried the leaders of Tanjore—some of the Company officers who influenced Tanjore's financial and political affairs. On 24 January 1787, Hudleston expected more

---

57 IOR/P/252/15, 183–185.
58 IOR/P/252/15, 183.
59 IOR/P/252/15, 185.
60 Subramanian: The Maratha Rajas of Tanjore, 19–20.

hardships for Tanjore and decided to return to England.[61] He stated that Tulāji's health condition remained grave and worrying; he obtained reliable information about Serfoji's pedigree from "an old, very intelligent inhabitant of Tanjore" and expressed his doubts about this adoption. He reported that until his adoption, Serfoji did not live in the palace; besides, the principal people of Tanjore disapproved of this adoption, adding a layer of uncertainty to the narrative.

The following day, on 25 January 1787, Hudleston sent Campbell another letter with these details.[62] Hippisley and Stuart did not wish to offend Tulāji. Therefore, they accepted Serfoji as Tulāji's heir. After Schwartz's return from Tranquebar, Hudleston showed him copies of his reports on Serfoji to Campbell. He opined that Schwartz did not want to recognise the adoption hurriedly, but he would write to Campbell. On 26 January 1787, Tulāji's health deteriorated. Hudleston showed no sympathy for Tulāji and asked Shiva Rao to pay 50,000 Pagodas to the Company. This amount was due in January 1787. Immediately, Shiva Rao sent 40,000 Pagodas.[63] Even in this grave situation, Hudleston thought only of procuring money for the Company.

Tulāji desperately wanted to consult Schwartz about his successor. He was so sick on 27 January that he could not speak. The following day, Schwartz spent time with Tulāji. At that time, Tulāji pointed to Serfoji and spoke to Schwartz: "This is not my son, but yours; I hand him over to your care." Immediately, Schwartz responded: "May this child become a child of God."[64] A strong cough prevented Tulāji from speaking further. Schwartz communicated his observation to Hudleston, who in turn informed Campbell on 29 January 1787:

> Mr. Swartz's visit yesterday [28/1/1787] to the Rajah was very short. The little boy was sent for and being brought. His Excellency desired Mr Swartz to look upon him as his son. Mr Swartz describes the Rajah's countenance as resembling what he called the *faceis hupocratia* [i.e. *hippocratic facies* = showing signs of imminent death] and thinks him very near the end. The Rajah sent for Mr. Swartz again today [29 January 1787]. The substance of what passed was this: his Excellency requested him to accept the Guardian of the Child office. Mr. Swarz declined and advised him as more proper and sensible to appoint his/ the Rajah's Brother to that office. The Raja objected but promised to consider it at last.[65]

Realising that the end of Tulāji's life was near, Schwartz visited him often. He met him around 1 p.m. on 30 January 1787 and reported the content of his discussion with him as follows:

> You know that I have served you as much as possible, but I cannot fulfil this request. As I have already heard, you have adopted a nine-year-old child, and you have not named a guardian. Therefore, the child's life will be in danger, and the people will be confused. More factions will arise than you can imagine. Considering our current circumstances, I cannot be your child's guardian. You must choose another method. At that moment, the king intervened

---

61 IOR/P/252/15, 187. For Schwartz's letter to John Hudleston's mother dated 3 February 1787, see section 7.1.

62 IOR/P/252/15, 188–189.

63 IOR/P/252/15, 91.

64 Pearson: Memoirs, Vol. 2, 134.

65 IOR/P/252/15, 223–224.

> and asked what I meant by another method. I responded: 'Appoint your brother as guardian. Hand over the country and its governance to him. Let him raise the child and prove himself to be his father. Thus, the child and the government will survive; he will accept and still be better; he must take care of the child because everyone will watch him.'[66]

Immediately, the king expressed his concern and wanted to reflect on it further.[67] Then, at midnight, he called Schwartz and Hudleston back. At 4 a.m., Tulāji invited the boy and his mother to come to him. He gave the boy and his country to his brother Ameer Singh and asked him to care for his servants and Serfoji. He reminded Ameer Singh to request that the Company protect the boy and himself by the existing treaty. He charged Ameer Singh to train Serfoji "according to rank." Before Ameer Singh's death, he and Serfoji should have considered the next course of action. Finally, Tulāji requested Schwartz and Hudleston to accept what he had said and arranged.[68]

On 30 January 1787, Schwartz reported on this matter to Governor Campbell, informing him that two days earlier, on 28 January 1787, Tulāji had appointed him Serfoji's legal guardian. On the following day, he placed Serfoji's hands in Schwartz's hands and confirmed Schwartz as Serfoji's guardian.[69] At that time, Schwartz prudently responded to Tulāji:

> 'You know, Rajah, that I have always been willing to serve you as far as I [possibly] could. However, this your last wish is above my power. You have taken this child as heir. You leave it without a Guardian, without a support. I am afraid that by doing so you do not consult the happiness of the child, neither [sic! = nor] the welfare of your country. Pabal [sic] & Animosities will ensure more than you may think of. As for me, I must beg [for] leave to disclaim all Guardianship for this reason because waiving all other considerations it would be impossible to [sic! = for] me to take care of the child in my situation. Another method must be used.'
> The Rajah asked: 'What method do you mean?' I replied: 'The child must be delivered to the care of somebody, e.g. your brother, to bring it up. If the child behaves well, treat him as his son. By this method, the child's health and life and the welfare of the country may be secured.' 'Well,' said the Rajah, 'I will consider all that you have said.' In the night, he sent for his brother Ramaswami and delivered the child to his care and his old servants. This the Rajah did in the presence of the principal people. All the people of the palace rejoiced at the step that Rajah had taken. [… Instead of fear and perplexity,] I have thought it my duty to give you this plain account without any disguise whatever [… so that you decide your next course of action].[70]

---

66 AFSt/M 1 C 29b : 6a. In addition to Schwartz's comments in German, an unnamed Company chronicler noted the following in IOR/H/285A, 625: At Schwartz's recommendation, Tulāji "appointed his Brother Ameer Singh to be the Guardian of Serfoji and Manager of Tanjore during the minority of Serfoji." He requested Ameer Singh, who had no son, to care for young Serfoji. The chronicler "asserted that if it had not been for Mr. Swartz's intercession, Tulajee would have bequeathed nothing to Ameer Sing."

67 IOR/H/571, 183: An unnamed chronicler of the Company summarised these events as follows: Schwartz knew that Tulāji's selection, adoption (on 22 January 1787) and appointment of the ten-year-old Serfoji as his successor would create problems among the rightful royal claimants to Tanjore's throne. To prevent civil unrest and possible loss of lives, Schwartz, as an envoy for peace and justice, recommended the appointment of Ameer Singh as the interim ruler. Tulāji adopted his cousin Serfoji. For this adoption, he correctly followed the principles of his religion and customs. Then he placed Serfoji's hands into Ameer Singh's hands and encouraged him to raise him, manage Tanjore as its interim manager and keep the Company's trust in him.

68 IOR/H/285A, 625: An unnamed Company historian summarised Schwartz's engagements

Then, Schwartz requested that Campbell show kindness to Tulāji by accepting Ramaswami, also known as Ameer Singh, and Serfoji, respectively, as the new and prospective rulers. Since all these events happened in the presence of senior leaders of Tanjore, Tulāji's words had credibility. Finally, Schwartz informed Campbell about a system for administering justice for the welfare of the country:

> Whatever salutary regulations for the welfare of the country & administration of justice should be made might now be introduced with great ease. As the Rajah's brother would cheerfully consent to all that might be proposed by you, Hon'ble Sir, or that the welfare of the country might now be grounded upon a solid basis. My wish has been and always shall be that your government may prove the greatest blessing to the country.[71]

Hudleston, Stuart, Hippisley and Schwartz stayed near the palace in Captain Brown's house. At 2 a.m. on January 30, 1787, Shiva Rao asked them to visit the palace. He told them that Tulāji had placed the hands of his adopted son, Serfoji, in the hands of his half-brother, Ameer Singh, also known as Ramaswamy, and requested him to take care of his son and heir. He also nominated Ameer Singh to govern Tanjore in the interim period. He placed a unique dress on Ameer Singh to symbolise the transfer of power and asked him to be kind to his old servants. Tulāji's mother and all the principal officers of the palace witnessed these events. They rejoiced that the king made these arrangements while he was still alive. Shiva Rao assumed the king might die at any time, so he conducted Hudleston, Hippisley, and Schwartz to a pavilion where Tulāji lay on a carpet. He introduced Ameer Singh and Serfoji to them and had the following message read: He had entrusted his adopted son Serfoji to his brother Ameer Singh for protection and education. As the guardian of his son, Ameer Singh should govern Tanjore. The Company should protect Tanjore, as they had been doing, according to the "solemn covenant between him and the Company, by which they had promised to maintain him and his heirs on the throne as long as the sun and moon should endure." When Stuart joined the meeting later, Shiva Rao and Schwartz acquainted him with the events.[72]

---

with Ameer Singh. If Schwartz had not proposed and stressed his appointment as an interim ruler, Tulāji would not have thought of Ameer Singh: "The Raja [Tulāji] afterwards consulted Mr. Swartz respecting the appointment of a Regent when Mr. Swartz opposed Ameer Sing Rama Samy as being the Raja's Brother, and the Raja made answer that as to his being his Brother he entertained doubts. On the following day, Tulajee called for Col. Stuart, Mr. Hudleston and Mr. Swartz and informed them that he had at the recommendation of Mr. Swartz appointed his Brother Ameer Singh to be the Guardian of Serfojee, and Manager of Tanjore during the minority of Serfojee, requesting that Ameer Singh who had no son of his own, would also adopt the youth who he had committed to his care. It is asserted that if it had not been for Mr. Swartz's intercession, Tulaja would have bequeathed nothing to Ameer Sing."

69 IOR/P/252/26, 2208: On 7 August 1788, the Company in Madras accepted Tulāji's appointment of Schwartz as the "Guardian to the adopted son of the late Rajah of Tanjore, and it is accordingly agreed that a copy of the forgoing letter is sent to Mr Petrice and that he be desired on his arrival at Tanjore to pay every attention to the subject contained in it." Archibald Campbell, John Holland, Casamajor, and Maunsell signed this decision.

70 IOR/P/252/15, 232–235.

71 IOR/P/252/15, 235.

72 IOR/P/252/15, 224–228.

An hour after this meeting, Stuart recorded his observation: Serfoji, Ramaswamy alias Ameer Singh, and "all the relations he had upon the earth" assembled around Tulāji, who lay there weak and exhausted. Ramaswamy should serve as "the guardian and protector" of Serfoji. He should treat the boy as his son. Tulāji expected the Company to support Serfoji and his family "in all their just rights and to see him and his descendants succeed to and help in quiet possession of the Tanjore Territories." Moreover, he requested that the Company treat his "adopted son and brother with every mark of tenderness, attachment, and affection."[73]

During Tulāji's last hours, several groups rushed to meet him, each with vastly different goals, creating a tense and complex situation. The Company pursued wealth and the territory of Tanjore, cloaking its greed as an expression of justice for the royal house and tranquillity for the people. They were willing to sacrifice the royal house for their gain. On the other hand, Ameer Singh was determined to ascend the throne at any cost, adding another layer of tension. Amid these conflicting interests, Schwartz tried to bring harmony between the groups, a daunting task in such a charged atmosphere. For example, at noon on January 31, 1787, Hudleston reported to Campbell about a meeting between Shiva Rao and Schwartz that had taken place shortly after midnight. In the name of his dying master, Tulāji, Shiva Rao requested confirmation from Schwartz of all matters that Tulāji had committed to the Company officers. Shiva Rao wanted to know whether Hudleston had communicated Tulāji's decision about Serfoji and Ameer Singh to the governor. Schwartz confirmed the communication about these matters. He assured the gathered people that as soon as they received the governor's decision, Shiva Rao and the Company officers should discuss and determine the best methods of publicising it.[74] As discussed later (Section 8.6), Serfoji's adoption posed challenges, and his relationship with Ameer Singh remained strained.

5.6 Tulāji's Death (31 January 1787)

The last years of Tulāji were politically and economically troublesome, with Tanjore facing a grave situation. A report by an unnamed Company chronicler describes Tulāji's plight in the years preceding his life: by September 1786, Tulāji was so ill that people expected his death at any time. To undermine Tanjore's agricultural revenues, Wallajah's servants deliberately destroyed the water channels of the rivers Kaveri and Vennār. Meanwhile, Tulāji attempted to raise sufficient funds to pay his tribute to Wallajah and cover the expenses of the Company's military in Nagapattinam and elsewhere. He appointed Baba as his chief revenue collector (*diwan*), who, in turn, began to oppress the inhabitants "by acts of injustice, cruelty, and oppression." The Company viewed him as "the pest and scourge of the Country." This exploitation by the Company led to many

---

[73] IOR/P/252/15, 230–232.
[74] IOR/P/252/15, 228–229.

inhabitants leaving Tanjore and settling in Pondicherry, Karaikal, Nagore, and Tiruccirāppaḷḷi.

The large southern and western regions of Tanjore remained uncultivated. Hence, the prospects of raising revenue for the Company remained bleak. Alarmed by these events, on 8 June 1786, Campbell required Tulāji to dismiss Baba and his officers. Tulāji resented Campbell's interference and took upon himself the consequences of Baba's action. He stated that Baba lowered the cost of buying paddy and raised its selling price. This action affected countless farmers and landless inhabitants. The farmers lost their marginal profit in cultivating paddy; landless inhabitants and workers (e.g., migrant labourers, mercenaries) starved. At the same time, Tulāji struggled hard to pay the 600,000 Pagodas as war debt to the Company, and the Company demanded this amount relentlessly.[75]

Not knowing Tulāji's death, Archibald Campbell, Alexander Davidson and James Henry Casamajor met on 31 January 1787 to discuss preventive measures for Tanjore. During Tulāji's death, they expected the new Resident of Tanjore, Alexander Macleod, to implement the following six measures: 1) Colonel James Stuart and his troops must safeguard the palace, its inhabitants, and possessions. 2) To prevent theft or embezzlement, all individuals entering or leaving the palace must undergo a thorough security check. 3) No one should become Tulāji's successor until the Company in Madras consents. 4) Convene the Committee of Inspection to guide Tulāji's ministers in undertaking calculated measures that would best promote the welfare of the people and the interests of the Company. 5) Gather the Committee of Inspection, "the Rajah's brother, one of the guardians or regents for the adopted child, if any such are appointed, and a public minister who is in office at the time of the Rajah's death" and then store Tulāji's treasures and belongings in a safe room, seal it and place guards before it. 6) Protect Baba, whom Tulāji had imprisoned for oppressing and exploiting the people. No one should take vengeance on him so that the Company could get "every information which may tend to illustrate the proper state of the Tanjore Country."[76] Before these instructions arrived in Tanjore, Tulāji passed away at 10 p.m. on January 31, 1787. His cremation took place on 1 February. Two of his widows wanted to burn themselves on his funeral pyre. However, they remembered his prohibition of *satī* and chose to live.[77]

Colonel Stuart reported that at 1 a.m. on 1 February 1787, i.e., three hours after Tulāji's death, Hudleston, Hippisley and Schwartz met in his house. They opened the governor's instruction and took the soldiers of the 72nd Regiment to protect the palace, "where the Rajah's brother, the adopted boy and the principal people were assembled." Schwartz translated the Governor's order to them. Stuart stated

75 IOR/H/285A, 620–628.

76 IOR/P/252/15, 210–212.

77 IOR/P/252/16, 81: On 10.04.1787, Archibald Campbell asked Ameer Singh to encourage the widows of Tanjore to emulate the example of Tulāji's widows and to abolish satī, the inhuman custom that "only serves to enrich the priests." These priests took away the jewels of the widows and sent them "cruelly and untimely [...] out of the world."

that the people were "perfectly satisfied" with what they heard. Then, he posted "two European officers, a European sergeant and a subaidar" to guard the palace and its sealed treasury.[78]

Colonel Stuart wrote another letter at 7 p.m. on 1 February 1787, summarising the noteworthy events of that day. Ameer Singh, Tulāji's relatives, and the palace's principal leaders cooperated with the Company soldiers at the palace gates and on the city streets. The soldiers prevented looting and ensured tranquillity. At 7 a.m. on February 1, 1787, the pallbearers carried Tulāji's remains from the palace to a cremation ground about a mile from the fort.[79] Colonel Mackenzie's soldiers ensured that the procession progressed peacefully. Ameer Singh and Tulāji's relatives conducted the last rites according to their customs and returned to the palace. Stuart's soldiers guarded each gate of the castle, checking every person who entered or exited. Stuart reiterated that everything "is quiet & all manner of persons are following their different occupations." When the Company soldiers sealed the treasury, jewels and other valuable effects, Tulāji's relatives were present, and they consented to what the soldiers had sealed. Stuart assured the governor that he would not allow anyone to proclaim Tulāji's successor and wait for the Company's instruction from Fort St. George.[80]

The news about Tulāji's death did not sadden the Company. Instead, they saw it as an opportunity to seize the material wealth of the palace and the Tanjore country. Their immediate focus was on ascertaining and securing Tulāji's treasures, jewels, and valuables, not out of respect for the deceased, but to claim the pending tribute and further their economic interests in the region.[81]

Alexander Macleod, the new Company Resident, reached Tanjore on the evening of 3 February 1787 and met with Ameer Singh. Schwartz could hear what these two men said to each other. He understood how the Company in Madras preferred Ameer Sing to be the rightful successor. Consequently, everyone was particularly kind to Ameer Singh.[82] Ameer Singh's role in the succession process was significant. He was a key figure in the palace and the Company's preferred candidate. His influence and the Company's support made him a strong contender for the throne, shaping Tanjore's succession process and future.

John Hudleston seems to have left Tanjore on 3 February 1787. Schwartz esteemed him for his Christian values, his compassionate yet firm interactions with responsible individuals, and his interventions for the benefit of Tanjore's inhabitants. He wrote a moving letter to Hudlestone's mother the same day and sent it through him. This letter still breathes Schwartz's respect for those who, under his tutelage, created a win-win situation for the inhabitants of Tanjore and the Company:

---

78 IOR/P/252/15, 236–237.

79 AFSt/M 1 C 29b : 6c: On 02.03.1787, Schwartz explained that guns were fired till Tulāji's body burned entirely. He could not bear the heat and dust clouds caused by the gunfire. Therefore, he rushed to his school and spent time with the children there.

80 IOR/P/252/15, 251–255.

81 IOR/P/252/15, 236–237.

82 AFSt/M 1 C 29b : 6b dated 4 February 1787.

Madam, Though I never have had the pleasure of being acquainted with you as to converse with you, yet is your way of thinking, your desire of pleasing our Maker, your hunger and thirst after the righteousness of Jesus, and your Christian wish to promote the welfare of your children [are] well known to me.
I have enjoyed the pleasure of both your sons' acquaintance. Your eldest son has been [a] Resident here at Tanjore, almost two years. From the very first day of our acquaintance, there has been a very cordial friendship between him and me. In all the multiplied transactions he was to take care of, he has been most open and candid, ever willing to hear and to ponder any advice, which I was able to give him, which is a rare case considering the self-conceit, which is lurking in all our breasts and hearts.
The Rajah of Tanjore [Tulāji] was particularly happy in having your son's support, without which he would have suffered severely more than once. But not only the Rajah, but the Honourable Company reaped great benefit from your son's conduct. Kind as he was to the Rajah, he was equally faithful to his employers. Nay, I can say consistently with the strictest truth that your son proved a blessing to the country, for when cruel oppression had driven the inhabitants to despair and emigration, your son, my friend, entreated the Rajah to become a father to his people and consequently to hinder and oppress those cruel methods, which his barbarous minister made use of. I had the pleasure of being present when this was done. I was his interpreter. As far as I know, your son has acted an upright and disinterested part. Had he followed another course, he might have heaped up riches, but that was a destructive way he detested. As he is now prepared to return, he promises himself much happiness in paying his filial respect to his religious mother.
Dear, as you are to both your sons, you are so to me, on account of your love to our Blessed Redeemer. Not all that are connected with him [are] dear to each other. As to your second son, he has invited me to correspond with him because he says that will please his venerable mother. So, it will rejoice me. God bless you, Dear Madam, throughout all Eternity, so wishes your most friend C. F. Swartz.[83]

On 3 February 1787, the Company Board in Fort St. George instructed Macleod, Stuart, Hippisley, and Schwartz to prepare, in the presence of Ameer Singh and four other principal persons of the palace, a detailed inventory of the treasure, jewels, and other valuable effects of Tulāji. These officers stored the valuable things in a sealed and guarded room. The Committee of Inspection readily assumed the responsibility for ensuring a safe and transparent succession process.[84]

In another account, dated 6 February 1787, regarding Tulāji's death, Schwartz provided additional information: as soon as he received Hudleston's urgent message to return to Tanjore, Schwartz left Tranquebar on 24 January 1787, travelled non-stop through the night, and reached Tanjore around 7 or 8 a.m. on 26 January. One of Tulāji's ministers informed him about the nine-year-old boy his master had adopted. On 28 January, Tulāji asked Schwartz to come to him and committed Serfoji to his care: "This is not my son, but yours." As Tulāji's health deteriorated, paymaster Hippisley devised an evil plot. Tulāji's half-brother, Ameer Singh, promised rewards. In the morning of January 31, Tulāji was extremely weak. After drinking milk in the evening, he looked better for a brief period. Then, he died suddenly at 10 p.m., just as a lamp stopped burning. He was 43 years old. His life had had difficulties. He possessed astute mental powers, but his addiction

83 Bodleian Library: 72290ind-box2, Document 17 dated 03.02.1787: Schwartz to the mother of John Hudleston about her eldest son. John Hudleston's father, William Hudleston, was the vicar of St. Cuthbert's near London. This congregation was part of the Church of England.

84 IOR/P/252/15, 237–239.

to sensual pleasures caused him sorrow and damaged his country. Just before his death, he presented large gifts to his senior servants and the Brahmins of Tanjore. Since Europeans mistreated him, he did not hold them in high esteem. After Pigot had restored him to his throne, he considered him a "fatherly friend." After Pigot's imprisonment and death at St. Thomas Mount near Madras, Tulāji no longer trusted other Europeans. He saw them as lawless people who had no conscience. Due to European mistreatment and exploitation, he thought of Christianity as a useless religion. Even when Schwartz spoke with him about Christianity, he remained silent and did not respond. Schwartz stated that Tulāji entered eternity to reap what he had sown.[85]

5.7 Interim Rule by the Committee of Inspection

Since Tulāji requested the Committee of Inspection on his deathbed not to dismiss Shiva Rao, his diwan, or his civil servants, on 2 February 1787, Campbell, not knowing of Tulāji's death, informed Governor General Cornwallis in Calcutta of Tulāji's impending death and communicated to him Tulāji's last wish: The Company should give his adopted son called "Surfogee Rajah" the same "favor and protection." Until his response, Campbell promised to "take care to protect good order in the Kingdom of Tanjore, and the right of succession be ascertained."[86]

On 3 February 1787, Campbell informed Cornwallis about Tulāji's death. He sent him an extract of a letter from the Court of Directors dated 12 April 1775. It outlined what Pigot should do when Tulāji died and how to consult Wallajah and appoint Tulāji's successor. Campbell requested Cornwallis's advice to move forward.[87] On the same day (February 3, 1787), the Committee of Inspection decided on the following measures until the appointment of a successor: Colonel Stuart proposed that his soldiers be tasked with guarding the palace. Schwartz opposed Stuart's unilateral decision and wanted the committee to consider "the sentiments of the Palace Managers" and determine whether they would accept the soldiers as peacekeepers. At Schwartz's request, the Committee invited Shiva Rao and Lala, the palace's two "principal Managers." These managers stated that "as all animosities have perfectly subsided, keeping the Europeans before the Palace" was unnecessary. They said the "sepoys, one sergeant & 2 officers, who are put over the treasury, may remain." The Committee advised these two managers "to continue their functions until further orders from the Government arrive." Thus, Schwartz's prudence safeguarded the dignity of the two principal managers of the palace, avoiding unnecessary expenses and conflicts. Later, the Committee of Inspection inquired of the palace managers about the soldiers' behaviour. The managers responded, "The troops have behaved with all possible civility, without

85 AFSt/M 1 C 27 : 24.
86 IOR/P/252/15, 213–214.
87 IOR/P/252/15, 240–242.

deviating from the Rules of Models, and, therefore, have perfectly obeyed the Colonel's orders."[88] The palace managers did not reveal the entire truth.[89] As Schwartz had indicated earlier to King Tulāji, they knew of the brewing rivalries and animosities within the palace. The Company soldiers ensured outward peace and harmony, but they were unaware of the internal controversies about the succession to the throne.

On 7 February 1787, Hudleston handed over his responsibility as Resident of Tanjore to Alexander Macleod and left Tanjore.[90] Macleod chaired the Committee of Inspection and reported in exaggerated terms the peaceful conditions of Tanjore. As far as they knew, every part of the Kingdom of Tanjore had the most perfect tranquillity. They expected this peace would not last long.[91] This Committee assured the Company in Madras that it would faithfully, "without diminution," hand over all rights, properties, treasures, and jewels which Tulāji had left behind to his successor. The Committee requested Schwartz's opinion on all administrative matters, especially on executing the Company's order in Madras, because his "judgment stands so high due to his long residency and complete knowledge of the people, respecting the most conciliatory mode of carrying the Government's orders into immediate execution." Then, the Committee of Inspection enlisted the support of Ameer Singh, four senior managers, and two "reputable sheriffs [...] exclusive of the usual servants of the Treasury" and assessed Tulāji's assets.[92]

Additionally, the Committee of Inspection requested Schwartz "to go before them to the Palace and explain privately to the late Rajah's brother the nature and object of the instructions of the Company in Madras." Then, the members of this Committee gave Ameer Singh a letter of condolence from the governor on the death of his brother. Schwartz explained the instructions to Ameer Singh, who expressed his "highest respect for and obedience to the will of Government, declaring that the Committee shall have access to every part of the Palace and secure every valuable effect of the late Rajah." Ameer Singh requested that the Committee keep the evaluators' names and identities confidential. Then, the evaluators assessed Tulāji's treasury on 7 February 1787 and confirmed that it had 12,485 Star Pagodas, 1,000 Rupees, 41,387 Tanjore Cakkarams and 1,035 Madras Cakkarams.[93] Thus, the Company had already and indirectly concluded that Ameer Singh was Tulāji's legitimate brother and future ruler, so they included him in their deliberations.

---

88 IOR/P/252/15, 305–307.

89 IOR/P/252/15, 318: On 08.02.1787, the new Company Resident Macleod informed Governor Campbell about Ameer Singh's disorderly government. Ameer Singh did not publicise his appointment of Shiva Rao and his other chief administrators. Therefore, ordinary officers of Tanjore did not know to whom they were answerable. Hence, they delayed executing many things, which caused damage on all fronts.

90 IOR/P/252/15, 311: As Hudleston retired from the Committee of Inspection, Macleod succeeded him.

91 IOR/P/252/15, 307–309.

92 IOR/P/252/15, 311–312.

93 IOR/P/252/15, 313–316; IOR/P/252/15, 627–628: On 07.03.1787, the evaluators of the Committee of Inspection assessed Tulāji's jewels: Three breast jewels valued respectively at

On 8 February 1787, Alexander MacLeod warned Governor Campbell that since there was no announcement of the successor to Tulāji, people remained confused. Shiva Rao could not work well because he did not know to whom he was accountable.[94] The farmers harvested paddy and assumed they did not have to surrender any part of their harvest to the king. The temptation for "fraud and embezzlement" was ripe among the Rajah's people, and there was no proper punishment for those who committed such offenses.[95] On the same day, Macleod sent another report to Governor Campbell, highlighting the severe financial dangers of mismanagement. He stated that the "real state of affairs" remained ruinous for revenue collection, emphasising the dire consequences of the current situation.

> No person employed in the collections from the Soubahdar [*cupētār*] and Amildar [*amiltār*] down to the Manager or inferior officers of the Circar knows or feels the authority under which he is to act. The existence of this present Government [i.e. Committee of Inspection], if it may be called Government, never having been publicly announced.
> The consequence of this need hardly be pointed out either the Cuthwals [*kottuvāl*] of the Land not knowing that the present administration [by the Committee of Inspection] have authority to punish offenders, will defraud the *circar*, or which is most probably, the amildars will cease the favorable occasion of enriching themselves at the expense both Ryots [farmer-tenants] and of the Government. The emigrations formerly dreaded but resided by the timely intervention of this Committee will take place.[96]

Then, Macleod extracted a portion of Governor Campbel's earlier letter to Ameer Singh and recommended its immediate publication: Until the Company in Madras considered the details of Tulāji's successor to the throne, Ameer Singh and Tulāji's ministers should stay in power, "promote the good of the country and the happiness of the inhabitants" and thus secure "the friendship of the Honourable Company and my protection."[97] Macleod explained that this interim arrangement did not endorse Ameer Singh's kingship. Instead, it asked him to "be part of the present temporary administration and exhorts him to such behaviour as may procure him the Company's friendship." Macleod urged Governor Campbell to make Ameer Singh a member of the Committee of Inspection because he had a "natural interest by blood" for the country's welfare. Besides, "his education has been good. The late Rajah thought he could conduct an administration during a long ministry. Is it not advisable that such a man should have at least an equal share in the temporary government of the Tanjore Country?" On 13 February 1787, John Chamier received Macleod's recommendation and did not pursue it.[98]

980, 696 and 1,225 Porto Novo Pagodas; a turban jewel for 1,080 Porto Novo Pagodas; two pairs of ear jewels respectively at 527 and 100 Porto Nogo Pagodas. Another turban-jewel for 1,226 Porto Novo Pagodas. A pair of bracelets for 1,300 Porto Novo Pagodas. A ring for the arm for four hundred Porto Novo Pagodas; two feathers for a turban for 80 Porto Novo Pagodas; two chains for the neck for 625 Porto Novo Pagodas; two sets of women's jewels, each for 598 and 258 Porto Novo Pagodas; a pearl dress for three hundred Porto Novo Pagodas. The total value of all jewels was 9,493 Porto Novo Pagodas.

94 IOR/P/252/15, 317–319.

95 IOR/P/252/15, 313–316.

96 IOR/P/252/15, 319–323.

97 IOR/P/252/15, 319–323.

The Committee of Inspection, a body established to oversee the administration of Tanjore, continued to manage the region. On 27 February 1787, they reported that sowing paddy had already begun in Tanjore. They asked the farmers not to sell paddy to anyone outside of Tanjore and curtailed the powers of Baba, the most vicious oppressor of the farmers. They decided not to tax the paddy before it was harvested. They raised the February *kist* of 90,000 Pagodas from non-agricultural sources. Macleod informed Campbell that he had initiated an inquiry to determine the annual consumption of rice throughout the Tanjore country and to estimate the quantities of rice from Tanjore at a fair price. Hippisley wanted a weekly record from the time of Tulāji's death; all officers in Tanjore who dealt with money and grains should mention the day and time of these transactions and send their records to the Committee of Inspection every week. This financial oversight would prevent deceptions and enable the Committee to raise three-fourths of all revenues for the Company. He believed that the managers had taken 700,000 Pagodas without keeping any accounts. This Committee, acting as trustees for the successor of Tulāji, aimed to instil trust in the Company among the people of Tanjore. The Committee also considered issuing orders (*cowles*) and leasing the uncultivated lands to farmers. For this purpose, the managers should collaborate with the Committee of Inspection. The Committee also decided to meet on Mondays and requested Schwartz to communicate this change to all concerned persons; finally, this Committee appointed Harrington to check the banks of the rivers and channels for uninterrupted irrigation. Thus, as an interim measure, the Committee of Inspection sought to increase revenues for the Company, primarily through the sale of agricultural produce. However, it was not as easy as the Committee of Inspection imagined. A problem arose along the banks of the river Cauvery. For example, Wallajah's deputy, Muhammad Lassier Cawn, did not permit the revenue collectors of Tanjore to enter the regions around the Akaṇda Cauvery.[99] Though Wallajah was an ally of the Company, he remained the enemy of the king of Tanjore. The people living in such conflict-ridden places suffered greatly.

By February 28, 1787, the members of the Committee of Inspection had developed differing opinions about their roles. Macleod was the Resident, and he wanted everyone to obey his decisions. The rest of the committee members thought of each other as equals. They wanted to admit at least one Indian manager to this Committee, but Macleod opposed this request. Hippisley believed that during the interim period, the normal representative functions of a Company Resident remained suspended because Tulāji had no successor. Therefore, Tanjore's managers disregarded the instructions from the Committee of Inspection. The tax collectors did not know to whom they should report and what penalties would apply for non-compliance. Each manager acted independently, and overall, the situation of Tanjore Country remained grave. The Committee knew it was a trust that would stay in effect until the new ruler assumed control of the

98 IOR/P/252/15, 323–324.

99 IOR/P/252/15, 433–446.

administration. Then, the Committee would dissolve, and the Company's Resident would resume his duties as the deputy of the Company.[100] Until that time, the committee members should have equal rights and powers.

On the contrary, Macleod attempted to assert his authority by insisting that, as the Company Resident alone, he had the power and privilege to send instructions to the managers and to meet Ameer Singh in the palace. When the members could not agree on their course of action, Hippisley requested Schwartz's mediation. Schwartz, a vital member of the Committee of Inspection, proposed to admit at least one Indian manager for deliberations. He left the question of access to the palace unanswered because Schwartz had unlimited access to Ameer Singh, Serfoji and other royal persons. Finally, Schwartz proposed a compromise. Whenever the committee discussed the grassroots realities of Tanjore and revenue collection, they could invite an Indian manager to give an update. Otherwise, the four European members could make all the decisions. Consequently, the Committee of Inspection invited Ramaiah, who had previously worked as the Palace Manager and was now the Country Manager, to answer Hippisley's questions about paddy cultivation and the custom of accepting tax in either money or in kind, such as grain.

Ramaiah explained that the managers had implemented all the articles of Tulāji's cowle to the farmers who had returned from their earlier diaspora. He further stated that the revenue collectors accepted the stipulated tax. Some paid cash. Others gave it in kind, such as paddy or other harvested goods. Hippisley wondered if the price of paddy remained low, the tax amount would also be less. Ramaiah prudently replied that the tax collectors could not collect the Company's share of the money because some farmers could only pay their share of the harvested goods. The Company should fix the paddy's buying and selling price so that Indian managers could work toward paying the stipulated *kists* on time.[101]

On 2 March 1787, Schwartz described the prevailing uncertainty of Tulāji's successor. He knew a reply from the Company in Bengal would need at least a month to reach Tanjore. In the meantime, three contending parties vied for the throne: Ameer Singh, the forerunner, the boy Serfoji, and a young man named Nana Sahib.[102] On 7 March 1787, Schwartz gave details about Nana Sahib in the genealogical line of King Tukkoji. The four sons of Tukkoji were 1) Anna Saheb, 2) Baba Saheb, 3) Nana Saheb and 4) Pratāpasimha, the father of Tulāji and Ameer Singh.[103] Nana Saheb died before Pratāpasimha became king, but Anna Saheb

100 IOR/P/252/15, 561, 563 and 566–568.

101 IOR/P/252/15, 576–78; IOR/P/252/15, 590: In their meeting on 8 March 1787, Schwartz changed his opinion about the representation of the managers: Ramiah did not tell the truth. Therefore, all managers should appear in person and share their views. Of course, "I [Schwartz] retract my former opinion."

102 AFSt/M 1 C 29b : 6c.

103 IOR/H/571, 183: A Company reporter stated that Tulāji wanted to get Serfoji married immediately. However, the news of his adoption "created a great deal of alarm at Tanjore because he was a distant relation." At the same time, Ameer Singh's party "was strong." Hence, Serfoji's marriage did not take place.

lived longer. When Tulāji died, his son, Nana Saheb, was twenty-five years old.[104] This Nana Saheb lived within the palace of Tanjore and hoped to succeed Tulāji.[105] Serfoji, whose family name was Bhonsle, was nine or ten when Tulāji adopted him. Ameer Singh, who was thirty-five years old, kept Nana Saheb's son close to him and appeared to love him because he had no son. Schwartz was also aware of the close relationship between Ameer Singh and Nana Saheb, and they would not want Serfoji to survive.[106]

On 21 March 1787, Schwartz's foresight clashed with the Company's unchecked greed at Fort St. George. He anticipated that their insatiable appetite and the rapacious behaviour of the Company's creditors and renters would ruin Tanjore's economy. He predicted drastic upheavals in Tanjore's political, military, and civil spheres. For instance, he envisioned a future where Tanjore's rulers would serve more as tax collectors for the Company than as true leaders. To meet the Company's exorbitant demands, the king's tax collectors imposed heavier taxes on the ordinary people, leading to their disillusionment with their rulers.[107]

Schwartz urged the Committee of Inspection to govern the people fairly during the interim period but had little success. Until then, Tulāji's revenue collectors had been taxing the agricultural produce before the farmers could harvest it. Schwartz proposed taxing only the harvested produce, but the Committee of Inspection continued with Tulāji's method. Simultaneously, the eldest son of Nawab Wallajah dispatched his Muslim tax collectors to Tanjore, believing that after Tulāji's death, Tanjore was rightfully his. One of these tax collectors aspired to become the king of Tanjore, promising Pohle that if he ascended the throne, he would pay the Nawab 200,000 Star Pagodas more than any ruler appointed by the Company. These conflicting groups of tax collectors made life unbearable for ordinary people.

On 7 March 1787, the Committee of Inspection debated the price of paddy harvested during the rainy season but was unable to determine its price.[108] Meanwhile, the farmers of Papanasam, a town twenty-five kilometres from Tanjore, found themselves in a dire situation. Faced with the relentless tax collector of the Nawab, "Mootiamoopeh" (Muttaiyā Mūppaṉār?), who sent his soldiers armed with matchets and pickaxes to evict them, they had no choice but to abandon their unharvested paddy in the fields and flee to safer places.[109] In their meeting on March 8, 1787, Macleod informed the Committee that he had rushed

---

104 IOR/H/285A, 864: Nana Saheb was a son of Pratāpasimha's older brother, also named Nana Saheb. When Tulāji died, Nana Saheb assumed he would be Tanjore's next king. On 27 January 1793, Ameer Singh declared his intention to adopt Nana Saheb's son as his successor.

105 IOR/H/571, 184: An unnamed Company reporter mentioned that King Tulāji imprisoned the twenty-year-old Nana Saheb and his diwan Baba for plotting to seize the Kingdom of Tanjore from Tulāji.

106 AFSt/M 1 C 29b : 6d.

107 AFSt/M 1 C 29b : 6e.

108 IOR/P/252/15, 552–556.

109 IOR/P/252/15, 594: Mootiamoopeh was responsible for overseeing seven districts in the Kumbakonam region. He forced the farmers "to withhold the circar share of grain," halted the paddy harvest and threatened to kill the farmers. Therefore, they fled to other places.

to Kumbakonam to meet the farmers and assure them of protection.[110] As a result of Macleod's intervention, some farmers found the courage to return, hopeful for a better future.[111]

At a critical juncture, the Court of Directors in London, exercising their authority, deemed it necessary to enforce their decision to extract more revenue from the Kingdom of Tanjore. On 9 March 1787, the Company in Madras deliberated on a significant directive from the Court of Directors, which proposed a treaty with the future ruler of Tanjore, thereby further solidifying external influence on Tanjore's governance.[112] The directors, pleased with the restoration of peace on the Coromandel Coast and Tanjore, put forth a "just and equitable Treaty, a Plan for the future Defence and protection of Carnatic, the Tanjore Country, and the northern Circars, on a solid and lasting foundation." This treaty included provisions such as the future ruler of Tanjore reimbursing the cost of maintaining a Military Peace Establishment in his country, which covered all war expenses, army maintenance, fort support, officer and civil administrator salaries, and more.

The first stipulation of this draft treaty proposed that, starting from 12 July 1787, the ruler of Tanjore should pay the Company annually 400,000 Star Pagodas: "November 20,000; December 50,000; January 50,000; February 90,000; March 90,000; and April 100,000." The second stipulation stated that this amount of four lakhs of Star Pagodas, based on ten lakhs, is the estimated gross annual income of Tanjore Country. If this income increased, Tanjore's king should pay more to the Company. The third stipulation was more brutal than it seemed in its calculated intent to occupy the Kingdom of Tanjore as soon as possible. It reads as follows:

> In case of failure in the punctual payment of the four lakhs of Pagodas already mentioned to the extent of fifty thousand Pagodas for the period of one month after the same shall become due, his Excellency the Rajah agrees that certain districts specified in the schedule [...] shall be made answerable for such failure and that the Company shall have power to appoint superintendents or receivers to collect from the Rajah and managers and *amuldar*s all the revenues, duties and customs of the districts and these superintendents shall exercise all necessary authority collecting such rents, revenues & giving regular receipts for all the monies that may be received by the said superintends who shall have full power to inspect and examine all cutcherry receipts and accounts of the lands and districts aforesaid as well as to ascertain the state of all other revenues which shall be collected annually within the said districts and when the total amount for which such districts stood answerable shall have been paid to the Company, the superintendents or receivers shall be immediately recalled.

---

110 IOR/P/252/15, 585.

111 IOR/P/252/15, 595: Alexander Macleod informed the Committee of Inspection on 08.03.1787: If the Company abolished Pilly Tax, i.e. either *pilanti*-tax or land-tax (*nilavari*), the farmers would return and cultivate the land. IOR/P/252/15, 621–622: On 12.03.1787, the managers of Tanjore sought to abolish the Pilly tax. They encouraged the farmers to harvest their paddy, to give what was due to the king of Tanjore and to keep what was due to them "according to Justice." They stated that the Company would punish the transgressors and thieves severely. IOR/P/252/15, 660: On 19.03.1787, the Committee of Inspection named the four managers of Tanjore District as "Shevarow, Baupanah, Suntapah and Pillynapah [sic. =Shiva Rao, Baupanā, Cāntappā and Paḻaṉiyappā]."

112 IOR/P/252/15, 454–516.

The fourth stipulation required the future ruler of Tanjore to ask his revenue collectors to answer to the Company-appointed superintendents. There was no other crueller method to exploit the economic resources of Tanjore. The fifth stipulation would impose a moral blow to the ruler: accordingly, the Company would not interfere with the civil administration; it would uphold and preserve the dignity of the ruler and his family, but the ruler would have no power to collect taxes and revenues from his own country. The sixth and seventh stipulations made cruel demands: in the event of war, not only in the Kingdom of Tanjore but anywhere along the Coromandel Coast, the Company's army would seize all power and conduct the war. However, the ruler of Tanjore should pay all war reparations. For this purpose, he should pledge to pay four-fifths of his total revenue. The eighth stipulation was dictatorial: if the ruler could not pay four-fifths of the revenues of Tanjore, the Governor in Madras would automatically appoint inspectors with full power to examine all incomes and expenses at local and regional levels. The ninth stipulation mandated that the ruler of Tanjore continue to pay four-fifths of his gross annual revenue to the Company, even after the termination of the war, until all debts and war expenses, as determined by the Company, were settled. The tenth stipulation promised that the Company would recall its superintendents from Tanjore to pay all debts and expenses. The eleventh and twelfth stipulations stated that the Company would gladly send more troops to Tanjore if the future ruler required and paid for them. The thirteenth stipulation obliged the future ruler of Tanjore to pay off the accumulated and pending tribute of 300,000 Pagodas to Wallajah, which Tulāji had refused to pay. Finally, the Company in Madras approved the draft and waited for an opportunity to impose it on the next ruler of Tanjore.

On 15 March 1787, the Committee of Inspection, in a profound show of respect, acknowledged Ameer Singh's self-perception as the regent of Tanjore. Ameer Singh's official letter, bearing his signature, "Sree Ram Pretaub [Sri Ram Pratab]," reiterated his presumed regal status.[113] The prefix 'Sri' indicated his royal attachment to his biological father, Pratāpasimha. This signature helped Hippisley understand why Governor Campbell respected Ameer Singh as a regent. At that time, he was just a member of the Committee of Inspection and a manager. As a result, the Committee requested that Schwartz persuade Ameer Singh not to claim royal status at this time. On the same day, Schwartz reported how often Macleod reminded Ameer Singh "not to look upon himself as the Rajah, but simply as one acting in conformity with the four managers and according to the wish of the Committee."[114]

On 24 March 1787, the four managers, namely "Shevarow [Sambajee], Baupanah, Suntapah and Gillinappah," asked the Committee of Inspection to give

---

[113] Ameer Singh alias Rama Swamy signed his letters as "Shree Ram Pretaub." IOR/P/252/15, 624: On 15.03.1787, Hippisley expressed unhappiness about Ameer Singh assuming the royal name and dignity because the Company in Madras had not yet named a successor to Tulāji. Ameer Singh should not view himself as a king; at that time, he was merely a Tanjore manager and a member of the Committee of Inspection.

[114] IOR/P/252/15, 624–626.

them during the brief harvest time more servants to reap the paddy not to take any money from the poor farmers but to be content with the share in kind as grains due to the government of Tanjore. The tax collectors should ensure that the farmers receive a fair price for their share of the government of Tanjore. Without these arrangements, the tax collectors could not collect the needed money for the *kists* to the Company.[115]

Consequently, on 26 March 1787, the Committee of Inspection discussed this letter, and Hippisley proposed making this concession. Schwartz concurred with Hippisley and added his views as follows: this "concession was requested by Ameer Sing and the four Managers and was the only difference between the cowle, which was approved of by the Committee and published, the other [measure] proposed by Ameer Singh and the four Managers — I therefore agree with Mr. Hippisley's proposition provided the Circar Paddy be forced upon none."[116]

On the same day (26 March 1787), the Committee of Inspection gave the managers the freedom to fix a fair price for the Circar Paddy that would be acceptable to the inhabitants: it "will be for the Managers to fix such a reasonable price on the Circar Paddy as to make it the interest of the inhabitants to take it and to keep them satisfied in this respect will be the true interest of the Circar."[117] Strangely, the Company Resident Macleod did not sign this reply. He was unhappy with this concession and abstained from signing it. Stuart, Hippisley and Schwartz supported this harmonious interaction between the Company and the people.

5.8 Ameer Singh as an Interim Ruler

As an interim ruler, Ameer Singh navigated a complex web of relationships, priorities, failures and reorientations. This period allowed the members of the Committee of Inspection to interact with Ameer Singh, assess his competencies, and gauge his willingness to cooperate with them in raising funds for the Company's army, which protected the palace and Tanjore Country. The Company's scrutiny of Ameer Singh's legitimacy was a significant factor in Tanjore's political dynamics. Ameer Singh, in turn, would have observed the Company's cooperation with Wallajah, Tanjore's archenemy, which could have influenced his political strategies.

5.8.1 Ameer Singh's Background

When Schwartz suggested Ameer Singh Ramaswamy (1738–1802) as a possible candidate to succeed Tulāji, questions arose about his father and the moral integrity of his mother. Most people who knew Ameer Singh believed that his father was King Pratāpasimha, and his mother was an unnamed concubine of Pratāpasimha. Others claimed that Ameer Singh's father was Vencana, a low-ranking servant

---

115 IOR/P/252/15, 678–679.
116 IOR/P/252/15, 677.
117 IOR/P/252/15, 679–680.

who bore a resemblance to Pratāpasimha. When Pratāpasimha learned of his concubine's pregnancy and the subsequent birth of Ameer Singh, he sought to kill Vencana, who fled. Draupadī Bāi Sāhibā, the legal wife of Pratāpasimha, ensured the safety of Ameer Singh's mother, allowing her to stay in the palace under the condition that she should not meet either the king or the queen. Thus, Ameer Singh grew up within the palace.[118] In 1787, he was about thirty years old. Most people in the palace recognised him as Tulāji's brother and assumed he would succeed Tulāji, even though he did not possess any exceptional skills in politics or administration.[119] They knew how Tulāji deputed him to receive Governor Pigot in 1776 when he came to Tanjore to free Tulāji from imprisonment and reinstall him as the king of Tanjore.[120]

The common notion that Ameer Singh was a son of Pratāpasimha and a half-brother of Tulāji persuaded Hudleston to prefer him to other claimants to the throne. Wallajah, too, insisted that Tulāji's successor should have a royal lineage. Shiva Row, who had not previously esteemed Ameer Singh, suddenly considered him and Serfoji the "nearest and dearest to him in the world." Soon after Tulāji's death, Shiva Row wanted to proclaim Ameer Singh as the king, but Schwartz persuaded him to wait for the Company's opinion on Tulāji's successor.[121] Schwartz did not immediately disclose the intimate link between Shiva Rao and Ameer Singh. Seven years later, in 1795, he stated that Shiva Rao was fully aware of Ameer Singh's illegitimate claim to the throne and how the former financed the latter to stay in power. As a result, Ameer Singh was always afraid of Shiva Rao and did not dare to challenge his wrongdoings.[122]

---

118 IOR/H/285A, 626–627: "The Raja afterwards consulted Mr. Swartz respecting the appointment of a Regent when Mr. Swartz opposed Ameer Sing Rama Samy as being the Raja's brother, and the Raja made answer that as to his being his Brother he entertained doubts. On the following day, Tuljajee called for Col. Stuart, Mr. Hudleston and Mr. Swartz and informed them that he had at the recommendation of Mr. Swartz appointed his Brother Ameer Singh to be the Guardian of Serfojee, and Manager of Tanjore during the minority of Serfojee, requesting that Ameer Singh who had no son of his own, would also adopt the youth who he had committed to his care. It is asserted that if it had not been for Mr. Swartz's intercession, Tuljajee would have bequeathed nothing to Ameer Sing. There existed a strong party in favor of Ameer Sing, residing in the Palace. He was supposed to be about 30 years old, a man of no abilities and supposed to have been of suspicious origin, and his illegitimacy was publicly talked of at this time. Ameer Sing was the son of a slave girl, a Concubine of Pratab Sing but his real father is said to have been Vencasia or Vencana, a slave whom he greatly resembled in person, and if recalled right, [...] Ameer Sing was very dark and Pratab Sing very fair. [...] Had Ameer Sing been legitimate, Serfojee's Rights by adoption would have been preferable to his. Pratab Sing would have sent Vencana to death, but he fled, and he would have killed the child also, but he was spared at the intercession of Dropada Baie Saheb, the lawful wife of Pratab Sing, from that time, the mother of Ameer Sing did not appear before the Raja or the Queen. A small house was given to him, and Ameer Sing could live there. Vencana was at Tanjore in June 1796 [sic] and was in the service of Ameer Sing."

119 IOR/H/571, 183.

120 IOR/H/571, 188.

121 IOR/H/571, 184–186.

122 Pearson: Memoirs, Vol. 2, 322–323: Towards the end of 1795, Schwartz wrote to Resident Macleod in Tanjore: "You know the unhappy cause of the rajah's attachment to Shevarow

On 26 February 1787, Cornwallis requested that the Company in Madras assess the opinion of the inhabitants of Tanjore and subsequently appoint a successor. He suggested that Serfoji become the next king, provided the Nawab and his successors unanimously supported him. Otherwise, Rama Swamy alias Ameer Singh should become the king. "Should they require an investigation and the matter remain doubtful, Rama Swamy is to be preferred."[123]

Governor Campbell aimed to achieve two goals: to ensure a higher and steady income from Tanjore for the Company. He believed that appointing a new ruler would provide a suitable opportunity for concluding a treaty that would benefit the Company. Therefore, on 9 March 1787, he presented a draft of the treaty to the Company Council in Madras. Upon receiving their approval, he announced his intention to travel to Tanjore on March 13, 1787. Secondly, he wanted to install Ameer Singh as Tulāji's successor for two reasons: Tulāji considered him his brother. As proof of his relationship with him, Tulāji permitted Ameer Singh to reside in a suitable house on the palace grounds.[124]

A fuller version of Campbell's two-fold purpose provides additional information: Firstly, Campbell wanted to appoint Tulāji's successor. Secondly, he wanted to conclude a treaty with him "for the General Defence and Security of the Carnatic," which the Company's Court of Directors in London had sent to their governor in Madras. This council read this letter on 9 March 1787. Campbell expected to receive the decision of the Governor General in Calcutta about the successor. If the decision did not reach him before he arrived in Tanjore, he wanted to know whether "the child or Brother Rama Swamy ought to succeed to the Rajahship of Tanjore." Then, he evaluated the merits and demerits of each claimant as follows:

> The adopted child claims his pretensions from the recited acts of the Rajah on his deathbed, and the brother claims it as the next heir from consanguinity. The abilities and legitimacy of Rama Swamy have been doubted, but as far as I can learn, he does not want for abilities and what is much to his credit, he bears the reputation of a virtuous honest man; as to his illegitimacy, the late Rajah never once to my knowledge, announced it; on the contrary, he considered him publicly as a brother for whom he had entertained considerable respect; for the Rajah assigned to him apartments of the best quality in the palace and deputed him to meet Lord Pigot, on his entering the territories of Tanjore every time his Lordship was sent to restore the Rajah to his kingdom. Whether, under 'all these circumstances, the late Rajah had a legal right to adopt a very distant relation to the prejudice of his brother Rama Swamy, or whether the adoption was in itself just and regular, is a matter which merits inquiry and may be very accurately ascertained.'[125]

---

and his whole family. It is not any regard he has for them: no—he is actuated only by fear. He is conscious of having no legal claim to the crown; and that insidious family know it likewise; and they have been so imprudent as to declare, that as he owed his elevation to their assistance, so they had it in their power to bring him down whenever they pleased. It is fear of losing his glory, or splendid misery. It makes him bear any insult to preserve himself in the possession of his throne. He has delivered the management of the whole country to that family, not daring to control them. Accordingly they took the accounts out of the palace and the treasures likewise."

[123] IOR/H/571, 190.

[124] IOR/H/571, 190.

[125] IOR/P/252/15, 544–552.

Although Campbell preferred Ameer Singh, he wanted to determine what Tanjore's prominent religious leaders thought about Serfoji's adoption. Therefore, all voting members should cast their votes. Otherwise, Ameer Singh would be the next king. He pretended to uphold Tulāji's adoption of Serfoji because, he claimed, "the Justice of our Government [in the UK and India]" would require it. He cunningly planned to control Ameer Singh for the benefit of the Company. He perceived Ameer Singh's installation would give the Company "a perpetual check" and "the surest pledge in our hands for his future good behaviour." Campbell resolutely wanted to keep "the claim of the Nabob to sovereignty" over Tanjore open, so that the Company could conveniently force Ameer Singh to obey the Company's dictates.[126]

5.8.2 Twelve Pandits Endorsing Ameer Singh

On 2 April 1787, Ameer Singh and Serfoji received Campbell in Tanjore. The following day, Campbell gathered the European inhabitants and leading Indian merchants in Tanjore who were "intimately acquainted with the laws and religious principles of the Hindus." He assumed that the gathered people supported Ameer Singh as the successor to Tulāji and considered Serfoji's adoption as "highly irregular and defective." These people suggested that the dying Tulāji lost his rational mind and adopted Serfoji. They believed that the nine-year-old Serfoji was the only child of Tulāji's distant relative. They accused Tulāji of adopting him without the consent of his parents. They declared that the entire adoption process was invalid. According to the "religious principles of the Hinduoos," one should not adopt the only son of a family. Likewise, the adopted child should not be older than five years.[127]

At 3 p.m. on the same day (April 3, 1787), Campbell visited Ameer Singh and Serfoji in the palace and informed them of Cornwallis's minute dated February 26, 1787. Accordingly, he wanted to consult twelve "pandits of the first character in Tanjore."[128] He also wanted to find out the religious appropriateness of Serfoji's adoption. He asked Ameer Singh to gather these pandits at 10 a.m. on April 4, 1787. Without consulting Schwartz or the palace priests, who had authorised Tulāji to adopt Serfoji, Ameer Singh identified the following twelve pandits: "1. Dada,

---

126 IOR/P/252/15, 544–552.

127 IOR/P/252/16, 31–32: Campbell's diary of 3 April 1787 reads as follows: Campbell inquired about the rights of Ameer Sing to succession and the legality of Serfoji's adoption. He gathered the leaders of European men in Tanjore, well-informed merchants and those "who were intimately acquainted with the laws and religious principles of the Hindoos." He asked their opinion about Ameer Singh's right to the throne. They asserted that Tulāji "never once publicly declared him to be illegitimate, but on the contrary, treated him with the respect and attention of a brother on whom he had placed as great a degree of confidence as Hindoo princes generally do to the most ostensible successor." After losing his senses, Tulāji adopted Serfoji, the only son of his family. Additionally, one could only adopt a five-year-old boy. However, Serfoji was nine years old when Tulāji adopted him. Hence, Serfoji's adoption was "adverse to the laws & religious practices of the Hindoos."

128 IOR/H/571, 192.

2. Bijenrow Krist, 3. Paulel Asary, 4. Appa Sastry, 5. Rama Sastry, 6. Narasinga Asary, 7. Sallia Nidy Asary, 8. Aiyen Asary, 9. Sey Asary, 10. Madava Asary, 11. Vija Asary [and] 12. Bhapana."[129]

At that time, neither Campbell nor the members of the Inspection Committee considered consulting Tulāji's priests, who had approved the adoption and performed the relevant ceremonies for Serfoji.[130] They also did not assess the competency of the newly selected pandits in either the Sanskrit scriptures or matters of adoption. They did not mind their age or religious affiliations, whether as Śaivites or Vaiṣṇavites. They convened the meeting hurriedly in a room within the palace. Campbell prohibited the pandits from consulting each other and charged them to give their opinion "according to truth and their conscience. They should write their answers and hand them over to Campbell. Thus, their opinion would be kept from each other and the public eye."[131]

Campbell handed over the answers of these priests to Schwartz. Appendix 2, found at the end of this biography, contains Schwartz's English translation of these answers in Tamil. Schwartz translated their Tamil answers quickly into English. These answers were elicited from Campbell's questions to favour Ameer Singh. For example, the first question asked whether "the late Rajah of Tanjore considered Ameer Singh as his brother & gave him apartments" in the palace. The answer of all pandits affirmed Tulāji's grant of a living place to Ameer Singh within the palace complex. However, they did not indicate that Tulāji had publicly acknowledged him as his brother.

5.8.3 Schwartz's Failure to Consult Sanskrit Law Books and Lawyers

Surprisingly, Schwartz failed to consult Tulāji's court priests, who had approved Serfoji's adoption. He would have known at least some of them. Likewise, he might have known at least some of the twelve Maratha Brahmin pandits who recommended Ameer Singh's customary religious fitness for enthronement, and he did not question their credibility or check the truthfulness of their answers. Don Wright, who studied Ameer Singh's enthronement, wondered how Schwartz, known for his careful and honest evaluations, could have failed in this regard.[132]

Schwartz did not read, speak, or understand Sanskrit. However, he could have consulted Nathaniel Brassey Halhed's *A Code of Gentoo Laws or Ordinations of*

---

129 For another list of these twelve pandits, see IOR/P/253/12, 1443–4 in Section 8.4.3. Tulāji's widows dictated these names from their memory.

130 Wright: Swartz of Thanjavur: A missionary in politics, 98: Wright rightly wondered why and how Schwartz chose these pandits and did not consult the head priest at the palace. Schwartz "must have known their reputation." It is also possible that Campbell's record is false because he wanted to impress his readers with his commitment to upholding justice. However, it was evident that even before he arrived in Tanjore, he had favoured Ameer Singh and rejected Serfoji.

131 IOR/P/252/16, 34–35.

132 Wright: Swartz of Thanjavur, 98.

the Pandits.[133] Its first section deals with "Inheritance from a Father, a Grandfather, a Great-Grandfather, and Such Kind of Relations." The properties of a man without a biological son, grandson or great-grandson belonged to his adopted son.[134] Its ninth section explains the adoption process: a man could adopt a child with the following conditions: The male child's ears must have no ornaments. The child should not have received the sacred thread of the Brahmins. He should not be married; he should be over five years old and have other brothers. Either the father or the mother, with the father's permission, could give up the child for adoption. Those wishing to adopt the child should perform religious rituals and give Gold and Rice to the Father of the Child. [...] He who has no Son, or Grandson, or Grandson's Son, or Brother's Son shall adopt a Son; while he has One adopted Son, he shall not adopt a Second."[135]

It is not understandable how the Company officers in Madras, too, failed to consult Halhed's *A Code of Gentoo Laws*. It is also incomprehensible how hastily Campbell accepted the answers of the twelve pandits. They gave him what he expected from them. He quickly declared Serfoji's adoption illegal and unacceptable. Then, he proceeded to enthrone Ameer Singh. He ironically referred to his action as a demonstration of "strict justice to the Tanjore family." At once, Ameer Singh expressed his high sense of "English justice" and declared that his brother, Tulāji, never intended to supersede his right to succession. He insisted that Tulāji's evil-minded courtiers "unhappily advised him to adopt this boy," especially "in the last hour of his affliction" and just before his death.[136]

5.8.4 Ameer Singh's Enthronement (7 April 1787)

Ameer Singh's enthronement occurred at 5 p.m. on Saturday, 7 April 1787, in the Grand Durbar Hall. Campbell, his military officers, the notable citizens of Tanjore, and other dignitaries were present. Ameer Singh, seated on the throne, made solemn promises to protect Serfoji and govern Tanjore with the utmost care and fidelity. His words, "I promise the most faithful compliance," resonated with a sense of trust and confidence in his ability to govern justly and righteously.[137] Then, Governor Campbell spoke on behalf of the Company:

> In the name of the English East India Company, having declared themselves to be the friends and protectors of the Tanjore Family, I have been sent to this metropolis to enquire about the

---

133 Nathaniel Brassey Halhed: A Code of Gentoo Laws, or Ordinations of the Pandits, from a Persian Translation, made from the Original written in the Shanscrit [sic = Sanskrit] Language. London: n.p. 1776.

134 Halhed: A Code of Gentoo Laws, 30.

135 Halhed: A Code of Gentoo Laws, 298–299.

136 IOR/H/571, 194; IOR/P/252/16, 41–42: Campbell noted in his diary that he met Ameer Singh and Serfoji on the evening of 5 April 1787. He was glad the twelve pandits confirmed Ameer Singh's right to the throne. He stated that he would enthrone Ameer Singh in the name of the English East India Company. Immediately, Ameer Singh appreciated the "English Justice" that enabled him to become the king of Tanjore.

137 IOR/H/571, 194.

> legal rights of those who claim succession to the Rajaship. Twelve pandits of the first character at Tanjore, men highly esteemed for their knowledge of the laws and religious tenets of the Hindoos, have been called together for the purpose of ascertaining these facts and from every information I can learn from them without exclusive of the public documents in my possession, I find that the adoption of Serfogee by the late Rajah has been irregular and defective; and that you, Amer Sing, are certainly the true and legal successor to the Kingdom of Tanjore.
> Such being the case and in the best confidence that you will merit the Government of Tanjore by a kind and fatherly attention to the welfare and happiness of the people and as strict regard to the general interest and security of the Carnatic, I rejoice exceedingly that it is in my power, in the name of the English East India Company, to place you upon the musnund of your ancestors and I hope and trust that these elements of distinction will be ever remitted on your mind a strong, unequivocal proof of the Justice, Integrity & Friendship of the English nation. I wish most sincerely that your reign may be long and prosperous, that your conduct may be marked with wisdom & liberty toward all mankind and that our subjects may be industrious and faithful and enabled by the kind fostering hand of their virtuous prince to rest in peace and affluence under the refreshing shade of your auspicious Government.[138]

Ameer Singh's declaration, read aloud by two Brahmins, affirmed his commitment to just governance. In a symbolic act, Campbell placed a chain made with costly gems around Ameer Singh's turban and bound a jewel around his arm, representing the royal insignia. These things symbolised the weight and legitimacy of Ameer Singh's rule. Campbell then requested Schwartz to read out the proclamation in the Tamil and Marathi languages:

> Let all people know that today, Ameer Singh sits on the throne of his ancestors, and according to the rules of this country, he is the legitimate King of Tanjore. Today, he publicly promised to rule this country and his subjects justly and righteously. Therefore, you are obliged to accept him as your king and obey him. God bless the King![139]

After the installation ceremony, Campbell gave Ameer Singh "a rich dress, an elephant, a horse and some jewels. [...] As the Governor had no proper horse or elephant to present to his Excellency, the Rajah supplied them from his stables so that the customs on such occasions might not be ostensibly omitted." Then, there was a grand celebration: "The Fort immediately fired a Royal Salute." The entire city celebrated the beginning of Ameer Singh's reign.[140] Then, Ameer Singh read aloud a response in Tamil and Marathi languages so that all people who had gathered could hear and understand its contents and implications:

> The repeated proofs which my family have experienced of the Justice, Friendship and Protection of the English nation have been early and strongly impressed upon my heart; the present instance is a perfect confirmation of all that is past and must convince the world of

138 IOR/P/252/16, 43–45.
139 NHR 3, 1790, issue 36, 1390–1391.
140 IOR/P/252/16, 46.
141 IOR/P/252/16, 45–46.
142 IOR/P/252/16, 29.
143 IOR/E/4/872, 611–613: On 13.071786, the Court of Directors instructed the Governor-General of Bengal and the Governor of Madras to treat ships "under the colours of the United States of America" like ships of any other nation, subject to the same rules and regulations.

> the value of such unbiased Friendship of which I shall entertain the warmest and most grateful sense as long as I live.
> Convinced that nothing can ever afford the English Company, or you, Sir, their Representative, so much satisfaction, as to the people of Tanjore happy under a mild & just government, it will be the study of my life; a strict regard to justice and to the particular interest and prosperity, to merit the continuance of your favour and protection.[141]

Ameer Singh requested that Governor Campbell and all those present proceed with him through the four main streets of the Fort, so that the people could see the new king. Campbell explicitly stated that Ameer Singh was a fair and reasonable man who knew how corrupt management had damaged his country. Therefore, he wanted to restore Tanjore to prosperity so that Ameer Singh could "discharge all his engagements without trying his people."[142]

5.8.5 Ameer Singh's First Treaty with the Company (1787)

Schwartz's prediction about the worst time for Tanjore became true. He had foretold that Ameer Singh would function more as a tax collector to help the Company flourish. Moreover, Schwartz feared that the cumulative burden of these large payments to the Company and Wallajah would ruin the country. Andrew Mackillop studied Archibald Campbell's life from a military historian's perspective and pointed out his limitless avarice for economic benefit that would solely benefit the Company army. He regretted the loss of British settlements in North America, so he did not want to lose their Indian trade to the Americans.[143] He planned to strengthen the Company's military with a continuous flow of money from Ameer Singh and Wallajah.[144] He was not worried about the possible negative impact of his plan on these men and their successors.

On 8 April 1787, Ameer Singh and Campbell wanted to conclude a treaty in the presence of Resident Alexander Macleod, Commander Colonel John Stuart, and the governor's secretary, Alexander Montgomery Campbell. They invited Schwartz as their interpreter. The first clause of their treaty was contradictory, unrealistic, and impracticable.[145] It stipulated that the "Friends and Enemies of

---

British officers should verify the credibility of their counterparts and ensure that no British citizen had navigated such a ship to conceal and transport British goods. The directors believed that vessels flying the flags of the United States of America would endanger the Company's trade.

144 Mackillop: Fashioning a 'British' Empire, 215–16: Archibald Campbell persuaded his friend Henry Dundas to grant him "civil and military governorships" as in the North American colonies. Campbell believed the new governors of Madras should possess expert knowledge in commerce and the military. Otherwise, the Carnatic would not soon be "in the hands of the British nation." In February 1787, he demanded that Wallajah increase his annual payments to the Company "from 16 to 21 lakhs of pagodas – a total of £840,000." He also required Ameer Singh to pay £160,000 annually to maintain the Madras Army.

145 IOR/P/252/16, 58–72. For a verbatim quote of this treaty, see Copies of Treaties concluded by Sir Archibald Campbell, Governor in Council of Fort Saint George, with the Nabob of Arcot and Rajah of Tanjore; together with Extracts of Letters to the Court of Directors, on Subject of those Treaties and also Extracts from Copies of Correspondence between the

His Excellency the Rajah of Tanjore and the English United East India Company" would be considered "the Friends and Enemies of both." Wallajah was a friend of the Company but an enemy of Ameer Singh. The second clause required Ameer Singh to annually contribute 400,000 Star Pagodas (in six instalments) to the Company for maintaining the Military Peace Establishment in Tanjore. The third clause stated that Tanjore's annual estimated income was ten lakh Pagodas. When Ameer Singh's revenues increased, he should pay the Company more proportionately. The fourth clause implied that if Ameer Singh could not pay the required amounts on time, the Company could take over Tanjore for the purpose of revenue collection. This clause would devastate Tanjore, and it reads as follows:

> In case of Failure in the punctual Payment of the Four Lacks of Pagodas already mentioned, to the Extent of Fifty thousand Pagodas, for the Period of One Month after the same become due, his Excellency the Rajah agrees, that the Company shall have Power to enter upon any of the Districts in the Tanjore Country that shall appear to them necessary to discharge the Amount of the Sum in Arrear; and that the Company shall have Power to appoint Superintendents or Receivers, to collect and receive from the Rajah's Renters, Managers and Amildars, all the Rents, Revenues, Duties and Customs of the said Districts; and these Superintendents or Receivers shall exercise all necessary Authority for collecting such Rents, Revenues, Duties and Customs of the said Districts, giving regular Receipts for all the Monies which may be received by the said Superintendents, who shall have full Power to inspect and examine all Cutcherry Receipts and Accounts of the Lands and Districts aforesaid, as well as to ascertain the State of all other Revenues which shall be collected Annually within the said Districts; and when the full Amount of the Arrears due shall have been paid to the Company, the Superintendents or Receivers shall be immediately recalled.[146]

The fifth clause required Ameer Singh to provide all information about the "Amildars, Renters, or Farmers of each District" to the Company's representatives. During the war, the ninth clause required Ameer Singh to pay four-fifths of Tanjore's revenues to meet the Company's military expenses. "For the more effectual Security of Four-Fifths of the Revenues" of Tanjore, the Governor of the Company in Madras would have the right "to appoint One or more Inspectors or Accountants to inspect and examine all Country and *Cutcherry* Accounts and Receipts of all the Countries and Districts" of Tanjore. The tenth clause repeated that even after the war had ended, Ameer Singh would continue to pay four-fifths of his revenues "to the Discharge of all Debts and Expenses that may be incurred or arise during the War." The thirteenth clause promised Ameer Singh more troops if he ever needed them. The fourteenth clause stated that Ameer Singh should pay Wallajah the outstanding tribute of 1,257,142 Star Pagodas because Tulāji had not sent his annual tribute to Wallajah for ten years, from 1777 to 1787. In 1788,

---

Governments of Bengal and Fort Saint George and the Nabob of Arcot, relative to the Government of Madras having assumed the Management of the Revenues of the Carnatic, Ordered to be printed 6 May 1791. London: n.p. n.d.

146 Copies of Treaties, 5; IOR/F/4/42, Document No. 1021, Paragraph 1 of the letter "Extract of Political Letter from Fort S. George dated 17.10.1797": As a predictable consequence of the treaty, Tanjore's political and economic life deteriorated, and the Company administrators worried about their inability to take over the entire administration. They lamented that an order from their "Supreme Government," i.e. the Governor-General of Bengal, prohibited

Ameer Singh paid 300,000 Star Pagodas annually as his tribute. Finally, this treaty concluded with a remark that implicated the successors of Ameer Singh in paying the pending dues to the Company: "And his Excellency Maha Rajah Ameer Singh, for himself, his heirs, and successors, has also subscribed and sealed the same instruments at Tanjore."[147] There was no clause for the Company to pay its dues to Tanjore if Tanjore's income decreased or ceased.

This treaty illustrates how the Company utilised Campbell, the remorseless exploiter. It did not hold the Company accountable for its failures and misdeeds. It did not consider the well-being of the ordinary people. Schwartz trembled at the consequences of this treaty and asked Ameer Singh why he had signed the treaty. Ameer Singh responded that he had no helper and stood alone before Campbell. Schwartz regretted how deeply the Company had insulted Ameer Singh's person and office. On 16 April 1787, he shared his deep disappointment with his younger colleague Jacob Klein in Tanjore: According to the *Treaty of 1787*, Ameer Singh should pay 400,000 Pagodas to the Company, 400,000 Rupees to the Nawab as tribute, an additional amount of 5,200,000 Pagodas to the Nawab as war reparations and 500,000 Pagodas to Company creditors. Then, he should pay the Company an annual amount of 700,000 for twelve years. Schwartz opposed this measure and told the Governor, "The king cannot pay the 700,000 Pagodas [other amounts to the Nawab. ...]. This is totally unjust. [...] You drown the man." The Governor replied angrily: "He must pay. This is the order of the Company and the Board of Control. I have not made this decision." Schwartz responded: "He cannot pay the money. He cannot raise it. Should he borrow it?" At this, the Governor replied: "No, No. If he cannot pay this year, he must pay it next year along with the due date." This cruel answer deeply disappointed Schwartz, and he sighed: "If he cannot pay the money this year, how can he pay it next year?" Alas!"[148] Governor Campbell was unempathetic and resolute in his opinion. From that time onward, he no longer esteemed Schwartz because he sided with Ameer Singh, attempted to uphold his royal dignity, and prevented him from incurring debts that he could not pay.

After signing this treaty, Ameer Singh met Campbell privately and praised his "impartial conduct." He voluntarily promised to adhere to Campbell's advice, asked him to suspend the Committee of Inspection, and allowed him "to correct the oppression of Bava during the days of the late Rajah's infirmities."[149] Campbell

---

them from engaging in local political meddling. On 17.10.1797, they wrote a letter to their Governor in Madras with the following content: "In our letter of 27 March last, we communicated to your Hon'ble Court the corruption, distraction, and confusion which pervaded the whole of the Tanjore Country, and we informed you, that by the Orders of the Supreme Government, we felt ourselves compelled to be tacit spectators of the approaching ruin of that valuable Country, while our only means of checking its progress was an expostulation with his Excellency the Rajah, through the means of your Resident at his Durbar, and a further reference to the Governor-General in Council."

147 IOR/P/252/16, 71.

148 AFSt/M 1 C 29 b : 7a.

149 IOR/P/252/16, 104: On 05.05.1787, Archibald Campbell wrote to Resident Alexander Macleod, Colonel James Stuart, John Cox Hippisley, and Schwartz to dissolve the Committee

responded that he would ask the Company's Council in Madras to suspend the Committee of Inspection. He assured him that the Company was determined "to make him happy and to support and protect him on all occasions." This sweeping promise for protection "on all occasions" would be detrimental to Ameer Singh and his country; at the same time, in financial terms, it would enrich the Company unimaginably. Ameer Singh agreed to repair the water reservoirs (*aṇaikkaṭṭu*), reclaim Hanumantagudi and maintain the "superior army" of the Company at a high cost. He asked the Company to return to him those regions (e.g., Mannārgudi) that the Company had previously taken for revenue purposes. Campbell did not promise to return to these regions. Then, both men discussed practical ways of reforming "public establishments and correcting abuses which had become enormous" and injurious.[150]

Without a sense of shame, Ameer Singh also requested Campbell to permit him to write a letter to his relatives in Pune, acquainting them with the Company's just manner of appointing him to the throne of Tanjore. He wanted to send an open letter to the Company's Resident in Poona (modern Pune), who would forward it to his relatives. Campbell gave permission.[151] Campbell's diary entry about this treaty mentions the following: Ameer Singh presented him with jewels, a rich dress, two finely caparisoned war horses, an elephant, and a richly carved state palanquin. Campbell declined these gifts, thereby disappointing Ameer Singh. Ameer Singh wondered whether this rejection amounted to enmity or dubious friendship. To minimise Ameer Singh's suspicion of the Company's true intentions towards him, Campbell used the palanquin and horses for a day and then returned them. He wanted Ameer Singh to know that "an English Governor, even after placing a Rajah on the *musnund*, could retire from the palace, as pure as he had entered it."[152] This statement of honesty concealed Campbell's ulterior motives, which were to exploit and ruin Ameer Singh and Tanjore for the exclusive benefit of the Company.

On 10 April 1787, Campbell advised Ameer Singh to function as the chief administrator of Tanjore. He was to be the Sirkeel and Prince, who heard and redressed complaints of all individuals and established a court of justice. He suggested that Ameer Singh appoint five "Natives" as superintendents of the five Subahs. Before leasing them out, he should evaluate the income of each *patukam* or lease land. He should reduce the salaries of the numerous dependents in the palace. He should not encourage "foreigners, priests and idle Fakeers" and reduce

---

of Inspection upon receiving this letter. He thanked them for their "zeal, abilities and exertions." IOR/P/252/16, 105: On the same day of 05.05.1787, John Chamier, the Military Secretary, informed Alexander Macleod that, at the request of Ameer Singh and his promise to obey the advice of the governor, he abolished the Committee of Inspection and appointed William Blackburn as Macleod's Marathi translator for the monthly salary of twenty Pagodas. Chamier appointed Blackburn because Ameer Singh did not trust Schwartz, who posed unpleasant questions to Ameer Singh and required him to work toward establishing peace and justice for the ordinary people.

150 IOR/P/252/16, 50–51.

151 IOR/H/571, 195–196.

152 IOR/P/252/16, 48–49 and IOR/H/571, 195.

their allowances. For example, "Ashruff Shah, the great fakeer," should pay rent for the village that he held. Ameer Singh should not allow the subaidars to make payments as they wish. Instead, he should adequately remunerate the "Amuldars, Managers and Simpetty [*cippanti*, 'servants']." Campbell also advised Ameer Singh to discontinue the practice of burning widows, lower the interest rate, and repair Tanjore's forts.[153] All these suggestions were good; however, the constant pressure to pay the stipulated dues on time weighed so heavily on Ameer Singh that he did not pay the required attention to matters concerning the welfare of the ordinary people in his kingdom. As expected, he often faltered.

Just before Campbell left Tanjore, Ameer Singh introduced his five-year-old daughter to Campbell. Campbell presented her with "dress and jewels, according to the country's custom, with which the Rajah seemed very much pleased." Ameer Singh accompanied Campbell "in his carriage to the Second River about six miles from Tanjore" and bid farewell. Campbell noted that Ameer Singh "seemed deeply afflicted at the parting."[154] In any case, Campbell was the winner because he had secured legal permission to check Ameer Singh and exploit the Tanjore country.

5.8.6 Ameer Singh's Extravagance

This *Treaty of 1787* delighted the members of the Company in Madras. For example, on 14 April 1787, Acting President Alexander Davidson and his colleague James Henry Casamajor noted that Campbell's unilateral imposition of his predetermined treaty on Ameer Singh was "the most impartial justice" done to the king of Tanjore and would bring "the most substantial benefits" for the Company. They also believed that Campbell's military and civil arrangements would enable the Company to place their possessions in the Carnatic and Tanjore on a "respectable footing" and that the Company President in Madras had received the power to defend these possessions from "any native prince or European enemy."[155]

Ameer Singh was aware of his mounting debts to the Company, Wallajah, and various landlords. He also understood how the revenue collectors in Subahs had exploited the political confusion just before and after the death of Tulāji. The consequences were dire: Many farmers either stopped farming their lands or moved elsewhere, unable to bear the burden of debts and taxes. This led to a significant decrease in revenue and an increase in the number of landless farmers, with no functioning court of justice. Ameer Singh faced the daunting task of maintaining his kingdom amidst mounting debts and exploitation, which led to a noticeable decline in Tanjore's revenues.

Amidst these massive troubles, Ameer Singh followed a separate way. At the beginning of September 1787, he and his party visited Kumbakonam and Tiruvaiyāru to celebrate his enthronement and birthday. Just before leaving

---

153 IOR/H/571, 197.
154 IOR/P/252/16, 54–55.
155 IOR/P/252/16, 26.

Tanjore, Ameer Singh asked whether Schwartz would join him. Schwartz politely declined this invitation and informed him about his intention to travel to Vallam near Tanjore, where he pastored a small congregation. In his characteristic style, Schwartz reminded Ameer Singh to pray to God and remain in God's service. Ameer Singh responded that he would perform these things and pursue worldly pleasures such as dance parties. Immediately, Schwartz replied that such an enthusiastic quest for carnal pleasure would inevitably undermine a person's devotion to God.[156]

For undeclared reasons, Daniel Pillay, the famous Tamil judge in the court of Tranquebar, joined Ameer Singh's processions to Kumbakonam for a few days. His letter to missionary Klein in Tanjore (February 1788) describes Ameer Singh's pomp and pageantry along the way. He reported on the composition and activities of the two large groups that followed Ameer Singh. The first group included the following animals and people: 1) an elephant bearing the royal flag mounted in its seat, 2) a camel carrying a pair of war drums, 3) some Company sepoys in formations, 4) a covered palanquin with the mother of the king; 5) two other covered palanquins with the wives of the king; 6) another covered palanquin with the daughter of the king; 7) two other covered palanquins with the concubines of the king; cavalrymen guarded all these palanquins. 8) a bullock cart with wooden canes for beating (*tadigal*); 9) many uncovered bullock carts with female servants; and 10) a leader of the cavalrymen.

According to Daniel Pillay, the second group that followed Ameer Singh contained the following animals and people: 1) a few elephants, on each of which a special flag was flying; 2) a camel with a pair of war drums; 3) a company of sepoys, 4) an elephant mounted with an open rack, in which a sixty-year-old dwarf man was sitting; 5) the royal bodyguards consisting of cavalrymen; 6) the royal musicians, *devadasi*s (lit. Tanzhuren, 'dancing prostitutes'), who were singing, playing and dancing; 7) the king riding a horse; around him were all kinds of dragoons and symbols of honour; on the right, slightly behind him, was his first minister; on the left, also, slightly behind him, was the Commander of Tanjore; 8) cavalrymen of different ranks and officers of the garrison; 9) *devadasi*s and players, 9) numerous servants, partly in palanquin, partly on bullock carts and partly on horses; 11) many hounds for hunting and many types of birds in beautiful cages; 12) porters, who had been carrying all kinds of things for comfort and provisions. When the king travelled during the night, many torches were lit; from a distance, they looked beautiful. Heralds walked ahead of the king and proclaimed his praises.[157]

A contemporaneous framed painting kept in the Victoria and Albert Museum in London, England, depicts Ameer Singh's stately profession; its appearance agrees with Daniel Pillay's portrayal of Ameer Singh's procession: Ameer Singh sat on a giant, caparisoned elephant. His companions rode three other elephants

---

[156] AFSt/M 1 C 29b : 7b.

[157] NHR 3, 1790, issue 36, 1392–1393.

that surrounded his elephant. Some European and Indian soldiers, dressed in white and red uniforms, rode four horses that were richly decorated in front of the elephants. A bullock cart, with two richly decorated bullocks, a driver, and two passengers, carried a dignitary.[158]

Organising, moving, maintaining and safeguarding all these people and animals required enormous coordination and involved tax money. Spending this money, when it was necessary for paying tributes to the Nawab and settling arrears for the Company, was nothing but extravagance, which affected the lives of countless poor people, especially farmers, who had to provide both grains and taxes to the king. Ameer Singh also donated lands and money to temples, Brahmins, *cattirams*, and his Indian and European creditors. These processions and philanthropic works increased his expenses and decreased his ability to pay off the dues to the Company on time. When Campbell learned about Ameer Singh's situation on June 14, 1787, he reminded him of their friendship. He expressed astonishment and sadness that Ameer Singh had already disregarded his promises. He wondered why Ameer Singh preferred "Pursuits of pleasure to the more rational advancement, which would result from a vigil and attention to the affairs of your country & the happiness of your people, who were but just beginning to raise their heads from the rod of oppression, under which they had laboured for many years."[159]

Campbell was disappointed that Ameer Singh did not maintain strict accounts of his financial transactions and failed miserably to make his people "easy and happy." He was sorry that Ameer Singh incurred "heavy expenses, far exceeding the resources" of his "impoverished revenues, which cannot fail to prove very inconvenient" to him and burdensome to his people. Campbell urged him to pursue "the paths of wisdom and justice. Let not the possession of power change the virtuous disposition of your own breast; on the contrary, let your mind be wholly turned to the good of your people." He advised Ameer Singh to improve the cultivation of fields using the river waters immediately and politely pointed out his dues (*kists*) to the Company. He also remarked that "irregularities in public affairs are very disagreeable, and I trust to the wisdom of your Excellency that you will carefully prove them." He concluded his letter: "May your days be long and prosperous and may your family and your people enjoy perfect happiness without interruption."[160]

On 16 June 1787, John Chamier, on behalf of the Company in Madras, required their Company's Resident in Tanjore, Macleod, to "enforce the agreement contained in the Governor's Letter by every means in your power & express to his Excellency in the strongest language, the prosperity of paying the utmost attention to the friendly advice given to him by the President." Chamier

---

158 Processional scene with Amar Singh, ruler of Thanjavur (Tanjore) and Serfoji (ca. 1797). Victoria and Albert Museum. URL: https://collections.vam.ac.uk/item/O17560/processional-scene-with-amar-singh-painting-unknown/ (accessed 29.01.2025).

159 IOR/P/252/16, 154 ff.

160 IOR/P/252/16, 154–157.

remarked that Ameer Singh should address the "welfare and prosperity of his country and his [earlier] assurances of everlasting fidelity & attachment." He informed Ameer Singh of the Company's appointment of Messer Garrow Webb & Landon to investigate his debts.[161] Despite this endearing yet warning advice, Ameer Sing displayed his royal power in various places. He neglected the felt needs of his subjects. On 27 June 1787, Macleod informed Campbell that Ameer Singh had begun renovating the water channels for irrigation and wished to establish a new system for administering the Tanjore region. He divided the Subahs into smaller administrative units, known as *Puddukkams*, for more accessible tax collection.[162]

5.8.7 Āyarpāṭi Village for Schwartz

On 18 October 1787, Schwartz informed his colleague, Jacob Klein, in Tanjore that on 14 April 1787, Ameer Singh had given him the village of Āyarpāṭi near Tranquebar. Schwartz hesitated to accept it for his personal use. He requested Ameer Singh to donate it not only to him but also to his successors. Schwartz could use its revenues for the church and schools. After the paymaster Hippisley had left Tanjore on 6 September 1787, Ameer Singh gave Schwartz the amended deed (*sāsanam*) for the village. On 15 September 1787, Schwartz sent three persons from the Bethlehem Church in Poṟaiyār near Tranquebar to take hold of Āyarpāṭi. They showed the deed (*sāsanam*) written in Marathi to Daniel Pillay, the much-respected judge in Tranquebar.[163]

Schwartz's letter of September 6, 1787, to Pasche contains additional information about Āyarpāṭi. Tulāji planned to donate a village to Schwartz. Schwartz was unhappy about accepting it from Ameer Singh, who neglected matters of justice in Tanjore. He was disappointed that Ameer Singh refused to appoint Daniel Pillay of Tranquebar as the chief judge of this court for a period of one to two years. The fact that Daniel Pillay was a Christian hindered his appointment.[164]

After a year, on 29 September 1788, the missionaries in Tranquebar informed Director Schulze in Halle about Schwartz's visit on 9 September. The main aim of his visit was to meet the newly arrived missionary Jänicke and persuade him to come to Tanjore. At the same time, he requested the Governor of Tranquebar to lease the village of Āyarpāṭi to him for an annual rent of 500 Pagodas.[165] We do not yet know what happened to this village afterwards.

---

161 IOR/P/252/16, 157–158.

162 IOR/P/252/16, 191–192.

163 AFSt/M 1 C 29b : 7a.

164 NHR 3, 1790, issue 36, 1398–1399.

165 AFSt/M 1 C 30 c : 7 = NHR 4, 1790, issue 37, 96. Editors of the *New Halle Reports* omitted the lease amount.

5.8.8 Decreasing Tanjore Revenues for the Company

Ameer Singh's extravagance, his inefficient management of financial matters and his increased payments to the Company and the Nawab depleted his treasury. Despite this, he dismissed his revenue collectors (*mujumutārs*), namely Ambāji Jaggarnat Pandit and Baba, and appointed the Brahmin Trimbach Sumbhajee, a vakeel from Madras, as his new revenue collector. Under the new regime, Ameer Singh found it challenging to meet the Company's and Wallajah's financial demands, but he was determined to do so.[166] The *Treaty of 1787* accelerated Tanjore's decline in revenue. Earlier wars, tributes, and interest in loans from various Indian and European creditors depleted the revenues and their sources.[167]

On 18 September 1787, Campbell answered Ameer Singh's twelve questions about administering Tanjore and collecting taxes for the Company:[168] Ameer Singh's increasing inability and failure to pay the promised money to the Company disappointed Campbell. He could not fully understand Ameer Singh's practical hardships in raising taxes. 1) The amildar of Tiruccirāppaḷḷi, accountable to Wallajah, prohibited Ameer Singh's officers from collecting revenues along the river Kaveri. Campbell responded that he had asked a Company engineer to inspect the dam (*anaicut*) and to survey the Island of Sri Rangam. 2) Ameer Singh stated that buying Star Pagodas cost him more commission, and he wanted to mint money in Tanjore instead. Campbell insisted on payment only in Star Pagodas. 3) Ameer Singh alleged that some poligars, who used to pay him tribute, had settled in Ariyalūr Udaiyārpālayam (lit. Airaloor Woddiarpollum); from there, they raided adjacent places of the Tanjore Country, destroyed houses, plundered the markets, took away harvested paddy and cattle. The farmers stopped cultivating their lands. Campbell assured Ameer Singh that he would discuss this matter with Wallajah and put an end to the atrocities. 4) Ameer Singh accused the Tondaiman of Ramanathapuram of raiding the border areas of Tanjore, plundering people and taking away their cattle. Campbell promised to ask the Tondaiman to stop "all differences and irregularities."

5) Ameer Singh wanted to supervise all the amildars of Tanjore country and their financial transactions. Campbell responded that his *Sardars* would not interfere with or interrupt his government. At the same time, he would empower the Company's Resident in Tanjore to keep a watchful eye on the amildars and their economic activities, so that the people would not suffer. 6) The Dutch rented Nagapattinam from Tanjore and paid an annual tribute of 5,000 Cakkarams. After the English captured this place during the reign of Tulāji, no income came. Ameer

---

166 IOR/P/252/15, 67–68: According to an estimate, the total annual income for the Company in January 1787 was 5,600,000 Pagodas, to which Wallajah contributed 2,400,000 Pagodas and the king of Tanjore 1,000,000 Pagodas. The Military Peace Establishment cost the Company 2,300,000 Pagodas every year. The Company spent hardly any money to maintain its army in southern India. Instead, it forced Wallajah and Ameer Singh to pay all costs.

167 Pratāpasimha and Tulāji fought against Wallajah and the British East India Company. They paid them significant tributes and war expenses. Tanjore's treaty with the Dutch in Nagapattinam and the Danes in Tranquebar did not generate the needed revenue.

168 IOR/P/252/16, 333–376.

Singh requested Campbell to reduce this amount from his annual *kist*. Campbell responded that he could not remedy this situation. 7) Ameer Singh pointed out a treaty between the Company and Tulāji in 1777 that stipulated an annual payment of 400,000 Pagodas to the Company. However, as soon as England and France concluded peace, the Company forced Tulāji to cede five *māhān*s that would yield 30,000 Pagodas as annual revenues. Hence, Ameer Singh requested Campbell to reduce this amount from the annual *kist* to the Company. Campbell refused because the peace treaty between England and France entailed mutual concessions and reciprocal advantages and losses. Tanjore had to bear its share of loss. 8) Ameer Singh demanded written acknowledgements for all Tanjore money paid into the Company's treasury. Until the end of the Company's war with Hyder Ali, the Company used to send the receipts; however, after the war, they stopped acknowledging them. Campbell concluded that this "request was proper and just" and would do what was necessary.

9) Ameer Singh requested Campbell to consider Tanjore's special relationship with the Danes in Tranquebar: The Nawab had plundered Tanjore and its Forts in 1773. As Tulāji had no money for the palace, he sent Vakeel Sumbhajee Pandit to borrow 50,000 Pagodas from the Danes and mortgaged four *māhāns* in the *patakkam* of Tirunellur to them. The Danes sent 35,000 Pagodas through Krishnaji Pandit, and Tulāji received that money. Later, the Danes sent 15,000 Pagodas again through Krishnaji Pandit; since Tulāji was by then in prison, Krishnaji Pandit used the money for his personal needs and died shortly after that. Krishnaji Pandit's brother succeeded him. Ameer Singh asked his brother to return 15,000 Pagodas, which Krishnaji Pandit had borrowed from him. Immediately, Krishnaji Pandit's brother left Tanjore and settled in Madras. Ameer Singh wanted Campbell "to punish him & obtain payment of that sum." Campbell promised to investigate this matter and requested Ameer Singh's agents in Madras to give him documentary evidence.

10) Ameer Singh wanted Campbell to instruct the Company Surgeon in "Viziamuntup," a place in the eastern part of Tanjore, not to hinder Ameer Singh's workers from preparing the procession and celebration of the Dasara Festival. Campbell agreed to help. 11) Ameer Singh requested Campbell to dismantle the iron arch over the bridge near the eastern gate of Tanjore, so that his elephants and processions could pass through it and proceed to Viziamuntup for the celebration of the festival Dasara, which typically occurs in September or October. Campbell agreed to help. 12) Finally, Ameer Singh requested Campbell to order his engineers not to throw earth around the Vīrabhadra Swamy Temple near the eastern gate rampart. Campbell agreed to help.

5.9 The Company's Treaty of 1787 with Wallajah

Having secured the treaty with Ameer Singh, Campbell returned to Madras with great joy and prevailed upon Wallajah to sign a more comprehensive treaty on 24 February 1787. This treaty, known as the *Treaty of 1787* with Wallajah, was a significant event in Tanjore's history. It marked a shift in power dynamics and set the stage for the East India Company's regional influence.[169] This "Treaty of perpetual Friendship, Alliance and Security" benefited only the Company. It confirmed the Company's efforts in establishing the "Blessings of Peace" on the Coast of Coromandel and the Carnatic, a strategic move to consolidate its power and influence in the region. It would provide for the "future Defence and Protection of the Carnatic and the Northern Circars" under the control of the Company and its Indian allies.

The first clause of the treaty, while seemingly straightforward, was a masterstroke of strategic cunning. The clause stated, "The friends and Enemies of His Highness the Nabob of the Carnatic and the English East India Company shall be considered the Friends and Enemies of Both." As we have discussed earlier, the Nawab of Arcot considered Ameer Singh his rebellious enemy, whom he wanted to remove. The Company, however, purposefully kept the enmity between Wallajah and Ameer Singh alive and benefited from both. The Company's divide-and-rule policy had significantly shaped the political landscape of Tanjore. It weakened the local rulers and strengthened the Company.

The second clause of the treaty was a heavy financial burden on the Nawab. It required him to pay annually, in two instalments, nine lakh Pagodas to meet the cost of hiring the Company's Military Peace Establishment. The third clause was even more complicated, and it could potentially destroy Tanjore. It stated that "the Honourable East India Company will in like Manner contribute and, with the Aid of Tanjore, shall pay and make good such further Sums as may be necessary to discharge the Expenses of the Military Peace Establishment, beyond the said Annual Contribution of his Highness." The fourth clause explained that the Company would submit an accurate account of all incomes and expenses to the Nawab.

The remainder of the treaty bore a resemblance to Campbell's treaty with Ameer Singh. If the Nawab failed to pay his due and the arrears amounted to one lakh Pagodas, the Company would assert its control by appointing its superintendents to collect revenues and taxes from farmers, renters, customs offices, zamindars, and poligars. Should a war break out in the Carnatic, the Company would direct all armies to apply "four-fifths of their whole Revenues in the Carnatic and the Northern Circars annually to the Military Expenses of the War." During a war, the Nawab could collect and retain an annual amount of 2,13,421 Pagodas for himself and his family, as well as 21,266 Pagodas for charity.

---

169 Treaty concluded by Sir Archibald Campbell with the Nabob of Arcot in February 1787; the Approbation transmitted by the Court of Directors of that Treaty; and the several Papers relative to it and to the Assumption of the Government and Revenues of The Carnatic, in the Year 1790, which were presented to the House of Commons in the last Session of Parliament. London 16 March 1792, here 3 & 5: The Nawab implicated himself, his heirs and successors. Besides him, his signatories included "Omdit ul Mulk, Unmeer ul Hind, Asoph Dowlah, Anewerdee Cawn Behauder, Zupher Jung, Sippa Salar, Sambabar of the Carnatic." The signatories were Governor Campbell, Alexander Davidson, James Henry Casamajor, and their witnesses. Their co-signatories were "John Macpherson, John Stables, John Chamier, Charles Binny and Alexander Montgomery Campbell, secretary to the Governor."

Otherwise, he should pay "Four-Fifths of his Revenue to the general Expense of such War."

If Wallajah failed to pay that amount, the Company's officers would occupy sections of his lands and collect necessary taxes. If the crops failed due to drought, flood, or other natural catastrophes, the Nawab could proportionately reduce the payment of dues. Previously, farmers had to pay taxes on crops they had planted, rather than those they had harvested. Now, they could pay taxes on the goods they harvested. While the Company did not promise any other assurance, they required Wallajah to vouchsafe this treaty for "himself, his Heirs and Successors." The partners signed the treaty on 24 February "in the Year of the Christian Æra" and "the Fifth Day of the Moon Jemmady, in the Year of the Hegyra [sic! = Hegira] Twelve hundred and One." The date of this treaty demonstrates interreligious sensitivity. The Company officers recorded the time according to their Christian calendar, while the Nawab kept to his Islamic calendar. This interreligious sensitivity had no economic implications. Acquiring monetary wealth or occupying new lands was not a religious act; it was a sign of the greed of both parties. The Company's Board in Madras required Wallajah and Ameer Singh to pay them cash for the sole benefit of the Company in India and Britain. Indian money supported the Company's armies, paid the salaries of the Company employees in India, maintained their establishments in the Carnatic and enriched the Company's shareholders and families in Britain.[170]

5.10 Agricultural Practices in Tanjore (1790)

In 1790, Samuel Christian John journeyed through Tanjore and detailed the agricultural practices he observed:[171] Paddy farmers faced formidable challenges. They relied on rain and irrigation, and as the ears emerged, they battled against crabs, rats, snakes, wild birds, and domestic animals. Crabs and rats would cut the straw, while snakes such as *nalla pāmpu* ('cobra') and *cārai pāmpu* ('rat snake,' *Ptyas mucosa*) would feed on rats, but also spoil the paddy plants. Sparrows would feast on paddy grains, while domestic animals, such as cows and goats, would devour the plants. Sometimes, thieves would steal the ripe paddy ears. Despite these adversities, the farmers persevered, demonstrating their resilience and determination in the face of such challenges.

Agricultural families called themselves *kudiyāṉavarkaḷ*, meaning 'those rooted in the soil.' They sowed the seeds, transplanted the saplings from nurseries into fields and tended them. However, they were unable to harvest the ripe ears. Instead, they had to wait for Ameer Singh's evaluators to assess the paddy before it was

170 Wallajah and Ameer Singh had their representatives in London for lobbying with the parliamentarians and the Court of Directors. Claims and counterclaims between these representatives and their British supporters affected the prospects of their family members and friends working in Madras, Arcot and Tanjore. At the insistence of these supporters, the British Parliament published Campbell's treaties with Wallajah and Ameer Singh in 1787.

171 NHR 4, 1792, issue 40, 360–363.

harvested. They called this process *puḷḷipārkkiṟatu* ('pointing, assessing'). Sometimes, the farmers waited for more than a month for this assessment. During this long waiting period, in a wet or hot climate, animals, birds and thieves consumed most of the paddy. Often, the evaluation was so high that the farmers could not pay it. Neither could they keep anything for their sustenance. Therefore, they habitually cheated or bribed the assessors.

The administrative provinces[172] and their subordinate villages[173] employed tax collectors who were primarily concerned with their welfare and position. Their main goal was to please the king by increasing revenue, often at the expense of the farmers. Pariah women and men usually harvested the paddy, bound it in stacks, dried it in the sun, and thrashed it against hard surfaces. Sometimes, oxen transported paddy. Depending on the type of paddy harvested, the farmers in Tanjore had to give the king 55% to 70% of their produce. This was a significantly higher tax rate than the farmers of Tranquebar, who gave the local government 25% to 55% of their produce. Even if the Tanjore farmers could not produce enough paddy, they still had to pay their taxes to the king. This system of taxation, imposed on impoverished farmers, only served to exacerbate social evils and economic oppression.

Amidst this situation, Ameer Singh required his tax officers to collect eighty per cent of the farmers' annual produce. He also imposed higher taxes on traders. His tax officers collected the revenue as cash or goods.[174] He needed a large amount of food for the soldiers and preferred paddy to money. For clarity and transparency, farmers and the royal accountants (*kaṇakkuppiḷḷai*s) jointly measured the produce, and the farmers paid taxes on the produce they could retain.

Royal officers who had collected paddy did not transfer it into the storage rooms. The heaped threshing floor stayed exposed for weeks and months. The farmers placed protective materials (e.g., straw, cow dung, wooden planks, and the like) on the heaps, posted specific signs of ownership, and left the heaps. They assumed that no one would steal the grain. However, thieves took at least some of

---

172 Madras District Gazetteer—Tanjore, 194: "When the British acquired possession of the country, it was divided into five subahs which with some modifications dated from the time of the first Marátha king. The headquarters were Tiruvádi, Kumbakónam, Máyavaram, Mannárgudi, and Pattukóttai."

173 NHR 4, 1792, issue 40, 362: In 1790, missionary John stated that Ameer Singh had created twelve *subas* out of the former five *subas*. He further divided each suba into *cīmai* (i.e. smaller territories and lands). An *awaldar* or *amuldar* oversaw each *cīmai*. Each *cīmai* was subdivided into *mākāṇams* ('province') and administered by a *mākāṇa maṇiyakkāraṉ* ('overseer of provinces'). Each *mākāṇam* consisted of several *kirāmams* ('villages'). A vaṭṭa *maṇiyakkāraṉ* (an 'overseer of circles') looked after each village. Each *maṇiyakkāraṉ* had two *cēvakaṉ* ('servants'), also known as *talaiyāris* ('headmen'). One of them was *aṅkacaṭṭai-cēvakaṉ* ('the one wearing a shirt'), and the other was *paṭṭaikāraṉ* ('the one who wears a belt') or *padaikāraṉ* ('soldier, security guard'). The *padaikāraṉ* protected the fields.

174 S. Chinnaiyan: Tax Structures in the Tanjore Kingdom under the Nayaks and Marathas (A.D. 1532–1799). In: Proceedings of the Indian History Congress 66, 2005–2006, 456–459, here 457–458: All Maratha rulers of Tanjore taxed the edible and non-edible things produced and sold in Tanjore. Many producers and sellers were unable to afford the high taxes. Notably, the farmers stopped cultivating their land. Ensuing famines impoverished the inhabitants of Tanjore even further. Many of these people migrated to other places.

the paddy away. When the king needed paddy, workers carried it in sacks daily from the threshing floors into the fort. There, rats ate up the paddy. Snakes abounded in the storage rooms because they fed on the rats, keeping their numbers down. Although the snakes spoiled crops, they helped farmers by eating rats and other harmful insects. For this purpose, the Tamils did not kill the snakes. Thus, the entire system of collecting taxes on agricultural produce was susceptible to corruption, deception, and decay, furthering Ameer Singh's difficulties in promptly paying the dues to the Company.

5.11 The Company Seeks to Occupy Tanjore (1790)

The Company in Madras remained unhappy that they could not extract more money from Ameer Singh. They tried to persuade Schwartz to help them exploit Ameer Singh and his subjects. Schwartz seems to have rejected their attempts. For example, on 19 January 1789, the missionaries in Tranquebar reported to Schulze in Halle that in November 1788, the Company in Madras had invited Schwartz to meet them in Madras and paid his travel expenses. They wanted him to impress Ameer Singh with the need for more revenue for the Company. The missionaries did not mention Schwartz's response.[175] He would probably have expressed his unwillingness to extract more money from Tanjore's inhabitants, who were already oppressed and exploited.

On 8 April 1789, the Company's Court of Directors in London expressed disappointment that Tanjore was "not in that train of prosperity which it is our most earnest wish." They asked the governor of Madras to continually remind Ameer Singh to adopt a more judicious system of management.[176] Then, they referred to Schwartz's description of the ruinous state of Tanjore. As mentioned in Section 6.3.1, the Court of Directors read the "alarming representations from the Revd Mr. Swartz" and agreed with him regarding the "ruinous tendency of the grants of lands that the Rajah [Ameer Singh] had made and was making." These grants reduced his income, and he could not fulfil his "engagements with the Company (as Mr Swartz very judiciously observes)."[177] The Court of Directors requested that the Governor of Madras compile a list of all land grants, including the details of the persons who held these grants and the amount of revenue lost to Ameer Singh and the Company.[178] On the same day, 8 April 1789, in a separate letter, the Court of Directors assured Ameer Singh of their "reliable friendship and the protection of the British Nation." The proof of their attachment to him was establishing "you [viz. Ameer Singh] on the Throne of your Ancestors."[179] Therefore, they urged him to pay the dues on time and without fail.[180]

---

175 AFSt/M 1 C 30c : 22. This is the verbatim copy of AFSt/M 1 C 30c : 21.
176 IOR/E/4/875, 359–360.
177 IOR/E/A/875, 361.
178 IOR/E/4/875, 361–363.
179 IOR/F/4/42, Document No. 1021, Paragraph 9 of the letter "Extract of Political Letter from Fort S. George dated 17 October 1797" repudiated this action and still called it British justice:

In any case, Ameer Singh's mismanagement of resources prevented him from paying the dues on time and in full. George Andrew Ram, the new Company Resident in Tanjore, made a concerted effort to settle these arrears. According to his report on 11 October 1789, he invited Schwartz to speak with Ameer Singh on his behalf. Ram was unhappy that Ameer Singh continued to employ Sirkeel Shiva Rao, who dissipated the revenues. Ram felt that Shiva Rao would never help Ameer Singh pay the dues.[181] Ram threatened Ameer Singh that if he did not pay all dues within eight days, he would arrange for the Company officers to collect the revenue. Simultaneously, Ram accused Ameer Singh of donating a *jaghir* (i.e., a district named "Samillee," valued annually at 40,000 Cakkarams, in addition to 20,000 Cakkarams as an annual salary) to his son-in-law.[182] Ram asked Colonel Stuart to prepare "Five Companies of Regular Sepoys and Two Battalions of Sibbendies" to collect the revenues.[183] Even this threat did not move Ameer Singh.

After repeated and failed attempts to get the arrears, Earnest William Fallowfield and George Andrew Ram, respectively, the Company Residents at Nagore and Tanjore, wanted to take over the entire Kingdom of Tanjore and administer it. On 16 August 1790, they attempted to persuade the Company Council in Fort St. George to occupy Tanjore and commence revenue collection. They proposed that if Ameer Singh would not positively pay off the arrears within five days from the date of their notification to him or would not "make a voluntary assignment of his Country to the Honorable Company," the Company should

---

"Under conviction of the invalidity of Ameer Sing's title, and that his possession of the Tanjore Government was derived from British Power, we were the more sensible to the calamities of that Country, and being satisfied, that the Dictates of Humanity and Justice will always have their due weight, in the deliberation of the Supreme Government we had no doubt, that a serious consideration of the question would lead to their honoring us with such instructions as might appear most conducive to the Interests of the Company and creditable to the British Nation in India."

180 IOR/E/4/875, 699–701.

181 Treaty concluded by Sir Archibald Campbell with the Nabob of Arcot in 1792. Petrie asked Ameer Singh to dismiss his diwan, Shiva Rao, who had pushed aside most senior officers, including Baupanah and Ganapathy Subbiah. Ameer Singh, however, defended Shiva Rao, stating that Shiva Rao had often consulted accountant Baupanah and performed his duties well.

182 Treaty concluded by Sir Archibald Campbell with the Nabob of Arcot 1792, 36; Cf. T Vol. 3449 B, 623–29: On 29.12.1790, Ameer Singh denied the allegation that he had donated the Jagir Swami Malai to his son-in-law. This jagir could annually generate 35,000 Cakkarams. Ameer Singh claimed that King Tulāji gave this land to his son-in-law, and he merely confirmed it. Later, Ameer Singh gave his daughter Gunavathy an *agraharam* to generate an annual income of about 25,000 Cakkarams. On 31.12.1790, he informed Schwartz that these donations to his family members were legal. Swami Malai should remain with Ameer Singh's son-in-law, and the *agraharam* with his daughter. He requested that Schwartz deduct 25,000 Cakkarams from his portion. He was ready to reduce the jagir to 4,000 Pagodas for his son-in-law. Ameer Singh urged Schwartz not to allow the Company servants to collect revenues from seven villages that exclusively belonged to him; additionally, he required the Company's revenue collectors to leave these villages immediately. He pleaded with Schwartz for one lakh kalam of paddy and a minimum of 20,000 Pagodas. He wanted to distribute these items as a half-month salary to his employees, who were preparing to celebrate the Pongal festival.

183 Treaty concluded by Sir Archibald Campbell with the Nabob of Arcot 1792, 36.

require "his consent to invest us with *Tasealdary* Authority." Suppose Ameer Singh did not respond to the Company's demands even after eight days of serving him the notice. In that case, the Company should require him to order the local tax collectors (*amuldars*) to obey the instructions of the Company Residents. If he continued to disregard the Company's notice, the Company should assume management of the Country by issuing a Proclamation.[184]

Understandably, Ameer Singh was furious and refused to accept the threat of the Company Residents. On 23 August 1790, he wrote a letter to the Company in Madras, requesting their intervention and protection. He acknowledged receipt of their letter of August 13, 1790, which Schwartz had given to him on August 18, 1790. Ameer Singh insisted that he had not broken the Company's agreement; by contrast, the Company in Madras had failed to acknowledge the dues of "68570 Pagodas, 31 Fanams, and 30 Kas" that he had paid in March 1790. He stated that the dues for April, namely one lakh Pagodas, were ready; he was willing to pay four-fifths of all Tanjore's revenues. He insisted that he wanted to maintain a good friendship with the Company; he did not offer to surrender Tanjore to the Company, even during times of war. Otherwise, he would appear "in the Eyes of all very low, nay, the Court of Directors would think that I failed in respect of the Treaty." By preserving his honour as king of Tanjore, he urged the Company in Madras to appoint accountants who could divide the revenue under the *Treaty of 1787*. He insisted that recently, he had not donated any villages as gifts (*inam*s) to anyone.[185]

The Company in Madras was not satisfied with Ameer Singh's claims. On 1 September 1790, they asserted that Ameer Singh had not paid them the four-fifths of Tanjore's total revenue. Therefore, they appointed their own *Tahsildar*s and other officers to collect revenues. They hoped to collect more revenue than the total amount Ameer Singh had given them up to that point.[186] In this dismal situation, Schwartz tried to save Tanjore for its inhabitants. He knew that the main reason for the problem was not Ameer Singh but the European renters and their Indian agents. The farmers paid high taxes to Ameer Singh and interest to the renters, who had leased some parts of Tanjore country in exchange for their loans to Ameer Singh. Like leeches, these renters sucked away all resources from the farmers. Impoverished and disappointed farmers left Tanjore. Those who chose to stay refused to cultivate. Some farmers requested Schwartz's intervention.

As a result, in November 1790, Schwartz expressed his displeasure about the renters to Governor Charles Oakley in Madras.[187] On 28 September 1790, Residents Ram and Fallowfield informed Governor Oakley that they had consulted Schwartz up to that time "upon every material step," and they were resolved to

---

184 IOR/P/252/48, 3368–3370.

185 IOR/P/252/48, 3454–3458.

186 IOR/H/285A, 903.

187 IOR/E/4/876, 925: On 03.06.1790, the Public Department of Company's Court of Directors in London appointed Charles Oakley as the Governor of Madras, and he replaced Major General William Meadows, who in turn would succeed "Government General of Bengal, upon the Death, Removal or Resignation of Earl Cornwallis, the present Governor General."

follow this "line of conduct" in future as well.[188] On 5 November 1790, he shared with Oakley the outcome of his interactions with Ameer Singh and Tanjore's inhabitants:

> Concerning this country, the income will be considerable; but you may be sure that, if the banks and water courses are properly repaired and the season proves favourable the revenue of the country of the next year will be much augmented. The probable account of the Revenue will be sent by today or tomorrow. [… Until now, Ameer Singh refused to share his financial accounts with us. Now we have received them.] In my last letter, I entreated the Hon'ble Board not to give the country to rapacious renters who mind nothing but their interest. This country is capable of very great improvements, and though I will not anticipate any future account, I may, however, safely say that, if the country be managed properly next year, you will find a wonderful increase in the Revenue at least in respect of paddy. As the poor people lost, for some years, almost all the benefit, which they had a right to expel from their labour, they became very dispirited.[189]

The farmers expected their pay because they remembered how Tulāji, Ameer Singh and the Company had cheated them in previous years. The rapaciousness of their senior officers and dubashes impoverished the people. People urgently needed a court of justice because many inhabitants who had "lost their fields and villages by the power granted by the rajah to some of his favourites" and lodged complaints were still awaiting justice. Their speedy redress would restore their rights, possessions and lands for cultivation. Additionally, the Company should fix the lawful interest rate on loans; otherwise, renters would be charged up to thirty percent annual interest, which almost no one could bear. Schwartz reminded Governor Oakley that proper governance, introduced and maintained by the Company in Tanjore, might "turn this country into a garden and make superiors and inferiors happy."[190]

Again, in November 1790, Schwartz sent a letter to Oakley with more profound contents: firstly, he had heard rumours that Oakley would permit various renters to administer Tanjore. He confessed frankly: "If this should be the case, I am afraid this poor country would still be more impoverished." Then, he provided an example from Tulāji's life, who had refused to listen to Schwartz's advice and employed "rapacious dubashes" to manage Tanjore. These dubashes had no moral principles to guide them. As soon as they had enriched themselves by ruining the country, its people and its king, these dishonest dubashes abandoned him. As he composed this letter, Ameer Singh was in great distress, being as it were, besieged by his servants, who had received no pay for seven months and were now very clamorous. Schwartz correctly recommended that Ameer Singh not be punished for his past mistakes. "To upbraid him now for his past misconduct would be cruel and altogether useless." Instead, the Company should convince him to establish a just administration system and encourage "industry and trade." In this context, he repeated the rumour. He highlighted its grave consequences for all stakeholders:

---

188 Pearson: Memoirs, Vol. 2, 212.
189 T Vol. No. 3449 B, 499, also in Pearson: Memoirs, Vol. 2, 218–219.
190 T Vol. No. 3449 B, 502, also in Pearson: Memoirs, Vol. 2, 220.

"But when I heard that the country might, perhaps, be given to renters, and very likely to Madras dubashes, who are well able to make supplements to Machiavelli's iniquitous scheme, my hopes vanished." Then, he asserted an impartial practice of justice as the "basis of the true welfare of a country." The renters would not be morally just and would not permit people to work justly. He pointed out that until then, renters, to whom the king had mortgaged entire districts, had been ruling Tanjore. The renters annexed their villages and fields if the villagers or farmers could not pay the expected taxes. Schwartz stated that many people had complained to him, and he could not deal with them without the help of an impartial court of justice. He recommended that Oakley consider appointing four or five judges. He stated further that a third part of Tanjore lay uncultivated because the oppressive dubashes exploited them. Before the rainy season began and the rivers overflowed with water, they forced the people to repay the money they had borrowed from them. Consequently, in the face of existential threats, the farmers stopped cultivation, and Tanjore lost more than ten lakh kalam of paddy. As more than 200 renters administered Tanjore, there was little hope for sufficient revenue collection. The Company in Madras should empower their Residents, Ram and Fallowfield, to work together and restrain the operations of these dubashes. Additionally, the Company should fix the interest rate for loans given for agricultural purposes. The lenders should have the assurance that they would receive their capital with due interest. Borrowers should be aware of the interest rate and whether they are required to pay it in cash or kind.[191]

Two chief dubashes, Shiva Rao and Subba Rao, submitted their complaints against Resident Ram. At the recommendation of Resident Fallowfield, Schwartz examined the merit of these complaints. On 30 November 1790, he responded to Fallowfield: Shiva Rao was the prime culprit. Most inhabitants did not trust him. Subba Rao was timid. He tried to rectify the mistakes that he had committed earlier. However, both men had no fixed moral principles, and no one would trust them.[192] Thus, Schwartz pleaded for more time to restore and cultivate the farmers' fields and regain people's confidence in their leaders and government. He did not favour the Company's plans to take over Tanjore. Instead, he insisted that the Company establish a just administration with rules relevant to the local conditions.

5.12 Ameer Singh's Second Treaty with the Company (1792)

Within five years, the Company and Ameer Singh recognized the impracticality of the *Treaty of 1787*; they amended it on June 11, 1793, by implicating themselves, their heirs, and their successors. They stated that this treaty should take effect retrospectively from July 12, 1792. On behalf of the Company, Charles Oakley and E.W. Fallowfield signed it:[193] despite the repeated and unsolvable troubles, the first article of this amended treaty reads as follows: The "friends and

---

191 T Volume No. 3449 B, 509–517 also in Pearson: Memoirs, Vol. 2, 213–218.
192 Pearson: Memoirs, Vol. 2, 222.

enemies of the contracting parties shall be considered the friends and enemies of both." While Wallajah was the enemy of Tanjore, he was the most ardent friend of the Company. The second article explained that the Company would provide a military force to safeguard the interests of Ameer Singh, and he had to pay for its expenses. The third article stated that during a war, the Company would garrison all forts in Tanjore and possess "full authority over the Tanjore country and shall collect the revenues thereof." Additionally, it would annually give to Ameer Singh 100,000 Star Pagodas, plus one-fifth of the total revenue. The fourth article required Ameer Singh to pay annually 350,000 Star Pagodas towards the military expenses, 114,285 Star Pagodas as tribute to Wallajah, and 60,000 Star Pagodas to discharge his debts to various creditors.

The remaining articles of the *Treaty of 1792* referred to minor concessions. However, they threatened the dire consequences for non-payment of stipulated sums by specific dates. These articles would solely benefit the Company. The Company would collect revenues from Tanjore and occupy the land. The ninth article prohibited Ameer Singh from "any negotiations or political correspondence with any European or Native power without the consent" of the Company. The tenth article was new: it required Ameer Singh to provide Serfoji with 11,000 Star Pagodas for his annual expenses. Likewise, he should provide 3,000 Star Pagodas to each of Tulāji's two widows. He should pay the money into the Company's accounts, which the Company would forward to Serfoji and the widows. The second schedule of this treaty named private individuals who had loaned money to Ameer Singh and designated a small portion of it as a donation to Schwartz's charitable works among the orphans. This sentence reads: "Mr. Swartz, for money subscribed by gentlemen to benefit orphans: Star Pagodas 1,000."[194]

In the meantime, Tanjore's socio-political and economic aspects worsened. Ameer Singh tried to raise money to pay the tributes to the Company by mortgaging and re-mortgaging villages, towns, and regions. On 15 January 1796, Schwartz translated a letter from Ameer Singh addressed to Resident Macleod. Accordingly, during the previous year, Ameer Singh mortgaged the subahs, other than Papanasam, to Nagappa Chetty to "pay the *kists* to the Company." Ameer Singh repossessed these subahs in 1796 and collected revenue from "the whole country" and would pay it to the Company "at the appointed time."[195] Five days

[193] IOR/P/253/58, 811–825. The opening words of this agreement reads: "Whereas by a Treaty between Sir Charles Oakley Baronet, President and Governor in Council of Fort St. George on the part of the Hon'ble English East India Company, their heirs and Successors – and his Excellency Ameer Sing, Rajah of Tanjore, in his own name, and for himself, his Heirs and Successors on the other part, dated the 12th day of July in the year 1792, it was stipulated and agreed by the 4th and 5th Articles of the said treaty, between the said contracting parties that during the time of public tranquillity in the Carnatic and its dependencies" that Ameer Singh should pay from 12th July 1795 to the Company 350,000 Star Pagodas and defray the costs. However, he did not pay it. For a printed version of this treaty, see William Hickey: The Tanjore Maratha Principality in Southern India: The Land of the Cholas; the Eden of the South. Madras [2]1874, here xxvi–xxxiv.

[194] Hickey: The Tanjore Mahratta Principality, xxxiv.

[195] IOR/P/253/58, 809–810.

later, on 20 January 1796, Macleod wanted to interview Shiva Rao about Tanjore's income and expenses. Ameer Singh did not permit Shiva Rao to appear before Macleod and stated that the sick Shiva Rao, as a Brahmin, lay in his temple and could not come out. Additionally, Ameer Singh clearly stated that Schwartz should not be present in the conversation because he did not appreciate Shiva Rao. When Ameer Singh finally met Macleod, Schwartz was present and expressed his opinion about Tanjore's mismanagement. Ameer Singh complained about this meeting to Governor Hobart in Madras:

> I have been dishonored by the extraordinary conduct of Mr Macleod towards me, my Dignity and Character has been diminished in the eyes of the world, and the revenue of my Country has been impaired. This will be the cause of much detriment to myself, as your Excellency is just, I rely upon the lofty sentiments of your own mind for a public reparation of those wrongs, which have been publicly offered me by Mr Macleod. I pray to God that your Excellency's justice may be prompt.[196]

Macleod and his colleagues informed the Court of Directors on 17 October 1797 about the impending collapse of public institutions and the state of life. They urged them to intervene fast. For example, they communicated the grave situation to the Court of Directors in London through their superiors: On 27 March 1796, they informed the Company about the

> corruption, distraction and confusion which pervaded the whole of the Tanjore Country, and we informed you, that by the Orders of the Supreme Government, we felt ourselves compelled to be tacit spectators of the approaching ruin of that valuable country, while our only means of checking its progress was an expostulation with his Excellency the Rajah, through the means of your Resident at his Darbar, and a further reference to the Governor-General in Council.[197]

Ameer Singh's negligence in controlling his moneylenders impoverished the country to such an extent that Macleod could not collect the revenues from the people or their king. On 27 March 1797, the Company Resident in Tanjore and his British colleagues wrote to the Court of Directors, stating that they had already informed the latter about the prevailing "corruption, distraction, and confusion" in the "whole of the Tanjore Country." In the meantime, they received orders from Bengal, their Supreme Government, not to interfere. Therefore, the Company Resident Macleod and his British colleagues lamented that they were "compelled to be tacit spectators of the approaching ruin of that valuable country."

These events unequivocally refute the unfounded accusations that Baman Das Basu has been accused of advocating.[198] Basu accused Schwartz and the Company

[196] IOR/P/253/58, 727–753, here 750.

[197] IOR/F/4/42, Document No. 1021, May 1799: "Extract of Political Letter from Fort S. George dated 17 October 1797."

[198] Baman Das Basu: Rise of the Christian Power in India. Calcutta [2]1931 ([1]1923). This book opposed the British Raj and viewed it as an extension of British rule. It equated Britain and the British Raj in India with Christianity. It interpreted the Company as "the Christian Government." This biased approach prevented Basu from examining the events as they unfolded.

Resident in Tanjore of misleading the Company in Madras. He cited the proverb "Give a dog a bad name to hang him" to underline his claim. At their insistence, the Company in Madras took Serfoji to Madras and blamed Ameer Singh for all the atrocious things occurring in Tanjore.[199] He did not bother examining any primary sources and followed H. H. Wilson's statement.[200] Basu's accusations against Schwartz and the Company in Tanjore are indirect and lack direct evidence. He acknowledged that Sanskrit pandits in renowned cities sometimes accepted bribes and rendered opinions that pleased the highest offer. Basu claimed that Schwartz and the Company in Tanjore bribed the pandits who declared Ameer Singh's rule an imposition, as they sought to exploit the new occupant of the throne, Serfoji.[201] By contrast, evidence gathered from primary sources has demonstrated Schwartz's honesty in dealing with public matters, such as his interaction with Ameer Singh and his successor, Serfoji, as explained in Sections 8.4 and 8.5.

5.13 Schwartz's Death

Schwartz's continuous work toward establishing peace, justice, and harmony among people of diverse identities, priorities, and occupations took a toll on his health. He also knew that he would die someday. Hence, he prepared himself for his death. One way that he prepared was to recruit, train, and appoint competent successors. Every time that he requested his authorities in Halle and London for successors, he expressed his anguish that he might suddenly die and all the works that he had initiated might not succeed as he had hoped. His neuropathy, pains and sores on his foot, knee pain resulting from the fall from a horse and poor eyesight reminded him of his impending death.

In April 1792, missionary Christoph Samuel John met Schwartz in Tirupālāṭuturai, not far away from Tanjore. Schwartz could not get out of his palanquin. John wondered how much weaker he had become and assumed he would not live much longer. Schwartz, too, confessed that he wanted to die soon and did not want to be sick for an extended period. His front tooth had become loose, and a golden thread held it attached. Otherwise, he was in pain most of the

199 Basu: Rise of the Christian Power in India, 353.

200 Basu: Rise of the Christian Power in India, 353: Basu cited H. H. Wilson's observations: "The cruel treatment of Sarbojee by the Raja was repeatedly brought to the notice of the authorities by the vigilance of his reverend guardian [Schwartz], and upon his representations and those of the Resident, the Madras Government insisted upon the removal of Sarbojee and the surviving widows of Tuljajee, who were also the objects of the Raja's oppression, to Madras."

201 Basu: Rise of the Christian Power in India, 353: After Serfoji's removal to Madras, "intrigues were carried on with him. An appeal was made to the Government against its former decision. It is a well-known thing in India that some learned Pandits of Benares and Nadia can be made to give any opinion on Hindu Law by presenting suitable gifts or fees to them. So now the adoption of Sarbojee, which had been very correctly declared invalid by the learned Hindu jurists, was to be enforced because some 'Pandits of learning and character, [...] interpreted the law in favour of adoption.'"

time, and he could not speak freely. However, he repeated his Sunday sermon to the Christians who came to see him near a wayside house of rest (lit. Ruhehaus). John considered Schwartz "a faithful and well-experienced brother" to whom he could share his profound thoughts until the early hours of the morning.[202] As time passed, Schwartz became increasingly fragile.

On 8 January 1796, Schwartz wrote to Pastor Uebele in London as follows: he was grateful to God that he had been able to celebrate his seventieth birthday three months prior. In October 1795, while he had children around him reading the Bible, he suddenly experienced suffocating pain in his chest. He assumed that his breathing would cease. This cramping pain continued until 3 a.m. When it stopped, he still felt the heavy pressure on his heart. He understood these signs as messengers, which his Saviour Jesus Christ had sent him to indicate that "the Lord Himself would soon visit him" (i.e., he would soon die). Therefore, Schwartz requested God's grace to watch and pray, and to always be ready for his imminent death.[203]

In the meantime, Schwartz continued his forenoon work at the Tamil and English congregations, schools and catechumen classes, which were integral to his missionary work. These institutions were not just places of learning and worship but also hubs for community engagement and spiritual growth. In the afternoon, he visited Christians living in nearby areas and conducted an evening prayer meeting from 7 to 8 p.m. He enjoyed this aspect of his pastoral work. He could not imagine himself sick and bedridden. In 1795, ninety people joined the Lutheran congregation in Tanjore; twenty-nine were non-Christians who underwent preparation and received baptism. Twenty-four Roman Catholics joined the Tamil Lutheran congregations. Thirty-seven children were born to Christian parents and were baptised. The Tamil school had fifty-three children, and the English school had fifteen children. The Provincial School in Tanjore had twenty students, and the one in Kumbakonam had fifteen children. The catechists engaged with Christians and non-Christians. Schwartz had paid the salary for these catechists and wondered whether the SPCK would pay them in future. He recommended a full-time missionary for the church in Pāḷaiyamkōṭṭai because Tamil Christian leaders needed supervision.[204]

On 2 February 1798, Pohle wrote that "our venerable father" was happy to meet Gericke, Gottfried Immanuel Holzberg and his family.[205] On 10 February 1798, Pohle's wife prepared a meal according to a Tamil custom, a gesture of respect and goodwill in the local culture. She fed people experiencing poverty in Tiruccirāppaḷḷi in honour of Schwartz, who began to show some signs of

---

202 AFSt/M 2 E 36 : 1 and NHR 4, 1794, issue 44, 706.

203 AFSt/M 1 C 37a : 4.

204 AFSt/M 1 C 25 : 33: On 8.10.1785, Schwartz wrote to Pasche that the two Tamil Lutheran pastors, Philip and Rāyappaṉ, were honest and competent. However, they needed supervision and guidance from German Lutheran missionaries. Leaving them alone would be dangerous because they might neglect their duties and gradually become disorderly. Therefore, Schwartz did not depute any of them to Cuddalore to replace Hüttemann or to Tiruccirāppaḷḷi to replace Pohle.

205 An Abstract of the Annual Reports 1814, 482.

improvement. According to local beliefs, his charitable activities and community involvement may have improved his health. Pohle requested that everyone who participated in the meal pray for Schwartz's recovery.[206] On 11 February 1798, John wrote from Tranquebar: The missionaries in Tranquebar heard that their worthy "Father Schwartz" seemed to be nearing the end of his life. Gericke and Gottfried Immanuel Holzberg were with him. John hoped that Holzberg would learn the art of leading Tanjore from Joseph Daniel Jänicke and Johann Caspar Kohlhoff after their death.[207]

Despite the intense and restless work among Christians in their schools and churches, and among non-Christians in the royal palace and the Company's administrative institutions, Schwartz's health weakened. In November 1797, he fell and injured one of his legs, which later became inflamed. All medical help failed to heal the legs. Two or three days after Gericke's arrival, Schwartz complained about pain in his right foot. Its inflammation did not heal, but his determination remained unwavering.[208] Kennedy, the Company's medical doctor, tried every remedy to cure it, but Schwartz's physical body was so weak that it did not accept the medicine. Kennedy wondered at Schwartz's patience during his illness and did not speak "one single word of impatience." Schwartz asked Gericke to inform his missionary colleagues in Tranquebar to "make the faithful discharge of their office their chief care and concern."[209]

Kennedy reported that during his illness, Schwartz read Edward Young's *Complaint or Night-Thoughts on Life, Death, and Immortality* (1742–45), his favourite book, which contained "weighty truths." This long poem paraphrased parts of the Book of Job. It did not ask anyone to abandon society or renounce their business. Instead, it asked its readers to consider the "emptiness of honours, the riches and pleasures of this world" and encouraged them to fix their hearts in the right place, "where true treasures are to be found." The medical doctor Kennedy remembered Schwartz's maxim not to mind "the things of this world as our chief good" but to contemplate "our eternal concerns."[210]

Schwartz's life in public as an ambassador for peace, justice, and social harmony earned him fame and brought blessings to the inhabitants of Tanjore and

---

206 NHR 5, 1801, issue 57, 748.

207 NHR 5, 1800, issue 56, 697.

208 Remains of the Rev. C. F. Schwartz, 8–14: Gericke, who had been with Schwartz since 02.02.1798, stated that the black spots on Schwartz's legs did not respond to any medical treatment. The medical doctor Samuel was with him. Schwartz's mouth was often dry, and he struggled to speak clearly, but he was able to recite a few words from hymns and remained calm. He stated that his suffering was not exceptional. God indeed helped him to bear it. He mentioned that many people had a good start in Christianity, but none were perfect. On the day of Schwartz's death, Gericke immediately informed the SPCK: it "pleased God to take from them their dear father, the Rev. Mr. Swartz, between four and five o'clock that evening." For further details on Schwartz's death, see Pearson: Memoirs, Vol. 2, 352.

209 An Abstract of the Annual Reports and Correspondence of the Society for Promoting Christian Knowledge from the Commencement of its Connexion with the East India Missions, A.D. 1709, to the Present Day together with the Charges Delivered to the Missionaries at Different Periods on their Departure for their several Missions, London 1814, here 482–483.

210 An Abstract of the Annual Reports, 481.

other places where he ministered. At the same time, he focused his mind on eternal things. Kennedy recollected what Schwartz told him two or three days before his death: "Doctor, in heaven, there will be no pain." The doctor confirmed it and stated that he wanted to keep Schwartz alive for the benefit of those around him. After a while, Schwartz spoke affectionately: "Oh, dear doctor, let us take care that we may not be missing there." His acceptance of his condition brought a sense of peace and tranquillity.[211]

Schwartz's unwavering commitment to the Tamil people was evident until his last breath. On 2 February 1798, he warmly welcomed missionaries Gericke and Holzberg, whom he held in high esteem as his patriarchs. At that moment, he urged them to show understanding towards the Tamil catechists, emphasising their loyalty and dedication to the cause. His commitment to the Tamil people was profound and unwavering, leaving a lasting impact on the audience.

> Of course, many a cross comes, but my brother, that is healing for us; it draws our hearts more to God, and we are kept in the humility that the stubborn and proud heart so quickly forgets. There is always more good than evil. Oh! When I consider how fatherly God has guided me up to this point, from what trouble he has rescued me, and how patiently he has borne and sustained me despite my many sins, I must exclaim: 'Blessed be his name! Believe me, the happiness is unspeakably great when you have forgiveness of sins in Christ. Oh! What my Savior has done for me, a poor sinner!'[212]

He recovered until Sunday, 9 February 1798, and the pain in his leg reduced. Gericke took leave from him on 12 February 1798 and left. On the morning of 13 February, Schwartz woke up but collapsed. Sudden spam gripped him so heavily that he could not breathe normally.[213] He spoke a few words. No one could understand them. Then he sang the hymn "Christ, He Is My Life" and committed all things into God's hands. As the Tamil catechists sang the last stanza of the hymn "Oh, Sacred Head, now wounded," he died peacefully around 4 p.m. on the same day, aged 71 years, three months and 21 days.[214]

Alexander Macleod, the new Company Resident in Tanjore, arranged for Schwartz's funeral on the evening of 14 February; in his attempt to know whether the sorrow-stricken Prince Serfoji would attend the funeral procession, he wrote this impressive message and underlined Schwartz's significance not only to the prince but to the world:

---

211 An Abstract of the Annual Reports, 484.

212 Germann: Missionar Christian Friedrich Schwartz, 380.

213 Remains of the Rev. C. F. Schwartz consisting of his Letters and Journals. London 1826, here 8–14.

214 Germann: Missionar Christian Friedrich Schwartz, 381. NHR 5, 1798, issue 53, Preface: On 29.9.1798, Director Schulze of the Glaucha Institutions informed the readers of the *New Halle Reports* about Schwartz's death: I share the sad news that "God has honoured his faithful servant, Missionary Schwarz in Tanjore, by a gentle death on the 13th February of this year to enjoy the reward of the loyalty he has demonstrated since 1749 in the service of the Gospel to non-Christians and Christians. His fellow brothers, who all honoured him as their father," observed that his vital strength had been diminishing for some time.

> My dear Sir [Serfoji]! I can well conceive of your affliction on hearing of the death of our invaluable and much-lamented Friend, Mr. Swartz. In his latter moments, he spoke of you with great regard and from what I have observed in your disposition. I am sure that you will always bear in remembrance the good precepts he taught and the Excellent Example he set to you and all the world. His corpse is to be buried at 4 O'clock this afternoon. I do not know that anything in the Hindoo Laws or Customs should deprive you of the consolation of seeing the last ceremonies performed over your valuable friend and benefactor. If those Laws and Customs should not forbid it, I make no doubt of your being present this afternoon. I shall be there, and if you shall be at your little Bungalow, [I] will attend you there a little before the time appointed.[215]

The evening of 14 February 1798 saw a congregation at the church within the fort (modern Christ Church) to pay their respects to Schwartz. Gericke, who was to speak, was overcome with emotion and could barely talk. Instead, a servant of Schwartz delivered the funeral sermon, which deeply moved both Christians and non-Christians present. His concluding words, declaring the loss of a father to the mission, the missionaries, the churches and schools, left those who knew Schwartz in tears.[216]

After the wake ceremony, Europeans carried Schwartz's coffin to the Tamil Lutheran Church in the garden (modern St. Peter's Church). Serfoji, accompanied by his courtiers, covered Schwartz's body with gold cloth and wept profusely. As the coffin was about to be lowered into the pit before the altar, the Tamil Christians sang a song, a poignant tribute to their beloved leader. Once the crowds had returned to the garden church, Gericke spoke about Schwartz, invoking Jacob's parting words to his sons in Genesis 49: 'I die, but God will be with you all.'[217]

On 14 February 1798, Jänicke, one of Schwartz's assistants, wrote a moving letter to Colonel Martinz in Ramanathapuram[218] and narrated Schwartz's death as follows:

> Dear Sir, Though never so unable to write a letter, I cannot omit acquainting you with the greatest regret that your old friend, Mr Swartz, is no more. He died yesterday at half after four o'clock in the afternoon & will be interred this afternoon at the chapel in his garden. He had entirely recovered from his long and severe indisposition and enjoyed good health except that his mental faculties were extremely weak, & his discourses often unconnected. When on the 2nd instance, we, to our great surprise, discovered eruptions & swellings on his right foot, which eruptions increased so rapidly, & shewed such symptoms that we had every reason to dread a mortification; but the application of bark & the use of it inwardly happily prevented it. However, we soon discovered that his feet and whole frame were disordered. From the fourth, he was confined to his bed. His disorder increased, and, at least four days before his departure, a fever ensued, which only terminated with the disposition of his life. Like the setting sun, which before was hid[den] by a cloud & afterwards appeared with redoubled splendour, the mind of our worthy Friend became the day before his dissolution perfectly

215 T. Vol. 4452, 6.

216 Germann: Missionar Christian Friedrich Schwartz, 382.

217 Germann: Missionar Christian Friedrich Schwartz, 382.

218 Julian James Cotton: List of Inscriptions on Tombs or Monuments in Madras Possessing Historical or Archaeological Interest, rev. ed. Vol. 2. Madras 1946, 164: The armies of the Company and Wallajah captured the Fort of Ramanathapuram in 1772 and appointed Colonel Martinz to supervise it. After Company and Wallajah withdrew their troops from Ramanathapuram in 1792, Martins commanded "the local corps of armed police, called the Revenue Battalion."

> serene & continued so till his great spirit was set at large. I never saw a man more patient and resigned. But my feelings are too severe to proceed. Wishing you therefore health and [paper broken] the manner of happiness. I am with the [... paper broken] regard. Dear Sir, Your most obedient and thankful servant, J. D. Janicke.[219]

On 14 February 1798, Pohle received the news of Schwartz's death and burial. Earlier, he did not esteem him much while he was alive. However, Pohle admired Schwartz as follows at his death: Schwartz was his worthy father and brother, who had gone ahead to God the Father. However, to deal with the grief, one should cry and let the tears flow to bear the loss. Pohle thanked God for the companionship, encouragement, and advice that Schwartz had given him.[220]

Jänicke attempted to take on Schwartz's unfinished tasks and contacted the individuals assigned to complete them. One of them was William Wheatley, whom Schwartz had educated (Section 4.6). At that time, he looked after the school in Ramanathapuram (Section 10.3). Before reminding Wheatley about his obligation to send him a report on income and expense, on 19 February 1798, he inserted the following note about Schwartz's death:

> My dear Friend, You have undoubtedly heard that the great and worthy Mr. Swartz, your father and teacher, is no more! His worth and greatness was always justly admired but never more conspicuous than in his last hours. His humility, his patience, his resignation, his relying solely on the Redeemer, his faith and hope, and other admirable graces, shewed their strength and splendour more than I can describe. May a gracious God prepare us that our latter end may be like to that of our dearest Father![221]

Pearson concluded that Schwartz's calm yet triumphant death complemented the "uniform tenor of his life," which was "eminently pious, consistent, exemplary, and holy." He felt that Schwartz's life had vividly demonstrated "tokens of the divine presence," which radiated "bright beams of divine consolation, hope, and joy" to all with whom he interacted.[222]

5.14 Schwartz's Estate

Schwartz entrusted Gericke with the management and execution of his estate. Gericke discovered how diligently Schwartz had invested in Company bonds, ensuring an annual interest rate of eight percent. In his undated will, Schwartz allocated the capital and its interest to further the missionary activities he had initiated in Tanjore and Pāḷaiyamkōṭṭai.[223] His will opens with his realisation of

219 SPCK D 36, Microfilm frames 36–37.
220 NHR 5, 1801, issue 57, 748.
221 William Taylor: A Memoir of the First Centenary of the Earliest Protestant Mission at Madras. Madras 1847, xvii–xviii. In a footnote, Taylor stated that William Wheatley later became the British Resident of Madurai and looked after the mission work in Pāḷaiyamkōṭṭai and other places in the south.
222 Pearson: Memoirs, Vol. 2, 377.
223 Germann: Missionar Christian Friedrich Schwartz, 383.

sin and an earnest prayer for God's forgiveness. He made this will in God's presence and with full awareness. He stated that using his Company salary, he built a house in the Big Fort, another home in the Small Fort in Tanjore, a church, and several tiny houses in the mission garden. He considered these properties as mission houses and intended them to remain so after his death. His missionary successors were to inherit and use his furniture and books without selling them.

Schwartz confessed that he did not spend his monthly salary from the Company. Apart from building the houses, he has entrusted the rest to his beloved brother, Gericke and friend, Breithaupt, in Madras for investment. The interest from these investments should benefit the mission work in Tanjore and Pāḷaiyamkōṭṭai.[224] Each missionary would receive an annual stipend of £50 and an additional salary of £50 from the SCPK. Although the wages from the SPCK were insufficient, any extra funds from SPCK and £100 from Schwartz's investment should benefit low-income individuals in the mission. The remaining interest could support his schools in Tanjore and Pāḷaiyamkōṭṭai, with three-fourths allocated to Tanjore and one-fourth to Pāḷaiyamkōṭṭai.

Schwartz's family members in Germany had no right to the money designated for the mission. As a token of his love,[225] he set aside five hundred Star Pagodas for his sister's children to share equally. He instructed his executors to sell the two golden watches he had received as gifts and distribute the proceeds to impoverished individuals. As a gesture of gratitude to his servant Joseph, he assigned 30 Star Pagodas to him. He also requested that his executors spend the interest from the estate to maintain the mission garden. The remaining interest should benefit the mission or individuals experiencing poverty.

As a sign of his affection for Johann Caspar Kohlhoff, Schwartz bequeathed all his silverware to him. If Joseph's character deteriorated, the thirty Star Pagodas would be reassigned to another servant of good character, especially during

224 AFSt/M 2 E 27 : 18 and NHR 6, 1807, issue 64, 268: On 03.07.1804, Christoph Samuel John reported that Cämmerer went to Tanjore to help Kohlhoff reduce the expenses. While interest in Schwartz's legacy remained the same, the salaries for catechists and schoolteachers increased. To maintain the missionary work, the co-workers in Tanjore agreed on a lower salary; they had to stop building a few chapels (lit. Bethäuser, 'prayer-houses').

225 Germann: Missionar Christian Friedrich Schwartz, 383–384: Schwartz helped his siblings and their children. He regularly assisted his sister, Maria Sophia Knospe. For example, on 13 March 1781, he sent money to her (AFSt/M 1 B 72 : 7). After her husband's death on 15.03.1787, Schwartz supported her young son, Christian Friedrich. He sent money to a widowed daughter of his other sister in Frankfurt and her sister, Mrs Kienast, in Pribrow. He was deeply concerned about the welfare of his half-sister, Martini (d. 1805), whose married life had been plagued by numerous problems. To ensure continued support, he had the house and field of his parents registered in the names of his children. He supported his half-brother, Carl Ludwig, although he caused him much heartache. Even after he had become a pastor of a local church, Schwartz paid off his student loans. Schwartz helped his maternal aunt, Mrs Rostin, who lived with her son, a Sergeant, in Berlin. In his will, he set aside five hundred Star Pagodas for the children of his siblings. AFSt/M 1 C 40a: 40: On 19 February 1799, Carl Ludwig Schwartz inquired with the Director of the Glaucha Institutions about his estate and requested a copy of his portrait. AFSt/M 1 C 40a: 38. On 25.02.1799, Christian Friedrich Knospe inquired of the same director about Schwartz's testament and his share of the inheritance.

Schwartz's death. Schwartz signed this will in the presence of Jänicke and Kohlhoff.[226] Gericke meticulously inventoried Schwartz's cash, bonds, advances, investments, and interest. His careful management revealed that Schwartz had invested 21,600 Pagodas, the largest amount, with the Hunter Hay and the Company receiving a 12% interest rate. On 1 November 1799, more than one and a half years after Schwartz's death, Gericke's calculations showed that Schwartz's investments had grown to 36,595 Pagodas, 33 Panam, and 76 Kas, demonstrating Schwartz's responsible stewardship.[227] Schwartz had bequeathed all his savings and possessions for missionary work in southern India. Penny noted that Schwartz's will did not mention Christ Church in Tanjore, instead leaving Rupees 85,600 to continue "the work at Tanjore and the branch missions."[228]

5.15 Schwartz's Character

Schwartz's life and work had a consistent pattern. His simple lifestyle and honest engagements with people at many levels of socio-political life earned him respect. The earliest description of his lifestyle and outlook dates to 1767, when he interacted with William Chambers in Tiruchirappalli. That year, William Chambers, the brother of Robert Chambers, the future Chief Justice of the Supreme Court in Calcutta, sought to learn Persian from a native Persian language teacher. For this purpose, he left Calcutta, came to Tiruccirāppaḷḷi, stayed there for two years and maintained a cordial spiritual bond with Schwartz.

William Chambers confessed that before coming to Tiruccirāppaḷḷi, he had already heard about Schwartz's missionary zeal, Christian piety, and commendable language skills; these were so extraordinary that he hardly believed what he had heard. However, he confessed that his first sight of Schwartz completely transformed him. Schwartz's dress seemed old, strange and "pretty well worn," but in "every other respect, his appearance" was not "forbidding or morose." He was a "stout well-made man, somewhat above the middle size, erect in his carriage and address, with a complexion rather dark, though healthy, black curled hair and a manly engaging countenance expressive of unaffected candour, ingenuousness and benevolence; and you will have an idea of what Mr Swartz appeared to be at first sight."[229]

Schwartz had learned the Hindustani language. For seven months, he had been learning Persian. The "Persian Gospels" that William Chambers possessed were

226 NHR 5, 1801, issue 57, 790–791.

227 AFSt/M 1 H 9 : 26.

228 Penny: The Church in Madras, 613: Schwartz "left a will; he mentioned a house in the greater fort, a house in the little fort, together with the Church and certain houses in the garden without the fort, which 'were erected out of the money which was assigned me monthly by the [East India] Company'; and he said of them 'I look on them, as I have ever regarded them, namely to be the houses of the mission.' He did not refer to Christ Church in Tanjore. He left Rs. 85,600 to continue mission works at Tanjore and its branches, including Pāḷaiyamkōṭṭai, Ramanathapuram, etc.

229 Pearson: Memoirs, Vol. 1, 163.

helpful to Schwartz. Learned Muslims read them "with profound veneration and attention." In his letter to his brother, William Chambers described Schwartz as a man of extensive learning, decisive judgment, regular conduct, cheerful disposition, and sincere piety.[230] Schwartz learned Persian to the extent that he could converse with Wallajah and later with Hyder Ali. Schwartz's missionary work, which involved spreading Christianity, promoting cultural exchange, and fostering understanding, had a profound impact on the local community, earning him respect and admiration.

Schwartz maintained warm Christian fellowship and correspondence, both in person and by letter, not only with William Cambers but also with his widow. For instance, on 19 November 1793, she summarised her esteem for Schwartz, his service to her husband and his comforting words. She explained Schwartz's lasting impact on her and her husband, and they sought to lead a Christian life amidst a group of British expatriates who prioritised secular matters higher than spiritual matters:

> Dear Sir, Your kind letter of the 5th of October reached me on the 6th instance [here in Calcutta] and was very acceptable. Such a mark of attention from so old a friend, as you are, of my ever-to-be-lamented husband was truly comforting. How much more so from a Christian friend of his, and that friend, one who had been the blessed means of showing him the true and only way to Eternal Life in the principles of Christianity, laid down in the Gospel which he was first convinced of and settled in at Trichinopoly. Blessed and praised be God! He ever remained fixed, and he was also made the happy instrument of leading others to the true Foundation of life, even Christ Jesus our Lord. His life was a life of mortification and self-denial; in his death, he evinced that his heart and affections were set on things above, not on the perishing things of this earth. His faith in his last hours was powerful to the enabling of him to lay all his care upon Him, who is mighty and willing to help in time of need, to the enabling of him to resign his soul in confidence into the hands of his blessed Redeemer. [...] I am anxious about nothing else either for myself or for my children but that we may be found in Christ Jesus.[231]

During his later years, Schwartz effortlessly interacted with military majors, colonels and generals, profoundly impacting them. As mentioned above, Major Wood, Major Stevens and General Munro became his friends. He also attracted the attention of the commanding officer, General William Fullarton, in Coimbatore. At that time, Schwartz was *en route* to meet Tipu Sultan. While waiting for Tipu Sultan's permission in Coimbatore, he accompanied General Fullarton in 1784. Three years later, in 1787, Fullarton acknowledged Schwartz's impact on him and others. He was confident that the "knowledge and integrity of this irreproachable Missionary [Schwartz] have retrieved the character of Europeans from imputations of general depravity."[232]

On 15 October 1788, William Petrie, the Company Resident at Tanjore, complained to the Council in Fort St. George about Ameer Singh's financial

---

230 Pearson: Memoirs, Vol. 1, 121–122.

231 Bodleian Library: 72290ind-box2, Document 27 dated 19.11.1793: Mrs Chambers, the sister-in-law of Sir Robert Chambers

232 Fullarton: A View of the English Interests in India, 183.

mismanagement and inability to pay the annual dues to the Company. Simultaneously, he was aware of Schwartz's role in advancing civil society. Both found it difficult to deal with Ameer Singh's untrustworthy administrators; they wished for public servants who were "men of Credit and responsibility." In this context, Petrie described Schwartz as a man whose "indefatigable exertions" astonished him and "to whose Zeal and Services" he could not do "sufficient justice."[233]

Schwartz's involvement in Tanjore's public affairs, particularly his stance on just practices, earned him high respect. Andrew George Ram, the successor to Petrie in Tanjore, wrote on 29 January 1790 about Schwartz to Governor John Holland in Fort St. George as follows: The "good Mr. Swartz having frequently lamented the mischiefs which are daily happening for want of a regular system of justice with that knowledge which his long acquaintance with the language and manners of the Country has given him."[234]

As Schwartz aged, his character became even finer and more impressive. Missionary Christoph Samuel John, who fell ill and required a peaceful recovery, travelled to Tanjore, where he stayed with Schwartz for eight days in February 1795 and observed his daily conduct. His contemporaneous description provides rare glimpses into Schwartz's character and his work in schools, in spiritual and temporal spheres:

> Kohlhoff met me at the banks of the Cauvery River. He was accompanied by fifty children, whom Schwartz currently maintained. I found him still as healthy and cheerful as he was several years ago, even though he is already over sixty-eight years old. He still teaches four hours daily to the English and Tamil school children and those preparing for Holy Baptism. Moreover, after work, he can still converse with others in a cheerful, instructive, and edifying manner. Admirable are his pure spirit, his unselfishness and conscientiousness, his activity and zeal for the preservation of the mission work, his faithful care to combine the spiritual well-being of Christians with the physical well-being and to provide them with means of sustenance, his wisdom in work, love of humanity and good job, his fervour in prayer, and his gift of speaking even in a mixed company in a way that attracts everyone's attention. Remarkably, he was skilled in expressing reproachable things with such friendly and cheerful facial gestures that even the most powerful and proudest person would not be offended. His other rare qualities must make him popular and appreciated by everyone. Furthermore, even his outward decency, silver-white curly hair, serene eyes, and facial features inspired awe and love towards him. I spent eight days with this patriarchal man in the most pleasant way, and in his company, I almost forgot that I was sick.[235]

This contemporaneous report portrayed Schwartz's final years of active work, both within and outside his missionary enterprise. Missionary John did not expect that Schwartz would die three years later. His death created a vacuum which other missionaries could not fill. For example, in December 1799, the missionaries in Tranquebar lamented his death. They highlighted aspects of his character they admired: They considered him their brother and cherished his affectionate

[233] IOR/P/252/27, 3075–3076.

[234] IOR/P/252/42, 414 quoted in Pearson: Memoirs, Vol. 2, 190.

[235] AFSt/M 2 E 27 : 13; NHR 5, 1797, issue 50, 151–152; Germann: Missionar Christian Friedrich Schwartz, 363.

fellowship with them. They stated that his memory remained afresh among them. They remembered his Christian wisdom, his glowing earnestness, and his unsurpassable example, which taught, strengthened, and guided them. They noted that he possessed a rare combination of talents. His conversations entertained and attracted Christians and non-Christians of various persuasions. Everyone felt strengthened. Some became Christians. Others understood that a faithful Christian like him was the happiest person. He was the same person in palaces, huts, and among the great and the poorest members of society.[236]

These missionaries knew that a faithful Christian would usually have enemies, but they made an exception to this general rule. They assured Schwartz that he had no enemy; even if a person became his enemy, that person would not remain his enemy for long. If he spoke in a group of people with diverse opinions, everyone listened to him eagerly because he kept his voice soft and often narrated about exciting things. He knew how to construct a speech and present religious and edifying matters so everyone would hear his position. He was never at a loss for words and ideas; he was never embarrassed by unexpected blame. He answered them with such presence of mind, sharp rationality and accuracy that they would learn to be silent in his presence. He combined humility with these competencies; he never shamed those who did not possess similar talents. He never weighed down on them; instead, he encouraged them to express their opinion. He listened to them intently and patiently, without interrupting them with unnecessary remarks. He confessed Christ to the high and low persons of society; he never left them without sharing Christ with them, and thus sowed an excellent seed in their hearts. He passionately believed this seed would germinate in the soil of their heart. The missionaries repeatedly confirmed the growth of this seed among the high and low of society. They explained how his words impressed them. If he had to express his disagreement to the high and low of society, he conveyed it to them with such dignity that they did not feel offended but understood what went wrong. The missionaries thought they could cite living examples for every aspect of their opinion about the unparalleled example of Schwartz. They refrained from it because otherwise, they would have to write a treatise.[237]

On 10 December 1801, Christian Pohle mentioned his emotional reaction on seeing a portrait of Schwartz: a major who had commanded the Company army in Tiruccirāppaḷḷi was a friend of Schwartz. He sent a picture of Schwartz to Pohle. Pohle opined that he had seen various portraits of Schwartz, but this portrait represented him accurately. It moved him so profoundly that he shed tears.

In February 1802, the English periodical *The Christian Observer* provided information on Gericke's (1799) visit to congregations that Schwartz had founded. Philochristos, a reader of this article, wrote to the editor of *The Christian Observer* that Schwartz merited more admiration than reported in SPCK publications and summarised his esteem for Schwartz: The simple and pious life of this "apostolic

---

236 NHR 5, 1804, issue 60, 1077–1078.

237 NHR 5, 1804, issue 60, 1106. Each copy of Schwartz's portrait cost ten Star Pagodas or twenty-five Royal Dollars.

man" impressed people. With equal earnestness, he urged Hindus, Muslims, and Christians to lead morally upright lives. He invited the English, Portuguese and Germans to embrace the Lordship of Jesus Christ. Amidst Europeans, whose lifestyle made the Hindus "suspect that the God whom Christians worship is Mammon," Schwartz represented an excellent, radiant form of Christianity. His "Christian character and conduct" subdued "prejudice and enforced conviction." The people loved and trusted him. The King of Tanjore revered him.[238]

As discussed in Section 5.6, John Hudleston seems to have left Tanjore on 3 February 1787 and took Schwartz's letter to his widowed mother in England. She was pleased that her son had cooperated with Schwartz, absorbed his teachings, and regarded him as a role model. After returning to England, he tried to gain a seat in the British Parliament. In that context, on 1 February 1802, his mother reminded him to imitate Schwartz's piety, character and lifestyle. Her letter uses language generally reserved for the Lord Jesus Christ: What would Jesus do if he were physically present before you? For Hudleston, Schwartz remained a moral example of truth and honesty, stemming from his Christian convictions.

> I feel myself extremely obliged to my friends, Captain Blackburn and Mr Torin for their kindness they have shown you and also to the Rev Mr Kohlhoff for his attention to your education. Your child was more fortunate than you were for several years under the kind care and instruction of the most pious and virtuous of men, the late Revd and lamented, how justly and deservedly lamented, Mr Swartz. The best advice I can give you is to remember his precepts, to have constantly in your kind his spottles example, and never to do or say anything that your conscience tells you: Mr Swartz if he were present, would disapprove. Keep always in your view the great lesson, which he taught and never cease to practise till he died, namely that the basis of everything worthy of your regard is religion [i.e. Christianity]. That is your best security against the temptations of vice, as no truly religious person will ever swerve from truth and honesty.[239]

In his letter of 13 February 1802 to John C. Kohlhoff, John Hudleston reflected on his time in Tanjore as the Company Resident (March 1785 – c. February 1787) and his association with Schwartz. He confessed that Schwartz was his "mentor and guide," who advised him about his interactions with King Tulāji and whose views had "encouraged and fortified him." Hudleston recalled how Tulāji, the night before his death, solemnly listened to Schwartz's advice, naming Ameer Singh as "the regent and caretaker of the affairs of his country" and entrusting his "child, Serfojee," to Schwartz for education and training until the latter became the ruler of Tanjore. Hudleston also remembered how Hyder Ali received Schwartz on his embassy to him and ordered his generals to respectfully allow the "venerable padre" to pass anywhere "for he is a pious, holy man and means no harm to my government." Hudleston affirmed that he valued Schwartz's friendship as the most treasured memory of his life.[240]

---

238 Philochristos: Particulars respecting the late Mr. Swartz. In: The Christian Observer 1, 1802, issue 6, 349–350.

239 Bodleian Library: 72290ind-box2, Document 18 dated 01.02.1802: John Hudleston to an unnamed recipient in Tanjore.

240 Bodleian Library: 72290ind-box2, Document 19 dated 13.02.1802: John Hudleston to J. C. Kohlhoff.

Another significant milestone in Schwartz's enduring legacy is the extraordinary marble monument in St. Mary's Church in Fort St. George, Madras. On 17 Sep 1806, James Cobb, Assistant Secretary of the Company in London, sent a letter to George Buchan, the Secretary of the Company at Fort St. George, about the decision of the Company's Court of Directors in London to erect a marble monument of Schwartz, which they had already prepared and loaded on the ship *Union*. The Company's Court of Directors felt that Schwartz had exhibited "Religion and Piety, and the exercise of the purest and most exalted Benevolence." They acknowledged the productive and transformative influence of his name and character on the inhabitants of Tanjore, who had shown him unbounded confidence and veneration. They also affirmed that Schwartz's exemplary life benefited the Company for years. Cobb stated that on "no [other] subject has the Court of Directors been more unanimous than in their anxious desire to perpetuate the memory of this Eminent Person and to excite in others an emulation of his great example." The Company's Court of Directors in London asked Reverend Dr Richard Hall Kerr (1768–1808), the chaplain at St. Mary's Church in Fort St. George, to erect the monument near the altar of the named church.[241] They further desired that "the Native Inhabitants by whom Mr Swartz was so justly revered may be permitted and encouraged to view the monument after it shall have been erected and that translations be made of the inscription into the country languages and published at Madras and copies be sent to Tanjore and the other districts in which Mr Swartz occasionally resided and established seminaries for Religious Institution." They also indicated Serfoji's desire to erect a monument in Tanjore. The sculptor Flaxman had prepared it, and the Court of Directors would arrange its free transport to Madras. Kerr should send it off to Tanjore.[242]

John Hudleston, the former Company Resident at Tanjore, who knew Schwartz well, prepared the inscribed text on this monument. It states that Schwartz promoted the "temporal and eternal welfare of others," and his Christianity was filled with a "graceful form and placid dignity." It mentions that Schwartz erected churches, seminaries and schools; he earned the respect of Europeans and Indians, who placed their "unbounded confidence in his Integrity and Truth." People experiencing poverty and those who were injured considered him their "unfailing

241 For a biography of Kerr, see Penny: The Church in Madras, 681–684.

242 IOR/E/4/898, 733–743. Papers Relating to East India Affairs (Resident Europeans–Police–MISSIONARIES–Weavers, and Investments). Ordered by the House of Commons, to be printed 14 April 1813. London 1813, here, 81–84: On 07.11.1807, Claudius Buchanan asked Minto, the Governor General of Bengal, why he and his officers deliberately discarded the directive of the Court of Directors to publicise the erection of Schwartz's monument in Madras and to circulate the translated text of the monument in local languages. He stated that the Christians in Bengal were eagerly waiting to receive "the honourable testimony to the apostolic Swartz," but they were disappointed that the Gazetteer of Bengal did not recognise "the venerable Missionary." Additionally, the Company in Bengal ridiculed the civilising works of the missionaries in other places (e.g. Greenland). Buchanan wondered why the servants of the Company in Bengal were indignant about Christian missionaries while "the honourable the East India Company were adorning the sepulchres of their Missionaries and embalming their memory in the South." Buchanan implored that the Company in Bengal should not oppose Christian missionaries and their good works to benefit the ordinary people.

Schwartz's Monument in St. Marys Church in Fort St. George. Private Copy friend and advocate." Amidst a devastating war, Hyder Ali ordered his officers "to permit the venerable Father Swartz to pass unmolested and show his respect and kindness, for he is a Holy Man and means no harm to my government." Tulāji entrusted him with "the administration of all affairs of his Country." This monument states that Schwartz had turned his house in Tanjore into an orphanage and educated children for twenty years. He urged all kinds of people to make Christianity "the first object of their care" and implored "with his last breath the Divine Blessing on their Labours. He closed his Christian Career in the 72nd year of his Age." Hudleston incorporated the wish of the Court of Directors into the monument: the Directors of the East India Company were committed "to perpetuate the memory of such transcendent worth and gratefully sensible of the Public Benefits which resulted from its influence, caused this Monument to be erected, Ann[o] Dom[ini]. 1807."

The Company's Court of Directors in London authorised Chaplain Richard Kerr to erect the marble monument near the altar of St. Mary's Church. This monument found its permanent place on the front portion of the wall on the left side of St. Mary's Church so that every preacher could see it from the pulpit. At the installation service, Kerr compared Schwartz's public ministry with that of the Lord Jesus Christ. Kerr stated that if the Lord Jesus Christ himself had lived in late eighteenth-century southern India, he would have

> Publicly declared his abhorrence, as Mr Swartz always did, of the base intrigues, the fraudulent loans, the cruel oppressions, which, during the early part of the good man's life and for many years after, made a land of misery, desolation and slavery, of one of the most fertile provinces of this part of India. Some of the Honourable Company's servants long since departed out of life, and others who are now virtuous and amiable members of the different communities in which they live have blessed the day when they became acquainted with this venerable man.[243]

Now, Serfoji also fondly remembered Schwartz's contribution to social peace and harmony. When he erected a monument in his honour at Christ Church in Tanjore, he highlighted his service to orphans, widows, and the distressed people of Tanjore, as well as his own contributions. In March 1826, Bishop Reginald Heber (1783–1826) visited Tanjore, just before his death on April 3 of that year. There, he met King Serfoji II, missionary Johann Caspar Kohlhoff and the poet Vēdanāyagam Sāstiriyār (1774–1864). Then, he preached the Easter Sermon in Schwartz's church. What he heard about Schwartz's person, character, work, and legacy changed his suspicious opinion and increased his profound esteem for him. Initially, he assumed that Schwartz was a "political prophet" and "there was too great a mixture of intrigue in his character." He could not believe why the non-Christians venerated him and "almost regarded him as a superior being, putting crowns and burning lights before his statue." After he went to Tirucсirāppaḷḷi on 1 April 1826, Heber confessed his uninformed thoughts about Schwartz to his

[243] The Life of C.F. Swartz: Missionary at Trichinopoly and Tanjore in India. New York 1800, here 106.

friend Robert John Wilmot-Horton (1784–1841), a politician in London, who was familiar with Schwartz's reputation in India. Heber stated that he had earlier suspected Schwartz's "admirable qualities" were full of intrigues. However, he articulated his changed esteem for Schwartz with these words:

> [Schwartz was] too much of a political prophet; the veneration which the heathen paid him and still pay him, and which almost regards him as a superior being, putting crowns and burning lights before his statue, was purchased by some unwarrantable compromise with their prejudices. I find I was quite mistaken. He was really one of the most active and fearless, as he was one of the most successful Missionaries who have appeared since the Apostles. To say that he was disinterested regarding money is nothing; he was perfectly careless of power and renown never seemed to affect him, even so far as to induce even an outward shew of humility. His temper was perfectly simple, open and cheerful and in his political negotiations (employments which he never sought for, but which fell in his way), he never pretended to impartiality but acted as the avowed, though, certainly, the successful and judicious agent of the orphan prince entrusted to his care and from attempting whose conversion to Christianity he seems to have abstained from a feeling of honour. His other converts were between six and seven thousand besides those whom his predecessors and companions in the cause had brought over.[244]

On 9 May 1829, Miron Winslow (1789–1864), a US-American missionary of the American Board of Commissioners for Foreign Missions and the famous compiler of the *Comprehensive Tamil and English Dictionary of High and Low Tamil* (1862), met the "venerable" Johann Caspar Kohlhoff and his colleagues in Tanjore to learn more about Schwartz. After visiting the churches, schools and other places associated with Schwartz, Winslow summarised Kohlhoff's narrative about Schwartz's character and habits: Schwartz was "altogether an uncommon man." Despite his exceptional talent acquisitions, he remained frugal and industrious. He read and meditated on a chapter in the Hebrew Bible or the Greek New Testament every morning. He walked a short distance, reached the chapel, sang a hymn, read and expounded a passage from the Tamil Bible and prayed. He returned home for breakfast, which consisted of "a little bread and tea." After that, he met with his catechists and pastors to review their work from the previous day and plan their current and future work. He then catechised the school children, attended to other business for an hour or two, ate rice and curry for lunch, took a brief midday nap, and read a book. Then, he attended to other pressing matters. He took his staff, visited the Tamil Lutherans in their homes and inquired about their welfare. At sunset, he returned to the chapel and sat on a chair on the steps. He spoke with Christians and non-Christians alike; around 7 p.m., he conducted a short worship service. After that, he met the sons of gentlemen in the hostel, who were learning English. He let them read a chapter from the Bible and prayed with them. After they had eaten their supper and rested, he had his dinner, which consisted of rice and either milk or buttermilk. He drank tea, read, meditated, and prayed before retiring for the night. His frugal lifestyle enabled him to save money,

---

[244] Reginald Heber: Narrative of a Journey through the Upper Provinces of India from Calcutta to Bombay, 1824–1825 (with Notes upon Ceylon). An Account of a Journey to Madras and the Southern Provinces, 1826 and Letters Written in India in Three Volumes. Vol. 3. London [4]1829 ([1]1828), here 459–460.

which he received as donations or stipends from different people. When he died, he possessed a "handsome property, which he willed to the mission. His language was, 'Let the cause of Christ be my heir.'"[245] The reviewers of Hugh Pearson's work on Schwartz expressed their astonishment as follows:

> We are literally in possession of nothing which tends to fix the slightest or minutest blot upon his name. His virtue, so far as is recorded, was (if we may so apply the word) *without spot, or wrinkle, or any such thing*. The nearest approach, which we have been able to detect, even to a momentary commotion of his temper, was occasioned by what he conceived to be a most pernicious abandonment of saving doctrine.[246]

Pearson knew that people like Bishop Reginald Heber did not initially appreciate Schwartz's political involvement. However, as soon as they observed his "wisdom, his prudence, his blamelessness, his sanctity, his acknowledged usefulness and beneficence," they learned to appreciate him. Schwartz's character and habits profoundly impacted his contemporaries and followers, shaping their perception of him and his work. The reviewers of Pearson's work on Schwartz, who were likely scholars or contemporaries of Schwartz, expressed their astonishment at the lack of any "dispositions, relations, or opportunities" that would have tarnished his excellent reputation during his lifetime or after his death. They acknowledged that Schwartz might have had opponents who resisted his ideas and actions. However, they found no just grounds of complaint against him.[247] Therefore, Pearson concluded his evaluation of Schwartz's life and work with these unusually astonishing remarks:

> It is, however, undoubtedly true that, whatever may have been the failings and infirmities of Swartz, they were known only to himself and to God. By his fellow mortals they have not only never been proclaimed, but never even conjectured. He was like the patriarch of old, 'perfect and upright in his generation' and, so far as the observation and scrutiny of man extended, exemplary and blameless. To whatever degree this peculiar excellence really belonged to him, he owed it, as he would gratefully have acknowledged, to the principles and motives of the gospel and to that grace of God which had made him what he was, by which he ennobled the name of missionary and displayed in these later days the virtues of the apostolic age.[248]

The reviewers of Pearson's biography on Schwartz recommended the example of Schwartz to the consideration of not only Christian missionaries but also every British citizen in India:

> [It] would be a blessed thing for India if the example of Swartz were constantly in the recollection, not merely of missionaries and clergymen, but of Europeans of every class and profession in that country. We are satisfied that a kind and considerate attention to the native

---

245 James Barton Longacre: The Life of Christian F. Swartz: An Early Missionary in India. Philadelphia 1830, 88–90.

246 Art. IV (i.e. A review of Pearson: Memoirs of the Life and Correspondence of the Reverend Christian Frederick Swartz). Ed. by Edward Smedley et al. In: The British Critic and Quarterly Theological Review and Ecclesiastical Record 15, 1834, issue 30, 363–392, here 366.

247 Pearson: Memoirs, Vol. 2, 433.

248 Pearson: Memoirs, Vol. 2, 434.

> peculiarities would do wonders to strengthen the attachment and confidence which our countrymen have already won by their attention to still weightier manners.[249]

In subsequent years, Schwartz's fame as a model missionary attracted the attention of various editors who published Christian magazines. They printed his biography. For example, in 1844, the weekly magazine *Littell's Living Age*, printed in Boston/USA, carried an essay on Schwartz. Its introductory remark on Schwartz demonstrates how the editors of this magazine perceived and presented his character to their readers:

> Many able and good men have devoted themselves to the cause and none more distinguished than he who has been called the Apostle to the East, Christian Schwartz. The saying of an eminent missionary who preached to a far different people, the stern and high-minded Indians of North America, is exemplified in his life, – 'Prayer and pains, through faith, will do anything.' For years, Schwartz laboured in obscurity, with few scattered and broken rays of encouragement to cheer his way. But his patience, his integrity, his unwearied benevolence, his sincerity and unblemished purity of life won a hearing for his words of doctrine, and he was rewarded at least by a more extended empire in the hearts of the Hindoos, both heathen and convert than perhaps any other European has obtained.[250]

In 1845, James Hough, who had worked as a Chaplain to the Company in Madras and Pāḷaiyamkōṭṭai, published a detailed description of Schwartz's life and work in Tiruccirāppaḷḷi, Tanjore, Pāḷaiyamkōṭṭai, Madras and other places.[251] He gave particular emphasis to Schwartz's *Defence of Mission* (1795). Hough constructed his arguments based on information from the SPCK publications and the writings of Claudius Buchanan, Hugh Pearson, and others. Hough's vivid presentation highlighted Schwartz's multifaceted interactions, which spanned individuals from diverse walks of life and various life stages, underscoring the breadth of his influence. In 1860, the weekly magazine *The Sunday at Home* carried a four-part biography of Schwartz and concluded it with this appeal to their readers:

> The history of Mr. Swartz proves that the purest and most uncompromising exhibition of Christian doctrines and Christian precepts, illustrated and adorned as they were by his own character and conduct, will be so far from exciting in the natives of India, of whatever rank, any feelings of aversion or distrust, that it cannot fail to attract their attention and conciliate their regard. It can never be too frequently repeated, or too constantly born in mind, that the triumph of this great missionary was that of Christianity itself, clearly and simply stated, assiduously inculcated and eminently and consistently exemplified.[252]

In 1847, William Taylor highlighted Schwartz's significance to the history and legacy of the Vepery Mission, where Schwartz's colleagues, Johann Philipp Fabricius, Christian Wilhelm Gericke, and Johann Peter Rottler, also worked. Taylor viewed Schwartz as "the Missionary Patriarch" and "an example to

---

249 Art. IV, 381.

250 Schwartz (From the Gallery of Portraits). In: Littell's Living Age. N.p. July 1844, 510.

251 James Hough: The History of Christianity in India from the Commencement of the Christian Era. Vol. III. London 1845, 549–569.

252 Life of Swartz. In: The Sunday at Home—A Family Magazine for Sabbath Reading 1860, 629–632, 644–648, 662–662 and 677–680, here 680.

missionaries in general." He further stated that Gericke and other Lutheran missionaries in southern India considered him their "good and venerable father." Taylor could not accept available accounts about Schwartz that presented him as "a man of God" and an "extraordinary man, raised up for an extraordinary time, and for very peculiar circumstances," but "without a fault." He believed that people ascribed his greatness not only to his celibacy, austere, and honest lifestyle, but also out of fear of the curse. For instance, a labourer reviled him during the construction of a church in Tiruccirāppaḷḷi, and Schwartz scolded him. Later, this labourer consumed alcohol, went to the terrace of his house to walk, fell to the ground, and died soon thereafter. From that time, Schwartz's hearers considered him possessed of supernatural powers. When Schwartz visited Ramanathapuram later, a Christian approached him on the street. Schwartz halted him and asked whether he should receive due punishment from the local ruler or himself. This Christian preferred Schwartz to the ruler and knelt before him. Schwartz "went through the appearance of giving him a caning" and told him to rise, go his way and lead a better life.[253] Taylor cited (now unverifiable) oral traditions to underscore his allegations. Likewise, Taylor alleged that Colonel Wood would not have entrusted money to Philipp Fabricius without Schwartz's knowledge and approval. Hence, according to Taylor, Schwartz's efforts to hold Fabricius alone accountable for the lost money (Section 7.10.1) were untenable.[254]

The first volume of Frank Penny's *Church in Madras* (1904) contains his remarkable assessment of Schwartz's ministry among Indians and Europeans and the respect he had enjoyed among them:

> The great and good Schwartz, the apostolic Schwartz, died in 1798. Gericke of Madras, Jaenicke of Palamcottah, J. C. Kohlhoff and Holtzberg of Tanjore were present when he passed away. The Rajah visited him on his deathbed both before and after the soul's departure. His body was buried in the garden chapel, and great was the universal grief. He worked to the end of his life at Tanjore as he began there, sharing his attention between the European exiles and the natives. His work was partly pastoral, partly evangelistic and wholly missionary in the old and best sense of the term. Natives of various nationalities responded as readily to his kindly and sympathetic ministrations as the European soldiers who were themselves from all parts of Great Britain and Ireland, from Hanover, Switzerland, Denmark and Holland. He always spoke and taught as one having authority, and, in the exercise of his excellent judgement, was always keenly alive to the limitations of human possibility in missionary work.[255]

In 1921, Jesse Page, the last English biographer of Schwartz, was delighted to revive Schwartz's story and present it to his readers. Having examined his teachings and deeds among Christians and non-Christians, the poor and rich, the young and the old, Page ended Schwartz's biography with this fitting conclusion:

---

[253] Taylor: A Memoir of the First Centenary of the Earliest Protestant Mission at Madras, 72–76.

[254] Taylor: A Memoir of the First Centenary of the Earliest Protestant Mission at Madras, 40–41.

[255] Frank Penny: The Church in Madras being the History of the Ecclesiastical and Missionary action of the East India Company in the Presidency of Madras in the Seventeenth and Eighteenth Centuries with illustrations. Vol. 1. London 1904, 612–613.

> No one can, however, read the letters and journals of Schwartz without recognizing that he solved the problem. A trained mind, an unwavering faith in God, a complete mastery of Brahmin literature, a still better knowledge of his Bible, the engaging art of winning the hearts of his hearers, a never flinching denunciation of idolatry and sin, a willingness to listen and to sympathize, an absolute fidelity to the Christian doctrine, a yearning love for the souls of men, a meek yet passionate love for the Saviour, these were the constituents of his character and service. Is it any wonder that they loved and trusted him? They gave him many titles of respect and honour, some very tender, but when with reverence they called him 'The Christian,' that name was the best of all.[256]

Schwartz's effectiveness as a missionary is evident in the respect and trust he earned from the people he served. His comprehensive understanding of the local culture, his unwavering faith, and his enthusiastic love for the Saviour endeared him to the hearts of his hearers, who reverentially called him "The Christian."[257] Santha Praburaj, a Tamil historian, examined the relationship between Schwartz and Serfoji. In 1999, he concluded his observations as follows: Schwartz's belief in the Lord Jesus Christ enabled him to work toward alleviating the sufferings of ordinary people. His interventions for justice and good governance cost him time, "but his eminence in the state never turned him aside from his supreme devotion to the task of a Christian missionary."[258]

5.16 Schwartz's Holistic Ministry

Schwartz's holistic ministry facilitated the contextual flourishing of people in body, mind and soul. He strove to create conducive spiritual, socio-economic and political conditions where all kinds of people could experience peace, justice and social harmony. He upheld holistic ministry from his first calling to become a missionary to the end of his life. For example, on 10 January 1760, Schwartz reflected on the freedom his parents had given him to serve in the place God had prepared for him. He was grateful to them for not slavishly clinging to him. If he had stayed in Germany, he could have been with his father at the time of his death. However, he remembered how his father had responded to those who had tried to prevent Schwartz's travel to India. They considered Schwartz's decision foolish. By contrast, Schwartz's father replied that interfering with his journey to India would only make him feel sorry on his deathbed. With deep faith in his missionary calling, Schwartz recalled the last lines of the German hymn "Oh, Lamb of God" ('O Lamm Gottes'), which he often sang during his missionary work: "Your blessing will fill that which is given up or lost." Schwartz never forgot his father and siblings. He provided them with financial assistance and directed it through G. A. Francke whenever possible (Section 2.1). For example, Schwartz thanked G. A. Francke for helping his father during his last days and for admitting his

---

256 Jesse Page: Schwartz of Tanjore. London 1921, here 200.
257 Page: Schwartz of Tanjore, 200.
258 Santha Praburaj: An Analysis of Schwartz materials, 111.

brother, Carl Ludwig Schwartz, to the Orphanage in Halle.[259] These events strengthened Schwartz's resolve and dedication to his missionary calling, inspiring his companions to a similar commitment.

On 1 February 1788, Schwartz's profound empathy towards the British soldiers of the Company was palpable. He reported a significant reduction in problems among the junior and senior soldiers who regularly attended his prayer meetings at the garrison in Vallam. Those soldiers who were conscious of their immoral behaviour[260] refrained from the Eucharist, while others found comfort and strength in it. The fear of war was a constant presence, leading the soldiers to often gather around the Word of God. Even when called to the battlefields, they promised to remember each other in prayer and fellowship. Schwartz provided them with valuable guidelines on forming a prayer group. Thirty-five soldiers joined the group and met thrice a week in the church. They even learned to read and write in school, which Schwartz had started for them.[261] He recruited fellow soldiers who served as co-teachers. Soon, Schwartz noticed how his catalyst role blessed these soldiers.[262]

In the same letter of 1 February 1788, Schwartz stated that some inhabitants of Tanjore recognised the untenability of image worship. At the same time, they were afraid of embracing Christianity because of the inevitable socio-economic sufferings that would result from their conversion. They could not easily overcome these existential difficulties. However, Schwartz assured them that he would continue preaching God's Word and hoped that someone would follow the Lord Jesus Christ.[263]

---

259 AFSt/M 1 B 49 : 19; AFSt/M 1 B 49 : 20: On 12.01.1760, Schwartz wrote to Benjamin Schultze in Halle and requested that he, as a father, look after his brother Carl Ludwig. He wished that Carl Ludwig would commit his life to God, who never rejected orphans and the destitute.

260 Immoral behaviour included cohabiting with women outside of legal marriage. For information on European soldiers who fathered children out of wedlock and had their children in the Lutheran Church in Tiruccirāppaḷḷi, see Bodleian Library: 72290ind-box1–2. The missionaries distinguished between natural children, who were born to European fathers and European or Indian mothers within wedlock and illegitimate children, who were fathered by Europeans outside the wedlock. Bodleian Library: 72290ind-box2, Document 31 contains a list of natural and illegitimate children baptised by Jänicke in Pāḷaiyamkōṭṭai and Ramanathapuram between 1794 and 1796.

261 Pearson: Memoirs, Vol. 2, 233: Schwartz stated that the soldiers at Vallam were friendly, attended "divine worship decently and took tracts. Nay, some learn to read, for which good purpose I have supplied them with spelling books."

262 AFSt/M C 29a : 5; AFSt/M 1 C 29a : 3. On 19.01.1788, Schwartz shared the content of this letter with his friend Pastor Sorge: 1,000 soldiers of the English Regiment were guarding Vallam, approximately five miles from Tanjore. Seventy to eighty soldiers attended prayer meetings. Thirty-five soldiers partook in the Eucharist in December 1787. They asked Schwartz to help them organise a society for prayer and singing, especially during the war, which might happen at any time. The English school for Christian children provided language training not only in English and Tamil but also in 'Mohrisch' (i.e. Persian). The students at the Provincial School were prepared for service in the Company. Schoolmaster David, a man of good character, taught the children at the Tamil School.

263 AFSt/M 1 C 29a : 5.

In the same letter of 1 February 1788, Schwartz informed Schulze in Halle that he had been preaching God's Word to the non-Christians of Tanjore, noting that not a single day had passed without recommending to someone the belief in the Lord Jesus Christ. Once a month, he could share God's Word with interested people in the palace. Ameer Singh, however, did not openly state his opinion about Christianity. During his upbringing, he had had no opportunity to gain valuable experience; hence, he had limited general knowledge. When his daughter suffered from smallpox, he conducted costly religious ceremonies that failed to affect her healing. At that time, Schwartz pointed him to the Source of all our spiritual and temporal well-being. Ameer Singh responded: "I know you are against our customs."[264] Schwartz implied that the reason for Ameer Singh's indifference to Christianity was not merely the wicked life of the European traders, renters and administrators, who systematically stole Tanjore's wealth, but also his greedy senior Indian employees at the palace who exploited him mercilessly and advised him not to listen to Schwartz's invitation to consider Christianity. It was evident that Ameer Singh could not freely express his opinion about Christianity in such a muddled context.

On 7 February 1788, Schwartz informed Pasche about his happiness in performing his duties. He spent his monthly salary of twenty Pagodas on the mission; until that time, he did not keep an account of his expenses. After Ameer Singh had granted him a village to benefit the schools and the needy Christians, he would ask Johann Kohlhoff, a trusted colleague and successor, to keep accounts. He mentioned that he had little time to write and keep accounts. From 6 in the morning till 1 p.m., he seldom had an undisturbed hour to read the Bible. He thanked God for making his work a sweet experience. Using the Latin phrase *labor ipse voluptas* ('labour is its own pleasure'), he expressed the joy of work. However, he quickly added that without Johann Kohlhoff's help with the church and school in Tanjore, he would not have been able to endure any longer.[265]

Schwartz never forgot his missionary calling. On 23 December 1788, for example, he informed Pasche about the Tamil people's resistance to the Gospel of the Lord Jesus Christ. They were aware of the reasonable nature of the Christian faith and life, but were unwilling to give up their ancestral ways. They feared the negative social consequences of embracing the Christian faith and lifestyle. Therefore, they avoided contact with Christianity. They believed the Gospel of the Lord Jesus Christ was less valuable than their worldly profits, honour and favour.[266]

Schwartz's ability to balance his missionary work with other activities, such as being an envoy for peace, justice, and social harmony, was impressive. His multitasking skills highlight his dedication and efficiency.[267] August Friedrich

---

264 AFSt/M 1 C 29a : 5.
265 AFSt/M 1 C 29a : 11.
266 AFSt/M 1 C 30c : 17 = NHR 4, 1790, issue 37, 113.
267 Memoirs of the Rev. Joseph D[aniel] Jænicke, a Fellow Labourer of Schwartz, at Tanjore, Interspersed with many original letters and notices of Schwartz. London 1833, here 113:

Cämmerer, a new Lutheran missionary, spent ten months (February to December 1791) with "Papa Schwartz"[268] learning Tamil. During this time, he observed Schwartz's missionary zeal and life in the church garden among the Tamil Lutherans. From morning until late evening, Indians of every rank sought his intervention to settle their disputes and differences. He prioritised worship services with the Tamil Christians in the morning and evening. They sang a hymn and listened to Schwartz's brief sermons. "Till this is over, everyone, even the most respectable, is obliged to wait." His solemn ways of conducting worship services or baptising individuals who voluntarily came forward and received his catechetical teachings attracted more people to him. Cämmerer unassumingly stated that even non-Christians "of the highest rank, who never intend to become worshippers of the true God and disciples of Jesus Christ, hear his instructions with pleasure." Some Christians sought his advice on establishing new worshipping congregations in their respective places. During his forty-eight years of service among the Tamils, he acquired a profound knowledge of the people's customs, manners, and character. He spoke with them in a manner befitting a Tamil person and addressed their questions convincingly. Some exclaimed: "We can lay nothing to the charge of this priest."[269]

Schwartz's uncompromising stand for his missionary calling remained fresh. In 1791, Cämmerer observed how deeply Europeans and Indians appreciated Schwartz's disinterested and equitable approach to public business. Indians from all social backgrounds, whether royalty or ordinary folk, "loved and respected him." People feared him because he "reproved them, without respect to situation and rank, when their conduct deserved animadversion [i.e. admonition, rebuke]." He advised "all persons without distinction" about what they should and should not do to promote their "temporal and eternal welfare."[270]

The SPCK advised the younger missionaries to visit India to imitate Schwartz's positive attitudes, exemplary lifestyle and enthusiastic missionary methods. For example, when the members of the SPCK appointed Päzold as a missionary to southern India on 23 January 1793, they requested Rector Samuel Classe, one of the court preachers and a member of the Royal Society of Sciences in London, to advise Päzold to follow Schwartz's example, the "champion of the Protestant Faith." Classe pointed out that Schwartz enjoyed the "affections of the ignorant and unlearned" and the "highest veneration and esteem" by those who were "blessed with superior light." Without consciously offending anyone, he pleaded for the missionary cause of Christianity. He preferred to suffer with God's people rather than "enjoy any pleasures or distinctions which this world could afford him." He esteemed "the reproach of Christ and the advancement of a despised religion, for greater riches than Indian treasures." The SPCK likened him to Moses, who

---

Schwartz's letters, like his life, are full of One Thing,' namely serving the Lord Jesus Christ in all his endeavours.

268 Germann: Missionar Christian Friedrich Schwartz, 364.

269 Pearson: Memoirs, Vol. 2, 248.

270 Pearson: Memoirs, Vol. 2, 246.

led God's people into the promised land. Similarly, Schwartz participated in God's work and focused solely on the "interests of a crucified Saviour and the propagation of His Gospel." Schwartz was indeed a "man *antiquâ [homo] virtute ac fide* ['a man of ancient virtue and fidelity']."[271]

On 5 January 1796, Schwartz revealed to Uebele in London the two-fold secret of his success: he described his eating habits, which were tailored to the local climate and work. Those who wished to lead a European lifestyle would ruin their health. Fatty food items were not suitable for the climatic conditions of Tanjore. For this reason, local inhabitants ate easily digestible things. Secondly, he described how missionaries could cultivate and maintain their psychological well-being: they should avoid depression and dissatisfaction. These negative dispositions would poison the body, ruin the soul and diminish one's faith, love and hope. Dissatisfied missionaries could not enjoy any spiritual work. Missionaries should not expect instant success, as sowing and harvesting have their own time. Meanwhile, they should live humbly, serve God faithfully and pray for God's blessings.[272] Schwartz encouraged them to engage in a holistic ministry, just as he did.

---

271 An Abstract of the Annual Reports, 366–367.

272 AFSt/M 1 C37a : 1: Memoirs of the Rev. Joseph D[aniel] Jænicke, 127.

Chapter 6

Schwartz's Written Documents

6.1 Schwartz's Linguistic Skills

From his early days in Germany to his service in southern India, Schwartz's life and ministry demonstrated remarkable adaptability and versatility. Born in the small town of Sonnenburg, where most inhabitants knew each other, he attended local schools. When he arrived at the Glaucha Institutions in Halle (Saale) in 1746, he was proficient in German, Hebrew, Greek and Latin. His journey into the Tamil language began with Benjamin Schultze, a veteran missionary who had worked among the Tamils in Tranquebar and Madras. Schwartz's multilingual proficiency was a personal achievement and a crucial tool in his mission work. It enabled him to effectively communicate Lutheran Pietist doctrines to the diverse linguistic communities in southern India, breaking down language barriers and fostering understanding.

Schwartz keenly observed how the Glaucha Institutions incorporated Pietism's theological and practical values into education and other humanitarian endeavours. In Tranquebar, he developed an appreciation for the Tamil people and their language. Additionally, he learned Portuguese, the language spoken by most people in the coastal regions. His work in Tiruccirāppaḷḷi, since 1762, introduced him to the importance of English and Persian. During his ministry in Tanjore, he learned Marathi, the court's spoken language and Mōḍi, the court's written language. These nine languages enriched his communication with people from various linguistic backgrounds.

Lutheran theological and pietistic convictions, missionary vocation and service, the realities of his living circumstances and his hopes for the future enabled Schwartz to carefully observe people's attitudes, behaviours, rituals and other ordinary events around him. His meticulous observations, recorded in both German and English for his European readers in India and Europe, demonstrate his profound understanding of the Tamil people and their language, literature, and cultural practices. They would have interpreted the contents of Schwartz's writings from their European perspectives and constructed the specific meanings that made sense to them at that time and in their life contexts.

6.2 Schwartz's Tamil Writings

While we may not have extensive evidence of Schwartz's Tamil writings, the following two works provide glimpses into the vocabulary and theology he communicated to the Tamil people. Although limited in number, these writings had a profound and lasting impact on the Tamil community, shaping their understanding of theology and vocabulary, and enlightening them about Christian doctrine and its teachings. The significance of Schwartz's writings for the Tamil community cannot be overstated.

6.2.1 Tamil Catechism

A catechism (Gk. *katēkhizen*, 'to instruct, clarify orally') contains, in summary form, the foundational theological principles of a Christian community's constitutive doctrines and practices, following a question-and-answer method between a teacher and a student. Typically, a catechism prepares enquirers for baptism, Holy Communion, renewal and confirmation of their earlier covenant with God and their church community. The catechist was (and still is) a called, trained and licensed lay teacher who worked (and still works) under the supervision of a clergyperson or a leader of a regular worshipping congregation. As discussed in Section 10.5, Schwartz regularly selected, trained, appointed and supervised Tamil Lutheran catechists. They assisted him in local evangelistic, administrative and mediatorial jobs. He prepared a Tamil catechism for them.

Thankfully, we have a preserved copy of Schwartz's Tamil Catechism.[1] Its title reads *kiṟisattamāṉa upatecattin viḷakkam* (a 'Description of the Teaching of Christian Religion'). An English title on the front page of this catechism states its origin and contents.[2] The British Library published this 382-page catechism online in 2018. Adjusted by its copyist, its Tamil is more polished than Schwartz's Tamil in the *Dialogues*. Its vocabulary is richer and more modern than that of the Tamil Lutheran Catechisms preceding Schwartz. Its copyist used a shorthand that contracts syllables in words and the words in a sentence.

When the German Lutheran missionaries began their work in Tranquebar in 1706, they found that the Tamil Roman Catholic Christians already had their catechisms prepared by the Jesuits. These included Henrique Henrique's *Tampirāṉ Vaṇakkam* ('worshipping the Self-Existing God,' printed on 20 October 1578 in Cochin) and *Kiṟisittiyāṉi Vaṇakkam* ('Christian Worship,' printed on 14 November 1579 also in Cochin). Ziegenbalg and his successors, including Schwartz, studied these Jesuit writings in Tamil and used them as a basis for their Tamil Lutheran catechism. For example, in August 1708, Ziegenbalg prepared a summary of

---

1 BL EAP971/2/3/1, i.e., Schwartz: kiṟisattamāṉa upatecattin viḷakkam. I, the author of this current biography of Schwartz, thank Dr. Mark Edward Balmforth, who brought this manuscript to my attention at Jaffna College in Sri Lanka in September 2017. He requested me to assess its significance and endorse his application to the Endangered Archives Programme. Accordingly, Columbia University digitised this manuscript. Since 2018, its scanned images have been available at the URL: https://eap.bl.uk/archive-file/EAP971-2-3-1 (accessed on 05.10.2024).

2 Catechetical Instructions, or An Explanation of Christian Doctrine written by Swartz: Copied from the MS in possession of Rev. G. H. Apthorp and rec[ive]d by him from Rev. Brotherton. Tanjore, March 1, 1841.

biblical teachings inscribed on strips of palm leaves. As he contemplated moving to Trichy in 1777, he recognised the need for a different kind of catechism to address the spiritual and practical needs of his followers and catechists. The inhabitants of Tanjore, exposed to diverse religious and intellectual traditions, required a catechism tailored to their specific contexts. With their deep theological understanding and empathy, Schwartz compiled a detailed catechism that interacted with his adherents' social, cultural, and religious milieu, connecting the present Tamil community to its historical roots.

Schwartz's catechism opens with a profound question: "What does each man [sic] desire and long for?" This question sets the stage for the entire document, as it leads to the fundamental answer: Every individual yearns for heavenly salvation (*uttama pākkiyam*), a state that offers eternal spiritual rest (*eppōtum uḷḷa iḷaippāṟutal*), joy (*cantōcam*), and peace (*camātāṉam*). The responder then asserts that God *Parāparaṉ* (the 'Supreme Being,' the Eternal One comprising the Beginning and the End) is the Ultimate and Noblest Being (*uccita poruḷ*). The goal of a blessed person is to understand, love and serve this Parāparaṉ. The subsequent sections of this catechism elaborate on this objective of knowing, loving and serving God.

Schwartz's catechism is also different. It includes paraphrases of Spener's catechetical explanation in certain places. For example, Schwartz's catechism states that God (*parāparaṉ*) gave three kinds of laws. 1) The ritual laws for Jews regarding their external duties, such as sacrifices, fasting, and ceremonies. These laws are no longer valid for Christians. 2) The laws governing Jewish life in the Promised Land guided their interactions with one another and with others. These laws, too, do not apply to the Christians. 3) The laws about duties and obligations for all human beings are summarised in the Ten Commandments. These commandments apply to Christians. God inscribed the third group of laws onto the human heart and consciousness at creation. Therefore, these laws regulate human attitudes toward God and fellow human beings, guiding human actions. They represented God's wisdom, holiness and justice. Secondly, God wrote these laws on two stone tablets on Mount Sinai when the Israelites came out of Egypt and wandered in the wilderness of Arabia. The first three laws were inscribed on one stone tablet and aimed to regulate human relationships with God.[3]

Schwartz's catechism emphasises the theological and ethical implications of the Ten Commandments. In the first Commandment,[4] for example, God addresses God's own Majesty as "We." Its singular nature has no peer. This monotheism prohibits expecting ultimate salvation from other beings. Jesus Christ is the only God who can give salvation to penitent sinners. Schwartz did not appreciate either polytheism or image worship. Secondly, Tamil Lutherans should not worship any being or anything, either in heaven or on earth. While they may honour a dead or

3 Schwartz: kiṟisattamāṉa upatecattin viḷakkam, 174–175. This section agrees with Philip Jacob Spener's teachings about the relationship between Law and Gospel in his Catechism Explanation. For further details see Philip Jacob Spener: Katechismuserklärung. Bielefeld 1984, here 22–25.

living person, they should not worship or revere them. Monotheistic belief should nourish their attitudes, behaviour patterns and habits that honour God. Thirdly, Christians should make informed ethical decisions by discerning good and evil. Fourthly, they should love God in two ways: They should not sin; they should not tolerate sin in their society; they can also resist those who commit sinful acts. Fifthly, Christians should fear the holy and just God in all circumstances by choosing to do good things and not following their evil passions. Sixthly, they should fellowship with God by doing beneficial works and enjoying God's peace. Seventhly, Christians should contemplate God's attributes, such as love. Thus, Christians recognise God, their Creator, as the source of all good things.[5] This example of Schwartz's exposition of the first commandment illustrates his theological inclination and how he would later apply it in his ministry among the Tamil people in southern India. Thus, Schwartz's Catechism helps its readers unlock the treasures of Christian theological thoughts in and through the idiom of the Tamil people. Although these Tamil idioms still carried their original meanings and implications, Schwartz taught his followers to understand Lutheran doctrines better and orient their lives accordingly. This catechism awaits further research to ascertain its embeddedness within the linguistic and socio-cultural milieu of the Tamil people.

Christian David (1771–1852), a student of Schwartz in Tanjore and then of Christoph Samuel John in Tranquebar, copied this catechism.[6] He adjusted Schwartz's Tamil language to the convenience of the missionary pastor G. H. Apthorp (Calthorpe?), who worked in Jaffna. David would have transcribed Schwartz's catechism from a copy which the missionary pastor Thomas Brotherton possessed.[7] Brotherton belonged to the Society for the Propagation of the Gospel in Foreign Parts (SPG), which took over Schwartz's congregations and schools in Tanjore in 1828. Johann Caspar Kohlhoff, the successor of Schwartz in Tanjore, joined the SPG and worked with Brotherton. At that time, Christian David, too, became a catechist of the SPG in Tanjore. Kohlhoff and David would have

---

4 Schwartz: kiṟisattamāṉa upatecattin viḷakkam, 176: Schwartz's text reads as follows: *uṉ tēvaṉākiya karttarāṉavar nāmē. namakku muṉpāka vēṟē tēvaṉillāmal pōkka-t takkatu* (We [the majestic plural of "I"] are your Lord God. There should be no other deity before Us [me]).

5 Schwartz: kiṟisattamāṉa upatecattin viḷakkam, 175–195.

6 Reginald Heber: The Life of Reginald Heber. Vol. 2. London 1830, here 168 & 358: The first Anglican bishop of India, Thomas Fanshaw Middleton (1769–1822) enquired about Christian David, a student of Schwartz. Tamil people in the Malabar Coast and Sri Lanka, who had known him as a catechist and teacher of the Society for Propagating the Gospel in Foreign Parts for several years, esteemed him "as an exemplary Christian" who "possessed considerable knowledge." Bishop Middleton invited him to come to Calcutta, ordained him as the first Indian Christian and admitted him to the episcopal order of the Church of England. Then, David served as the "colonial chaplain at Jaffna" under the Company's rule. For additional information on Christian David, see Mark Edward Balmforth: A Tamil Pietist in Ceylon: The Educational Experiments of Christian David. In: International Journal of Asian Christianity 3, 2020, issue 1, 44–68.

7 Arthur Westcott: Our Oldest Indian Mission: A Brief History of the Vepery (Madras) Mission. Madras, 1897, pp. 98–99: Brotherton worked in Vepery, Madras, from 1850 to 1854 and

acquainted Brotherton with Schwartz's catechism, who introduced it to G. H. Althorp of Jaffna. Finally, this manuscript has been archived at Jaffna College in Sri Lanka, and its scanned copy is now available online for further study.

6.2.2 Eighteen Dialogues (1777 and 1790)

In the Spring of 1771, Archdeacon Congreve of the Anglican Church in Ireland sent £100 to Schwartz through the Society for Promoting Christian Knowledge and requested that he translate into Tamil the book *Short and Easy Method with the Deists* by Charles Leslie (1650–1722).[8] Schwartz responded that all Tamils were theists, and they would need help understanding the dialogues between a Christian and a deist in Ireland. Instead, Schwartz offered to translate Bishop Wilson's theological teachings from English into Tamil. In February 1773, Congreve left the translation to Schwartz's discretion. However, the translation process took an unexpected turn when Michael Ziegenhagen, the influential Lutheran court preacher in London, intervened and recast Leslie's texts into seven dialogues between Christians and non-Christians, which he then sent to Schwartz.[9]

On 18 January 1776, Schwartz informed Ziegenhagen that he had already translated these dialogues. Fabricius would proofread and print them in Madras.[10] On 20 August 1776, Fabricius reported that he had proofread Schwartz's Tamil manuscript and appreciated how these dialogues introduced the divine nature of Christianity to the Tamils. In 1777, Fabricius printed these dialogues as a book in Madras. That year, King Tulāji encouraged Schwartz to learn the Marathi language for diplomacy. By contrast, Schwartz sought to use this language to introduce Tulāji to Lutheranism and its practical implications. On 25 September 1777, Schwartz informed Director Freylinghausen in Halle that, at the request of Tulāji, he had been studying the Marathi language for six months.[11] He composed ten dialogues between Christians and non-Christians in Tamil and translated them into Marathi. He also compiled a treatise on Christianity.

All my efforts to locate these ten dialogues have failed thus far. However, Pearson gives the titles of these ten dialogues: 1) God's being and infinite majesty;

---

toured the surrounding areas. During his visit to the Sawyerpuram Seminary in Tirunelveli (now in Tuticorin District) in 1853, he impressed the renowned Tamil Christian Poet H. A. Krishnapillai. In 1856, Brotherton became the principal of the Vepery Mission Seminary, which later evolved into the SPG Theological College. In 1859, he moved to Nazareth, one of the villages of refuge in Tirunelveli and served there until 1870.

8 Germann: Missionar Christian Friedrich Schwartz, 240; Charles Leslie: A Short and Easy Method with the Deists, wherein the Certainty of the Christian Religion is demonstrated by infallible Proof from Four Rules, which are incompatible with any Imposture that ever yet has been, and that can possibly be. London: George Strahan, [9]1745 ([1]1694).

9 An Abstract of the Annual Reports, 116–117.

10 AFSt/M 1 B 66 : 55; NHR 2, 1771, issue 16, 491–92 and AFSt/M 1 B 66 : 58.

11 AFSt/M 1 B 67 : 71; Germann: Missionar Christian Friedrich Schwartz, 243 and 361 AFSt/M 1 B 67 : 99: On 17.11.1778, Freylinghausen expressed his joy over Schwartz learning the Marathi language. He was happy that his eight co-workers were also well.

2) God's attributes; 3) God's creation and providence; 4) God's goodness towards the first parents by creating them wholesome and happy; 5) the sin, fall from grace and misery of the first parents; 6) God's mercy in promising and sending a Saviour to redeem the fallen humans; 7) Characteristics and deeds of the Lord Jesus Christ; 8) God's method of redeeming fallen humans via "repentance, faith and holiness"; 9) God's method of strengthening repentance through prayer and the sacraments of baptism and Eucharist. 10) The unspeakable happiness of those who walk in the path of faith, ordained by God, and keep His commandments. The treatise discussed the truth of Christianity.[12] On 23 January 1778, Schwartz stated that he handed the treatise and dialogues to Tulāji, and Tulāji began reading them.[13]

Schwartz and his followers used these dialogues in their evangelistic work. As the copies of the first Tamil edition sold out, Schwartz arranged for its second edition to be printed in Tranquebar in 1790. Its title reads as follows: *A Dialogue between an Image Worshipper and a Christian* (*Vikkiraka Patti Kāra̱nukkum Ki̱risatava̱nukkum Uṇaṭā̱na Camapāṣa̱nai*). This title page also references two paraphrased Bible verses. They reveal Schwartz's intention in publishing these dialogues: a) 1 Timothy 2:3–4: God (*parāpara̱n*, 'the Supreme male Being') desires that all people are saved (*iraṭcikkappaṭutal*, 'to be saved') and wants them to attain knowledge of the truth; b) Turn to me all ends of the earth because there is no other true God (*mey-parāpara̱n*).

A second edition of this book is available in the August Herrmann Francke Study Centre library at the Francke Foundations in Halle (Saale), Germany.[14] It contains 216 pages and eighteen dialogues. Appendix 3 of this biography provides a summary of these dialogues. They contain the ten dialogues I could not find as a separate set in India or Germany. The first page of this dialogue book includes the title and a quote from 1 Timothy 2:3–4. Its title reads: *Dialogue between an image worshipper and a Christian* (*vikkiraka pattik kāra̱nukkum ki̱risatava̱nukkum uṇaṭā̱na camapāṣa̱nai*).[15] According to 1 Timothy 2:3–4, God (*parāpara̱n*, 'the most Supreme {male} Being') desires the salvation of all people and wants them to attain the knowledge of the truth. Therefore, God invites all people to turn around from who they are and what they have to the Lord Jesus Christ, besides whom there is no other true God (*mey-parāpara̱n*).

The eighteen dialogues underline the basic theological themes that were dear to Schwartz. In the first dialogue, the Christian mentions that the one God has created the world and sustains it. All human beings (lit. *cāti* from Skt. jāti, 'birth group, caste') should know, love, worship, and belong to this one God only. The Bible, the *True Veda* (lit. *satya vetam*), shows how individuals can attain salvation

---

12 Pearson: Memoirs, Vol. 1, 320.

13 Pearson: Memoirs, Vol. 1, 325.

14 The call number of this book is E523a. Germann: Missionar Christian Friedrich Schwartz, 241: Germann stated that the Tract Society in Madras reprinted it twice in 1826 and 1832.

15 Christian Friedrich Schwartz: vikkiraka pattik kāra̱nukkum ki̱risatava̱nukkum uṇaṭā̱na camapāṣa̱nai ('Dialogue between an image worshipper and a Christian'). Tranquebar: Mission Press, [2]1790 ([1]1777).

(lit. *karaiyērutal*, 'to get ashore' from the ocean of birth and rebirth). It teaches how God created everything in six days, ranging from the moon and the sun, and "from an ant to an elephant." The same God created the first humans from soil, instituted marriage and taught them to sanctify married life.

The following three dialogues repeat the biblical narratives about the fall of Adam and Eve through their deliberate choice of disobedience and the loss of God's likeness (lit. *tēva cāyal*). Their fall affected their generations negatively. God gave them commandments, sent preachers and prophets and allowed monarchs to rule the land. None of them could lead a holy life by adhering to the one God only; they embraced the worship of other deities. Consequently, God permitted them to live as captives in Egypt, Assyria, Babylon, Persia, Greece and Rome. Finally, God sent his son Jesus to die on behalf of all humans and secure God's forgiveness for all people. Schwartz did not explain the intricacies of understanding the Triune God (Father, Son and Holy Spirit), the divine and human natures of the Lord Jesus Christ, or the personality of the Holy Spirit. He strongly opposed the worship of multiple deities. He invited his readers to place their trust squarely in the Lord Christ, whose birth, life, teachings, miracles, death and resurrection ensured forgiveness of sin and eternal life in God's presence.

The fifth and tenth dialogues convey the same truth in different ways: The religious rituals of the Tamil, such as ritual baths, digging bathing tanks, building temples, growing matted hair, wearing beads, reciting mantras, and self-mortification, do not grant forgiveness of sins. Conscious and voluntary belief in the Triune God alone would confer forgiveness of sin because the Lord Jesus died vicariously for human sins and met God's justice. Biblical narratives of creation, fall, redemption through the Lord Jesus Christ and the future life for all Christ-believers oppose discriminatory practices based on caste and its untouchability.

Four dialogues (11, 12, 13, and 14) emphasise the importance of the Lord's Prayer and the two sacraments of baptism and the Eucharist. These three types of spiritual medicine can cure the sick, i.e., those who are sinful. These dialogues urge the readers to become Christ-followers. They reiterate the truth that all people die once, and then they will face God's judgement. God would welcome and receive Christ-followers into God's presence. Therefore, there is neither reincarnation nor transmigration of souls.

The last four dialogues (15, 16, 17, and 18) provide three proofs of Christianity's divine origin: Lord Jesus Christ alone guarantees forgiveness of sin; in fact, He is God. Secondly, the Lord Jesus Christ fulfilled all the prophecies of older times. His extraordinary teachings on God and humanity reiterate the divine origin of the Christian faith. Thirdly, God did not choose supernatural angelic beings to spread the good news about the Lord Jesus Christ; instead, God chose ordinary human beings, such as Moses, to communicate His will. When the people did not listen to these chosen messengers, God sent God's son to die on the cross on behalf of all human beings and to grant forgiveness of sin to them. Ultimately, these dialogues encourage readers to embrace the Lordship of Jesus Christ and become God's children.

6.3 Schwartz's Writings for Europeans

Schwartz's letters, reports, and diaries, written in both German and English, were intended for European readers; they contained his views on people, places, events, and socio-political changes of his time. They reflect the complex contexts of Schwartz and his readers. Unravelling these contextual realities requires linguistic skills and knowledge of noteworthy events in India, Germany, England and, to an extent, Denmark. Schwartz's significant public work, which engaged with both elites and ordinary people, was paramount. He translated the work diaries of his catechists into either German or English, enabling us to hear the voices and to know the conditions of those mainstream people with whom he had interacted.

6.3.1 Schwartz's Addressees

Schwartz corresponded with a diverse array of recipients, including mission authorities in Germany, Denmark, and England; his relatives, friends, and acquaintances in India, Germany, and England; company officers in Madras and Tanjore; Prince Serfoji II and his caretakers in Madras; fellow missionaries in Madras and Tranquebar; as well as Tamil catechists and schoolteachers in various Tamil towns and villages. He adeptly tailored the tone and content of his letters to reflect the nature and level of trust in his relationships with each recipient. For example, his letters to friends were rich in personal language. At the same time, his communications with company officers or the kings of Tanjore took on a more formal and professional tone, carefully restraining emotional expression. Schwartz's varied writings revealed his multifaceted intentions: to inform, persuade, express gratitude, and sometimes even apologise. Despite these differences, all his correspondence maintained a respectful tone, honouring the dignity of his correspondents. They reflected his efforts to promote peace, justice and social harmony among those with whom he lived and worked.

Schwartz sought to fulfil his job descriptions, which authorities in Copenhagen, Halle, and London gave him (Section 2.3). He diligently kept his superiors informed about his missionary activities. In Copenhagen, he corresponded with the secretaries of the Mission Board, including Johann Finckenhagen (1694–1778) from 1738 to 1765, Christian Friedrich Ursin (d. 1802) from 1765 to 1776, and Christen Hee Wadum (1733–1814), who succeeded him. Wadum's anti-missionary stance disappointed Schwartz. Wadum resigned from his duties in 1792. Jacob Gude (1754–1810) became the secretary and upheld the original purpose of the Mission Board.[16]

Schwartz's addressees in Halle included the directors of the Glaucha Institutions: Gotthilf August Francke (1696–1769) directed them from 1739 to 1769. Johann Georg Knapp (1705–1771) followed him and led the Glaucha

[16] Anders Nørgaard: Secretaries of the Mission Board in Copenhagen 1714–1868. In: Halle and the Beginning of Protestant Christianity in India. Vol. III: Communication between India and Europe. Ed. by Andreas Gross et al. Halle (Saale) 2006, 1565–1567.

Institutions for two years until 1771. Gottlieb Anastasius Freylinghausen (1719–1785) succeeded him and directed the Glaucha Institutions until 1785. German Rationalism and Enlightenment ideologies swept through academic institutions such as the University of Halle during his tenure.[17] However, he managed to maintain the Pietistic spirit of his predecessors. Johann Ludwig Schulze (1734–1799) directed these institutions from 1785 to his death in 1799. His successor, Georg Christian Knapp (1753–1825), directed them until 1825 and depended on August Hermann Niemeyer (1754–1828), the great-grandson of August Hermann Francke. Knapp and Niemeyer leaned towards rationalism and shaped the Glaucha Institutions in line with the prevailing social and intellectual currents. Knapp was responsible for the *New Halle Reports*, which, during his tenure, contained more information about Tamil culture, history, and educational systems. He also published drastically edited versions of missionary reports from India. Under Niemeyer, the Glaucha Institutions became the Francke Foundations.[18]

Besides Copenhagen and Halle, Schwartz kept the Secretaries of the Society for Promoting Christian Knowledge (SPCK) in London fully informed of his ministries. He communicated with the SPCK through three German Court Preachers in London, namely Friedrich Michael Ziegenhagen (1694–1776), Friedrich Wilhelm Pasche (1728–1792) and John Christian Christoph Uebele (1767–1846). Originally, Ziegenhagen intended to serve as a missionary in Tranquebar; however, in 1722, he became a court preacher in London, where he remained until he died in 1776. Schwartz admired his spiritual teachings and theological convictions. Pasche succeeded Ziegenhagen and held the position until he died in 1792. Schwartz particularly liked Pasche and revealed to him more critical information about the events in Tanjore than to anyone else. Uebele followed Pasche and corresponded with Schwartz until Schwartz died in February 1798. During Uebele's time, interest in the Tranquebar Mission declined, and the Danish Government tried to place the missionary enterprise under the direction of the Danish Lutheran Church.[19]

Whenever Schwartz reported on socio-political matters that negatively impacted ordinary people's lives, he sent them to Pasche. For example, on 11 October 1784, Schwartz informed Pasche that Indian soldiers had not received

---

[17] Christian Thomasius (1655–1728) and Christian Wolff (1679–1754) initiated this movement in Halle (Saale). Immanuel Kant made human reason (Vernunft) the central authority in knowing natural laws and human morality. The philosophical currents of the "Storm and Stress" movement (Sturm und Drang, until the late 1780s) emphasised emotions over reason and empirical knowledge.

[18] Jürgen Gröschl: Directors of the Francke Foundations. In: Halle and the Beginning of Protestant Christianity in India. Vol. III: Communication between India and Europe. Ed. by Andreas Gross et al. Halle (Saale) 2006, 1551–1556.

[19] Jürgen Gröschl: Lutheran Chaplains in London. In: Halle and the Beginning of Protestant Christianity in India. Vol. III: Communication between India and Europe. Ed. by Andreas Gross et al. Halle (Saale) 2006 1557–1559. Daniel O'Connor: Secretaries of the Society for Promoting Christian Knowledge (SPCK) [...]. In: Halle and the Beginning of Protestant Christianity in India. Vol. III: Communication between India and Europe. Ed. by Andreas Gross et al. Halle (Saale) 2006, 1561–1564.

their salary from the Company for more than sixteen months.[20] Governor Macartney refused to pay the soldiers their allowance known as *batta*; the disheartened soldiers rebelled violently. Many of them joined Hyder's army. Schwartz fed some of the starving Company soldiers. He narrated how a civil officer in Madras resisted Maccartney. In the ensuing battle, another Company officer shot that civil officer dead. Macartney's assistant, the third-ranking member of the Company's Council in Madras, disagreed with Macartney and accused him of being a liar. Macartney challenged him to a duel but was wounded by a bullet wound under his chest. His assistant left the Council. After narrating these things, Schwartz asked Pasche:

> How do you feel when you hear these things? My heart and hands tremble. We are waiting for better regulations. Until now, we have heard nothing about them. I have written these things with great sorrow and fear in my heart. You know how to utilise this information. At least I have written it with that intention.[21]

There is clear evidence of the impact that Schwartz's reports had on the Company's Court of Directors in London. For example, as already stated in Section 5.11, on 8 April 1789, they informed the Governor and Council in Madras about the "alarming representations from Rev Mr Swartz," demonstrating the significant influence of his work[22] on the deplorable condition of the Kingdom of Tanjore. Consequently, the Court of Directors required Ameer Singh to practice justice for all inhabitants.[23]

Due to the challenges of shaking hands, poor eyesight, and rapidly changing political situations, Schwartz wrote concise letters and reports. In one instance, after reviewing Schwartz's letter, a biographer informed Uebele on 4 February 1794, "The brevity with which he dispatches his answers excites a natural regret that one who had seen and been an actor in so many exciting events had not committed more to writing." Immediately, the biographer added where Schwartz's importance lay: "But the Mission was all in all to him; and the important part he

---

20 AFSt/M 1 B 75 : 29: On 12.10.1784, Pohle had a bitter colonial critique. He requested the editors of the *New Halle Reports* (NHR) not to print these details: Pohle was happy to have peace after several years of war. Unlike the European practice of giving thanks to God for victorious wars, the English in Madras forgot everything. All kinds of suffering, like famine, persisted. The hands of the blood-sucking leeches and tyrants were not bound. They freely exploited the poor people. There was no shortage of money for the Company in Madras. They dismissed sepoys who had not received their salary for twenty-two months. The army officers were paid poorly. Hence, several internal rebellions occurred. The Company in Madras tried harsh methods to silence those who demanded just payments, but the European soldiers did not like the harsh treatment. They usually locked the rebelling sepoys to the poles in rooms. If they paid their rightly earned wages, they paid them in Fano, which the sepoys had to convert into Pagodas. Due to conversion rates and commissions, the sepoys incurred a considerable financial loss. People used Kas, but its value changes every month. As a result, people suffered greatly.

21 AFSt/M 1 B 75 : 24 quoted in Germann: Missionar Christian Friedrich Schwartz, 320–321.

22 IOR/E/A/875, 361.

23 IOR/E/A/875, 699–715.

occasionally took in public transactions, which he submitted to rather than sought, was only for the sake of promoting the work that lay so near his heart."[24]

Besides these official and semi-official writings, Schwartz kept his relatives and friends in Germany and England informed about his ministry and its challenges regarding the moral integrity of the Company officers and soldiers in Madras, Tiruccirāppaḷḷi and Tanjore, his travel experiences, the growth of Tamil Lutheran congregations and the need for more European missionaries and Tamil co-workers. He corresponded with his former roommate Johann Friedrich Backe (1730–1805), his friend Johann Friedrich Sorge (1727–1788) and others. He regularly wrote to his family members, especially his half-brother Carl Ludwig Schwartz (1743–1811). In 1758, Carl studied at one of the schools affiliated with the Glaucha Institutions in Halle. Later, he became a Lutheran pastor. Likewise, Schwartz corresponded with the children of Colonel John Wood, who had entrusted his estate to him and requested him to mentor his children after his death.

6.3.2 Extracts of Schwartz's Texts in German (a selection)

The journal *Halle Reports* (1710–1772) was a pioneering Lutheran Pietist missionary magazine, published and distributed by the Glaucha Institutions across major European cities. These reports include excerpts from letters, reports, and treatises written by missionaries in southern India. Until the middle of the eighteenth century, missionaries described how they learned the Tamil or Telugu languages, religions, and cultures, how they and their Indian adherents established worshiping congregations, how they overcame obstacles, and what European readers should know about various groups of people in India. Thus, these reports remain a primary, unparalleled source for scholars who wish to examine the significant languages, cultures, religions, and histories of Christians about their dominant non-Christian neighbours.

By the mid-eighteenth century, German intellectuals and the readers of the *Halle Reports* faced a changed mood. They preferred reports about the natural world of Indians to their religious conversions. As mentioned above, Georg Christian Knapp (1753–1825), the new director of the Glaucha Institutions, understood the changed mood of Europeans and introduced the *New Halle Reports*,[25] which retained some aspects of the *Halle Reports*. The *New Halle Reports* did not focus on conversions, baptisms, or church growth but on Tamil culture, history, educational systems, and other branches of knowledge.

Wilhelm Germann, a renowned German biographer of Schwartz, rightly noted that the editors of the *Halle Reports* and the *New Halle Reports* received letters

---

24 Memoirs of the Rev. Joseph D[aniel] Jænicke, 115.

25 New Halle Reports: Neuere Geschichte der evangelischen Missionsanstalten zu Bekehrung der Heiden in Ost-Indien aus den eigenhändigen Aufsätzen und Briefen der Missionarien ('Recent History of the evangelical missionary institutions for the conversion of Gentiles in East India from the missionaries' own essays and letters'). Vols. I–VIII. Halle: Waisenhaus, 1776–1847.

and reports from missionaries and preserved them in the archives. They consciously chose to publish only their relevant extracts, which would inform their readers about the missionaries' lives, works and achievements that were theologically and politically non-contentious. Honouring the ethical codes of conduct about the privacy of the missionaries, the editors did not print those matters that were confidential, private, or personal.[26] As the author of this biography, I can attest that the contents of the *Halle Reports* and the *New Halle Reports* remain trustworthy and authentic. However, researchers who wish to gain a fuller picture of what the missionaries wrote about themselves, their colleagues, personal and practical challenges, their work and achievements must study the entire manuscripts and determine what the *Halle Reports* and the *New Halle Reports* included and what they excluded.

This principle of critically engaging with the entire manuscripts and their published excerpts applies to this biography. Instead of relying on published materials, which all existing biographies, except Wilhelm Germann's, have followed, this biography rests on Schwartz's manuscripts. It is true that the *Halle Reports* and the *New Halle Reports* either quoted or faithfully paraphrased his manuscripts. Nevertheless, his manuscripts contain more relevant details for this biography. Occasionally, he requested that the editors of the *Halle Reports* and the *New Halle Reports* refrain from publishing certain sensitive materials, for which his European readers were not yet prepared. For instance, he asked the editor not to publish anything about William Chambers, Mrs. Wood, and a man named Scott in Tiruccirāppaḷḷi.[27] These individuals were associated with the Company but became Schwartz's spiritual followers. Schwartz, aware of the potential repercussions, requested that the editors respect his wishes, and they did so, demonstrating their consideration of Schwartz's concerns and their thoughtful editorial decisions.

Additionally, Schwartz requested that Pasche in London not publish Wallajah's repeated refusal from 1773 to 1775 to permit Schwartz to construct a new church building in Tanjore. Schwartz travelled twice from Tanjore to Madras to meet Wallajah, but Wallajah refused to allow him to erect a church building. Schwartz informed Pasche on February 20, 1775, about this refusal and requested that he keep this matter confidential. The editors of the *New Halle Reports*, exercising discretion, chose not to publish this information, thereby maintaining the sense of security and trust their readers had in them.[28]

Similarly, details on the behaviours of the Company officers remained secret. On 11 September 1783, Schwartz described to Pasche in London the immoral and

---

26 Germann: Missionar Christian Friedrich Schwartz, 392.

27 Germann: Missionar Christian Friedrich Schwartz, 203.

28 Germann: Missionar Christian Friedrich Schwartz, 204–205 and 234: For example, on 17.09.1773, Wallajah and the Company captured Tanjore. Wallajah's son Umdat ul-Umra (1748–1801) began ruling Tanjore from Nagore, known as *Nagore Āndavar Dharga*. Schwartz met him in Nagore and asked for permission to build a church. He already knew Ul-Umra's opposition to Christian centres of worship because he had already burnt the hut in Uraiyur, which Schwartz had set up for prayer and where his catechists stayed. Ul-Umra also disliked the Christian schools in Tiruccirāppaḷḷi.

unethical behaviour of the Company officers in Madras and Tanjore. He stated how their misbehaviour and maladministration caused famine in Tanjore and impoverished the Company. As a Pietist missionary, he noted that the English in India, who did not fear God, committed more evil acts. He felt comforted that a few people took their Christian faith seriously amidst the raging misery. He believed God was patient with the Company in India. He wondered what God would do to enable the people to embrace the Lordship of Jesus Christ in their life and work. He prayed that the Company would send spiritual teachers to India soon. Otherwise, the Company could reckon on its demise. Then, he requested Pasche to acquaint the Company leaders in London with the Company's situation in Madras and Tanjore and advise them to intervene.[29] The editors of the *New Halle Reports* did not print these details. Even Germann, who otherwise included verbatim quotes from Schwartz's writings, omitted parts of Schwartz's message.[30]

The *New Halle Report* did not publish Schwartz's disagreements with his missionary colleagues. For example, Christian Pohle did not wish to serve as a chaplain to the Company's soldiers in Tiruccirāppaḷḷi. Pohle shockingly failed to respect the Tamil people[31] and he neglected the Tamil Lutheran congregation and school there. His limited English and Tamil knowledge hindered his communication. Often, he treated the Tamil Lutheran catechists harshly, and they complained about this mistreatment to Schwartz. Once, to establish discipline and peace among the Tamil Lutheran catechists, he raised his stick to beat Catechist Jōtināyakkaṉ, who then fled to Schwartz in Tanjore.[32]

On 27 September 1779, Pohle reported that Catechist Ñāṉapirakācam and teacher Sāntappaṉ fought among themselves so severely that Sāntappaṉ was sentenced to one hundred lashes, while Ñāṉapirakācam and each of those who assisted them received eighty lashes. Wilhelm Germann stated that on hearing this news, mission friends in Tranquebar, Halle (Saale), and Wernigerode were horrified and deleted these details from Pohle's diary. Germann explained further that Schwartz personally went to Tiruccirāppaḷḷi and reconciled them.[33]

Published records do not contain details about the failures of Fabricius in Madras, Hüttemann in Cuddalore and Johann Zacharias Kiernander (1711–1799) in Calcutta.[34] Despite various attempts, Schwartz was unable to resolve the

---

29 AFSt/M 1 B 74 : 33.
30 Germann: Missionar Christian Friedrich Schwartz, 319–320.
31 Germann: Missionar Christian Friedrich Schwartz, 336.
32 Germann: Missionar Christian Friedrich Schwartz, 260.
33 Germann: Missionar Christian Friedrich Schwartz, 260–262.
34 Kiernander was the first Swedish Lutheran Pietist missionary in Calcutta. He left Cuddalore and went to Calcutta in 1757, hoping his friend Robert Clive would support his missionary work. AFSt/M 1 B 47 : 7: The missionaries in Tranquebar reported the death of their colleague Poltzenhagen in the Nicobar Islands. They also stated that the English armies in Bengal had taken away Chandranagar and other factories; after a massacre, they humiliated the Nawab of Bengal and took his lands away from him. AFSt/M 1 B 47 : 33. On 12.07.1757, a German military officer who witnessed Clive's victory at Plassey provided a detailed report. Kiernander established a Portuguese-medium school, educating students from diverse social backgrounds. In January 1762, he reported that 109 students had found good jobs. After the death of his wealthy wife, Ann, in 1773, Kiernander sold her jewels and expanded the school

regrettable problems of Fabricius and Hüttemann. Likewise, he could not help Kiernander or his assistant, Johann Christmann Diemer, in Calcutta, to perform their missionary work faithfully. In February 1775, Diemer accused Kiernander of ruining the church and school as his private business, refused to collaborate with him, left the mission, married the daughter of the wealthy English businessman Charles Weston and lived with his in-laws. The tension between Diemer and Kiernander endangered the mission work. With the help of his friend William Chambers, Schwartz attempted in vain to reconcile the two.[35] Gradually, Kiernander's problems increased.[36] After the death of his son Robert in 1791, Kiernander left Calcutta and lived as a refugee in the Dutch settlement, Chinsura, near Calcutta. From 1795, he received an annual pension of £40 from the SPCK.[37]

The *New Halle Reports* were cautious about Schwartz's political engagements and did not publish all the details. At times, Schwartz explicitly requested that the editors not publish certain information. For example, on 14 March 1780, he informed Freylinghausen that he had forgotten to mention to Pasche the gift of Rupees 300/- from Hyder Ali towards his travel expenses. He confessed to

---

to accommodate two hundred children. Forty-nine Christians follow him. Two Roman Catholic priests who had embraced Lutheranism joined Kiernander. One was Bento de Souza; he was fluent in Portuguese, French, Bengali, and Hindustani. On 12 January 1769, Bento wrote a letter to G. A. Francke (AFSt/M 1 B 58 : 33), and Francke sent him a reply as well (AFSt/M 1 B 58:63). In 1770, Kiernander dedicated the House of Prayer (*Beth Tephillah*) for worship. This church is called the Red Church (*Lal Girija*) or the Old Mission Church.

35 Germann: Missionar Christian Friedrich Schwartz, 291–292: Germann found Becker's unpublished report of 13.10.1778. It painted a grim picture of Kiernander's failed business attempts. Becker claimed that Kiernander's wife, Ann, was not as wealthy as the mission friends in Halle (Saale) believed. He could barely survive. Upon his arrival in Calcutta, many officers entrusted their money to him as their proxy, expecting him to deposit it into bank accounts. He also charged them a 5% commission for this service. Thus, he earned 30,000 Rupees annually, equal to 20,000 Thaler. By October 1778, he had accumulated 600,000 Rupees and lived pompously for a monthly rent of 1,500–2,000 Rupees. His church building and mission house should have cost him 130,000 Rupees.

36 In 1783, Kiernander endowed his church, *Beth Tephillah* ('House of Prayer'), with a substantial amount of money. However, in 1788, he began to lose his wealth and tried to generate income to support his ministry. At that time, he met a military officer who had bought land and built many houses for sale and rent. Likewise, Kiernander borrowed money from creditors, purchased land and built luxurious dwellings. As he tried to sell them for a higher price, the Company lowered the cost of land and buildings. Kiernander lost all his investments, could not pay many of his creditors and was impoverished.

37 Kiernander's creditors wanted to turn his church, school and house into storehouses. Kiernander sold them to Charles Grant, William Chambers and David Brown to avoid this misfortune. All three of them were Schwartz's friends. Brown oversaw the English services, while Pastor Frenzel oversaw the Portuguese services. Gerlach administered the sacraments. After Grant left Calcutta in 1790, he became a member of the Court of Directors of the Company in London. Kiernander continued to stay connected with him. At Grant's request, Brown pastored *Beth Tephillah*. The SPCK continued to seek new missionaries for Calcutta and sent Holzberg and Ringeltaube to the city in July 1796. Kiernander was active till the end of his life. Around June 1799, Kiernander fell, broke his leg and succumbed to the injury. The mission work did not end with him. After the arrival of William Carey in Calcutta in 1793 and his settlement in Serampore in 1800 under the administration of Schwartz's friends, such as Governor Ole Bie, a new chapter in the history of the Protestant mission began in Calcutta.

Freylinghausen how Hyder Ali appreciated Schwartz's Persian knowledge and his journey to establish peace between him and the Company. He was happy that Schwartz, a priest by vocation, undertook this political task. Nevertheless, Schwartz was unsure how the readers of the *New Halle Reports* in Europe would view his political involvements. After reporting these things, Schwartz added this note to Freylinghausen: "I request you to keep this paragraph secret."[38]

The *New Halle Reports* did not report Schwartz's bitter critique of the European Enlightenment and its perception of the Bible and Christianity. On 9 October 1780, he responded to a letter from his friend Johann Friedrich Sorge, who described the adverse effect of the European Enlightenment on Pietistic Christianity in Germany. Schwartz expressed his deep aversion towards the prevailing European Enlightenment ethos that rejected the Lordship of Jesus Christ and made fun of Christ's sin-atoning death. Schwartz wondered how these "satanic blasphemies" could exist in Germany, the land of Luther's Reformation. He believed that those Europeans who were under the sway of the Enlightenment had become "worse heathens" than the non-Christians of Southern India. He urged Sorge to remain watchful, pray faithfully, uphold God's righteousness, and value and cherish the treasures of the Gospel of the Lord Jesus Christ (e.g. forgiveness of sins, a meaningful life here and now, and eternal life after death).[39]

The editors of the *Halle Reports* and the *New Halle Reports* did not publish everything Schwartz wrote, and Schwartz did not intend to have all his writings published. By publishing accurate and reliable details, the editors respected Schwartz's ethical standards, integrity and accountability. They drew on the most significant aspects of his writings to inform their more comprehensive portrayal of missionary activities by diverse German Lutheran Pietists and Tamil Lutherans in southern India. Additionally, the editors did not wish to embarrass their European readers, most of whom were supporters of the missionaries in India, with unedifying stories and their complex contexts. Without knowing the entire context of these troubles, they would be confused. Therefore, whatever the editors published was authentic and trustworthy. Comparing these published materials with the unpublished parts of the manuscripts in archives yields a fuller picture of the events. Much of this current biography rests on previously unknown or lesser-known insights gleaned from unpublished archival materials in Germany, the United Kingdom, Denmark, and India.

6.3.3 Extracts of Schwartz's Texts in English (a selection)

This biography delves into documents related to Schwartz and their association with his adopted son and successor, Johann Caspar Kohlhoff, in Tanjore and their associates. Two notable men, Chaplain Claudius Buchanan of Calcutta and Bishop

---

38 AFSt/M 1 B 70 : 45.

39 AFSt/M 1 B 71 : 30. Its extract, found in NHR 3, 1783, issue 55, 152–157, does not contain these details. Germann: Missionar Christian Friedrich Schwartz, 283. Germann, too, did not quote Schwartz's full letter.

George Spencer of Madras, requested copies of these documents from Kohlhoff. On 7 February 1810, Buchannan received Kohlhoff's assurance that he would send the copies, but for some unknown reason, Kohlhoff was unable to do so. Nevertheless, Buchanan obtained the transcripts of Schwartz's four sermons from another unnamed source and forwarded them to Hugh Pearson.[40] Bishop George Spencer later requested John Schwartz Adolphus Arthur Kohlhoff, the son of J. C. Kohlhoff, to compile all documents concerning his father's relationship with Schwartz. Spencer successfully received these copies, although he did not personally write anything about Schwartz. Eventually, these copies were archived at the Bodleian Library in Oxford, England. Nowadays, their digital versions are available via the British Online Archives. This biography of Schwartz has benefited significantly from two boxes of materials. Box 1 consists of Schwartz's notes about the lectures he attended at the University of Halle in 1749. He preserved and consulted these notes on biblical studies, systematic theology, moral theology, and the like throughout his missionary career among the Tamils.[41] Box 2 presents a more comprehensive and fresh perspective on Schwartz's travels, interactions with schoolchildren, church members, coworkers, and ambassadorial functions, as well as visits to various places and institutions.[42] The remaining archival documents in seven boxes entitled *India General Papers* contain copies of manuscripts covering the development of Protestant Christianity in the Tanjore and Tirunelveli regions up to 1842.[43]

In 1814, the SPCK published *An Abstract of the Annual Reports and Correspondence*, which included extracts of Schwartz's letters, diaries and reports from his joining them in 1762 to his death in 1798. It describes how King Tulāji and his court officers invited Schwartz, listened to his exposition of Christian teachings, and requested him to live in Tanjore as a mediator between the king and the Company. It narrates Schwartz's perspectives about Wallajah and his attempts to build places of worship and education. It includes laudatory comments about Schwartz and his character by various Company officers who had returned to England. Reviewing these reports can provide a reasonably accurate picture of Schwartz, which the SPCK believed would appeal to their readers.

In 1847, William Taylor, who had written about the history of the Vepery Mission, briefly discussed Schwartz's association with Fabricius, Breithaupt, and Gericke, who lived in Vepery and were involved in caring for the mission. In an envelope given to him by Jänicke, Taylor unexpectedly found eleven letters addressed to Governor Charles Oakley, Colonel Martinz, and the schoolteacher William Wheatley in Ramanathapuram, all written by Schwartz.[44]

---

40 Pearson: Memoirs, Vols. 2, 40–79.

41 Bodleian Library: 72290ind-box1.

42 Bodleian Library: 72290ind-box2.

43 These documents include copies of baptism and marriage registers, deliberations about caste within Christian congregations, and visits by missionaries such as Gericke, Jänicke, SPG, and CMS, as they took over Tamil Lutheran congregations. These documents, now available at British Online Archives (https://britishonlinearchives.com/, accessed on 27.01.2025), await further research.

Besides the English biographies of Schwartz (Section 6.4.2), historians of missions seldom took note of Schwartz. In 1908, Julius Richter (1862–1940) pointed out Schwartz's "unassuming and simple faithfulness, the frank straightforwardness of his relations with both the great and the humble." These characteristics were not just personal traits but instrumental in enabling him to enjoy "the general confidence of the community as perhaps no other missionary in India has ever done."[45]

Seventy-nine years later, in 1981, Don Wright published two essays on Schwartz's political involvements. His first essay, *Swartz of Thanjavur: Raja Guru?*, does not consider Schwartz's biographies written "for hagiographic and didactic purposes."[46] It narrates how Schwartz continued the missionary practices of his predecessors in Tranquebar, Tanjore, and Madras, and highlights his simple and effective communication skills, employing a "conciliatory tone."[47] It states that Schwartz presented "Christianity in its loveliness" and invited the listeners to "attention and reflection." Although he critiqued non-Christian Tamils' religious beliefs and practices, he was "more attuned than most to the sensitivities of his hearers."[48] It mentions that Schwartz often explained the parable of the Prodigal Son to non-Christians, stressing the "sinfulness of man and the saviorhood of Christ."[49] It states that Schwartz did not neglect his missionary duties even though he participated in politics.[50]

Don Wright's second essay, *Swartz of Thanjavur: A Missionary in Politics*, examines Schwartz's political involvement's fundamental purposes and methods.[51] Contrary to the assumed knowledge that Schwartz undertook his political work unwillingly, this essay argues for his conscious, determined participation in politics. Schwartz's interactions with the Company did not align with their colonial objectives. For instance, he accompanied the Company army to Madurai (1763–64) not to further their conquest but to assist the wounded and secure supplies from the Tamil people for the Company army.[52] Secondly, Schwartz met Hyder Ali as an ambassador of the Company because Governor Rumbold had promised him brick and lime for his church in Tanjore.[53] Thirdly, Schwartz also preferred the Company government to that of Tulāji or Hyder Ali. Therefore, Schwartz assisted the Company soldiers in Tanjore with a regular food supply. When Tulāji could not pay the Company soldiers in Tanjore, Schwartz loaned him the money

44 Taylor: A Memoir of the First Centenary of the Earliest Protestant Mission at Madras, viii–xvii.

45 Richter: A History of Missions in India, 116–117.

46 Don Wright: Swartz of Thanjavur: Raja Guru? In: Indian Church History Review 15, 1981, issue 2, 123–144, here 126.

47 Wright: Swartz of Thanjavur: Raja Guru?, 129.

48 Wright: Swartz of Thanjavur: Raja Guru?, 129–130.

49 Wright: Swartz of Thanjavur: Raja Guru?, 134.

50 Wright: Swartz of Thanjavur: Raja Guru?, 125–126.

51 Don Wright: Swartz of Thanjavur: A missionary in politics. In: Journal of South Asian Studies 1981, 94–105.

52 Wright: Swartz of Thanjavur: A missionary in politics, 95.

53 Wright: Swartz of Thanjavur: A missionary in politics, 96.

on the guarantee of John Sulivan, the Company's resident in Tanjore.[54] Fourthly, Sulivan needed Schwartz's help in persuading the rulers of Ramanathapuram to establish English-medium schools for two reasons: These schools would train Tamil elites for better communication with the Company, and they would minimise Tamil prejudice against Christianity. Finally, Schwartz's participation in the Committee of Inspection of Tanjore, his dealings with Ameer Singh as a successor to Tulāji, his training of Serfoji II for enthronement, his role as the Company Resident of Tanjore for two years and his favourable correspondence with the Company governors in Madras show his cheerful disposition towards the increasing power of the Company.[55] Wright concluded that Schwartz undoubtedly "connived at the expansion of Company power because he believed that British rule would provide better conditions for the mission's work than were otherwise possible."[56] While Wallajah and Tulāji did not help Schwartz to establish churches, British officers in Tiruccirāppaḷḷi, Tanjore, and Vallam assisted him. Schwartz could realise his primary purpose of being a missionary to the Tamils.

In 1985, the second volume of the *History of Christianity in India (1707–1858)* by Stephen Neill (1900–1984)[57] appeared. It confesses that Neill could not identify the reasons for Schwartz's "extraordinary esteem in which he was held by Indians and Europeans alike." His letters and sermons demonstrated conventional pietist theology. Neill assumed that people appreciated Schwartz's "beauty of holiness." The "superlative purity and integrity of his life" impressed people, and Schwartz "left an impression of perfect and transparent sincerity on all." They could see how he overcame his "inner conflicts and temptations" and managed "painful experiences" with different people. His life radiated "an atmosphere of quiet tranquillity," and his "joyful and confident faith" attracted people to him.[58]

In 1992, Justus highlighted Schwartz's political engagement and mediatory services.[59] He correctly affirmed that during Schwartz's time, the Company controlled more territories on the Coromandel Coast than ever before. Nevertheless, he incorrectly claimed that Schwartz was "an imperialist" who "ably assisted the English."[60]

---

54 Wright: Swartz of Thanjavur: A missionary in politics, 96.

55 Wright: Swartz of Thanjavur: A missionary in politics, 98–100.

56 Wright: Swartz of Thanjavur: A missionary in politics, 102.

57 Neill worked as a lay missionary among the Tamil people of Tirunelvēli (1925–1944) and then became their bishop. He acquired a profound understanding of the history of Christianity in Southern India. For additional information on Neill, see Stephen Neill: God's Apprentice: The Autobiography of Bishop Stephen Neill. Ed. by Eleanor M Jackson. London 1991, and Dyron B. Daughrity: A Worldly Christian: The Life and Times of Stephen Neill. Cambridge 2021.

58 Stephen Neill: A History of Christianity in India (1707–1858). Vol. 2. Cambridge 1985, here 45–56.

59 M. Justus: Schwartz: A Missionary in Politics 1750–1798. In: Indian Church History Review 27, 1992, issue 1, 36–49.

60 Justus: Schwartz: A Missionary in Politics 1750–1798, 49. British imperialism began after Queen Victoria was declared Empress of India in 1858. The Company records written during Schwartz's lifetime, which I consulted, do not use the term "colonialism." Their preferred terms were "Government" for the Company Councils in Madras and Bombay, and "Supreme Government" for the Company Council in Calcutta.

In 1998, the author of this present work organised a conference on Schwartz's ministry among the Tamil people and published twenty edited essays.[61] These essays reflect on various Indian perceptions of Schwartz and his ministry. The essayists derived their insights from secondary materials in English that were available to them at the time. These included *Memoirs on Swartz* by Hugh Pearson[62] and G. H. Lamb,[63] a biography of Schwartz by Jesse Page,[64] and shorter descriptions of Schwartz in other English sources. Tamil essays in this book describe two of Schwartz's students, namely Poet Vēdanāyagam Sāstiriyār and Prince Serfoji II, and they compare Schwartz's theological teachings with the basic principles of the Tamil bhakti religions, such as Śaivism and Vaiṣṇavism.

In 1999, Professor Robert Eric Frykenberg summarised Schwartz's life and ministry among the Tamil people.[65] He praised his knowledge of classical languages (Hebrew, Greek, and Latin), European languages (German, Portuguese, and English), and Indian languages such as Tamil, Marathi, Modi, Hindustani, and Persian.[66] Frykenberg's essay acknowledges Schwartz's contribution to English-medium Provincial Schools, which the rulers of Tanjore and Ramanathapuram, as well as the Company, supported and subsidised. Students in these schools learned "biblical and Christian texts, as well as the principles and sciences of the Enlightenment, including English literature and European philosophy."[67] Later, young Brahmin men trained at these schools would occupy the highest civil ranks of the Company. Frykenberg's essay points out Schwartz's role in laying the "foundations for what was to become the largest and strongest evangelical Christian community in India,"[68] namely the Nadar Christians in Tirunelveli and Kanyakumari. It also highlights Schwartz's character in glowing terms: "In a world awash in corruption and injustice, both European and Indian, the personal integrity of Schwartz was never questioned. To the very last, he showed indifference to personal power or wealth."[69] As a result, young missionaries should emulate "that worthy man and labourer in Jesus Christ who established such a reputation of candour, integrity and disinterestedness among both natives and Europeans, as cannot fail to recommend the cause of Christianity to men of every description who have ever heard his name."[70] This essay ends with a lament that soon after his death, Schwartz's legacy faded away from the memories of Christians in India and Europe.

---

61 Christian Frederick Schwartz: His Contributions to South India. Ed. by Daniel Jeyaraj. Madras 1999.
62 Pearson: Memoirs, Vols. 1 and 2.
63 G. H. Lamb: Memoir of Christian Friedrick Schwartz. Madras 1948.
64 Jesse Page: Schwartz of Tanjore.
65 Robert Eric Frykenberg: Legacy of Christian Friedrich Schwartz. In: International Bulletin of Missionary Research 23, 1999, issue 3, 130–135.
66 Frykenberg: Legacy of Christian Friedrich Schwartz, 131.
67 Frykenberg: Legacy of Christian Friedrich Schwartz, 132.
68 Frykenberg: Legacy of Christian Friedrich Schwartz, 132.
69 Frykenberg: Legacy of Christian Friedrich Schwartz, 133.
70 Frykenberg: Legacy of Christian Friedrich Schwartz, 133.

In 2008, Professor Frykenberg expanded his essay to a chapter entitled *The Raja-Guru and Sishiyas of Thanjavur: Christian Friedrich Schwartz and his Disciples*.[71] This chapter examines how Schwartz combined his German Enlightenment learning with the ideals of Lutheran Pietism and helped his Tamil followers advance in life. Again, Frykenberg highlights Schwartz's linguistic proficiency, which made him a much-desired interpreter,[72] a successful chaplain for Company soldiers,[73] an exemplary diplomat,[74] an efficient secretary of State for Tanjore,[75] a celebrated Raja Guru,[76] and a teacher for influential Tamil leaders.[77] All these English essays and book chapters kept Schwartz's memory alive among English readers worldwide.

6.3.4 Schwartz's English Sermons

English was Schwartz's sixth language. By the time he could speak and write, he was proficient in five languages: German, Hebrew, Greek, Latin, and Tamil. His language skills reveal his insatiable thirst for knowledge and his longing for more effective communication of the Gospel of the Lord Jesus Christ to others. He began to grasp English during his time in England in 1749. Still, it was in Tranquebar, Tirucciräppaḷḷi, and Tanjore that he refined it through his daily interactions with English-speaking Europeans and Indians. In 1847, William Taylor, who had published a few of Schwartz's letters, commented on Schwartz's English proficiency:

> I had observed in Swartz's life that his letters appeared in [the] polished language and not like the idiom of a foreigner. Upon the whole I have thought it my duty not to polish these very familiar letters of his; but to give them *verbatim*: whence it will appear that, though he wrote very good English, there was still a something foreign about it, and pertaining to the German idiom. But the simplicity, piety, and good sense, of the writer are exceedingly conspicuous.[78]

This biography, however, contains verbatim quotes of relevant phrases and sections from Schwartz's English letters and reports. They still communicate Schwartz's intended messages. Whenever and whatever he wrote to his close relatives, friends, students, and others who had trusted him, for example, as the

---

71 Robert Eric Frykenberg: Christianity in India—From Beginnings to the Present. New York 2008, here 152–165.

72 Frykenberg: Christianity in India, 152.

73 Frykenberg: Christianity in India, 154–155.

74 Frykenberg: Christianity in India, 155–156.

75 Frykenberg: Christianity in India, 156–157.

76 Frykenberg: Christianity in India, 157–158.

77 Frykenberg: Christianity in India, 159–165: These leaders included Serfoji, Vēdanāyagam Sāstiriyār, Clarinda, Satyanātan Pillay, Chinnamuthu Sundarānantham David, Mahārasan Vēdamānickam of Mayilādi in Travancore (modern Kanyakumari).

78 Taylor: A Memoir of the First Centenary of the Earliest Protestant Mission at Madras, x of the appendix.

executor of their will or requested him to guide their children to navigate in life, he, without fail, pointed out the preeminent position of the Lord Jesus Christ as the only One who could forgive human sin and grant eternal life in God's presence. He pleaded with them to read their Bibles regularly and to reflect the characteristics of the Lord Jesus Christ in their speech and daily lives.

It seems that Schwartz preached extempore. His sermon notes have not survived. Nevertheless, Hugh Pearson obtained a copy of Schwartz's four English sermons from Claudius Buchanan, which he gave to an English audience in Tiruccirāppaḷḷi or Tanjore.[79] One of these four sermons, partly quoted by Pearson,[80] is available as a manuscript in Schwartz's handwriting.[81] It interprets Jesus's parable about the Great Banquet through the lens of German Lutheran Pietist theology, a perspective that emphasizes personal piety and practical service. This interpretation reflects not only on the poor, whom the Glaucha Institutions cared for and educated, but also Schwartz's ministry among the poor and social outcasts in Tiruccirāppaḷḷi and Tanjore. It highlights God's grace, which is prepared and offered to humankind, despite prevailing human indifference to it and the consequences of their negligence. For Schwartz, the Lord Jesus embodied God's grace and offered forgiveness of sins to humankind. The Lord's Supper, instituted and commanded by the Lord Jesus Christ, serves as the sacramental medium through which a repentant sinner can receive God's grace. Those who had received this eternal blessedness should lead a life of self-sacrifice and serve the poor and needy among them. As evident in his life and sermons, Schwartz's piety was a guiding light for those seeking a deeper spiritual connection.

> He [the Lord Jesus Christ] is my greatest gain. If I have Him, I have every thing: pardon, peace, joy, reconciliation with God, eternal life. Happy was Paul in his choice, and happy shall we be if we follow him. May the Spirit of Jesus incline our hearts to consider the things which belong to our peace. Amen.[82]

Like the sermons of the German Lutheran Pietists, Schwartz's sermons were rooted in biblical texts. He interpreted these texts as Christ-centred and applied their vital lessons to increase the hearers' personal piety and practical service to the poor and needy. With their timeless message, Schwartz's sermons still have the power to warm the readers' hearts and encourage them to cultivate personal piety, matched with tangible service, to make the world around them a better place for all. His sermons uphold his virtues of peace, justice and social harmony, leaving a lasting impact on those who read them.

---

79 Pearson: Memoirs, Vol. 2, 40–79.

80 Pearson: Memoirs, Vol. 2, 58–67.

81 Bodleian Library: 72290ind-box2, Document 1 without a date: Schwartz's sermon on Luke 14:16–24, i.e. Jesus's parable of a Great Banquet. An accompanying note on the front page of the sermon reads: "The accompanying manuscript is in the handwriting of our beloved Father Swartz and was in the possession of the Rev. John Caspar Kohlhoff, his adopted son, for many years. It then belonged to the Rev. C. S. Kohlhoff, who gave it to his son-in-law, the late Rev. John Hamshaw."

82 Pearson: Memoirs, Vol. 2, 67.

6.4 Biographies of Schwartz

6.4.1 Biographies of Schwartz: Failed Attempts

Johann Christian Christoph Uebele, the German Lutheran Pietist pastor at St. James's Palace in London and a member of the SPCK, was aware of Schwartz's popularity among the British who had returned from India. The SPCK, a key player in the spread of Christianity, held Schwartz in high regard and trusted his words. Therefore, on 22 October 1797, when he was still alive, Uebele suggested that Johann Ludwig Schulze (1734–1799), the director of the Glaucha Institutions, should publish a biography of Schwartz. A year later, Uebele could not understand why Schwartz's biography was still unavailable. The missionaries in southern India and the officers at the Glaucha Institution had been unable to gather the required information about Schwartz's life and work. Tragically, Schwartz passed away. On 1 April 1799, Uebele conveyed the news of Schwartz's death to the SPCK leaders. The presiding bishop authorised the SPCK to arrange a memorial for this "invaluable man" in Madras. Simultaneously, John Owen (1766–1822), a former chaplain in Calcutta, prepared a Latin text for the memorial.[83] The initial enthusiasm of the SPCK did not yield any tangible results.

Consequently, based on Schwartz's autobiography of December 1749, Georg Christian Knapp (1753–1825), the new director of the Glaucha Institutions, published a short biography of Schwartz.[84] This autobiography, a first-hand account of Schwartz's life and experiences, provided valuable insights.[85] Excerpts of letters and diaries published in the *Halle Reports* and the *New Halle Reports* provided other vital information. Knapp's version of Schwartz's biography summarises Schwartz's life in his parental home and at schools, his travels from Halle to Tranquebar via London and Cuddalore, his chaplaincy, and his work in Tanjore. It underlines how Schwartz used his annual salary of £100, paid by the Company, for mission purposes, supporting Johann Caspar Kohlhoff and Tamil catechists. It praises Schwartz for his joyful and sacrificial services to the Tamil people and his respect among Indians and Europeans. It discusses how his missionary colleagues esteemed him as their father, advisor and pioneer. It narrates how his cheerful attitude and nature impressed people around him. It states that in November 1797, three months before his death, Schwartz contracted a cold, and his health deteriorated rapidly.

At this point, Knapp added Gericke's report on Schwartz's last days.[86] On 7 February 1798, Gericke and Gottfried Immanuel Holzberg arrived in Tanjore, where they were concerned about Schwartz's impending death. Medical treatments did not help him. He faced the end of his life fearlessly; despite his weakness, he

---

[83] AFSt/M 1 C 40a : 28 quoted in NHR 5, 1799, issue 55, 658–662; Germann: Missionar Christian Friedrich Schwartz, 385.

[84] NHR 5, 1799, issue 55, 637–640.

[85] AFSt/M 1 K 10 : 71.

[86] NHR 5, 1799, issue 55, 640–645.

sang songs, maintained peace, advised his disciples, and died on the morning of February 13, 1798. He was buried the following day. After comforting Tulāji's widows and Serfoji, Gericke reviewed Schwartz's papers, located his last will, and executed it. He was surprised to find that Schwartz had left his inheritance to bless the missionary institutions in Tanjore. He admired Schwartz's honesty and wished it would enliven all missionaries in India to extend Christ's reign there. Immediately, he expressed his desire for a biography of Schwartz:

> I think it my duty to write the life of our late worthy friend, Mr. Swartz, though he was against it and never would consent to commit to paper any particular passages in his life, which Dr John and I often begged him to do; but my time is too much taken up, both with the business I always had and with the care which I have, since Mr Swartz's death, of his congregations between Tanjore and Cape Comorin. I intend, however, to do it still if God spares my life. In the meantime, I have satisfied my German friends with a narrative of his last days and dying hours. I had only to write what I saw and heard, being then with him at Tanjore.[87]

Gericke did not fulfil his promise. His long travels to visit the Tamil Lutheran congregations, combined with his failing health, did not permit him any spare time.[88] Therefore, on 18 June 1799, Knapp requested that the missionaries in Tranquebar and Madras compose Schwartz's biography, but they, too, did not write one.[89] In his response to Knapp, dated April 12, 1800, Karl Wilhelm Päzold (1764–1817) asked Knapp to advise Kohlhoff and Jänicke, who had worked with the "admirable" Schwartz for a more extended period, to write Schwartz's biography. Päzold asserted that the fearless and morally upright Schwartz was extraordinary in understanding things quickly and correctly. He considered Schwartz the second Martin Luther because his fifty years of exemplary ministry were unprecedented. He served as a redeemer, a benefactor, a father, and a protector of many thousands of poor and needy people, both Christians and non-Christians. He ministered to them not only in peaceful times but also in times of bloody wars. His acquaintances honoured him. He used his salary for missionary purposes. He designated the interest of his investments to continue the missionary work in Tanjore.[90] The reports from Gericke and Päzold did not satisfy Knapp. On 4 January 1801, he urged Gericke[91] and Päzold[92] to send him a more comprehensive account of Schwarz's life. Before receiving Knapp's letter, Gericke responded on 28 February 1801 that he had been working on a biography on Schwartz.[93]

---

87 Pearson: Memoirs, Vol. 1, viii–ix.

88 AFSt/M 1 C 41 : 89 quoted in NHR 5, 1801, issue 57, 799: On 12.04.1800, Gericke informed Knapp that he, at the earlier request of Schwartz, visited the Tamil Lutheran congregations in Pāḷaiyamkōṭṭai, Madurai, Ramanathapuram, Tiruccirāppaḷḷi, and Tanjore at least once a year. These long journeys required time, resources, energy, and personnel, so he was unable to write the biography.

89 AFSt/M 1 C 40b : 61b: Knapp directed his request to Christian Wilhelm Gericke, Karl Wilhelm Päzold, Johann Caspar Kohlhoff, Christian Pohle, Joseph Daniel Jänicke and Immanuel Gottfried Holzberg.

90 AFSt/M 1 C 41 : 88 printed in NHR 5, 1801, issue 57, 800–801.

91 AFSt/M 1 C 42a : 54a.

92 AFSt/M 1 C 42a : 54b.

93 AFSt/M 1 C 42a : 22, not printed in NHR 5, 1802, issue 58, 913–914.

On 10 December 1801, Christian Pohle mentioned a new, accurate copper portrait of Schwartz, accompanied by an endorsement. The Company's commanding officer in Tirucciráppaḷḷi, a great friend of Schwartz, gave it to him. Pohle confessed that he had seen Schwartz's other portraits, but this copper portrait moved him emotionally so profoundly that he shed tears of joy.[94] His reference to other portraits of Schwartz could refer to the image printed on the title page of the third volume of the *New Halle Report* in 1790. Schultze, its editor, commented that someone in Germany made this portrait based on an accurate drawing that Schwartz had sent. Schultze was convinced that the friends of the mission would welcome the picture of a man who "had been living to glorify God and for the benefit of his fellow people."[95]. Additionally, Pohle may have been aware of Schwartz's portrait in the palace of Serfoji II. For example, on 29 January 1804, Serfoji showed Christoph Samuel John the portraits of Schwartz and Gericke, whom he addressed as "fathers."[96]

In the meantime, on 5 October 1801, Päzold informed Knapp that he had been working on Schwartz's biography. Five months later, on 27 March 1802, he sent him an unfinished biography. Knapp used it and other source materials to draft a biography on Schwartz. However, he was unable to complete the project due to a lack of sufficient materials. Although Christoph Samuel John did not send to Knapp what he had written about Schwartz, he indicated in 1804 that he, too, had worked on Schwartz's biography.[97] But he did not send Knapp what he had written. The missionaries disappointed Knapp in this matter, and he was unable to fulfil the mission friends' requests for a copy of Schwartz's biography. For example, on 27 November 1805, Johann Tobias Strubell requested Knapp to send him Schwartz's biography.[98]

In the meantime, Päzold had accepted a teaching position in the newly established college of Fort William in Calcutta. On 26 January 1806, he described why he could not write Schwartz's biography:

> It will not be easy to write a complete and comprehensive biography of the missionary Schwartz. He never maintained a diary with records of events in his personal life or public office. His fundamental dictum reads as follows: according to Luke 10:20 and Philippians 4:3, our names and deeds should be written in the book of life in heaven rather than in the books of humans on earth. The older missionaries in Tranquebar, who had known Schwartz for over twenty years, could write more about him and the specific characteristics that made him distinct. Particularly, Johann Caspar Kohlhoff, whom Schwartz raised and trained as a missionary, could describe the significant aspects of his beloved mentor. Schwartz resembled August Hermann Francke, the incomparable founder of the Orphanage in Halle. I did not dare to write the biography of a man whom I knew no longer than seven months. However, I could collect a few details and send them to Pastor Ubele; his role in translating these details into English is crucial to our understanding of Schwartz's life and work.[99]

---

94 NHR 5, 1804, issue 60, 1106.
95 NHR 3, Preface, xvii.
96 NHR 6, 1807, issue 63, 259. Available records do not contain the names of the artists who prepared these portraits.
97 AFSt/M 1 C 45 : 95.
98 AFSt/M 1 C 46 : 21.
99 AFSt/M 1 K 5 : 19a.

Päzold's reference to Johann Caspar Kohlhoff (1762–1844) merits attention. Johann Caspar was born in Tranquebar to Johann Balthasar Kohlhoff in Tranquebar (1736–1790).[100] When he was eight, Schwartz adopted him (1770), educated him first in Tiruccirāppaḷḷi and then in Tanjore, and appointed him his assistant. He ordained him as a missionary on January 23, 1787, and officially affiliated him with the Society for the Propagation of the Gospel in Foreign Parts (SPG). Johann Caspar was more at home with Tamil than with German. In 1806, Claudius Buchanan (1766–1815), the evangelical chaplain of the Company in Calcutta from 1797 to 1808, visited Tanjore. At that time, he requested Johann Caspar to write Schwartz's biography. He could not fulfil Buchanan's request because he was unable to read German manuscripts. However, he and his colleague Christoph Heinrich Horst (1761–1810)[101] consulted published materials and provided Buchanan with a summary of Schwartz's life from 1726 to 1758. On 4 January 1809, Buchanan expressed his renewed hope that Horst would write a fuller version of Schwartz's biography.[102] However, the Lutheran missionaries could not fulfil Buchanan's wish. At that point, all attempts to persuade the missionaries in India to write a biography of Schwartz failed. One should look to American and English authors for a fuller biography.

6.4.2 Schwartz's Biographies in English

The American Tract Society in New York published the first comprehensive biography of Schwartz.[103] This biography appears to have been published in 1800. It contains details found in the annual *Account of the Society for Promoting Christian Knowledge*. This seminal work offers a detailed account of Schwartz's life and work. Its first chapter chronicles Schwartz's life and work until his embassy to Hyder Ali and the construction of the Christ Church in Tanjore in

---

100 Johann Caspar's parents were Johann Balthasar Kohlhoff (1711–1790) and Pernille Kohlhoff (born Thors, 1727–1807). Johann Balthasar was first married to Margaretha Wilhelmina Wiger, who died on 18.11.1751. Then, on 21.7.1760, he married Pernille, who had arrived in Tranquebar a month earlier on 15.06.1760. He studied with Schwartz and Christian Pohle. Then, he received his ordination as a missionary. On 01.07.1811, Johann Caspar married Christina Magdelena Horst. Johann Caspar's other siblings, Elias Eobanus Kohlhoff, Daniel Friedrich Kohlhoff, Christian Daniel Kohlhoff and Dorothea Elisabeth Kohlhoff, went their own way.

101 Horst was a trained theologian, teacher, medical practitioner and soldier. After reaching Madras in May 1787, he worked there in various capacities. In 1792, he became a reader of the Mission Church in Cuddalore, where he also founded an English school. Then, he moved to Tranquebar in 1803 and was trained as a missionary until 1806. Christian Pohle ordained him on 30.11.1806 and appointed him an SPCK missionary in Tanjore.

102 72290ind-box3: Document 42: Buchanan's letter of 04.01.1809 from Bristol to missionaries Kohlhoff and Horst in Tanjore: "I have heard that Mr. Pazold was once thinking of writing a Life of Swartz. I dare say he will be willing to furnish you with whatever may be in his possession. If I hear that Dr. Rottler is in distress from the relinquishment of the Society [i.e., SPCK], I shall order him some pecuniary aid. He also may assist you in the design. Be pleased to inform me particularly of your circumstances."

103 The Life of C.F. Swartz—Missionary at Trichinopoly and Tanjore in India.

1799.[104] It emphasises his role as "the great and disinterested friend of his adopted country and mankind."[105] The second chapter presents a unique perspective on Schwartz's life from 1781 to 1790, focusing on key events such as the establishment of the Provincial English Schools, Johann Caspar Kohlhoff's ordination, and Schwartz's *Defence of Mission* (1795).[106] The third chapter covers Schwartz's life until his death on 13 February 1798, narrating the history of marble monuments by Serfoji and the Company. It concludes by noting the blessings bestowed upon those who "became acquainted with this venerable man."[107]

In 1826, an unnamed author published *The Remains of the Rev. C. F. Schwartz*.[108] This 316-page book consists of his letters and journals from 1768 to 1772. Its engagement with Schwartz's visit to Hyder Ali in 1779 is noteworthy. As it summarises published materials on Schwartz, it provides no new insight for this current biography. Another biography of Schwartz appeared in 1831 by E. W. Grinfield, who derived parts of his insights from his study of SPCK's archival materials.[109] He wove them into his book *Sketches of the Danish Mission on the Coast of Coromandel* and devoted fifty-seven pages to Schwartz.[110] He highlighted Schwartz's emotional struggles in becoming a missionary of the SPCK and enthusiastically narrated his visit to Hyder Ali in Seringapatam in 1779. In Hyder Ali's army, Schwartz was surprised and pained to meet "Englishmen, Germans, Portuguese," as well as some Tamil Lutherans whom he had taught in Tiruccirāppaḷḷi. He received permission to pitch a tent on the glacis of the Fort in Seringapatam and conducted worship services "without any impediment."[111] Grinfield stated further that most of the 120 members of the church in Pāḷaiyamkōṭṭai were merchants, artisans, farmers, and a few soldiers. They worked and earned their livelihood, and did not expect any charitable assistance from others. Denoting their economic well-being, they put tiles on the church roof. Their

104 The Life of C.F. Swartz—Missionary at Trichinopoly and Tanjore in India, 5–25.

105 The Life of C.F. Swartz—Missionary at Trichinopoly and Tanjore in India, 22.

106 The Life of C.F. Swartz—Missionary at Trichinopoly and Tanjore in India, 26–66.

107 The Life of C.F. Swartz—Missionary at Trichinopoly and Tanjore in India, 67–106.

108 Remains of the Rev. C.F. Schwartz, consisting of his Letters and Journals. London 1826.

109 E. W. Grinfield: Sketches of the Danish Mission on the Coast of Coromandel. London 1831, here 5: Grinfield's dedicatory remark to the SPCK reads as follows: "As whatever is curious or valuable in the following narrative is drawn from the manuscript records of the Society for Promoting Christian Knowledge, the Author deems it right to return his thanks to the Committee of that Society, for their liberal permission of access to its archives. Kensington, Nov. 25, 1830."

110 Grinfield: Sketches of the Danish Mission, 77–134.

111 Grinfield: Sketches of the Danish Mission, 112; Pearson: Memoirs, Vol. 1, 354 & 358. Pearson provides a different and fuller narrative of the same event: Schwartz pitched his tent in Seringapatam and kept it open for all soldiers, especially the Germans, French, and Tamil. Some Tamils were Christians whom Schwartz had educated in Tiruccirāppaḷḷi. Schwartz was sad to find those Tamil Christians there. When more soldiers joined, Captain Buden, the commander of the German troops, lent him his tent. Schwartz conducted Sunday worship services there. Though he did not ask for any permission, no one hindered them. The gathered worshippers sang and prayed aloud. They listened to Schwartz's sermons. Schwartz considered these happenings as God's.

leader was a Brahmin woman named Clarinda. Schwartz's Catechist, Sattiyanātaṉ, assisted her, and astonishingly, her schoolteacher paid Sattiyanātaṉ's salary. A Tamil Lutheran pastor visited them annually to administer the holy sacraments. Before the sermon, they used the Tamil version of the "English Liturgy."[112] Grinfield further observed how German rationalism and Enlightenment opposed the missionary interest of the Pietists in Germany.[113] Some Anglicans in England eventually came to realise their missionary consciousness. In 1813, their leaders introduced the Pious Clause into the Company's Charter Act. As a result, Thomas Fanshawe Middleton (1769–1822) became the first Anglican Bishop to Calcutta, and he was aware of the Anglican Church inheriting vital Lutheran congregations in India.

In 1833, John Carne published a short biography of Schwartz.[114] It coincided with the Company's renewal of its Charter with an enlarged version of the previous Pious Clause. This Clause allowed Protestant missionaries from Euro-American countries to work in the Company's territories. Carne described Schwartz's work in Tranquebar, Tiruccirāppaḷḷi, Tanjore, Madras and other places. Another vital work, *Memoirs of the Rev. Joseph D[aniel] Jænicke*, appeared in London in 1833.[115] It illustrates the close bond between Schwartz and his trainee missionaries, such as Joseph Daniel Jänicke and Johann Caspar Kohlhoff in Tanjore, Christian Pohle in Tiruccirāppaḷḷi, Christoph Samuel John and others in Tranquebar.

In 1834, Hugh Nicholas Pearson, the Dean of Salisbury Cathedral in England and a Member of the Royal Academy of Sciences, published his most influential two-volume *Memoirs of the Life and Correspondence of the Reverend Christian Frederick Swartz*. Based on the published and unpublished materials he had collected from Britain and Germany, this work played a crucial role in preserving

112 Grinfield: Sketches of the Danish Mission, 117–118; Pearson: Memoirs, Vol. 1, 159: About 120 members belonged to the congregation in Pāḷaiyamkōṭṭai. Many of them were "inferior traders, some artificers, some farmers and a few native soldiers or sepoys, all having their respective employments and none, as far as he knew, living upon the charity of others, much less of the church." Catechist Sattiyanātaṉ guided these Christians excellently. The Tamil liturgy, until the beginning of the sermon, was translated from the *English Book of Common Prayer*.

113 Memoirs of the Rev. Joseph D[aniel] Jænicke, 122: On 11.04.1795, Schwartz expressed his deep disappointment over Germany's decline of pietistic ideals. He lamented the nominal spiritual condition of many Christians in Tanjore and found the new theological trends in Germany horrific. He stated that some Germans "invented a Gospel that Paul and the other apostles knew nothing about. The precious atonement of Jesus Christ and the powerful operations of the Holy Ghost are rejected."

114 John Carne: Lives of the Eminent Missionaries. Vol. 1. London 1833, here 96–184 for a brief biography of Schwartz. Additionally, this book features short biographies of John Eliot (1604–1690) in Boston, Massachusetts, Hans Egede (1686–1758) in Greenland, John Zacharias Kiernander (1710–1799) in Calcutta, and William Hocker and John Antes (1740–1811) in Egypt.

115 The unnamed author of this Memoir, who worked at that time in St. Alban Hall at Oxford, was probably Hugh Nicholas Pearson (1776–1856). Pearson: Memoirs, Vol. 1, xix: Pearson stated that as he had been working on the *Memoirs of the Rev. Joseph D[aniel] Jænicke,* he could not publish Schwartz's biography earlier. Both works contain Schwartz's writings and provide a fuller picture of Schwartz's life and work.

Schwartz's legacy.[116] For example, Pearson could consult Schwartz's letters addressed to William Chambers from 1769 to 1793, John Sulivan from 1784 to 1785, and William Duffin; however, he could not obtain Schwartz's letters from John Hudleston, who was an earlier Company resident at Tanjore.

Pearson dedicated this biography to the Anglican Bishop Daniel Wilson in Calcutta (1832–1858), who tried to abolish caste consciousness among Indian Christians. Pearson knew that when John Thomas James was the Bishop of Calcutta from 1827 to 1828, he desired to give a copy of Schwartz's memoirs to each student at the Bishop's College and each missionary in his diocese.[117] Bishop James asked whether Kohlhoff could write Schwartz's biography. On 15 May 1828, Kohlhoff responded to the bishop from Tanjore: "There is scarcely a scrap of his writings left in the mission." Schwartz "had a great deal to do in civil and political matters, as well as in the more interesting part of missionary labour." Kohlhoff stated further that, due to his multifaceted work, Schwartz did not keep copies of what he wrote. Then, he informed Bishop James that German publications contained vital details about Schwartz that were unavailable in English. Kohlhoff had limited knowledge of German, so he requested Sperschneider translate some of these German writings into English. Sperschneider was so busy with his work that he could not translate all of Schwartz's writings.[118] After Bishop James left Calcutta, Bishop John Matthias Turner officiated in Calcutta for three years (1829–1831), and Daniel Wilson succeeded him. Pearson fulfilled Bishop James's desire by writing a two-volume biography and dedicating it to Bishop Wilson.

The editors of the prestigious *The British Critic and Quarterly Theological Review* wrote positively about Pearson's work and described Schwartz as an exemplary missionary and a role model for Europeans. They opined that Schwartz would have rejoiced to know "the Legislature of England awakened to a sense of its responsibilities, the Church of England expanding herself to the East."[119] Soon,

---

[116] Pearson: Memoirs, Vol. 2, xii: Pearson did not know German. Therefore, he requested Carl Friedrich Adolf Steinkopf (1773–1856) to help translate Schwartz's writings from German into English. Steinkopf served as the pastor of the German Lutheran congregation in Savoy, London, and was associated with the British and Foreign Bible Society since its inception in 1804. Steinkopf appointed Mr. Falcke to translate Schwartz's materials and contacted Director Knapp of the Glaucha Institutions for help. Finally, Steinkopf provided Pearson with an English version of Schwartz's writings, as published in the *Halle Report* and the *New Halle Report*.

[117] Pearson: Memoirs, Vol. 2, 435. Pearson got this information from James 1830, 108. "The Bishop used to say at his table at Calcutta, that he wished 'a copy of the Memoirs of Schwartz might be placed in the hands of every student at Bishop's college and every missionary throughout the diocese' and he took the opportunity of an official communication with Mr Kohlhoff, of Tanjore, the same who had been a missionary there when Bishop Middleton visited the place." Middleton wanted to know whether any of Schwartz's writings remained in Tanjore.

[118] Edward James: Brief Memoirs of the late Right Reverend John Thomas James, D.D. Lord Bishop of Calcutta, Particularly During his Residence in India Gathered from his Letters and Papers. London 1830, 109–110.

[119] Smedley: Art. IV, 384: This reference alludes to the Anglican Bishops in Calcutta and their efforts to educate Indian clergy in the Bishop's College. These Anglican bishops included

Pearson's *Memoirs* gained popularity in the United States, proof of the global impact of Schwartz's work. Within a year, in 1835, a single-volume edition appeared in Boston, Philadelphia and New York, demonstrating the widespread recognition of Schwartz's legacy and the inspiration he continues to provide to missionaries worldwide.[120] These publishers considered the American missionaries in Sri Lanka and Madurai as Schwartz's direct successors, highlighting the enduring influence of his work and the strong connection between his legacy and the current generation of missionaries.

> [On] the very ground where Swartz and Gerické laboured and prayed [...] The influence of Swartz and his associates was so diffused among the Tamul race that all [US American] missionaries now among that people are his successors. These missionaries continued Schwartz's ministries. This biography portrayed Schwartz 'as no other Christian missionary ever was before. He was called to sustain the twofold character of a political adviser and a missionary of Jesus.'[121]

In 1855, a 272-page biography of Schwartz, based entirely on Pearson's Memoir, appeared anonymously.[122] It confessed that "any attempt to construct a different account [of Schwartz] would naturally fail" because Pearson "had gathered the choicest materials and had most judiciously arranged them." It esteemed Schwartz as a "devoted Christian Missionary," "the truest follower of the Apostles," and "the first of the missionaries of modern times."[123] Twenty years later, in 1874, J. J. Higginbotham, who resided in Bangalore, included Schwartz in his list of men who had made an impact on India.[124] He highlighted Schwartz's frugal lifestyle in Tiruccirāppaḷḷi. For example, in 1765, Schwartz was satisfied with a monthly salary of 10 Pagodas, which amounted to £24 per year. Higginbotham evaluated that this money was sufficient for a decent life in England, but not in Tiruccirāppaḷḷi. An army commander had given Schwartz a single bedroom for accommodation. Like the Tamils, he ate rice and vegetables, wore a black dress and led a simple lifestyle, gradually attracting people to him. The rest of this biography tells of Schwartz's visit to Hyder Ali, interactions with Governors Rumbold and Pigot and Tanjore's rulers. It describes how the merchants and officers of the Company, including Paul Benfield, exploited the Tamil people and took their wealth to Britain.

Thomas Fanshawe Middleton (1814–1822), Reginald Heber (1823–1826), John Thomas James (1827–1828), John Matthias Turner (1829–1831) and Daniel Wilson (1832–1858).

120 Hugh Pearson: Memoirs of the Life and Correspondence of Swartz, to which prefixed, a Sketch of the History of Christianity in India. First American Edition. Boston and Philadelphia 1835.

121 Hugh Pearson: Memoirs of the Life and Correspondence of Swartz, to which prefixed, a Sketch of the History of Christianity in India. New York 1835, here iv.

122 Life of Christian F. Swartz: Missionary at Travancore [sic! = Tanjore], A.D. 1750–1798, London 1855.

123 Life of Christian F. Swartz: Missionary at Travancore [sic! = Tanjore], iv–v.

124 J.J. Higginbotham: Men Whom India Has Known—Biographies of Eminent Indian Characters, 2nd ed. Madras 1874, 388–392.

In 1921, Jesse Page published a biography of Schwartz in London. He based his observations on the archival materials of the SPCK, the *Remains* (1826) and Pearson's *Memoirs* (1834) and claimed to have redeemed Schwartz's memory from obscurity.[125] Page stressed Schwartz's political and missionary involvements. People trusted him because he refused to accept bribes and maintained a clear conscience. His missionary successors derived valuable lessons from his handling of thorny issues, such as caste sensitivities among Christians, education, and literature.[126]

In 1923, C. B. Gohdes introduced Schwartz as "the Apostle of India," who believed in the life-transforming power of the Gospel of the Lord Jesus Christ. Schwartz's example provided an alternative way of thinking in European academic institutions, where Voltaire's scepticism and general disregard for the Gospel prevailed. Gohdes hoped Christians would appreciate Schwartz's "old Gospel" and his conviction that "God buries his workers, but his work goes on."[127]

1948 marked the 150th anniversary of Schwartz's death. To commemorate that occasion, missionary H. G. Lamb published a 50-page biography of Schwartz, which described his work in Tranquebar, Tiruccirāppaḷḷi, and Tanjore. The biography refers to Schwartz's successful meeting with Hyder Ali (1779), his failed attempts to visit Tipu Sultan (1784), his role in protecting Serfoji and his stepmothers, and his training of younger missionaries.

6.4.3 Schwartz's Biographies in German

As mentioned earlier, the first half of the nineteenth century saw several unsuccessful attempts by German scholars to write a comprehensive biography of Schwartz. Despite these failures, occasional chapters on Schwartz did appear in missionary magazines and books. Michael Bergunder examined them and identified their strengths. He questioned Schwartz's treatment of caste as *jāti*, a social etiquette that defines a person's social rank, status, and identity. Bergunder highlighted the impact of Schwartz's unmarried status on his followers.[128]

In 1836, Karl Christian Gottlieb Schmidt, a teacher at the Cathedral School in Naumburg near Halle (Saale), described the *Life and Work of the Lutheran Missionary Schwartz*.[129] Schmidt derived his ideas solely from Pearson's two-

---

125 Page: Schwartz of Tanjore, iv: Despite raging wars, Schwartz and his colleagues "quietly pursued their sacred duties and, with weapons not carnal but spiritual, fought their good fight of faith." Schwartz's contributions should be studied alongside the contributions of famous men such as Robert Clive, Warren Hastings and Charles Cornwallis. Schwartz is indeed also "entitled to a niche of honour as one who laid the foundation of that reign of the Kingdom of God, which thousands of faithful missionaries are promoting throughout the Indian Empire today. It is the sacred office of the Church to preserve the blessed memory of her standard-bearers and confessors."

126 Page: Schwartz of Tanjore, v.

127 Gohdes: Schwartz—The Apostle to India, 176.

128 Michael Bergunder: Christian Friedrich Schwartz (1726–1798) in German Mission Literature. In: Christian Friedrich Schwartz: His Contributions to South India. Ed. by Daniel Jeyaraj. Madras 1999, 36–57.

volume biography of Schwartz (1834) and appreciated Schwartz's apostolic spirit. Otherwise, it did not contain any of the latest information on Schwartz.

In 1843, Johannes Ferdinand Fenger (1805–1861), Secretary of the Danish Missionary Society, published a chapter entitled *C. F. Schwarz i Trankebar, Tiruschinapally og Tanjour* ('Schwartz in Tranquebar, Tiruccirāppaḷḷi and Tanjore').[130] He derived his insights from unpublished archival sources in the Danish Mission College in Copenhagen and published materials such as the *Halle Reports*, the *New Halle Reports*, Schmidt's biography on Schwartz, and information on Schwartz found in the *Abstract of the Annual Reports and Correspondence* of the SPCK (1814). Nevertheless, his chapter on Schwartz did not contain details that would enrich this current biography. Later, Emil Francke translated this chapter into German[131] and English.[132]

In 1846, Christian Gottlieb Blumhardt (1779–1838)[133] paraphrased Pearson's work and published a single-volume biography of Schwartz.[134] This biography tried to redeem Schwartz's 'Germanness' because the English had already regarded him as their missionary; the Congregationalists in Boston, New York and Philadelphia considered him a predecessor to their missionaries in India. By contrast, Blumhardt attempted to reclaim the person and work of Schwartz to his German readers. By 10 December 1834, he had drafted a manuscript that covered the life and work of Schwartz up to 1771. Twelve years later, in 1846, Blumhardt's successor, Wilhelm Hoffmann (1806–1873), summarised the remaining parts of Schwartz's life and work from 1772 to 1798 and presented Schwartz as a model missionary for the Germans.

In 1851, Reinhold Vormbaum, a Lutheran pastor in Kaiserwerth, published a 199-page biography on Schwartz. He derived his ideas from the SPCK publications, Buchanan's writings and Pearson's biography. He understood Schwartz's closing years as undeniable evidence of his worthy life. He highlighted Schwartz's role as Serfoji's guardian and how Serfoji honoured Schwartz by erecting a monument in Tanjore and speaking about him with European visitors.

In 1860, Gotthilf Heinrich von Schubert (1780–1860) published an 88-page-long biography of Schwartz twice in the same year. Its first appearance viewed

---

129 Karl Christian Gottlieb Schmidt: Kurzgefaßte Lebensbeschreibungen der merkwürdigsten evangelischen Missionare. Vol. 1. Leipzig 1836, 71–101.

130 Johannes Ferdinand Fenger: Den Trankebarske Missions-Historie. Kjøbenhavn 1843, 213–252.

131 Johannes Ferdinand Fenger: Geschichte der Trankebarschen Mission. Transl. Emil Francke. Grimma 1845, 171–202.

132 Fenger: History of the Tranquebar Mission, 199–236.

133 Blumhardt was a close friend of Carl Friedrich Adolf Steinkopf (1773–1856), who assisted Pearson in obtaining English translations of Schwartz's German writings, which were found in the *Halle Report*s and the *New Halle Reports*. Blumhardt succeeded Steinkopf as the secretary to the German Christian Society, which had played a vital role in forming the Basel Missionary Society, commonly known as the Basel Mission. He also served as the Extraordinary Professor of Theology at the University of Basel.

134 Christian Gottlieb Blumhardt: Christian Friedrich Schwartz: der deutsche Missionar in Südindien nach dem Englischen des Hugh Pearson, Basel 1846.

Schwartz as a role model for Christians and Christian missionaries.[135] Its second edition[136] begins with a reference to God's extraordinary intervention in the life of Schwartz's mother, who, on her deathbed, dedicated him to God's work. This conviction that his mother dedicated him to God's service manifested itself in and through Schwartz's life and work. Otherwise, this work offers no fresh information for this current biography.

In 1868, Hermann Gundert (1814–1893), a renowned missionary of the Basel Mission in modern Kerala, published a brief biography of Schwartz. It recounts Schwartz's fall from a horse and his subsequent bedridden state for a few weeks in 1776. Schwartz used that time to learn the Marathi language and compose eleven dialogues between an image-worshipper and a Christian in Tamil (Section 6.2.2). According to Gundert, these dialogues appeared in Madras in 1777. They reflected Schwartz's understanding of Halle Pietism and Natural Theology.[137] Gundert's biography of Schwartz shows his long-lasting influence among soldiers. For instance, when Gericke visited Seringapatam in 1802, he met people who remembered meeting Schwartz in 1779. This enduring influence demonstrates the respect and admiration Schwartz commanded among those he served.[138]

Two biographies appeared in German in 1870. Julius Pauli presented the life and work of Roberto de Nobili[139] and Schwartz.[140] This is a unique comparison. It was intended to inspire German interest in a missionary vocation. Schwartz would not have appreciated this comparison because he disliked the Jesuits and their accommodation of Tamil socio-cultural etiquette. He opposed the missionary works of the Jesuits and their Tamil followers (Section 5.2).

The other biography, published in 1870, became a reliable resource for understanding Schwartz's life, work, and legacy. Wilhelm Germann (1840–1902), the compiler, devoted the later years of his life to exploring the rich archival holdings of the Danish-Halle Mission Archives at the contemporary August Hermann Francke Study Centre of the Francke Foundations in Halle (Saale). He had already published biographies of Johann Philip Fabricius, Bartholomäus Ziegenbalg, and Heinrich Plütschau[141]. Now, he presented Schwartz as a convinced German Lutheran Pietist. Even after becoming a garrison chaplain of the Company in 1768 and drawing an annual salary of £100/- from the Company, Schwartz

---

135 Gotthilf Heinrich von Schubert: Christian Friedrich Schwartz. Erlangen 1860, 99–212. Heinrich von Schubert's role models included Captain Hedley Vicars, Sir Henri Havelock, Gregorius Lopez, Christian Friedrich Schwartz, Christian Gottlob Krafft, David Spleiß and Johannes Rudolf Roth.

136 Gotthilf Heinrich von Schubert: Christian Friedrich Schwartz, der Sendbote des Evangeliums in Indien—Aus dem zweiten Bande der vermischten Schriften besonders abgedruckt. Erlangen 1860.

137 Gundert: Arbeiter in der Tamil-Mission, 231.

138 Gundert: Arbeiter in der Tamil-Mission, 235.

139 Julius Pauli: Roberto dei Nobili und Christian Friedrich Schwartz: zwei Missionare in Ostindien. Nürnberg 1870, 7–46.

140 Pauli: Roberto de Nobili und Christian Friedrich Schwartz, 47–100.

141 Wilhelm Germann: Ziegenbalg und Plütschau—Die Gründungsjahre der Trankebarschen Mission—Ein Beitrag zur Geschichte des Pietismus nach handschriftlichen Quellen und ältesten Drucken. Two Vols. Erlangen 1868.

remained a Lutheran. Germann contended that Schwartz remained a "son of the Lutheran Church, indeed of the Lutheran Church in Germany."[142] He lamented that no Germans ever set up a marble monument for him in Germany. At the same time, he acknowledged the later erection of a memorial plate in the Lutheran church at Sonnenburg, Schwartz's birthplace.[143] Germann blamed the British missionaries of the SPG for usurping the Schwartz's institutions in Tiruccirāppaḷḷi, Tanjore and Kumbakonam. They did not hold the German Lutheran missionaries in high esteem in these regions.[144] He appreciated those Lutheran missionaries from Germany and other countries who worked among the Tamil Lutherans in southern India. He wished that Schwartz's example, as a leader and predecessor, would encourage all Lutheran missionaries, whether they worked in or outside of Germany, and that they would imitate the Lord Jesus Christ, the originator and perfecter of their faith.[145]

Twenty-four years later, in 1894, Armin Stein (1840–1929), a resident of Halle (Saale), published a biography of Schwartz.[146] Four years later, in 1898, P. Richter celebrated Schwartz's 100th death anniversary with a brief biography of Schwartz.[147] It quotes Schwartz's conversations with diverse groups of the Tamil people. In 1901, Julius Hardeland (1828–1903), who worked for the Leipzig Evangelical Lutheran Mission from 1860 to 1891, published an 81-page biography of Schwartz. He felt that the Germans did not recognise Schwartz sufficiently and were unaware of his Lutheran, ecumenical relationship with the Reformed Anglicans. Since the Leipzig Evangelical Lutheran Mission sent its missionaries to work in places where Schwartz had ministered earlier, Hardeland presented him as a fruit of Lutheranism.[148] In 1946, Hans Lilje published a novel about Schwartz and attempted to introduce his readers to him.[149] Eight years later, in 1954, Walther Ruf published a 16-page biography of Schwartz.[150] It relies heavily on Pearson and Germann's biographies of Schwartz. Ruf highlighted how Schwartz worked to minimise the sufferings of the ordinary people in Tranquebar.

---

142 Germann: Missionar Christian Friedrich Schwartz, 395.

143 Germann: Missionary Christian Friedrich Schwartz, 395: This plate had the following message: "In memory of the missionary of East India, the departed Christian Friedrich Schwartz, born in Sonnenburg on 22 October 1726 and died in Tanjore on 13 February 1798, erected by the mission friends in and around Sonnenburg on 22 October 1855. Daniel 12.3." Germann noted further that an essay in the journal *Biene* ('Bee') of February 1868, which was fixed above the memorial tablet in the Lutheran church at Sonnerburg, contained a remarkable observation: "Schwartz, the great missionary, was also the great statesman, who in both functions remained an envoy of peace."

144 Germann: Missionar Christian Friedrich Schwartz, 395.

145 Germann: Missionar Christian Friedrich Schwartz, 396.

146 Armin Stein: Christian Friedrich Schwartz: der Apostel Indiens – Ein Lebensbild. Halle (Saale) 1894.

147 P. Richter: Christian Friedrich Schwartz. In: Geschichte und Bilder aus der Mission 16 (Der Ostindischen Missions-Nachrichten – Neue Folge. Ed. by W. Fries), 1898, 1–15.

148 Julius Hardeland: Der Königspriester von Tandschāur: Lebensbild des Gesegnetesten unter den alten halleschen Missionaren. Leipzig 1901, 3.

149 Hans Lilje: Der Königspriester: eine indische Novelle. Tübingen 1946.

150 Ruf Walther: Christian Friedrich Schwartz: der Königspriester von Tanjore. Stuttgart 1957.

In 1955, Arno Lehmann presented Schwartz as the *Rajaguru*, or a 'royal teacher.' He observed how Stephen Neill understood Schwartz as a prince, bishop, and patriarch and exaggerated the saying about Schwartz: "Whom Father Schwartz blesses, is blessed; whom he curses remains cursed." Lehmann reckoned 8 October 1726 as Schwartz's correct date of birth. He also calculated that Schwartz had baptised more than 2,000 persons. He discussed Schwartz's work in Tranquebar as a teacher and counsellor, his journey to Ceylon in 1760, his refusal of marriage, his poor health, and his unwavering loyalty to the beliefs and practices of the Pietist pioneers in Halle (Saale). He summarised Schwartz's ministry in Tiruccirāppaḷḷi and Tanjore, including his training of young men such as Johann Caspar Kohlhoff, Vēdanāyagam Sāstiriyār, and Serfoji, as well as the fame he received from English bishops like Reginald Heber. Like Germann,[151] Lehmann also concluded that Schwartz was a son of the Lutheran Church, yes, the Lutheran Church of Germany. Praise God that he has given us such leaders and pioneers in the mission work!"[152]

6.4.4 Schwartz's Biographies in Other Languages

In 1825, an Italian version of Schwartz's biography appeared in Malta, based on *The Life of C.F. Swartz: Missionary at Trichinopoly and Tanjore in India.*[153] Likewise, in 1839, Henry Bower (1812–1885), the famous modern translator of the Tamil Bible, published a 92-page biography of Schwartz in Tamil. He derived his insights entirely from Pearson's biography of Schwartz.[154] In 1894, a Dutch version of Armin Steins's work on Schwartz appeared in The Hague.[155] Four years later, in 1898, a Danish biography commemorated Schwartz's first death centenary.[156] And in 1924, a Swedish version of Schwartz's biography also appeared.[157] Though not offering any new insight for this current research work, these biographies demonstrate the breadth and depth of Schwartz's impact. In addition to what Pearson and Germann offered, this current biography explores Schwartz's contributions to peace, justice, and social harmony in southern India.

---

151 Germann: Missionar Christian Friedrich Schwartz, 395.

152 Arno Lehmann: Es begann in Tranquebar: Die Geschichte der ersten evangelischen Kirche in Indien. Berlin 1955, 262–273, here 273.

153 Vita del Rev. C.F. Swartz: Missionario nelle Indie Orientali, etc. (Italian: 'Life of Rev. C.F. Swartz: Missionary in East India'). Malta 1825.

154 Henry Bower: Caṅkai Poruntiya Cuvāccu Aiyyar Carittiram ('History of the Venerable Reverend Schwartz'), Madras 1839.

155 Armin Stein: Christian Friedrich Schwartz: De Apostel von Indië: Een Levensbeeld uit de vorgie eeuw [Dutch: 'Christian Friedrich Schwartz: The Apostle to the Indies—A Portrayal of a Life in the last century'). Gravenhage (i.e. The Hague) 1894.

156 A.C.L. Grove-Rasmussen: Christian Friedrich Schwartz: Anledning af Hundredårsdagen for hans Død (Danish: 'Christian Friedrich Schwartz: On the Occasion of his first Death Anniversary'). Copenhagen 1898.

157 Elin Silen: Christian Friederich Schwartz. Stockholm 1924.

Chapter 7

Schwartz as an Ambassador for Peace and Justice

7.1 Schwartz as the Company's Moral Conscience

During Schwartz's time, the Company in Madras and Tanjore functioned as a Company State. It made "sovereign" agreements with Tanjore's kings, maintained armies at the expense of these kings and interfered in local administration. Most Company servants in Madras and Tanjore traded freely and lent substantial amounts of money to the kings of Tanjore at exorbitant interest. The kings, unable to repay the capital and interest, mortgaged large parts of their land to the Company servants. These servants, in turn, employed their interpreters, revenue collectors, accountants, record keepers and armies to exploit the local people. The cooperation between Company business and private trade, as Menon asserted, occurred at every level, and the Governor in Madras could not do anything about it. This exploitation was not an isolated incident but a systematic and widespread practice that had a profound impact on the local population.[1]

Amidst this context, Schwartz, a Pietist missionary, emerged as a pivotal figure, mediating for peace and highlighting the exploitation and injustices faced by the local people. His role as a mediator for peace and justice, standing against exploitation and injustices, meant that he had a comprehensive understanding of the historical and current contexts of the people of Tanjore. He intimately knew how the employees of the kings of Tanjore and Wallajah seized every opportunity to exploit the ordinary people, especially the farmers. He observed with a heavy heart and deep empathy how these employers treated the Tamil farmers and artisans, who refused to work to enrich the European creditors. The king of Tanjore and the Nawab deserted them so miserably that these Indians could no longer care for their families, a stark example of the injustice faced by the local people.

On 6 October 1768, Schwartz bravely expressed his profound anguish about the Company's exploitation in his neighbourhoods. He fearlessly declared that the unjust wealth of its representatives was nothing but the "sweat and blood of the poor people." His words resonated with the plight of the farmers, their toil and suffering not in vain but for the prosperity of others. A few days later, on 28 October 1768, he explained the extent of the exploitation: The king of Tanjore had 6,000 cavalrymen and 2,000 foot soldiers. A rider-master should have one hundred horses.

1 Minakshi Menon: Medicine, Money and the Making of the East India Company State: William Roxburgh in Madras, c. 1790. In: Histories of Medicine and Healing in the Indian Ocean World. Ed. by Anna Winterbottom and Facil Tesfaye. Vol. 1. London 2015, 151–178, here 151.

The renters of lands had to pay the salary of these soldiers. If these renters did not pay, the soldiers became poorer. Typically, renters were required to pay 50% of the rent in advance. Those who could not make this advance payment borrowed it from Indian or European moneylenders at an annual interest rate of 40% or more. To recover the capital and its interest, the renters oppressed the farmers. Often, the farmers could not take care of their own families. Schwartz's critique of the Company's exploitation, with its stark revelations and undeniable truths, is a powerful testament to his moral stance and the ethical issues of the time.

Schwartz was shocked and saddened to learn how unjustly and cruelly the renters mistreated and exploited ordinary people to amass great wealth for themselves. For example, a renter wanted to lease a piece of land from the king of Tanjore for 10,000 Pagodas. Immediately, another renter would offer the king 11,000 Pagodas and get the land. This renter would force the farmers to cultivate their land for a meagre wage. Should the harvest fail, the renters confiscated the houses and goods of the farmers. Typically, the renters would collect 60–70% of their produce for the king. With the remaining 30 to 40% of the harvest, they had to cover the costs of seed, sowing, labor, and all other expenses. If the king needed money for his army, he would take away 100% of the harvest. In such instances, the farmers had nothing to live on. Typically, such farming families would relocate to other areas to ensure their survival. This cycle of exploitation and poverty was a harsh reality for the local people. Schwartz's detailed account of these practices is a powerful testament to the moral and ethical issues of the time.

Additionally, Schwartz lamented the prevalence of bribery in Tanjore. He stated that those who paid and received bribes could accomplish anything. In this context, no leader attempted to raise the living standard of people experiencing poverty and persisted in their proverbial behaviour: "Let a donkey remain a donkey." By neglecting the ordinary people and bribing local judges and elites, the wealthy inhabitants of Tanjore distorted justice, pretending it was justice. Schwartz vehemently condemned this perversion of justice. He noted how the king of Tanjore, European renters and creditors used Brahmins as intermediaries to give and receive bribes. These Brahmins, who were traditionally respected as the intellectual and spiritual elite, had become complicit in the exploitation and injustice, using their influence and knowledge to further the interests of the ruling class. Schwartz's critique of this system of exploitation and the role of the (*Deśastha*) Brahmins[2] was morally powerful and courageous.[3]

On 11 September 1783, Schwartz critiqued the Company in bitter terms, stating that its officers led a spiritually miserable life. As their dealings had no place for God, whom Jesus Christ had revealed, their lifestyle became immoral and pathetic. As they supported the Company's affairs, they developed their private business enterprises more aggressively and profitably. This dual business activity

---

2 These men were probably Deśastha Brahmins, who or whose ancestors hailed from the modern regions of Maharashtra, especially from Pune and became these residents (*deśastha*) of Tanjore.

3 AFSt/M 1 B 58 : 41.

compromised the Company's economic prospects for personal gain. Some British merchants did not restrain their avarice and thievery. They believed they could swim away on a plank if the ship were to break apart. However, if they lost their business, they would also lose their capital and interest. Additionally, the disunity among the chief administrators of the Company hindered and damaged the performance of their naval and military operations. French armies and Hyder Ali benefited from this disunity. Schwartz did not want to cite more examples; otherwise, Pasche might assume that Schwartz had exaggerated the Company's "wickedness" and added that most Company leaders realised the urgent need for fair trade and law courts that upheld justice. They also knew that without these reforms, the Company would not "remain in this country for long." People would discard it as rubbish (lit. unflath, meaning 'filth'). Schwartz, as a Pietist missionary, assessed the vices of the Company leaders (e.g. gambling, drinking and adultery) as "the worst acts of wickedness." He blamed the Company's Court of Directors in London for sending such immoral persons to India. The British society could not tolerate these vicious people and got rid of them, at least temporarily, by sending them to India. He concluded his remarks about the Company's unjust administration in Tanjore with his characteristic "*Aiyō*" (lit. 'Eheu', 'Alas'). He tried to be the Company's moral conscience but was distressed that the Company officers failed to concur with him.[4]

On 19 March 1784, Schwartz informed Pasche about the cruelties of the Indian and British administrators in Tanjore. In 1783, the civil servants of the king of Tanjore treated their fellow Indian inhabitants far worse than Hyder Ali. The Company officers mistreated Tulāji so harshly that he felt "suffocated" physically and emotionally. The Company officers did not help either Tulāji or his people. A new Company officer from Britain arrived in Tanjore and thought of nothing but accumulating tons of gold. Such officials wanted to return to Britain with immense wealth. As they made their fortune, they disregarded the welfare of the inhabitants of Tanjore. Schwartz repeated that the British in Tanjore consumed nothing but the "sweat and blood of the people" and that he could fill more than 1,000 pages with the misdeeds of the British among the Tamil people. He wondered what would happen to the young British employees who came to Madras and Tanjore, amassed material wealth, and neglected their spiritual lives.[5]

Schwartz knew that some Company officers maintained false accounts and pocketed money from the Company for their private use. In his letter of 11 October 1784, addressed to Pasche in London, Schwartz critiqued the Company officers, who sent the wrong accounts to the Company and stole three to four million Pagodas for their personal use.[6] He stated that the Company officers, merchants, money lenders and interpreters abused their powers. They exploited the people of Tanjore and increased their suffering. He also mentioned that they looked to him

4 AFSt/M 1 B 74 : 33 and Germann: Missionar Christian Friedrich Schwartz, 319–320.
5 AFSt/M 1 B 74 : 28.
6 Germann: Missionar Christian Friedrich Schwartz, 316–317.

to redress their problems. At that time, a certain Burck, a representative of the British Crown, lived in Tanjore. He admired Schwartz's life and service, praising him as "an apostolic man."[7]

On 20 December 1786, Schwartz again questioned the brutal exploitation of the people of Tanjore by the Company administrators in Madras.[8] He stated that Governor George Macartney's administration of Tanjore was evil and vicious.[9] He and his subordinates threatened Tulāji and demanded large bribes. They were unsatisfied with the large bribe that Tulāji gave them, so they demanded much larger bribes from him. Schwartz appreciated that Governor-General Cornwallis of Bengal did not accept bribes, and Governor Campbell did not openly solicit bribes. Still, he was not free from avarice and exploited Ameer Singh as much as possible.[10]

On 23 December 1788, Schwartz acquainted his trusted friend Pasche in London with his determination to oppose the Company's plot to exploit Tulāji. By that time, Schwartz considered Tanjore as "our Tanjore" because he had fully identified himself with the people of Tanjore. Its welfare was his welfare. Tulāji could not manage his transition from imprisonment to the throne of Tanjore effortlessly. In Schwartz's estimation, he wandered aimlessly, went on hunting expeditions, engaged in childish activities, and wasted money. He listened to Schwartz's warnings but chose not to act on them. He could not enforce a just government because he associated himself with senior officers, who, through flattery, exploited him even more than the Company did. In this context, Schwartz learned about the Company's plan to take over the kingdom of Tanjore from Tulāji and became more concerned. Tulāji agreed to donate gold and money to the Company; however, they should not take the land away from him. Consequently, the Company in Madras deputed a commissioner, whom Schwarz referred to as "Mr. P," and requested Schwartz's assistance to exploit Tulāji further. Immediately, Schwartz pointed out two serious concerns. Since the Company demanded more money than Tulāji could afford, Schwartz had urged Tulāji not to sign the agreement which the commissioner had brought. He had noticed how Tulāji, overcome by worries and fear, signed the deal. Immediately, Schwartz walked out of the room. Secondly, he reprimanded the commissioner, stating that he had no right to consider

---

7 Germann: Missionar Christian Friedrich Schwartz, 317: Mr. Burck wrote to the Lutheran missionaries in Tranquebar about Schwartz and stated that against the widespread belief that "nowadays no apostolic person lives. But in truth, Schwartz is an apostolic man."

8 AFSt/M 1 C 27 : 25.

9 Macartney was the president of the Company in Madras from June 1781 to February 1785. Following *Pitt's India Act of 1784*, he served as the Governor of Madras from February to June 1785. An interim administration by Alexander Davidson (June 1785 to April 1786) followed. Then, Archibald Campbell served as the Governor of Madras from 06.04.1786 to 07.02.1789.

10 Suresh Kumar: The Carnatic Wars, 191: Campbell asked Ameer Singh to pay two lakhs of Pagodas to maintain the Company's army to protect Tanjore. Ameer Singh was unable to raise this money. Hence, he borrowed it from rapacious agents, who would collect revenue from the territories assigned to him. Ameer Singh considered it a kindness that Campbell granted him a subsidy of 460,000 Rupees in nine monthly instalments, namely "November 20,000, December 50,000, January 50,000, February 90,000, April 100,000, May 50,000, July 40,000, August 30,000, [and] September 30,000."

taking the land away from Tulāji. In this context, the commissioner requested that Schwartz supervise and adjudicate matters that required justice. Schwartz remarked that he had not asked the Company servants to decide on court issues and concluded his report: "Only time will tell how things develop from now on."[11] Thus, Schwartz seized every opportunity to promote the welfare of ordinary people by upholding the virtues of peace, justice, and social harmony.

7.2 Mediation with Hyder Ali

Schwartz's life and work coincided with two powerful groups of people: On the one hand, the rulers of Tanjore and Mysore increasingly lost their political, economic and military power. On the other hand, the Company expanded its powers and raised sufficient funds from its Indian sources to support its military operations against Indian rulers. Indians paid the salaries of the British administrators, who enriched their stakeholders in Britain. For example, the Second Carnatic War (1749–1754), waged by the Company's Robert Clive against the French, demonstrated the Company army's superior military power and discipline. The Battle of Ambur (August 1749) marked the Company's resolution to occupy critical areas in southern India. The ensuing wars rendered the English more powerful than the French. The Battle of Plassey (1757) marked a significant turning point, making the Company *de facto* ruler of the Bengal Presidency, and it began collecting revenues to meet its expenses. This victory tempted British soldiers and traders in Madras to become even greedier. They secured Fort St. David at Cuddalore and won the Battle of Vandavasi on January 22, 1760, under the guidance of General Eyre Coote. Coote led the Company's army against the French in Pondicherry. Though the Company had defeated the French on 4 September 1760, the French surrendered to Coote on 15 January 1761. These military victories strengthened the Company Raj in the Carnatic.[12]

In this context, the people of the Carnatic coped with unexpected and destructive invasions by the armies of Hyder Ali (c. 1720–1782) and his French supporters. In 1761, Hyder Ali established himself as the ruler of Mysore.[13] He hindered the Company's expansionist attempts. Initially, his weak army was unable to defeat either the Company or Wallajah. He made several agreements with the Company and the French to buy time. The French supported Hyder Ali and fought against the Company on several fronts. On 7 January 1760, the missionaries in

11 AFSt/M 1 C 30c : 17 = not printed in NHR 4, 1790, issue 37, 113.

12 Innes Munro: A Narrative of the Military Operations on the Coromandel Coast: Against the Combined Forces of the French, Dutch and Hyder Ally Cawn, From the Year 1780 to the Peace in 1784. London 1789.

13 Hyder Ali's imprisonment of King Krishnaraja Wadiyar II (d. 1766) of Mysore infuriated the royal family. Queen Lakshmi Ammani Rao immediately requested help from Governor Macartney of Madras (Section 7.3). However, it was only after Tipu Sultan's murder on 04.05.1799 that Wadiyar's successor, the five-year-old Krishnaraja Wadiyar III, came to power on 30.06.1799.

Tranquebar informed the King of Denmark about the destructive impact of the wars between the English and the French.[14] For example, in 1758, the English took away the forts at Cuddalore and Devakottai from the French, causing significant disruption to the local population. The French recaptured them and occupied Arcot, Wallajah's capital city. At that time, the Company's navy under Admiral Pocock defeated the French navy near Tranquebar and forced them to return to Pondicherry.[15] As victors, the Company began to renege on their agreements with rulers like Hyder Ali. For instance, according to the Company's agreement with Hyder Ali in July 1766, the Company was supposed to assist Hyder Ali in repelling his enemies, namely the Nizam of Hyderabad and the Marathas. However, when the time came, the Company did not uphold their end of the bargain, leaving Hyder Ali feeling betrayed. Three years later, in 1769, Hyder Ali and the Company agreed not to attack each other. However, due to mutual distrust, both armies recruited more soldiers and planned to conquer each other.

On 30 April 1769, Schwartz stated that the Company initiated the First Anglo-Mysore War (1767–1769) against Hyder Ali, who had dispatched his soldiers to capture the Cauvery Delta.[16] They attacked Sri Rangam, Karur and Cauvery Puram. This army would have captured more areas if it had not rained heavily for three days. In April 1769, the Company in Madras and Hyder Ali concluded a treaty that would exchange people and places between them, helping each other against their common enemy. As the Company broke this treaty, Hyder Ali's soldiers attacked several places near Madras in October 1769.[17]

By 1770, the Company in Madras refused to assist Hyder Ali in defeating the Maratha army under Madhav Rao. After this incident, Hyder Ali no longer trusted the Company. Nevertheless, on 23 March 1778, Thomas Rumbold suggested to Warren Hastings that the Company in Madras should enlist Hyder Ali's support and assist the Company's army in Bombay in defeating the Marathas, the common

---

14 AFSt/M 2 D 36 : 1.

15 AFSt/M 1 B 49 : 7: On 08.01.1760, all missionaries in Tranquebar reported to Francke that the French had captured Sri Rangam. On 10.09.1759, the French and the English fought at the pier of Tranquebar. The French fled to Pondicherry.

16 AFSt/M 1 B 58 : 37. In 1761, Hyder Ali deposed Krishnarāja Wadiyar II (1734–1766). Five years later, in 1766, he declared himself the sovereign ruler of Mysore.

17 Penny: The Church in Madras, 354: In August 1767, Hyder Ali sent 70,000 soldiers into the Carnatic. Some of these soldiers were French and Swiss mercenaries. General Joseph Smith defeated Ali's army at "Chengamah" on 02.09.1767 and "Tirumalai" on 03.10.1767. Between those dates, Ali's cavalry reached Madras, plundered the Company's garrison at St. Thomas, burned several villages nearby, and rapidly departed. The war between the Company and Hyder Ali continued through 1768 along the bordering territories. Ali's cavalry attacked Madras (1769) because the Company had broken their peace agreement with him. BL MSS Eur D 1208, 16: By 04.04.1769, Hyder Ali and the Company in Madras made a treaty. Its first article reads: "That all hostilities shall immediately cease, on the conclusion of this treaty, which is set to be perpetual, or as long as the Company may exist; that peace and friendship shall take place between the contracting parties, particularly including therein the Rajah of Tanjore, the Marawer, Ram Rajah, and Murari Row, who are friends and allies to the Carnatick Payen Gatte; also all others, the friends and allies of the contracting parties, provided they do not become the aggressors against either of them; but if they are aggressors, not to be assisted by either party."

enemies of Hyder Ali and the Company. Rumbold assumed that such cooperation with Hyder Ali would enable him to overcome his enmity towards the Company and prevent him from seeking help from the French. He also confessed that the Company in Madras could not expect any military help from Nawab Wallajah because his twelve hundred horsemen had not received their pay for a long time and had become disorderly. He also stated that the treasury of the Company in Madras was "at a very low ebb, nor is there any likelihood of reserving any considerable sum for some time." He also knew the King of Tanjore would not pay four lakhs of Pagodas within the next eight months.[18] In this context, Hyder Ali's help to the Company would minimise their war expenses.

Hastings, whose involvement in the cruel and expensive Rohilla War (1774) to support the Nawab of Awadh did not please the Court of Directors, did not respond to Rumbold's urgent suggestion. Rumbold, feeling the weight of the situation, informed Hastings on 15 April 1778 that he had received "the most pressing letter from Hyder Ally to enter into a negotiation with him" and that "a firm alliance with him" would ensure "the security of the Carnatic" and prevent the French from establishing their foothold in India afresh.[19]

Ten days later, on 25 April 1778, Rumbold renewed his urgent appeal to Hastings for permission for the Company army in Madras to secure help from Hyder Ali's large army. He warned that if this were not done, Hyder Ali would strengthen his ties with the French, potentially leading to a war between England and France in Europe, putting the Company in India in grave danger.[20] Hastings did not consider Rumbold's appeal, and as a result, Hyder Ali deepened his relationship with the French and significantly strengthened his army on all fronts, intensifying the tension between the Company and Hyder Ali.

Towards the end of 1778, Rumbold wanted to meet Tulāji personally in Tanjore and extract more money from him. At that time, George Burghall, sympathetic towards Tulāji, advised him not to fall into Rumbold's trap. On 10 December 1778, he sent him a lengthy letter that described how Wallajah's agents in Madras, Calcutta, and London had persuaded his supporters to work against Tulāji and his restoration by Pigot. The Court of Directors, persuaded by justice, listened to Tulāji's requests and rejected Wallajah's unjust claims. In this context, Burghall urged Tulāji to "establish a character for firmness" so that no one would presume upon him and "a character for punctuality" so that everyone would trust him.[21] Then, he warned him not to trust Rumbold and to reject his demands respectfully:

> The treatment you have hitherto received from Mr Rumbold gives me little reason to hope that he intends to be your friend or that it is a disinterested desire of serving you that now leads him to Tanjore and I assure that he cannot be much your enemy if you will but exert that resolution which has more than once preserved you amongst greater difficulties than you have at present to apprehend.[22]

---

18 BL ADD 29140, folios 221v–222v.
19 BL ADD 29140, folios 260r–260v.
20 BL ADD 29140, folios 310–312.
21 BL MSS Eur D 1208, 279.
22 BL MSS Eur D 1208, 276.

As Rumbold was bent on raising more money for himself, he ignored Hyder Ali's preparations for war. In March 1779, Rumbold permitted the Company's armies to capture Hyder Ali's most important seaport, Mahé, on the Malabar Coast. This action enraged Hyder Ali, who planned to avenge the Company. During that time, General Hector Munro, "the oldest King's Officer upon the Coast" of Coromandel,[23] wanted the Company to honour Schwartz for his services as a chaplain to the English soldiers in Tanjore and as a Marathi translator for the Company officers and King Tulāji of Tanjore. Munro observed the respect and trust that Schwartz enjoyed among the local people. He appreciated Schwartz's knowledge of Tamil, English, Marathi and Persian. Munro had noticed how Schwartz functioned without an interpreter and how quickly and inexpensively he had performed his role. Munro admired Schwartz's unassuming, simple lifestyle and honest service to the welfare of needy people. Therefore, Munro persuaded Governor Thomas Rumbold in Madras to send Schwartz as the Company's envoy to Hyder Ali. Rumbold, known for his insatiable greed for money, material wealth, and political power, sought to defeat Hyder Ali and secretly plunder his wealth.

At this time, without income from Tanjore, Wallajah could not cover the growing expenses of the Company in Madras. The English believed he depended solely on the Company for his safety and for governing the entire Carnatic.[24] However, his inability to support the Company greatly alarmed English officers like John Whitehill (1735–1812), who informed Warren Hastings about their vulnerable situation.[25] Whitehill noted that King Tulāji of Tanjore could not bring the promised tribute of four lakh Pagodas to the Company and demanded that he pay the same amount in instalments.[26] At the same time, the English in Madras received secret messages from Hyder Ali's vakeel in Pondicherry, stating that he

---

23 BL ADD 38404, 32: On 01.02.1780, Eyre Coote, the Commander-in-Chief of the King's army in India, then stationed in Lucknow, authorised Sir Hector Munro, "the oldest King's officer" on the Coast of Coromandel, to oversee all army affairs.

24 BL ADD 13612, folios 18–19: John Whitehall's details were extracted from Fort St. George Military Consultations dated 16.01.1778 and referred to Wallajah as follows: Our Friend and Allay Nawab Wallajah "has lately reduced his own troops considerably and instead of seven Regiments of Cavalry which he before kept up he has now only four. The Revenues of his Country may be reckoned at from 25 to 30 Lakhs of Pagodas annually. The Nabob has no connection but with the English. We believe him sincerely. [... As] far as we can judge, he has no views independent of their Friendship and Support." The Company in Madras could not fulfil his repeated demands to return the Kingdom of Tanjore to him because the Court of Directors in London ordered Pigot to return it to King Tulāji.

25 BL ADD 13612, folios 10–17: In 1778, the Company's annual income amounted to 12,00,000 Pagodas. Wallajah refused to give Poonamallee near Madras to the Company because he had assigned most of his domains to his private creditors, known as renters.

26 BL ADD 13612, folio 20: Whitehill reported: King Tulāji "represented his inability to complete the payments of so considerable a sum from his revenue in less than six months having besides this money 3 lakhs of Pagodas to pay in the course of the next four months on account of his annual subsidy to the Company, we therefore agreed to receive the deposit from him in the following payments, viz: on the 30th January Pagodas 50,000; 28 February Pagodas 100,000, 30th March Pagodas 50,000; 30th April 50,000; 30th May 50,000; 30th June 100,000."

possessed "three crores" (3,00,00,000) of Rupees and concentrated his efforts on keeping the Maratha armies away from his borders. Pressed for more money to meet the Company's growing expenses, greedy Rumbold requested Schwartz to discover Hyder Ali's intentions about wars against the Company.[27] As an envoy of peace, justice and harmony, he believed that Schwartz could discover and convey Hyder Ali's intentions to the Company.

7.2.1 Schwartz's Embassy to Hyder Ali (5 June – 24 August 1779)

Schwartz accepted Rumbold's invitation for four noble reasons despite his initial hesitation. First, he saw an opportunity to avert bloodshed and promote peace for all the region's inhabitants. Second, he passionately desired to preach the gospel of the Lord Jesus Christ to the people living as far as Seringapatam. Third, he hoped that this journey would persuade Wallajah to repay the debt he had borrowed from Philip Fabricius, which his son-in-law had earlier. Finally, he wanted to thank those Company officers who had assisted him.

With these considerations, Schwartz left Tanjore on 5 June 1779. After spending time with Hyder Ali in Seringapatam, Schwartz returned to Tiruccirāppaḷḷi on 30 August 1779. From there, he proceeded to Madras.[28] On arrival in Madras, Schwartz informed Rumbold that Hyder Ali wanted to live peacefully with them. If the Company dealt with him peacefully and beneficially, he would honour them.[29] Schwartz reported that Hyder Ali invited him to sit beside him, listen intently, and observe his daily activities.[30] He lamented how often the Company had broken "their solemn engagements and promises, but that he was willing to live in peace with them, provided ***."[31] Then he dictated a letter to the Company and gave Schwartz this message: "What I have spoken with you

---

27 AFSt/M 1 B 70 : 43.

28 AFSt/M 1 B 70 : 42.

29 AFSt/M 1 B 74 : 31.

30 BL ADD 57313 folios 37–42v: "When I [Schwartz] sat near Hydernaik, I particularly observed in what a regular succession and with what rapid dispatch his affairs proceeded one after the other. Whenever he made a pause in speaking, an account was read to him of the districts and letters received. He heard it and ordered the answer immediately. The writers ran to write the letter and read it, and Hyder affixed his seal. Thus, in one evening, a great many letters were expedited [sic! = expedited]. Hyder can neither read nor write, but his memory is excellent. He orders one man to write a letter and read it to him. Then, he calls another to reread it. If the writer has in the least deviated from his orders, his head pays for it."

31 Pearson: Memoirs, Vol. 1, 361: Colonel Mark Wilks noted: "But of these mysterious provisions, nothing can now be ascertained." Wilks: Report on the Interior Administration, 439–440: "Although I [Mark Wilks] had the pleasure of Mr Swartz's acquaintance many years afterwards and have heard him narrate many facts connected with the subject of this mission, he died long before my attention was directed to historical pursuits; but I had hoped that a journal might be found among his papers; and his worthy successors kindly complied with my request [footnote entry reads: Through my friend, Colonel Blackburn, political resident at Tanjore] to examine them for that purpose; no such document was found; but the extracts were made from his correspondence, which unfortunately interposes a mysterious blank at the very point on which our information is defective." Wilks: Report on the Interior Administration, 523–528: Appendix VIII in Wilks' book contains an English version of Schwartz's embassy to Hyder Ali.

about, I have shortly mentioned in the letter. You will explain the whole more at length,"[32]

As Schwartz departed from Seringapatam, Hyder Ali asked him to speak with him in Persian, which he understood but could not speak. Schwartz spoke with him in Persian and said that, as a priest, he had accepted a political assignment to preserve peace. He wanted to avoid the great "misery and horrors attendant on war." He wanted to cement a "durable Friendship between the two governments" and thus to secure "the Blessings of peace" for all. Hyder Ali responded "with great cordiality: 'Very well! Very well! I am of the same opinion with you, and I wish that the English may be as studious of Peace as you are. If they offer me the Hand of Peace and Concord, I shall not withdraw mine.'"[33] Schwartz delivered a letter from Hyder Ali to Rumbold, which the annals of the Company in Madras did not record and practically ignored. However, an online version of a letter attributed to Hyder Ali reveals his intentions.

> I [Hyder Ali] had the pleasure of receiving your letter by Mr. Schwartz, containing friendly assurances towards me and a desire that the friendship between the Company and me may be firmly established. Before this, when a friendship confirmed by a solid treaty existed between the Company and me, I imagined it would increase daily and would not be broken through. You, setting aside all faith and treaties of the Company, have lately sent troops against Mahe, a French factory situated within my territories and plundered it; and besides this, [you] have committed depredations in the countries of Calicut and Cabingury, belonging to me. There are, in my countries, many factories belonging to the English, Germans, Dutch, Portuguese, Danes and others; among those was one belonging to the French, and there was no person in it who bore [i.e. led] the procession of arms; it was no more than a factory, such as the English, on many places of the seacoast. Notwithstanding the friendship subsisting between the Company and me, you, without any regard or consideration for it, sent your troops and destroyed the factory of the French and pillaged the countries belonging to me. What property was there in this? You wrote to me besides that you were sending a body of your troops to the Nawab Basalat Jung, from which I conceive you pay no regard to the friendship between the Company and me but do whatever your inclination leads you to and are determined at any rate to break with me. I was convinced that the king of England and the Company were one and that there would not be the smallest deviation from the treaties made by the Company, but I now think otherwise from your proceedings. Having a consideration for the friendship of the king of England and the Company, I have made no reprisals or taken any revenge till this time; it is no matter, but if you, henceforth forgetting all treaties and engagements of the Company, still are intent on breaking with me, what advantage can attend writing to you? You are acquainted with everything; it is right to act in all things with prudence and foresight. Mr. Schwartz came here some time ago and brought me a letter from you, to which I have written an answer containing all the particulars and sent it to you by him. He also will acquaint you with several matters which I have charged him with (28th September 1779).[34]

---

[32] BL ADD 57313, folios 37r–42v.

[33] BL ADD 57313, folios 37r–42v; AFSt/M 1 B 70: 45. On 14 March 1780, Schwartz wrote to Director Freylinghausen about his visit to Hyder Ali, stating that at their departure, Hyder Ali told him, "Very good, very good. I will not take my hand back if the English extended a hand of friendship to me." Immediately, Schwartz added this note: "Please keep this paragraph confidential." Hence, Freylinghausen did not publish it.

[34] George Gray's embassy to Hyder Ali, 1780. In: Notes on Indian History. 16.01.2018. URL: https://www.notesonindianhistory.com/2018/01/george-grays-embassy-to-hyder-ali-1780.html (accessed on 20.11.2024).

Mark Wilks, who examined the Company's military history in Madras, tried to identify official references to Schwartz's embassy to Hyder Ali. However, he could not find a single record. He expressed his astonishment as follows:

> [About Schwartz's visit to Hyder Ali,] no entry was made on the record of the information from Mr. Swartz, thus directly and officially referred to; nor a single line of report, or a journal, or communication, in any form, from a person who had been charged with a political mission of the greatest importance. In a period, abounding with themes of wonder, it is impossible to repress our astonishment, that no individual charged with public authority in India or England, ever suggested the examination of Mr. Swartz on these points or called for a journal or report of his proceedings. A Committee of the House of Commons, subsequently charged with the investigation of these transactions, simply reports the fact of no such entry having been made; but adds no suggestion regarding the obvious means of supplying the defect.[35]

Such was the general respect Schwartz enjoyed not only in Madras but also in England. As discussed in Section 7.2.1, the Court of Directors received Schwartz's report about Hyder Ali's intention to wage a war against the Company. Hyder Ali understood the Company as the representatives of the British king and nation. He accused them of repeatedly breaking their treaty with him and urged them not to provoke him. He treated Schwartz respectfully.[36] When Schwartz took leave, Hyder Ali sent Rupees 300 to defray his travel expenses. Schwartz gave this money to the Company in Madras, which they asked him to keep as a gift. Schwartz used that money to support the orphans of Europeans in Tanjore. In his assessment, Hyder Ali outperformed the Company because he upheld strict discipline, was passionate about justice, and worked for the welfare of the weakest and poorest people in his territories.[37] Schwartz's letter to his close friend Pastor Sorge in early 1780 compared Hyder Ali with King Frederick William II (1786–1797) of Prussia:

> I wish I could write more about Hyder Ali's person, governance, army, country, income and many other things; I cannot write long letters. However, I wish to convey this information to you. In my mind, I compared Hyder Ali with your great king. He is accurate in his dealings. He is quick to punish those who disobey his commands. Daily, he tries to regulate and

---

35 Mark Wilks: Report on the Interior Administration, Resources and Expenditure of the Government of Mysoor under the system prescribed by the Orders of the Governor General in Council dated 4th September 1799. Fort William (Calcutta) 1805, here 339.

36 George Gray's Embassy to Hyder Ali, 1780: this report contains rare details about Hyder Ali and Schwartz: "According to Colonel Lindsay, when Schwartz approached the throne, Hyder rose and advanced to receive him, declaring that he was now sensible the Company wished his friendship, by sending such a man to communicate with him. The prince parted with the priest highly satisfied with the assurances he had received of the Company's amicable feelings, acquiesced in the measures offered to his consideration, and, as a token of his esteem, Hyder pressed Mr Schwartz to accept a valuable diamond and a sum of money. These proffered presents were refused, with dignity tempered with respect, Mr Schwartz observing that he could not receive them in his ambassadorial character, but duly appreciating the kindness and generosity of the donor, he would appropriate the money to the erection of a church he was about to build at Tanjore if his highness would permit him to put it down as a benefaction of the Mysore prince in the promotion of that undertaking. Hyder answered, with a smile, 'Be it, my friend, as you please,' and his name now stands, or ought to do so, at the head of the list of benefactors of the Christian church at that place."

37 AFSt/M 1 B 70 : 43.

> improve the function of his army. Every day, he answers all letters that he receives most strictly. These are some aspects of my comparison. By contrast, the most surprising difference is this: your king is a learned prince, but Hyder Ali cannot read. Nevertheless, no one could deceive him. In his strict governance, he is often tyrannical. However, he welcomed me and listened to what I had to convey. When he asked me to speak in Persian, I told him of his desire to promote the best for the poor inhabitants; otherwise, I would not have accepted this assignment. He approved my travel and its purpose and promised to have the mind towards the ordinary people. Then he told me the English are dishonest. Eheu! [*aiyō*!, 'Alas!'].[38]

Despite Hyder Ali's reputation for tyranny, Schwartz portrayed him as a dignified warrior who genuinely sought peace with the English. This unexpected message, which urged restraint and a diplomatic solution, was not well-received by Rumbold and the Nawab. Their preference for war over peace was evident in their decision not to publish Schwartz's report.[39]

Another reason for not recording Schwartz's report might have been its frequent reference to worship services and evangelistic discussions with Christians and non-Christians. For example, on 8 August 1779, they met a German named Landsknecht in Kurumudi. His family was also with him. Schwartz spent a Sunday with him. Several Tamils joined this worship service. A mendicant (*Pandaram*) discussed various themes related to God, the sin of the first humans, the redeemer Jesus Christ, the Order of Salvation, and prayer with Schwartz. This mendicant could not reconcile the material body of humans with the spirit of Jesus Christ. During his stay in Seringapatam, Schwartz had his separate tent on the palace grounds and engaged with European and Indian Christian soldiers. According to his report, a Frenchman commanded Hyder Ali's European soldiers. Several Germans were among them. One of them was Captain Buden from Württemberg, who had lent Schwartz his tent for Christian gatherings, prayers, singing and worship services in German and Tamil. These and other references to Christian faith and mission seemed abhorrent to Rumbold and his allies, who chose not to record Schwartz's embassy to Hyder Ali.[40]

Hayavadana Rao, who had examined Mark Wilk's notes about Schwartz's embassy to Hyder Ali and other relevant documents in Madras, asserted that Wallajah had frustrated the Company's "hopes of peace" and persuaded Rumbold to reject Schwartz's message of peace and friendship between the Company and Hyder Ali. He confirmed that he could not trace Schwartz's report among the Fort St. George records either.[41]

---

38 AFSt/M 1 B 71 : 30 and NHR 3, 1783, issue 26, 153–4.

39 Pearson: Memoirs, Vol. 1, 366: "Swartz himself was not deceived as to the probability of an approaching rupture. He clearly foresaw and in subsequent letters to his friends plainly adverted to the intrigues of the nabob and the misconduct of other persons, as the causes of this calamitous event. May it not, therefore, be conjectured, that the report of the result of his mission to Hyder was not recorded, because it little coincided with the prevalent views of the Madras government?"

40 AFSt/M 1 B 74 : 31: Schwartz wrote his 38-page report entitled *Short report on my travel to Seringapatam in 1799* later. It reached Halle only on 10.11.1784. Schwartz's earlier report on the same journey (AFSt/M 2 E 17 : 13) appeared in NHR 3, 1783, issue 27, 283–296.

41 Conjeevaram Hayavadana Rao: History of Mysore 1399–1799. Vol. 3: 1766–1799. Bangalore 1946, here 502.

I, too, the author of this present biography, searched for Schwartz's report in the Danish-Halle Mission Archives at the August Herrmann Francke Study Centre of the Francke Foundations in Halle (Saale), Germany, and in the contemporary Company records at the British Library in London, but I could not find it. However, there is a reference in which the Company's Court of Directors in London relied on Schwartz's report to punish Thomas Rumbold (discussed at the end of section 7.2.3).

7.2.2 Gray's Embassy to Hyder Ali (1780)

Rumbold did not welcome the message of peace that Schwartz brought from Hyder Ali and waited for an opportunity to send another envoy to him. In the meantime, Hyder Ali arrested six British men and a woman who had reached Calicut on a Danish ship. He deported them to Seringapatam, hoping the men could serve him as his gunners.[42] Rumbold seized the opportunity presented by the plight of the British prisoners to dispatch another envoy to Hyder Ali. This time, he chose George Gray, a former civil servant in Bengal, to persuade Hyder Ali to release the English prisoners and foster a better relationship with the English. However, Hyder Ali's response to Gray differed from his welcome of Schwartz. He treated Gray as an unwanted spy and promptly sent him away.[43]

Gray's long journey, from 14 January to 19 March 1780, produced no noteworthy results. Gray's diary highlights the contrast between Hyder Ali's welcome to Schwartz and his subsequent rejection by Hyder Ali. For example, Gray's diary ends as follows:

> [When I met Hyder Ali,] I was rather received and treated as a spy than as an ambassador, rather confined and lodged. He never allowed me to [have] a confidential audience, although I frequently solicited it. He never allowed me to enter his city by daylight; he kept me at a distance from his person as if he suspected I had a design upon his life, and he watched me as narrowly as if he thought I had come to pry into his affairs or to carry on some secret plot with his people. I was by no means sorry to leave so inhospitable a region. I set out the following day and arrived in Madras in ten days.[44]

While Hyder Ali rejected Gray, he respectfully interacted with Schwartz. Rumbold was unhappy with Hyder Ali. In this context, Schwartz discovered Rumbold's dishonesty and became more critical of Rumbold's attempts to exploit the impoverished people of Tanjore. On 10 October 1780, Schwartz reported to Freylinghausen about the Company's cruel exploitations in Madras and Tanjore by repeatedly pointing out how the officers of the Company oppressed Tulāji. These

[42] Wilks: Report on the Interior Administration, 440.

[43] Wilks: Report on the Interior Administration, 440: Hyder Ali made Gray wait long at Ambur, where his territory started. After allowing him to travel, he arranged Gray's lodging in a shed two hours away from Seringapatam. This shed was "half filled with artillery ropes." A subedar often came into that shed, sat beside him and asked, "impertinent questions."

[44] IOR/H/250, 1–19: This diary, George Gray's Journal of his Embassy to Hyder Ally in January 1780, is a copy that Thomas Rumbold furnished on 3 June 1782.

cunning officers exploited Tulāji and his subjects as if exploitation were their "religion." Senior and junior Company officers were greedy for money and wealth. They sailed for England when they had gathered enough money to satisfy them. They showed no concern for the welfare of the people of Tanjore. For example, whenever Tulāji paid his annual dues to the Company, Rumbold expected large bribes from him. Sometimes, Tulāji could not bribe Rumbold. When that happened, Rumbold intimidated Tulāji through his agents in Tanjore. Schwartz lamented the immoral and unethical behaviour of the Company officers. He was concerned that such unjust practices hindered the spread of Christianity in Tanjore.[45]

7.2.3 Hyder Ali's Invasion of the Carnatic (1780)

Schwartz informed Freylinghausen on 10 October 1780 about Hyder Ali's intelligence in discerning Rumbold's original plan for war with him and extracting money from him.[46] People who had heard about Hyder Ali's imminent invasion of Arcot and his determination to capture Tiruccirāppaḷḷi abandoned their homes. Some Company soldiers ran away. At that time, Schwartz learned that Hyder Ali had ordered his generals to permit Schwartz to pass through the places under his control unmolested, as he, being a priest, did not pose a threat to his reign.[47]

Schwartz knew that Rumbold had retracted his promises to Hyder Ali and neglected the welfare of the inhabitants of Tanjore. Instead, he focused his energy on raising more money for himself. He remained unprepared for Hyder Ali's devastating invasion of the Carnatic in June 1780. By July 1780, his armies had launched attacks on numerous parts of the Madras Presidency, marking the beginning of the Second Anglo-Mysore War (1780–1784). His army damaged the northern parts of Madras.[48] Another part of his army joined the soldiers of the Marudhu Brothers and Māppiḷḷai Tēvar of Ramanathapuram and defeated Wallajah's army. Consequently, Hyder's armies captured most of Tanjore, Sri Rangam, Madurai and the southern regions up to the borders of Travancore.[49] General Munro was unable to contain Hyder Ali's armies in Kanchipuram.[50]

---

45 AFSt/M 1 B 71 : 32.

46 AFSt/M 1 B 71 : 32.

47 Schwartz's monument in St. Mary's Church in Fort St. George in Chennai contains this statement: "The late HYDER ALLY CAWN, amid a bloody and vindictive war with the CARNATIC, sent orders to his Officers to Permit the venerable FATHER SWARTZ to pass unmolested and shew him Respect and Kindness, for he is a Holy Man and means no harm to my Government." Germann: Missionar Christian Friedrich Schwartz, 316: Germann noted that Hyder Ali's generals did not follow this order. Once, they confiscated all written materials from Schwartz.

48 K. Sasikala: Tipu Sultan's Invasions in Tamilnadu 1782–1799: A Study. Diss. phil. Annamalai 2015. URL: http://hdl.handle.net/10603/181671 (accessed on 10.11.2024), here 111: Sasikala reported that in July 1780, Hyder Ali's army of 83,000 soldiers "came down on the plains like an avalanche." Some of his soldiers reached St. Thomas Mount. They burnt the villages along the way and killed many people. Ali wanted to possess the territories between Pullicat and Pondicherry. He had no intention of attacking Fort St. George.

49 Elangovan: Colonial Acquisitions, 75–77.

On 20 May 1781, missionaries in Madras, Fabricius and Breithaupt, explained how General Eyre Coote rushed from Calcutta and defeated Hyder Ali at Fort Tripasore. This war demoralised the inhabitants of the Madras Presidency so badly that Fabricius and Breithaupt could not foresee a better future. They could not correspond with Schwartz either.[51] According to another report by the missionaries in Tranquebar, dated 20 July 1781, Coote captured the Dutch who had assisted Hyder Ali, thereby breaking his four-month blockade of Tiruccirāpālli and Tanjore. The missionaries in Tranquebar were concerned about Schwartz and his colleagues in Tanjore, as they had lost all communication, and their worries grew with each passing day.

At the same time, Schwartz reported Rumbold's negligence to his friends at the SPCK, who forwarded his reports to the Company's Court of Directors in London. Consequently, they held Rumbold responsible for a breach of public trust and war crimes and imposed a heavy penalty on him.[52] Accordingly, on 12 April 1775, the Court of Directors ordered Rumbold to settle Tanjore's problem, to "deliver the Inhabitants from Oppression, and to improve the Company's Revenues." Rumbold rejected Hyder Ali's offer to cooperate in Guntur. On 23 September 1779, Rumbold authorised Colonel Harpur to lead his army to Adoni by passing "through the Country of Hyder Ally without his previous Licence" and thus committed "an Act of Hostility against that Prince" and contributed to "the Causes of the subsequent War with Hyder Ali." Rumbold breached King George III's order that prohibited the Presidencies of Madras, Bombay and Bengal "from making any Order to commence Hostilities against any Indian Prince or Power without first obtaining the Consent of the Government of Bengal, except in Cases of imminent Necessity, or of a special Order from the said Company." Rumbold also did not punish military officers and spies, such as Samuel John, who had failed to learn from Hyder Ali's invasion of the Carnatic.[53]

The most convincing account that the Company Directors in London considered against Rumbold was Schwartz's confidential report on his visit to Hyder Ali in mid-1779 (Section 7.2.1). Accordingly, Schwartz warned Rumbold

---

50 BL ADD 38404. Liverpool Papers. Vol. CCXI. East India Papers. 1780. Presented by Henry Berkeley Portman, 223: On 14.10.1780, General Hector Munro reported from Fort St. George that Hyder Ali's armies had begun attacking the Carnatic in July 1780. In August 1780, they besieged Madras and Arcot. On 26 August 1780, Munro led His Majesty's 73rd Regiment and approximately 4,000 Indian soldiers from Madras to free Arcot. He expected help from Colonel Baillie. Heavy rain at Kanchipuram halted Munro's armies. A wounded soldier informed Munro that Hyder Ali's armies defeated Baillie because his "three tumbrels of Ammunition" had blown up. Hyder Ali took away to Seringapatam as war captives: thirty-two British officers, three hundred Europeans and 1,000 Indian soldiers.

51 AFSt/M 1 B 72 : 47.

52 A Bill for Inflicting certain Pain and Penalties on Sir Thomas Rumbold, Baronet, and Peter Perring, Esquire, for certain Breaches of Public Trust, and High Crimes and Misdemeanours, committed by them whilst they respectively held the Offices of Governor and President, Counsellors and Members of the Select Committee, of the Settlement of Fort Saint George, on the Coast of Coromandel, in the East Indies. London 1782.

53 A Bill for Inflicting certain Pain and Penalties on Sir Thomas Rumbold, 1–2, 21, 34–35.

of Hyder Ali's resolve to fight against the Company and Wallajah. The Company Directors in London were displeased that Rumbold ignored Schwartz's warning and articulated their opinion as follows:

> The heaviest and the clearest charge in the bill is the unprepared state of the Carnatic at the time that it was invaded by Hyder Ally in June 1780. For as early as October 1779, in consequence of the hostile stile [sic. i.e. style] of Hyder's letters, Sir Thomas Rumbold sent the Rev. Mr. Swartz to his court to learn the real disposition of that Prince & he then informed the Board that the issue of this secret negotiation left him no room to doubt of the hostile intentions of Hyder, both to the Company & to the Nabob. On the 10th Nov. 1779, Mr Smith moved that vigorous measures should be adopted & submitted to the Board the propriety of collecting troops at Vellore & Conjeveram [modern Kanchipuram], to be in readiness to act as occasion might require. At the time of Sir Thomas Rumbold's departure, appearances became still more threatening & notwithstanding the imminent danger of his invasion, the neglect to prepare for defence still continued.[54]

Those policymakers who weighed against Thomas Rumbold considered his close link with the detested banker Paul Benfield in Madras,[55] who had loaned large amounts of money to influential elites like Wallajah and Tulāji and forced them to rent him vast regions for revenue collection. For instance, on 1 November 1781, he wrote from London to Benfield in Madras about the abuses and accusations he had endured up to that point. He asserted that he depended on Benfield's "good offices" in anything that concerned his interests or affairs at Madras, and assured him that he would never neglect any opportunity that might arise of showing his attachment to him here in London, where policymakers were evaluating Benfield's wealth and influence.

The penalties against Rumbold had challengers. For example, Horace Rumbold described the relationship of the Rumbold Clan with the Company in India, beginning with Thomas Rumbold's father, William Rumbold, in 1709.[56] He claimed that Thomas Rumbold solved the Tanjore problems created by Pigot and should be viewed in the same light as Robert Clive, a founder of Britain's "Eastern domain." For this purpose, posterity should be grateful to him.[57]

7.2.4 Hyder Ali's Invasion of Tranquebar (1781)

On 14 October 1780, Hector Munro wrote from Madras about Hyder's invasion of the Carnatic in July of that year, accompanied by many cavalry and foot soldiers. He captured Arcot, the capital of the Carnatic, in August 1780. Munro commanded

---

54 BL ADD 35381, folios 94r–107v: Abridgement of the Bill of Pains and Penalties, here folios 105v–106r.

55 The Writings and Speeches of Edmund Burke. Ed. by Peter J. Marshall. Vol. 5: India: Madras and Bengal. Oxford 1981, 127: On 17.01.1781, Burke accused Benfield of not producing any vouchers for the loans he had given to Wallajah and quoted everything from memory. He alleged that Pigot had received a bribe, but he could not prove his allegation with any documents. He arranged for Pigot's arrest and used Wallajah's Black Horse, the name of an Indian battalion, to guard Pigot for eight months. Pigot rejected Tulāji's restoration in 1776 and expected to get more money from Tanjore.

56 BL ADD 57939, folios 81–92.

57 BL ADD 57939, 1–15 of the printed booklet.

His Majesty's 73rd Regiment and moved 4,000 Company soldiers toward Kanchipuram. Heavy rain prevented Munro's army from proceeding faster. On 28 August 1780, a wounded soldier, suffering from rheumatic attacks in his hands, told him how Hyder's army had defeated Colonel Baillie because his three tumbrels with ammunition had exploded and how he took away thirty-two British officers and 1,000 Indian soldiers.[58] Thus, Hyder's army could freely wander into the Carnatic and devastate large regions for several months.

An eighteen-page unpublished manuscript describes how Hyder Ali's army devastated the areas in and around Tranquebar in 1781.[59] On 16 February 1781, Hyder Ali's army set ablaze the areas along the Collaran River. The following day, they reached Tirumullaivācal and burned unharvested and harvested paddy fields, a temple car (*tēr*) and several straw-thatched houses. The inhabitants of Tiruviṭaikkāṭu and Tirukkaṭaiyūr, despite their fear, took their temple elephants and left the places. However, Hyder's army overtook them at Yāṉaikkōvil and captured many of them. The elephants valiantly fought back, but one suffered a deep injury on its back caused by a spear. Some people found refuge in the city, but the invasion had already had a profound impact on the local population.

On 18 February 1781, the missionaries in Tranquebar and their congregations gathered in the Jerusalem Church for morning worship from 7 a.m. to 9 a.m. Despite the imminent threat, they continued their worship services, a testament to their unwavering faith. At that time, they heard the sound of gunshots. Tamil Pastor Philipp closed the church in Poṟaiyār; his catechist Arulappan hid himself in a bush, and Hyder's soldiers did not find him; thus, he survived. The Danish Governor stood near the closed city gate door, speaking with Hyder's soldiers through a hole in the door, and sent his Tamil interpreter, Daniel Pillay, and his Persian interpreter to negotiate peace with them. When Daniel Pillay visited Karaikal and Tirumalai Rājapatnam on 21 February 1781, he saw terrible suffering and many dead bodies lying around.

Hyder's army returned to Tranquebar on 26 February 1781; their commander, Lalla Sahib, requested that the Governor of Tranquebar permit his army to pass through Tranquebar and attack the French territories of Karaikal and Nagore, where Wallajah's army was stationed. The governor sensed the danger. He sent his interpreter, Daniel Pillay, to Lalla Sahib and asked him to give the commander five hundred Pagodas. Daniel Pillay's diplomatic intervention saved Tranquebar on that day. However, Lalla Sahib led his army through Tranquebar on 28 February 1781. This army wounded a Tamil Lutheran Christian who was carrying a palm leaf letter to the church. Later, the injured Christian and eighty other victims received their medical treatment in a hospital in Nagapattinam. By 1 p.m. on 28 February 1781, Hyder's soldiers reached Sāttaṉkudi and destroyed the gardens and houses there. They plundered the Muslims and the French. On 29 February 1781, Hyder's army captured Tranquebar. Fire and smoke billowed from the houses, which they had plundered and set on fire. Thus, they devastated many

---

58 BL ADD 38404, 223.

59 AFSt/M 1 B 72 : 10.

parts of the Coromandel Coast. Schwartz's mediation with Hyder Ali did not avert the war mainly because Rumbold did not respect the Company's earlier treaties with Hyder Ali. However, Schwartz's portrayal of Hyder Ali and Hyder Ali's esteem for Schwartz's interventions for peace, justice and social harmony were genuine. They highlighted the humane aspects of both men.

7.3 Mediation for the Wadiyars of Mysore (1782)

The senior members of the Wadiyar Dynasty, whom Hyder Ali had deposed, made a concerted effort to restore their kingdom. Particularly, Queen Lakshmi Ammani Rao, the widow of Krishnaraja Wadiyar II (d. 1766), requested that Governor Macartney of Madras assist her in regaining the Company's government. She promised him that she would repay him for all expenses incurred by the Company in restoring her to the throne. To achieve this purpose, she authorised her trusted agent, Tirumala Rao, to meet with the group of men deputed by Macartney. This group included Resident John Sulivan of Tanjore, Assistant Resident J.C. Hippisley and C.F. Schwartz. Before the men met in Tanjore, Macartney cunningly drafted an agreement on 27 September 1782 with thirteen stipulations that singularly favoured the Company. On 28 October 1782, the committee members met in Tanjore and discussed the *Rana Treaty*. John Sulivan, the Company's primary representative, led the negotiation. Out of desperation and outwitted by John Sulivan and Hippisley, Tirumala Rao agreed to the stipulations of the *Rana Treaty*.

Unsurprisingly, this treaty viewed Hyder Ali as a usurper. The deposed Queen voluntarily invited the Company to fight against Hyder Ali on her behalf; according to the stages of victory, she agreed to reward the Company with money and lands. Once she was on the throne of Mysore, she expected the Company not to interfere in her administration and not to station any Company soldiers in Seringapatam, which was a centre of religious significance for her. If the Company could not defeat Hyder Ali, she sought the Company's protection for her and her successors. She fixed the stages of rewarding the Company. When the Company drove Hyder Ali away from Coimbatore, she would pay them 300,000 Kanthiriyi Pagodas. No sooner did the Company conquer the regions of Balaghat, Barandanahalli, and Vijayapuram than she would have 100,000 Pagodas and another 100,000 Pagodas at Hyder Ali's surrender. When the Company captured Seringapatam, she would pay them 500,000 Pagodas. As soon as the Company proclaimed her the Queen of Mysore, she would pay the Company not only 500,000 Pagodas but also give them a region for revenue collection. Finally, she requested the Company to maintain their army, artillery, officers, guns and stores "in the same manner as given to the Rajah of Tanjore" and the "Government of Mysore must engage to pay whatever the charges of such an army as may exceed the sum of five lakhs of Pagodas."[60]

---

60 For a fuller version of the Rana Treaty, see Hayavadana Rao, History of Mysore, 1399–1799, 1181–1187.

The reason for Schwartz's involvement in this committee is unknown. He served as the official interpreter of the Company and an impartial witness to both parties. An unpublished handwritten copy of the introduction to these stipulations throws some light on the role of Schwartz's mediation. This introduction states that these stipulations stand "irrevocably as fixed." Only the queen and the Company could discuss and agree on altering them for mutual benefit. This introduction states that all articles of this treaty were "authenticated by the Revd Mr Swartz and interchanged with Tirumulrow." It also mentions that John Sulivan and J.C. Hippisley signed and affixed the seal of the Company "in the presence of the Almighty God." Then comes the astonishing remark: "Signed and sealed in the presence of C.F. Swartz."[61] This introduction does not state the reason for Schwartz's involvement. He was not only the official interpreter of the negotiators but also an impartial witness. The fact that this treaty was sealed and signed in his presence signified its sacredness and binding authority on both parties. The Company capitalised on the queen's desperation to defeat Hyder Ali and establish her rule over Mysore.

Within three months after signing this treaty, Hyder Ali died suddenly of cancer in Cittūr on 7 December 1782.[62] To prevent unwanted uproar, his ministers, Purnaiya and Krishna Rao, managed to keep his death secret and sent his body secretly to Kōlār. Hyder Ali's son, Tipu Sultan, succeeded his father and ruled with even greater vigour and violence. Only after his murder in 1799 did the Wadiyar family claim the throne of Mysore. Mummadi Krishnaraja Wadiyar III (1799–1831), a great-grandson of Queen Lakshmi Ammani Rao, ascended the throne at the age of five. Krishnacharya Purnaiya (1746–1812), the same diwan of Hyder Ali, administered Mysore on behalf of the boy king; however, the British residents in Mysore and Bangalore managed all political and economic affairs for the benefit of the Company.

7.4 Mediation Attempt with Tipu Sultan (15 December 1783 – 26 January 1784)

In July 1783, Tipu Sultan's soldiers surrounded the region of Mangalore and forced the Company soldiers there to starve. At that time, he expected help from France, but the *Treaty of Paris* (1763) prohibited the French from aiding him. In November 1783, Governor Macartney of Madras dispatched three negotiators, namely Anthony Sadlier, George Leonard Staunton and John Hudleston, to meet Tipu Sultan in Seringapatam and to make a peace treaty with him. To solve many

---

61 Bodleian Library: 72290ind-box2, Document 8 dated 18.10.1782: A copy of the Rana Treaty.

62 Anglo Mysore Wars: Second Anglo Mysore War–Treaty of Mangalore. In: Notes on Indian History, 13.05.2016. URL: https://www.notesonindianhistory.com/2016/05/anglo-mysore-wars-second-anglo-mysore.html (accessed on 29.10.2024): The sixty-year-old Hyder Ali died of cancer on 07.12.1782 near Chittoor. His ministers, Diwan Krishnacharya Purnaiya and Krishna Rao, kept his death secret. Later, they sent Hyder Ali's body to Kolar "in a chest resembling some valuable spoil."

problems along the way, they requested Macartney to persuade Schwartz to accompany them as their interpreter. By that time, Schwartz could speak not only Persian but also Hindustani. The deputies were aware of Schwartz's accurate and impartial translation of the details.

Consequently, at their request, Schwartz left Tanjore and reached Sattiyamaṅkalam on 15 December 1783. As he waited there, he received a personal letter from Governor Macartney dated 16 December 1783:

> To the Rev Mr Swartz, Dear Sir, I received with great pleasure your letter of the 9th instance informing me of your acquiescing with the request I made to you to proceed to the Mysore Country in order to lend your assistance to our commissioners towards the completion of the important business entrusted to their charge. I beg leave to express to you how much I think myself & those whom I have the honour to serve obliged to you for your readiness in undertaking a service which on many accounts could not be desirable to you. Enclosed I send a letter to Tippoo Sultan, which you will be pleased to deliver to him yourself. The charge of this letter, together with my own passport, which I sent to you, would render any other Cowle unnecessary. *Integer vitae, scelerisque purus, non eget Mauri iaculis, nec arcu*, ['The man who is of pure life and free from sin does not need bows and arrows of the Moor.']. In warmth, very great esteem and regard, Dear Sir, Your most obedient & most humble servant, Macartney. Fort St. George, 16th December 1783.[63]

This letter demonstrated the respect and trust that the Company had in Schwartz. He waited in vain to receive Tipu's permission. Without citing any reason, Tipu politely asked Schwartz to return to Tanjore. He would not have forgotten Rumbold's disregard for Schwartz's message for peace with Hyder Ali. Secondly, Tipu might have been aware of Schwartz's earlier involvement in the Rana Treaty, which had worked against his rule. Thirdly, he might have been aware of Schwartz's role as the Company's interpreter, who would have sought a harmonious agreement.

Disappointed by the circumstances that prevented Schwartz from meeting Tipu, he arrived in Tanjore on 27 January 1784.[64] However, the Company's negotiators proceeded and met with Tipu, not as envisaged in Seringapatam, but in Mangalore and signed a peace treaty with him on 6 April 1784.[65] This treaty ended the Second Anglo-Mysore War; subsequently, the Company obtained vast regions for tax collection.

---

63 SPCK D 36, Microfilm Frames 40–41.

64 Germann: Missionar Christian Friedrich Schwartz, 318.

65 Selections from the Letters, Despatches and Other State Papers Preserved in the Bombay Secretariat—Home Series. Ed. by George W. Forrest. Vol. II. Bombay 1887, 314–316: "Treaty of perpetual peace and friendship between the Honourable the English East India Company and the Nabob Tippoo Sultan Bahadur, on his own behalf; for the countries of Seringapatam Hyder Nagur etc. and all his other possessions settled by Anthony Sadlier, George Leonard Staunton and John Hudleston Esquires, on behalf of the Honourable English East India Company for all their possessions and for the Carnatic Payen Ghaut, by virtue of powers delegated to the Right Honourable the President & Select Committee of Fort St. George for that purpose, by the Honourable the Governor General & Council appointed by the King & Parliament of Great Britain, to direct & control all political affairs of the Honourable English East India Company in India, by the said Nabob agreeably to the following Articles, which are to be strictly and invariably, observed as long as the Sun &

A month after his return to Tanjore, on 20 February 1784, Schwartz stated the following: Tipu Sultan wanted to live in peace with the Company, but the Company sent General Fullarton from Tiruccirāppaḷḷi to march towards Mangalore with his army of 1,500 European soldiers and 8,000 Indian sepoys. Fullarton had captured Coimbatore. Tipu was unhappy about the Company's aggression. Consequently, Tipu and Fullarton did not permit provisions for each other's army to pass through the areas under their control. Schwartz was sarcastic about this mutual transgression: The "people name it political wisdom. Others name it rottenness and treachery."[66]

As the negotiators approached Seringapatam, Governor Macartney requested that Schwartz meet them and participate in the peace negotiations. Schwartz was aware of the dangers along the way, yet he decided to travel there and assist the suffering people in the lands controlled by Tipu and the Company. He wrote a letter to Tipu's General Rauschen Chan, revealing the purpose of his travel and stating that he would leave Tanjore on 15 December 1783. He passed through Tiruccirāppaḷḷi, Vadamadurai, Dindigul and Dharapuram. He noticed how sepoys dismantled the huts' roofs and used the wood to cook their meals. They robbed the farmers of their agricultural produce and fed on their "sweat and blood." The sorrowful condition of these suffering people saddened Schwartz. On 30 December, he joined General William Fullarton near Yāṉaimalai, also known as „Elephant Mountain." As Fullarton and Schwartz travelled in their palanquins, they watched with sadness how the sepoys ran through the agricultural fields, destroyed the crops unnecessarily, and caused deliberate damage. Therefore, Fullarton ordered horse riders to force the sepoys to march along the roads and not to destroy the crops; however, this did not have much effect, as numerous people, including children, followed the army. Ten thousand soldiers were marching, but those who followed them were nine or ten times more.[67] As soon as the military set up their tents, the mobs ran through the nearby villages and plundered the houses and fields. Fullarton even arranged for the hanging of a few violent plunderers. Several leaders of the surrounding places came and requested Fullarton's protection, and he sent a guard to each village.[68]

Moon shall last, by both parties, that is to say, by the English Company & the three Governments of Bengal, Madras and Bombay and the Nabob Tippoo Sultan Bahadur."

66 AFSt/M 1 B 75 : 27.

67 Peter Joseph du Plat: Brief vom 29. März 1784. In: A Great War in South India: German Accounts of the Anglo-Mysore Wars, 1766–1799. Ed. by Ravi Ahuja and Martin Christof-Füchsle. Berlin 2020, 345–356, here 349: "The English employ porters to carry their wine, palanquins and torches. The army must pay higher wages for these people. Another evil plagues the army as well: every sepoy or black soldier is accompanied by his wife, his parents and children, the parents of his wife and other relatives. The EIC [i.e. the English East India Company] must pay for their food and maintain them. Their love to the sepoys is great and the sepoys feel happier when their own people are around them. Therefore, the Company does not force them to leave their families back. These many people increase the expenses of the army and cause more work in procuring and providing all necessary things for them. However, a sepoy is happy with a bowl of rice, pepper water and some butter. They do not eat meat."

68 AFSt/M 1 B 75 : 27 and NHR 3, 1785, issue 29, 560–576.

Schwartz, fellow Christians in the army and Fullarton celebrated the end of the old year and the beginning of the new year. After hearing the songs and the predictions of prosperity in the year, Fullarton astonishingly critiqued the Company. He questioned the Company's vain attempts to enrich themselves by oppressing Indians. Schwartz recorded this critique: During the past eight months since he had last seen Schwartz, Fullarton had not witnessed anything that had delighted him. He confessed to Schwartz that fighting was the duty of the soldiers. However, no Company officer worked for the country's and its people's welfare. Therefore, he heartily wished the Indians would drive the Company out of India. He stressed that their departure would mean a better life for the people. Schwartz intervened and asked whether anything good would result from the proper institutions the Company could establish for the country's benefit. Fullarton responded that the Company officers were deeply corrupt. No officer worked in one place for three years; therefore, these officers were unstable and unreliable. Should an intelligent person occupy a responsible position, that person would not stay there long. A successor tore down what his predecessor had built. Fullarton stated further that the Company was so corrupt that an honest person could not manage the corrupt personnel. If someone reported on the country and its governance, they exaggerated everything and presented their embellished accounts as truth. Fullarton asserted that he would not tread the path of his predecessors. Contrary to custom, he did not levy any tax on goods sold in his barracks. Other officers criticised him for it. However, he gladly and willingly accepted the blame rather than harbouring an evil conscience.[69]

On 1 January 1784, Schwartz took leave from Fullarton, met General Rauschen Chan in his place and celebrated the New Year under a tree. A village leader (*jamadar*) approached Schwartz and thanked him for the worship service, songs and prayers. Schwartz opined: "If Europeans would honour God, the inhabitants of this country would honour and esteem them." In the meantime, Rauschen Chan sent Schwartz and his people the necessary provisions, including rice, butter, spices, sheep, fruits and some wheat flour for baking bread. Fullarton sent Rauschen Chan three kinds of wine, namely "Bouteille Branntwein, Madeirawein and Claret," and received Rauschen Chan's feedback. It was unusual for this Muslim military general to enjoy and comment on different kinds of wine. Rauschen Chan provided a travel permit to Schwartz and his party, allowing them to proceed. Schwartz then went to Tipu's other camp, which General Navas Beg commanded. While waiting several days for Tipu's permission, he shared God's word with some people there. Finally, Schwartz did not receive Tipu's permission to proceed and decided to return.

On 30 December 1783, Schwartz neared Coimbatore, where he met Colonel William Fullarton, the Company's Southern Army commander. Fullarton lamented that he had received orders from his superiors to leave Coimbatore and proceed to Dindigul. This news disappointed Schwartz deeply. He could not understand

69 AFSt/M 1 B 75 : 27 and NHR 3, 1785, issue 29, 567.

how Fullarton's superiors could ask him to leave the wealthy region of Coimbatore before the Company's negotiators could establish peace with Tipu. If Fullerton had stayed in Coimbatore, Tipu would have listened to the negotiators more readily and willingly. Schwartz wondered how the Company in Madras would "manage the beast. The colonel said, 'I could not help it.' I have written in strong terms to the Government."[70]

On Sunday, January 4, 1784, Schwartz conducted a worship service for all who were willing to participate. At the end of the service, several villagers informed him about Tipu's soldiers, who had taken away everything they had for sustenance. On January 5, Schwartz and his team arrived in Sathyamangalam. The fort commander (*killadar*) asked Schwartz to stay in his tent until he had received Tipu's permission. As he waited, he could walk out of the fort and meet people; they narrated to him many kinds of cruelties, including hangings by Tipu and his generals.

On 18 January, two horse riders, sent by Rauschen Chan, accompanied Schwartz back to Sathyamangalam and requested that he return to Tanjore. As he returned, several people in Vadamadurai expressed their disappointment that he had not brought them the news of peace. He celebrated the Sunday worship service in Maṇappāṟai and reached Tiruccirāppaḷḷi on January 26, staying with Pohle. Two days later, on 28 January, the young Kohlhoff welcomed him to Tanjore.

The Company officers in Madras were unhappy that Tipu did not allow Schwartz to meet him. They requested that Schwartz again consider joining the negotiators in Thalasseri (in modern Kerala). Schwartz politely declined the request for health reasons: He had developed a scorbutic rosary (i.e., painful tenderness of anterior ribs) that made travelling in a palanquin difficult. He could neither sit nor lie in the swaying and shaking palanquin.

Schwartz lamented the dishonesty on both sides: the Company and Tipu blamed each other for violating the ceasefire. Company officers met Tipu Sultan in Mangalore and signed the *Treaty of Mangalore* on March 11, 1784, with him. This treaty ended the Second Anglo-Mysore War. Total peace, however, did not return because Tipu Sultan and the Company did not trust each other.[71] After the *Treaty of Mangalore*, the Company handed over the fort of Mangalore not to establish peace but to avoid being starved by Tipu. Tipu had taken the best soldiers with him; nobody knew whether he would strike. Schwartz ended his report by praying to God for peace in the land. He believed that following the Lord Jesus Christ seriously was the only way to establish peace for all people.[72]

A popular tradition holds that in February 1784, Tipu Sultan captured numerous Roman Catholics of Mangalore and ordered them to move to Seringapatam. Many thousands of them died on the way. He forced most of those who arrived in Seringapatam to embrace Islam. Those who resisted forced conversion suffered a

---

70 BL ADD 41622, folio 153: "Copies of the letters from Mr Swartz to J[ohn] Sulivan Esq. dated 30 & 31st Dec. [17]83."

71 NHR 3, 1784, issue 28, 401–402.

72 NHR 3, 1785, issue 29, 576.

great deal. Xavier Koodapuzha mentioned that the atrocities of Tipu Sultan against the Christians in the northern regions of modern Kerala provoked a protest; for example, on 2 February 1787, Christians of eighty-four parishes assembled in Angamaly Padiyola to protest that Tipu Sultan's armies had destroyed their church buildings.[73] Despite the setback of a failed mediation, Schwartz's unwavering commitment to matters related to Tipu remained steadfast.[74] In 1792, Tipu learned of the Company army's advance under Cornwallis's command and came forward to offer peace. This treaty was a blow to Tipu Sultan's pride because he lost half of his territories to the Company, paid a large amount of money as war reparations, and surrendered his son as a hostage. However, he preferred suffering this loss rather than risking the storming of the place.[75]

At the request of Cornwallis, Schwartz visited Tipu's sons in Madras and found the younger son "full of animation." He read several Persian verses to Schwartz "concerning the providence of God and our duty to submit without repining to His allotment. The elder boy was silent."[76] He probably stammered and was unwilling to speak before strangers.[77] Schwartz, acting as an intermediary, made efforts to assist the Company negotiators as their interpreter. However, his repeated attempts to establish peace, though remarkable, did not produce any tangible results because Tipu Sultan, who respected Schwartz, chose not to meet him.

The Company continued to attempt to defeat Tipu Sultan, annex his territories, and plunder his wealth. Finally, in April 1799, Tipu Sultan's general, Mir Sadiq, betrayed his master and helped Major General David Baird to breach the wall of Seringapatam. On 4 April 1799, Company soldiers shot Tipu Sultan dead, celebrated this murder,[78] became supreme rulers in southern India, enriched the treasuries and museums of India and Britain, and entertained the British public for a long time.[79]

---

73 Xavier Koodapuzha: Christianity in India. Kottayam 1998, 101–102.

74 AFSt/M 1 C 26 : 1: Many rumours about Tipu Sultan's death circulated. For example, on 28.01.1785, Schwartz reported to Pasche that he had heard from Gericke about Tipu Sultan's death. Tipu was a more terrible tyrant than his father. It was alleged that as he made a broad road through a forest along the Malabar Coast, he was gravely wounded one evening and died. The following day, his people carried him to Seringapatam. This rumour was untrue. Tipu was killed on 04.05.1799 in Seringapatam.

75 Memoirs of the Rev. Joseph D[aniel] Jænicke, 112.

76 Memoirs of the Rev. Joseph D[aniel] Jænicke, 113: The book's editor inserted the following footnote: Schwartz did not record many things that might interest his readers. However, his "letters, like his life, are full of One Thing," namely, serving the Lord Jesus Christ as an ambassador for peace, justice and social harmony.

77 Schwartz died before the Fourth Anglo-Mysore War (1798–1799) ended. BL ADD 13663: The Nizam of Hyderabad and the Marathas supported Cornwallis's war against Tipu Sultan.

78 BL ADD 13663, 96–165: Journal of the Mysore Campaign, here 140: "Thus fell Tippoo Sultan, the son of the renowned Hyder whose life has been a continued career of ambition & cruelty and whose death will afford to the haughty Princes of the East an awful lesson of instruction; his treaties with the French Directory, his intended plans of cooperation with Buonaparte, have all come to light, and formed a part of the great combination with Herman Shaw, the Marathas, & other Indian powers; for extirpating the English from the land, and he seems to have had imbibed the same eternal enmity to them that the son of Amilear [sic! = Hannibal, the son of the Carthaginian General Hamilcar Barca] had to the Romans; his

7.5 Mediation with Tanjore Farmers (1783)

Tulāji did not recover well from his imprisonment (16 September 1773 to 11 April 1776), ill-treatment, and looting by Wallajah and his English creditors.[80] The socio-economic conditions in Tanjore during the late 18th century were dire. Wallajah, Tulāji, and the Company robbed ordinary people so thoroughly that they had little or nothing to survive. The invasions by Hyder Ali and Tipu Sultan from 1780 further impoverished these people. Tipu's war policies were more destructive than those of his father. Wars and relentless exploitations by Wallajah, Tulāji and the Company created a devastating famine in Tanjore.[81]

On 12 September 1783, Schwartz wrote to Pasche that finding a healthy person during the famine was challenging. The famine, which resulted from the war policies and practices of Hyder Ali and Tipu Sultan, severely affected the people of Tanjore. People looked like walking skeletons. After his return from Seringapatam in 1779, he knew that Rumbold would wage a war against Hyder Ali. Schwartz bought massive quantities of paddy at a lower price to help his catechists feed some starving people on the streets.[82]

In the same letter of 12 September 1783, Schwartz described another problem that affected the farmers of Tanjore and their king. He stated that every inhabitant felt compelled to lie and steal. For example, the farmers bribed the revenue officers so that the latter would lower the value of the unharvested crops. Otherwise, the farmers should hand over three-fourths of their harvest to the revenue officers, who might resell it for a higher price. The farmers could keep only one-fourth of their harvest. Thus, Schwartz felt that the farmers and the revenue collectors impoverished the royal treasury.[83]

During this famine, the farmers were reluctant to sell their paddy because they feared the buyers would not pay them. The famine severely affected the Company soldiers stationed within the city of Tanjore. Most of them did not receive their salaries for about sixteen months and starved. Some of them died miserably, highlighting the dire consequences of the socio-economic conditions. Their superiors in Madras focused on looting Tanjore and returning to Britain with a

---

character, as far as our knowledge extends, is chiefly marked for his harshness to prisoners, & the number of his murders; among those who have survived captivity, General Baird himself is an instance."

79 For details about this long-term impact, see Anne Buddle, Pauline Rohatgi and Iain Gordon Brown: The Tiger and the Thistle—Tipu Sultan and the Scots in India 1760–1800. Edinburgh 1999.

80 After his reinstatement, Tulāji, an ardent Vaiṣṇavite, built new Viṣṇu temples such as Nīlakaṇṭa Perumāḷ Kōvil and Naraciṅka Perumāḷ Kōvil. He helped repair older temples. Therefore, people called him the "Servant of Viṣṇu Temples" (*Viṣṇu-ālaya-t-toṇdaṉ*). He richly endowed Brahmin communities and settlements. He patronised Telugu and Sanskrit poets such as Ālūr Kuppana.

81 Love: Vestiges of Old Madras. Vol. 1. 558: Hyder Ali's war plunged the Carnatic region into acute famine. Numerous people died in the city of Madras. Many famine-stricken left Madras.

82 NHR 3, 1785, issue 29, 515. AFSt/M 1 B 74 : 33: By 18.03.1784, Schwartz fed 120 poor people daily. He picked them up from the streets of Tanjore.

83 AFSt/M 1 B 75 : 25 and NHR 3, 1785, issue 29, 516.

large fortune. They neglected their soldiers, either employed by Wallajah or hired by Tulāji. For example, since 1766, the Company in Madras reduced the allowance (*batta*) to their field officers and soldiers. Discontent was brewing among the Company soldiers.

As the famine worsened, Schwartz requested several Europeans in Tanjore to donate money to purchase enough paddy to feed the starving people. The trust the people, especially the farmers, placed in Schwartz was evident when Tulāji and the Company Resident in Tanjore requested his help. Aware of the people's confidence in him, Schwartz asked his catechists to persuade the local farmers to sell their paddy and lend their oxen to carry large quantities of paddy into the city.

> During the paddy harvest in February 1783, the people of Tanjore were afraid of a war. The soldiers in the fort had few provisions. The king's servants lamented that they could not hire oxen to bring paddy into the city. However, the real reason for not obtaining oxen was people's distrust of the king and the Company officers. They believed that if they sent their oxen to transport paddy, they would lose them because the king and the Company officers would keep them and not pay them any money. Finally, the king and the Company officers requested Schwartz to write to the inhabitants, assuring them of payment and protection and urging them to send their oxen to transport grains into the fort. The inhabitants trusted Schwartz's promise, sending over a thousand of their oxen and transporting more grain into the fort than was needed. Schwartz ensured that they received their just payment. His catechists paid the owners of the oxen and their paddy honestly and gave them a wage for their work for 1½ months. The farmers went away happily. Schwartz reiterated that he had deputed his catechists to perform this work; they went into the countryside and oversaw the entire job. Simultaneously, they preached God's Word to the inhabitants. Schwartz expected this sowing of God's Word would bring blessings.[84]

On 11 October 1784, Schwartz informed Pasche that he thanked God for protection from the wars of 1783. In that year, more English traders, creditors and renters came to Tanjore, increasing the suffering of the soldiers. The European soldiers received small quantities of rice, which was insufficient. The Indian sepoys did not receive their salary for more than sixteen months. Hunger drove them to arrest some of their senior officers. When the Mysore armies attacked Tanjore, the Company in Tanjore had no ammunition in store. Neither did the soldiers receive cooked rice for meals. Food grains were available in the countryside. However, no one was willing to send bullocks into the city. Again, King Tulāji and the Company residents in Tanjore requested Schwartz's help to save the town from hunger and starvation. Schwartz wrote letters to the farmers, and one of his catechists took his letters to the oxen owners and requested that they send their oxen. The catechists also persuaded the farmers to sell paddy. Consequently, 1,200 bulls brought 70,000–80,000 kalam of rice into the fort. Schwartz stated that he paid the farmers and the oxen owners well, and they departed happily. A Company officer observed these events and exclaimed as follows:

---

84 AFSt/M 1 B 74 : 31.

> It is a new method of paying people correctly and fully. We are not used to this. According to our customary procedure, which these thieves follow, the Company would have paid 4,000 Pagodas more, and the people would not have received even half of it. They say, 'We charge the Company in such and such a manner. This is customary.'[85]

Schwartz's mediation with the farmers of Tanjore was not just a timely intervention but a significant act of dedication that saved many people's lives within the city. His services to the ordinary people during times of crisis remained impactful and noteworthy.

7.6 Mediation with Tanjore Emigrants (1786)

On 17 July 1786, Schwartz informed his friend Sorge about his mediatory services to the emigrants of Tanjore:[86] The Second Anglo-Mysore War impoverished the inhabitants of Tanjore to such a miserable condition that they failed to respond to Schwartz's preaching. Many left Tanjore and emigrated to neighbouring Nagapattinam, Karaikal and other places.[87] The time for sowing paddy seeds arrived; rivers and irrigation channels were full of water, but there were no farmers in Tanjore. Schwartz exclaimed that he had never witnessed such horrid conditions. Governor Campbell feared that he would not get the necessary revenues from Tanjore. To remedy the situation, Campbell organised a Committee of Inspection, appointed Schwartz as one of its members, and charged it with overseeing cultivation, harvest, and revenue collection. This Committee terrified Tulāji, and he secretly requested Schwartz to ensure his dignity as king and justice for the ordinary people of Tanjore. Immediately, Schwartz proposed seven conditions and requested Tulāji to accept them:

1) Schwartz wanted the assessors to evaluate the unharvested produce fairly. They should not impose a high tax on poor people. Earlier, they behaved differently; they overestimated the harvest and levied higher taxes. For example, the assessors estimated 150 kalam of paddy for a field producing a maximum of 100 kalam of paddy. Two-thirds of the produce belonged to the king. Sometimes, the royal assessors would take away the entire harvest of 100 kalam paddy, leaving nothing for the farmers. Schwartz demanded that the king stop exploiting the people, and the king agreed. 2) The royal assessors should assess only the

---

85 AFSt/M 1 B 75 : 24 quoted in Germann: Missionar Christian Friedrich Schwartz, 317.

86 AFSt/M 1 C 27 : 5.

87 Germann: Missionar Christian Friedrich Schwartz, 342–343: The Company's peace agreement with Mysore did not significantly benefit the people of Tanjore. Tulāji could not bear the sudden death of his only son and heir to his throne. He also lost other relatives. Depressed, he shut himself within the palace. His senior officers used this opportunity to exploit the people of Tanjore. Notably, the greedy minister suffocated the people. The farmers left their fields uncultivated. Sixty-five thousand people emigrated from Tanjore. The Company officers and Tulāji tried to bring them back. After their efforts had failed, Tulāji requested Schwartz to persuade the emigrants to return to Tanjore and cultivate their lands. The Company officers noticed Schwartz's impact on the people and began to seek his advice more often than before.

harvested, thrashed and measured paddy. They should leave one-third of this paddy to the farmers. Schwartz believed that this measure was sufficient for the farmers, as they could cultivate their fields twice a year and thus sustain themselves adequately. 3) Earlier, the farmers paid a special tax of one Fano for every 100 kalam of paddy that the royal assessors bought from them. Schwartz felt this tax was unnecessary and illogical, so he persuaded the king to cancel it. 4) If the royal assessors, on behalf of the king, wished to sell some paddy back to the farmers, the farmers should pay ten Fano for every 100 kalam of paddy. This price was 30% less than the average price of paddy. Schwartz advised the king to stop this unjust practice, and the king abolished it. 5) If the king decided to sell the paddy back to the farmers, the farmers would have to pay one Pagoda more than the market price for one hundred kalam. 6) The king paid half the salary of his assessors; the assessors took the other half of their salary from the farmers. As a result, there were deceptions and oppressions. Schwartz persuaded the king to abolish this practice and arranged for the entire salary to be paid from the royal treasury. Additionally, earlier, the king leased the entire salt production to influential persons of Tanjore for a high price. When these people harvested salt, they sold it for a much higher price. As a result, ordinary people could not afford to buy salt. Schwartz persuaded the king to cancel all these unjust lease agreements and to offer goods and services at a fair price to the ordinary people.

Schwartz did not mention the seventh condition, but he added that, until that time, people survived the struggle in three ways: some stole, some ran away, and some sold what they had possessed. As an envoy for peace, justice, and social harmony, Schwartz convinced King Tulāji to cease unjust and unreasonable dealings and implement measures that helped ordinary people live as well as they could.

Schwartz knew that King Tulāji agreed to these conditions because he was afraid of the Committee of Inspection, which might otherwise take over the entire administration of Tanjore. At that time, whole towns and villages were deserted, with no inhabitants or farmers. The farmers outside Tanjore did not want to believe Tulāji or the Company's assurances. By contrast, they trusted Schwartz and his assurance of fair treatment. Consequently, 7,000 farmers returned; soon, more emigrant farmers joined them. Although the right season for sowing paddy seeds had passed, these farmers worked harder and sought to achieve better harvests than before. Schwartz did not miss an opportunity to speak with them about the Gospel of the Lord Jesus Christ. He believed his works to establish spiritual and temporal peace and social harmony would bear fruit in time.[88]

Sometimes, Schwartz mediated between different groups of weavers. For example, in July 1790, the weavers of Kumbakonam complained against Resident

---

[88] AFSt/M 1 C 27 : 8: On 02.10.1786, Schwartz described this episode to Pasche and included additional information: the servants of the king, the Nawab and the Company oppressed the people so much that many of them left the towns and villages. The agricultural field remained uncultivated; all main businesses ceased to function. For further details, see An Abstract of the Annual Reports, 254–255.

George Andrew Ram, who had appointed a Company representative of the weaver villages of Kumbakonam. This person sold low-quality indigo and clothes for a higher price, which the weavers could not afford. For example, earlier, the weavers sold a dyed cloth for thirty Panam. Ram's agent asked the weavers to pay forty Panam for low-quality dye and clothes. Earlier, these weavers received customers from the south and the north. After Ram's intervention, they did not come to them because they did not want to buy low-quality goods for a higher price. This intervention destroyed the lives of several weavers. The representatives approached Ameer Singh for intervention. Ameer Singh did not help them because he had borrowed 20,000 Pagodas from Ram. The weavers asked Suburau Gopal Rao, the leader of all weavers in Kumbakonam, but he was unable to convince Ameer Sing to intercede with Ram. Gopal Rao had loaned 9,000 Pagodas to Ameer Singh. Finally, the leaders of all the weaver villages met with Schwartz, submitted their complaints, and requested that he intercede with the Company in Tanjore and Madras.[89] These weavers trusted Schwartz and believed he would secure justice for them.

7.7 Mediation with Tranquebar

7.7.1 Regarding Tranquebar Emigrants in Tanjore

From 1620, the governors of Tranquebar paid the king of Tanjore their annual tribute of 2,000 Cakkarams on a special occasion. This tribute symbolised the king's political, economic and ritual significance and was a significant part of the financial relationship between Tranquebar and Tanjore.[90] Otherwise, they managed their political and mercantile affairs independently. When the kings of Tanjore demanded more money from Tranquebar, or the inhabitants of Tranquebar and Tanjore settled in each other's territories, conflicts between Tanjore and Tranquebar surfaced. For example, on 7 September 1756, the missionaries in Tranquebar reported an armed conflict in the territory of Tranquebar. Perumāḷ Nāyakkar, an employee of the king of Tanjore, guarded the boundaries between Tranquebar and the Kingdom of Tanjore. He disagreed with the governor of Tranquebar on specific issues, and in June 1756, he dispatched his soldiers to attack and plunder villages such as Erukkañcēri and Āṉantamaṅkalam. His soldiers stole cattle and troubled the inhabitants, leading to a significant armed

89 IOR/P/316/89, 269–328. Schwartz's translations of these letters merit a separate study.

90 Strandberg: The Moḍī Documents from Tanjore, 20 and Rastén: The Tranquebar tribute, 42: On *Dasara* (i.e. *Vijayadaśamī*, 'the victorious tenth day' at the end of the nine-day festival of *Navaratri*, the 'nine nights'), the kings of Tanjore received their annual tributes from the governors of Tranquebar in the Grand Audience Hall. Since the Vijayanagar Empire, this day has been considered the most auspicious day for kings and princes to organise processions and worship the goddess Durga. This day symbolically affirmed the sovereign status of the kings and princes, who awarded grants and titles to subordinate nobles, property owners and dignitaries.

conflict.[91] Diago, one of the Tamil Lutheran pastors, reported on 11 October 1756 that the Tanjore soldiers had destroyed his house in Tillaiyāṭi.[92]

After the enthronement of Ameer Singh in April 1787, Schwartz mediated between Tanjore and Tranquebar. On 29 May 1787, Ameer Singh invited Schwartz to meet him in Kumbakonam. He informed Schwartz how Governor Campbell of Madras did not recognise the dignity of his kingship (lit. Stolz, 'pride') and disregarded his negotiations with the governor of Tranquebar. He asked him to speak with Campbell about this matter.[93] Schwartz's efforts to mediate these delicate negotiations were commendable.

Schwartz interceded with the governors of Madras and Tranquebar, arranging the annual tribute payment by the Danes to Ameer Singh. Ameer Singh was pleased with this arrangement and desired to reward Schwartz. On his return to Tanjore, he gave Schwartz the village of Āyarpāṭi (lit. *Aidpari*) bordering Tranquebar. Schwartz refused to accept it as private property because people could easily interpret it as a bribe. He requested Ameer Singh to issue a royal deed in favour of him and his successors, so that it would belong to the Lutheran Church and schools in Tanjore.[94]

On 5 September 1787, Hippisley, the Company's paymaster in Tanjore, met Ameer Singh to announce his permanent departure from Tanjore. Schwartz served as Hippisley's interpreter. Ameer Singh requested Hippisley to hand over the royal deed for Āyarpāṭi to Schwartz. This deed named Schwartz its perpetual owner and stated that he could use its annual income of 1,000 Rupees in any way he liked. Schwartz decided to use it to support three English-medium schools in Tanjore: one for the children of Tamil Lutherans, a second for the children of English soldiers, and a third for the Provincial School for Brahmin youth in Tanjore.[95]

On 29 September 1787, Schwartz informed his friend Pasche in London about the extreme poverty that affected the inhabitants of Tranquebar. Some left Tranquebar and settled in the adjoining places that belonged to the Kingdom of Tanjore.[96] A few days later, on 8 October 1787, the missionaries in Tranquebar informed Director Johann Ludwig Schulze of a devastating storm that had occurred from 17 to 21 May 1787, which had destroyed the houses and

---

91 AFSt/M 1 B 46 : 2 and 3.

92 AFSt/M 1 B 47 : 27.

93 AFSt/M 1 C 29b : 7.

94 Germann: Missionar Christian Friedrich Schwartz, 346.

95 Germann: Missionar Christian Friedrich Schwartz, 345–346. Ī. Ē. Cellatturai: "Tañcai Marāttiya Maṉṉarkaḷum Kiṟistavarkaḷum [Tamil: 'The Marathi Kings of Tanjore and Christians']," Māmaṉṉar Carapōji. Ed. by Catācivam. Tañcāvūrar 1990, 23–40, here 25: In 1794, Ameer Singh gave the village of Sadayangal (nowadays, approximately twenty-five kilometres from Tanjore, postal code 614302 in Pāpanāsam Taluk) to Schwartz in exchange for the village of Āyarpāṭi near Tranquebar. German Lutheran missionaries and their Tamil followers were unable to reach Āyarpāṭi quickly. Sadayangal encompassed an area of 30 vēli and yielded 1,000 kalam of paddy annually. At that time, a kalam of paddy was priced at 0.75 Paisa, and the missionaries earned an annual income of 1,750 Rupees from this village. Additionally, Ameer Singh donated the land where the current *Makarnōmpu Cāvaṭi* in Tanjore is located to the Tamil Lutherans to build their houses.

96 AFSt/M 1 C 28 : 72.

possessions of many inhabitants. Most survivors fled into the nearby territories of Tanjore. At that time, some members of the "Salupper Caste" (The *saluppa ceṭṭiyārkaḷ*) mistreated their domestic servants and agricultural labourers in Tranquebar.[97] Despite this oppression, these brave individuals also left Tranquebar and settled in the nearby territories that belonged to the Kingdom of Tanjore, showing remarkable resilience in the face of adversity.

The departure of these people increased the suffering in Tranquebar because agricultural work nearly came to a halt. Governor Peter Hermann Abbestée (1779–1783, 1785–1788) implored them to return, but they did not listen. Ameer Singh also attempted to send these people back to Tranquebar to maintain a peaceful relationship, but they refused to go. On 10 December 1787, Ameer Singh requested an assurance from Abbestée that he would welcome the emigrants back to Tranquebar and provide for their care. He advised Abbestée to send his assurance through Schwartz. As soon as he received it from Schwartz, he would immediately allow the emigrants to return to Tranquebar.[98] In December 1787, Sivarāya, Ameer Singh's *Sarakhela* (equivalent to a Prime Minister), wrote another letter to Schwartz, whom he addressed as Pādri (a spiritual „father"). Sivarāya reminded Schwartz about Ameer Singh's earlier request to Abbestée and urged Schwartz to intervene. Strandberg's English version of this letter reads as follows:

> To the priest, Mr. Schwartz, many greetings are sent by Sivarāya. Moreover, in accordance with what you yourself said, a letter from the Honourable Mahārājā [Ameer Singh] to the Governor of Tranquebar, [Peter Hermann] Abbestée, has been written, prepared, and sealed. The sealed letter has been put into a bag and sent to you by messenger: you must see it to that it is handed over to the [official] interpreter [of Tranquebar], Dāniye Pile [i.e. Daniel Pillay, 1740–1802] and brought to Tranquebar. In order that the inhabitants of Tranquebar may go from here, you had been told that a warrant from Governor Abbestée should be produced. Get that done and the rest of the (Tranquebar) inhabitants will go (home from here). Where there is friendship, what need is there for writing more? Many greetings. To be forwarded to the priest Schwartz.[99]

On 1 February 1788, Schwartz recorded the following circumstances that necessitated his visit to Tranquebar in January 1788: Schwartz accompanied many

---

97 AFSt/M 1 C 29b : 29. These missionaries included Jacob Klein, Johann Friedrich König, Christoph Samuel John, Johann Peter Rottler, and Peder Rubek Hagelund. They mentioned Ameer Singh, who, instead of Serfoji, became the king. They also referred to Kiernander's visit to Friedrigsnagar (i.e. Serampore) near Calcutta. And they recommend starting a new centre of missionary activities there.

98 Strandberg: The Moḍī Documents from Tanjore, 319: Ameer Singh's letter is written in *Moḍī*-script. Strandberg's English version of this letter reads as follows: The "inhabitants of Tranquebar have in big numbers gone out of that place and come into our territory. We have told some things to the priest Mr. Schwartz, to get them to go by (you) giving them satisfaction through issuing a *cowle* ['agreement']; you will be informed by what he writes to you. When you have sent the cowle by the hand of Mr. Schwartz and we have made a strong injunction to the inhabitants (of Tranquebar), we shall send them all together with some of our people."

99 Strandberg: The Moḍī Documents from Tanjore, 321. A facsimile of this *Moḍi*-letter kept in the Royal Archives of Denmark in Copenhagen with the Call Number AsK 2183(d) is reproduced and transliterated on pages 182–183.

protesting inhabitants of Tranquebar from Tanjore country back into Tranquebar. They alleged that in June 1787, the Government of Tranquebar ill-treated them; hence, they left Tranquebar and settled six miles away from its borders in the Tanjore country. All attempts to persuade them to return failed. Many rogues joined them in raiding Tranquebar, damaging agricultural fields, vandalising properties and committing shameful things. They prevented the farmers of Tranquebar from sowing seeds, planting, and cultivating their fields. If any farmer disregarded their warning, vandalising mobs of emigrants plucked the plants, and they stopped all travellers from and to Tranquebar. Therefore, the inhabitants of Tranquebar, living within the walled town, could not hire any washermen, shoemakers, or fishermen. They did not have firewood to cook their meals. Schwartz stated that this protest affected everyone, and his missionary colleagues in Tranquebar shared this suffering. Simultaneously, the people of Tanjore, among whom these Tranquebar emigrants resided, encouraged them to stay with them for an extended period.[100]

Neither Abbestée nor Ameer Singh persuaded the emigrants to return to Tranquebar. They sought Schwartz's intervention. He discovered that the leaders of the emigrants from Tranquebar wished to pay Ameer Singh 12,000 pagodas and requested that he permit them to remain longer within the Tanjore territory.[101] This agreement alarmed Schwartz, and he urged Ameer Singh not to accept this bribe. Finally, the same leaders approached Schwartz and asked for his mediation between Tanjore and Tranquebar. He rebuked them for the evils they had committed; in particular, he scolded them for destroying the agricultural fields and thus sinning against God. After speaking with them, he wrote to Abbestée and requested his assurance to forgive the emigrants' evil deeds, to hear their complaints, and to redress them impartially according to the rule of law. The governor promised to carry out Schwartz's recommendations.

At that stage, the emigrants feared retaliation and hesitated to return. They requested that Schwartz go with them. Therefore, Schwartz went ahead of them and led them to the governor's house, where he told him, "Now you have your sheep that had gone astray." Then, each one returned to their homes. The governor appointed a committee to hear their complaints and solve their problems in court.

---

100 AFSt/M 1 C 29a : 5; AFSt/M 1 C 29a : 3: On 19.01.1788, Schwartz shared some additional details of this event with his friend Pastor Sorge: Having brought emigrants back to Tranquebar and attended to their needs, Schwartz returned to Tanjore on 14.01.1788. Most of the city's inhabitants of Tranquebar left and settled in Tanjore Country. The governor of Tranquebar made a concerted effort for six months to bring them back. The emigrants were stubborn and remained in Tanjore. Finally, their leaders requested that Schwartz serve as their mediator. Accordingly, Schwartz wrote to the governor of Tranquebar and asked him to forgive all the evils they had committed against the people of Tranquebar. On receiving the governor's written assurances, Schwartz led the people and went ahead of them. They followed him. Along the way, he preached about God's grace and forgiveness of sins. He stated that the governance of Tanjore was so pitiable that Schwartz feared a total takeover by the Company. He encouraged Sorge to live a Christian life in Europe, which had become increasingly non-Christian.

101 AFSt/M 1 C 29a : 5.

Schwartz sat in the court for some time and witnessed the redressal of their complaints. Concurrently, he shared with the people the right way to find life and worship God. He prayed to God for justice for the people who suffered without it.

On 29 September 1788, the missionaries in Tranquebar informed Director Johann Ludwig Schulze in Halle about Schwartz's mediatory role and Schulze, for some undisclosed reason, did not print this part:

> The unrest and disturbances that the Tamil inhabitants of Tranquebar caused last year have ceased. Those who had taken refuge in Tanjore have been invited back to Tranquebar for peaceful living. Towards the end of last year, Schwartz, appointed as the mediator, led many returnees into Tranquebar. Nowadays, these people remain content and quiet because they fear dire consequences if they disturb the city of Tranquebar.[102]

Thus, Schwartz, as a mediator, promoted peace, justice and social harmony, which neither the king of Tanjore nor the Governor of Tranquebar could ensure.

7.7.2 Regarding Tranquebar Loans to Tanjore

The Company did not appreciate Tranquebar's existence as a Danish colony. They did not want Ameer Singh to rent or mortgage any new villages or towns to the Danes and receive loans from them. Ameer Singh thought it was his right to deal with the Danes on his terms. By contrast, the Company opposed him in this regard. Both requested Schwartz's mediation to resolve the problem. In 1778, the Danish East India Company (DEIC) underwent significant changes.[103] The reign of the sickly King Christian VII (reigned 1766–1808) remained a troubled period. His short-lived marriage to Caroline Mathilde, the sister of King George III of Great Britain, in November 1766 cemented the commercial relationships between Denmark and Great Britain in Europe and Tranquebar. Even after he had divorced Mathilde in 1772, the relationship between the two countries continued. In 1772, private merchants and investors from Denmark and Norway intervened to save the Danish Asiatic Company from near extinction. Five years later, in 1777, King Christian VII nationalised this company, freed it from administering Tranquebar

---

102 AFSt/M 1 C 30c : 7, partly printed in NHR 4, 1790, issue 37, 95–96.

103 Despite the well-intended trade treaty of 1620, trade between Tranquebar and Copenhagen did not flourish. It ceased to function from 1648 to 1670. King Friedrich IV (reigned 1699–1730) restored the DEIC, but it struggled to make profits for its shareholders. King Christian VI (reigned 1730–1746) revived the Danish East India Company (DEIC) on 12 April 1732, for a period of forty years, expanding its scope beyond Tranquebar and beginning to trade in Chinese and Indian goods, especially cotton cloths, pepper, cinnamon, and other spices. His son, King Friedrich V (reigned 1746–1766), recognised the validity of the second DEIC. Under his rule, small Danish trading centres were established in Calicut (1752), the Andaman and Nicobar Islands (1754) and Serampore (1755). King Christian VII (reigned 1766–1808), the son of King Friedrich V, remained sickly and unstable for most of his life. His physician, Johann Friedrich Struensee, was an influential figure in Denmark until his arrest and execution in 1772. Hereditary Prince Frederick, the son of Friedrich V and Queen Juliane Marie, ruled Denmark from 1772 to 1784. In 1784, Crown Prince Frederick VI checked the influence of Ove Høegh-Guldberg, who tried to lead the Danish government.

and Serampore and permitted private merchants to compete with its trade with Tranquebar and Serampore.[104]

Ole Feldbæk, who examined the India Trade under the Danish Flag 1772–1808, concluded that the success of the Danish trade with India depended on two strands of business: both the Asiatic Company and the Danish private merchants sold ammunition, guns, and other weapons to various Indian stakeholders, who either cooperated with or opposed the Company's unstoppable growth in India.[105] They bought pepper and other spices for their customers in Denmark.[106] The second strand of Danish business was more subtle: Anglo-Indian traders and civil officers in India, who were unable to send their ill-gotten riches to their families in Britain via English ships due to strict regulations, used Danish ships to transport their wealth illegally. This illicit trade significantly contributed to the financial success of the Danish trade in India.[107] At the same time, some members of the Company liked the Danish Asiatic Company, but the Company, as an organisation, preferred not to exist in its current form.[108]

In this context, Ameer Singh's mounting debt to the Company compelled him to borrow money from various lenders, including the Governor of Tranquebar. He mortgaged certain parts of his country to Tranquebar and borrowed more money. For example, on 27 January 1786, Jacob Klein stated that Ameer Singh had mortgaged the district of Tiruvidaikali to Tranquebar for 35,000 Pagodas. Its main town lay just half an hour from Sirkāli.[109] The Company was unhappy about this mortgage. They did not want farmers and other manual workers of Tranquebar to settle in the newly mortgaged places. Ameer Singh was unable to regulate people's movements across borders and sought Schwartz's intervention. Strandberg described the social, economic, and political background of this letter: due to continuous wars with the Company and the Nawab of Carnatic, the kings of

---

104 George Howells and A.C. Underwood: The Story of Serampore and its College. Serampore 1918.

105 Ole Feldbæk: India Trade under the Danish Flag 1772–1808: European Enterprise and Anglo-Indian Remittance and Trade. Copenhagen 1969, here 19: For example, in 1773, Nawab Wallajah purchased from the Danes in Tranquebar a "very large order of guns, muskets and ammunition." The Danes sold weapons to Wallajah's opponent, Hyder Ali, through their trading centre in Kozhikode (earlier: Calicut).

106 Feldbæk: India Trade under the Danish Flag 1772–1808, 20 and 48: in 1773, Danish merchants agreed to sell weapons to the King of Travancore through their trading centre in Colachel in Kanyakumari. They required the king to pay the price of firearms with pepper.

107 Feldbæk: India Trade under the Danish Flag 1772–1808, 239: The Danish traders in Tranquebar and Serampore acted "as the Anglo-Indian community's safety valve for remittance and trade." Between 1772 and 1808, the Danish traders transported on their ships "Anglo-Indian capital and goods to the value of about 55 million of current rupees." They obtained a decent commission for their illicit services.

108 The Company and Wallajah possessed Tanjore from 1773 to 1776. Later, the Company occupied Tranquebar twice, from 1801 to 1802 and from 1808 to 1815. These occupations weakened Tranquebar to such an extent that it never recovered. Finally, the Company bought Tranquebar and Serampore in 1845.

109 AFSt/M 1 C 27 : 4; IOR/P/252/16, 193: On 27.06.1787, resident Macleod of Tanjore informed Governor Campbell that "the Danes have refused the offer of granting the lease of the lands to an individual." He stated further that such an agreement might have existed before Tulāji's death, and he did not want it during Ameer Singh's rule.

Tanjore were under pressure to obtain more money from all sources. They constantly approached the Danes in Tranquebar for their usual annual tribute and occasional loans. The Danes seized this opportunity to lease additional lands from the kings and permitted some of the inhabitants of Tranquebar to settle in these newly acquired territories. Due to Ameer Singh's persisting financial troubles and inability to pay off previous loans, the people of Tranquebar remained in the territories of Tanjore.[110] They became a burden to Ameer Singh, and he wanted them to return to Tranquebar.

On 10 December 1787, Ameer Singh requested that Governor Abbestée settle the disputes between two bankers in Tranquebar and Tanjore and recall the settlers from Tranquebar who were in the mortgaged places of Tanjore back to Tranquebar.[111] As Abbestée did not respond to Ameer Singh's requests, Ameer Singh informed Governor Abbestée on December 24, 1787, that he had appointed Schwartz as his mediator for the settlers.[112]

On 29 May 1787, Schwartz informed his missionary colleague, Jacob Klein, in Tranquebar that Ameer Singh had appointed him as a mediator between himself and the Dutch East India Company.[113] In the meantime, Sivarāya, one of Ameer Singh's most senior officers, contacted Daniel Pillay (1740–1802), the official Tamil interpreter (1760–1802) for the Danish administrators in Tranquebar, for help.[114] As already discussed, towards the end of December 1787, Sivarāya requested Schwartz's intervention with Abbestée. Schwartz's negotiations with Abbestée did not produce any tangible result acceptable to the Company. The Company in Madras blamed Resident William Petrie for inaction and inefficiency. On 19 September 1788, he requested information from Schwartz about his interventions in these matters. He believed that Schwartz's response would save his reputation and job:

> I desire to know if I did not repeatedly declare to the Rajah [Ameer Singh] and his Sirkeel through your interpretation that I would not tolerate any acts of oppression or injustice to any person whatever in the Rajah's domains under the pretence of raising money on account of his arrears to the Honourable Company, assuring him at the same time that I would never

---

110 Strandberg: The Moḍī Documents from Tanjore, 17.

111 Strandberg: The Moḍī Documents from Tanjore, 319.

112 Strandberg: The Moḍī Documents from Tanjore, 322: Document No 28: "By the hand of the priest, Mr. Schwartz the cowle [i.e. a written agreement] carrying your seal was sent to your inhabitants who have come here and dwell on our territory, that they may all in trust come (back) to you; the cowle, being according to specification, we were very satisfied to read. In conformity with the cowle written by you, the inhabitants being pardoned for whatever offence that they may have committed should be dealt with in agreement with what is proper. On this account the priest, Mr. Schwartz has been appointed mediator for them and he is coming to you together with our hircarras [i.e. messengers carrying and delivering unique messages]. We are full of trust that you will listen carefully to the purport of what the inhabitants have to say and decide in such a reasonable way that they may be satisfied. If in some way or other the priest Mr. Schwartz has to come back here quickly because of some matter, then we shall also be satisfied with his brother (missionary) called [Christoph Samuel] John to go there in his place."

113 AFSt/M 1 C 29b : 7b.

114 Pillay served as an uncontested elder of the Tamil Lutheran community in Tranquebar, and he remained in touch with Schwartz.

> consent to the liquidation of his debt by such disgraceful and ruining measure? I request you will do me the favour to say if, since my arrival at Tanjore, to the best of your knowledge, I have not done everything in my power to prevent measures of rapacity, oppression and injustice and whether or not you have approved of the manner in which I have conducted my negotiations at the durbar or if in your opinion I could have pursued any other measures more likely to have attained the object of my commission or that were better adapted to the real welfare of the Rajah and the interest of his country?[115]

On 3 October 1788, Governor Archibald Campbell in Madras cautioned Abbestée about the potential risks: the loss of the villages of Tranquebar that he had mortgaged to Tanjore, and the possibility of losing the entire loan to Ameer Singh, including its interest. This warning was significant as it set the stage for the subsequent actions and decisions. In this delicate situation, Schwartz's diplomatic role in mediating the negotiations remained indispensable.

> I beg leave to acquaint you that the English East India Company have formed a Treaty with the Rajah of Tanjore by which he is bound to pay them annually a certain sum of money for their Protection and Support and has engaged in default of such Payments to assign his Country for the purpose of making good the failures. Thus, the whole Tanjore Country is eventually mortgaged to the English Company.
> Such being the Case, your Excellency must be sensible that it is not in my Power from the Public Station I hold to sanction any mortgages upon the Tanjore Country as it might to a certain Extent, deprive this Government of the advantages to be derived by their Constituents from the Articles of the Treaty. [... You may give him the loan if you so wished].
> The Rajah of Tanjore is his own Master so long as he continues to fulfil his Engagements with the English Company without pursuing measures that cannot fail to prove destructive to his Revenues and oppressive to the Inhabitants, this Government can never interfere in the affairs of his Country.[116]

Neither Ameer Singh nor Abbestée took this warning seriously. Unable to bear it, Robert Maunsell, a member of the Company Council in Madras, reprimanded resident William Petrie on 28 October 1788 for allowing Ameer Singh to borrow 40,000 Pagodas from Mr. De Souza in Tranquebar.[117] Maunsell wondered how Ameer Singh would repay this money and other loans to the Danes, who had no authority to possess new territories in Tanjore. He wanted to know whether Petrie had directly or indirectly assigned any part of the Tanjore country to the Danes. On the same day, the Company Council in Madras resolved that Ameer Singh should not pledge any part of "Tanjore Country" to the Danes, as Danish

---

[115] Bodleian Library: 72290ind-box2, Document 21 dated 19.09.1788: William Petrie to Schwartz

[116] IOR/P/252/27, 2852–2853.

[117] Bodleian Library: 72290ind-box2, Document 21 dated 19.09.1788: William Petrie to Schwartz: "I beg to know if any other terms were then mentioned or if at that time, you had any idea that the Danes were to require any alienation or gift of territory to their settlement, or that the simple negotiation of the loan was to be clogged with any demand or expectation with respect to tribute, or any other matter whatever, and did you ever communicate to me that the Danes intended to make such demands? On what terms did Mr De Souza offer to lend 40,000 Pagodas to the Rajah? Did he ask for any sanctions from me or from the Company's Government? Did he require any mortgage or security on the country, or did he load his offer with any other demands than merely the interest of 12 per cent per annum?"

possession of new territories in Tanjore might endanger the Company's security. The Council also informed the Danish creditors in Tranquebar of the Company's readiness to invoke the penal clauses of their treaty with Ameer Singh that prohibited him from mortgaging any part of Tanjore to anyone. The same Council warned the Danish creditors that they would lose all credits given to Ameer Singh.[118]

Having already noticed the displeasure of the Company Council in Madras, William Petrie wanted to meet Ameer Singh in the presence of Colonel Stewart and Schwartz. Ameer Singh, too, knew the reason for this meeting and was unwilling to attend it. On 27 October 1788, he sent a messenger to Schwartz to inform Petrie that he was indisposed and could not meet anyone. Petrie understood Ameer Singh's refusal not as an excuse but as his mindfulness of maintaining religious customs regarding auspicious and inauspicious times for performing certain things.[119] In the meantime, on 31 October 1788, Governor Campbell conveyed to Petrie the Company's determination not to permit Ameer Singh to enter into any new agreement with the Danes in Tranquebar that might compromise the Company's security in Tanjore.[120]

On 16 November 1788, Petrie requested that Schwartz give his opinion on Ameer Sing's land mortgage to the Danes at Tranquebar. He believed that Schwartz's response would save his reputation for professionalism, honesty and integrity. He wanted to know whether Schwartz was aware of Sirkeel Bava's land mortgage under Tulāji's instructions. He expected that Schwartz's response would shed "fuller light" on a mortgage of Tanjore lands to the Danes of Tranquebar and that he would "lay the Subject completely before the Madras Government."[121]

On 23 November 1788, Petrie confessed to the Company Council in Madras that he had communicated the Company's will to Ameer Singh and his ministers via Schwartz. With the influential help of Schwartz, Petrie obtained copies of the leases for the villages from Ameer Singh, which he and Tulāji had concluded with the Danes. Accordingly, the Danes did not own any of the villages; when Ameer Singh paid the borrowed money and its interest, they would return the villages to Tanjore. Petrie assured the Company Council in Madras that he had persuaded Ameer Singh not to lease any new parts of the country to the Danes or anyone else.[122]

On 18 November 1788, Schwartz translated Ameer Singh's letter, which explained the reason for taking large loans from the Danes: he sought those who would lend him enough money to pay off all arrears to the Company. The Danes provided him with the necessary loan at an annual interest rate of 12%. This strategic move led Ameer Singh to lease "several villages" to them. Schwartz also noted that Ameer Singh was not the first to borrow money from the Danes. He

---

[118] IOR/P/252/28, 3158–3162.
[119] IOR/P/252/28, 3265–3266.
[120] IOR/P/252/28, 3208–3209.
[121] Bodleian Library: 72290ind-box2, Document 22 dated 16.11.1788: William Petrie to Schwartz.
[122] IOR/P/252/28, 3563–3566.

pointed out that when Baba was the *Sirkeel* (the most senior officer, next only to the king), he mortgaged a few villages to the Danes and obtained 30,000 Star Pagodas with an annual interest rate of 12%. As soon as Baba paid the capital and its interest, the Danes restored the villages to Tanjore. Schwartz further noted that farmers cultivated these leased villages successfully and generated more revenue than Tanjore.[123]

On 21 November 1788, Schwartz produced a copy of the lease agreement between Tulāji and Governor Abbestée of Tranquebar. Accordingly, Tulāji leased fourteen villages to the Danes for ten years and received 32,500 Star Pagodas. He estimated that of the fourteen villages, ten alone would produce enough money for the Danes to get their capital and interest quickly. At the end of the lease period, they would also get the loan along with its interest.[124]

On the same day, i.e. 21 November 1788, Schwartz also produced a summary of a lease agreement between Ameer Singh and Governor Abbestée that they had concluded on 29 September 1788. Accordingly, Ameer Singh obtained a loan of 60,000 Star Pagodas from Abbestée. As surety, he had rented forty-four villages to the Danes for a period of twelve years. This lease agreement named these villages: thirty villages belonged to Māyāvaram Suba, ten villages were located within the "Tiraklasheri Maganum," and four villages were in the "Aakur Maganum." The Danes could take all produce except the shares that belonged to the inhabitants; likewise, they should not take any produce from the lands that belonged to the local temples. They could expect to get 16,983 Cakkarams as their annual income, which was indeed the yearly interest of the loan. The lease reiterated that the Danes were merely renters, not owners of these villages. When Ameer Singh paid 60,000 Star Pagodas at the end of the twelfth year, the Danes would return the villages to Tanjore. If any invasion from an enemy army would hinder the cultivation of these villages, Ameer Singh would pay the loss. The Danes were free from paying customs for the grains and wood they might transport from these villages to Tranquebar.[125]

Over time, the relationship between the Danes in Tranquebar and the Company became troublesome. Governor General Wellesley sought an opportunity to remove the Danish Asiatic Company's trading privileges and possibilities in Tranquebar and Serampore.[126] After the Company had established itself in Tanjore, they were interested in discovering more about the territories that the former rulers of Tanjore had leased to Tranquebar. For example, on 23 February 1791, William Collins Jackson (1754–1814), Secretary to the Madras Military Department at Fort St. George, requested that Schwartz verify the following facts: why did the Governor of Tranquebar loan 32,500 Pagodas to the king of Tanjore? Have they

123 IOR/P/252/28, 3572–3573.

124 IOR/P/252/28, 3574.

125 IOR/P/252/28, 3574–3577.

126 Feldbæk: India Trade under the Danish Flag 1772–1808, 211: Wellesley found the prevailing uncertain conditions of Tranquebar and Serampore irritating. He viewed Ole Bie, the Governor of Serampore, "as a ridiculous person" and arranged for the British occupation of Serampore in 1801.

had the Governor, in exchange, receive the right to collect revenue from fourteen villages for a period of ten years? Jackson assumed that Schwartz would have been aware of the circumstances surrounding these past transactions and their current validity. Therefore, he requested Schwartz to apprise the Company in Madras about these dealings between Ameer Singh and the Governor of Tranquebar.[127]

Jackson's request to Schwartz reflected the Company's unarticulated resolve to control all Tanjore country territories and collect revenue. They could not accept Ameer Singh's transaction with Abbestée. After Serfoji became the king of Tanjore in 1798, the Company in Madras granted him a special privilege to collect and keep the annual rent from Tranquebar. The following Tenth Article of the Treaty of the Company with Serfoji reads as follows:

> Whereas a certain annual pishcash amounting to Pagodas [...] is payable by the Danish Government of Tranquebar for lands held of the Rajah of Tanjore in the vicinity of that place. It is stipulated and agreed that the said *pishcash* shall continue to be received by His Excellency the Rajah [Serfoji] without any deduction from His Excellency's proportion of the revenue as hereinbefore stipulated.[128]

Eventually, the Company accused the administrators of Tranquebar of assisting the French during both peacetime and wartime, occupying Tranquebar from 1801 to 1802 and again from 1808 to 1815.[129] These measures led to Tranquebar losing its trade. The subsequent economic and political decline of Tranquebar led to its sale to the Company in 1845. The fact that the Company did not wage a war against Tranquebar during Schwartz's political activities is noteworthy; instead, they requested him to mediate between themselves and the governor of Tranquebar. As Schwartz mediated various parties with divergent goals, he promoted peace and justice. Otherwise, no one would have trusted him with weighty mediatory responsibilities.

7.8 Mediation with the Poligars

In 1771, Tulāji waged a war against the ruler of Sivaganga, Vēṅkaṉ Periya Udaiyāt Tēvar (reigned from 1790 to 1801) and wanted to return Hanumangudi to Tanjore. Later, in 1784, John Sulivan and Schwartz met this leader and discussed their plan

---

127 IOR/P/252/58, 949–950, also quoted verbatim in Bodleian Library: 72290ind-box2, Document 24 dated 23.02.1791: W. C. Jackson to Schwartz about Ameer Singh mortgaging villages to the Danes in Tranquebar: "To the Reverend Mr. Swartz at Tanjore, Sir, The Governor of Tranquebar having represented to the Board that the late Rajah of Tanjore mortgaged to the Danes fourteen Villages in the Tanjore Country for the Term of ten years, on account of a Loan of 32,500 Pagodas, I am directed to request you will explain to the Board such Circumstances may have come to your knowledge regarding this Transaction, stating at the same time the present footing on which it stands. I am, W. C. [William Collins] Jackson, Secretary [of the Military Department], Fort St. George."

128 IOR/H/457, 126.

129 Rastén: The Tranquebar tribute, 44: The Napoleonic wars led the British to occupy Denmark and the Danish settlements in India twice, from 1801 to 1802 and from 1808 to 1815. The

to start a Provincial School in Ramanathapuram. On 20 January 1790, missionary Jakob Klein reported that the leader of Sivaganga, who did not trust any other European due to their conflicting interests, requested Schwartz to be his envoy between himself and the Company. He could not bear the troubles caused by the Nawab and believed that Schwartz's intervention, given his impartiality and understanding of European and local perspectives, would persuade the Company officers in Madras to assist him. In this context, Klein wished that God would protect and equip Schwartz as the "ambassador of the country."[130]

7.9 Mediation as Executor of Estates

7.9.1 Dealing with Money Matters

Schwartz's unshakable commitment to his role as an executor and guardian is evident in his actions. His honesty in public dealings and disinterest in accumulating material wealth for non-selfish use led some of his close European acquaintances to appoint him as their executor. The following three representative examples vividly demonstrate Schwartz's serious efforts in fulfilling his executorship, underscoring the weight of his responsibilities. In the first instance, Schwartz's letter of 20 September 1774 reports on Lieutenant Sioeffartz, who died in Tiruccirāppaḷḷi in 1773. He had appointed Schwartz as the executor of his will. After the death of this lieutenant, Schwartz tried to send 2,000 Pagodas (equal to 4,000 Royal Dollars in Copenhagen) to his widow. The Mission College in Copenhagen agreed to hand over the money to her. Schwartz attempted to contact the lieutenant's friend to forward the designated funds to them. Despite reminders, no one claimed it even after a year. In another instance, Schwartz referred to Rätzel, a company employee in Tiruccirāppaḷḷi, who passed away towards the end of 1773. Schwartz transferred 1,000 Pagodas of Rätzel's estate to Philip Fabricius in Madras, who in turn agreed to send a bill of exchange to Freylinghausen, the director of the Glaucha Institutions. Freylinghausen would pay the money to the Rätzel family.[131]

Similarly, in 1774, Schwartz agreed to be the executor of Colonel Wood's estate in a two-fold manner, demonstrating his compassion towards Wood's family. By that time, he had known Wood for at least nine years.[132] The Company's Court of Justice in Madras accused Colonel Wood of failing to assist his fellow officers in defeating Hyder Ali. Wood dreaded the outcome of this inquiry and became

British occupation of Tranquebar had a minimal impact on the people of Tranquebar. Following the peace treaty in Kiel, Germany, signed on 14.01.1814, the British restored Tranquebar to the Danes on 20.09.1815. Danish Governor Gerhard Sievers Bille took charge of Tranquebar.

130 NHR 4, 1791, issue 38, 202.

131 AFSt/M 1 B 65 : 41.

132 Germann: Missionar Christian Friedrich Schwartz, 156–158: In March 1765, the Company in Madras permitted Schwartz to erect a school building. Wood laid the foundation of the Wood on 13.03.1765 and supervised its construction. Wallajah visited it in October 1765. Schwartz dedicated it on 18.05.1766 and named it Christ's Church.

seriously ill. On his deathbed, he appointed Schwartz as the guardian of his children.[133] Just before his death on 3 July 1774, the 48-year-old Wood appointed Schwartz and William Chambers[134] as the joint executors of his estate.[135] After William Chambers had returned to Calcutta, Schwartz became the sole executor of Wood's will.

In August 1774, Schwartz travelled from Tanjore to Madras to execute Wood's will. It included the recovery of two loans that Wood had made. Schwartz's persistence in recovering these loans is evident. Firstly, in 1767, Wood had loaned money to Tulāji's army. At that time, he commanded 1,000 cavalrymen in Nāmakkal. Suddenly, Hyder Ali's cavalry surrounded them and cut off their supply lines. To rescue the cavalrymen from starving, Wood loaned 14,400 Pagodas to three cavalry leaders: On 17 May 1767, he loaned 5,400 Pagodas to "Wenget Row Gade." On 12 June 1767, he loaned 5,000 Pagodas to "Socke Wenkaji." On 26 August 1767, he loaned 4,000 Pagodas to "Socke Wenkaji" again. These three men promised to return the money and its interest within a month, wrote bonds and gave them to Schwartz.[136] When these men did not return the money and its interest, Tulāji agreed to return the loaned money to Mrs. Wood with an interest rate of ten to twelve percent. In the meantime, Wallajah and the Company occupied Tanjore in 1773. Schwartz brought this matter to Wallajah, who agreed to pay this debt to Mrs Wood. However, when Tulāji became the king of Tanjore in 1776, he and Wallajah refused to pay anything and blamed each other. Schwartz persisted in his efforts, persuading Tulāji to return the capital and interest to Mrs Wood, and he agreed to "pay every year the third part of the debt" and clear the entire debt in three years.[137] Despite the challenges, Schwartz's efforts bore fruit, and Mrs Wood

133 Germann: Missionar Christian Friedrich Schwartz, 237: Since then, Schwartz proved himself an affectionate father to these semi-orphan children.

134 Germann: Missionar Christian Friedrich Schwartz, 202–203: Wood's family accommodated William Chambers in their house, who had arrived in Tiruccirāppaḷḷi in October 1768 and desired to learn Persian from the aged Muhammad Panah. Schwartz advised the Woods and Chambers not to focus on accumulating worldly wealth, but to prioritise their spiritual well-being. Whenever Major Wood went on business to meet Tulāji in Tanjore, he took Schwartz as his interpreter. The king asked Schwartz to explain the meaning of the Christian Sabbath and the differences between the Catholic and the Protestant Church traditions. He also permitted him to preach to his servants about Schwartz's understanding of the true God. The Woods liked Schwartz's approach to God and human life.

135 Germann: Missionar Christian Friedrich Schwartz, 220 and 234; Pearson: Memoirs, Vol. 1, 308. While Germann named only Schwartz as the executor, Pearson confirmed that William Chambers was also a joint executor of Wood's will.

136 IOR/P/252/16, 159–190.

137 Pearson: Memoirs, Vol. 2, 165: Wallajah had looted Tulāji's treasury; Hyder Ali's army ravaged Tanjore. Amidst these troubling events in early 1780, Schwartz informed William Chambers in Calcutta that Mrs Wood would not get any money from Wallajah. Hyder Ali had taken away most of Tanjore's wealth. Tulāji promised to pay Mrs Wood the 14,500 Pagodas her husband lent him. However, as his people ran away from Tanjore, he might be unable to spend the money. Schwartz remained a faithful proxy to Mrs. Wood. Nine years later, in 1789, he informed William Chambers that the Company assessors had included Wood's money in Tulāji's private debts. Therefore, whenever the Company paid a dividend to other creditors, Mrs Wood would also get her share. Schwartz was so taken by this mediating work that he was finally exhausted.

received a sizeable portion of the loans. This example demonstrated how earnestly Schwartz pursued his mediatory role and worked for justice, achieving a positive outcome.

Schwartz's persistence in recovering Wood's loan to Philip Fabricius in Madras demonstrated his determination and perseverance. As discussed below (Section 7.10.1), Fabricius loaned this money to an unnamed poligar. A son-in-law of Nawab Wallajah enticed this poligar to give him all the money. As Fabricius could not recover any money from the poligar, he was unable to repay Wood's money. Schwartz persuaded Governor Campbell and his wife to intercede with the Nawab on behalf of Mrs Wood, other widows and orphans who had lost money. The Campbells contacted the Nawab and urged Schwartz to approach him directly. When Schwartz met the Nawab, he sent his eldest son to receive Schwartz. This son promised Schwartz that he would inform his father about it. Schwartz felt these words were "*verba* [et voces], *praetereaque nihil* ['words and voices and nothing else' = empty words]." He wanted to appoint Gericke as his power of attorney because the burden of being the executor of Wood's estate weighed heavily on him.[138] Schwartz did not give up his mediatory efforts.

After twenty years, Schwartz had a glimmer of hope: On June 6, 1787, he requested that Governor Campbell forward Mrs. Wood's plea for repayment to the Committee for Investigating the Debts of His Excellency, the Rajah of Tanjore.[139] Three months later, on 30 September 1787, Edward Garrow, William Webb and James Landon, who had investigated all matters about this loan, concluded the following:

> Mr. Swartz, having delivered in Colonel Wood's original bonds with an account of the sum, which has been paid on each, we have calculated the interest due on them from their respective dates to the 12th July last at 12 per cent agreeable to the orders of your Honour in Council and now beg leave to enclose a statement of them.[140]

Accordingly, Mrs Wood should receive 45,389.15 Pagodas. This example, however, demonstrates Schwartz's faithfulness in pursuing a task that he had agreed to perform.

7.9.2 Dealing as a Guardian

Though Schwartz could not recover Wood's money, he took his role as a guardian of Wood's children seriously and fulfilled it to the best of his ability. After Colonel Wood died, his widow moved to England with her three daughters and son, who were between six and eleven years old. Just before their departure, Schwartz provided them with practical guidelines for study and offered advice on how they could grow holistically.[141] He corresponded with the Woods for several years. His

---

138 Pearson: Memoirs, Vol. 2, 165.
139 IOR/P/252/16, 159–190.
140 IOR/P/252/16, 435–436.

letter to the Woods in January 1778 is filled with filial love and spiritual longing. It requests them to pray for Schwartz so that he could "preach the gospel of my Saviour faithfully [... and] win immortal souls unto Christ and that I may finish my course with joy and enter into the joy of my Lord."[142]

On 22 February 1780, Schwartz wrote to Wood's son, expressing his joy over the boy's spiritual, intellectual, and social growth. Schwartz praised this boy's schoolteacher and advised him to acquire both theoretical and practical skills in diverse subjects, becoming "useful in human society."[143] Simultaneously, Schwartz wrote a separate letter to Wood's daughter, encouraging her to be mindful of her physical, mental and spiritual growth. She should learn to overcome all worldly temptations and limitations. Schwartz assured her of his prayers for her and wished that she would receive "all the riches of grace, strength, and comfort, which are to be found in Jesus." He requested her to pray for her "old friend," who lived in Tanjore's spiritual wilderness.[144]

On 9 March 1792, Schwartz wrote a letter to the Woods. He was pleased that the oldest and youngest daughters were married and had families of their own. The youngest daughter was married to Basil Wood, an Anglican clergyman and an avid supporter of the Church Missionary Society. Schwartz fondly inquired about the whereabouts of Wood's second daughter and son. He reminded Wood's children to lead a Christ-centred life. He informed them about the frailty of his old age and his determination to preach "the glad tidings concerning a Redeemer, who came to save that which was lost" because the Lord Jesus Christ was the "Consolation of the nations." He urged them to seek comfort and wisdom in Jesus

---

141 Pearson: Memoirs, Vol. 1, 312–314. Pearson reproduced two letters dated 16.01.1775 and 08.09.1775.

142 Pearson: Memoirs, Vol. 1, 331.

143 Pearson: Memoirs, Vol. 1, 371–373. The following quote demonstrates Schwartz's delicate and empathetic art of teaching Wood's young son John in a faraway place: "You learn Latin, geography, arithmetic, French, drawing; all which may be very serviceable to you and beneficial to your fellow creatures. I entreat you, therefore, to be very diligent and to spend your time in the best manner. I remember that when I learnt vocal music in my younger days, I did not think that I should use it much; and behold now, every morning and evening when the Malabar children come to prayer, I teach them to sing in praise of their Redeemer. Every week, they learn one hymn, for they are slow. Now, I am well pleased that I was instructed in vocal music; all things may become useful to us and others. But then, my dear friend, our intention, our duties, must be well managed; or in other words, our hearts must be truly mended. As you have spent many months and years learning useful things, let your heart now be given over to your God. Otherwise, your learning will not prove beneficial; nay, which is deplorable, it may be abused to your detriment. [...] Rest not till you find rest to your soul. Having obtained pardon and peace through Jesus, watch and pray that you may not lose what you have gained but that you may rather grow daily in faith, love and hope. In your conversation with young people, be very cautious. Their thoughts and speeches are often too frothy, aye and even dangerous. Above all, try to gain strength – divine strength, to overcome that sinful bashfulness, whereby many are ashamed to confess or practise what they otherwise approve of in their heart. If you read your Bible and pray heartily to God, you will get strength every day to go on and prosper in his way. Our time is but short; eternity, awful eternity, is at hand. Let us, therefore, not trifle away our time, but let us seek the Lord and his grace, his blessing and his strength."

144 Pearson: Memoirs, Vol. 1, 376–378.

Christ, who was "a full and atoning righteousness." He urged the children to live a life of loyalty to the Lord Jesus Christ. He reiterated that worldly "riches and honours are not sinful in themselves." They should use them "with thankfulness to God" and "care and vigilance, lest they become a snare to us."[145]

7.10 Mediation with Fellow Missionaries

7.10.1 Johann Philipp Fabricius

In July 1778, Schwartz travelled to Madras to assist his fellow missionary, Johann Philipp Fabricius (1711–1791), with his financial affairs. On 9 October 1778, he notified Freylinghausen about Fabricius's perilous situation. Fabricius, who had suffered a life-threatening head injury, had lost all the money entrusted to him by the Tamil Lutherans, European orphans, men like Mr Hagemeister, and widows like Mrs Wood. Fabricius had invested their money for interest in his self-chosen role as a banker and money changer. Still, his financial decisions, negatively affected by the local economic and political changes, led to significant losses.[146]

According to Schwartz, Fabricius committed three grave mistakes that ruined his credibility. Several years earlier, Fabricius had lent 50,000 Royal Dollars to a local poligar in exchange for a lease of a small piece of land. Fabricius did not know that this poligar was a vassal to Wallajah. When Wallajah compelled this poligar to pay him his customary tribute, he borrowed the money from Fabricius and absconded. Fabricius asked Wallajah to help him recover this money from the poligar, but Wallajah refused to assist him. Not learning from this mistake, Fabricius again loaned 50,000 Royal Dollars to one of Wallajah's sons-in-law, who took advantage of Wallajah and escaped with Fabricius's money in 1774. Fabricius asked Wallajah for help recovering his money, but Wallajah refused to assist him. When Schwartz heard about these financial losses, he was unable to believe them. He viewed the allegations as blasphemous. However, at the request of his colleagues in Tranquebar, Schwartz rushed to Madras and interceded with Wallajah and his eldest son. He, too, could not receive any help. The arduous journey from Tiruccirāppaḷḷi, combined with mental stress and various disappointments, had a profound impact on Schwartz's nervous system. His body shook involuntarily, and he was unable to sleep.[147]

---

145 Pearson: Memoirs, Vol. 2, 254–257.

146 AFSt/M 1 B 69 : 45 and Germann: Missionar Christian Friedrich Schwartz, 305.

147 AFSt/M 1 B 69 : 46: On 24.02.1779, Schwartz wrote to Freylinghausen that Fabricius had loaned more than 50,000 Pagodas to a Muslim man and a non-Christian man (lit. Heide, 'heathen'). This money belonged to orphans and widows such as Mrs Wood. Wallajah gave him some money that belonged to Mrs Wood. He loaned 25,000 Pagodas from that money to a borrower who then absconded. Likewise, he loaned 1,700 Pagodas that belonged to a friend of Mr. Rätzel. These actions shocked Schwartz beyond description. He wondered how a missionary, supposed to be a beggar in this world, could spend such substantial amounts of money.

Schwartz regretted that Fabricius had spent 1,000 Pagodas belonging to the Lutheran mission in Madras. He did not consult his colleagues, Breithaupt and Schwartz, for four years and executed things independently.[148] Schwartz doubted whether Fabricius would ever return these enormous amounts of money to his creditors. On 23 February 1779, he informed Pasche that Fabricius's mismanagement of funds damaged the reputation of the missionary enterprise in Madras and threatened its existence. He stated that Fabricius realised his mistake, humbled himself in front of everyone, and begged mercy and forgiveness. Schwartz confessed to Pasche that he had not informed the SPCK about this saddest event and requested that he update the SPCK suitably. He stated further that Fabricius was not greedy but failed to calculate the risk and endangered the missionary work.[149] Fabricius's misdeed disappointed Freylinghausen. In February 1780, he informed Schwartz that he had urged Fabricius to accept his sin and to humble himself before God.[150] Additionally, Schwartz stated that the missionary, Fabricius, dedicated to voluntary poverty, became covetous and involved in money-earning business activities.[151]

Despite Schwartz's requests to Wallajah and the Company officers in Madras, Fabricius was unable to recover his money. On 14 January 1785, he confessed that the gravity of Fabricius' debts plagued and drained him physically, emotionally and morally. For his own sake, he maintained a clear record of all incomes and expenses and presented it to the Company officers for verification. He noted that clear, transparent and accurate bookkeeping freed a missionary from temptations. Nobody could blame him for not disclosing what he received, how he spent it, or for what purpose. Since he raised Fabricius' matter with the Company officers and the Nawab, they could not plead innocence either.[152] However, their inaction to help Fabricius deeply disappointed Schwartz for a long time. His mediatory role as an envoy for peace and justice did not have the desired effect. It was still remarkable that he tried to redeem a fellow missionary labourer from public disgrace.

148 AFSt/M 1 B 69 : 45 and AFSt/M 1 B 69 : 47.

149 AFSt/M 1 B 70 : 40. AFSt/M 1 B 69 : 46. On 24.2.1779, Schwartz stated that Fabricius had loaded 50,000 Pagodas for Hindus (lit. Heiden, 'heathen', 'polytheists') and Muslims. Ordinary people, like Mrs. Wood, requested Fabricius to invest the money on their behalf in Company bonds. On another occasion, Fabricius loaned 25,000 Pagodas to another person, who had absconded with that money. Fabricius also loaned 1,700 Pagodas to those who had also left Madras. Neither Fabricius nor Schwartz would be able to find these men.

150 AFSt/M 1 B 69 : 108; Westcott 1897, 18: Arthur Westcott blamed Fabricius' Tamil assistants for losing this money. He also stated that Fabricius used to borrow and lend money. He lost a considerable sum of money when the French army under Lally plundered the mission premises at Vepery. From that time, things worsened. Only in 1791 did he hand over mission responsibilities to Gericke, and he died. His grave is now located in the St. Matthias Churchyard in Vepery, Chennai.

151 AFSt/M 1 C 30c : 22 = partially printed in NHR 4, 1790, issue 37, 100–101.

152 AFSt/M 1 B 75 : 25.

7.10.2 Christian Pohle

Before joining Schwartz in Tiruccirāppaḷḷi, Christian Pohle (1744–1818) gathered varied work experiences in Germany. He completed his theological studies at Leipzig and worked as a teacher. Then, he became a catechist at the palace in Wernigerode in 1774. After two years, on November 1, 1776, he received his ordination in Copenhagen and arrived in Tranquebar on June 6, 1777. Six months later, he joined Schwartz in Tiruccirāppaḷḷi and became a missionary of the SPCK. Schwartz taught him the Tamil language and helped him become acquainted with Anglicans from England and Tamil Lutherans in Tiruccirāppaḷḷi. Pohle felt uncomfortable in Tiruccirāppaḷḷi and secretly longed to work in Tranquebar.

On 17 February 1778, Schwartz informed Pasche that Pohle had reached Tiruccirāppaḷḷi about ten days earlier. He had already written two sermons in Tamil. Schwartz found his pronunciation acceptable and hoped Pohle would work happily in Tiruccirāppaḷḷi.[153] On 9 October 1778, Schwartz reported to Freylinghausen about Pohle's encouraging development in acquiring the Tamil and English languages and his ability to preach and catechise. Schwartz felt that if Pohle continued his ministry in Tiruccirāppaḷḷi, he could concentrate on developing his missionary work in Tanjore.[154] In February 1780, Freylinghausen expressed happiness that Schwartz had an excellent coworker in Pohle.[155]

On 10 October 1780, Schwartz informed Freylinghausen that he had visited Pohle that year and appreciated his work.[156] The ripple effect of Fabricius's debt also affected Pohle. For instance, he did not receive any salary from the SPCK for two years (1779 and 1780) as the SPCK used his salary to pay off Fabricius's debt to Mrs Wood. Schwartz shared his salary with Pohle for 1779, but he was uncertain how to raise Pohle's salary for 1780. This financial uncertainty strained the relationship between Schwartz and Pohle, adding to the emotional toll of the situation.

On 11 February 1785, Pohle accused Schwartz of gullibility, stating in a conference of missionaries in Tranquebar that Schwartz trusted his Tamil catechists, who had cheated him. For example, according to Pohle, Sattiyanātaṉ, Schwartz's beloved catechist, was a hypocrite and a cheat. He accused Schwartz of not condemning his behaviour. Klein supported Pohle's views. Pohle and Klein wrote about Schwarz's views on Sattiyanātaṉ to Director Schulze of the Glaucha Institutions. On 6 September 1787, Schulze admonished Schwartz about his carelessness. This letter deeply saddened Schwartz.. He forwarded it to his colleagues in Tranquebar and asked them to prove their allegations. They responded that they had not written to Schulze, but Schwartz could not believe their statement.[157]

---

[153] AFSt/M 1 B 67 : 73.
[154] AFSt/M 1 B 69 : 45.
[155] AFSt/M 1 B 69 : 107.
[156] AFSt/M 1 B 70 : 46.
[157] Germann: Missionar Christian Friedrich Schwartz, 328–330.

Schwartz explained to his colleagues in Tranquebar that Sattiyanātaṉ was honest and deeply devoted to teaching spiritual matters. His passion for sharing the gospel of the Lord Jesus Christ with others was remarkable, and his unselfish behaviour stood out. Schwartz admitted that Sattiyanātaṉ's conversations in clear and eloquent Tamil with non-Christians often humbled him. Sattiyanātaṉ presented the Gospel's contents impressively. Schwartz's observations of Sattiyanātaṉ's conversations with non-Christians, his daily activities, and his dedication to Lutheranism enabled him to defend Sattiyanātaṉ against false allegations. He was pleased that Sattiyanātaṉ promoted a better understanding between catechists and missionaries.[158] Eventually, Schwartz's assessment of Sattiyanātaṉ proved to be accurate,[159] Sattiyanātaṉ indeed became an impactful leader.

On 26 February 1785, Schwartz informed Pasche that he had sent his assistant, Kohlhoff, to oversee the church and schools in Tiruccirāppaḷḷi for a month, as Pohle wished to visit his colleagues in Tranquebar for a few days. However, after reaching Tranquebar, Pohle informed Schwartz that he would permanently stay in Tranquebar and train future missionaries by teaching them natural sciences and the classical languages of Europe, namely Hebrew, Greek and Latin. He believed this school would benefit missionary children and competent Tamil students. This unexpected news shocked Schwartz to the core. Schwartz affirmed that the idea of the new school was good; he defined missionary education as follows: firstly, missionary education should teach the students the entire "mind of God." Secondly, it should lead students to internalise the Word of God and demonstrate true repentance, faith, and a holy life. Thirdly, missionary education should help students interact with a diverse range of people and should not require proficiency in Hebrew, Greek, and Latin. Instead, students should be proficient in Tamil. Finally, Schwartz reiterated that Pohle's desire to work in Tranquebar would deeply disappoint the SPCK, which was already unhappy with the poor performance of Fabricius in Madras and Johann Christmann Diemer in Calcutta. They might stop supporting even the existing work in Tiruccirāppaḷḷi, Thanjavur, Ramanathapuram, Pālaiyamkōṭṭai, and other places, and the work in these centres might disappear.

On 8 October 1785, Schwartz reiterated to Pasche about Pohle's plan to leave Tiruccirāppaḷḷi to settle in Tranquebar and to start a Latin school with the help of

---

158 AFSt/M 1 C 27 : 26 and Germann: Missionar Christian Friedrich Schwartz, 330: On 01.02.1788, Schwartz sent a letter to his colleagues in Tranquebar and asked them not to doubt Sattiyanātaṉ's behaviour and diligence. He stated how the King of Travancore had welcomed Sattiyanātaṉ and desired to know more about Lutheranism. Both Sattiyanātaṉ and the king were happy. Schwartz lamented the shortage of missionaries. If only more missionaries were there, they could travel freely into many regions in southern India and share God's word.

159 Satthianadhan 1871, 360–361: W. T. Satthianadhan praised his namesake Sattiyanātaṉ, as Schwartz's "Timothy," who could converse well with non-Christians. People appreciated his honesty, humility and selflessness. They acknowledged his "love for Christ" and his determination to serve fellow Indians. He was a gifted preacher. He was content with "his scanty stipend" of three Star Pagodas per month and did many good things. Additionally, he managed his family well and set a good example for all.

other missionary colleagues: Pohle had grudges against the English. Additionally, he disliked working with the Tamil people because he struggled to speak Tamil fluently.[160] Pohle disagreed with Schwartz's views about caste. He secretly went to Tranquebar and started working in John's school. Schwartz had great difficulty persuading Pohle to return to Tiruccirāppaḷḷi and work peacefully with his Tamil catechists and schoolteachers. Once Pohle had decided to remain in Tiruccirāppaḷḷi, he flourished there and became a blessing to many people. For example, his admirers and beneficiaries established a settlement near Tuticorin in southern India and named it in his honour *Polaiyarpuram* ('Pohle's Hamlet'). Finally, Schwartz's mediatory role as an envoy for peace and reconciliation worked for Pohle.

7.10.3 Christoph Samuel John

Schwartz met with his fellow missionaries in Tranquebar as needed and shared details of his expanding ministries with them.[161] He and Christoph Samuel John (1747–1813) maintained cordial and collegial relationships. In 1776, after an illness, John stayed with Schwartz in Tiruccirāppaḷḷi. As he recuperated, he dedicated himself to working among the Tamil Lutherans and the Anglicans. Schwartz appreciated John's mastery of English despite his unique accent. On 21 January 1777, Schwartz informed Pasche that his frequent travels necessitated his requesting that his Tranquebar colleagues depute John to come to Tanjore and assist him.[162] Since John was married, Schwartz could not pay him enough to support his family there. Therefore, in 1777, he accepted Pohle as his colleague, and the Company appointed him their chaplain. John kept a good relationship with Schwartz and visited him occasionally in Tanjore.[163]

---

160 AFSt/M 1 C 25 : 33.

161 AFSt/M 1 B 63 : 28: After a visit in December 1773, Schwartz reported on 11.01.1774 that Johann Balthasar Kohlhoff (1711–1790) was well but extremely weak, and Oluf Maderup (1711–1776) was lively but had problems with his foot. Daniel Zeglin (1716–1780) was fragile, but he visited Christians regularly and discussed spiritual matters with non-Christians; he should be careful not to catch a cold. Other missionaries, such as Jacob Klein (1721–1790), were well and lively. Schwartz shared with them the details of his ministry in the countryside and the necessity of missionaries living there. He insisted that the Tamil Lutheran catechists appreciated encouragement from missionaries. They could accompany them on their tours to visit rural congregations. Otherwise, the catechists performed their ministry well.

162 AFSt/M 1 B 68 : 45 and Germann: Missionar Christian Friedrich Schwartz, 405. AFSt/M 1 B 66 : 4: On 04.01.1776, Schwartz reported John's arrival in Tiruccirāppaḷḷi to recuperate from sickness. AFSt/M 1 B 66 : 58: On 18.01.1776, Schwartz informed Pasche about John's stay in Tiruccirāppaḷḷi. He considered John a good man who had learned the Tamil language well, and he would be a helpful instrument in God's work. AFSt/M 1 B 66 : 60: On 29.01.1776, Schwartz stated that John was an able and dedicated missionary. AFSt/M 1 B 66 : 20: On 28.02.1776, John shared his joy with Freylinghausen and stated that Schwartz had taken him on his missionary tour to Vallam. AFSt/M 1 B 68 : 42 and Germann: Missionar Christian Friedrich Schwartz, 402–403: On 14.10.1776, Schwartz mentioned that John had visited him twice; during his second visit, he stayed in Tiruccirāppaḷḷi for a few months and worked. Schwartz opined that John was an excellent fit for the role of missionary. Due to his late-night study, he became sick with *Malum hypochondriac* ('sickness hypochondria') and

John should have discussed his plan for a new school in Tranquebar with his colleagues or Schwartz. Wilhelm Germann explained the background for John's private school more fully: Missionary Zeglin died in 1780. The newly arrived missionary, Lorenz Friedrich Rulfsen (1753–1780), died one month after he arrived in Tranquebar. In 1777, Christoph Samuel John married the Danish woman Christiana Sophia Guldberg. He did not receive the additional salary which other married missionaries had. John revived Gerlach's school plan and tried to establish a boarding school. While missionaries König, Zeglin and Schwartz did not welcome this plan, missionaries Kohlhoff and Klein wanted to put their children to study in this new school. Despite this enduring conflict, John devoted himself more to the school, with missionaries Rottler and Wilhelm David Becker joining him as teachers. Johann Daniel Mentel, the missionary who reached Tranquebar on 28 June 1781, joined John's school.[164] Christian Pohle was willing to join John in Tranquebar. As conflicts and disunity increased, the senior missionaries in Tranquebar requested Schwartz's intervention.

On 17 June 1782, all missionaries, including Schwartz, met in Tranquebar. Schwartz expressed his assessment and reminded them about their original vocation to work for the benefit of the Tamil people.[165] On 30 November 1782, he recalled memories of this meeting. He informed Freylinghausen about it: the sad examples of Fabricius and Hüttemann had convinced him not to remain silent about troubles among colleagues. Instead, he wanted to establish peace, trustworthiness and harmony among colleagues. He was unhappy that John's school attracted the younger missionaries, who would not engage in conventional missionary activities. This school did not require the new missionaries to learn the Tamil language well, a point of contention that led to a conflict between Schwartz and John. Schwartz felt that worldly needs and aspirations should not determine missionary priorities. A man who knew three or four languages could easily find employment that would pay him four times as much as he would otherwise receive in the mission. Without love for God and a simple lifestyle, it would be difficult to carry on missionary service. To avoid misunderstanding, Schwartz shared this letter with Pohle and Klein. Klein regretted supporting John's school.[166]

Jacob Gude (1754–1810), the secretary of the Mission College in Copenhagen, did not endorse John's school project. Gude's disagreement with Schwartz added another layer of conflict to the situation.[167] Freylinghausen might have known Gude's position. However, he informed Schwartz that he did not oppose John's

---

suffered from it during the scorching summer months. John himself worried about being ill with this disease.

163 AFSt/M 1 B 67 : 19: On 04.02.1778, John wrote to Freylinghausen about his plan to visit Schwartz in Tanjore.

164 Germann: Missionar Christian Friedrich Schwartz, 294.

165 Germann: Missionar Christian Friedrich Schwartz, 297–299.

166 AFSt/M 1 B 72 : 58 dealt in Germann: Missionar Christian Friedrich Schwartz, 294–295.

167 Anders Nørgaard: Secretaries of the Mission Board in Copenhagen 1714–1868. In: Halle and the Beginning of Protestant Christianity in India. Vol. III: Communication between India and Europe. Ed. by Andreas Gross et al. Halle 2006, 1565–1567, here 1565.

new school because he could not understand the local circumstances that led John to establish it. He advised Schwartz and Gericke to assess these circumstances and ensure unity among the missionaries in Tranquebar.[168]

On 22 June 1783, Schwartz expressed to Freylinghausen his disappointment about Pohle's intention to leave Tiruccirāppaḷḷi and join John's school in Tranquebar. Pohle presented his desire as an effort to restore his health. He claimed that the climate and the work atmosphere in Tiruccirāppaḷḷi were not conducive to his health. Schwartz did his best to persuade him to remain in Tiruccirāppaḷḷi and continue the ministry. Then, Schwartz repeated to Freylinghausen the three principles he had already discussed with John: 1) He did not oppose John's new school because it might give the children of the mission a good education. 2) The school should become an integral part of the missionary endeavour in Tranquebar so that it does not cause disagreements, divisions and disunity. 3) This school should employ Tamil teachers. Then, Schwartz repeated John's assurances to him: John wanted to integrate the new school into the Tranquebar Mission, but his colleagues were not interested in it. Therefore, John tried to start it independently. John assured Schwartz that he had never forgotten his vocation as a missionary. He felt that the non-availability of competent teachers might prevent him from starting the school anyway. Schwartz recommended that John follow his example: while performing his missionary outreach, he spent twelve years teaching in a school in Tranquebar. Similarly, John's missionary colleagues there could dedicate one or two hours to this new school and then fulfil their missionary duties. All children would have benefited if John had started this school in cooperation with his colleagues.[169]

On 20 October 1783, John had five students – four girls and one boy – in his school. Some of the children paid seven to ten Pagodas. Schwartz assumed this income would not sustain the school for a prolonged period. If this school had been part of the entire mission, there could be a single account. A married missionary could receive his salary from the school's income. The remaining income should be allocated to the mission. As this was not the case, Schwartz disagreed with the purpose and administration of this school.[170] On 16 February 1784, he reminded John of Nicholas Dal's work principle, which was not to allow new missionaries to work among the Tamil people until they had learned the Tamil language, emphasising the importance of cultural adaptation in missionary work.[171]

Consequently, on March 30, 1787, John sent a detailed report to Christen Hee Wadum, the secretary of the Mission College in Copenhagen, regarding his resolve to delay his school project. He expressly stated: "Schwartz, whom we all honour as our father, told me: 'Brother, do we want to bury the mission? Should we allow God's holy judgment to lead the mission into ruin?" Schwartz advised John to learn from Johann Balthasar Kohlhoff, who, despite being unable to work for

---

168 AFSt/M 1 B 72 : 66.
169 AFSt/M 1 B 74 : 32.
170 AFSt/M 1 B 74 : 34 quoted in Germann: Missionar Christian Friedrich Schwartz, 300.
171 Germann: Missionar Christian Friedrich Schwartz, 299.

several years, remained faithful in serving God, and Jacob Klein, who, despite having completely lost his hearing, faithfully served in the Portuguese school and church. The newly arrived missionary Hagelund had "no heart for mission." As a result of his discussion with Schwartz, John changed his mind and decided to continue his work, at least tentatively.[172]

On 15 October 1792, John informed Director Schulze of the Glaucha Institutions that his school would not teach the whole Bible but only a few excerpts. His educational curriculum omitted biblical narratives on creation and the necessity of one's spiritual birth. Instead, John proposed structuring his catechism with biblical sayings alongside those of the non-Christian religions in India. John wanted to print a Bible containing only his selected passages. He considered Christianity sectarian and sought to develop a pedagogical system that catered to humanity's everyday needs. Schulze confessed that John's intentions and decisions pained him, and he could not endorse his school project.[173] John persisted and developed his school. On 9 January 1794, John informed Director Schulze that his European School had admitted a boy from Cochin and a girl from Indonesia. John was happy about his link with Indonesia.[174]

Heike Liebau, who examined the genesis and function of John's school, stated that John wanted Indian teachers to teach reading, writing, and expounding vernacular literature. European teachers should teach the English language, mathematics, astronomy, geography and history. Students would learn from mathematical tables and books. Each class should have ten to twelve students of similar abilities. The most competent and responsible student should be appointed as their preceptor. Teachers would decide what to teach and when to teach it. This innovative approach to education, where the missionaries adapted to the local resources and needs, demonstrated their resourcefulness. Soon, John's schools spread to twenty villages in and around Tranquebar.[175]

On 23 March 1801, John wrote to the Editor in Halle: If only the mission agencies in Europe would send their new missionaries to Tranquebar for a short training period at his school, the missionaries would become more confident in their knowledge about "Indostan." Christians and non-Christians would value them. From Tranquebar, they could go to other places. John had already received applications from prospective missionary candidates. He regretted that he could not admit them all. If the missionary candidates studied natural sciences, mathematics and chemistry, Europeans in India would esteem them. Besides academic disciplines, there was a great demand for skilled carpenters, watchmakers

---

172 AFSt/M 1 C 29b : 24. This letter remains unpublished.

173 Germann: Missionar Christian Friedrich Schwartz, 333.

174 NHR 4, 1794, issue 45, 839.

175 Heike Liebau: Christoph Samuel John's Essay on Education Policy. In: Halle and the Beginning of Protestant Christianity in India. Vol. III: Communication between India and Europe. Ed. by Andreas Gross et al. Halle 2006, 1323–1332. For John's views on India, Indian culture and civilisation, see Christoph Samuel John: On Indian Civilization In: Halle and the Beginning of Protestant Christianity in India. Vol. III: Communication between India and Europe. Ed. by Andreas Gross et al. Halle 2006, 1467–1491.

and other professionals.[176] John felt that caste, which had previously hindered the spread of the Gospel, was gradually losing its influence in areas under the Company's control. Missionaries could achieve more in these changed circumstances. Political changes also occurred under God's rule; these changes influenced heavenly matters, even though their human agents were unaware of them. John concluded his report with a note of hope for a better future.[177]

John obtained insights and moral support for his English-medium school from educational scholars such as Andrew Bell (1753–1832) in Madras. He also communicated his intentions for a new school to his readers in England. One of these readers, John Carne, stated that soon after he arrived in Tranquebar, he began seeking an opportunity to teach young people differently. Three years later, certain families living in the modern regions of Nagapattinam, Sri Lanka, Jakarta, and Indonesia requested that John educate their children. They believed that his educational principle would "polish and civilise the native character" of children, and they would emulate European manners and learn new languages and sciences. Besides, John's school would benefit "country priests, teachers of English to native families, organists, merchants, draughtsmen, interpreters, captains, mates, schoolmasters, &c."[178]

In his later years, John's life reflected the influence of Schwartz. At the beginning of the nineteenth century, the missionaries in Tranquebar did not receive any funding to continue their work due to European wars. John hoped that admitting more students from India and neighbouring countries would generate funds to support himself, his family, and his colleagues. However, the shortage of teachers and school space prevented him from accepting more students.

Those who knew John admired his "Christian simplicity and integrity," which reminded them of the character of the venerable Swartz. He understood that his fifteen Tamil and five English schools were meant to develop Indian civilisation. His pedagogical experiments demonstrated that "neither Civilization nor Christianity is opposed in India in the manner represented by ignorant infidels [i.e., European Company servants] who prefer Heathenism to Christianity."[179]

It was remarkable that John rekindled his earlier passion for mission and strove to help both his Christian and non-Christian students understand and appreciate

---

176 A footnote entry on this page refers to John's undated letter to his unnamed friend in London: "Trusting in the Almighty and employing best means, we must befriend local regents, collectors, residents and other notables of good character and influence; in our good schools, we should train translators and servants for these people. In the absence of English pastors in our office (as preachers), we can serve them unselfishly; we can promote and help them run institutions for the poor. Through civilised and modest dealings, through acquaintance with the sciences, we can lead informed conversation[s] about all kinds of useful blessings so that they can learn to love and trust us. This was the endeavour of the blessed Schwartz, and it is also ours. Thus, much good has been achieved to further our main purpose."

177 NHR 5, 1802, issue 58, 896.

178 Carne: Lives of the Eminent Missionaries, 183.

179 Thomas Thompson: The Gods of the East Indies: Or, an Account of the Religion of the Hindoos, with a Short Vindication of the Attempts to Propagate Christianity in India. London 1810, 14–15.

one another, fostering growth and unity for the common good of India. Thomas Thompson (1754–1828), a businessman in Hull, England, summarised the purpose and impact of John's schools in Tranquebar:

> [John] considered himself as sent chiefly to offer the light of the Gospel to the Heathen, although he added to his missionary duties a boarding school and a separate private school for the instruction of Tamul youth. To the separate school, he added Heathen children, and he endeavoured to instruct them and to diffuse the knowledge of Christianity among them. Of these, the greater part of whom were children of beggars, some became country priests, catechists, schoolmasters, writers, merchants, and country captains."[180]

Most of John's students were children of "principal persons in several villages." He admitted them only with their parents' consent. Brahmin parents sent their sons to John's schools. Like Schwartz, John believed that his schools were agents of positive societal transformation, ushering in "gradual civilisation and the enlightenment of the nations [i.e. kingdoms or princely states] of India." Prejudices based on caste and religion would gradually disappear. John hoped that all persons and institutions who aimed for the "glorious object of enlightening India, by preaching the Gospel, and distributing the Scriptures"[181] would join him. Thus, he had imbibed from Schwartz not only the characteristics of simplicity and integrity but also the value of English-medium schools, which Schwartz had pioneered.

7.10.4 Georg Heinrich Conrad Hüttemann

Georg Heinrich Conrad Hüttemann (1728–1781), David Poltzenhagen, and Schwartz sailed together and reached Cuddalore on 17 July 1750. In 1751, Hüttemann married Elisabeth, who died on 22 September 1773, a union that brought him closer to the local community. Three years after the death of his first wife, on 16 February 1776, he married Françoise de Marchis, a Dutch widow from Amsterdam. He had seven sons and two daughters.[182] His growing family's needs remained a constant concern for Hüttemann, and his inability to meet them caused him great distress. His bitter disappointment with the Tamil mendicant Arunachalam, who had faked his conversion to Lutheranism, also disappointed Hüttemann.[183] Hüttemann initially extolled the mendicant's conversion in his reports to his European friends, and they publicised it widely. However, when the mendicant renounced Lutheranism and returned to his ancestral faith, Hüttemann

180 Thompson: The Gods of the East Indies, 16.
181 Thompson: The Gods of the East Indies, 18.
182 Hüttemann's sons were Christian Friedrich (born on 05.04.1755), Johann Heinrich, Carl (1778), Samuel (1781), Georg Heinrich Conrad (died on 17.07.1781), Andreas (1788) and Ernst Georg Friedrich (1795). His daughters were Anna Sophia and Gracy Dorothea (1756–1768). On 31.07.1769, Anna Sophia married the missionary Christian Wilhelm Gericke, who came to Cuddalore in 1767 and worked with Hüttemann until 1782. When the French invaded Cuddalore, Gericke and his family, who were dedicated to their service, moved to Tranquebar. They served in Nagapattinam from 1784 to 1788 and then moved to Vepery in Madras.
183 AFSt/M 1 B 53 : 30, as of 12.01.1769 and AFSt/M 1 B 54 : Ad32.

was deeply disappointed. This fraud shook his faith in the local population, leading him to assume that all Tamils, including the Tamil Lutherans in his congregation in Cuddalore, resembled this dishonest mendicant and viewed them as poverty-stricken beggars and cheats. This marked a significant shift in his attitude toward the people he was trying to minister to.

For example, on 17 February 1778, he wrote to Kiernander in Calcutta about Indians, whom he knew as "beggars" and "rascals," for whom the "honest people of Europe" should not raise money. He was content with his "beggarly salary to instruct the children of beggars and vagabonds." He recommended the establishment of an "English College" in either Madras or Calcutta, following the plan of the Irish Bishop George Berkeley (1685–1753), to train future missionaries for India. The students at this college should learn "English, Latin, Greek, French, Theology, Philosophy, Mathematics," and the like. Their annual tuition fee should be £15; each teacher should receive £200 as their annual salary. He believed that God's law and the laws of England forbade stealing, begging, cunning and forgery, but then these Laws commend in the most robust manner that no man must labour for nothing. He proposed that European missionaries should not learn the languages of their students, "and as fools ape their pronunciation, as the fanatical Ziegenbalg and Schulze introduced."[184] Instead, the students at the English College should "learn our language, Latin and Greek," "get acquainted with our books" and "learn the wisdom of Religion." European missionaries should not waste their time and energy learning the miserable languages of their students. Instead, the students should learn the languages of their teachers and rulers. For example, the Romans imposed Latin on the conquered people, thereby stabilising their empire. Once the students at the English College were "deemed qualified, then they must receive a mission and call to preach the Christian Religion to their countrymen."[185]

On 9 October 1778, Schwartz reported to Freylinghausen that Hüttemann had ceased his missionary work a few years earlier, still receiving money for the mission in Cuddalore but keeping it unused. He refused to help those in economic need, and his son-in-law, Gericke, who collaborated with him in Cuddalore, found it impossible to discuss mission matters with him. Schwartz, who had previously refrained from commenting on his colleagues' work, felt compelled to discuss Hüttemann due to the adverse effects of Fabricius's financial debt and subsequent imprisonment. He requested Pasche to empower Gericke to look after the mission account in Cuddalore.

On 23 February 1779, Schwartz informed Pasche that the misdeeds of Fabricius and Hüttemann were so dangerous that they jeopardised the mission and its reputation. While Fabricius regretted his mistake, humbled himself and asked

184 AFSt/M 1 B 69 : 72: On 15.01.1778, Hüttemann wrote a similar letter to the secretary of the SPCK. He doubted the linguistic abilities of his predecessors: "Here was the Rock, where Ziegenbalg and Schultze split, when they had stuffed their memories with a sufficient number of words, they ventured into the streets and held forth as charlatans and mountebanks." Ziegenbalg, the pioneer missionary in Tranquebar, interpreted the attention of the Tamil as their interest in his Christian doctrines. In this regard, he was "greatly mistaken."

185 AFSt/M 1 B 71 : 43.

for forgiveness, Hüttemann remained “unwilling, murmuring and hostile” and considered the mission futile. The attitudes and misdeeds of Fabricius and Hüttemann affected Schwartz’s mind and body severely, and he became sick.[186] On the following day, 24 February 1779, Schwartz informed Freylinghausen of Hüttemann’s opposition to missionary work and how Hüttemann had tried to prevent others, including his son-in-law Gericke, from engaging in missionary work.[187]

Hüttemann’s educational plan[188] disappointed Schwartz so much that he informed Pasche. Pasche sent a warning letter to Hüttemann, and Schwartz received a copy of it. In an unpublished letter dated March 14, 1780, he expressed his displeasure about Hüttemann’s bitterness towards the Tamil people and missionary endeavours. Instead of enumerating Hüttemann’s faults, Schwartz stated that, on his part, he was happy with his own divine vocation as a missionary, and he could already witness “traces of God’s gracious reign.” Schwartz’s positive perspective on missionary work was unwavering, unlike Hüttemann’s contempt, and would have inspired other missionaries and Tamil catechists. Furthermore, he firmly believed that God would bless and ultimately make the mission great. Then, Schwartz cited the encouraging words of a faithful catechist at Vallam, probably Sattiyanātaṉ, to those non-Christians who were afraid to embrace Christianity. These non-Christians had stated that if they became Christians, they would lose their ties with their relatives and friends, and they would not be able to find marriage partners for their children. The catechists responded, “Do not fear! God has done many great things during the past fifteen years. He will still extend his reign.”[189] It was the conviction of a Tamil catechist, whom Hüttemann had despised, that Schwartz allowed to respond to Hüttemann’s allegations.

In the same letter, Schwartz rejected Hüttemann’s comparison of the Tamil people to nomads. Schwartz argued that even Europeans who did not value the Tamil people would never label them as nomads. Instead, these Europeans knew the Tamil people were well-built and carried themselves with dignity. These Europeans also appreciated their keen, rational minds. Schwartz believed that even the most intelligent Europeans, without a transformed spiritual life, were not superior to the ordinary Tamil people.[190] These positive perspectives about the Tamil people, often ignored in missionary discussions, significantly influenced Schwartz’s views and actions, contributing to his lasting fame.

---

186 AFSt/M 1 B 70 : 40.

187 AFSt/M 1 B 69 : 46.

188 AFSt/M 1 B 70: 45: Hüttemann recommended training Tamil catechists in English and the natural sciences of Europeans. Schwartz judged this training foolish and harmful. If missionaries, even to teach English and natural sciences, did not learn the Tamil language, the Tamil people would not heed their teachings. Schwartz wanted to ask Hüttemann whether he had ever trained Tamil catechists or schoolteachers during his thirty years of ministry. His greed and pride made him lazy and unfaithful. He even forced his Catechist Tiruciluvai (the ‘Holy Cross’) to engage in trade for profit.

189 AFSt/M 1 B 70 : 45.

190 AFSt/M 1 B 70 : 45.

Germann noted that Hüttemann showed little interest or time to engage with the non-Christian Tamils, assuming widespread disdain for Christian missionaries from both Indians and Europeans.[191] He opined that the Company valued Schwartz only for his historical, political, and topographical knowledge, not his missionary efforts. Schwartz spoke many languages so that he could speak with diverse people. Despite Schwartz's linguistic abilities, which enabled him to communicate with diverse groups, Hüttemann claimed that the Company officers appreciated Schwartz primarily for his captivating stories, such as his daring attempts to meet Tipu Sultan outside the Company's territories and his return alive. Hüttemann saw Schwartz as an excellent adviser in times of need and asserted that no Company officer cared about his missionary service.[192] While Schwartz embraced a broader mission involving political interventions for peace and justice, Hüttemann's perspective was much narrower. Hüttemann died disheartened in Cuddalore on 17 July 1781, leaving Schwartz saddened by the perceived lack of value in his work as an envoy of peace, justice, and social harmony.

7.10.5 Johann Wilhelm Gerlach

Johann Wilhelm Gerlach (1738–1791) was an experienced teacher and preacher. For example, in 1767, he taught in the Latin School of the Glaucha Institutions. For another eight years (1767–1775), he taught at the school known as *Pädagogium* within the same Glaucha Institutions. This school catered to the needs of children from aristocratic backgrounds. Upon receiving a missionary call, Gerlach was ordained on 3 November 1775 in Copenhagen and then sailed to Tranquebar, arriving there on 5 August 1776. Soon after his arrival, he became dissatisfied with the educational system in Tranquebar and desired to establish a separate school under his own leadership. His teaching experiences in the *Pädagogium* made him unfit to teach in the mission schools, where children from poorer and less educated backgrounds studied.

When Schwartz visited Tranquebar on 2 February 1777, he met Gerlach and listened to him explain his new school plan. Schwartz immediately foresaw grave problems with Gerlach's plan, which did not prioritise Christian knowledge and experience. Instead, Gerlach aimed to educate competent citizens for the common good without the need to learn Indian languages.[193] Schwartz disapproved of his school plan, but he impacted Gerlach's attitude. Two weeks after meeting with Schwartz in Tranquebar, Gerlach expressed his admiration for Schwartz's simple lifestyle and trustworthiness on February 17, 1777.[194] Gerlach decided not to work in Tranquebar, and, hence, in August 1778, he travelled to Calcutta to assist Johann Zacharias Kiernander (1711–1799).

---

[191] Germann: Missionar Christian Friedrich Schwartz, 288.
[192] Germann: Missionar Christian Friedrich Schwartz, 354–355.
[193] AFSt/M 1 B 68 : 46 dealt in Germann: Missionar Christian Friedrich Schwartz, 407.
[194] AFSt/M 1 B 68 : 20 dealt in Germann: Missionar Christian Friedrich Schwartz, 248.

Schwartz remained in touch with Gerlach, and on 20 October 1783, he recalled his memories of their interactions: Gerlach did not want to start at the bottom and work his way up. He wanted to start with students who could study mathematics and astronomy at higher levels. Schwartz, showing his determination, felt that his attempts to persuade him to abandon his idea about the new school had failed. Gerlach did not know which language he would teach in. He was proficient in German, but Indian children did not typically learn German. He did not know English, Dutch, or Portuguese. Consequently, he was unable to teach the children.[195] He could not open a new school in Calcutta and left the mission (c. 1784). Schwartz's efforts to help him reset his priorities did not yield the expected result.

195 AFSt/M 1 B 74 : 34 dealt in Germann: Missionar Christian Friedrich Schwartz, 248–249.

Chapter 8

Schwartz as a King Maker

The epithet *Rajaguru* ('royal teacher') has become synonymous with Schwartz's relationship with his adopted son, Prince Serfoji. As a mediator and mentor, Schwartz prepared him to become Tanjore's legitimate and competent king. However, it is not yet widely known that he was the chief cause for the selection, enthronement and impeachment of the interim king Ameer Singh. Schwartz was their kingmaker, not only for Serfoji II but also for his predecessor, Ameer Singh. This role underscored Schwartz's importance in the political dynamics of the time and his deep bond with Serfoji.

8.1 Ameer Singh's Enmity Towards Serfoji and Schwartz

Just before his death, Tulāji appointed and celebrated Serfoji as his heir to the throne of Tanjore. As discussed in Section 5.5, Schwartz nominated Ameer Singh, also known as Ramaswami, as the interim ruler of Tanjore. He was indeed a son of King Pratāpasimha, but his mother was not married to his father. Ameer Singh bribed twelve pandits to prove his legitimacy to the throne and got their approval. This political manoeuvring and the subsequent events had significant implications for the succession of the Tanjore throne.[1] The pandits declared Serfoji's adoption as illegal and non-customary. Accordingly, Governor Campbell enthroned Ameer Singh. At that time, Schwartz urged Campbell to get a written assurance from Ameer Singh that he would care for and protect Serfoji. Campbell rejected this request and advised Ameer Singh orally not to neglect Serfoji's welfare. Of course, Ameer Singh promised to look after the young boy in the governor's presence. Schwartz, however, knew Ameer Singh would not keep this promise.[2]

In the meantime, on 28 September 1789, John Chamier of the Company, which collected revenue from Tanjore and indirectly ruled it, stated that Ameer Singh's chief secretaries Shiva Row, "Bapana," and "Gunna Pilly Soubiah" failed to pay the stipulated tribute to the Company. The Company, a powerful entity in Tanjore's political landscape, directed the resident George Andrew Ram of Tanjore to keep the

---

1 Germann: Missionar Christian Friedrich Schwartz, 356: Schwartz observed Ameer Singh's harsh treatment of Serfoji and arranged for a secret investigation of his dealings with the twelve pandits. He discovered that these pandits received bribes from Ameer Singh and voted in favour of his enthronement. Shiva Row, Ameer Singh's most trusted but greedy minister, kept Serfoji in prison and tried to kill him. Schwartz alerted the Company officers about this danger; they freed Serfoji and requested that Schwartz protect, raise, and educate him.

2 Germann: Missionar Christian Friedrich Schwartz, 344–345.

three secretaries under custody and to collect revenues from the entire Tanjore. He insisted that the Company's representative in Tanjore should collect revenues from the territories that Ameer Singh had given to others, either as *jaghir*s or in other forms.[3]

Soon after his installation, Ameer Singh disregarded the interim nature of his administration, grew hostile towards Serfoji, made his life difficult, and refused to provide him and his stepmothers with adequate rice for their sustenance. He confined Serfoji in a dark room without the flow of fresh air, a cruel act that deprived him of fundamental human rights. He did nothing to educate and prepare him for the throne, an apparent injustice. He also did not care for Tulāji's seventy-year-old mother, Draupadī Bāi Sāhibā, and two widows, Sulochanā Bāi Sāhibā and Mohana Bāi Sāhibā. Ameer Singh withheld their annual allowances, causing them to feel offended and tarnishing their dignity. They informed Ram and Schwartz about it, seeking justice and protection. One of their undated letters contains the following information: Tulāji requested that they care for his adopted son, Serfoji. For this purpose, they should not commit *satī*. When Ram saw this letter, he saved Serfoji and appointed the Company's soldiers to guard their rooms. Thus, he ensured Serfoji's well-being. Serfoji and his stepmothers requested that the Company provide them with regular stipends for their sustenance and security. They praised the Company for making and acting on "true decisions."[4] Upon receiving this complaint, the Company's Residents, George Andrew Ram and Earnest William Fallowfield, who valued Schwartz's expertise and influence, requested that he assess their situation and recommend the sum to which Serfoji, the mother, and the widows were entitled.

On 11 October 1789, Ram reported that he had sent Schwartz to gather more details about Serfoji's condition and mentioned that Ameer Singh wanted Serfoji to get married. Until that time, he should remain in his room. He did not want him to visit his adoptive mothers because "it would be highly repugnant to their Customs for a Youth of Serfogee's Age to visit the Apartment of the Widow of the late Rajah." Ram disagreed with Ameer Singh because Serfoji, as a child, should not be confined to a room without "freedom, Benefits of Light, and Air." Ram could not prevail over Ameer Singh; therefore, he requested Schwartz to intervene. Ameer Singh knew that the Company's Governor placed his "utmost confidence in Mr Schwartz's Direction and Zeal for the service." However, Ameer Singh had many excuses not to meet Schwartz; when they finally met, Schwartz demanded the release of Serfoji from the "present dark and dismal Place of his Confinement," and Ameer Singh agreed.[5]

Based on Schwartz's report, on 27 October 1789, a significant date in Tanjore's history, George Andrew Ram informed the Governor of Madras that he led Serfoji by the hand away from the presence of Ameer Singh into a newly renovated house in the palace grounds. He placed twelve sepoys to guard him continuously.[6] Following

---

3 BL IOR/P/252/37, 2897–2900.

4 BL IOR/P/316/89, 196–198.

5 Treaty concluded by Sir Archibald Campbell with the Nabob of Arcot 1792, 36.

6 IOR/H/571, 200: On 16.10.1792, Schwartz requested that the Company consider granting this family an annual subsidy of 30,000 kalam paddy for their sustenance (IOR/P/253/2, 5455–5456). Tulāji's widows requested that Schwartz intercede on their behalf with the

Schwartz's recommendation, Ram appointed Dada Row, a Maratha Brahmin, to teach Serfoji the "alphabet," i.e., the basics of reading and writing in Marathi, possibly also Tamil and English. He permitted Serfoji to receive his food and other provisions from his adopted mothers. He did not permit Shiva Row, the *diwan* (prime minister) of Ameer Singh, to exert any evil influence on Serfoji.[7]

Consequently, Ameer Singh grew more hostile towards Serfoji and his adoptive mothers.[8] For example, in 1790, Queen Mother Draupadī Bāi Sāhibā wrote a letter to Schwartz, requesting that he translate it into English for the Company's Resident, Ram, in Tanjore. The Company officers in Madras and the Company's Court of Directors in London expressed favourable support to Serfoji. This support caused Ameer Singh to inflict more hardships on Serfoji and his adoptive mothers. The Queen Mother stated that Tulāji took "a boy of our caste, adopted him according to our Shaster, delivered the Government to him in the presence of our God and delivered that adopted boy to the Honorable Company because he knew that the Honorable Company was faithful." She narrated further how Tulāji persuaded his three wives not to burn themselves to death on his funeral pyre. He charged them to care for the boy Serfoji. She lamented that Ameer Singh "got the Government by various means." She was convinced she could expect "justice" from the Company for Serfoji, whom Ameer Singh had confined. She explained further how Ameer Singh had taken away the jewels of her three daughters-in-law, withheld their monthly allowance, stopped funding for their charity houses at *Nitya Mangalam*, and taken away the village of "Ambapoor" from Sulochanā Bāi Sāhibā, while also supporting three local poligars who plundered the charity house at "Ambapoor." The Queen Mother stated that these and other atrocities vexed the three widows so intensely that they wished to die. She urged the "faithful and just" Company to intervene within eight days and save Serfoji, the widows and herself. She concluded her letter with this remark: "As I am the Eldest of all, must I see all this Injustice? Who is Amersing [sic!] that He should do all this to me?"[9]

Ameer Singh's treatment of Serfoji grew worse. In an undated letter, written in September or October 1790, Resident Alexander Macleod informed Governor Archibald Campbell of Serfoji's miserable condition. Macleod stated that he and Schwartz had attempted to rescue Serfoji, but Ameer Singh had thwarted their earlier efforts. Finally, Macleod passionately appealed to Campbell:

Company. On 12.11.1792, Schwartz wrote a letter to the Company explaining the hardship of Serfoji and his stepmothers. He requested Cornwallis, who happened to be in Madras at that time, to "interpose his authority" on the fate of Serfoji and his adopted mothers. IOR/H/571, 211–212: An unnamed officer summarised Schwartz's letter of 12.04.1793, which described Serfoji's confinement as follows: "For four years, the Raja continued to behave cruelly towards Serfoji." Mr. Swartz remonstrated." Soon after occupying the throne, Ameer Sing confined Serfoji in a dark room with a small oil lamp and did not arrange for his education. He did not permit him to meet his adopted mothers. As the room was full of insects, Serfoji was unable to sleep that night. Schwartz moved the Company to issue necessary orders to free Serfoji.

7 IOR/P/252/37, 3169–3178.

8 Chidambaram Srinivasachari Ramanujam: British Relations with Tanjore (1748–1799). Diss. phil. London 1968, 398.

9 IOR/ P/316/89, 196–198.

> [Serfoji] remains still deprived not only of all education, but likewise of free air, exercise and attendance. There being no prospect of a favourable change in his situation, humanity induces me to hope that some effectual mode of interposition may suggest itself to you, Honourable Sir, by which the Boy may receive the Protection he so well merits from the Justice of the Honourable Company. I beg leave to add that the Reverend Mr. Swartz whom Tulajah on his death bed appointed Guardian to Sherfogee [sic], might with propriety be constituted the Judge of the Boy's condition, and while he approved of the Treatment shewn by his Excellency the Child would be secure of every protection The Honourable Company could wish to obtain from him.[10]

In the meantime, on 22 October 1790, Schwartz received an alarming letter from Tulāji's widows. They stated that during the recent Dasara Festival, Ameer Singh tried to kill Serfoji. During the festival, it was customary in Tanjore to slaughter sheep and goats. By contrast, the widows alleged that Ameer Singh kept a monkey for beheading. In the pretence of slaughtering that monkey, he wanted to behead Serfoji secretly. He assumed that after killing Serfoji, he would have no rivals. Firmly convinced that he would get rid of Serfoji, Ameer Singh reduced Serfoji's monthly allowance to sixty Pagodas, whereas Schwartz had suggested 1,000 Pagodas earlier. As soon as Macleod received news about this sinister plot for murdering Serfoji from "Govendarow Englay, a man of Reputation," he requested Schwartz to stay day and night with Serfoji. Accordingly, on 21 October 1790, when Schwartz was with Serfoji, Ameer Singh's people attempted twice to abduct Serfoji. Macleod confessed that "the propriety of that Gentleman's conduct [i.e. Schwartz's conduct] and the prudence of the Boy himself" prevented a tragedy.[11] This murder attempt alarmed the Company's officers in Tanjore and Madras, and they arranged for Serfoji's release.

In the meantime, the Company's senior officers counted on Schwartz's intervention in all matters related to Serfoji and the general welfare of all Tanjore inhabitants. For instance, on 18 November 1790, Governor Charles Oakley recognised Schwartz's unabated "zeal for the prosperity of the Tanjore country" and admired his "benevolent purposes." He promised Schwartz that he would instruct his colleagues in Tanjore "to pay the greatest regard to your advice upon the subjects." He stated that he had forwarded Schwartz's suggestions about Tanjore's management to the Board of Revenues and would "have every consideration given to them."[12]

The Company focused on getting as much revenue as possible from Ameer Singh. Concurrently, Ameer Singh's priorities lay elsewhere. In early December 1790, Ameer Singh requested that Schwartz obtain cash from the Company to support the maintenance of temples, their rituals, and charity houses in Māyāpuram, Shiyāli, Mannārgudi, and Sithāmangalam. Ameer Singh claimed that his ancestors paid "for the performance of religious rites to [sic! = for] some 10 & 12 months." Tulāji supported these temples fully until Hyder Ali's army invaded Tanjore in 1780. During the war,

---

10 IOR/P/316/89, 174–175.

11 IOR/P/316/89, 176–179.

12 Bodleian Library: 72290ind-box2, Document 23 dated 18.11.1790: Charles Oakley to Schwartz. Oakley also mentioned to Schwarz about erecting an epitaph: "I have spoken to Mr Chance, about Mrs Horne's Representative, concerning the monument, and he consents to its being placed without the church. You will be pleased therefore to give the necessary directions accordingly."

Diwan Baba provided partial support. Ameer Singh provided them with substantial amounts of money, but these were insufficient to cover the running costs. After the Company began administering Tanjore revenues, these temples did not receive sufficient subsidies. Therefore, Ameer Singh wanted Schwartz to receive sufficient funds from the Company to support the temples, rituals, and institutions. He requested that Schwartz show him details of all Tanjore's revenues so that he would be aware of them and receive his annual grant of one lakh Pagodas and one-fifth of Tanjore's revenues. He expressed his sense of insult when Ram and Fallowfield wanted him to obtain prior permission to pluck fruits and vegetables from his private garden. He reminded Schwartz to respect his royal dignity when representing him to Ram and Fallowfield.[13] The tone of this long letter indicated Ameer Singh's displeasure over Schwartz's relationship with him.

On 8 December 1790, Ameer Singh lamented that his enemies, Schwartz and Ram, had removed Serfoji from his protection, thereby causing the Company's displeasure. He blamed Ram for wanting to see Serfoji and then forcefully led him away from his presence. He accused Ram of insulting and disrespecting him, feeling belittled "in the eyes of the world." He claimed that this mistreatment harmed his dignity and informed the Company officers in Madras that it was "highly improper" for the Company servants to attempt to "interfere with the private concerns of my family and household."[14] In any case, Schwartz and Ram freed Serfoji from Ameer Singh's direct control and arranged a separate accommodation for Serfoji on the palace grounds.

At the request of the Queen Mother, Schwartz reported on 14 December 1790 to the residents that the Queen Mother considered herself the matriarch and employed several female assistants. He recommended 1,000 Pagodas for her monthly expenses. He felt that each of the three widows should receive an annual subsidy of 500 to 600 Pagodas. The four widows viewed Ameer Singh not as a king but as a usurper of the throne of Tanjore. Schwartz recommended that the Company directly pay the money to the widows and Serfoji and permit Serfoji to visit his adoptive mothers whenever he desired.[15] Consequently, the Military Department of the Company approved Schwartz's recommendation on 21 December 1790, and the Company began paying them. The Queen Mother received 1,000 Pagodas monthly, and the three widows received 1,500. Serfoji got 1,300 Pagodas monthly.[16]

---

13 T Vol 3450 A, 253–257.

14 IOR/P/252/52, 5378–5387.

15 T Vol. 3449 B, 565–568: Schwartz consulted Baba, Tulāji's former diwan and found the following stipends suitable, especially during exigencies. Then he sent the following message to Residents Ram and Fallowfield, who later forwarded it to the Company: Tulāji's "mother is a Lady of 70 years and looks upon herself as the mother of the whole family. She takes pride in maintaining many relatives. I wish, therefore, that she may get monthly 1,000 Pagodas. As for the other 3 widows, I thought at the beginning that they did not need so much and that 500 or 600 Pagodas each month would be sufficient to maintain them. This is my opinion, which, however, is and ought to be submitted to the superior wisdom of the Hon'ble Board. As to Serfojee's allowances, His Excellency [Ameer Singh] himself doth not make any objection against it. The main point and principal request of those Ladies is that they may receive their allowance from the Hon'ble Company and not from His Excellency, for by this means all complaints will cease."

16 T Vol. 3449 B, 614. T Vol. 3450 A, 38: In March 1791, Jackson requested that Schwartz inform the widows about their increased monthly allowances: accordingly, the Queen Mother

However, Military Secretary W.C. Jackson did not want the widows to consider Ameer Singh a usurper because Governor Archibald Campbell had observed the due procedures of ascertaining the successor to Tulāji. Therefore, Ameer Singh was a lawful king. Jackon did not want the widows to call Serfoji their Maharaja (the 'Great King').[17] After releasing Serfoji from Ameer Singh's control, Macleod stressed the Company's obligation to protect and educate him under Schwartz's tutelage and guidance. In the meantime, they wanted to avoid unnecessary gossip about their support for Serfoji. Hence, they decided not to visit Serfoji all too often. Macleod mentioned that he thought Serfoji could not write any script when freed from confinement. However, under Schwartz's guidance and teaching, Serfoji made considerable progress in reading and writing. Macleod and Schwartz knew why Jackson did not want anyone to address Serfoji as their "Maharaz" (i.e., Maharaja, "great king"). Macleod concluded his letter: Neither Schwartz nor Macleod believed "any person under our Orders ever addressed the Boy as Maharaz."[18]

At the same time, Macleod requested that Schwartz find details about two land donations and their annual revenue from Ameer Singh. These land donations, made by Tulāji and Ameer Singh, were significant as they contributed to the yearly revenue of the Tanjore region. Earlier, Tulāji donated the region of Swami Malai (nowadays a suburb of Kumbakonam) to his son-in-law. This region would yield approximately 35,000 Cakkarams annually. Later, Ameer Singh donated the village of Ganapathi Agraharam (now in Papanasam Taluk, Tiruchirappalli District) to his son-in-law. This village would annually yield 25,000 Cakkarams.[19]

On 31 December 1790, Ameer Singh responded to Schwartz regarding these two places, which were part of his private domain. However, if the Company insisted that they would add the income of these two places to Tanjore's total revenue, he would lose the two amounts. Additionally, he requested Ram and Fallowfield to deduct 4,500 Cakkarams as the tax value of seven other smaller villages. In this case, he would not have any money left to pay half-salary to his employees, who would soon celebrate the Pongal Festival. Therefore, he requested that Schwartz urge Ram and Fallowfield to immediately grant him one lakh kalam of paddy and 25,000 Cakkarams. He further

---

would receive 5,000 Star Pagodas, each of the three widows 3,000 Star Pagodas, and Serfoji and his other relatives 11,000 Star Pagodas. Jackson also requested that Schwartz update Ameer Singh about this revision and hoped that "both parties will be induced to consent to it on the Principle of Impartiality."

17 T Vol 3450 A. 32–33: On 31.03.1791, Jackson sent to Schwartz the following information: "Whatever might have been the original cause for the Rajah's ill-will to the family of his late Brother, the Board are inclined to believe, that the Homes of Discord have been kept alive and perhaps considerably heightened, by their appeals to Government. More especially, if by any means, his Excellency should be in the Knowledge of the Contents of the Letters, in which they assert that he is a 'Usurper' and that Serjogee (whom they improperly stile 'Maharaz') is the lawful Prince of the country. These expressions must naturally excite alarm and jealousy in the Rajah's breast—they are, besides, extremely disrespectful to the Company, who, from motives of Justice, placed the present Rajah on the *musnund* in preference to the adopted son."

18 IOR/P/316/89, 180.

19 T Vol 3449 B, 623–625: This document mentioning these two land donations bears the date as 29.12.1790.

stated that he wanted to help his distressed employees, and his duty was to help them at this critical time.[20] It must have been humiliating for him to request a small portion of the significant Tanjore revenue from the Company.

By then, the Company had tried to reform their administrative structure. They did not want the residents to collect taxes. Instead, taxes would become the prerogative of collectors. Consequently, on 5 January 1791,[21] Jackson informed Ram that his post as a resident had ceased, and he had become one of two new revenue collectors in Tanjore. Jackson further stated, "Whatever intercourse with the Palace is deemed necessary in the future is to be carried out solely through the channel of the Reverend Mr. Swartz."[22]

On the same day, Jackson wrote another letter to Schwartz, emphasising his crucial role as a mediator between the Company and Ameer Singh's palace. As a trusted advisor and mediator, Schwartz played a vital role in facilitating open communication and understanding between the two parties. The Company officers sought to benefit from Schwartz's experiences and acquaintance with the Kingdom of Tanjore. Jackson acknowledged Schwartz's commitment to furthering the "mutual Business of the Honorable Company and His Excellency the Rajah [Ameer Singh]," and he reiterated that the Company officers had entrusted Schwartz "solely with such communications as they may have to make to the Rajah in future." He was convinced that Schwartz was the only person capable of managing the complex tasks the Company officers found daunting.

On 16 March 1791, Governor Charles Oakley wrote a private, confidential letter to Schwartz requesting his mediatory role between the Company and the royal household of Tanjore. This letter illustrates the esteem and respect which the Company accorded to Schwartz:

> Revd Sir, From the letter which you have lately written, and which I have laid before the Board and from the general complexion of things at Tanjore, I am inclined to believe that a considerable amendment has taken place in the Rajah's politics. He seems better disposed to listen to advice, and there are even marks of consideration towards the boy Serfojee. It is happy for all parties that we have struck at the root of intrigue by removing spurious people from the country, but above all by placing your virtue as the only medium between us and the Rajah, I feel now perfectly easy in the conduct of all affairs. I hope by degrees and with your assistance that something effectual will be done for the benefit of the poor inhabitants, and you may rely upon us. The collectors shall have every support in carrying your ideas upon this point into execution. I am sensible that great reforms cannot be suddenly accomplished, but you have the satisfaction, I hope, already of seeing the attention to general justice in the administration of the revenue. I beg now and then to be favoured with your opinions, which will always have great weight with me. I am Revd Sir, your faithful and humble servant, Charles Oakley, Fort St. George, 6 March 1791.[23]

On the other hand, Ameer Singh was unhappy with the Company officers collecting revenues through their servants, as revealed in his letters to the Company. Jackson

20 T Vol 3449 B, 627–630.

21 By September 1790, outstanding arrears enabled the Company at Fort St. George to begin collecting revenues directly in Tanjore.

22 IOR/P/252/57, 77.

23 Bodleian Library: 72290ind-box2, Document 25 dated 16.031791: Sir Charles Oakley's private letter to Schwartz.

found Ameer Singh's letters "disrespectful to the Government and unbecoming his Dignity." He requested that Schwartz explain to Ameer Singh the impropriety of such Language in his Public Letters. As a result, Ameer Singh was to communicate his future wishes only through Schwartz.[24] Likewise, on 31 March 1791, Jackson informed Schwartz that the Company had appointed him as their sole representative to transact business on their behalf with the palace. The Company's decision to appoint Schwartz as its sole representative demonstrated its trust in his judgment and ability to maintain impartiality. Neither Ameer Singh nor Tulāji's widows should contact the Company directly, but only through Schwartz. Schwartz should convey the Company's desire to do justice to each member of the royal household by following the Principle of Impartiality.[25] As an effective mediator, Schwartz should receive the necessary funds directly from the revenue collectors and pass them on to Tulāji's widows and Serfoji.[26]

The Company's direct management of Tanjore's economic and political affairs through the revenue collectors significantly reduced Ameer Singh's ability to pay 5,000 Pagodas for the annual maintenance of Tulāji's family. Schwartz's undated letter to Governor Charles Oakley, which the Company's council members read on April 19, 1791, revealed that Ameer Singh had willingly accepted 20,000 Pagodas, which the two revenue collectors had sent him for support. However, he refused to accept the 5,000 Pagodas the revenue collectors sent to support Tulāji's family; he opined that this family deserved only one thousand Pagodas as subsidies, not five thousand Pagodas. In response, the Company instructed the revenue collectors to pay the subsidies to Schwartz, who would then distribute them to Ameer Singh and Tulāji's family.[27]

Over time, Schwartz envisaged three ways Ameer Singh would try to establish his legitimacy to the throne of Tanjore. On 27 January 1792, he explained these possibilities to Governor Oakley: The 43-year-old Ameer Singh could marry one or more wives and beget a son. Secondly, if he does not have a son, he might adopt the son of his concubine, named Nana Saheb. Thirdly, he might induce "many people well versed in the Shaster of the Hindoos," as with the twelve pandits, who declared Serfoji's right to the throne illegal and invalid. He assumed that Oakley would assess these options.[28]

Schwartz attached an English version of a letter to his request, which was written by Tulāji's mother, Draupadī Bāi Sāhibā, and his widow, Mohana Bāi Sāhibā, on 9 November 1792. They reported that Tulāji's other widow, Sulochanā Bāi Sāhibā, who had passed away on 14 October 1792, regarded Serfoji as her son. The two widows asked Ameer Singh to permit Serfoji to light the funeral pyre of Sulochanā Bāi Sāhibā. Ameer Singh rejected their plea and arranged for a different person to light her funeral pyre. This act deeply offended the widows and Serfoji. Soon after that, Ameer Singh

---

24 IOR/P/252/57, 78–79.

25 T Vol 3450 A, 31: The Company wanted to do "every Justice" to Tulāji's widows. However, they would no longer receive any of their requests directly but "through you [Schwartz], who are appointed to transact the Company's Business at the Palace."

26 IOR/P/252/57, 364–365.

27 IOR/P/252/60, 1851–1852.

28 IOR/P/253/10, 482–485.

accused Mohana Bāi Sāhibā of practising witchcraft against him and his son-in-law, who had died recently. He tried to vacate her from the Company's house within the palace. To evict her, Ameer Singh linked the theft of jewels in the home of the Company's officer, Strange, two days earlier, on 7 November 1791[29] and accused her of orchestrating it. However, further inquiries revealed that a priest (*pūcāri*) stole those jewels. Yet, Ameer Singh insisted that Mohana Bāi Sāhibā organised that theft through the priest. He had that priest caught and paraded him through the streets of the Fort; he asked his servants to read out this message: Mohana Bāi Sāhibā "has paid a great deal of money to the pūcāri by her slave girl desiring the pūcāri to kill the Raja and his son-in-law of which witchcraft Raja's son-in-law died. Therefore, I, Raja, order him to be hanged."[30]

Immediately, Strange sent his dubash Venkatachalam to recover the jewels. Venkatachalam flogged the pūcāri and found a tiny key tied around his waist. Upon opening the box with the key, Venkatachalam found a note offering a reward for committing the theft. Ameer Singh immediately blamed Mohana Bāi Sāhibā for secretly sending that note and persuading the priest to steal the jewels.[31]

When Schwartz enquired about this event, Ameer Singh seemed stressed and disoriented. Soon thereafter, Ameer Singh dismissed Serfoji's attendants, including his Brahmin teacher, cooks, washermen and other servants. When Ameer Singh's wife could not sleep, he blamed the widows for using witchcraft against her. To ward off evil, he performed a religious ceremony by burning chillies and other ingredients near the widows, where Serfoji and his servants were staying. They felt suffocated and ran out, panting for fresh air.[32] In this context, Tulāji's widows requested protection from the Company. Schwartz intervened and reminded Ameer Singh of his obligation to protect, educate and train Serfoji. He asked him to recall the Company's orders and the Court of Directors' decrees in London on 6 May 1791.[33] Ameer Singh did not respond to Schwartz's advice and continued to trouble Serfoji and his adoptive mothers.

---

29 It is unclear whether this Strange was James Charles Stuart Strange (1753–1840), the fur trader, or Thomas Strange, who later became the Chief Justice of the Company's Court in Madras.

30 NHR 5, 1797, issue 50, 151: During his travel from February to May 1795, Christoph Samuel John saw in an open space just before Tanjore city, gallows with the skeleton of a priest (*pandaram*, 'mendicant'). His legs were broken so that his soul could not wander around like a ghost. Ameer Singh believed that two years earlier, this priest had killed his son-in-law through witchcraft. He refused to listen to any rational argument and ordered his murder. John sighed at the power of such strong superstition.

31 IOR/H/571, 201–203.

32 This ritual, often seen as superstitious, appears to be the *tiruṣṭi-cuṟṟu* ('waving round' to counteract the perceived effects of the evil eye) or *tiruṣṭi kaḻi* ('repelling' the evil eye). Typically, a woman performs this ceremony to protect against the harmful influence of the evil eye. She waves a small bundle of cloth containing three or five dry red chillies and sea salts around the afflicted person's head or body parts and then burns the bundle at a road junction. As the salts crackle and the chillies burn, it is believed that the sound and smoke expel the evil spirit, aiding the person's recovery. In this specific instance, Ameer Singh's people burnt the salts and chillies beneath the widows of the room where Serfoji and the widows of Tulāji were staying, hoping that the smoke would suffocate them and lead to their deaths.

33 IOR/H/571, 201–203.

Based on the evidence produced by Schwartz, the Company requested that Schwartz translate their letters from English into Marathi and personally deliver them to Ameer Singh on 16 November 1792. They also assured Schwartz that the commanding officer in Tanjore would assist him in rescuing Serfoji if the need arose and that the revenue collectors would provide the necessary funds. On the same day, Governor Charles Oakley expressed his displeasure to Ameer Singh and urged him to show "every mark of attention and respect" to Serfoji and the widows. He informed Ameer Singh that the Company had empowered Schwartz to execute their decisions.[34]

8.2 Serfoji and Tulāji's Widows Rescued

On 19 November 1792, W.C. Jackson asked the Company's Commanding Officer in Tanjore to assist Schwartz "to take measures for the immediate removal of Serfoji, the adopted son of Tujajee" to Madras and to protect the "whole family of the late Rajah, who are exposed to imminent danger from" Ameer Singh. Jackson urged the Commanding Officer to address this urgent matter prudently and respectfully, safeguarding the concerned persons.[35] Accordingly, the Commanding Officer arranged for the rescue of Serfoji and the widows. On 19 November 1792, Schwartz informed the officer that Ameer Singh had ordered his employees not to supply water to Serfoji and his adopted mothers the previous day so that they "had no water to drink." As the situation worsened, Captain Wallace sent two companies of European soldiers to the palace, "put double guards before Serfojee's door and double guards before the entrance which leads to the Ladies' Quarters." Simultaneously, he sent a messenger to Ameer Singh in the "Bahanan's Garden, two miles from the Fort" and informed him of his rescue operations. Once freed, Serfoji and the widows were "unspeakably happy." They requested that Schwartz accompany them not only to Cuddalore but also to Madras. They also asked him to thank the Company for the timely help.[36]

8.2.1 Serfoji's Move from Tanjore to Madras

Two days later, on 21 November 1792, Schwartz wrote to Governor Charles Oakley about the departure of Serfoji and his adopted mothers as follows:

> I have the honor to acquaint your Honor that Serfojee and the widows of the late Rajah quitted the palace this morning and were conducted by Captain Douglas to the Little Fort. They live in the Pagoda, where they collect their baggage. To protect the baggage, where it is carried out, sepoys are left in the palace. All the Europeans who were posted in the palace have left it and are again in the Little Fort. I acquainted His Excellency [Ameer Singh] with all this and entreated him in the name of the Ladies to be so kind as to let them have their former palanquins. His Excellency has promised to send me an answer.[37]

---

34 IOR/H/571, 204–205.
35 IOR/P/253/3, 6092–6094.
36 IOR/P/253/3, 6420–6421.
37 IOR/P/253/3, 6422.

On the following day, on 22 November 1792, Schwartz communicated to the Company another practical problem: The widows had numerous female servants who lived in their own houses. They could stay there if the Company's commanding officer could protect them in Tanjore. "To take them all to Madras would be very expensive."[38] Two days later, on 24 November 1792, Schwartz dealt with yet another unexpected event. Unnamed persons in the Fort and the town of Tanjore had spread a rumour that the widows desired to return to their palaces.

To dispel this rumour, Schwartz requested that Captains Wallace and Douglas accompany him to the Great Temple in Tanjore, a significant religious and cultural site where the ladies were staying. Ameer Singh's favourite dubash and a Brahmin writer went with them. After drawing a large curtain between the ladies and the men, the ladies loudly dictated their views in Marathi, which the writer noted. Its English version can be summarised as follows: The two queens, namely Rajesh Bāi Sāhibā and Mohana Bāi Sāhibā declared that they did not "wish to stay an hour here at Tanjore, whether we have our signs or marks [of dignity] due to us or whether we have them not, we will go to Madras; should we go back to the palace, we both and our son, Serfojee, would sacrifice ourselves." Schwartz attached the original Marathi letter, which the Brahmin writer wrote and sent to the Company. This board received Schwartz's message and forwarded it to the Governor General in Bengal.[39]

On 7 December 1792, Jackson communicated the pleasure of the Company regarding Schwartz securing the personal statements of the widows: it was "perfectly sufficient for the Board that the widows of the late Rajah declared their wish to come to Madras in your presence." The Board did not consult Ameer Singh. Jackson informed Schwartz that he should be the official communication channel between Ameer Singh and the Company and that the Company would not trust anyone else. Jackson updated Schwartz that he had ordered Captain Wallace to expedite the departure of Serfoji and the Ladies, agreeably to their wishes.[40] Finally, Schwartz accompanied Serfoji, the Queen Mother Draupadī Bāi Sāhibā and the two widows and reached Madras in December 1792.[41] By 10 January 1793, they had settled there safely.[42]

---

38 IOR/P/253/3, 6423; IOR/P/253/3, 6423–24: On 27.11.1792, Jackson communicated to Schwartz the Company's decision not to transport the "train of servants." The ladies should take only those servants who were essential to them. Others would be protected in Tanjore itself. Schwartz could decide to accompany Serfoji and the ladies to Cuddalore or Madras. If he came to Madras, he could help them settle down properly.

39 IOR/P/253/3, 6454–6455.

40 IOR/P/253/3, 6482–6483.

41 NHR 4, 1795, issue 47, 998, Memoirs of the Rev. Joseph D[aniel] Jænicke, 115–116 and Germann: Missionar Christian Friedrich Schwartz, 357: On 04.02.1794, Schwartz informed Uebele in London these details: "You ask whether the King [Ameer Singh] has had Tanjore restored to him. Certainly, but the inhabitants do not rejoice at the change. For two years, I have discharged the duties of a RESIDENT [from January 1791 to the end of 1792]. A Resident usually receives 7,000 Star Pagodas or 3,000 Sterling." Schwartz stated that he did not ask the Company to pay him any money for his service as a Resident of Tanjore. As Serfoji's legal guardian, he paid for his journey to Madras. There, he met Governor General Cornwallis, who assured him that Serfoji would soon become the king of Tanjore. At that time, King Ameer Singh was only forty-six, but he appeared sixty.

42 NHR 4, 1795, issue 47, 998: On 04.02.1794, Schwartz reiterated that as Serfoji's legal guardian, he paid all travel expenses from Tanjore to Madras. He reiterated that this was

8.2.2 Serfoji's Stay in Madras

The settlement of Serfoji's adopted mothers and their relatives in Madras soon became contentious. According to Dattajee's letter to Schwarz on 12 November 1793, the Queen Mother, often referred to as the 'Great Lady' due to her influential position, and the two widows requested additional funds from the Company to support their 65 relatives. The Queen Mother, often referred to as the Great Lady, required Dattajee to obtain 1,000 Pagodas monthly from the Company. Her voice (*cattam*, 'noise') was so loud that it "could break the dike of a river." She asserted that if she did not receive this money, she would move to another place of her choice. Serfoji had to prevail on her tactfully. Annually, the Company gave 5,000 Star Pagodas to support Serfoji and the three widows. This money included 1,311 Cakkarams (= 582 Pagodas and 15 Panams) to support the sixty-five relatives. Dattajee claimed this amount was sufficient for only eight months and eighteen days. Most relatives did not do anything useful. They roamed Madras aimlessly. Occasionally, they met various Company officers and complained about a lack of financial support. Some servants even switched their allegiance from Serfoji to Ameer Singh and returned to Tanjore.[43] Unable to bear the multiple problems, Mr Haliburton of the Company wondered why the ladies chose to live in Madras. He asked whether it was "in vain that Mr Swartz brought" them there. He recommended they consider returning to Tanjore and receiving their pension directly from Ameer Singh. He spoke about this matter with Sambajee Baroh, the Tanjore *Vakkīl*. The followers of the Queen Mother responded that they could not return to Tanjore until the Company settled their request for more money; they also asserted that they could not expect any help from Ameer Singh.[44]

On 21 October 1793, Serfoji informed Schwartz that the Queen Mother was impatient and wanted to visit Kanchipuram and "made several troubles which cannot be expressed." However, Serfoji persuaded her to stay in Madras till the "monsoon is over, and she is now content to go to one of the villages in the neighbourhood. The Rev. Mr. Gericke is always instructing me." Serfoji concluded this letter with a request

---

morally correct. He stated further that Serfoji's life in Tanjore was in great danger. Now, he was in Madras and would learn to read good books. Schwartz was convinced that the One, who examined the hearts and minds of people, would know how these (unnamed) good books would impact Serfoji in the future. Cornwallis was pleased with Serfoji and would have immediately made him the king. Cornwallis also wondered why Ameer Singh, who was only forty-six years old, looked like a sixty-year-old person. Before Schwartz left Madras, he ensured that Gericke would care for Serfoji and his family in Madras. Cornwallis was pleased with Schwartz's arrangements.

43 T Vol. 4448, 76–77: On 06.02.1794, Schwartz informed Serfoji that Dada Rao's accountant met him in Tanjore two days earlier and informed him about his accidental meeting with two female servants of the Queen Mother in Tiruvidaimaruthur, where Ameer Singh camped. One of them was Mīnāṭci ('the fish-eyed woman'). They decorated the local *Catram* with colourful hangings (*tōraṇam*) and "offered a whole basket of fruits to the Rajah." These servants told Dada Rao that Mohana Bāi Sāhibā and the Queen Mother might return to Tanjore after visiting Tirupati. Schwartz advised Serfoji to remain in Madras.

44 T Vol. 4448, 5–8; T Vol. 4448, 72: Schwartz was sympathetic to the needs of the Queen Mother's servants and Tulāji's widows. On 28 December 1793, he informed Dattajee of this proactive information: "Concerning the eldest Lady, I have written to Mr. Gericke, who will talk to the Governor and ask him whether 9- or 12-month" pay should be paid to the children.

for regular updates on Schwartz's health.[45] The Queen Mother and the widows felt bored in Madras and insisted they return to Tanjore. Serfoji informed Schwartz about this situation. On 28 December 1793, Schwartz strictly admonished him not to give in to the widows' requests and to stay in Madras for his safety and education. Despite the challenges and the pressure, Serfoji remained resilient and committed to his stay in Madras, inspiring those around him.

> My dear Friend [Serfoji], Your kind letter I have received & am happy that you enjoy good health. The eldest Lady is mistaken if she thinks that by staying away, she will oblige the Government to fulfil her desire. She does not know the temper of the Europeans. I have heard that they both intend to return to Tanjore. Surely, they will repent of it. I hope that you will not be taken in by their idle talk. They do not know the present happy situation. If they will return, let them do as they please. But it would be best if you stayed where you are. Here, you could not live with any safety.[46]

Tulāji's mother and widows demanded that Dattajee and Serfoji give them more money. Additionally, a few former servants came from Tanjore to Madras and demanded higher pay. For example, on 30 December 1793, Schwartz advised Serfoji against his relative Bhapana, who had been deceiving Serfoji earlier. Schwartz's letter contains harsh admonitions that would work like a bitter medicine necessary for healing a sick person. It reads as follows:

> To Serfoji Rajah. My dear Friend, in my last letter I have entreated you not to make any extraordinary expense. I have rebuked Dattajee very sharply for spending more than he ought to. Now I hear that Bhapana, and other people desire a salary. Bhapana has formerly imposed upon you & your family. He must not get any pay because he is a deceiver. Mahadie Row is with you to no purpose. If you increase the pay of such people, I tell you that all your relations will pay you a visit & rob you of all your money & when the Governor hears of it you will suffer severely. Admit none of these people. Here are some of your relations that intend to go to Madras because they hope that you will give them double pay. Be upon your own guard. We are all well. May God bless you by giving a truly pious obedient heart. I am Your sincere friend, C.F. Swartz. Tanjore, December 30, 1793.[47]

---

45 T Vol. 4448, 4.

46 T Vol. 4448, 73. T Vol. 4448, 85–86: On 15.07.1794, Schwartz repeated the same advice to Serfoji: he was sorry for the troubles the Queen Mother had caused. Serfoji should not listen to her in this regard. Otherwise, she would trouble him even more. "Should she threaten to go to Tanjore, do not be alarmed. If she comes [to Tanjore], the Rajah's people will make her repent, and her going away cannot hurt you. Therefore, be not afraid." T Vol. 4448, 87: Again, on 06.08.1794, Schwartz underlined this crucial point again: "My dear Friend, your kind letter I have received. It seems that the eldest lady will hardly become satisfied. Though her servants, I believe, are as such to be believed, who stir up her mind to make so many unreasonable demands." T Vol. 4448, 90: On 20.11.1794, Schwartz wrote to Serfoji: "I am glad to hear that the eldest lady is quiet & behaves kindly to you. As she grows older, I wish she may grow wiser." T Vol. 4448, 27: On 16.12.1795, Serfoji again informed Schwartz that "the Great Lady always asks leave of me to go to Tanjore to which I never give an answer." T Vol. 4448, 29–30: On 10.01.1796, Dattajee wrote to Schwartz about the same intensified problem: The "Great Lady always plagued us to go to Tanjore. Soon after she was informed of this present affair, she makes an interruption, pretending that she will never set out from hence."

47 T Vol. 4448, 74; T Vol. 4448, 75–76: On 07.01.1794, Schwartz wrote to Serfoji: your relatives in Tanjore know that some met you in Madras and got your money. "Therefore, they will all go & trouble you. Pray, send everyone away. Why will you keep them there? [...] Do not

On January 7, 1794, Schwartz wished Serfoji "divine mercy and blessing" for the new year. Simultaneously, he admonished him to "fear and adore him who has created heaven and earth, who has loved mankind and sent them a Redeemer who is willing to mend our hearts and make us happy forever." At the same time, he chastised Serfoji for making useless expenses. He also stated that he was "very angry with Dattajee" for spending substantial money without speaking with Gericke.

On 15 January 1794, Serfoji acknowledged Schwartz's four letters (28 and 30 December 1793 and 7 and 9 January 1794) and informed him that he would not heed the impractical demands of the Queen Mother and the two widows. When one of his former servants asked him for wages, he characteristically responded, "I cannot give you anything without Mr. Swartz's order, because he knows that you were discharged from the service." Gericke and Dada Rao taught him valuable lessons. At the end of this letter, Serfoji identified himself as Schwartz's "dutiful scholar."[48] This kind of open and confidential letter exchange between a prospective Indian ruler and Christian missionaries is rare.

Serfoji found it challenging to refuse the Queen Mother's repeated demands for more money from the Company for her private travel to Kanchipuram. Mohana Bāi Sāhibā insisted on visiting Tirupati. On 22 January 1794, Dattajee informed Schwartz that the Queen Mother had stayed in Nungambakkam and sent her agents, such as Subbarao Bhavana and Bhavana Jetro, to Tanjore to explore the possibility of her speedy return to Tanjore. Dattajee reiterated how Serfoji firmly rejected the requests of the women. Dattajee explained how Serfoji, with Gericke's permission, visited Nawab Wallajah's sons in Madras and how Gericke would teach Serfoji sacred music.[49] Likewise, he became cautious about the servants. Dattajee concluded his letter by

---

increase the pay or allowance of your relations. If you do, they will ruin you. They have no mercy. May God preserve and guide you in the way of true piety. I am, Your affectionate friend, C.F. Swartz." T Vol. 4448, 77: On 06.02.1794, Schwartz advised Serfoji: You have already too many servants. "Do not [take] any into your service. God bless you and grant you grace to adore and obey him. I am, Sir, Your most affectionate friend, C.F. Swartz." T Vol. 4448, 83: On 02.05.1794, Schwartz advised Dattajee why he should be prudent in spending: "Take great care of your master. Do not make useless expenses. As the Government will have great expenses on account of the war, you may perhaps not be paid very regularly. If Government should write to the Rajah exhorting him to reduce the jewels, it must be done very poignantly. Otherwise, it will have no effect. May God guide you and your master. May you trust him who alone can help you!"

48 T Vol. 4448, 9: Serfoji requested Schwartz to forgive him for buying wicked [sic! = an unruly] horse without seeking Gericke's advice. "As soon as I bought, I made it known to him, but it is my fault that I did not do it before. For the future, I will follow the advice of the Reverend Mr Gericke even in the least things. I beg leave to conclude with my best respects. I deliver over myself to the Lord God, and I firmly trust in him expecting his grace & kindness."

49 T Vol. 4448, 79: On 11.03.1794, Schwartz wrote to Serfoji: Mohana Bāi Sāhibā's journey to Tirupati "will cost her a great deal of money and will do her no good. But stubborn people [are] intractable refusing to hearken to salutary advice." T Vol. 4448, 14: On 15.03 1794, Serfoji informed Schwartz about the young widow who had gone to Tirupati. The Governor give her "24 Sepoys and a Havildar. One Naig, two marches, seven Sepoys' tents, bamboo boys, lascars and bullocks." T Vol. 4448, 15: On 22.03.1794, Dattajee reported to Schwartz: "I have received this morning a letter from the young lady. She has ascended the Trippatee Mount and will set out from thence tomorrow to Calahasty [modern Srikalahasti in Tirupathi District]."

referring to his faith in God, whom he could trust.[50] When the Queen Mother realised that she would not get a monthly allowance of 1,000 Star Pagodas from the Company, she pestered Serfoji and Dattajee for more rice paddy.[51]

Serfoji and Dattajee continued to encounter more problems from the relatives of Queen Mother Draupadī Bāi Sāhibā and the widows. They repeatedly insisted on returning to Tanjore. Serfoji, Dattajee and Gericke alerted Schwartz to the irritating situation. On 17 February 1794, Schwartz communicated to Serfoji his deep disappointment over the behaviour of these ladies:

> [If the Queen Mother Draupadī Bāi Sāhibā and two widows] should be so imprudent as to come to Tanjore, they will lose all protection of Government & repent of [their] choice. However, their former sufferings which I hope they have not yet forget [sic, i.e. forgotten] will teach them better things. One thing I pray you to observe viz. whatever those ladies may propose, let Government decide all & then they cannot accuse you.[52]

The Queen Mother and the widows continued to demand more money and provisions such as paddy. On 2 May 1794, Schwartz advised Dattajee to persuade the Queen Mother to accept 2,500 Pagodas as her allowance. This amount was equal to the cost of 15,000 kalam of paddy. Serfoji should keep it with him if she refused to take it. He could give it to her when she needed it.[53] Additionally, Schwartz dealt with other matters related to the royal family, as by 31 June 1794, Serfoji could no longer bear the troubles of the Queen Mother and the young widow. He reported his annoyance to Schwartz and sought his guidance.[54]

While conveying Governor Hobart's greetings to Schwartz, Serfoji stated on 7 December 1794 that he practised reading and writing. He exercised his horse as advised by Schwartz and signed his letter as "Your affectionate and dutiful scholar." Three days later, on 10 December 1794, Dattajee informed Schwartz that a relative of the deceased widow, Sulochanā Bāi Sāhibā, had pressed Annojee Panth, an agent of Serfoji and Dattajee in Tanjore, to immediately provide either two hundred kalams of paddy or its equivalent value. Annojee Panth feared for his life and requested two or three

---

50 T Vol. 4448, 11–13.

51 T Vol. 4448, 15.

52 T Vol. 4448, 77–78.

53 T Vol. 4448, 83.

54 T Vol. 4448, 16–17: "Reverend Sir, Your kind letter of the 16th of June I have received on the 23rd June. I thank you for the kind admonitions you [have] given me in that letter. As I improve, I shall endeavour to write you the letters without the assistance of others. I always give my best attention to my learning which the Rev. Mr. Gericke will acquaint you with. The Great Lady refuses to accept the third part of the sum of the 2,500 Pagodas of the Paddy and desires as much as she got last year, about 6,000 kalam of paddy. She had got them, as you know, a thousand times more by quarrelling than she should have gotten. Likewise, she insists on us to give 150 Pagodas out of my allowance every month, to which I answered strictly not a cash can be allowed by the Government more than we have received and that we must take it patiently. She never leaves off troubling and perplexing us and saying that she shall go anywhere as she shall choose. The young Lady demands as the Great Lady shall be allowed by us. You know all this more particularly by the letter of Dattajeeapah. Gadiasalam arrived here 15 days ago. No more at present than that. I remain your affectionate scholar, Serfojee Rajah. Choultry Plain, 31 June 1794."

sepoys as his bodyguards. Likewise, a servant of the deceased Sadasivarow Maitra met Dattajee in Madras and demanded "the allowance by the deceased wife's name."[55]

The complex and convoluted relationship between the Queen Mother, the two widows and their numerous servants posed many challenges. Throughout their stay in Madras, the Queen Mother and the widows were safe, but they expressed discontent on diverse matters. They lamented that they did not have the customary luxuries and services in Tanjore. The Queen Mother and the widows preferred Tanjore to Madras and wanted to return to Tanjore as soon as possible. In these circumstances, Schwartz served as an envoy of peace, justice and social harmony. He was the main point of reference and contact for Tulāji's family members and the Company.

At the same time, Serfoji requested Schwartz to guide him in his learning and maturing. After thanking God for his safety and opportunities to experience new things, on 8 March 1795, he requested Schwartz: "I read and write and exercise of the horse every day and wishing to hear your health continually with good advice which reforms me daily."[56] Schwartz's guidance reformed his attitudes and behaviour. His letter of 30 March 1795 to Schwartz revealed the influence of Christianity on his style of writing letters. He confessed that "By the grace of God," he and his adopted mothers were well. He requested that Schwartz write to him more often and admonish him, which afforded him "great joy."[57]

8.3 Serfoji's Education in Madras

It is common knowledge that Schwartz and his friend Christian William Gericke, the German Lutheran Pietist missionary in Vepery in Madras, educated Serfoji.[58] The details of how these two missionaries facilitated his education and the subjects he studied remain unexplored. Schwartz and Gericke guided Serfoji to be cautious in his interactions with Europeans in Madras.[59] Schwartz promoted Serfoji's education in diverse disciplines despite his pressing demands in Tanjore. He regularly corresponded

55 T Vol. 4448, 21.

56 T Vol. 4448, 22.

57 T Vol. 4448, 22.

58 V.S. Radhika: Development of Sadir in the court of Raja Serfoji-II (1798–1832) of Tanjore. Diss. phil. Hyderabad 2011, here 52: "Serfoji-II received his early education in English, Arithmetic and instruction in Bible from European scholars Rev. William Gerrick and the Christian missionary Rev. Schwartz. His interest for western learning was cultivated by these eminent teachers, especially the latter in whose company and protecting care, Serfoji spent his childhood and who was instrumental in restoring the throne of Tanjore to his worthy student. It was Rev. Schwartz who appointed Dada Rao a pundit to impart knowledge to young Serfoji in indigenous subjects." Graham Shaw: The Tanjore 'Aesop' in the Context of Early Marathi Printing. In: The Library 5:3, 1978, 207–214, here 208–209: Since 1778, Schwartz lived in Tanjore and assisted King Tulāji. He translated into Marathi a dialogue between Christians and non-Christians and gave it to the king. In 1787, the king nominated Schwartz as the guardian of his adopted son Serfoji. Schwartz was a linguist. Serfoji learned from Schwartz a taste for European literature and science." Serfoji collected "an air-pump, an electrifying machine, an ivory skeleton, astronomical instruments" and books on medicine for his museum. Around 1805, he established a printing press in Tanjore.

with Serfoji, encouraging him to uphold Christian values and excel in English education. Schwartz's care and guidance from Tanjore helped Serfoji to advance his studies rapidly. For example, he learned to write letters in English within ten months.[60]

The relationship between Schwartz and Serfoji was not just one of teacher and student but of mutual respect. Schwartz addressed him as "Serfoji Rajah" and viewed himself as his friend and humble servant. Serfoji, in turn, addressed Schwartz primarily as "Reverend Sir" and ended his letters by stating that he was Schwartz's most obedient, affectionate or dutiful scholar, "Serfoee Rajah." This mutual respect is evident in the surviving letters between Schwarz and Serfoji, as well as between Serfoji and Gericke, which provide valuable insights into his education.

8.3.1 The Military Male Orphan Asylum

The Vestry of St. Mary's Church in Fort St. George established the first orphan school in Madras to care for the European children orphaned by the Company's wars in 1761 and 1762 against Pondicherry, Karaikal, Vellore, Nellore, Gingee and "several other posts held by the French." Additionally, the explosion of an ammunition depot in Tiruccirāppaḷḷi in 1762 orphaned more European children. Similarly, the Company's siege of Madura in 1763 and 1764, as well as the poligar war of the latter year, vastly increased the number of widows and orphans to be provided for by the Church Stock.[61] Moreover, Indian mothers gave birth to boys whom British army officers, in and out of wedlock, had fathered within the Madras Presidency. As some of these officers died, their sons became destitute.

In this context, Governor Hobart requested on 27 June 1787 that the vestry at St. Mary's Church in Fort St. George establish a school for male orphans. Consequently, the Vestry met on 13 July 1787, consulted with Schwartz about his charity schools in Tiruccirāppaḷḷi, and decided on the establishment of the Military Male Orphan Asylum

---

59 T Vol. 4448, 11–13: When Lady Oakley invited Serfoji to a concert on Sacred Music, he requested Gericke's permission to attend it. T Vol. 4448, pp 17–18: On 31.07.1794, Serfoji reported to Schwartz that to practice speaking English, he visited Gericke, Mr. Ince and Col. Braithwaite in their homes. He also learned to ride a horse. T Vol. 4448, pp 18–19: On 09.11.1794, Serfoji wrote to Schwartz that Governor Hobart and his secretary visited him and gave him three books by Samuel Johnson. T Vol. 4448, 19–20: On 07.12.1794, Serfoji informed Schwartz about his recent meeting with Governor Hobart, who wanted to know when Schwartz would revisit Madras. Hobart asked: Has "Mr. Swartz no mind to come here? I answered that he will come whenever your Lordship will be pleased. I read and write and exercise the horse as you advised."

60 T Vol. 4448, 2–3: "Sir, after you set out from hence [Madras to Tanjore] the Reverend Mr. Gericke came four times until the 1st October by whom I was instructed in the Bible & by whom my writing was corrected. Three days once I personally paid my visit to the ladies and I am exercising the horse two day once (though I have a mind to exercise every day). I have none but one meek horse at present also the mare that was as quiet as a lamb is dead. I behave in my reading & writing as you advised & for the other affairs you will particularly know by the letter of the Reverend Mr. Gericke. I was sorry to hear that your foot was sprained a little, but I am now glad to hear it is a little better. I shall be exceedingly happy to hear frequently of your good health continuing. I am, Your most obedient scholar, Serfogee Rajah, Choultry Plain, 3. Oct. 1793."

61 Penny: The Church in Madras, 350.

for one hundred orphans, which was founded at Egmore in Madras in 1789. Andrew Bell (1753–1832), a chaplain at St. Mary's Church in Fort St. George, became its superintendent and served in that role for eight years.[62] This school aimed to instil the "principles of religion and morality" in the hearts and minds of young people so that they could form the "habits of diligence, industry, veracity and honesty." By gaining "useful knowledge," they would better serve themselves and the state.[63]

In 1796, Andrew Bell explained how beginners practised writing the alphabet on the sand, following the method of learning to write that was used in Tamil schools.[64] Older boys learned to read, write, and perform basic accounting tasks. Depending on their age and competencies, students learned the art of formal writing.[65] The Military Male Orphan Asylum curriculum was comprehensive and covered diverse subjects. Students learned grammar, mathematics, geography, navigation, the 'art of measuring things,' navigation and astronomy, morality, and the Anglican form of Christianity. Mathematics included 'Arithmetic vulgar and decimal,' bookkeeping, geometry, and tables. All students read the Bible, the Catechism, and *The Speaker*[66] by William Enfield (1741–1797), a Unitarian minister in Warrington, England. Those older students who excelled in these areas taught younger students in a caring and responsible manner.[67]

---

62 In 1797, Bell transplanted this Madras System of Education to Aldgate in London. Soon, charity schools in White Chapel and Lambeth adopted it. The Royal Military Asylum in Chelsea benefited from it. It spread to other places in the UK and equipped older students to teach younger ones. Penny states that at the instruction from the Company's Court of Directors in London, the Company opened the Male Asylum in June 1787, the same money when Andrew Bell reached Madras on his way to Calcutta. In July 1787, a letter from Gericke persuaded the Company to enable Bell to stay in Madras and to help them develop the asylum. They also appointed him a chaplain to their armies, but he was not required to travel. For six months, Bell stayed in the house of Andrew Ross, an influential free merchant of Madras, who was an ardent member of St. Mary's Church in Madras (Penny: The Church in Madras, 524–525).

63 Andrew Bell: An Experiment in Education made at the Male Asylum of Madras suggesting a System by which a School or Family may teach itself under the Superintendence of a Master or Parent. London: Cadell and Davies, 1797, here 5–9.

64 Bell: An Experiment in Education, 11: Beginners learned to write the alphabet. "I had, at first sight of a Malabar [Tamil] school, adopted the idea of teaching the letters in sand spread over a board or bench before the scholars, as on the ground in the schools of the natives of this country." Bell: An Experiment in Education, 17: The "school is thus rendered a scene of amusement to the scholar and a spectacle of delight to the beholder."

65 Bell: An Experiment in Education, 19: Children used the "Great and Small Alphabets," "Child's First Book and Figures" and "Child's Second Book, Stops, Marks and Hymns."

66 William Enfield: The Speaker or Miscellaneous Pieces selected from the best English Writers and disposed under proper heads with a view to facilitate the Improvement of Youth in Reading and Speaking, to which is prefixed an Essay on Elocution. London: Joseph Johnson, 1774, vii–xxii: The eight rules for elocution are 1) "Let your articulation be distinct and deliberate." 2) "Let your pronunciation be bold and forcible." 3) "Acquire a compass and variety in the height of your voice." 4) "Pronounce your words with propriety and elegance." 5) "Pronounce every word consisting of more than one syllable, with its proper ACCENT." 6) "In every sentence, distinguish the more significant words by a natural, forcible, and varied EMPHASIS." 7) "Acquire a just variety of pause[s] and cadence." 8) "Accompany the Emotions and Passions which your words express, by correspondent tones, looks, and gestures."

Schwartz stayed in Madras in 1793 and was responsible for Serfoji's safety and education. He also requested that his trusted friend Gericke educate Serfoji. At that time, Gericke oversaw the Tamil Lutheran Church in Vepery, Madras. From 1786, he supervised girls' education at the Military Female Orphan Asylum, which Lady Campbell, the wife of Archibald Campbell, had established. Schwartz's initiative for the Provincial Schools in Tanjore and Tiruccirāppaḷḷi (since 1784) and the success of the Military Female Orphan Asylum seem to have persuaded the Court of Directors in London to permit schools for European orphans in Calcutta (14 March 1786), and they encouraged a similar orphan school in Madras.

Serfoji joined this school in 1793 and left it after three years in 1796.[68] Furthermore, he learned about and understood the British perspective on Tanjore.[69] He noticed how senior students at the Military Male Orphan Asylum taught their junior students. Serfoji was drawn to English literature and the lifestyle of the British in the diaspora. He observed how they discussed and adhered to virtues such as fairness, justice, respect for tradition, and obedience to rules and authorities. He would have also noticed the British and their armies' unjust and immoral trade practices in Madras. He would have begun to acquire professional competencies in trade and political negotiations, measurements, navigation, and the administration of vast territories using Indian personnel. He would have also recognised the importance of studying both the humanities and the natural sciences.[70]

8.3.2 Learning English

On 3 October 1793, Serfoji shared with Schwartz his joy of learning under the tutelage of Gericke. This is his earliest English letter addressed to Schwartz. Its peculiar diction and tone betray his elementary level of learning the English language:

> Sir, After you set out from hence, the Reverend Mr. Gericke came four times until the 1st October, by whom I was instructed in the Bible and by whom my writing was corrected. Three days once I personally paid my visit to the ladies and I am exercising the horse two days once (though I have a mind to exercise every day). I have none but one meek horse at

67 Bell: An Experiment in Education, 19. See also Andrew Bell: The Madras School or Elements of Tuition comprising the Analysis of an Experiment in Education made at the Male Asylum, Madras. London ^{4}1808, here 85: The catechism included *Church Catechism*, Mrs Trimmer's *Teacher's Assistant* and *Scripture Catechism*.

68 P. J. Thomas: History of Education in Madras. In: The Madras Tercentenary Commemoration Volume. London: Oxford University Press, 1939, 439–457, here 441: Serfoji, the "son and successor of the Rajah of Tanjore was educated from 1793–1797" in this school.

69 Bell: An Experiment in Education, 19–20: Serfoji's mentors would have included not only Andrew Bell but also Francis Johnson (principal), Richard Taylor (head of classroom activities) and James Blood (head of activities outside the classrooms) and teachers Charles Hancock, George Stevens, William Faulkner, Robert Kenrich and John Friskin. In 1796, this school had two hundred students.

70 Bell: The Madras School, 110–111: Bell helped his students discover the natural world's patterns. He likened the natural world to a "book of God. Students should allow the Son of Righteousness to rise on it. Then, they could gain knowledge by studying every grove, valley, mountain and sea and advance their knowledge of the mineral, vegetable and animal world."

> present, also the mare that is as quiet as a lamb is dead. I behave in my reading and writing as you advised & for the other affairs, you will particularly know by the letter of the Reverend Mr Gericke. I was sorry to hear that your foot was sprained a little, but I am now glad to hear it is a little better. I shall be exceedingly happy to hear frequently of your good health continuing. I am, Your most obedient scholar, Serfogee Rajah, Choultry Plain, 3. Oct. 1793.[71]

Serfoji's caretaker, Dattajee, apprised Schwartz about Serfoji's well-being, learning and interactions with other Indians and various Company officers. According to his letter of October 14, 1793, Serfoji, with the governor's permission, attended a gathering on October 4, 1793. He met Governor General Cornwallis, Governor Oakley, and other officeholders there. Dattajee informed Schwartz about the Queen Mother's demand to visit Kanchipuram. Oakley, Gericke and others opposed this move. Finally, Serfoji persuaded her to remain in Madras for the time being. Gericke visited Serfoji once in three days, corrected his English drafts, and taught him the art of speaking English. Before Cornwallis left for England on 8 October 1793, he received Ameer Singh's long letter and did not act on it. Dattajee promised to keep Schwartz updated.[72]

On 21 October 1793, Serfoji communicated the exact details to Schwartz and added this final sentence: "The Rev Mr. Gericke is always instructing me as you did, wishing to have frequently your kind advice to hear often of your health." Again, its diction and tone reveal the learner's attempts to grasp the English language and its nuances. Gericke's efforts to help him improve were significant.[73]

On 24 October 1793, Schwartz expressed his delight about Serfoji's progress in acquiring proficiency in English and reminded him that knowing English alone would not be enough. He should learn to write excellent and elegant letters in English and his native language, Marathi, because this skill would advance his governance and please his correspondents. Schwartz encouraged him to honour the Queen Mother and the widows of Tulāji "notwithstanding their infirmities."[74] With the same tone, he advised Serfoji to heed Gericke's teaching. Finally, Schwartz urged him to "seek the favour of the only true God. If he is your friend, all will be well. If you leave and provoke him, all [things] will go wrong. Pray to Him daily, for He hears our prayers and helps us.[75] This example illustrates Schwartz's gentle approach to expressing his missionary vocation to Serfoji.

Serfoji's meeting with the Company's senior officers required a good knowledge of English, which Serfoji had not yet acquired. Therefore, on 14 April 1794, Schwartz asked Serfoji to write a letter in English "without having it dictated by others" and concluded his letter with an earnest wish that Serfoji would give his "heart to God," his "Creator and Divine Benefactor."[76] Two months later, on 16 June 1794, he inquired about his improvement in English: "It has now been a long time since I left you. Have

---

71 T Vol. 4448, 2–3.
72 T Vol. 4448, 3–4.
73 T Vol. 4448, 5.
74 T. Vol. 4448, 9: Serfoji's letter of 15.01.1794 to Schwartz: "I and the two Ladies are well by the grace of God, hoping to hear the same from you. I obey the Ladies when they give me good advice, not when their advice is bad."
75 T Vol. 4448, 69–70.
76 T Vol. 4448, 82.

you improved in the English Language? Can you write a letter about your composition?" Then he concluded his letter with his usual reference to God's providence: "May God bless you in every respect. Look up to Him who has made heaven and earth and who will be your Father, if you choose His way and humbly seek His mercy."[77] On 15 July 1794, Schwartz inquired further about his knowledge of English:

> To Serfoji Rajah,
> My dear Friend, I have received your kind letter, which my friend Rev. Mr. Gericke has corrected. I entreat you to read and write every day. A language cannot be learnt but by assiduous application. As the Malabar [i.e. Tamil] boy is now with you, let him not be idle as he is inclined to be. He used to make excuses, but do not allow him to stay away. The Governor would wonder about your progress in the English Language. I wished you had somebody near you with whom you could talk. By conversation, one improves. When you send me a letter, I wish to see your composition without being corrected. Then I shall be fully convinced of your progress.[78]

Schwartz was convinced that Serfoji's English knowledge would help him communicate directly with English speakers without interpreters and govern his country more effectively. Therefore, he insisted on learning this language as much as he could. On 9th October 1794, he urged Serfoji to improve his English language even further and highlighted his rationale for it:

> [The] English are fond of their language & like everyone who speaks it with a tolerable propriety. If Lord Hobart sends you books, he will enquire whether you have read them and will ask whether and how you have read them and what improvement you have made by the perusal of them. However, above all, be careful to have the gracious God on your side; his loving kindness is better than life. Pray to him, fear him. Do not dare to do anything against his will & he will be with you.[79]

Now and then, Serfoji received English visitors. Some of them invited him to accompany them on various occasions. These interactions provided him with opportunities to practice his English and learn about their culture. He often received letters from these Company officers. He needed to respond to any problems quickly, accurately and diplomatically. Gericke helped him on separate occasions. Schwartz learned that Governor Charles Oakley had sent a letter to Serfoji, and Serfoji sought Gericke's help in writing a reply. In response, Schwartz wrote to Serfoji on November 20, 1794, emphasising the importance of developing his reading and understanding of English letters. At the same time, he prudently advised him not to rely too heavily on his acquaintance with senior officers, such as the governor, because he could not know their hidden motives. Therefore, he directed his attention to rely on God and wrote the following letter:

> To Serfoji Rajah,
> My dear Friend, I have received your kind letter & expect according to your promise a copy

[77] T Vol. 4448, 84–85.
[78] T Vol. 4448, 85.
[79] T Vol. 4448, 88–89.

of Sir Chares Oakley's letter to you. You plainly see that studying the English language with more assiduity will be very necessary. My good brother, the Reverend Mr. Gericke, cannot always attend to you. If the Governor or any other gentleman visits you unexpectedly, you must be able to converse with them without the assistance of any friend. Sir Hobart and his lady show you civility, which is very pleasing. None will despise it. However, do not make too much of it. The friendship of the world is often very precarious. But the love of God is permanent & immutable. David says in one of his Psalms: 'Thy loving kindness, O God, is better than life.' […] If you think proper, present my humble respects to Lord Hobart. Wishing you true happiness in time and eternity. I am, my dear friend, Your affectionate friend, C.F. Swartz.[80]

Upon receiving Schwartz's encouragement, Serfoji invested more effort into improving his language skills. Schwartz was pleased with this development, as it demonstrated Serfoji's potential for growth. He also aimed to indirectly teach Serfoji the seriousness of governing a country, advising him to avoid the depraved model of Ameer Singh's governance. To convey this, on 15 December 1794, he wrote the following letter to Serfoji:

To Serfoji Rajah,
My dear Friend, your kind letter I have received and rejoice at your health and happiness. The copies I likewise received, viz: The copy of your letter to Sir Charles Oakley & the copy of his answer to you. May a merciful God direct all to his praise and your eternal happiness. I am very glad that you improve in knowledge, wishing that all useful knowledge may have a proper effect on your heart. Our knowledge is like a light in which we are to walk so that we are lit and influenced by the knowledge of what is good. Just now, I have examined the children who are instructed in the Malabar School, fifty in number. All received a new cloth which they put on with joy. When I am dead, you will, I hope, clothe them. But when we look upon the Author of all blessing, we must humbly acknowledge, that it is the God who feeds & clothes us all. May we adore his holy name & serve him faithfully. […] The Rajah [Ameer Singh] is still at Combaconum, hunting, playing & trifling. To him, trifling is living, but he will find that dying is no trifle. Forget not him who is the Source of all blessing. Ask, and it shall be given. Seek, you shall find. Knock, and it shall be opened to you. May we finish this year in the fear and favour of our Almighty Maker. I am sincerely, Your affectionate friend, C.F. Swartz.[81]

was not entirely satisfied with the quality of Serfoji's learning. While he acknowledged his limited progress, he also expressed his disappointment that Serfoji's relatives in Madras hindered his learning. In contrast, on 29 December 1794, he expressed his frustration to Dattajee, who was supposed to assist Serfoji in learning more quickly and effectively. Since he failed in this regard, Schwartz did not hesitate to chide him:

To Dattajee, Sir, English letter I have received & rejoice at your improvement in the English language. However, I am sorry that your master is not very desirous to improve in the language & other useful knowledge. His lazy relations sit with him and make him indolent, too. He ought not to allow them to rob of him of his time. If you love your master, you ought to cheer him up. But you neglect it which grieveth me very much. […] May God bless you. May he give you in the New Year a new heart & new mind to fear, love and obey him. Give my respects to your master. God bless you all. I am, Sir, Your sincere friend, C.F. Swartz.[82]

---

80 T Vol. 4448, 89–90.
81 T Vol. 4448, 91–92.
82 T Vol. 4448, 93–94.

8.3.3 The Art of Writing and Networking

Dattajee, as the primary contact person for Serfoji in Madras, was not just a facilitator but a key player in Serfoji's interactions with influential figures. On 14 Oct 1793, Dattajee informed Schwartz that Cornwallis had invited Serfoji to the Ball House. With Gericke's permission, Serfoji met Cornwallis, the Governor of Madras, and other leading Company officers in the Ballroom on 4 October 1793. He also met the sons of Tipu Sultan and watched the fireworks of the Company's army. Gericke came once in three days and taught Serfoji the art of writing; he also corrected his draft texts. Just before Cornwallis sailed from Madras, Ameer Singh sent him an eight-page letter, which he refused to accept. However, Oakley received it from his agent, Bavah. Dattajee promised to inform Schwartz if he received further information about this letter.[83] Exactly a month later, on 14 November 1794, Dattajee informed Schwartz that Ameer Singh had requested Cornwallis to reverse his decision about Serfoji's adoption, namely, that Serfoji was "the son of his own father, but not to be considered as a son of the late Tulja Maha Rajah." It was obvious that Cornwallis did not respond to Ameer Singh. In this context, Schwartz's mentorship involved teaching and shaping Serfoji's understanding and decisions, as well as creating opportunities for him to engage with Indians and Europeans, with whom he would later work.[84]

8.3.4 Mathematical Skills

Another person who privately taught Serfoji was the aged Dada Row, who had earlier sided with Ameer Singh, accepted his bribe and repented of this grievous mistake. Schwartz appointed him Serfoji's mathematics teacher because Dada Row possessed admirable mathematical skills. He was familiar with the customary accounting practices in Tanjore. Serfoji should also have learned from him the art of making, reading, and verifying account books. These vital insights would have enabled him to effectively supervise his government's income and expenses and create realistic budgets.[85]

Unexpectedly, Dada Row was often sick. On 12 November 1793, Dattajee informed Schwartz that Dada Row had become "very weak from the torment of fever, cough, and phlegm, which prevented him from coming to my master."[86] Gericke, too, informed Schwartz about Dada Row's sickness. On the following day, 13 November 1793, Schwartz immediately wrote to Dattajee, expressing his sorrow over Dada's life-threatening illness. He cared about Dada Row's temporal health and spiritual welfare and pointed him to the divine redeemer, Jesus Christ: "To Dettajee. Sir, [...] I am sorry

83 T Vol 4448, 3–4.

84 T Vol 4448, 6; T Vol. 4448, 70–71: On 07.11.1793, Schwartz wrote to Dattejee: Ameer Singh mortgaged most Subahs of Tanjore to Europeans and Indian dubashes, who had promised to pay five lakhs Star Pagodas to the Company on his behalf. "All are well and in good health, the Country is well cultivated. Some fields have been damaged by floods, however, not very much."

85 T Vol. 4448, 69.

86 T. Vol. 4448, 5.

that Dada is as weak as Mr. Gericke has written to me. Oh, that he would take refuge in God and that divine Redeemer who alone can save us. [...] God bless you all. [...] Your friend, C.F. Swartz."[87]

A few days later, he died. On 28 December 1793, Schwartz expressed his sadness about Dada Row's death and reminded Dattajee that all humans should always be ready to die and enter "eternal happiness." He knew that Dada Row's death would have worried Dattejee:

> To Dattajee.
> Yesterday I received your letter, which filled my mind with sorrow. Dada is no more. May God help us to be ready at all times that when we die we may enter into eternal happiness. I can easily imagine how your master must have suffered by the death of Dada. You are now alone with your master. You are to help him faithfully & to see that he may daily improve in learning. [...] God bless you & all who are with you. Your sincere friend, C. F. Swartz.[88]

Although Schwartz stayed far away in Tanjore, he closely monitored Serfoji's progress and supported his teachers, not as their superior but as a friend. He continuously mentored Serfoji, providing him with personal and emotional guidance. In this regard, Schwartz remained an exemplary teacher.

8.3.5 Spending Money Prudently

Schwartz's advice to Serfoji on financial prudence was not just a passing comment but a crucial lesson in governance. He was deeply concerned when Serfoji spent money on unnecessary things and advised him to exercise discernment and frugality. As a ruler, it was essential for Serfoji to understand the value of money and the importance of prudence. For example, on 28 December 1793, he "scolded" Serfoji, his adopted son, for overspending:

> I am sorry that you make more expenses than are necessary. I have often told you that you do not know what may happen. To throw away so much money upon the lazy Brahmin is not prudent. I hope you consult with Mr. Gericke on the Article on expenses. I have rebuked Dattajee very much. Surely, he ought to follow the example of Dada[row].[89]

Schwartz's guidance and Serfoji's willingness to learn led to this transformation. Serfoji realised Schwartz's concern for his economic welfare. On 15 January 1794, he apologised to Schwartz for spending more money on one of the widows and purchasing a "horse without the Rev. Mr. Gericke's advice. As soon as I bought, I made it known to him, but it is my fault that I did not do it before. For the future, I will follow the advice of the Reverend Mr. Gericke even in the least things."[90] On 7 January 1793, Schwartz expressed his disappointment over Serfoji's horse: "I am truly sorry that you bought a bad horse without asking Mr Gericke's advice, which would have consulted

---

87 T Vol. 4448, 71.
88 T Vol. 4448, 72.
89 T Vol. 4448, 73.
90 T. Vol. 4448, 11.

proper people. By neglecting the advice, you have bought a wicked beast which you cannot mount. Alas!"[91] On 15 January 1794, Serfoji requested Schwartz to forgive him and promised to follow his advice.[92] Gradually, Serfoji took Schwartz's admonition seriously and concentrated on learning. On 22 January 1794, Dattajee reported to Schwartz that Serfoji, his master, "writes copies, reads the grammar and Bible, etc., as usual."[93] On 26 May 1795, Schwartz became impatient because Serfoji had not sent his accounts, which showed his income and expenditures for the entire year. He was concerned about the responsible use of public money in governance. He pointed out how Ameer Singh had spent the money of his "poor subjects" most extravagantly and how he placed "his confidence in idle ceremonies & will, at last, find himself disappointed." Then, he concluded this letter by asking Serfoji to explain how he had spent his money, as he had not seen any account for a year. Serfoji should send his account to him as soon as possible.[94]

Accordingly, on 1 July 1795, Serfoji sent Schwartz a copy of his account for six months. He wrote it in English, and Schwartz was delighted to receive it. However, he was not fully satisfied with its content. To demonstrate his dissatisfaction, he quoted three examples and permitted Serfoji to draw practical lessons for his future governance. Firstly, Schwartz stated that Ameer Singh knew "no account except what his servants are pleased to give him." His ignorance and blind trust helped his unscrupulous advisors and accountants cheat him and inflict suffering on his people. Ameer Singh's case served as a stark reminder of the consequences of financial mismanagement in governance. Secondly, Ameer Singh did not wish to be accountable to anyone. According to Schwartz, Ameer Singh did not have monitors to give him realistic and responsible advice. Ameer Singh was unwilling "to hear or receive good advice & which is still worse, betrays those who offer him good advice. He & [the] country suffer & will suffer as long as he is hostile to a monitor." Immediately, Schwartz reminded Serfoji of King Solomon of the Hebrew Bible, who stated, "Whosoever hears good advice, nay, rebuke, will become wise. But a fool rejects advice & rebuke.'" Thirdly, Schwartz narrated a brief story with deep meaning for good governance:

> To confirm this, give me leave to tell you a short story. There was a great Emperor in ancient times, the richest man in the world, whose name was Gorses. In his time lived a wise man called Solon, who would now & then offer good advice to that rich Emperor. No doubt, the advice contained some truth, which the rich people do [sic! did] not like to hear. The proud Emperor, therefore, hated the wise man. But the possession of riches and worldly greatness is very unstable. The emperor commenced a war, lost the battle [and] was taken a prisoner,

---

91 T Vol. 4448, 75–76.

92 Santha Praburaj: An Analysis of Schwartz materials, 110: "I beg of you to forgive me. My fault that I have bought a horse without the advice of Rev. Mr. Gericke. As soon as I bought, I made it known to him. But is my fault that I did not do it before. For the future, I will follow the advice of the Rev. Mr Gericke even in the least things."

93 T. Vol. 4448, 13.

94 T. Vol. 4448, 96 and Santha Praburaj: An Analysis of Schwartz materials, 109: "Let me ask you how you spend your money. I have not seen any account for the space of a year. Be so kind as to send me an account of the expenses which you have made to convince me that you are and always will be a good Economist."

> & lost not only his liberty, but his riches likewise. In this sad condition he remembered the wise speeches of Solon (for Solon would and could not flatter), but, when he had lost his worldly grandeur & riches, then, he looked upon Solon as a wise counsellor. That you may never be ensnared by the deceitful flatterer, but have your ear & heart open to wholesome advice is the sincere wish of Your affectionate friend, C.F. Swartz.[95]

This story serves as a cautionary tale, emphasizing the importance of heeding good advice and the consequences of ignoring it. It highlights the importance of financial prudence and accountability in governance. Keeping a good account of income and expenditure is a mark of an envoy for peace, justice, and social harmony. Careful planning and spending of public money would benefit more people. Schwartz's methods of teaching these principles, both directly and through stories, remain admirable.

8.3.6 Geography

On 31 July 1794, Serfoji informed Schwartz that Colonel John Braithwaite (1739–1803)[96] had presented him with a globe.[97] In his reply to Serfoji on 6 August 1794, Schwartz expressed his joy over the globe and encouraged him to familiarise himself with the world's geography. In his characteristic manner, Schwartz directed Serfoji's attention to the God of Geography, the creator of everything. He, as a prince, should have sound knowledge about the contemporary understanding of the world and its geographical factors:

> As Colonel Braithwaite has given you a globe, you ought to know something of geography; as you live in the world, you ought to know something of the world which God has created that you may get some idea of the great God, the Creator of the heaven & earth. It is ignorance of the work of God that inclines us to value the creature more than God. A good prince is obliged to imitate God. But how can he imitate him if he does not know him and his goodness, wisdom, power and justice? God complains that the heathen [peoples] have not worshipped worthily though they might have known it by the works of creation and providence. A great king, therefore, prayed to God, saying: 'Open thou mine eyes that I may see the wonders of works and words.' That you may be happy here & hereafter is the wish of our affectionate friend C.F. Swartz.[98]

Before Gericke started his journey to Cuddalore, he appointed a European, Mr Ross,[99] to teach Serfoji. Serfoji met with Ross daily, which improved his learning and expanded his fields of interest. On 16 December 1795, he informed Schwartz that he intended to meet Michael Topping (1747–1796) in his house and to "see the stars and some other curious things." Topping had founded the Survey School in Madras in 1794 to educate

---

95 T Vol. 4448, 100–101.

96 During the Second Mysore War, Tipu Sultan imprisoned Braithwaite in Seringapatam in 1782 and later released him. By 1793, Braithwaite oversaw the Company's siege of Pondicherry and became an interim Commander-in-Chief of the army of Madras.

97 T Vol. 4448, 17.

98 T Vol. 4448, 87–88.

99 T Vol. 4448, 53: On 15.02.1793, Gericke wrote from Sadras to Serfoji in Madras: Mr Ross "must regulate his hours in attending his new master [i.e. Serfoji] in the study of the Malabar [= Tamil] language as not to neglect any part of what he has to do with you."

gifted students. He aroused Serfoji's interest in technical and engineering subjects. Serfoji stated further that he had read "the Bible & Farmer Simkin's *Tale* once through & some other books also."[100] This was the beginning of Serfoji's interest in astronomy. This scientific study of the universe would have challenged the prevalent mythological understanding of the universe.

8.3.7 Astronomy

In May 1795, Christoph Samuel John visited Madras for medical treatment and stayed with Gericke for two months. At that time, whenever his health permitted, he met with Serfoji and discussed with him diverse matters:[101] John could quickly meet Serfoji in his home, which occupied the central place of a vast garden. His adoptive mothers lived in the side houses. At that time, Serfoji was about nineteen years old and had a pleasing appearance. His facial complexion was a rare mixture of white and light yellow. John communicated with him in English to teach spoken English; when he had trouble understanding the full meaning, John explained the details in Tamil. One of his servants translated the meaning into Marathi so that he could understand the subject well. John read him history books that he could understand easily. He showed Serfoji the most recent map of southern India and explained various places. He also expounded on the solar system, which contradicted the commonly held mythological views of the Tamil people. John showed him the relationships between planets and the sun, as well as how they rotated around the sun once a year. He taught him details about the warm and cold climates, the four seasons in Europe in contrast to the two seasons in southern India, how the Earth rotates daily on its axis and various timings of sunrise and sunset in different eastern and western countries. As Serfoji could not grasp the concept of the Zodiac, John used a room with twelve doors and windows to demonstrate it. The room represented the Zodiac. He asked Serfoji to stand in the middle to symbolise the sun, his first servant as the moon and John himself standing as the earth. As John circled him, his servant circled John. They could see various Zodiac symbols as they went around, such as the Ram (Aries) or the Bull (Taurus) and the like.[102]

John used a globe to illustrate geography to Serfoji. He showed on modern maps how navigators like Lieutenant James Cook, the discoverer of Australia for Europeans in 1770, sailed around the world. It was new for Serfoji that these navigators did not come across the sea of milk or butter or the enormous Mount Meru resting on the [thousand-headed] snake Ādiśeṣa as taught in Indic cosmologies. John demonstrated that it was not the poison of this snake that created solar and lunar eclipses, but the movement of the sun and moon. John's lessons and practical demonstrations deepened Serfoji's curiosity in astronomy (e.g. Serfoji's *Devendra Kuravanji* discussed in Section 8.8).

100 T Vol. 4448, 27.

101 NHR 5, 1797, issue 50, 167–168.

102 Preetha Nair, 2012, xxix: "John often functioned as Serfoji's Tamil translator, he also regularly copied out for the Raja news from *The Madras Courier* and instructed him in astronomy and geography with the aid of instruments and globe."

8.3.8 Good Governance – Schwartz's Advice

When Schwartz learned of Serfoji's desire to learn, he was overjoyed. On 26 May 1795, he sent a letter emphasizing the importance of effective communication in English for governance, as Serfoji would be interacting with the Company's officers. The letter also highlighted the relationship between religious faith and its impact on one's moral attitudes and habits, the responsibility of handling public funds, the importance of keeping promises, and the need for transparent records of income and expenditure. The tone and style of the letter underscore its practical advice:

> To Serfoji Rajah, my dear Friend,
> Some time ago, I received your letter, which gave me great pleasure being thereby informed of your health and willingness to improve. It is the duty of everyone to improve in knowledge, but we ought likewise to take care that our knowledge may produce good fruits. In short, by our improvement in knowledge, we ought to grow wiser and [more] obedient to do the will of our Creator and become beneficial to mankind.
> The Rajah Amer Singh, having spent his money or the money of his poor subjects in the most extravagant manner, is to return in four or five days. He places his confidence in idle ceremonies and will, at last, find himself disappointed. However, let me ask you how you spend your money. I have not seen any account for the space of a year. Be so kind as to send me an account of the expense, which you have made to convince me that you are and always will be a good economist.
> Here at Tanjore is all confusion. They increase their debt, not considering whether they can pay them off. Of course, they must tell many falsities, constantly promising and seldom performing, by which the mind is sadly corrupted. I hope you will detest such horrid practice. The word of every good man should be equal to an oath. This is one of the fundamental rules which ought to be strictly observed.
> I hear that a European reads and talks with you in English, by which means you will soon improve in speaking English. Let me advise you to endeavour to write a good letter in English. May you be happy truly, nay eternally happy which is the sincere wish of Your affectionate friend, C.F. Swartz.[103]

A month later, Schwartz was delighted to receive Serfoji's response in English. He had also enclosed a few copies of the letters which he had received from the Company. At once, Schwartz asked Serfoji (on June 24, 1795) not to take vain compliments to heart. The more he expected compliments, the more likely he was to be disappointed. Simultaneously, Schwartz attempted to direct Serfoji's attention to God, stating that "true and genuine hope in God Almighty never disappoints us. Whosoever trusts in him shall not be ashamed." Schwartz was happy that Serfoji had an Englishman as his tutor, who would teach him both "pronunciation and tone" of the English language. Schwartz was deeply concerned with equipping Serfoji as a trustworthy ruler who could write and maintain confidentiality regarding certain matters. To exemplify this principle, he narrated the following details:

> But now I have one request to make, viz: I wish that you may exercise yourself in writing English letters. It may be of the utmost importance to you. Should you once correspond with Government you may, you will wish that the contents of some letters should be known to none. In that case, you must be able to write it yourself. To say to the writer, you must not

---

[103] T Vol. 4448, 96–97.

> disclose the contents of the letter and must keep it a secret, will be useless. There at Tanjore, everything that is said or written in Palace is known within a brief time throughout all the streets.
> Learn from your youth to keep your secrets within your own breast. It is related of Alexander [the Great] that he told a secret to his friend enjoining him secrecy. His friend, unable to keep the secret, disclosed it. Alexander, hearing of it was very wrath, called for his teacher and asked him what punishment he ought to inflict on the man who had revealed his secret. The teacher said: 'Don't punish him, rather punish yourself, for if you could not keep your own secret much less will others keep it.'[104]

In his letter to Serfoji on August 19, 1795, Schwartz revealed that his health had recently deteriorated. He considered his sickness as a messenger from God, announcing that "his time upon earth would not be long" and that he ought to prepare himself for departure. Then he narrated his most profound theological conviction, which had been sustaining him, as follows: "If we have the pardon of our sins & are reconciled to God by that blessed Redeemer Jesus Christ, we have no reason to be afraid of dying & quitting the world." Then, he stated that our "whole life ought to be a preparation for death." Schwartz viewed eternity without the forgiveness of sin as "awful." Finally, he wished the following for Serfoji and himself: "May God give us grace daily to die to sin, to the wicked practices of the world & to live to his glory that when he calls us away, we may be found prepared for that great Change."[105] The fact that all life has a limited duration should alert Serfoji to aspire for a good, just and beneficial administration.

The English letter, which Schwartz wrote to Serfoji on 26 November 1795, is the last surviving specimen. It reveals Schwartz's deep love for Serfoji, his adopted son. He respectfully addressed him as "Serfoji Rajah, my dear Friend" and viewed himself as his "affectionate friend." The opening line of this letter demonstrates Schwartz's care and concern for Serfoji's welfare: "I am always anxious to hear of you, your health, your conduct, your disposition of mind, your diligence, and your improvement in all." Then, this letter recommends self-examination because God should help us to regulate the many passions hidden in our hearts. The rest of this letter condemns pride as a vice, as it remains the leading cause of all sins. By contrast, true humility is the root or foundation for all virtues. A happy person is not prone to pride.

To illustrate this principle, Schwartz drew Serfoji's attention to the Babylonian King Nebuchadnezzar, who reigned from 605 to 562 BCE, in the Book of Daniel. He was known for erecting magnificent buildings in his capital city and took great pride. As a result, he lost his reason; after humiliating experiences, he regained his rationality and thanked God for it (Daniel 4:34–37). The same letter continues to reiterate the importance of getting rid of pride and to warn of the consequences of inefficient governance under Ameer Singh:

> Pride hinders us to hearken to a good advice which our friends offer us. Pride makes us deaf. But true humility enables us to make the best use of friendly instructions. Our pride makes us indolent so that we are loath to exert ourselves. We become useless & unprofitable people. We grow angry with those, who intend to stir us up, as a sleeper becomes angry with the man,

[104] T Vol. 4448, 99.
[105] T Vol. 4448, 102.

> who wakes him. All these reflections occurred to me when I observed the calamity under which the Country groaneth.
> Last Saturday, those inhabitants who had left their villages appeared before the Rajah [Ameer Singh]. Many of them spoke very boldly exclaiming against the Rajah's indolence & inattention to the welfare of the Country, of his inactivity & lameness when he plainly saw that his servants plundered the country.
> Oh, my dear Friend, do not imitate such [a] bad example. This poor Rajah has often been warned, but he refused to hear the friendly advice of well-meaning people. He was deaf, indolent & stubborn. But why do I mention this to you? To rouse you, to excite you, to press you, to become humble, diligent & willing to hear & accept good advice. I shall be happy to hear from the Rev. Mr. Gericke that you hate & detest stubbornness, idleness and haughtiness. If you read & ponder the Proverbs written by King Solomon, you will be fully instructed in the points above mentioned.
> God is willing to make us happy, but he desireth likewise that we should choose the path that leads to happiness. Be not ashamed to call upon him. Only wishing you true happiness here & hereafter, I am, my dear Friend, Your affectionate friend, C.F. Swartz.[106]

It is remarkable how Schwartz acknowledged Serfoji's right to make an informed choice in religious matters and refrained from pushing him into Lutheran Pietism, demonstrating a profound respect for Serfoji's beliefs and autonomy.

8.3.9 Good Governance – John's Advice

Missionary Christoph Samuel John also shared his ideas on good governance with Serfoji.[107] He showed Serfoji a large map of the world and pointed out the locations of different countries. He concentrated on England, Denmark, the Netherlands, and France, probably because these countries had significant trade relations with India. He indicated that traders from various countries set up their business centres within Tanjore. He also described what these traders imported into the Coromandel Coast and what they exported from Madras. He commented on the relationships between these countries and how each governed its people. While explaining these things, he pointed out God's power, wisdom, glory, and goodness, as well as their impact on these countries. He informed Serfoji about the duties of a good ruler and exemplified them by comparing the political situations of various Indian rulers with those of rulers in different European countries. He demonstrated how a virtuous ruler made their subjects happy and content. This ruler should be wise, live an exemplary life and have excellent ministers to administer all matters effectively. A prince should seek and respect their advice, especially when they point out his failures. These ministers should not remain silent; they should not affirm anything they could not endorse. He exemplified these solemn principles with France as an example. The French nation fell because its rulers were addicted to licentiousness. On the one hand, they allowed women to mislead them. On the other hand, they succumbed to flattery by cunning and selfish ministers.

---

106 T Vol. 4448, 103–105.

107 NHR 5, 1797, issue 50, 168–170.

John illustrated how socio-political turmoil was fermenting in France for a long time and broke out as a revolution. If only King Louis XVI had listened to the demonstrators rationally and justly, he could have averted the revolution that had ruined him, his family and his country. He should not use force to execute his decisions. John advised Serfoji that a ruler should not believe what his subjects would think of him. He should find out what the rest of the world would think about him. He should avoid those who flattered him. His subjects should be free to share their opinions with him about what they thought of his rule. Otherwise, they would love him superficially but secretly hate him. The ruler would know that after his death, he would be accountable to God, the Great Lord. Therefore, he should uphold the law and judge each person's behaviour impartially; he should then either reward or punish that person according to what his character and deeds merited.

Finally, John encouraged him to thank God's providence for bringing him to Madras, where he could enjoy the teachings of Gericke and benefit from Schwartz's fatherly correspondence. Serfoji showed him the copies of all letters he had received from Schwartz and those he had written to Schwartz. It was evident that Schwartz's letters contained many guidelines for his future governance of Tanjore. Simultaneously, John urged him to observe how the Company governed various places in India and to select only those principles that would help him and his people. John advised him to familiarise himself with the productivity of every region of Tanjore, including the names of all fruit trees and machines. John recommended that when Serfoji went for a walk, he should observe all happenings around him. His administrative policy should focus on benefiting his people the most. After giving similar instructions on other subject matters, John returned to Tranquebar.

8.3.10 Religious Faith and Public Life

Schwartz, gently and prudently, shared his religious opinions with Serfoji without imposing or demanding his embrace of the Christian faith. For instance, on 4 January 1794, he sent his New Year greetings to Serfoji and entreated him to consider this thought: "May you fear and adore him who has created heavens and earth (Gen. 14:19) who has loved mankind and sent a Redeemer (1Jn 4:10), who is willing to mend our hearts and make us happy forever."[108] Two months later, on 23 March 1794, Schwartz recommended that Serfoji consider God's warning to the Israelites in the Hebrew Bible. Revering God and keeping God's commandments would safeguard them. Their disobedience would merit God's punishment. Likewise, Schwartz requested Serfoji to make an informed choice to honour the true God and incline his "heart towards that which is truly good."[109] Again, on 22 May 1794, Schwartz requested that Serfoji consider his recommendation: "Your welfare, believe me, depends entirely on God,

[108] Santha Praburaj: An Analysis of Schwartz materials, 111–112.
[109] Santha Praburaj: An Analysis of Schwartz materials, 113.
[110] Santha Praburaj: An Analysis of Schwartz materials, 112.

who governs all things. If He is your God and Father, all will be well. But that He may be your protector and benefactor, you must honour, adore and fear him."[110]

Schwartz did not mention the beneficial relationship between Serfoji's religious affiliation and public life. In his New Year greeting on 5 January 1795, Schwartz explained Jesus's parable of a good tree that bears good fruits and the fate of the trees that do not bear good fruits (Matthew 3:10 and Luke 3:9). This letter is worth quoting fully because it reveals Schwartz's affection towards Serfoji and how he instructed him in spiritual and temporal matters:

> To Serfojee Rajah,
> My dear Friend, At present, I have no letter to answer. The season of the New Year puts me to wish you true happiness. Hitherto, God has preserved us. To this moment, we enjoy his mercy. But surely we do not know how long we are to enjoy it. We are planted by God as trees. These trees are to bring good fruits by which God is to be honoured. What sort of fruits we have borne, we are to enquire by searching our hearts. If we do not bear good fruits, we shall at last be cut down. I heartily wish and beseech God to make you a good tree, which bears good fruits to the praise of God, your Maker and Benefactor. Besides the welfare of our souls, which ought to be our first concern, we are obliged to prepare us likewise for the wise exercise of every duty to which God may call us. You, in your station, are to learn all virtues by the exercise of which you may become beneficial to mankind. Justice, benevolence, patience and resignation to the will of God. I wish you may read History by which you may be instructed in every necessary point. History shows us how many princes have exercised justice, benevolence, and diligence by which they made a whole nation happy. But History informs you likewise how many princes have indulged in wickedness and impiety and sloth and cruelty by which they have ruined even their lives. In short it is and will always be true what was said to an Israelite King: Thou has forsaken God; Therefore, God will forsake thee. Do not, my dear Friend, indulge in sloth and idleness; be diligent in every laudable thing. I have rebuked Dettagee for neglecting you. He learns the English language very well but [page 59] doth not, as it seems, care for you. Dada's son has not acquainted me how far you have advanced in arithmetic. Tell him not to be slothful. His father was a faithful friend to you. As for his son and your other servants, I am afraid that they mind their own interest more than yours. My love to you inclineth me to write in this manner. I wish to hear from the Reverend Mr. Gericke that you improve in all that is good. I am, Your faithful friend, C.F. Swartz. Tanjore, January 5th, 1795.[111]

Santha Praburaj further points out how Schwartz reminded Serfoji on 26 November 1795 to familiarise himself with the Book of Proverbs in the Hebrew Bible. Schwartz expressed his desire as a request and a recommendation, leaving it to Serfoji's discretion.[112] He was aware of Serfoji's deep devotion to his ancestral faith and his unspoken commitment to upholding it. Once he ascended the throne of Tanjore, he would be the protector and benefactor of the numerous temples, temple-related institutions and their businesses in Tanjore. Therefore, Schwartz encouraged Serfoji to make his own choice and be responsible for the outcome of his actions.

---

111 T Vol 3455, 57–61.

112 Section 8.8 of this biography describes Serfoji's rootedness in his ancestral religious traditions, contributions to renovate temples and his pilgrimages to various holy sites.

8.4 Serfoji as Heir to the Throne of Tanjore

8.4.1 Schwartz's Additional Contributions

On 15 January 1793, Schwartz thanked Governor Charles Oakley for allowing him to bring Serfoji and the royal widows to Madras. He urged Oakley to proclaim Serfoji as the presumptive heir to the throne of Tanjore because he had "an undoubted right" to it, "according to the law of the Hindoos contained in the Shaster. He was legally adopted by the late Rajah [Tulāji]." Without disclosing how he obtained these insights into the teachings and practices contained in the Sanskrit *śāstras*, Schwartz stated that the *śāstras* did not permit the adoption of the firstborn son. Serfoji was not the first son. His two elder sisters were still alive. Schwartz asserted that, according to the *śāstras*, the property of a man without either a son or a grandson should belong "to his adopted son. The son of a concubine has no right to inheritance, but the adopted son has a right to inheritance." Schwartz claimed that the pandits who invalidated Serfoji's adoption did not derive their opinion from the *śāstras*. Instead, they received bribes from Ameer Singh and supported him as the proper heir to the throne of Tanjore. Some pandits had confessed their mistake to Schwartz and mourned it. Schwartz knew that Ameer Singh could ruin Serfoji and urged the Company to declare Serfoji as the "presumptive successor." He believed such a declaration would deter creditors from lending more money to Ameer Singh, as it would invalidate "all grants of fields and villages" that Ameer Singh "might make from the time Serfoji was proclaimed as presumptive successor." The new successor would be responsible for all royal servants, including those who had brought the country to ruin.[113] The Company welcomed Schwartz's candid assessments and decided to proclaim Serfoji as the presumptive heir to the throne of Tanjore.[114]

---

[113] IOR/P/253/10, 311–315; IOR/H/571, 207–8: A reporter of the Company in Madras summarised the exact details: On 15.01.1793, Schwartz answered the Company's questions about Serfoji's safety and status as the presumptive heir to the throne. The Company promised to safeguard Serfoji. Schwartz requested the Company to plan Serfoji's enthronement carefully. Schwartz knew that Ameer Singh would claim that Serfoji was the only son of his father. Therefore, his adoption was invalid. In his response, Schwartz pointed out that Serfoji had two older sisters still alive. Moreover, Ameer Singh bribed the Brahmin Pandits to vote for him. Finally, Ameer Sing could do anything to get rid of Serfoji. Thus, Schwartz alerted the Company officers of scenarios and prepared them to help enthrone Serfoji.

[114] IOR/H/285A, 652–662: An unnamed chronicler summarised Schwartz's recommendation to declare Serfoji as the heir to the throne of Tanjore. "In a letter dated 12 April 1793, Mr. Swartz informed Lord Cornwallis of the circumstances surrounding the appointment of himself as the Guardian of Serfojee and of Ameer Sing to the Regency of Tanjore by Tuljajee on his deathbed. Mr. Swartz expressed his regret that, through ignorance of the Shaster, he had been deterred from opposing the 12 Pundits when they voted against Serfojee in April 1787. The Pundits ought to have quoted the words of the Shaster. After reading the translations of the Hindoo Laws published in Bengal, Mr. Swartz was astonished to find what an unjust decision the Pundits had come to, but as Ameer Singh had been established, he was unwilling to disturb his government. Mr. Swartz then mentioned the subsequent ill treatment of Serfojee and the Baie Sahebs by the Raja of Tanjore. He assured that Serfojee was entitled to the succession by Birth as well as by adoption. He transmitted a paper demonstrating Serfojee's Lineage and a letter from the two Widows of Tuljajee. As the Pundits consulted by Sir A. Campbell

8.4.2 Serfoji Declared as Heir and Ameer Singh's Opposition

On 30 January 1793, Oakley forwarded Schwartz's recommendation regarding the "Tanjore Succession" to Governor-General Cornwallis in Bengal and awaited his response.[115] Cornwallis and his team scrutinised Schwartz's recommendation and the circumstances of Ameer Singh becoming the ruler of Tanjore. On 11 February 1793, Cornwallis declared his thoughts as follows:

> We must confess that Mr Swartz's sentiments, in addition to other circumstances, have created great doubts in our minds of the just right of the present Rajah [Ameer Singh] of Tanjore to the succession to the Raj and we are entirely persuaded that he is personally very unworthy of that station. But it is necessary to proceed with great circumspection and delicacy in impeaching a right that has been sanctioned by a solemn Decision passed in consequence of answers that were made by fifteen [sic! = twelve] pandits to the questions that were referred to them. We, therefore, can only recommend to you, at present, to proclaim Serfoji presumptive heir to the Raj, but we shall, in the meantime, without mentioning the names of the parties, call upon learned pandits in this place and at Benares for answers to the substance of the questions that were put to the Pandits at Tanjore after the death of the late Rajah [Tulāji], and it will also be proper in [sic! = for] you to endeavour to establish, in a clear and authentic manner, whether the opinion of any of the Tanjore Pandits was obtained by means of bribery and corruption.[116]

The Company received Cornwallis's letter and discussed it on 5 March 1793. On the same day, W.C. Jackson issued the following proclamation:

> Whereas considerable detriment has arisen to the affairs of the Tanjore Government, by reason of the uncertainty which exists with regard to the succession to the Raj and whereas it is expedient for the tranquillity of the country and the prosperity of every class of the inhabitants that all doubts upon this point should be removed without delay, the Honorable the President in Council with the sanction of the Governor General in Council of Bengal has resolved that Serfojee the adopted son of the late Tulajee Maharaz, be declared presumptive Heir to His Excellency, the Present Raja, Ameer Sing and he is hereby declared and proclaimed presumptive Heir accordingly. All Acts and Proceedings, therefore, relative to the Government and Interests of the said Province are henceforth to be made with due attention to the Rights of Serfojee as presumptive Heir aforesaid and used as shall in anywise tend to impair or encumber his Inheritance will be considered in no shape binding upon the said presumptive Heir or entitled to any countenance or respect whatever from the Honorable Company's Government. Given under the Seal of the said Company in Fort St. George on the day of 8/93. By order of the Honorable the President in Council. [Signed] W.C. Jackson.[117]

On the following day, 6 March 1793, the Governor of Madras sent a letter with identical content to Ameer Singh. This letter stated that after mature consideration, the governors of Madras and Calcutta concluded that Serfoji was the rightful successor to the throne

---

in 1787 did not quote any legal authority in support of their assertions, the Company proposed that Serfojee should be proclaimed Heir apparent to the Musnud of Tanjore, [... barring] the succession of any son that might be born to Ameer Singh, and they admonished the Raja not to adopt one which he intended to do and was told that under such circumstances, it would not be necessary to incur such large expenses as he had so improperly incurred, such as building a large Palace under an assumption that his own title to the Raja of Tanjore was indisputable."

115 IOR/P/253/10, 571–572.

116 IOR/P/253/11, 1186–1188.

117 IOR/P/253/11, 1189–1191.

of Tanjore. The Governor sent his proclamation letter to the Commanding Officer in Tanjore, removing doubts about Serfoji's enthronement.[118]

On the same day, the Company sent a copy of Cornwallis's letter to Schwartz with the following request: Cornwallis appreciated Schwartz's efforts of ascertaining whether the Tanjore Pandits received bribes and supported Ameer Singh.[119] Ameer Singh, too, received a copy of the letter of 6 March 1793 and the directive from Cornwallis. Consequently, Ameer Singh became anxious. On 26 March 1793, he expressed disappointment in not being consulted about his successor. He claimed that Serfoji's adoption was "contrary to the Shaster, Sir Archibald Campbell set it aside as of no avail." He repeated that "Tulza Maharaz adopted Sherfogee on the 22nd January 1787" just before his death. At that time, he was suffering severe pain; his mind was confused, and his understanding was affected. Ameer Singh insisted that Serfoji's adoption was illegitimate. He stated that he "remained in silent confidence of the English faith and justice." Consequently, Archibald Campbell stayed in Madras for one and a half months longer, "informed himself, particularly on the laws of the shaster" and came to Tanjore on 5 April 1787. There, he obtained the report of the twelve pandits "on the law and custom of the Hindoos according to the Shaster." After consulting Colonel John Stuart and three other English officers, he rejected Serfoji's adoption:

> Upon the following grounds, because a child to be adopted should be of five years old, whereas Sherfogee was nine; 2nd because the adoption should be made with the consent of all the relations and friends; but this was not the case. 3rd because it is expressly written in the shaster that the eldest son of another cannot be adopted; and in all these particulars was Sherfogee's adoption deficient.[120]

In the same letter, Ameer Singh requested that the Company reverse its decision regarding Serfoji. He appealed to his perception of their just and impartial treatment of people: "As your Excellency is even and just, I trust that you will prevent my *rajya* ['kingdom'] and palace from passing over to the strangers." He wondered why the Company did not send him copies of the complaints "his enemies" had raised. After promising to inform the Company of his activities, he surrendered himself to the Company: "I have no support but from the English. Upon them, I rely in all respects. It, therefore, rests with Your Excellency to treat me with attention and favour. Believe me, always. Your sincere friend."[121]

8.4.3 Ameer Singh's Bribery of the Pandits – Perspectives of Tulāji's Widows

The Company officers received Ameer Singh's letter containing conflicting information and sent a copy to the Governor General in Bengal for consideration. To establish clarity and to prove Serfoji as the legitimate heir to the throne of Tanjore,

---

118 IOR/P/253/11, 1191–1192.
119 IOR/P/253/11, 1193.
120 IOR/P/253/12, 1667–1671.
121 IOR/P/253/12, 1667–1671.

Schwartz obtained from Tulāji's widows the names of the twelve pandits. On 11 March 1793, he acknowledged Governor Charles Oakley's request of 3 March 1793 for his mature opinion about whether any of the twelve pandits had accepted any bribe or was corrupt in any other way.[122]

At that time, Schwartz was staying in Vepery and from there, he responded to Oakley: "Hopes and fears" influenced the twelve pandits to support Ameer Singh. The first four pandits received honours and reasonable payments. Hence, they would not openly admit to accepting bribes. Four pandits received rent-free *sarvamāṉiyam* fields. They would have to surrender them if they admitted to accepting bribery. The 11th and 12th pandits could not be considered because Dada Row "declared his guilt before me long ago. I asked him whether he had received anything. 'No,' said he, 'I had hopes.'" After he had become Serfoji's teacher, his written testimony had "no weight." Schwartz stated further that the opinion of Tulāji's two widows seemed "rational."[123]

Additionally, Schwartz suggested that if the twelve pandits could not "prove their opinion from the Shaster." Evidently, "something else has influenced them in giving their opinion." He wondered whether Ameer Singh's earlier position as the Tanjore Country's treasurer and the fame he had enjoyed would have persuaded the pandits to answer the seven questions "sent from Bengal"[124] in the way that they did. They were carried away by "hopes and fears. [... Disinterested] integrity was a point by far too difficult for them. I will not draw a conclusion from the preceding remarks but leave it to your Honor's judgement."[125]

Schwartz enclosed his English translation of the widows' declaration in Marathi on 11 March 1793. This declaration represents the rare voice not only of women but of the widows in a legal debate. It also provides fresh insights into the process of selecting and appointing Serfoji as the heir to the throne of Tanjore:

> Tulja M[aha] Rajah of Tanjore, considering the necessity of having a successor to govern the country and to perform the funeral rites and looking upon Amer Sing, the son of a concubine unfit for those purposes, consulted his principal Priest, Progiden [= purōkitaṉ from Skt. purōhita, 'a family priest'], and his relations about the propriety of adopting a son. The result of this consultation was that it was proper to adopt a son.

---

[122] IOR/P/253/12, 1443–1444: On 11.03.1793, Tulāji's two widows mentioned the names of these twelve pandits; Schwartz added his remarks about each of them as follows: 1) Madava Chari, 2) Madavai and 3) Rama Shastri were Ameer Singh's employees. 4) Biying Rao was the servant of Ameer Singh's "female favourite." 5) Pattala Chari was dead (by 1793). 6) Satta Nidi Achari, 7) Ayena Chari, 8) Narasingha Chari and 9) Jeyachari accepted their wrongdoing, favouring Ameer Singh. 10) Appa Chari was "not seen and therefore not consulted." 11) Dada [Row] confessed "his guilt." Since he was Serfoji's servant, his opinion had no weight. 12) Bapina knew "nothing of the Shaster. He has, therefore, followed others. In writing, he observed [what] others had written."

[123] IOR/P/253/12, 1437: "The proposal, therefore, made by the ladies seems to me a rational one." They assert that Tulāji's adoption of Serfoji was legitimate. The twelve pandits failed to give scriptural references to support their opinions.

[124] It seems that neither Governor Archibald Campbell of Madras nor the Company's Residents in Tanjore drafted these seven questions. Instead, Schwartz implied that the Company officers in Calcutta sent them to Campbell, who, through Schwartz's agency as interpreter from English into Marathi, passed them to the twelve pandits.

[125] IOR/P/253/12, 1435–1437.

> Accordingly, Tulja M[aha] R[aja] called for the parents of Serfojee and the whole family & made known his design. Moreover, all relations, and particularly Serfojee's uncle, were called likewise. The principal priest and many Bramins [sic! = Brahmins] who were versed in the Shaster, the Managers of the country [Diwan] and Shevarow [Shiva Rao], who now opposes us, before this whole company the ceremonies appointed to be performed when an adoption takes place, were performed, and the name Serfojee was given to the young boy, and he was put upon the Throne & all who were present were desired to pay their respect to Serfojee. Shevaraow likewise acknowledged him respectfully and mentioned the same to the Government. Serfojee's uncle Babajee Bhonsle announced the adoption through all the streets with the usual solemnity. Serfojee's parents were called to an entertainment & presents were given to them. Likewise, all relations received presents. At last, Tulja M.R. delivered Serfoji to the English gentlemen who served the honorable Company.
> When Sir Archib[ald]. Campbell came, and after he went away, Serfojee suffered much trouble, but after that Amer Sing M[aha] R[aja] confined Serfojee, as Serfojee was young, Amer Sing was appointed to govern the country & when Serfojee should be of proper age, he was to deliver the government to him. Whatever had then [taken place], Amer Sing to confirm Serfojee.
> When we heard that 12 Pandits incited by covetousness and partly by fear had declared Amer Sing to be the true governor of the country, we were very sorry. Tulaja M[aha] R[aja] was well acquainted with the Shaster and all other laws and customs of the country. He knew that the son of a concubine, whose mother's character was not good, was unfit[tted] to succeed in the government according to the declaration of the Shaster and custom. He knew that according to the Shaster Serfojee was a proper person. When Serfojee had been adopted according to the tenets of the Shaster and our consent, 12 false Pandits made a decision by answering some questions which were sent from Bengal, of which questions we knew nothing, neither were we consulted.
> We have therefore declared in our letter that the 12 pandits have made a false decision being moved by covetousness and fear. If you require of us to prove our assertion, we think that those Bramins employed by Tulja M[aha] Raja] who declared the adoption be conformable to the Shaster & the 12 Bramins who made false decision should be called and ordered to prove their opinion by a paragraph of the Shaster. If the 12 pandits cannot prove their opinion or sentence by a passage from the Shaster, it is plain that they have been influenced by desire or fear.
> Besides, three of those 12 pandits have been honored by Amer Sing with high stations and elegant equipage, which glory they had not before they had given authority to Amer Sing. It is therefore plain that they enjoy the fruit of their false decision.
> The other Bramin who voted for Amer Sing have *Saruvamaniam* fields, free from taxes. It is true that they have confessed in the audience of some people their guilt, but if they now publicly confess it, they lose their fields. It will be better therefore to order them to prove from the Shaster the opinion given by them. This is our opinion. March 11th, 1793.[126]

The two widows mentioned the names of the twelve pandits who had favoured Ameer Singh. The Company received this letter from Schwartz, but it did not recognise it as essential and did not consider its claims. They had already forwarded Schwartz's representations to Bengal and were waiting for the Governor General's binding order.[127] In the meantime, on 9 May 1793, Governor General Charles Cornwallis acknowledged his receipt of Schwartz's letter and expressed his respect for Schwartz:

> Revd Mr Swartz, Sir, I have received your letter dated the 12th ultimo, and am much obliged to you for the candid manner in which you have communicated your sentiments to me respecting the adoption of Serfojee and the succession of the Raje of Tanjore.

126 IOR/P/253/12, 1438–1443.
127 IOR/P/253/12, 1444.

> From the respectable character which you have always borne, I entertain no doubt of your having recalled the attention of our Government to the Claims of Serfojee, from your perfect conviction of them being founded on justice and may be assured that in order to guide the judgement of the Supreme Government, I shall call upon the Pundits of the highest reputation in Bengal and Banaras for their opinions upon this important question. I am, Sir, your most obedient, humble Servant, Cornwallis. Fort William, 9 May 1793.[128]

Schwartz did not require any better or higher authorisation than Cornwallis's. Astonishingly, Cornwallis acknowledged Schwartz's moral reputation and just and impartial assessment. He would have been aware of the preeminent position of Maratha Brahmin pandits in Banaras, who networked with fellow Marathi Brahmin pandits in other centres of political and economic influence, such as the court of Tanjore. Like the Maratha Brahmin pandits of Tanjore, they were also not immune to receiving undue favours for pronouncing their opinion on contested issues.[129] Schwartz might have been aware of these transregional connections of the Marathi Brahmin pandits. After exposing how the Maratha Brahmin pandits, whom Ameer Singh had recruited for his favour, accepted bribes, Schwartz independently began collecting compelling documentary evidence for Serfoji's enthronement.

8.4.4 Ameer Singh's Bribery of the Pandits – Perspectives of Schwartz

Schwartz's support for Serfoji angered Ameer Singh, who sought to eliminate Schwartz. He engaged his astrologers and magicians to work against Schwartz. They predicted that Schwartz would fall into a river on the return journey and drown. Therefore, Ameer Singh did not expect Schwartz's return. However, his safe arrival on 2 November 1793 astonished and angered Ameer Singh. The Company was aware of the threat to Schwartz's life. Therefore, they sent their soldiers to guard him, his house and his movements.[130]

Soon after he arrived in Tanjore, Schwartz found out how Ameer Singh's pandits, who had earlier accepted bribes, tried hard to nullify Serfoji's adoption. In his attempts to obtain first-hand information on adoption, he received a copy of Halhed's *Code of Gentoo Laws*.[131] The ninth section of its twenty-first chapter[132] described who could adopt whom. Accordingly, a man who wishes to adopt a child should inform the local

---

[128] Bodleian Library: 72290ind-box2, Document 27: Lord Cornwallis to Schwartz

[129] O'Hanlon: Letters Home–Banaras pandits and the Maratha regions in early modern India, 237: In "the 1720s, an effective network of functioning Maratha courts had developed in Satara, Kolhapur, Tanjore, and in Pune—the administrative and banking centre of the new Maratha state under the new leadership of the Chitpavan Bhatta family. A new constellation of judicial authorities was emerging. The Pune court increasingly took over the burden of trying to inculcate unity amongst Maharashtrian Brahmans, and under the leadership of Ramasastri Prabhune developed its own sophisticated judicial apparatus. In Banaras itself, there was a new kind of Maratha presence, now characterized by lavish building projects and direct charitable grants to Brahmans."

[130] Germann: Missionar Christian Friedrich Schwartz, 358.

[131] Nathaniel Brassey Halhed: A Code of Gentoo Laws, or Ordinations of the Pandits, from a Persian Translation, made from the Original written in the Shanscrit [sic = Sanskrit] Language. London: n.p., 1776.

[132] Halhed: Code of Gentoo Laws, 298–299.

magistrate of his intention and then perform the stipulated religious sacrifice (*yāga*). He should give gold and rice to the child's father. If they had not already pierced the child's ears, he should arrange for the child's ceremonial ear piercing. He should also verify whether the child had received a sacred thread from a Brahmin priest and whether the child was already married. The child should not be older than five years. It should not be the only child of the family. While a man could adopt a child, a woman had no independent right to adopt any child. A Shudra man should first request a Brahmin priest to conduct a *yāga* on his behalf and then adopt a child. Finally, the man "who has no Son, or Grandson, or Grandson's Son, or Brother's Son, shall adopt a Son; and while he has One adopted Son, he shall not adopt a Second."[133]

This explanation was enough for Schwartz and the Company administrators to authorise Serfoji as the legal heir to the throne of Tanjore. Additionally, on 8 April 1794, Schwartz sent Cornwallis authentic proofs of how Ameer Singh had bribed the pandits and Company officers in India and England.[134] Four days later, on 12 April 1794, an unnamed Company officer in Madras summarised Schwartz's report on the pandits: In April 1787, Campbell summoned twelve pandits. At that time, Schwartz was present. These pandits did not search their religious books. Instead, they voted for Amer Sing and excluded Serfoji. Schwartz felt "sorry that he did not call upon them to produce their authorities. The matter ended in haste. After this, Mr Swartz translated the Hindoo Laws published in Bengal and was astonished to find that the Pandits had made an unjust decision."[135]

In the meantime, on 19 September 1794, Governor Charles Oakley informed Schwartz about his agreement with Serfoji as the legitimate heir to the throne of Tanjore. He also expressed satisfaction with Schwartz's effort to promote "peace and goodness" for all inhabitants. Then he confessed that the "Court of Directors entirely approve the steps we have taken relative to Serfojee" and he would render his services as far as he could to enable Serfoji's enthronement. He concluded his letter with this remark: Serfoji "is a very well-disposed young man and conducts himself with great modesty and propriety."[136]

---

133 Halhed: Code of Gentoo Laws, 299.

134 IOR/H/571, 209 quoted in Pearson: Memoirs, Vol. 2, 316: "Your Lordship [Cornwallis] wished to have authentic proofs of the 12 Pandits having been bribed. Five of them who formerly had no office are taken into the Rajah's service; others have fields, which they would immediately lose if they confessed. One of them is here who declared that hope and fear had influenced him that he was conscious of having done wrong, but he said, as the present Raja before he was proclaimed was already in possession of the country and of the treasure, everyone had hope and fears. You had no reason to expect a just decision from us under these circumstances. His money has made him King, but if you desire us to confess publicly, you must protect us publicly. This is in some degree confirmed by a declaration which the present Raja made in the presence of Mr. De Souza, a Portuguese gentleman, Sir A. Campbell's Dubash, Shevarow and me. At that time, Mr. Petrice was sent to Tanjore to oblige the Raja to pay the arrears – the Raja then said: 'If they press me too much, I will reveal all and raise a stench all over England for they have all got money from me, expect Mr. Swartz.' Whether those who were present would choose to confirm this declaration, I know not, but I would confirm it most awfully and solemnly."

135 IOR/H/571, 210.

136 Bodleian Library: 72290ind-box2, Document 29 dated 19.09.1794: Charles Oakley to Schwartz as Serfoji as the prospective heir.

8.4.5 Serfoji's Return to Tanjore

By the beginning of 1796, Serfoji, now approximately twenty-one years old, felt ready to return to Tanjore and become acquainted with the events there. On 10 January 1796, Dattajee requested that Schwartz arrange for Serfoji's safe travel from Madras to Tanjore: "My master is entirely trusting you and Rev. Mr. Gericke." He requested bodyguards to protect him both inside and outside the palace in Tanjore. He expected sufficient room for himself as the prince and the widows. Dattajee asked Schwartz to arrange these matters with Macleod, the Company's Resident in Tanjore.[137]

Schwartz consulted the Company officers and arranged for Serfoji's safe return to Tanjore. Macleod promised to protect Serfoji in Tanjore, prescribed his travel routes, and persuaded Ameer Singh to instruct his officers at Kumbakonam to allow Serfoji and his entourage to pass through respectfully.[138] On 25 January 1796, Governor Hobart wrote to Schwartz that he had spoken with Gericke and other "respectable authorities" about Serfoji's intended return to Tanjore and allowed him to leave Madras.[139] Since Macleod was a friend and supporter of Ameer Singh, he was not there in Tanjore to welcome Serfoji. Instead, he remained in Kumbakonam to settle a court case.

On 18 March 1796, Dattajee informed Gericke that he, Serfoji and his servants had reached Tanjore on 16 March 1796. Schwartz met them and exclaimed, "Serfoji left Tanjore as a fugitive, but he returned as a prince!" Serfoji and his companions quietly entered the Company's house within the palace. They did not wish to provoke Ameer Singh, who was not feeling well that day.[140] On 21 March 1796, Gericke wrote a letter to Serfoji, encouraging him to meet the officers of the Company at Nagore, Cuddalore, Tranquebar, and Pondicherry. He reminded him of his meeting with Colonel Braithwaite in Madras, the globe he had given him for geographical lessons and the guidelines for an influential prince. Gericke asked Serfoji to remember Braithwaite's advice: accordingly, Serfoji should surround himself with kind and wise companions because lazy and naïve companions would easily make him lazy and naïve. Gericke always asked Serfoji to remain "diligent, industrious, vigilant, prudent and wise."

Gericke reminded Serfoji of Braithwaite's observations about the military major stationed in Pondicherry who had met "idle and ignorant" princes in northern India. Their naïve companions made the lives of those princes so miserable that they could no longer "manage the affairs" of their countries. By contrast, Braithwaite wanted Serfoji, who had received suitable lessons from Schwartz and was still learning from him, to be "the best Prince that ever was in the Country." Gericke endorsed this wish and replied: "So be it. I will always pray that the Lord God may make you the best of Princes."[141]

On 9 April 1796, Gericke replied to Dattajee's letter of 18 March 1796, thanking God for both the pleasant and unpleasant events in Serfoji's life, as they were seen as

137 T Vol. 4448, 29–30.
138 T Vol. 4452, 1.
139 Bodleian Library: 72290ind-box2, Document 29 dated 25.01.1796: Hobart to Schwartz about Serfoji's return to Tanjore.
140 T Vol. 4448, 31–32.
141 T Vol. 4448, 103–105.

teaching tools to help him discern God's will. Gericke stated that he had already spoken with Governor Hobart about Serfoji's allowance and bodyguards to protect him when we went out. Then Gericke expressed his shock and sadness over the sudden death of Dattajee's first child. In this context, he reminded him of the Book of Job in the Hebrew Bible:

> You have read the Book Job, that good man lived several thousand years ago; at the death of his children, he said: 'The Lord gave, and the Lord has taken away' and added, 'Blessed be the name of the Lord.'
> May God make us so piously resigned like that good man was. Speak of pious Job to your Father & Mother, to your wife & relations and may God comfort you in every sorrow.[142]

8.4.6 Schwartz's Scriptural Evidence Supporting Serfoji's Adoption

Schwartz collected scriptural evidence from Sanskrit legal treatises to endorse Serfoji's adoption. On 26 August 1796, he sent his findings to Governor Hobart, who on 2 September 1796 placed them before the Company, and this board made the following remarks:

> As His Excellency the Rajah [Ameer Singh] has made some objections concerning the legality of Sherfojee's adoption, particularly on account of his being the only Son, who might not be adopted according to the Hindoo law, I have consulted the most learned Pandit at Tanjore on that subject and have received some extracts (in Duplicate) from the Shaster, which will I hope, elucidate that point. I therefore beg leave to offer them to your Lordship's perusal.
> According to the Shashter of *Samscara Kowsluvam*,[143] the adoption made by Tulaji Maja Rajah is right or legal.
> If you say that an only child cannot be adopted by another, this (Sherfogee) is not an only child, for he has two sisters, the one older and the other younger than he. Therefore, he is neither the only nor the first child. But if you still stay, is he not the only child, tho' there are two sisters?
> In the *Kowsluvam Shaster*, it is said that girls may be adopted as well as boys. If there is a proof or a speech concerning this, the Shaster says, that as a boy may be adopted so likewise a girl. As the word child [*piḷḷai* or *kuḻantai*] belongs equally to girls as to boys. Both may be adopted. Therefore, if there is a sister, at the same time, you cannot call the boy the only child. As Sherfojee has sisters, he cannot be called the only child. An adopted son and an adopted daughter are equally regarded.
> In the *Shaster Rama Krittee Ditto Mimamstse* [the śāstra entitled *Rāmakṛṣṇa Dhatta*'s *Mīmāṃsā*?][144] it is written: if one gives his only child to be adopted, he commits a sin, but to him that takes such child, it becomes his child. The child that has been adopted with the consent of the father, cannot return to the father, viz. to sell salt is not good; the seller is guilty, but he that takes or buys it, is not guilty. The seller of that salt cannot take it again. It becomes the property of the buyer whosoever has something as his own property, he has power to give it to another. He may give, sell, or exchange his own child, but he has no power to sell his brother or grandson – these he cannot give, sell, or exchange.

---

142 T Vol. 4448, 110–111.

143 Despite many efforts, I have not been able to identify this treatise (*śāstra*). It could refer to *saṃskāra kucavam* (?) and mean a summary of the purifying or refining ritual(s), by which an adopted son becomes the legal son of a family.

144 I am grateful to Professor Richard Fox Young for suggesting a conjectural reading of the Sanskrit legal treatise *Śāstra Rāmānujīya Mīmāṃsā*.

> Another Shaster says that an only child must not be given to be adopted, but if one disregards the Shaster and will take the guilt upon him, and so gives his child to be adopted he commits a sin, but he who takes the child to be adopted is guiltless The child belongs doubtlessly to him who had adopted it.
> *Gowloma Shaster* says whoever has no sister to be adopted, whether he that takes the boy knows it or whether he does not know it (viz. that the boy is the only child, without having a sister and performs the ceremony of tying a string about him & that boy belongs to the person who has adopted him, he belongs no longer to the father. Whether a child may be adopted lawfully or not must be considered before the Ceremony of Omam [Skt. Homa, a 'Vedic ritual,' burnt offering, any sacrifice] is performed. When the ceremony has been performed, and the child is adopted, it belongs to him who has adopted it.[145]
> *The Shaster Weganesere*[146] says: Who has adopted a girl, whether he had no child and afterwards gets a child of his own, both are to share equally in the inheritance. Therefore, boy and girl are equal children, when these are sisters, the boy is not to be called the only child.
> *Hematri Shaster*[147] says: A child may not be given or be adopted by a strange tribe, but in the proper tribe or family, it may be given, and it is his child who has adopted it.[148]

Immediately, the Company forwarded these proofs to the Governor General in Bengal:

> Honorable Sir,
> We have the honor to transmit a copy of a letter from Reverend Mr Swartz enclosing further extracts from the Shaster with respect to the Hindoo Law on the subject of adoption, which we consider of very material importance as it may affect the question as if one between Sherfogee and the present Rajah at Tanjore and calculated to remove any doubts that may possibly remain concerning the person in whom the real right of inheritance actually exists. To your directions, we have transmitted the original papers.
> Should you already have communicated your sentiments to the Court of Directors upon this subject we should hope you will not on that account judge it inadvisable to transmit the documents we have now the honor to forward, since they are of a nature so essential to the purposes of substantial justice. We have the honor to be with great respect, Hobart, Fort St. George, 2nd September 1796.[149]

On 20 September 1796, Schwartz sent two more scriptural passages to Hobart with the following note:

> The teachers of the Shaster have been searching for the various volumes of the Hindu Shaster and have thought the enclosed 2 paragraphs a very great confirmation of the legality of Serfogee's adoption. I therefore beg leave to offer them to your Lordship's judgement. I have the honor to be C.F. Swartz. Tanjore, September 20, 1796.
> *Rama kritta Detta Mimamse Shastra* [*Rāmakṛṣṇa Dhatta*'s *Mīmāṃsā Śāstra*?]: father and mother cannot give their first-born child or only child to be adopted to a strange tribe. But

---

145 Despite many efforts, I could not locate this *śāstra*. However, I am grateful to Professor Richard Fox Young for suggesting a conjectural reading of the Sanskrit legal treatise *Gautama Dharmashāstra* or *Gautamīya*.

146 Despite many efforts, I could not locate this *śāstra*. However, I am grateful to Professor Richard Fox Young for suggesting a conjectural reading of the Sanskrit treatise *Shāstra Vaiṣṇavīśeṣa* or *Shāstra Vaiṣṇavīśeṣaṭīkā* or *Shāstra Viṣṇusmṛti*.

147 Despite many efforts, I could not locate this *śāstra*. However, I am grateful to Professor Richard Fox Young for suggesting a conjectural reading of the Sanskrit *Hemādri Śāstra* (also known as *Hemādri*). This work engages with morality and legal issues.

148 IOR/P/253/64, 3647–3651.

149 IOR/P/253/64, 3651–3652.

> they may give their first child and only child to be adopted to their own tribe. There is no guilt in it.
> *Warada Rajeya Shastra*:[150] as he, viz. the father, is, so is the male child. As the male child is, so is the female child. As the children may increase by a male child, so likewise from a female child. Therefore, if there are sisters, the father may give his only male child to be adopted.
> Ordered that a copy of the foregoing letter with the two original extracts from the Shaster be sent immediately to Bengal.[151]

Schwartz believed these scriptural proofs would sufficiently underline Serfoji's legitimacy to the throne of Tanjore. He thought of Serfoji till the end of his life and wished him well. For example, on 10 February 1798, August Friedrich Cämmerer, who had been with Schwartz during the last days of his life, informed us of how Schwartz had asked Serfoji to come to him. When they met, Schwartz was extremely weak but alert. Cämmerer reproduced Schwartz's last words to Serfoji:

> God will soon take me to himself. I have spoken with you many things and given you hearty admonitions. I cannot speak with you at length. However, I want to share with you four important things: when you begin your rule, keep away from pomp, extravagant expenditure, [and] sensual pleasures because they corrupt your heart. In all humility, consider what would please God. Make sure that justice and righteousness are practised throughout your country and that your subjects are happy. Appoint officers with whom you meet once a week to hear and read how justice is practised and how the country is governed. When you begin your reign, remember to protect the Christians in your country. Help them and keep them away from all oppression. If they make mistakes, punish them. However, let them live undisturbed in their faith. Finally, he raised his hands towards heaven and said: 'May the gracious God show mercy to you and guide your heart and mind to Christ so that at the end you would strand before his throne as a true disciple of Jesus.' Cämmerer concluded his remark: 'The prince was deeply touched because he considered Schwartz his father.'[152]

8.4.7 Schwartz Acquainting Serfoji with Tanjore

On 13 April 1796, Dattajee shared additional information about Serfoji's return with Gericke: The young widows could reside in the same apartments where they had previously lived. Only the Queen Mother preferred to stay in Tiruvaiyāṟu.[153] Dattajee stated that on 6 April 1796, Serfoji met Schwartz in his garden and the missionaries Jänicke and Kohlhoff in their homes. In discussion with these missionaries, Serfoji identified nine areas where the Company should make immediate changes. On 25 May 1796, he requested that Gericke communicate the nine concerns to the Company. 1)

---

150 Conjecturally, this text might have been the *warada rājeya śāstra* (the 'science of governance, kingship of the Waradas,' 6th – 14th century). The Waradas ruled the geographical areas that covered the modern districts of Bidar, Gulbarga, and Raichur in Karnataka.

151 IOR/P/253/65, 4061–4062.

152 NHR 5, 1799, issue 54, 552.

153 Tiruvaiyāṟu is one of the holy places for Śiva. It stands on the banks of the fifth branch of the River Cauvery in Tanjore. It houses the most famous Śaivite temple, the *Taṭciṇa Kailācam* ('southern abode'). Poet Thiyāgarāja (1767–1848) lived in this place. Later, Serfoji built the *Kalyāṇa Mahāl* for lodging twenty royal women he had married or kept. He also kept forty-eight royal women in the building named *Maṅgaḷa Vilācam* (the 'auspicious address') adjacent to the palace.

The Company should immediately repair the dam (*aṇaikkaṭṭu*) on the River Cauvery so that the three Subahs, namely Kumbakonam, Tiruvaiyāru, and Māyāpuram, can receive irrigation water. 2) Separating these three subahs from other subahs would make cultivation, tax collection and other administrative matters easier. 3) The Tanjore Toll Tax (*cuṅkam*) was always the king's prerogative; it should no longer be in the hands of *Panjayam*. 4) It was necessary that Resident Macleod should not merely come to the palace to translate the Marathi letters from Madras, as his predecessor, Ram, had done. He should also consult Schwartz, "who is well acquainted with the Tanjore Country." 5) It would have been better if Ameer Singh had not met Macleod in the palace garden. Schwartz prevented this meeting because he knew of Ameer Singh's "malicious temper." 6) Mrs. Macleod and her Tamil nurse should not interfere in the function of the judges in Tanjore. They should not be involved with the Company's business in Tanjore. 7) Dattajee wondered why Resident Macleod, his wife, their nurse and the wife of another captain visited Ameer Singh's wife in the palace. Macleod's nurse served as an interpreter for both parties. 8) Colonel Baird, John Butler, Captain Ince, Vengadachala Pillay, an agent of the influential Ciṉṉaiyā Mudali and the brother of the deceased Chana Saheb, came from Madras. They were Ameer Singh's advisors. They should not interfere in any matters involving Serfoji. 9) Serfoji wanted to know about the country's business and justice, but everything remained disagreeable to the Reverend Mr. Swartz's opinion. Therefore, my master cannot be well acquainted with the country's business.[154]

The Kingdom of Tanjore, which Serfoji saw on his return from Madras, changed significantly from what he had seen before his journey to Madras. Dattajee described the kingdom's miserable situation to Gericke on 18 September 1796: Diwan Ciṉṉaiyā Mudali oversaw the entire kingdom and supervised revenue collectors whom he had appointed. Shankar Row, the brother of the former Sirkeel Shiva Rao, was among the most significant of these revenue collectors. Shankar Row supervised revenue collectors of the entire kingdom. He hindered Sirkeel Bagavati's works and caused great confusion. At that time, Colonel David Baird, who had celebrated Ameer Singh's installation as king with a twenty-one-gun salute, prevented the sepoys from accompanying Serfoji when he left his home to go for a walk. As an intimate friend of Ameer Singh, he insisted that the sepoys could only guard Serfoji's house. The young widow, Mohana Bāi Sāhibā, yielded to the counsel of her female servant, met Ameer Singh in his house, and attempted to obtain the revenues from the villages that her deceased husband, Tulāji, had assigned to her. In this context, Serfoji was unable to visit her at all. Additionally, Ameer Singh was happy that he could prevent Serfoji from going around the kingdom. Consequently, Serfoji lived like a prisoner in his room. Dattajee reiterated his earlier request for regular payment of allowances directly by the Company's paymaster in Tanjore. Finally, he implored Gericke to intervene with Governor Hobart on behalf of Serfoji.[155]

In the meantime, Schwartz acquainted Serfoji with the local law court (*cutcherry*). Serfoji once went there when Macleod settled the claimants. He asked Macleod to assign

154 T Vol. 4448, 34–36.
155 T Vol. 4448, 41–42.

soldiers to protect him in his residence and during his travels, and he instructed the Company's paymaster to pay his allowances directly to him (and not through the office of Ameer Singh). He informed Doctor James Anderson about the plants he had received from him.[156] Serfoji stated that those were growing well in Tanjore. He concluded his letter with greetings from his "two mothers."[157] This was the first time Serfoji categorically recognised the widows as his mothers, not merely as the "two ladies."

Serfoji's situation in the palace did not improve significantly. His house became a trouble spot. Either the Company or Ameer Singh could terminate his employment at any time. As he did not have bodyguards, he could not take different routes outdoors, even for exercise. On 6 August 1796, Dattajee blamed Macleod as the primary cause for Serfoji's departure from Madras. He promised all help and protection but failed to deliver them. Hence, Serfoji weighed whether to return to Madras, but he understood that his return would shame him "among all Nabobs." The gates to the house of the young widow Mohana Bāi Sāhibā had no guards. Hence, Ameer Singh used to visit her secretly. It would be a disaster if Serfoji were to meet Ameer Singh at the young widow's house. Dattajee believed that Gericke could convince Governor Hobart to arrange for Serfoji's protection and travel into the kingdom.[158] Gericke discussed these matters with Governor Hobart, who advised Serfoji to resolve all issues locally with Resident Macleod. He would also instruct Macleod to pay the allowances directly to Serfoji. Gericke, often sick and weak, inquired about what Serfoji's "sick father," i.e. Schwartz, was doing. He concluded his letter with good wishes to Serfoji and his relatives.[159]

8.5 Serfoji's Enthronement

In the meantime, the Secret Committee of the Company's Court of Directors in London, a group responsible for overseeing the company's operations and making critical decisions, reviewed the reports about Serfoji's adoption, Ameer Singh's enthronement and rule and the declining state of the Kingdom of Tanjore. In October 1797, they astonishingly concluded that they and Archibald Campbell, their representative as Governor in Madras, were "authors of the unjust succession of Ameer Sing." They were sorry that Ameer Singh's "misrepresentation and corruption" misled their officers in Madras. They wanted to "repair the injury" urgently by enthroning Serfoji. Immediately, they informed their Governor in Madras that King Tulāji had appointed Ameer Singh only as Serfoji's guardian.[160] Similarly, they updated John Shore, who would soon sail to Calcutta as the new Governor-General and asked him to ensure Serfoji's enthronement.

---

156 T Vol. 4448, 101: Gericke introduced Serfoji to Doctor James Anderson on 256.1795. Anderson gave Serfoji a "copy of my father's picture at that time." Neither Serfoji nor Gericke disclosed the identity of this deceased person.

157 T Vol. 4448, 36–37.

158 T Vol. 4448, 39–41.

159 T Vol. 4448, 43.

160 IOR/F/4/80, 18a–18d.

Meanwhile, Serfoji's situation in Tanjore was far from promising. After his guardian, Schwartz, fell ill and became immobile, Macleod appeared to have temporarily sided with Ameer Singh, withholding the allowances meant for Serfoji and his mother. On 2 February 1798, he forwarded a letter from Rājes Bāi Sāhibā to Governor Hobart, in which she detailed the injustice they were facing:

> Before our friend and guardian of my son, Rev Mr Swartz, fell sick, we found by the account of the Rajah's treasurer that Mr Macleod received for us from the Rajah 4000 Star Pagodas. We sent a copy of that account to Mr Swartz, who sent it to Mr Macleod and requested that he pay these sums to us. Mr Macleod answered Mr Swartz that he had received no money from the Rajah [Ameer Singh. On learning about this matter, Macleod and his Dubash Rayaloo met Serfoji and requested that he have some patience. They asked:] Why do you speak of these things to Mr Swartz? [...Finally, Rājes Bāi Sāhibā requested Hobart] to take us again under your protection at Madras. We were happy there, and found a friend in Mr Gericke, who did for us what my son's guardian would have done had he remained with us at Madras.[161]

Two days later, Serfoji repeated the same request to Hobart and added further details. His letter of 4 February 1798 reads as follows:

My dear Sir, I am ashamed to address you on the subject of this letter. But my circumstances oblige me to do it. My allowance for the last eight months is not yet paid. My creditors and my servants are troubling me. My distress is very great. I shall be, therefore, exceedingly obliged to you if you will order the payment of the 6663 Star Pagodas you have received on account of my allowance and to oblige the Rajah [Ameer Singh] to pay the 3577 Star Pagodas which is still due from him. Be so kind as to favour me by an answer to this. I have the honour to be Serfogee. Tanjore, 4 Feb 1798.[162]

Serfoji's letter of 4 February 1798 seems to have infuriated the newly arrived Governor Harris.[163] He wanted the Company to examine Macleod's delay in paying Serfoji further, because "a charge of so offensive a nature as that imputed to Mr. Macleod requires the fullest enquiry." He wanted to send an extract of Serfoji's letter to Macleod so that "he may be prepared to justify himself from the imputation."[164] Eventually, Alexander Macleod received information about his resignation, and Benjamin Torin (1762–1839) became the new Company Resident in Tanjore. On 8 March 1798, Serfoji sent a letter to the new Governor, Lieutenant-General George

161 IOR/F/4/48, Document 1102, 7–12.

162 IOR/F/4/48, Document 1102, 20 and repeated on page 22.

163 IOR/F/4/48, Document 1102, 21: On 01.03.1798, the Company wrote the following letter to their resident Torin in Tanjore: "The Governor in Council has considerable mortification in charging you with an enquiry, which, however, is indispensable. By the enclosed copy of an address Sherfogee, you will observe that a considerable sum of money is stated to have been received by Mr Macleod from the Rajah on account of the allowance granted for the maintenance of the late Rajah's Family, but that it had been withheld from them to the greatest convenience of the Family." This letter contained the order for Torin to collect evidence and submit a report.

164 IOR/F/4/48: In October 1798, the Examiner's Office compiled a 93-page document numbered 1102, which included an acknowledgement from September 1799 regarding the payment of money to Serfoji and his family. IOR/F/4/48, Document 1102, 20. This statement is a footnote on this page.

Harris, and welcomed him. He was sad about Hobart's sudden departure to England and viewed Harris as his "Friend and Protector."[165] Torin prepared a detailed report of the money payments made to Serfoji and his family from May 20, 1796, to January 18, 1798. He also received two accounts: One set dealt with money collected for Serfoji from Ameer Singh. The other accounts showed the periodical payments to Serfoji, which Schwartz countersigned.[166] On 15 April 1798, the Examiner's Office in London concluded that Serfoji's charges against Macleod seemed "without foundation." Till they received further confirmation from Serfoji, they reserved their final judgment.

Simultaneously, however, conscious efforts were underway to install Serfoji as the legal king of Tanjore. John Shore reached Calcutta on 17 May 1798 and assumed control of the Bengal Government the following day. He was aware of the urgent desire of the Secret Committee of the Court of Directors in London to install Serfoji as the legitimate ruler of Tanjore. Immediately assuming the duty on 18 May 1798, he ordered the Governor of Madras to dethrone Ameer Singh and enthrone Serfoji without delay.[167] John Shore's order forced Governor George Harris of Madras and Benjamin Torin of Tanjore to act swiftly. On 2 July 1798, Torin described in meticulous detail the unfolding process of Serfoji's enthronement.[168] On 25 June 1798, he received the necessary orders from John Shore and the Governor of Madras to depose Ameer Singh and install Serfoji on Tanjore's throne. Immediately, he charged Colonel Aston to gather the soldiers of Major Allan with His Majesty's 12th Regiment and Major Innes with the Company's 36th Battalion and post them at the palace from 4 a.m. Torin persuaded Dattajee, "an old confidential servant" of King Tulāji, to show him "the places of most consequence," such as the treasury, Rajah Mahal, and the Offices of Records and Accounts, and secure them with the Company's seal. Torin also requested that Jänicke "wait on the young" Serfoji and inform him of the planned events.

In a display of respect, Torin and his military colleagues met with Ameer Singh, assuring him of "personal safety to himself and family" and presenting him with the orders of the Governor General. Ameer Singh, a man of strong opinions, expressed his disagreement with the pandits of Bengal and Banaras regarding adoption. He found the amended views of the pandits of Tanjore and the quotations from various Shastras to be "partial, imperfect, and susceptible to perversion." The Company's decision not to consult him puzzled him. Despite these concerns, he submitted to the Company's justice, promised to obey their commands, and agreed to have his minister and other principal officers of his *durbar* arrested.

---

165 IOR/F/4/48, Document 1102, 25–27.

166 IOR/F/4/48, Document 1102, 40–50, 57–61, 79–89, of which some receipts bear Schwartz's countersignature.

167 IOR/F/4/42, Document No. 1021: "Extract Public Letter from Bengal dated the 2nd July 1798." Point 2: "The Governor-General [John Shore], shortly after his arrival [on 17 May 1798], communicated to us [on 18 May 1798] the letter from your Secret Committee announcing their decision in favor of the claim of Sherfogee to the Musnud of Tanjore. [... Point 4] We issued orders to the Government of Fort St George to place Sherfogee on the Musnud without delay."

168 IOR/P/254/20, 4731–4750.

Then, Torin and Major Wheatley met the anxious Serfoji under Jänicke's supervision. On receiving the orders from the Governor General, Serfoji confessed that "he would be ever mindful of the admonition of his friends, the Honorable Company, that he would ever look up to the Benefactors for Protection and Support." Torin assured him that the Company would treat him according to his "Interest and honour." He then read the six stipulations in English, as Serfoji could follow them to some degree. Later, Jänicke explained them to Serfoji in Tamil. People celebrated this event till late evening, marking a significant historical moment.

The next day, Serfoji happily signed both the English and Tamil versions of the stipulations and requested Torin to arrange his installation according to the "customs and usages at Tanjore" in the Durbar Hall of the Palace with the necessary "regalia and trappings of state." While the preparations were underway for the installation ceremony, Torin made a brief public proclamation about Serfoji's enthronement "by the beat of the Tom-Tom."

By this time, Ameer Singh realised that the time of his rule was over; hence, when Torin met him, he requested permission to stay in the "two suits of apartments" within the place where "he had resided unseen for near 40 years of his life before his elevation to the *musnud*." Torin wanted to consult Serfoji for a solution. At the same time, he asked Ameer Singh for the state "seals, serpoose [sic!] and other jewels and insignia" that belonged to Tulāji. Ameer Singh declared that he did not have all the jewels; several years ago, he mortgaged some of them and sold the rest to raise money to pay off parts of his debts. This answer did not convince Serfoji, and he urged the Company to find these missing things for him. Soon, celebrations of his installation began with several processions and ceremonies. The actual installation took place early in the morning of 29 June 1798:

> [Serfoji's people] were most active in their decoration at 4 o'clock. The gentlemen and all the principal inhabitants assembled at the Rajah's House and at five we proceeded to the Durbar where we had the honor to place His Excellency [Serfoji] on the *musnud*. In the presence of his people, I put the seal of state upon the fourth finger of the right hand and delivered the sword to Colonel Aston to be presented by him while we were paying the usual honors, the cannon and musketry from the palace yard and the walls of the Fort proclaimed to the people and the public at large the Instalment and Restoration of Serfoji Maja Rajah to the *musnud* of Tanjore. Then Proclamations were then read both in English and Malabar by the Reverend Mr Jaenicke and his people testified their happiness and approbation by repeated shouts and acclamations.[169]

It was evident that the enthusiastic reaction of the people to Serfoji's installation demonstrated widespread support for his rule and a hope for a better future under his governance. Torin congratulated Serfoji "on being restored to the throne by the virtues

---

[169] IOR/P/254/20, 4745. Charles Lawson: Memoirs of Madras. London 1905, 257–258: "The old Rajah [Ameer Singh] was deposed while [Captain George] Elers [of the 12th Regiment of Foot] was at Tanjore, and Suffrajeh [sic! = Serfoji], educated by Schwartz, the German Missionary, was affected without bloodshed or confusion. The young Rajah, then about twenty-four years of age, entertained the Military and Civil Officers at a grand banquet. When he appeared so splendidly attired that Elers was reminded of the Sultans, Caliphs, and Princes described in the Arabian Nights Entertainment. His Highness made presents to all his guests, and Elers received a cloth of gold sufficient for a dress."

of the Honorable Company's Power and Justice, to the Government of his kingdom, and to all the original rights that pertain to the *musnud* of Tanjore." At that time, Torin reminded Serfoji to publicly accept the *Treaty of 1792* (Section 5.12), which Ameer Singh concluded with the Company. This treaty, a significant document in the history of Tanjore, outlined the terms of the relationship between the Company and the Tanjore kingdom. On receiving Serfoji's consent, Torin lamented the "maladministration of the country for the past 10 years" that had "reduced it to a divided and distracted state" and expressed the hope of the Company that Serfoji's government would "soon recover its original prosperity." In this context, Torin reported that Serfoji immediately referred to his youthful age and inexperience in governance. He needed help with practical ways to face and overcome administrative difficulties. Therefore, he requested "assistance from the Honorable Company." Torin did not promise anything, but he opined that the Company "would think it their duty to afford the Rajah every assistance in their power, but as he was now in full possession of his lawful authority, it was for him to express the nature and extent of that assistance, as no interference could take place, but what was formally and explicitly specified by himself."[170]

Torin encouraged Serfoji to reflect on his needs and get back to him after a few days. Afterwards, Serfoji presented Torin and Colonel Ashton with a breast jewel; he gave "dresses, shawls, and gold cloths" to the rest of the gentlemen. He also distributed a few thousand Rupees to the soldiers. He went to the temple within the palace "to return thanks to his God for this great event, then to his adoptive mother, the Dowager Queen, where he made his obeisance." After these events, he visited the people gathered in the principal streets of Tanjore. The Commanding Officer ensured his safety.

Finally, Torin thanked his military colleagues and all others who had assisted him in this installation ceremony. He particularly thanked Jänicke, "in whose service and attachment the Rajah has a perfect confidence. Mr. Jaenicke is the successor of the deceased Mr. Swartz. The Rajah repeatedly lamented that his most Excellent Guardian and Friend had been called away before he had witnessed this event."[171] Torin concluded his report by thanking Major Allan and Major Innes for "sealing and securing the various apartments of the Palace and Captain Butler the Fort adjutant" and the Company in Fort St. George for guidance. Governor General John Shore received news about Serfoji's enthronement from the Governor of Madras. He expressed his deep satisfaction that "this signal act of justice [i.e. enthroning Serfoji] took place without occasioning any disturbance at Tanjore."[172]

On 7 July 1798, Torin sent another report to Governor Harris in Madras Fort St. George, along with an English translation of Serfoji's Marathi letter.[173] This new report includes Torin's cautious discussion with Serfoji. Since Serfoji was the sovereign ruler "with all the rights and authorities of his kingdom," the Company would not interfere in the management of Tanjore. Therefore, to better understand the actual realities of the

---

170 IOR/P/254/20, 4747.
171 IOR/P/254/20, 4749.
172 IOR/F/4/42, Document No. 1021, "Extract of Governor-General's Letter to the Court of Directors dated 21st Nov 1798."
173 IOR/P/254/20, 4750–4763.

people, Torin advised Serfoji to "consult with his relations, his friends and the principal landholders of his country" on important administrative matters. Serfoji expressed his views in a letter written in English. Upon seeing it, Torin advised him to write all his official letters in Marathi to communicate his views more clearly and nuanced. Since the state seals were with Ameer Singh, Serfoji's letters did not have his seal. According to Torin, Serfoji placed his "entire confidence in the friendship and honour of the Honorable Company" and hoped that his local knowledge was sufficient. However, he needed the "Company's civil and military authority" to remove all obstacles from those who would oppose his policies and decisions. At the conclusion, Torin highlighted the urgent need for a new administrative system to prevent government servants (of Serfoji and the Company) from exploiting the farmers mercilessly.

Torin also included J. Webbe's English translation of Serfoji's Marathi letter of July 2, 1798, addressed to Benjamin Torin. Serfoji wrote this letter personally. Referring to his administrative inexperience and desire to learn through involvement in day-to-day governance activities, he asked the Company to administer his country for an additional two years. This letter shows his drastically changed self-understanding, and he has designated himself "Maharaz Rajashree Serfogee Rajah." Webbe's English version of Serfoji's Marathi letter reads as follows:

> As I have not yet attained years of maturity, as the Country is to a great degree in a state of derangement and as it will therefore be a work of such difficulty to reduce it to order. I entreat you [i.e. Resident Benjamin Torin] will represent to the [Madras] Government that I pray that the Company will favor me and take upon themselves the burthen [sic! = burden] of managing my country for one or at farthest for two years. In order to give the Honorable Company pleasure, to provide that my *ryots* may live in the enjoyment of plenty and to make myself fit to conduct the government. I also request you to give orders that I may be present and inspect the transactions of the public business of Tanjore, the 2nd July 1798.[174]

Torin's letter to the Company clarified the implied meaning of Serfoji's English expressions, such as his desire to "inspect the transactions of public business." Torin explained that Serfoji meant "to inspect, but not to control." Torin asserted that Schwartz's education impressed Serfoji's mind with "honourable principles" and turned it into serious business. Otherwise, in Torin's estimation, Serfoji was "not quick and lively to a sense of pleasure, but sedate and attentive to business, as the support of his future Dignity." Torin requested that his superiors in Madras consider his character to be unlike "the generality of Indian princes" and recommended Serfoji to their "highest consideration."[175]

On 28 August 1798, Gericke reported to Johann Ludwig Schulze at the Glaucha Institutions about Serfoji's installation: Schwartz's death had created a vacuum in Tanjore, which worried Gericke. He stated that Ameer Singh and the Company Residents did not like Christians. He sighed in relief when he heard of Benjamin Torin's appointment as the new resident of Tanjore. Collector Torin and missionary Jänicke had worked in Pāḷaiyamkōṭṭai and knew each other. During Serfoji's installation as king of Tanjore, Kohlhoff and Jänicke served as official interpreters. They translated various

---

174 IOR/P/254/20, 4763–4764.
175 IOR/P/254/20, 4757.

negotiations and documents from English into Tamil and vice versa. Gericke mentioned that Serfoji would protect Christians and immediately recalled Schwartz's advice: "I believe that God will establish and expand his reign here. It will, however, happen under much tribulation. We should always reckon with tribulations from inside and outside." Gericke confessed that Schwartz's effective presence protected everyone in Tanjore because he did not tolerate any evil, even if the kings defended it.[176] Thus, Schwartz's life and work had a profoundly positive impact on the lives of the inhabitants of Tanjore.

Basu did not examine these primary sources about Ameer Singh's impeachment and Serfoji's enthronement. Nevertheless, he alleged that Resident Alexander MacLeod and Schwartz conspired against Ameer Singh. He claimed that no European Christian writer of Indian History did any "justice to that unfortunate" Prince Ameer Singh.[177] Basu further alleged that the government in Tanjore was indeed a "Christian Government," and Ameer Singh was a victim of their deliberate injustice. He insisted that "the Christian Government of the day did not remove Amar Singh from the *musnad* of Tanjore and place Sarbojee on it out of disinterested motives." Basu stated that this government forced Serfoji to sign a new treaty, which allowed him to become a pensioner and look after the city only.[178]

Alternatively, available primary sources give a different picture of Ameer Singh and his interactions with the Company. Without citing any verifiable evidence, Basu alleged that Schwartz's reports about Ameer Singh's "cruelties and oppressions" were unreliable. He further alleged that Resident Alexander Macleod supported Schwartz in his plot against Ameer Singh.[179] He illogically connected Schwartz with specific arrogant missionaries of the late nineteenth century in Africa and branded him untrustworthy.[180] As stated above, the reliable details in the primary documents regarding Ameer Singh and Serfoji strongly contradict Basu's account.

8.6 Serfoji's Unreconciled Relationship with Ameer Singh

A palpable distance marked the relationship between Serfoji and Ameer Singh. On 15 March 1797, Ameer Singh's reflections on Serfoji's return to Tanjore underscored this: On 1 March 1796, Serfoji, Maya Bāi Sāhibā and Mohana Bāi Sāhibā arrived at Trivady near Tanjore. That day, Macleod asked Ameer Singh to prepare accommodation for the two ladies. Serfoji would occupy John Sulivan's house, and "there would be no intercourse between him" and Ameer Singh. On 11 March 1796, Serfoji arrived from Trivady and began living in John Sulivan's house. While Maya Bāi Sāhibā stayed in

176 AFSt/ M 1 C 39b : 36 = printed in NHR 5, 1800, issue 56, 701–702.

177 Basu: Rise of the Christian Power in India, 354.

178 Basu: Rise of the Christian Power in India, 353–354.

179 Basu: Rise of the Christian Power in India, 357.

180 Basu: Rise of the Christian Power in India, 357: Basu alleged that Schwartz did not care for the welfare of the dark-skinned people. Basu blamed Christian missionaries for causing "little wars" such as the Cetewayo Cruelty (1879 in the Zulu Kingdom), the Abyssinian Affair (1935–1936, when Italian soldiers invaded Ethiopia), and the Zulus' contempt for the Sabbath day. Basu believed that the Company's Madras Government should not permit Christian missionaries to be involved in politics or government affairs.

Trivady, Mohana Bāi Sāhibā occupied the same apartment in the palace of Tanjore she had lived in before her move to Madras. Ameer Singh accused Macleod, his dubash, Schwartz, and Serfoji's servant, "Dullajee," of disturbing the peace of the palace.[181] It was evident that neither Serfoji nor Ameer Singh attempted to reconcile, underscoring the enduring nature of their rift.

Another reason for Serfoji's detachment from Ameer Singh was the sudden shift in Mohana Bāi Sāhibā's loyalty to Ameer Singh. She vehemently denied the legality of Serfoji's adoption in a four-and-a-half-page letter (A4 size) addressed to Governor Hobart. The letter, written early in 1797, informed him about the illegality of Serfoji's adoption and the necessity of maintaining Ameer Singh on the throne.[182] At the risk of repetition, I summarise Mohana Bāi Sāhibā's views about Serfoji's adoption below. She stated that when Tulāji and she ruled Tanjore, she bore him two children. The two children, however, "unexpectedly went to Heaven." Their death plunged Tulāji into extreme despair. Eight days before his death, those "near him brought a youth from among our relatives" and introduced him to Tulāji (as discussed in Section 5.5). Tulāji did not accept the boy and found their recommendation to him incorrect. Therefore, he confidentially asked Mohana Bāi Sāhibā's opinion, and she replied: "Are not the two children born from me gone? What is the use of adopting a boy to you in the Seventh Generation? Their affair does not appear proper to me." On hearing this, Tulāji consulted his brother, Ameer Singh, "whose life he had preserved and into whose hands he had delivered" his mother, Draupadī Bāi Sāhibā. Despite his hesitation and resistance from others, Tulāji adopted Serfoji and asked his mother, two wives and servants to protect him. Three days later, Tulāji "went into heaven." Serfoji and his adopted mothers lived in Tanjore for three years. Finally, "the padre [Schwartz]" and others close to him wanted to train and raise Serfoji "to power." They demanded that Ameer Singh give Serfoji a separate apartment. Mohana Bāi Sāhibā opposed this demand and expressed her views as follows:

> Although I believed the suggestion of my Mother [in-law] to be improper yet compelled by the duty of submitting to my Elder and being without resource[s], I joined them and separated myself from Brother-in-Law Amer Sing. Sometime after this, my mother-in-law, Dropeda Bhaie Saheb, went to reside in heaven. This event was soon followed by the death of Sulochana Bhaie Saheb, my good adviser. While I was thus plunged in grief by the loss of my husband, my mother-in-law and my companion, some ill-disposed persons about Sherfogee joined themselves with Padre Swartz and having made, I know not what representation to Madras, obtained an Order from Sir Charles Oakeley authorizing us to come if we wish to Madras. Sherfogee and my Summatee [*sampati*, 'one connected by marriage'] using every persuasion and threatening me with the fear of much distress if I should remain here, took me with them to Madras. Upon my arrival there, I continued for some time in the same sentiments. But Sherfogee did me much injustice and plundered some of my property & destroyed me in many respects. My mind being unsettled by this induced me to think of leaving Madras at this time. Sherfogee gave orders to his people to prevent me from going to Tanjour. This brought me into much sorrow, and in this condition, you did us the favour of giving us the leave and of sending us thither. After my departure from Madras and arrival at

---

181 IOR/F/4/42, Document No. 1021, "Extract Fort St George Military & Political Consultations, the 18th April 1797."

182 IOR/F/4/42, Document No. 1021, "Translation of a Letter from Mohana Bhaie Saheb" to Hobart.

> Tanjour, I have with my own consent attached myself to my father-in-law [sic!] Ameer Sing according to the directions which had before been given by my husband and have remained happy in my own apartments. I have no wish for any future connection with Sherfogee and the rest. [I have been receiving through] the Company's means 3.500 Star Pagodas for my annual expenses. This sum, I continue to receive from my brother-in-law Ameer Sing. I have written this at my own pleasure for your information. The burthen of shewing [sic! = burden of showing] me favor rests upon you. If the ill-disposed people here offer me any inconveniences, I shall send to inform you of them & I trust that you will do me the favour of punishing them. To a friend, why should I write more?[183]

Thus, Mohana Bāi Sāhibā representatively communicated the voices of Serfoji's opponents and Ameer Singh's proponents. Their unwavering belief that Serfoji's adoption and enthronement were illegal and invalid underlay their conviction. As they could not dethrone Serfoji, they became vexed. On 7 April 1797, Ameer Singh wrote a letter to Governor General John Shore in Calcutta to complain about the misrule of the Company in Tanjore and concluded it with an unusual reference to Schwartz: "I entreat you in the most earnest manner that I may be permitted to live in happiness & and that the Padre [Schwartz], & the Company's servants may be prevented from interfering with my affairs."[184]

Ameer Singh, who deeply resented Schwartz's guardianship over Serfoji, found it increasingly intolerable. Three months later, on 26 July 1797, Mohana Bāi Sāhibā sought the intervention of Governor Hobart. She expressed her disappointment that Hobart had not responded to her letter of 17 April 1797, delivered through Ameer Singh's vakeel in Madras, Sambhaji Trimbak. She attributed all the family problems to the influence of the "evil stars," which had compelled her to move to Madras. Upon her return to Ameer Singh's family, her problems ceased. She was content to receive her annual allowance from Ameer Singh, but she did not want to have any connection with Serfoji.[185] On the following day, on 27 July 1797, Ameer Singh echoed the contents of Mohana Bāi Sāhibā's letter. He also accused Schwartz of instigating domestic problems, a betrayal that deeply wounded him.[186] In the same letter, he accused Macleod of stationing a soldier in front of Mohana Bāi Sāhibā's house, effectively isolating her from her relatives. Furthermore, Ameer Singh accused Schwartz and Macleod of asking Mohana Bāi Sāhibā to vacate her horse stable to store food grains for Serfoji, further separating her.[187]

---

183 IOR/F/4/42, Document No. 1021, "Translation of a Letter from Mohana Bhaie Saheb" to Hobart.

184 IOR/F/4/42, Document No. 1021, "Translation of a letter [of 7 April 1797] from the Rajah of Tanjore to the Honorable Sir John Shore Bahadur, Governor General of Bengal."

185 IOR/F/4/42, Document No. 1021, "Translation of a letter from Matashree Mohana Bhaie Saheb to the Right Honorable Lord Hobart Governor & dated 26 July 1797."

186 IOR/F/4/42, Document No. 1021, "Translation of a letter from the Rajah of Tanjore to the Right Honorable Lord Hobart Governor, &, dated 27 July 1797: "Upon a former occasion Mr Swartz and the rest by evil advice to Mohana Bhai Saheb etc. excited disputes in my family, after the return of Matasree Mohana Bhaie Saheb to this place. She re-joined my family, in consequence of which I have continued to pay her annual allowance of 3,500 Pagodas and have her receipts accordingly."

187 IOR/F/4/42, Document No. 1021, "Translation of a letter from the Rajah of Tanjour to Mr Macleod dated 22 July 1797." During an earlier dispute, Ameer Singh showed the entire place to "the Padre's Dada [i.e. Dattajee, the servant of Serfoji, whom Ameer Singh perceived as

During this time, Ameer Singh received an annual pension of 25,000 Pagodas from the Company and lived at a palace in Mahdearjune near Tanjore. On 14 April 1802, William Blackburn informed the Company about Ameer Singh's sudden illness on 11 April 1802. His chest pain was so severe that his Tamil doctor doubted his survival. When Ameer Singh was conscious, he dictated a brief note to Blackburn, committing his "son and family to the care and protection of the Honourable Company." Knowing the prevailing animosity among Ameer Singh's relatives, Blackburn sent his soldiers as a precautionary measure to safeguard Ameer Singh's only infant son and secure his movable wealth. He assured Ameer Singh that "his wives and children will always be treated with the utmost respect and kindness and remain under the immediate protection of the Government."[188] Ameer Singh expressed his gratitude to the Company.

Eight days later, Ameer Singh died at 10 a.m. on 19 April 1802. Blackburn informed the Company that people cremated Ameer Singh on the same day, "agreeable to the forms of his religion." Two of his wives, Pārvatī Bāi and Sāvitrī Bāi, insisted on "accompanying him, and after a strenuous but unavailing resistance on the part of their relatives and many servants, had been suffered [i.e. allowed] to consummate the horrid sacrifice."[189] As Ameer Singh's family had no adult member to carry on responsibilities, Blackburn became their interim custodian. Then, he appointed two trustworthy servants of Ameer Singh, "Totobey Mohilik and Arunachalam," to look after the widowed queen Bhavānī Bāi, her daughter and her infant son.[190] Blackburn's decision and appointment of servants sheds light on the complex power dynamics and the Company's role in managing the affairs of Ameer Singh's family after his death.[191] After his enthronement, Serfoji had no further dealings with Ameer Singh and his family. Hence, Blackburn did not mention that Serfoji cared for either of them.

Likewise, in July 1806, Blackburn observed that feuds, jealousies and hatred spread among Ameer Singh's relatives and senior officers after his death. The reasons for these conflicts, which included personal ambitions, power struggles, and the desire for control, were deeply rooted in the family's history and the political landscape of the time. Initially, Ameer Singh's widow, Bhavānī Bāi, favoured her brother, Govinder

---

Schwartz's servant] and proved it to him. This is well known to the Padre [Schwartz] himself. Under the circumstances of my furniture being in those apartments sealed and locked up, Sherfojee has broken those seals and taken away some of the furniture."

188 IOR/F/4/136, 11–17.

189 IOR/F/4/136, 21; IOR/H/571, 197: An unnamed reporter, who prepared this summary sometime after the death of Ameer Singh in 1802, stated that the "widows of Tuljajee were not burnt with him. NB: when Ameer Singh died in 1802, his two widows could not be prevented from burning themselves." IOR/F/4/136, 3–5: Following Ameer Singh's death, the Court of Directors granted a generous stipend to his son, whom they referred to as "Prince." They appreciated William Blackburne, their resident in Tanjore, for being "judicious and humane" to Ameer Singh during the latter's sickness and death. They were happy about the "means, adopted, under the authority of the British Government, to dissuade the sacrifice [of *satī*], made on that occasion by the devotion of two of that Prince's consorts, to the flames in conformity to the tenets of the Hindu Religion."

190 IOR/F/4/136, 19–34.

191 IOR/F/4/136, 51: On 11.05.1802, the Company granted an annual allowance of 25,000 Pagodas to Ameer Singh's son. It was the exact amount Ameer Singh had previously received from the company.

Row Gady, and her cousin, Raout Row Nerwall, with special favours and bounties. After they had molested her female servants, Bhavānī Bāi dismissed them and appointed Appaneh Gady, her other first cousin. Shortly after that, Appaneh Gady turned against Bhavānī Bāi, his lover, and tried to oppress her. Consequently, the Company's Resident Blackburn removed Appaneh Gady and his accomplices from the palace. Blackburn's report did not mention Serfoji's involvement in solving the problems in Ameer Singh's family, probably because they lay beyond his remit.

8.7 Serfoji Surrendering Tanjore to the Company (1799)

After Serfoji became the king of Tanjore, he observed the complex power struggle within the palace. Likewise, he would have noticed how the various officers in distant places failed to collect enough revenues to pay the dues that he had agreed upon with the Company. Additionally, he visited the separate locations and land-holding families in other parts of Tanjore. Therefore, he voluntarily planned to surrender the Kingdom of Tanjore to the Company and request an annual allowance instead. On 14 October 1799, Benjamin Torin informed Governor Clive in Madras that Serfoji "relinquished with less difficulty" than Torin had expected "his demand for augmentation of the proportion of the Revenue stipulated to be paid to him." He negotiated for his sovereignty over the palace and the Fort. He asked the Company to "supply him annually with a certain quantity of gram and other articles as well as rice."[192] Torin reported triumphantly that Serfoji "carefully abstained from all demands which tended to impede their full operation." According to a Company's report, Serfoji also

> Abstained from keeping in his own hands the lands which had been offered to Him by the original propositions; that his situation was now materially changed, and he should be entirely dependent on the Company in future for many accommodations which he had hitherto drawn immediately from His Country.[193]

Authorised and empowered by the Governor General, "Mornington Bahadoor" of Calcutta, and the Governor, Charles Oakley of Madras, Benjamin Torin and Serfoji negotiated a new treaty, which they concluded on 25 October 1799.[194] Its first article confirmed their friendship. Its second article annulled all provisions of the previous treaties as inadequate. It introduced a permanent system for collecting revenue and

---

192 IOR/H/457, 26–27: On 14.10.1799, Serfoji and Torin agreed on this draft clause about grains that should be added to the *Treaty of 1799*: "Additional Article respecting supplies of grain: And whereas it is necessary to the convenience & comfort of His Excellency the Rajah [Serfoji] that certain supplies of Rice, Gram, & other Grain should be supplied for the use of His Excellency, the Company bind themselves to furnish the said supplies as often as the Rajah shall find it necessary to obtain for this purpose, His Excellency binding himself to pay for the said Grain with the charges of transportation at the rate of the current prices for the time being." This draft became the fifteenth article of the *Treaty of 1799*. In other words, Serfoji put himself at the mercy of the Company even for his daily sustenance! It is lamentable that he voluntarily became a beggar in his own country, despite having a plentiful income.

193 IOR/H/457, 17–24.

194 Hickey 1874, xxxix–xxxiv.

administering justice. The third article stipulated that the Company would have the freedom "to ascertain, determine, and establish property rights and to fix a reasonable assignment upon the country's several subahs, pergunahs, and villages, and to secure a fixed and permanent revenue." The fourth article established a court or courts "for the due administration of Civil and Criminal Justice, under the sole authority of the judges and other personnel of the English East India Company." The Governor of Madras was to be the final deciding authority. Serfoji had no "control, authority or interference" in this court system. The Company would formulate "such ordinances and regulations (framed with due regard to the existing laws and usages of the country) as shall from time to time be enacted and published by the said Governor in Council." The fifth article ensured that Serfoji had no power over the Company officers outside Tanjore. The sixth article proposed that Serfoji did not have to pay the Company any revenue; instead, the Company would be responsible for the income and expenses of the entire Tanjore.

Article ten promised that the Company would vacate its troops from the Fort of Tanjore, and Serfoji was entirely free "to garrison the said Fort in such manner as he shall see fit." However, in case of an invasion by an enemy into the "territories of the Company or their allies or in the event of any failures in the due performance of the engagements contracted" by Serfoji, the Company would occupy the fort "as a military post, for the protection and mutual interests of the contracting parties." Article eleven of the *Treaty of 1799* required Serfoji to agree that "the said Fort shall in no case whatever become an asylum for public offenders or for persons desirous of escaping from the jurisdiction of the Courts of Civil and Criminal Justice, from the authority of the Revenue Officers, or any other branches of the authority" of the Company.

Article twelve required that the inhabitants within the Fort should apply for justice directly to Serfoji. Someone who complains about Serfoji's relatives or friends should approach the Company's resident in Tanjore for redressal. The resident would speak with Serfoji about this complaint and recommend it to the courts.[195] Article thirteen proposed a transparent method of accounting: Serfoji was free to "inspect the accounts of the Head Cutcherry or the Collector's treasury from time to time, or to station a vakeel or accountant at his own expense." Article fourteen promised that Serfoji could continue to receive from the Danish Government in Tranquebar the annual rent of 2,000 Cakkarams "for lands held of the Rajah of Tanjore in the vicinity of that place" and keep it without any deduction. Serfoji was particularly pleased with this provision: he could ceremoniously receive the annual tribute from Tranquebar without any deduction, as described above in Section 7.7.1. Article fifteen promised that the Company would supply Serfoji with "certain supplies of rice, gram and other grain." However, he should pay for these things and their transport. The Secret Committee of

[195] Serfoji's handing over his country to the Company for administration and collection of revenues posed a legal problem for the law courts. Astonishingly, he and Torin agreed that the law courts could not function well under the "the double authority" (of Serfoji and the Company). Therefore, Serfoji did not wish to retain any part of his country that would be exempt from his authority. The Company happily acknowledged this power transfer to them and stated that this arrangement would keep Serfoji away from "much personal inconvenience and vexation" (IOR/H/457, 27). In other words, Serfoji authorised the Company to control his country's legal systems and law courts.

the Company's Court of Directors in London appreciated this treaty because it provided a "permanent system" for collecting revenues and administering justice in the best interest of the Company. They were pleased that the Company officers in Tanjore oversaw both "civil and criminal justice." Their judges should consider not only British law but also local customary regulations. The members of the Secret Committee knew that the Company would appoint officers who were not answerable to Serfoji.[196]

As time passed, even within his palace and the walled city of Tanjore, Serfoji thought and behaved as if he were a dependent on the mercy of the Company. For example, in April 1806, a Maratha chieftain named Chintaman Row Putwardan visited Tanjore to purchase elephants. Serfoji welcomed him and his messengers into the palace without informing the Company Resident, Blackburn. Immediately, on 21 March 1806 and 30 April 1806, Blackburn reported Putwardan's presence and purpose to his superiors in Madras.[197] The Company directed Blackburn on 6 May 1806 to advise Serfoji to distance himself from Putwardan, as the "injurious effects" of his "turbulent disposition" would disturb the "public tranquillity" of Tanjore.[198] Consequently, William Blackburn discussed these matters with Serfoji, who, according to Blackburn's letter of 21 May 1786, "[wholeheartedly] declared himself particularly obliged" to the Company. He informed Blackburn:

> [...] without the least reserve and with a very animated countenance that the wish of his heart was to have no connections, but such as should be agreeable to the Government that he relied solely on them and that it was his firm determination to keep no secret from them and to admit of no foreign intercourse with himself or Court, but what had at first been imparted to you as Resident. [... Serfoji] prides himself much on the plan he has adopted of informing you of all foreign communications before he has anything to do with the Parties.[199]

In October 1806, Serfoji requested that the Company permit him, "after the Peace with the Maratta Chieftains," to garrison the Little Fort with his soldiers. On 6 October 1806, the Company reminded Serfoji of the tenth clause of the treaty they had signed with him on 25 November 1799. Accordingly, the Company army would take over the Little Fort in an emergency. Until then, he should store enough food and weapons in the Great Fort.[200] It was unfortunate that Serfoji made himself powerless in his ancestral homeland and became the Company's puppet.

8.8. Serfoji's Indebtedness to Christians

Schwartz faithfully discharged his guardian duties and raised Serfoji. He guided him to develop his mental capabilities and to become a better ruler than his predecessors. Schwartz established a professional network for Serfoji, comprising the German Lutheran missionaries in India, the leaders of the Company and Tanjore, and the Tamil

196 IOR/F/4/80, 55–56.
197 IOR/F/4/218, 1–11.
198 IOR/F/4/218, 12–14.
199 IOR/F/4/218, 21–22.
200 IOR/F/4/218, Document 4786, 1–3.

Lutherans. These diverse kinds of people broadened his knowledge horizon. Under the direct influence of German Lutheran missionaries and Tamil Lutherans, Serfoji enriched the palace library founded by the Nayak rulers and previously maintained by Marathi rulers. Serfoji's interactions with Christian missionaries and Company officers in Madras opened new avenues for enriching knowledge, cross-fertilising ideas, and applying practical skills to improve the lives of ordinary people in Tanjore. He acquired maps of the world and various countries, manuscripts and books in different European languages, scientific instruments like globes, paintings and portraits, and diverse museum artefacts. Under Schwartz's influence, he began collecting multiple types of cotton and silk textiles,[201] later boosting the local textile manufacturing units in Tanjore. After hearing about the curiosity cabinets in the Glaucha Institutions in Halle (Saale), Serfoji created curiosity cabinets for the palace library and added new things.[202] His contributions to this library were so significant that it is named Thanjavur Maharaja Serfoji's Saraswathi Mahal Library.

Serfoji built the Dhanvantari Mahal (i.e., Taṉvantiri Mahāl, the 'hall of the healer-Viṣṇu') in Tanjore, appointed skilled medical doctors, produced Siddha medicine, and promoted healthcare. This hospital was primarily known for its eye care.[203] He appreciated European music and astronomy. He supported court poets, artists and entertainers.[204] He established a tuition-free school, *Navavidyā Kalāniti Sālā*, a "treasure house of new knowledge," to teach subjects in the arts and humanities.[205] His liberal education in Madras, his interactions with various English and German intellectuals and his indebtedness to Schwartz's pedagogical methods led him to initiate vital developmental programs for Tanjore. To celebrate the English victory over Napoleon (1814–1815), Serfoji built the 120-foot hexagonal Maṉōrā Tower in Carapēntira Rājā

---

201 Vijaya Ramaswamy: Historical Dictionary of the Tamils. Lanham/Maryland [2]2017 ([1]2006), here 309: "The idea of developing the Saraswati Mahal Library came to Sarfoji because of the strong influence of his Danish [sic! = German] mentor Father Rev. Schwartz. Because Schwartz was also an expert on Indian textiles and wrote extensively on it, the library also came to acquire some rare textile pieces."

202 India Viswanathan Peterson: The Cabinet of King Serfoji of Tanjore: A European Collection in early nineteenth-century India. In: Journal of Historical Collections 11, 1999, issue 1, 71–93.

203 Savithri Preetha Nair: Diseases of the Eye: Medical Pluralism at the Tanjore Court in the Early Nineteenth Century. In: Social History of Medicine 25, 2012, issue 2, 573–588.

204 For further details on Serfoji, his rule and contributions, see Mu. Catācivam (ed.): Māmaṉṉar Cracapōci— Āyvukkōvai Tokuti 3 ('The Great King Serfoji—Collection of Research Essays'). Tanjore 1990. Tulajendra Rajah P Bhonsle: Raja Serfoji II with a Short History of Thanjavur Mahrattas. Tanjore [2]1999. Indira Viswanathan Peterson: Multilingual Dramas at the Tanjavur Maratha Court and Literary Cultures in Early Modern South India. In: The Medieval History Journal 14, 2011, issue 2, 285–321. Indira Viswanathan Peterson: Tanjore, Tranquebar and Halle: European Science and German Missionary Education in the Lives of Two Indian Intellectuals in the Early Nineteenth Century. In: Christians and Missionaries in India: Cross-Cultural Communications since 1500. Ed. by Robert E. Frykenberg. Grand Rapids 2003, 93–126. Preetha Nair: Raja Serfoji-II.

205 Radhika: Development of Sadir in the court of Raja Serfoji-II, 54–55: This *Navavidya Kalanidhi Sala* had provisions for girls and boys to learn subjects such as "Arts, Philosophy, Astronomy, Fine Arts and Linguistics (Persian, Arabic, Telugu, Sanskrit, Marathi and English)" free of cost. Additionally, he established a separate Vedic School to teach the *Vedas* and *Purāṇas* to those who were permitted to learn them.

Paṭṭiṇam on the seacoast facing the Bay of Bengal, approximately ten miles from modern Pudukkottai. He encouraged arts such as painting, music, dance, etc.

Serfoji authored books in Sanskrit,[206] Marathi,[207] Telugu and Tamil. Two of his representative writings illustrate the impact of his upbringing under the tutelage of Schwartz and his Christian missionary colleagues. The Sanskrit booklet *Kumarasambhava Champu* ('The Birth of Kumaran in Champu-meter') narrates the courtship between Śiva and Pārvatī, Śiva overcoming the temptations of Kāma, Pārvatī's devotion to Śiva and the birth of Kumaran to defeat all evil spirits. Its reviewer, Subramanya Sastri, lauded it as Serfoji's best Sanskrit writing, which was easy, flowing, and elegant. It resembled "Bhojadeva's Ramayanacampu."[208] This booklet does not reflect the teachings of Schwartz or his missionary colleagues.

By contrast, Serfoji's other work, *Devendra Kuravanji*, written in Marathi, describes world geography in the popular Tamil poetic genre of *Kuravanji*.[209] This work reflects the astronomical, geographical, and cartographical lessons he received from Schwartz, Christoph Samuel John, other German Lutheran missionaries in Tanjore and Tranquebar, as well as his European teachers, including Colonel Braithwaite in Madras. The *Kuratti*, a wandering woman, informed the hero of this narrative that she had circumnavigated Earth and visited the world of deities (*devaloka*). Her description of the solar system agrees with Christoph Samuel John's demonstration. According to Jatavallabhar, the editor of *Devendra Kuravanji*, the Kuratti

> [Narrates] in detail the natural phenomena, the cyclic movements of the Earth and the Moon, the effects of such movements and the like. She goes on relating, at great length, details about all the continents she had visited and the important countries, towns, rivers and mountains therein. Since nothing is said about the continent of Australia, it can be presumed that, perhaps, Serfoji did not have the right kind of map of Australia for his reference or that he had no time to include it in his work. [... The] musical narration of world geography [in verses] in the form of a Dance-Drama [...is] sweet, simple, emotional and instructive. Elegance and easy flow of language are the keynotes of Serfoji's work. He has avoided descriptive diffuseness, and there is no doubt about his meaning.[210]

The Marathi index of this book contains English equivalents. Accordingly, the Kuratti visited various places, rivers and mountains in and around Africa, North America, South America, Europe, Asia, and India, providing a comprehensive and accurate

---

[206] Serfoji: Kumārasambhavachampū [in Sanskrit] by Śrī Śarabhoji Mahārāja of Tanjore. Ed. by T. K. Balasubramanya Aiyar. Srirangam 1939, here i–ii: P. P. Subramanya Sastri, a Professor of Sanskrit at Presidency College in Madras, stated that Serfoji authored four Sanskrit works: "Smritisarasamuccaya, Smritisangraha, Mudraraksasacchaya and Kumarasambhavacampu."

[207] Serfoji: Sarapēntira Vaittiya Ratṉāvaḷi (Tamil: 'A Collection of Medical Treatments by King Serfoji'). Transl. and ed. by A. Krishnasamy Madikrow. Tanjore [8]2008, here iii: Serfoji authored twelve works in Marathi. Among them are stories about *Umāmakēsvari*, *Nīlakaṇṭa Kulā Lavar*, *Sivarātri*, *Gaṇēṣh*, *Rādā-Kirṣṇa*, and the like.

[208] Serfoji: Kumārasambhavachampū, i–ii: P. P. Subramanya Sastri opined that "Kumarasambhavacampu is *par excellence* his best work."

[209] For a brief discussion about *Kuravanji* in Tanjore court, see Radhika Seshan: From Folk Culture to Court Culture: The 'Kuravanji' in the Tanjore Court. In: Proceedings of the Indian History Congress 65, 2004, 331–334.

[210] Serfoji: Devendra Kuravanji [in Marathi] by Serfoji Raja. Ed. by T. L. Thyagaraja Jatawallabhar. Kumbakonam 1950, here iv.

account of the Earth's geography:[211] North America,[212] South America,[213] Europe,[214] Asia,[215] and India.[216] It is praiseworthy that Serfoji enabled a woman from an otherwise marginalised background to serve as the principal spokesperson and teacher, educating her listeners in international geography. Her presentation, which challenged her listeners' religious cosmologies, proves the lasting impact of missionaries like Schwartz on Serfoji's writings.

The royal house of Tanjore maintains Schwartz's memories alive to this day. For example, in 1998, the Senior Prince Bhonsle Chattrapath at the Palace of Tanjore revealed a hitherto unknown habit that Schwartz and Serfoji had practised: he acknowledged that the clergyman Schwartz was behind the success and fame of Serfoji. He credited Schwartz with imparting education and a "thirst for knowledge," and moulding "the raw man Serfoji into a great king of fine qualities." When Schwartz lay on his deathbed, Serfoji came to visit him. At that time, as was customary between them, they shook hands. Their handshake was a "communion between the two noble hearts because, in the human body, the heart is on the left side." This handshake was also Serfoji's promise to "his tutor that he would support and save Christianity even after Schwartz." The stone marble, which Serfoji erected to honour Schwartz within the Fort Church in Tanjore, provides compelling evidence "that Serfoji worshipped Schwartz and his motto. Hats off to these two great men."[217]

Preetha Nair has assessed the processes and outcomes of Serfoji's various projects, from collecting books for his library to eye care.[218] It is evident that throughout his

---

211 The Kuratti referred to geographical areas that included Algeria, Azorees Island, Egypt, Madagascar, Madeira Island, Mauritius, Loango, St. Michael Island, San Salvador and St. Helena Island.

212 The Kuratti spoke about the Appalachian Mountains, Edenton, Bahama Island, Bermuda Island, California; Canada, Kingston, the Conche River, Charleston; the Colorado River, Georgia; Jamaica, and the Dakota River; Delaware River, Santo Domino, South Carolina; the Greet Pedis; the Penoscrotal River, East Florida, Pennsylvania; Pensacola, the Boise River; the Moose River, Maryland; the Mohawk River, New Orleans, New England, New Jersey, New Brunswick, New Briton, New Mexico, New York, the Nepisiguit River, the Newfoundland Island, the Restigouche River; the Rupert River, Louisiana, Virginia; Savannah River, the Severn river, the Santee River, Tobago Island, and the Hudson River, etc.

213 The Kuratti mentioned the Andes Mountains, the Amazon River, the Guajahu River, Guiana, the Grande River, Chile, Terraform, Darein, the Dela Plata River, Brazil, the Magellan Strait, Rio Grande, Argentina, Santiago Island, etc.

214 The Kuratti described France, Spain, England, Russia, Switzerland, Scotland, Ireland, Hungary, Portugal, Poland, Italy, Bohemia, Germany, Flanders, Sweden, etc.

215 The Kuratti explained Kandy in Ceylon, Gilolo Island, Guaham in Ladonna Island, India, Japan, the Yenisei River in Tartary, the Jordan River, Turkey, Malacca Island, China, and Pegu in India-China.

216 The Kuratti spoke about the Indus River, Udaipur, Cauvery River, the Caso (Kousiki) River, the Krishna River, the Godavari River, the Ganges River, the Gandaki River, Madras, Jaipur, Jodhpur, Tanjore, the Rapti River, the Tamraparani River, the Tungabhadra River, Delhi, Poona, the Purna River, the Burda River, the Buin Ganga River, Bharatpur, the Bhogavati River, the Mahanadi River, the Mahi River, Multan (now in Pakistan), the Yamuna River, Lahore, the Weni River, the Vaigai River, the Saraswati River, the Son River, etc.

217 Raja Senior S. Babai Rajah Bhonsle Chattrapathy: The King [Serfoji] and the Clergy Man [Schwartz]. In: Christian Friedrich Schwartz: His Contributions to South India. Ed. by Daniel Jeyaraj. Chennai 1999, 117–118, here 118.

218 Preetha Nair: Raja Serfoji II and Diseases of the Eye.

life, Serfoji acknowledged Schwartz's decisive role as his cherished guardian, who protected him from political dangers and trained him in various disciplines to the best of his ability. He considered Schwartz his father and appreciated his firmness, humility, wisdom and honesty. His eulogy for Schwartz (Appendix 6b and c) remains unmatched. Notably, the eulogy in Christ's Church (Appendix 6 b) is incredibly moving.[219]

8.9 Serfoji's Indebtedness to Ancestral Habits

Schwartz imparted to Serfoji his Christian faith in God the Creator and Jesus Christ the Redeemer. He urged Serfoji to derive his ethical and moral principles for both his private and public engagement from his understanding of God as the Creator, who is omnipresent, omniscient, and omnipotent. This God is a God of order who holds all persons accountable for their thoughts and actions. He introduced Serfoji to the central beliefs and practices of Lutheran Pietism. However, he refrained from requiring Serfoji to embrace Lutheran Pietism as a mark of his outward identity. He respected Serfoji's freedom to remain "an orthodox Hindu."[220]

Simultaneously, Serfoji carefully observed how the Company officers practised their Christian faith. Their form of Christianity, filled with indifference to God, theological beliefs and religious rituals but overwhelmingly passionate about amassing significant material wealth irrespective of its negative impact on Indians, did not appeal to Serfoji. He remained "an orthodox Hindu, who did not convert to Christianity despite his close relationship to Schwartz, as well as a devoted keeper of Indian traditions,"[221] especially the religious and ritual traditions of the Śaivites and Vaiṣṇavites. He was indeed the custodian of the temples in Tanjore, including the Great Temple.

The missionaries in Tranquebar did not know how to relate to Serfoji in his capacity as a ruler, who was sympathetic towards Christians. For example, on January 1, 1799, Christoph Samuel John, Johann Peter Rottler, and August Friedrich Cämmerer (1767–1837) stated that King Serfoji showed kindness to missionaries serving in and outside Tanjore. The leaders of local districts and small places knew of Serfoji's cheerful attitude towards Christians, especially missionaries. Therefore, they treated the missionaries with kindness and respect. John, Rottler and Cämmerer asserted that Serfoji appreciated their selfless service, focusing on enhancing the quality of life for all people in Tanjore Country. They willingly provided their advice whenever he needed it.[222] On 24 April 1799, missionary John wrote that Serfoji was kind but lacked

219 Cotton: List of Inscriptions on Tombs or Monuments in Madras Possessing Historical or Archaeological Interest, Vol. 2, 241: Serfoji composed this eulogy and had it engraved on an epitaph covering Schwartz's grave in St. Peter's Church in Tanjore.

220 Simon Rastén: The Tranquebar tribute: Contested perceptions during the reign of Rajah Serfoji II of Tanjore. In: Review of Development and Change 14, 2009, issue 1&2, 41–60, here 44.

221 Simon Rastén: The Tranquebar tribute: Contested perceptions during the reign of Rajah Serfoji II of Tanjore. In: Review of Development and Change 14, 2009, issue 1&2, 41–60, here 44.

222 NHR 5, 1800, issue 56, 674.

firmness in resisting "temptations," i.e., he permitted Śaivite and Vaiṣṇavite religious activities, as well as pompous and expensive processions. Johann Kohlhoff knew that Serfoji could not stop these renewed forms of spiritual expression. However, he was convinced that Serfoji would gradually reform his country. He hoped to meet Serfoji privately and discuss his cheerful disposition towards Christians.[223]

As far as Serfoji's religious identity and belonging were concerned, he remained an ardent follower and supporter of Śaivism. To demonstrate his religious affiliation, soon after he ascended the throne, he gifted precious jewels to Śiva, the presiding deity of the Great Temple, also known as *Peruvuṭaiyār Kōvil* and Brihadisvara Temple. He installed 108 *Liṅga*s carved in granite stone there. He loved to worship in the Bangaru Kamatchi Amman Temple in Tanjore and the Tiyagaraja Temple in Tiruvarur. He undertook pilgrimages to various temples in the Tamil country, including Palani and Rameswaram. In October 1820–1821, he and his entourage of 3,000 men visited Kāśī (i.e. Varanasi, also known as Banaras) for worship, learning and collecting Sanskrit manuscripts.[224] He honoured the *Ācharya* of Kanchipuram and interacted with other Śaivite and Vaiṣṇavite teachers. He began his daily activity by worshipping Śiva.

As Serfoji had surrendered his kingdom, except the city, its fort, and its administration, to the Company, he did not have to worry about raising money for his upkeep and manifold expenses. He was satisfied with his annual allowance of 100,000 Star Pagodas and twenty percent of the revenues from the entire Tanjore. The wars of the Company with neighbouring states did not affect him as he did not have to pay any war reparations. Every year, he received a fixed allowance from the Company and one-fifth of the total revenue from Tanjore Country. Besides, he could keep the entire annual rent of Tranquebar. He could live in his palace rent-free. The Company provided him with everything he needed to sustain and run his city government. These arrangements increased his wealth.

Soon, Serfoji became famous as the first English-educated ruler of Tanjore. He networked with the officers of the Company for his visits, travels, and accommodations in and outside the Madras Presidency. He had the time and means to devote his energies and activities to learning, philanthropy and pilgrimages to holy sites in and outside of Tanjore. He either built new temples or repaired old ones. He established charitable institutions and educational establishments. He employed poets in his court for literary compositions. He sponsored personal priests who put Sanskrit-based Brahmanical traditions into practice in Tanjore.

Serfoji's interactions with the German Lutheran missionaries did not impact his marital relationships. Jeetendra Hirschfeld, who had examined the marital practices of the Maratha kings of Tanjore, discovered that in 1796, Serfoji fell in love with Soubhagyavati Muktambal Bāi Sāhibā, likely a dancer attached to a Thiruvaiyaru Temple,[225] and he brought her to his palace. The pandits at the palace advised him not to marry her because her horoscope did not match his. The Company, too, warned him not to marry her. Otherwise, he would forfeit his throne. Despite these warnings, Serfoji

---

223 NHR 5, 1801, issue 57, 786.

224 Savithri Preetha Nair: Raja Serfoji II: Science, Medicine and Enlightenment in Tanjore. London 2012, 107–112.

married her in 1797 through a Sword Marriage (*Katti Kalyāṇam*, a form of arranged marriage commonly associated with concubinage).[226] She died after giving birth to a child.[227] On 26 February 1799, Serfoji officially married another woman and, a few years later, two more women. These women bore him "five daughters and three sons." Before he died on 8 March 1832, he asked his wives and concubines not to commit *satī*. Nevertheless, Queen Srimant Akhand Mohana Chatrapati Maharani Bāi Sāhibā (1761–1833) and Queen Srimant Akhand Soubhagyavati Avu Bāi Chatrapati Maharani Sāhibā (1789–1864), along with six concubines at Kalyāṇa Mahāl in Tiruvaiyāṟu, wished to commit *satī*.[228] The Company officers, senior palace administrators and relatives had difficulty persuading them to avoid jumping into Serfoji's funeral fire. Consequently, after his death, Serfoji's twenty-four concubines lived in the *Kalyāṇa Mahāl*.[229]

Serfoji exemplified a unique blend of pragmatic governance, guided by his capabilities, religious devotion, and a commitment to preserving Tanjore's culture. He did not permit his intensive interactions with the German Lutheran Pietist missionaries and Tamil Christians, as well as his extensive education in European arts and sciences, which were available to him, to sway him away from his ancestral religious beliefs, practices, and traditions. He knew the art of navigating between the necessity of a progressive ruler and, simultaneously, the protector and promoter of local religious and cultural traditions. He was sympathetic and respectful towards Christians. However, as custodian of local temples and traditions, he endowed them with lavish financial gifts for repairs, decorations, regular functions and occasional festivals. He helped the local people develop schools, libraries, and temples, bridging the old and new ways of life, as well as Indian and European values, to foster harmonious coexistence. His life and work demonstrate the strength of embracing beneficial, catalytic values for social change from outside while maintaining one's ancestral roots.

---

225 Jeetendra Hirschfeld: Seraglios of the Tanjore Mahārājahs: Sword Wives of the Kalyāṇa Mahāl and Vijayā Maṅgala Vilāsam Mahāl. In: Sathir Dance Art. 2 May 2009. URL: https://sathirdance.wordpress.com/2009/05/02/seraglios-of-the-tanjore-maharajahs-sword-wives-of-the-kalya%E1%B9%87a-mahal-and-vijaya-ma%E1%B9%85gala-vilasam-mahal/ (accessed on 20.11. 2024).

226 A *cumaṅkali* (an 'auspicious woman'), the wife whose husband was alive, tied on behalf of a royal man represented by a sword (*katti*), the *tāli* (a marriage badge either a gold chain or a cord smeared with turmeric paste) around a woman's neck. Hence, this marriage was known as the sword marriage.

227 At the request of the dying Muktambal, Serfoji built an ornate *catram* in Orathanadu and dedicated it on 16 January 1802. He endowed this *Mukatambal Catram* with lands and cash reserves.

228 Hirschfeld: Seraglios of the Tanjore Mahārājahs.

229 Hirschfeld: Seraglios of the Tanjore Mahārājahs, Footnote 16: Two of Serfoji's eighteen women, who lived in Tiruvaiyāru in 1855, were "Soubhagyavati (Matusri ['widowed queen']) Sonabhadra Bāi Sāhibā and Soubhagyavati (Matusri) Bhavani Bāi Sāhibā."

Chapter 9

Schwartz as a Social Reformer

9.1 Empowering Justice in Tanjore

Schwartz, though not the originator of the Tanjore justice system, played a crucial role in highlighting its shortcomings. He proposed a more pragmatic and efficient system to serve the affluent and the underprivileged, marking a significant step towards societal equity. He tried to bridge the gap between the privileged and the disadvantaged in Tanjore's judicial system.

In 1995, K. Manamalar provided a detailed account of the localised judicial system of the Nayak rulers.[1] The Maratha rulers followed it until King Pratāpasimha appointed a judge and placed him in Tanjore City, centralising the judicial system.[2] His son, Tulāji, turned it into a graded system.[3] However, after Tulāji's demise, this court system deteriorated significantly under Ameer Singh's interim rule, adversely affecting the people of Tanjore. Manamalar's account of the legal system and its failure aligns with Schwartz's critique of the dysfunctional court system under Ameer Singh.[4] To fully appreciate Schwartz's efforts in establishing a better-functioning judiciary for ordinary people, it is essential to understand Tanjore's agriculture-based economy and the introduction of British laws in the Company-administered territories.[5]

---

1 K. Manamalar: Administration and Social Life under the Marathas of Thanjavur. Diss. phil. Trichy 1995, 60: "The subedars, amuldars and the karbar exercised judicial authority." The village panchayats settled the local disputes. In the city, Brahmin Pandits assisted the king in resolving problems. These Pandits followed the teachings of their *smrities* ('that which is remembered,' i.e., Sanskrit scriptures such as itihasas, puranas, and the like) and relevant legal literature.

2 Manamalar: Administration and Social Life under the Marathas of Thanjavur, 60: Pratāpasimha established a regular court, appointed a judge (with an annual salary of thirty Pagodas), and assigned him an accountant to record the decisions. This court could decide many cases. However, it referred the difficult ones to the king. Often, the king deputed his diwan to attend to these cases.

3 Manamalar: Administration and Social Life under the Marathas of Thanjavur, 60: "King Tulaja established four graded courts at the capital, namely: 1. *Nyaya sabha* or criminal court; 2. *Mudirtha sabha* or civil court; 3. *Dharma sabha* or religious court, and 4. *Nyaya Dhisa Sabha, Prathistha Sabha*, or the Supreme Court.

4 Manamalar: Administration and Social Life under the Marathas of Thanjavur, 61: Ameer Singh neglected the judiciary. He tolerated bribery and corruption, as well as interference by influential individuals, which prevented the judges from carrying out their duties impartially. Notably, Shiva Rao's tyranny endangered the court and its function. Finally, the influential people bought or sold justice.

5 For an overview of the British administration of justice, see A. T. Markose: Judicial Control of Administrative Action in India–A Study in Methods. Madras 1956, 76.

9.1.1 Tanjore's Agriculture-based Economy

Chinnaiyan has explained that the cultivable lands of Tanjore belonged to the major temples.[6] The authorities of these temples distributed the land primarily to certain Brahmins and *Veḷḷāḷars*, who were large-scale cultivators. After Hyder Ali invaded Tanjore and besieged the city (1766–1769), many land-owning Brahmins and Veḷḷāḷars entrusted their lands to hereditary landowners (*mirācutār*) belonging to three communities: Kaḷḷars, Paṭaiyāccis, and Mūppaṉārs. The *mirācutār* employed two types of farmers: the permanent residential tenant cultivators (*uḷkuṭi*) were responsible for the cultivation. The occasional and non-residential farmers called *puṟakkuṭi* ploughed the fields, sowed the seeds, transplanted the seedlings, and returned to harvest the yields. The lives of the non-residential, wandering farmers remained miserable. Without land and permanent work, they and their families could barely survive.

Tanjore's agricultural produce was the Company's and Wallajah's primary source of revenue. After capturing Tanjore in 1773, Wallajah established the *amáni* system of taxation: his officers, under the leadership of Dabír Pandit, monitored the amount of crops harvested. They taxed the harvest and collected the taxes. The actions of these officers were so cruel that many farmers stopped cultivation and migrated to other places. After the Company restored Tulāji in 1776, he raised taxes to satisfy the greedy Company officers. Wallajah's tax collectors and the consequences of Hyder Ali's invasion in 1781 ruined the farmers' prospects in the Kumbakonam, Sīrkāli, and Tiruvady regions. They emigrated to other places.

Tulāji appointed Bāvanna Pandit to invent a new system to remedy the situation. Bāvanna Pandit divided the Kingdom of Tanjore into *patakkam*s by joining deserted and impoverished villages and towns with other wealthier villages and towns. He also appointed a *patakkakkār* ('pendent-wearer') as the chief tax collector for each *patakkam*, which consisted of impoverished and wealthier villages. The *patakkakkārs* collected taxes from all towns and fields of their *patakkam*.[7] Bāvanna Pandit's method raised enough revenue for Tulāji to pay the mandatory tribute to the Company on time. However, Bāvanna Pandit's subordinates committed mistakes and injustices that hurt the farmers, and they cried out for justice. Schwartz listened to their cries and attempted to establish a system of justice that would alleviate their suffering.

9.1.2 British Laws in the Company Territories

The Mughals administered justice through their courts (*adalats*), each with its standards or procedures. Since 1661, the Company Council in Madras had its Mayor's Courts. Indians did not fully appreciate the new law court in Tanjore, and its lawyers threatened to leave. After the victory at Plassey in 1757 and acquiring the *Diwani* rights over Bengal, Bihar, and Orissa from the Mughal Emperor in

---

6 Chinnaiyan: Social History of Thanjavur 1532–1799, 133.
7 Madras District Gazetteer—Tanjore, rpt. Ed. by F. R. Hemingway. Madras 1915, 169–170.

1765, Robert Clive and his successors in Bengal began settling legal disputes over movable and immovable properties, socio-cultural privileges (e.g. caste), rites of passage (especially marriage alliances, divorce, inheritance questions and adoption),[8] religious loyalties and the like. With sufficient legal and parliamentary authorisation, the thirteenth clause of the *Regulating Act of India* (1773) empowered the Company in Calcutta to establish a Supreme Court. It consisted of a chief justice and three other justices "to exercise all civil, criminal, admiralty and ecclesiastical jurisdiction and appoint such clerks and other ministerial officers, with salaries as shall be approved of by the said Governor-General and Council."[9]

The English judges, unfamiliar with the local customs, traditions, and religions, faced significant challenges in administering justice. They believed their laws were fair, accurate, honest, and dignified. However, they remained under pressure to enrich themselves and their shareholders in London. In the name of maintaining justice and peace, they applied their laws to extract the maximum amount of money from Indians to finance their operations and to exploit Indians. In the Carnatic, the English judges faced additional challenges: since the *Treaty of Paris* (1763), Nawab Wallajah considered himself the sole sovereign over the Carnatic. On the other hand, the Company also claimed sovereignty over the same region mainly because it had better trade powers and a superior military. Schwartz was aware of these conflicting interests and operational methods of diverse groups in Tanjore. He admired those British judges, like Robert Chambers, the Chief Justice of India, for introducing "justice into this desert."[10].

9.1.3 Reforming the Court System of Tanjore

As discussed in Section 5.8.5, the *Treaty of 1787* required Ameer Singh to establish a law court in Tanjore. This court should remove injustices and oppressive measures. Governor Campbell accused Bāvanna Pandit, also known as Bava, of being responsible for all losses in Tanjore. Tulāji had appointed him, an ordinary man, as Tanjore's prime minister (*sirkeel*). Campbell also alleged that Bāvanna Pandit did not permit the court of justice to function for an extended period. To remedy the situation, Campbell advised Ameer Singh to choose "five honest, able, discreet men" as civil heads of the administrative districts, who, in turn, would work for the welfare and happiness of the people. He even suggested five persons: "Sembuga Pandiden" had already served as the inspector of the southern districts. "Manapa" worked in Tiruvarur. The Brahmin Dada was well known. Lala worked in the palace. Finally, Campbell believed that the son of the deceased Dobeer

---

8 Embree: British East India Company Raj, 171. The Company's judges could not codify personal laws that applied to people of various religions and diverse traditions within these religions. They found that these laws were incompatible with British personal laws.

9 John William Kaye: The Administration of the East India Company – A History of Indian Progress. London ²1853, 329.

10 Pearson: Memoirs, Vol. 1, 334–335.

would be a fitting administrator. He required Ameer Singh not to lease any land to anyone and recommended a three-member committee to assess the value of the king's leased properties. This committee should consist of a competent leader, a member whom Ameer Singh would nominate and another member whom Schwartz would propose. Campbell proposed that if agreeable to Ameer Singh, "the Resident of Tanjore may accompany the Reverend Mr Swartz during the valuation." Then, he suggested various reform measures, including withholding support for religious priests and mendicants who received their sustenance from various charity organisations.[11] On the same day, April 10, 1787, he handed over to Ameer Singh the Regulations for the Court of Judicature at Tanjore, which Schwartz had previously drafted. The text below reproduces the original English:

> 1) To introduce a better System of Justice at Tanjore, the Court in which the Judges are to sit ought to be an open place to which every person, whether rich or poor, may have free and ready access.
> 2) Four respectable persons of tried abilities and integrity ought to be appointed to hear the people's complaints and to decide upon them according to Law and strict impartial Justice.
> 3) The judges should have competent salary to put them above the meanness and infamy of accepting any bribe – such, who shall dare to disgrace the character of an upright judge by taking any fee or reward on account of their judgements, ought to be severely punished and disqualified from ever sitting afterwards as a judge.
> 4) All monies recovered by fines ought to be kept as a separate fund to be applied as your Excellency may think best, but the judges ought never to have any share in it.
> 5) No verbal complaints ought to be listened to. Complainants should write complaints under their proper signatures, imploring justice and stating their names and witnesses.
> 6) Three or four writers should note and regularly record the lawsuits brought by the judges. They ought also to register and pen all supplications for justice.
> 7) The judges should give [...] on the last day of every month a summary of the lawsuits that came before them and their decisions upon them.
> 8) When any person is convicted of bribery, the punishment should be exemplary and public.
> 9) Expedition should be recommended to the judges in the most peremptory measures when they are tedious in their decisions. A class of people is constrained to quit their cases on this principle: that it is much better to give them hopes of success than to incur the most enormous expense by tedious delay.
> 10) No intercession of great men or less of the women of the palace should be received by the judges, for justice and truth should prevail untainted with the threats and supplications of others.
>
> This last article has been so shamefully neglected that the judges have often declared that they could not do common justice because such powerful advocates support the great criminals.[12]

Campbell asked Ameer Singh to follow these guidelines and improve the socio-economic conditions of his subjects. He also advised that "if any two contending parties should agree to have their affair decided by arbitration, they should have full permission to do so." Then, he referred to Daniel Pillay, the well-known interpreter at the Danish government in Tranquebar. Schwartz must have

---

11 IOR/P/252/16, 74–82.

12 IOR/P/252/16, 83–85; AFSt/M 1 C 29 a : 5: On 01.02.1788, Schwartz mentioned to Schulze that he had drafted these guidelines at the request of Archibald Campbell.

recommended his friend Daniel Pillay to Archibald Campbell. Hence, Campbell advised Ameer Singh to appoint Daniel Pillay, "who is at the head of the Law" under Governor Abbestée at Tranquebar. Campbell characterised Daniel Pillay as "so respectable" that Ameer Singh should appoint him "the head of your judges here, even for twelve months, as he would arrange the proceedings in your Law Courts" satisfactorily.[13] An unnamed employee of the Company in Madras, who had summarised the official proceedings about Tanjore, stated that Campbell proposed to appoint Daniel Pillay as the head of the Court of Judicature and five Indian leaders as the heads of each Subah. This summary reiterated Campbell's advice to regularise the salaries of palace employees and to reduce subsidies for charities, where priests and *fakirs* (e.g., "Ashraff Shah") did not engage in gainful work.[14]

9.1.4 Ameer Singh's Failure

According to Hemingway, Ameer Singh disregarded these suggestions for two reasons: firstly, the judges of Tanjore raised their own salaries and incidental expenses by levying a five percent fee on all claims of money and a fine on real property in dispute. Secondly, the judges could not function effectively because the contending parties were engaged in different arbitrations. Most influential persons received bribes and made recommendations on behalf of their parties. Contending parties who lived in far-off districts (*zilla*) approached their regional arbitrators (*zilladars*) rather than coming to the judges in the city of Tanjore. The regional arbitrators bypassed the judges and sent their reports directly to Ameer Singh.[15]

On 1 February 1788, Schwartz informed Schulze that Ameer Singh agreed orally to establish a law court according to Schwartz's plan, which Campbell had endorsed.[16] However, Ameer Singh ignored Schwartz's plan for a law court and remained faithful to his system, which was favourable to the Company's traders, renters, and officers, who freely stole the wealth of Tanjore and vanished. They failed to make any contributions to local development. Schwartz could not tolerate these Europeans, who professed to be Christians yet did not practice Christian virtues towards the local people. Their hypocritical lifestyle pained Schwartz considerably.

Schwartz informed Governor Petrie in Madras about Ameer Singh's failure. Consequently, Petrie recommended on 3 November 1788 the necessity of administering justice in all aspects of Ameer Singh's transactions. He informed the Company in Madras of Ameer Singh's willingness to allow Schwartz to superintend the proceedings of the Court of Justice in Tanjore. Accordingly, the Court should prepare a weekly report of all proceedings and give it to Schwartz for examination. He could then forward this report and his views to the Resident,

---

13 IOR/P/252/16, 85.
14 IOR/H/571, 197.
15 Madras District Gazetteer—Tanjore, 202.
16 AFSt/M 1 C 29 a : 5.

who would apprise the Company in Madras. Additionally, Petrie ascertained that Shiva Row, the most senior administrator in Ameer Singh's government, was responsible for various transactions. Replacing him with more capable men like Baba was difficult because Ameer Singh defended Shiva Row and disliked Baba. Petrie pleaded to honour Ameer Singh's sentiments for the time being. Instead, he proposed improvements in agricultural production, civil administration, and the functioning of the Court of Justice.[17]

9.1.5 Schwartz's Interventions

As injustices and exploitations increased, Schwartz became restless. In 1789, he condemned Ameer Singh's failure to address these injustices and reported them to the Company in Madras. Consequently, this board dispatched Petrie to supervise legal matters. Upon arrival, Petrie persuaded Ameer Singh to dismiss his minister, Shiva Row, who, as the sirkeel, had caused much of the suffering in Tanjore. He also convinced Ameer Singh to establish a Court of Justice and asked Schwartz to supervise its day-to-day activities. Thus, Schwartz actively represented justice and embodied Tanjore's public consciousness.

Over time, Ameer Singh failed his people and continued his oppressive measures. In February 1790, Schwartz drew up eighteen specific principles of justice and gave them to the Company's Resident, who forwarded them to the Company in Madras.[18] On behalf of Tanjore's inhabitants, on 20 August 1790, Schwartz urged Governor John Holland and the Company in Madras to administer justice to the ordinary people and prevent all exploitation. The opening words of his letter illustrate how he had identified himself with his adopted country:

> Permit me humbly to address you on behalf of this country, of which you are constituted guardians and defenders and whose prosperity or distress you are concerned. Every government is to be supported by a rational administration of justice, without which the king and subjects cannot prosper. This proposition needs no proof, being self-evident. All nations confirm it, at least in theory; experience, nay, all history, gives us the strongest proof that a country without justice is a ruined country.[19]

Schwartz further explained the reasons for his well-considered intervention: a few years prior, he could not tolerate Tulāji's cruel treatment of his subjects, who had no recourse to a court of justice. They hated how he, through his officers, habitually deceived and oppressed them, and accordingly, they stopped trusting

---

17 IOR/P/252/28, 3292–3299.

18 Pearson: Memoirs, Vol. 2, 190: When Resident George Andrew Ram forwarded these guidelines to his superiors in Madras, he expressed that "the want of such regulations is daily before my eyes. Any man in the Tanjore country (who has the power) ties up and tortures whomsoever he pleases, on the most frivolous pretences."

19 T Vol. 3449 A, 23–26; Pearson: Memoirs, Vol. 2, 191. Robert Fulton's statement: "The foundation of our empire in India rests on the principle of justice and England retains its supremacy in India mainly by justice. Without justice we could not hold India for a moment," quoted in J. T. Sunderland: India in Bondage: Her Right to Freedom. New York 1929, 105.

him. Therefore, at one time, Tulāji empowered Schwartz "to publish his promise in writing and to be responsible for its accomplishment." Consequently, "the people rejoiced and returned from their emigration to their native country." Though the sowing season had passed, they hurried to cultivate their lands. They averted a famine and harvested a rich crop. Just after Tulāji's death and just before Ameer Singh's enthronement, Schwartz discussed with Governor Campbell the urgent necessity for an impartial administration of justice. Campbell agreed with Schwartz and requested him to draft a plan to administer justice according to the laws and customs of the local inhabitants.[20]

Campbell requested that Schwartz draft guiding principles and supervise the court proceedings. Schwartz noted that the judges could not function freely because Ameer Singh's agents constantly interfered, preventing them from carrying out their work impartially. Schwartz named the atrocities of the moneylender Ciṉṉaiyā Mudali as intimidating, confining, and physically harming those who stood up for justice.[21] These injustices corrupted the judges. Revenue collectors forced the farmers to pay exorbitant rent for their fields. Worse yet, they did not even wait for the harvest. The judges' negligence in performing their public duties in a just manner plunged many farmers into deeper debt.[22] Finally, Schwartz intervened on Serfoji's behalf due to Ameer Singh's mistreatment of him. Schwartz urged the Company in Madras to protect Serfoji and concluded his letter with this wise statement: A regular and impartial administration, according to "the laws of the Hindoos, would enhance Ameer Singh's happiness, the Company's honour and the quality of life of Tanjore inhabitants. Schwartz hoped that the Company in Madras would approve of his plan because, like his contemporaries in Tanjore, he, too, lived "under the protection of the English Government."[23]

The following selection of Schwartz's eighteen principles of justice is noteworthy:[24] 1) Ameer Singh should empower these judges "to decide all complaints according to justice." 2) The Court of Justice should be in an open room separate from the palace. One or two soldiers should be stationed at its entrance. The present room, located in a corner of the palace, was notorious for its corruption and bribery. The palace officers were the "mortal enemies to equity

---

20 T Vol. 3449 A, 23–24.

21 Pearson: Memoirs, Vol. 2, 193: The dubashes lent money to Ameer Singh and acted as his master. They could confine and punish anyone. They manipulated justice and emerged as winners. The practice of justice collapsed in Tanjore. Ciṉṉappā Mutali, the most significant moneylender to Ameer Singh, committed unjust acts. Even Ameer Singh's diwan Shiva Rao could not do anything to stop him. Once he sighed: "What can I do when Chinnia intercedes for the unjust party?"'

22 Pearson: Memoirs, Vol. 2, 194: Farmers could not cultivate their lands; those who could cultivate found it challenging to protect the fields from natural calamities and robberies. Most farmers were fed up with the broken promises of their rulers. For example, before the farmers could harvest, they were required to pay half of their taxes. They borrowed money from preying dubashes at exorbitant interest. They could not repay their capital and the annual interest of 12 percent. "No country, though the most fertile, can bear such oppression."

23 T Vol. 3449 A, 26.

24 Pearson: Memoirs, Vol. 2, 196–200.

and justice." 3) The judges should be familiar with the "customs of this country and its laws."[25] Otherwise, even an honest judge, "without much knowledge of their laws, would be very improper to decide in their disputes." 4) Judges should not accept bribes. 16) The Court of Justice should regulate the rate of interest because "taking high interest and premiums" had already ruined many families. Other rules specify the roles of writers, accountants, and other minor officers necessary for speedy hearings on behalf of all contending parties. They demonstrate how Schwartz was far ahead of his time. He did not reveal the sources of his legal insights. He likely received help from William Chambers, the brother of Robert Chambers, the Chief Justice of Calcutta and the Company's Persian translator in Calcutta. As discussed in Section 5.15, William Chamber was Schwartz's admirer and follower.

Neither the Company in Madras nor Ameer Singh acted on Schwartz's recommendations. On 8 May 1790, Schwartz wrote that Ameer Singh had entrusted the administration of his country and the collection of revenues to five or six "rapacious agents," who oppressed and impoverished the "100,000 people" because Ameer Singh was unable to read or calculate. Ameer Singh's diwan, Shiva Rao, cheated him mostly. Schwartz felt that God did not create Tanjore's inhabitants to enrich the few rapacious Indian agents and European moneylenders of the Company unjustly.[26]

Upset with the mounting exploitation, Schwartz recommended that the Company in Madras appoint Baba, a former sirkeel, as the inspector of all revenues and their accounts. Baba was not without mistakes. When he was the head (*subaidar*) of a region (*subah*), he committed crimes, but later repented; he was familiar with the local villages, regions, systems, and customs. Therefore, other agents could not easily cheat him. Schwartz also urged the Company in Madras to establish a court of justice where people could lodge their complaints and receive impartial judgments. The Company officers in Madras and Tanjore, along with Ameer Singh and his agents, were unconcerned with the welfare of the people. By contrast, Schwartz was worried about the welfare of the whole population of Tanjore.

Schwartz's firm commitment to establishing a properly functioning court of justice is evident in his continuous efforts. On 29 January 1790, he shared a copy of his draft proposal entitled "Establishing a Court of Justice at Tanjore and inferior *Cutcharee* Courts in the Districts." His dedication to this cause is truly inspiring.[27]

---

25 Like Schwartz, Wilks also underscored the importance of upholding the local customs that defined their identity. Mark Wilks: Report on the Interior Administration, Resources and Expenditure of the Government of Mysoor under the system prescribed by the Orders of the Governor General in Council dated 4th September 1799. Fort William 1805, 22: The Company administrators should pay close attention to "the ancient institutions of the country; and to the doctrines of the Hindoo law," especially to the established precedents known as *mamūl* ('customary usages') in dispensing justice.

26 IOR/P/252/45, 1644–50 quoted in Pearson: Memoirs, Vol. 2, 201–204.

27 IOC/P/252/52, 5484–5485: On 04.12.1790, Residents Ram and Fallowfield forwarded Schwartz's proposal to John Charmier, the Military Secretary of the Company in Madras. They highlighted how Schwartz set forth "the advantages that would result from a more

Eleven months later, on 28 November 1790, he forwarded the same draft to Ram and Fallowfield. The first paragraph of this draft states that "an impartial administration of justice" is necessary for a country's "prosperity and happiness." As soon as the Company began managing the affairs of Tanjore in September 1790, "the Inhabitants entertained the hope that a more regular system of Justice would be introduced." The circumstances were an opportune time for the Company to fulfil their expectation by establishing a Court of Justice in Tanjore and Cutcherry Courts in adjoining districts. Contemporary arbitration practices were insufficient to do justice to those who were "deprived of their houses, fields, or property through the oppression of those in power," as the arbitrators' decisions lacked legal validity. The existing Cutcherry Courts were inefficient in handling weighty matters. The new legal system of justice must be based on the established laws of the Country or its ancient Customs, which have obtained the sanction of a Law. To introduce European Laws would confuse and inconvenience people, thus creating a general uneasiness throughout the Country.[28]

9.1.6 Schwartz's Sensitivity to Local Etiquette

Schwartz's respect for local etiquette in legal matters, shared by allies like the orientalist Nathaniel Brassey Halhed (1751–1830) and Judge Francis Workman-McNaughton (1763–1843), demonstrates his cultural sensitivity. His proposal to follow local laws and customs in settling court matters not only helped the people of Tanjore protect their customary laws and practices but also fostered a renewed awareness of their cultural heritage.[29] Schwartz's draft required that the judges be upright, disinterested, and qualified for office; their goal should be "the welfare of the Country." Then Schwartz introduced a judge in Tranquebar, his friend Daniel Pillay, as a competent judge:

> One person I am acquainted with, of uncorrupted morals and disinterested principles [...,] is a Christian and [he] has been employed as a judge at Tranquebar for these 25 years. He is indeed in the service of the Danish Government. However, the governor of Tranquebar would willingly permit him to assist, at least for some time, in the Establishment and necessary regulating of a court. For this man's integrity, I will be responsible. He was once sent to Tanjore by the Danish Government, and at that time, many people chose him as an arbitrator in their tedious suits and willingly submitted to his decision. His being a Christian would be no objection to his being employed, as there are even Brahmins willing to acknowledge him a capable and good man.[30]

---

regular administration of Justice being introduced into this Country." The Company in Madras discussed this proposal on 24.12.1790.

28 IOC/P/252/52, 5487 quoted in Pearson: Memoirs, Vol. 2, 223.

29 P. Perumal: The Sanskrit Manuscripts in Tamilnadu. In: Aspects of Manuscript Culture in South India. Ed. by Saraju Rath. Leiden 2012, 157–172, here 165: Serfoji composed religious works entitled *Kumārasaṁbhavacampu*, *Mohinīmaheśa-pariṇaya* and *Rādhākṛṣṇavilāsa-nāṭaka*. He appointed to his Court of Justice those pandits who were well versed in *Dharmaśāstra*. These judges "compiled *Vyavahāra-prakāśa* from various *smṛti* texts for day-to-day use in the conduct of administration and justice."

30 IOC/P/252/52, 5487–5488 quoted in Pearson: Memoirs, Vol. 2, 224.

Schwartz's draft concludes with an earnest plea for an impartial administration of justice. He believed that the change of government in Tanjore provided an opportune time to introduce this change for the better. He expected the Company in Madras to concur with his opinion and support the "necessary and useful undertaking."[31] August Friedrich Cämmerer, who stayed with Schwartz to learn the Tamil language in 1791, mentioned two additional matters where Schwartz served as an adjudicator. Once, two temple priests lured a young boy "splendidly adorned with gold and precious stones" into a temple, took the jewels and killed him. When this murder came to the attention of the Company officers in Madras, they requested Schwartz to "investigate this horrid deed. He accordingly examined the murderers in the king's palace and brought them to confess the crime. They were afterwards executed."[32]

The second instance involved Schwartz's attempts to abolish the age-old practice of *satī* among those within his sphere of influence. Cämmerer reported in 1791 that he had seen Schwartz conversing with an aged, landed Brahmin in Kumbakonam. At his death, his wife immolated herself on his funeral pyre. She presumed that she would thus go with her husband into heaven (*svarga*) instead of suffering the social stigma of being a widow (considered a *muṇṭam*, a 'headless body,' an angry wandering spirit). Cämmerer believed that if Schwartz had known the woman's intention to commit *satī* beforehand, he would have exerted "his utmost influence to prevent it."[33]

9.1.7 Schwartz's Opposition to the Company's Extortion

As an ardent proponent of justice, Schwartz opposed the Company's plan to allow renters to occupy Tanjore and extort high rents from farmers and others who used their lands. He feared that the renters would make the lives of ordinary people miserable. Notably, he disliked the Madras dubashes, who, as renters, were crueller than Machiavelli's ubiquitous schemes. Schwartz believed that the oppressive behaviour of the renters was so immoral that they could never render justice to anyone. They looted the people of Tanjore by imposing heavy taxes, taking away their lands and villages, and even driving them out of their native places.[34]

Hemingway, the accomplished editor of a gazetteer on Tanjore, acknowledged Schwartz's "approach to a systematic administration of civil justice" before the

---

31 IOC/P/252/52, 5488 quoted in Pearson: Memoirs, Vol. 2, 225.

32 Pearson: Memoirs, Vol. 2, 247.

33 Pearson: Memoirs, Vol. 2, 248. Cämmerer would have known how the English Colonel Lyttleton, a follower of Schwartz in Tanjore, saved Clarinda (1746–1806), a Maratha Brahmin widow, from the funeral pyre. He would have also known Tulāji's widows who chose to live.

34 Pearson: Memoirs, Vol. 2, 215–216: Dubashes and renters managed Tanjore. They and their friends wanted to extract money from the inhabitants. If they could not pay, they took away their possessions. Most of these victims lodged their complaints with Schwartz. Using force and fraudulent methods, some dubashes obtained two to six villages. Schwartz warned the

British acquired Tanjore and appointed British Commissioners in 1798.[35] Schwartz knew that his stand on justice would have costly consequences for his Christian followers. On 15 October 1795, he reported that after the Company had transferred the administration of justice from the regional arbitrators (*zilladar*s and *patakakkārar*s) to Ameer Singh's officers. These officers made the lives of many Christians in the countryside miserable and wrested their land from them."[36]

On 7 July 1796, Schwartz expressed his distress to Schulze in Halle and stated that the Court of Directors in London had accepted his principles for administering law and justice in Tanjore. Consequently, the Company and Ameer Singh had transferred some persons to establish law and order in Tanjore. These individuals did not take their work seriously because they were motivated by selfish and greedy interests. Schwartz found it challenging to combat the systemic corruption within the Company. The appointed officers discarded the concerns, miseries and cries of low-income people. Schwartz wondered whether the "faithless and godless" Europeans would bring God's judgment on Tanjore.[37]

9.2 Upholding the King's Dignity

Following the attacks by Hyder Ali and Tipu Sultan on various parts of the Kingdom of Tanjore in the 1780s, the social, political, and economic conditions in Tanjore deteriorated significantly for its people. Many British traders and others loaned money to Nawab Wallajah at a high interest rate. When he was unable to pay the loan and its interest, he gave them large strips of land. These greedy British creditors extorted high taxes from the farmers, impoverishing them.[38] During this time, Tulāji's son, the prospective successor to the throne of Tanjore, passed away, and Tulāji became so depressed that he neglected the welfare of the people. On 15 October 1785, Schwartz described Tulāji's deplorable condition: He could not pay the annual tribute of 400,000 Pagodas to the Company, and the Company pressured him to pay all arrears. For instance, in 1785, the Company required him to transfer 600,000 Pagodas into their treasury annually. As the Company

Company officers that these deceitful dubashes and renters hindered formal enquiries. He advocated the establishment of a court of justice.

35 Hemingway: Madras District Gazetteer—Tanjore, 58.

36 Memoirs of the Rev. Joseph D[aniel] Jænicke, 125.

37 AFSt/M 1 C 37a : 66 = not mentioned in NHR 5, 1797, issue 51, 284–285. Hemingway: Madras District Gazetteer—Tanjore, 202–203: Schwartz's dream came true eight years after he died in 1806. The Company established the first District Court in Kumbakonam and appointed a collector to look after it. This court was bifurcated to meet the growing judicial need, and another Zilla Court was established in Tranquebar in 1860. This branch court in Tranquebar was moved to Tanjore in 1884 and became the District Court.

38 Tulāji, too, borrowed money from various British creditors. For example, according to a report of the Court of Directors dated 12.04.1786 (IOR/E/4/872, 343–343), during the outbreak of war between the Company and Hyder Ali in the 1780s, Tulāji borrowed from British creditors "3 Lakhs and a half of Pagodas, or thereabout; and that the sums so due were bonafide lent to be punctual in the payment of this annual subsidy to the Company." By 30 October 1781, this debt and its interest amounted to six lakhs Pagodas.

oppressed Tulāji, Tulāji oppressed his people with high taxes. Schwartz wondered how long this oppression would continue.[39]

On 31 October 1785, Schwartz informed Resident John Hudleston about a significant loan he had made to King Tulāji. This loan was a crucial support for his Indian soldiers, who had planned a mutiny due to unpaid wages. With the consent of the vestry members of his former church in Tiruccirāppaḷḷi, Schwartz borrowed 2,500 Porto Novo Pagodas, loaning the money to King Tulāji at an annual interest rate of 12% during the war and 10% during times of peace. The former resident, John Sulivan, witnessed this transaction. After the war ended, Schwartz asked Hudleston to pay him both the capital and its interest. Hudleston agreed to pay an annual interest of 8%. Immediately, Schwartz requested that he forward his request for a 12% interest to the Company in Madras, so that he could help the orphan children.[40] John Chamier, the Military Superintendent of the Company in Madras, played a crucial role in Schwartz's request. He considered it favourably and recommended the capital with interest, thereby showing the Company's support for Schwartz's initiative.[41] W.C. Jackson, the Company's attorney, deeply appreciated Schwartz's financial assistance to Tulāji. His recognition of Schwartz's efforts led him to reward him with a higher interest rate. On 9 November 1785, he instructed Hudleston to exchange Schwartz's bonds at 8% interest. He stated further that Schwartz aided Tulāji, who was, at that time, unable "to pay his subsidy" to his soldiers. Therefore, he asked Hudleston to get

---

39 AFSt/M 1 C 26 : 3.

40 T Vol. 3443 B, 659–661: "To J[ohn] Hudleston Esq., Resident at Tanjore, Sir, Permit me to lay before you a case, wherein I am concerned & which has caused some uneasiness in the minds of others. During the war, our Sepoys could not be regularly paid. A mutiny was dreaded; nay, in some degree, it began. I, seeing the calamity coming upon this place, offered to procure the orphan money, which was in the hands of the vestry at Tiruchirapally, provided the Company would pay the same interest, which the vestry had received hitherto, viz. 12 per cent. Mr Sulivan engaged in using his best endeavours to procure that interest and promised to beseech the Honourable Board after the war was ended, either to give a Bond at 10 per cent or to pay off the Capital. But when I applied to you, Sir, to be so kind as to pay the interest, you told me that you were not authorized to pay more than 8 per cent on the 2500 Porto Novo Pagodas. I declared to you my apprehension that, in this case, the vestry would not be able to maintain the usual number of Children. As the vestry lent the money upon my mentioning the promise made by Mr. Sulivan, the members of it are not only disappointed, but what is more, the orphans will suffer. I therefore humbly entreat you to represent this case to the Honorable Board in the best manner, hoping they will consider the necessities of the Orphans and decide it in favour of them. I am respectfully, Sir, Your most obedient servant, C.F. Swartz. Tanjore, October 31, 1785."

41 T Vol. 3443 B, 667–8: "I [John Chamier] have the honour to present you a copy of a letter, which I have received from the Reverend Mr. Swartz on the subject of his loan to the late Resident of 2,500 Star Pagodas belonging to the Church at Trichinopoley. Because of the peculiar circumstances under which the money was lent on a promise made to Mr. Swartz by Mr. Sulivan, now the Hon'ble Board will permit one to allow interest upon it at the rate of 12 per cent during the War and 10 per cent from the period of the conclusion of the Peace, as requested by Mr. Swartz. I enclose Mr. Sulivan's note, the Vestry wishing to have it exchanged for a bond bearing date the 14th October 1785, to which day I shall, with the approbation of the Honourable Board, discharge the interest."

42 T Vol. 3443 B, 661; T Vol. 3443 B, 727: The secretary of the Military Department of the Company in Madras informed Resident John Hudleston in Tanjore of their decision to

an additional 4% interest from Tulāji to pay off all "arrears due to Mr Swartz."[42] Thus, Schwartz assisted Tulāji in maintaining his royal dignity and preventing a mutiny among his soldiers.

9.2.1 By Securing the King's Consent and Ensuring Justice for Farmers

One of Tulāji's ministers oppressed the farmers of Tanjore by extracting additional taxes from them. As a result, most of them stopped cultivating their fields; about 65,000 farmers left Tanjore and settled in other places. Neither Tulāji nor the Company's representatives could persuade them to return. They approached Schwartz for help, their trust in him unwavering. Schwartz's deep empathy towards the plight of the farmers convinced them to return and cultivate their land. They knew he would not desert them. Their response to Schwartz, their beacon of hope, convinced Governor Archibald Campbell to appoint Schwartz in 1786 as a voting member of the Inspection Committee of Tanjore. This decision gave the committee members "a sense of security."[43]

Schwartz was pivotal in ensuring that this Committee recognised Tulāji's authority and dignity, securing the King's position and influence.[44] By then, he had sufficiently addressed the needs of the farmers. If any members began supervising the farmers, their actions would offend the king. Therefore, along with Hudleston, Schwartz opposed any attempt by the Inspection Committee "which might unnecessarily irritate the rajah [king] or infringe upon those principles of justice by which the British government ought to be actuated upon all occasions."[45]

On 2 October 1786, Schwartz informed Pasche about the Committee of Inspection and how he persuaded it to wait until he had spoken with the king; otherwise, this Committee would undermine his authority and dignity. Schwartz discussed with the king the urgency of inviting the "emigrants," who had left Tanjore for distinct reasons, to return to Tanjore. He promised the king that he would act not in the name of the Committee of Inspection but in his capacity as the friend of the king and the people of Tanjore. The king, in turn, entrusted Schwartz with a significant task, authorising him to interact with the emigrants on his behalf.[46] Consequently, Schwartz drafted a moving, undated letter to Governor Archibald Campbell revealing his passionate, well-considered determination to defend Tulāji's dignity and to maximise the benefit for Tanjore's inhabitants:

---

exchange Schwartz's loan for Company bonds at the usual annual interest rate of 8%. They believed that Schwartz's loan aided King Tulāji, who was unable to pay his subsidy at the time. Hence, the Company directed Hudleston to ask King Tulāji to pay Schwartz an additional annual interest of 4% and "to liquidate the claim conformably to his opinion."

43 This committee consisted of Schwartz, Resident John Hudleston, Major John Stuart and Paymaster John Coxe Hippisley.

44 Germann: Missionar Christian Friedrich Schwartz, 342.

45 Pearson: Memoirs, Vol. 2, 117.

46 AFSt/M 1 C 27 : 8.

> To the Honourable Sir Archibald Campbell, President and Governor
> Convinced of the multiplicity of your important business, I have hitherto refrained from troubling you with my writing. But, as you have mentioned [of] me twice in your letter, written to Mr Hudleston, [… it would be ingratitude on my part to remain silent], particularly as you have been pleased to desire me to sit in the Committee as an honorary member. [… I would be happy], if I were able to contribute anything in the smallest degree to the welfare of the poor inhabitants of this country to the satisfaction of Raja and honour of the Company. I rejoiced when I read in the orders given by you to the Committee to take care, not to hurt the feelings of the Raja. This line comforted me in the midst of my apprehensions that by the Committee, the dignity and authority might be taken from the Raja, which would have affected me very much. Not as if I looked upon the 3 members of that Committee, [… as the Raja did]. Far from it. But I dreaded the poor Raja's disposition. Being educated by people who constantly flatter his vanity, he is become impatient of hearing [the] plain truth. This dangerous disposition, I feared, might induce the Committee to propose coercive means. He has suffered greatly in his life. He is now, as it seems, almost a candidate for eternity. Let me, Honourable Sir, beseech you in the humblest manner to let him depart in peace.
> If I had the honour of conversing with you for an hour, I should use the freedom, which your generous heart would willingly grant to me, […to] lay open what I now must keep in my heart. This much I may say: Should this country [not] be governed by gentlemen, it must, of course, become a prey to the rapaciousness of dubashes. Woe to that country. I have seen so much of it that I shall take the afflicting thoughts into the grave. In order to fulfil your benevolent desire, which is not to hurt the feelings of the Raja, I offered myself to wait on the Raja to induce him by all possible arguments to treat his inhabitants better. The result of which you will hear from the contents of that conversation. May almighty God make you a glorious instrument for promoting the welfare of this country.[47]

This persuasive letter demonstrates Schwartz's respect and humility toward individuals in positions of power and appeals to their sense of justice and benevolence. His manner of defending the king's dignity, meeting with him, ensuring maximum benefit for ordinary people, and honesty in telling the truth with a tempered tone is noteworthy. He believed that the Company, as a considerate government, would work for the welfare of the long-suffering inhabitants in Tanjore.

In this Committee, Schwartz must have had a tough time; Major John Stuart was the same person who had arrested Pigot, who opposed the restoration of Tulāji to his throne and sided with Nawab Wallajah. Schwartz, however, attempted to uphold the best interests of ordinary people as much as possible. He was deeply concerned about the dignity and welfare of Tulāji on the one hand and the just treatment of the farmers on the other. Finally, Tulāji and the members of the Committee authorised Schwartz to deal with the farmers. The farmers, in turn, trusted Schwartz, returned to Tanjore, and cultivated the land.[48] The plentiful harvest of that year delighted the Company. This success impressed the Company

---

47 Bodleian Library: 72290ind-box2, Document 12 without a date: Schwartz to Archibald Campbell.

48 Pearson: Memoirs, Vol. 2, 120: Tulāji feared the consequences of the Company taking over the Tanjore administration and reluctantly announced specific reforms. Ordinary people did not trust his words, so he requested that Schwartz intercede on behalf of the emigrants. At his word, seven thousand emigrants returned, and others followed them. They knew that the best season for sowing seeds was over. Nevertheless, they replied to Schwartz: "As you have shown kindness to us, we intend to work night and day to manifest our regard for you." Their hard and sincere labour yielded a more abundant harvest than in the previous years.

officers in Madras so profoundly that they appointed him as their translator and awarded him an annual salary of £100, along with £20 for his transportation. They also asked Hudleston to convey to Schwartz their highest respect. They wished that under Schwartz's guidance, Tulāji and his people would flourish. Some people stated that they had "a prospect of seeing this country better managed, that is, with more justice, it is to be hoped that it will have a beneficial effect upon the people." Even during his public activities, Schwartz spoke with people about the Lord Jesus Christ and the eternal salvation He offered to all those who trusted Him.[49]

9.2.2 By Trying to Remove the Rapacious Dubashes

Raghavan, who edited the *Sarva-Deva-Vilāsa*, asserted that the Company conducted its business through several "local gentlemen of standing" whom they referred to as Indian dubashes. The governor, officers in the military and commercial departments of the Company and all other notable Europeans had their Indian dubashes as their trusted private agents.[50] However, it was not easy for them to find Indian dubashes who were fluent in Tamil, Telugu, Marathi, Persian, and English. Ordinary people in Madras spoke Tamil or Telugu. The rulers and elites of Tanjore communicated in Marathi. All those who dealt with Nawab Wallajah and other Muslim elites conversed in Persian. The English relied on their Indian dubashes, who lacked sophisticated and nuanced knowledge of the English language. They did not fully understand other Indian languages. An English person often spoke with an Indian dubash who knew only Persian. This Indian dubash spoke with another Indian dubash who knew Persian and Tamil. This second Indian dubash talked to the third Indian dubash, who was fluent in Persian, Tamil, or Marathi. Thus, the sequence of translation remained complex. Most of the time, the English and their translators did not fully understand each other. On 10 October 1776, a Company officer recorded the difficulty of finding a competent Indian dubash:

> There is no person about Mr Stratton but the Vakeel, who speaks the Maratta language, and he cannot converse in English on the most common subject. He renders the Maratta letters into Malabars, from which they are translated into very bad English by a Brahmin of my acquaintance, and they corrected by Mr Stratton himself; so sensible was this gentleman of the faults in translation they were subject to by coming through so many hands, that he was at last obliged to trust the Vakeel's own account of them, as appears by his letter to the Rajah.[51]

Tulāji's dubashes, also known as *vakkīls*, "Triumbuch Sambajee and Rudragee Punt," wrote their letters in Marathi and sent them to William Ross, the Company's official interpreter in Madras, who was fluent in English and Tamil. Hence,

---

49 Pearson: Memoirs, Vol. 2, 121.

50 Raghavan: The Sarva-Deva-Vilāsa, 70. Dubashi Kaliṅgarāja was so influential that the English feared him. Dubashi Colla Ravanappa Chetti was a wizard in dealing with the English. In addition to these people, the Company recruited Brahmins, "a wizard in dealing with the English." Besides these people, the Company recruited Brahmin dubashis, such as the highly learned Giryappa and Venkaṭanātha, for various kinds of work.

51 IOR/T 663. Extract of a letter from a Gentleman at Fort St. George, 2.

someone who knew Marathi and Tamil translated Tulāji's Marathi letters into Tamil, and Ross translated them into English. Nobody could vouch for the accuracy of their translations.[52] In any case, Indian dubashes, without whom the Company officers could not engage with Indians, held significant power. They could either make or break any transaction, and their positions in the Company administration remained unchallenged. They determined what the British should know and what they should not. They also explained to the British the ways of extracting more taxes from their fellow Indians. Schwartz knew how these Indian dubashes in Madras tricked the British and opposed them.

For instance, on 8 May 1790, Schwartz wrote a detailed letter to Resident Andrew Ram, expressing his reservations about the Company's desire to collect four-fifths (i.e. 80%) of Tanjore's revenues.[53] He lamented that Ameer Singh lacked reading and calculating skills. Hence, Sirkeel Shiva Rao, who as Madras dubash, exploited him. Schwartz concluded that Shiva Rao had "neither intellect nor integrity." He had thwarted Schwartz's plan for a better civil administration and the establishment of a new court system in Tanjore. Shiva Rao persuaded Ameer Singh to disregard the charitable deeds of his deceased brother, Tulāji, to the farmers, and to impose additional taxes on them. As a result, more revenue came into Tanjore's treasury. However, Shiva Rao squandered it. He sent his servants to collect more money from the impoverished inhabitants. With profound empathy for the ordinary people, Schwartz explained the situation to Andrew Ram as follows:

> [Ameer Singh had delivered Tanjore's management to] five or six rapacious dubashes. These people, having lent some money to the Rajah, exercise a most arbitrary power in confining and beating the inhabitants and employing their creatures. The inhabitants are obliged to take the *circar*'s share of paddy and to pay 4 Fano for a kalam when they can hardly sell it for 3 Fano. The money which the inhabitants are to pay for the circar's share of paddy was formerly collected in April. However, now it is exacted 2 or 3 months before. The inhabitants, not having ready money, are directed to borrow that money from the *dubashes* or those are connected with them. They pay 8, 9 and even 10 per cent premium and 3 or 4 per cent per month interest. This money is afterwards exacted by the peons to whom the poor inhabitants must pay *batta*. All this is done in contradiction to the orders of taking no more than 12 per cent. Not being able to bear such an oppression the inhabitants have often quitted their houses. Even a few days [later] many of the principal people addressed you [Resident Andrew Ram] and [are] imploring the Company's protection. The present Sirkeel Shivarow has neither intellect nor integrity to manage the country. The revenue is spent or squandered away so that at least they can give no account of it. As the Rajah is not versed in reading and arithmetic, he knows nothing but what his servants or minions are pleased to tell him.[54]

Fed up with this mismanagement and being empathetic to the suffering people of Tanjore, Schwartz pleaded to contain the dubashes. Their mismanagement plunged the country into a state of melancholy. Schwartz estimated that Ameer Singh could not pay 760,000 Pagodas from May 1790 to June 1791. He could borrow enough

52 IOR/T 663. Extract of a letter from a Gentleman at Fort St. George, 11–13.
53 IOR/P/252/45, 1644–1650.
54 IOR/P/252/45, 1644–1645.

money from his greedy dubashes and pay off his dues to the Company. However, Schwartz feared that Ameer Singh would impose more taxes on ordinary people. He wrote he trembled "at the consequences, as the poor inhabitants must pay all the exorbitant interest on those advanced sums." He feared that Ameer Singh's borrowing money from dubashes would not help the "welfare of the country and the dignity of the Rajah." Then, Schwartz made a startling statement: "Surely, so many as 100,000 were not created to satisfy the rapaciousness of plundering dubashes."[55]

Schwartz suggested a better way of administering Tanjore. He proposed dismissing the senior administrators, such as Shiva Rao and Shankar Rao, whom Ameer Singh had employed, and appointing more experienced and knowledgeable officers, like Baba. Earlier, Baba was unfaithful towards Tulāji. But by now, Baba had realised his past mistakes, repented, and expressed his willingness to work for the betterment of Tanjore.[56] Schwartz felt that the repentant Baba would demonstrate more integrity and compassion than Shiva Rao,[57] and as the Sirkeel of Tanjore, he could contain the activities of the rapacious dubashes.[58] Schwartz knew how Baba was acquainted with the conditions, cultivation practices and produce of every village in Tanjore and could inspect all of them. He was

55 IOR/P/252/45, 1646 quoted in Pearson: Memoirs, Vol. 2, 202.

56 IOR/P/252/26, 2393: On 30 August 1788, William Petrie wrote to Archibald Campbell: "From the universal complaints of the inhabitants of this place and the neighbouring districts of the most flagitious abuses in the administration of Justice [by Shiva Rao], confirmed by the testimony of Mr Swartz I desired this Gentleman whose sanctity of character is equally respected by natives and Europeans to represent this alarming evil to the Rajah [Ameer Singh] and I have the satisfaction to inform you that a proclamation was this day published which Mr. Swartz is of opinion will be attended with the most beneficial consequences." By recommending Baba to replace Shiva Rao, Schwartz seems to have chosen the lesser evil.

57 IOR/P/252/45, 1649–1650: But On 8 May 1790, Schwartz wrote to Ram: If "the Honorable Board [in Madras] should be pleased to remove Sheverow & Chenniah Moodely from the administration, the Rajah [Ameer Singh] might be persuaded to admit Baba as Inspector of the Revenues. Should those 2 people remain in power, they and their friends would frustrate the design of [the Company] Government [in Tanjore]. But, Sir, how shall they be removed by arguments? That will be impossible. Nothing but a most Peremptory Order, sent by the Government, will or can affect it. If they both were called to the Presidency, all would go well, without any considerable objection or opposition. But having been favoured with a perusal of your letter to the Government, I heartily agree with you in the point of detaining those 2 persons here [in Tanjore] in case their accounts are to be inspected."

58 IOR/H/285A, 880–886: Shiva Rao was a native of Madras. He took his brother Shankar Rao, Ciṉṉaiyā Mudali and another man as his assistants. On 26.02.1787, Ameer Singh removed Sirkeel Baba and appointed Shiva Rao. By 15.01.1790, Shiva Rao and Shankar Rao had squandered public funds and oppressed the inhabitants of Tanjore. To check their atrocities, the Company asked Ameer Singh to dismiss Shiva Rao and appoint "Baupanah" and Ganapathy Subbiah instead. These two men promised the Company they would pay their tributes on time. The Company officers requested Schwartz to superintend "the proceedings of the Court of Justice at Tanjore." Ameer Singh rejected the Company's proposal and protected Shiva Rao. To save Tanjore from total collapse, on 16 September 1790, Ram and Schwartz recommended the reappointment of Baba as the Sirkeel of Tanjore. However, Ameer Singh did not heed their advice. On 21.01.1791, they repeated their recommendation. At that time, Ameer Singh complained to the Company in Madras about Ram and his corrupt dealings. Consequently, the Company required Ameer Singh to consult with Schwartz before writing anything to them.

convinced Baba would usher in a better administration to help the people flourish. Ameer Singh's dignity would be "founded on its proper basis." Therefore, Schwartz urged the Company in Madras to require Ameer Singh to dismiss Shiva Rao, his brother Shankar Row and their friend Ciṉṉaiyā Mudali from the administration of Tanjore. The Company took note of this letter but deferred its response. They wanted to hear the opinion of the Governor General in Calcutta about this matter. In the meantime, they urged Ram to collect the tributes from Ameer Singh.[59] The Company did not like Schwartz's drastic efforts to curb the impact of the exploitative dubashes.

Ameer Singh ignored Schwartz's repeated admonition to hear his subjects' complaints and "restrain the injustice of his servants."[60] Instead of reprimanding them, Ameer Singh trusted his dubashes more than anyone else. In November 1790, Schwartz informed the Company in Madras that Ameer Singh relied on the rapacious dubashes, who managed the country.[61] They enriched themselves by impoverishing the country. They ruined Ameer Singh and then abandoned him. "Surely, they might have extricated him if the least principle of honesty had been in their hearts."[62] Ameer Sing regretted their treachery and was deeply distressed. He could not pay his servants for seven months because his dubashes had spent the money as they wished.

Ameer Singh trusted Shiva Row and his family members more than anyone else. According to Macleod's letter of 19 December 1795 to Governor Hobart, Shiva Row felt emboldened and defied the Company's orders.[63] Schwartz could not tolerate Shiva Row's injustices. On 19 December 1795, he described the complex interdependence between Ameer Singh and Shiva Row. They were not just allies, but also mutually afraid of each other. Shiva Row knew that Ameer Singh had no legal right to the throne and exploited Ameer Singh to benefit himself and his family. Ameer Singh had entrusted the "management of the whole country" to Shiva Rao. Consequently, Shiva Row raised money for Ameer Singh, but he did not pay the salaries of Ameer Singh's employees. He did not provide money to buy fodder for the horses. Ameer Singh's judges accepted bribes and judged in favour of those who gave them more money. People could purchase offices from Shiva Row. He did not hold them responsible for any failures. His employees monopolised trade with cloth, spices, oil and *ghee* (melted butter). His brother Shankar Row made a secret contract with the taxpayers; accordingly, they paid half the taxes to Shankar Row himself. Most inhabitants suffered, but Ameer Singh did not listen to their complaints. Schwartz pleaded with the Company in Madras to emancipate Ameer Singh from the clutches of his dubashes, who had kept him as their "slave" and prevented free trade. The inhabitants grew desperate, and some

59 IOR/P/252/45, 1647–1650 quoted in Pearson: Memoirs, Vol. 2, 202–204.
60 Pearson: Memoirs, Vol. 2, 143.
61 Pearson: Memoirs, Vol. 2, 213–218.
62 Pearson: Memoirs, Vol. 2, 214.
63 IOR/P/253/57, 103.
64 IOR/P/253/57, 105–109.

left Tanjore.[64] Despite Schwartz's impassioned pleas, the Company callously ignored his recommendations, biding their time for an opportunity to seize Tanjore. As Ameer Singh struggled to meet his financial obligations, the Company saw their chance to coerce him into surrendering Tanjore. In the face of this indifference, Schwartz did his utmost to preserve the king's dignity and the welfare of the people.

9.3 Managing Caste Distinctions

9.3.1 Caste as Varṇa and Jāti

The European word 'caste' confusingly represents India's two interrelated socio-religious systems, namely *varṇa* and *jāti*. The system of *varṇa* (lit. 'colour' or 'category') refers to the unchangeably fixed, fourfold socio-religious, political, and economic hierarchy of being human in India, known as *caturvarṇa*.[65] The Brahmins, as priests, teachers, and custodians of professional Sanskrit knowledge, occupy the highest position.[66] Next come the *Kṣatriyas*, who wage wars and govern society on terms set by the Brahmins.[67] The *Vaiśya* constitute the third *varṇa*. They make, own and distribute material wealth.[68] The male individuals of these three *varṇa*s can undergo the investiture ceremony (*upanayana*), receive the sacred thread, and have their spiritual birth (*dvija*, meaning 'twice-born'). The fourth *varṇa* consists of *Śūdras*, who are expected to serve the people of the three upper *varṇas*.[69] There is no fifth *varṇa*. Therefore, people who fall outside the

---

65 One of the earliest references to the origin of this fourfold division of Indians is found in the *Puruṣasūkta* of the *Ṛgveda* (10.90 verse 12). Accordingly, when the primal cosmic person, *Puruṣa*, created the universe, the *Brahmins* arose from his mouth, the *Kṣatriyas* from his arms, and the *Vaiśyas* from his thighs. The *Śūdra*s were made from his feet. As such, the *caturvarṇa* belongs to the created order of the universe and human society in India.

66 The six-fold ideal works of the Brahmins (*antaṇararutoḻil*) are *ōtal*, *ōtuvittal*, *vēṭṭal*, *vēṭpittal*, *ītal* and *ēṟṟal*: Accordingly, 1) the Brahmins learn and recite the four Vedas. 2) They recite and teach the four Vedas to others, specifically learners among fellow Brahmins. 3) They offer sacrifices (*yagas*) for themselves. 4) They offer sacrifices on behalf of others. 5) They offer things such as holy water and sacred ash (*vibhuti*) to others. 6) They accept gifts such as gold, cows, houses and lands from others.

67 The six-fold ideal occupations of the *Kṣatriyas* (*aracararutoḻil*) are *ōtal*, *vēṭṭal*, *ītal*, *paṭaikkalam payiṟal*, *palluyi rōmpal* and *pakaittiṟan teṟutal*. Accordingly, 1) *Kṣatriyas*, as rulers, recite the four Vedas. 2) They offer sacrifices on behalf of others. 3) They give alms (to the Brahmin priests). 4) They learn the art of waging successful wars against enemies. 5) They protect living beings. 6) They inform themselves about the strength of their enemies.

68 The six-fold ideal duties of the *Vaiśyas* (*vaṇikararutoḻil*) are *ōtal*, *vēṭṭal*, *ītal*, *uḻavu*, *niraiyōmpal* and *vāṇikam*. Accordingly, 1) the *Vaiśyas* can recite the Vedas. 2) They offer sacrifices on behalf of others. 3) They give alms (to the Brahmin priests). 4) They can cultivate their lands. 5) They breed their cattle. 6) They undertake gainful business.

69 The six-fold ideal tasks for the *Śūdras* (*cūttirararutoḻil*) are *pacu kāttal*, *poruḷīṭṭal*, *payiriṭal*, *purāṇātikaḷ ōtal*, *ītal* and *antaṇar mutaliyōrkku aṉukūlattoḻil ceytal*. Accordingly, the *Śūdras* are responsible for protecting the cows. 2) They earn material wealth. 3) They cultivate their lands. 4) They can recite the *Purāṇās*. 5) They give gifts (to the Brahmin priests). 6) They serve the Brahmins pleasingly.

four-fold categorisation are the *avarṇa* people.[70] They are unequal to the *varṇa*-people in terms of their genealogy and in matters of religion, spirituality, ritual, and humanity.

Secondly, caste as *jāti* refers to the birth-based, blood-related families within and outside the *varṇa*. Each *jāti* has its family lineage. Its social rank, compared to other *jātis*, is hierarchical. Each *jāti* jealously maintains its characteristic socio-cultural, religious, political, and economic etiquettes that govern its private and public life. These etiquettes encompass notions of social respect (*matippu*) and standing (*antastu*), as well as civility and reverence (*mariyātai*), honour and dignity (*māṉam*). Each *jāti* maintains its eating habits, conditions for contracting marriages and conducting funeral rites. Deviation from *jāti*-etiquette and identities invites punishment, such as the cessation of family relationships and imposition of social ostracism.

9.3.2 Jāti during Schwartz's Times

During the times of Schwartz, *varṇa* and *jāti* played a significant role in the personal and social life of the Tamil people. For example, in April 1792, Christoph Samuel John observed caste-based attitudes that led to oppressive social discrimination in Kanjanur (in modern Thiruvidaimarudur taluk of Tanjore district) and in "Tererhendur" (Tērūrntavūr?). He noted that, unlike in rural areas, awareness of caste identities in European settlements (e.g., Tranquebar and Nagapattinam) was less pronounced. Christians in the countryside coped with the realities of *varṇa* and *jāti* prejudices. For example, taking leave from Schwartz in Tirupālāṭuturai,[71] John met the Pariah catechist Kailasam, who followed the local etiquette and lived harmoniously with others. The term 'Pariah' here refers to a social group historically considered the lowest in the *varṇa* and *jāti* hierarchy, often subjected to severe discrimination and social ostracisation. When John met the Tamil Lutherans in "Tererhendur," he observed the cruelty of *varṇa*-based social discrimination: the Sudras did not permit the Pariahs to live in fertile areas. They forced them to settle in dry, unproductive regions. They did not allow the Pariahs to plant fruit or shady trees. If they planted these trees in defiance of the prevailing customs, the Sudras felled them. They did not permit the Pariah women

---

70 According to https://www.learnsanskrit.cc/, the Sanskrit masculine noun *avarṇa* can mean "speaking ill of," "no praise," "blame," "colourless," or "having no outward appearance" (accessed on 20.11.2024).

71 AFSt/M 1 C 29 a : 5: On 01.02.1788, Schwartz reported that he could not easily find a catechist for the Tamil Lutheran congregation with Sudra-Christians in Tirupālāṭuturai. Expecting its future growth, he bought a house for this congregation and deputed a Tamil pastor and the catechist Ñāṉapirakācam ('Spiritual Brightness') to minister among them. Tirupālāṭuturai had a separate Tamil Lutheran Pariah congregation, led by a humble, pious, and effective Pariah catechist. This catechist was accountable to the missionaries in Tranquebar. This congregation welcomed Schwartz and received his teachings with great pleasure. Schwartz witnessed how boldly the Pariah Christian women there answered his questions.

to cover their upper bodies with any cloth. Therefore, the Pariah women crossed their hands over their bare chests and struggled to maintain their modesty and decorum in public places. The mistreatment of these Tamil Lutherans pained him.[72]

John explained further that the Tamil Lutherans adhered to *varṇa* and *jāti* norms out of existential necessity. All attempts by the missionaries to eradicate these prejudices proved fruitless.[73] They pointed out the irrationality and destructive consequences of these prejudices. For example, if a Christian from a higher *varṇa* and *jāti* tried to get his daughter married to an able Pariah Christian, his whole community would break their social ties with him, ostracise and despise him. This Pariah Christian might perform better and more skilled work in a European household than a Sudra man. He might work as an able dubash and help Europeans to make weighty decisions. However, a Sudra would not respect a Pariah.

Likewise, Tamil Lutherans faced additional discrimination based on *varṇa*- and *jāti* norms. For example, a Tamil Lutheran from a Vellalar community who wished to marry into a Telugu family had to endure harsh family conflict. To marry a spouse from a similar *jāti* background, some Tamil Lutherans returned to their ancestral faith. Otherwise, they married close relatives. Additionally, no Tamil Lutheran would ever dine with a European who ate beef.

Varṇa- and *jāti*-prejudices were so strong that the Tamils hesitated to embrace Lutheranism and interact with Europeans. Once, Rayappan, the Lutheran Pastor for the rural congregations, ate with a European because no other Tamil person was with him at the time. However, he refused to eat beef.[74] Many years previously, the missionaries used two chalices to administer Holy Communion to the Sudra and Pariah Christians. This practice horrified the non-Christian Tamils, who refused to embrace Lutheranism. Due to numerous objections from non-Christian Tamils, the missionaries and Tamil Lutherans discontinued using two chalices. Still, they agreed to serve the Holy Communion first to the Sudra Christians and then to the Pariah Christians. Consequently, many Tamil Lutherans completely abstained from the Holy Communion. Earlier, the missionaries and the Tamil Lutherans spread a single mat that covered the entire floor of the church. Both Sudra and Pariah Christians sat together and worshipped God. When the non-Christian Tamils observed this practice, they objected to it so vehemently that the

---

72 AFSt/M 2 E 36 : 1 and NHR 4, 1794, issue 44, 707–708.

73 AFSt/M 1 C 22 : 49: On 17 October 1779, Christoph Samuel John reported his previous attempts to remove the *jāti* prejudices among the Tamil Lutherans. He brought two Sudra boys, David (Christian?) and Piragasam, to Tranquebar with their parents' permission. He trained them, along with a few Pariah boys, to serve as catechists in the countryside. Additionally, he requested that the Tamil Lutheran pastors take these Pariah boys along on their evangelistic itinerary in the countryside. However, the pastors, except Pastor Philip, hesitated to ask this because they could not eat with these Pariah boys.

74 AFSt/M 1 C 22 : 49: On 17.10.1779, C.S. John reported that an English officer in Ramanathapuram invited Philip, the Tamil Lutheran pastor, for a meal. When he saw beef on the table, he did not want to eat with the officer. However, he managed to sit with him at the table. John considered this gesture as a breakthrough in overcoming caste-and racial prejudice.

Tamil Lutherans cut the mat in half – one part for the Sudra Christians and the other part for the Pariah Christians.[75] Thus, *varṇa-* and *jāti*-based prejudices and practices determined the social life of all Tamils, and the Tamil Lutherans could not escape from this social reality.

9.3.3 Schwartz's Approaches to caste in Urban and Rural Settings

Most human traditions, customs, rites, mores, and taboos are contextual, habitual, and specific to a particular people, place, and time. They have no universal relevance and require prudence and tolerance.[76] The tenth chapter of the *Formula of Concord* presents the Lutheran position on adiaphora, or 'indifferent things'. Its first paragraph defines *adiaphora* as "ceremonies and church rites which are neither commanded nor forbidden in God's Word but are introduced into the Church with a good intention, for the sake of good order and propriety, or otherwise to maintain Christian discipline." These traditions and habits do not contribute to the Lutheran doctrine of justification by faith.[77] Schwartz probably knew how Christians in diverse socio-cultural and political environments struggled to agree on time-tested and honoured human habits and rituals that defined their identity and confirmed their social status.[78] Therefore, he appears to have found Lutheran teachings on adiaphora a possible lens through which to perceive, interpret, and tolerate the caste system as an institution unnecessary for the salvation of a Tamil individual, yet deemed essential for their dignified local existence and social recognition.

---

75 AFSt/M 2 E 36 : 1 and NHR 4, 1794, issue 44, 708–710.

76 The New Testament contains conflicting views and practices about fasting, eating, Sabbath rituals, Christian freedom and legalism. For example, contemporaries of John the Baptist blamed him for abstaining from eating and drinking and of Jesus for eating and drinking (Luke 7:31–35). Some people of Jesus' time observed Sabbath rituals (Mark 2:24). At the same time, Jesus felt that these Sabbath rituals did not bind him because God set aside the Sabbath for the benefit of human beings (Mark 2:27). Likewise, the Apostle Paul recommended observance of special days to honour the Lord Jesus (Romans 14:6) and yet in the Lord nothing is unclean (Romans 14:14). A Christian could eat anything with thanksgiving, yet should give it up, if it would cause a fellow Christian to stumble (Romans 14:20). He also stated that not all lawful things are helpful (1Corinthians 6:12). These and other biblical passages allow the observance of certain traditions and customs according to individuals' consciousness and usages.

77 For an excellent overview of the evidence of adiaphora in the New Testament, the Early Church, among the Reformers and modern Christianity, see Gottlieb Werner Luetkehoelter: Adiaphora. Consensus 12, 1986, issue 1, 117–135.

78 Christians entertain different opinions and practices about feasting and fasting, marriage and celibacy, wealth and poverty, luxury or simple lifestyle, the status of married or unmarried women and widows in and outside of the church, mode of consecrating and receiving Eucharistic elements, giving and receiving baptism by infants or adults, purity codes, dress codes, church hierarchy and administration with or without a bishop or a superintendent, growing beard, eating loaves or unfermented bread or fish during Lent, celebrating or ignoring festivals like Christmas, Easter and Pentecost, nationalism and patriotism, worship services with or without music, hymns translated from European or North American sources or locally composed lyrics, and the like. The list of possible disagreements among Christian habits is indeed endless.

On 14 February 1788, Schwartz explained how he dealt with the Tamil Lutherans who harboured *jāti*-prejudices: He requested that the men sit on one side of the nave and the women on the other. He encouraged the Sudra or Pariah Christians to interact with each other as they pleased. The Sudra catechists Ñāṉapirakācam and Ñāṉamuttu, and the Pariah catechist Gabriel, modelled good behaviour and interacted with each other as equals. Consequently, Pariah Christians and Sudra Christians accepted the Eucharist elements on a first-come, first-served basis. On Sundays, all Christians maintained cleanliness. The Pariah Christians abstained from eating the meat of fallen animals.[79]

However, when Schwartz was among the non-Christian Sudras in the countryside, he employed a different approach. For example, on 14 February 1788, he cited an incident in Tirupālāduturai: At that time, he visited a non-Christian Sudra man in his house. At the same time, the Pariah Catechist Gabriel, who had previously spoken freely with Sudras in the city, came to meet Schwartz. Immediately, Schwartz asked the catechist to stay away and went to meet him at a distance. This expression of Schwartz's socio-cultural sensitivity resonated with the people around him. They treated the catechist with more extraordinary kindness. Schwartz explained that the Sudras had not yet learned to be humble and chose to remain proud, sinful individuals. He advised Christian missionaries to be patient with such people.[80]

In the same letter, he mentioned another incident: when he visited a non-Christian Sudra house owner, many people thronged to see and hear him. The house owner, too, sat at his feet. Schwartz catechised, prayed and worshipped God with them all. People from different *jāti* backgrounds listened to the gospel message. Schwartz wished that if missionaries could spend more time with non-Christians, they would accept people of all *jāti*-backgrounds as equals. By quoting 1 Corinthians 1:30, Schwartz concluded his letter with his remark: "We preach to the people of higher and lower *jāti*s that Jesus Christ remains our wisdom and justice, sanctification and redemption."[81]

9.3.4 Schwartz's Two Chalices

Christian Pohle reached Tranquebar in the summer of 1777. He became unhappy about using two chalices, one for the Sudra Christians and the other for the Pariah Christians. He accused the older missionaries of being fearful and indecisive. On 19 September 1778, he informed Director Freylinghausen in Halle that the Sudra Christians wished to avoid drinking from the same chalice as the Pariah Christians. Older missionaries used two chalices in specific large German Lutheran

---

79 AFSt/M 1 C 29a : 11: Schwartz did not explain what (ritual) cleanliness meant for him or his followers. First, they ate the meat of fallen animals. Second, the Pariah Christians adjusted their social etiquette to that of the Sudras. Third, all Christians fasted before accepting the Eucharist so that their lips and saliva (*eccil*) would not ritually defile the chalice.

80 AFSt/M 1 C 29a : 11.

81 AFSt/M 1 C 29a : 11 and NHR 3, 1790, issue 36, 1403.

congregations, one chalice for women and the other for men. To avoid conflicts, the older missionaries allowed the Sudra Christians to participate in the Eucharist first, and then the Pariah Christians came forward.[82] After Pohle moved to Tiruccirāppaḷḷi, Freylinghausen wanted to know whether Schwartz had used two chalices. Pohle responded that, unlike Schwartz, he did not permit Sudra Christians or Pariah Christians to drink from their chalices. Instead, he had only one chalice for all Christians.[83]

A year later, on September 27, 1779, Pohle wrote that the members of his congregation, hailing from diverse caste backgrounds, drank from the same chalice. As a temporary measure, Pohle permitted the Sudras to participate in the Eucharist initially. Later, he gave the Eucharistic elements to whosoever came first. Pohle taught that partaking in the Eucharist did not resemble eating *sōru* ('cooked rice') and drinking *kañji* ('broth of the boiled rice'). The Eucharist did not make them either better Sudras or better Pariahs. The Eucharist did not affirm their caste pride. Instead, it challenged them to become better Christians, realise their equal membership in the same Body of Christ and demonstrate the equality of all humans in their attitude and behaviour. To illustrate his teaching, Pohle drank from the same chalice as the last person, after Sudras and Pariahs had already drunk from it earlier. This gradual change from separate chalices to a shared one symbolised the patience and perseverance of the missionaries in promoting equality among the Tamil Lutherans of Tiruccirāppaḷḷi.

9.3.5 Schwartz's Two Settlements

In January 1791, Schwartz informed Pasche that the Tamil Lutherans from Sudra- and Pariah backgrounds learned to kneel together for Holy Communion. They ate from the same bread and drank from the same cup, symbolising their unity in worship. Schwartz thanked God for the shrinking and dwindling impact of caste among the Tamil Lutherans in Tanjore, fostering community and togetherness.[84] Eight months later, on 5 September 1791, he reported to Pasche on the Sudra- and Pariah settlements he had established around his large garden in Tanjore. He rejoiced in this breakthrough, as Sudra and Pariah Christians agreed to live closer to each other and meet frequently in the church for prayer and worship.[85] However, they did not entirely give up their *jāti*-related prejudices and practices.[86] Schwartz's contribution to this (limited, yet praiseworthy) social integration attracted the

---

82 AFSt/M 1 B 67 : 74 and Wilhelm Germann: Johann Philipp Fabricius–Seine fünfzigjährige Wirksamkeit im Tamulenlande und das Missionsleben des achtzehnten Jahrhunderts daheim und draußen nach handschriftlichen Quellen dargestellt. Erlangen 1865, 205–206.

83 Germann: Johann Philipp Fabricius, 206.

84 NHR 4, 1792, issue 40, 386.

85 AFSt/M 1 C 32b : 66.

86 For a detailed analysis of caste biases and practices among Indian Christians, see Duncan B. Forrester: Caste and Christianity: Attitudes and Policies on Caste of Anglo-Saxon Protestant Missions in India. London 2018.

attention of Friedrich Max Müller (1823–1900), the famous German Indologist at Oxford University. Max Müller appreciated Schwartz's tolerant, fair and respectful approach to overcoming *jāti*-based prejudices and practices among his followers.[87]

9.3.6 Schwartz's Two Schools

On 13 September 1787, Schwartz, in a letter to John Sulivan in London, expressed his gratitude for Sulivan's efforts in securing financial and moral support from the Company officers for the Provincial Schools. This support was crucial for the schools' operations and further underscored Sulivan's dedication to education.

According to John Sulivan, Schwartz's letter of 13 September 1787 assured that the provincial schools would maintain the caste-related status quo, hierarchy and even untouchability. The students would learn the English language and develop their reading skills in English literature. At the right time, they would come to know the truth of Christianity, probably because English concepts required an explanation of the background of Judeo-Christian influences on Britain. According to John Sulivan, Schwartz's letter reveals his questionable approach to avowedly maintaining caste distinctions in imparting English education:

> Your caution not to take into the provincial schools, children of a low cast[e], shall be observed: — nay, one could not venture it, as the prejudices are so strong; but the lower sort of people will not so much as wish to learn the English language. Moreover, you may be sure that though our intention is to lessen their prejudices and so to prepare them for the reception of the truth, nevertheless, in those schools, the English language is taught and not the Christian doctrine. Everything has its proper time and place.
> Concerning the provincial English schools, we have one at Ramanadaporam [sic! = Ramanathapuram] and one at Tanjore. The last we have re-established two months ago. You would absolutely think it impossible, that the scholars should have made so great a proficiency as they have done, in so short a time. At present, all the scholars are Brahmins, but others desire to come. None but the higher castes are received into this school. As to force them into the acknowledgement of the Christian doctrines, that will, I hope, never enter a missionary's mind. If, hereafter, they should read English books of various kinds, they may perhaps quit some of their prejudices. Truth shall work its own way.[88]

9.4 Transforming the Kaḷḷar-Community

It was customary for the British Parliament to review the Charter of the Company once in twenty years. When the Charter came up for review in 1793, evangelical parliamentarians such as Charles Grant (1746–1823) and William Wilberforce (1759–1833) attempted to persuade the Board of Control in the British Parliament

---

87 Germann: Missionar Christian Friedrich Schwartz, 267.

88 John Sullivan: Tracts Upon India written in the years 1779, 1780 and 1788 with subsequent observations. London: W. Bulmer and Co., 1795, here 48–49.

to create a legal framework for British missionaries to work among the Indians. Henry Dundas (1742–1811), the President of the Board of Control from June 1793 to May 1801, realised the significance of this proposal and requested more time to review its merits. The Company's renewed Charter Act of 1793 did not include the Pious Clause, as he chose not to review it.

During that debate, Montgomery Campbell opposed the proposal put forth by Grant and Wilberforce. He misquoted Schwartz's work among the Kaḷḷar followers of Schwartz in the small town of Būdalūr in 1774.[89] Montgomery Campbell alleged that most of Schwartz's followers came from despised Pariah communities and behaved worse than non-Christian Indians. On 24 May 1793, the London-based newspaper *Courier* reported Campbell's opinions as follows:

> Montgomery Campbell gave his decided vote against the clause and reprobated the idea of converting the Gentoos. It is true that missionaries have made proselytes of the Paraiars [i.e. the Pariahs] but they were the lowest order of people and had even degraded the religion they professed to embrace. Mr. Swartz, whose character was held so deservedly high, could not have any reason to boast of the purity of his followers: They were proverbial for their profligacy. An instance occurred to his recollection, perfectly in point. He had been preaching for many hours to this caste of proselytes on the heinousness of theft and, in the heat of his discourse, had taken off his stock when that and his gold buckle were stolen by one of his virtuous and enlightened congregation. In such a description of natives did the doctrine of the missionaries operate. Men of high caste would spurn the idea of changing the religion of their ancestors.[90]

Montgomery Campbell began working with the Company in Madras at a low level. After his relative, Archibald Campbell, the Governor of Madras (1786–1789), appointed him as his secretary, he rose in rank and served as Postmaster General for some time. Finally, he served Wallajah for an annual salary of £2,100 and assisted him in drafting the *Treaty of Arcot*, which the Directors of the East India Company in London deemed faulty. Therefore, they called Montgomery Campbell back to London in 1789.[91]

Schwartz knew Montgomery Campbell as Wallajah's servant. On 11 March 1789, he stated that he had requested Montgomery Campbell to intervene on behalf of the missionary Philip Fabricius in Madras and recover the money that Fabricius had loaned to Wallajah's eldest son. Still, Montgomery Campbell did not intervene, and Fabricius did not recover his money.[92] Montgomery Campbell's strong association with Wallajah may have been the reason he misquoted Schwartz during the debate in the British Parliament in 1793.

Schwartz read Montgomery Campbell's allegation in 1794, composed an impressive reply, and sent it to the SPCK for publication. This response stated that

---

89 The Kaḷḷar, also known as the *Kollaries*, were (are still) a caste group. The noun *Kollaries* is a European corruption of the Tamil noun *koḷḷaiyar* ('robbers'). They were known for professional thievery, cattle raids, and looting in the eighteenth century. They even paid taxes on their loot to the kings of Tanjore.

90 Christian Friedrich Schwartz: Defence of Missions in India by the late Venerable Mr. Swartz. London: H. Brayer, 1796, here 1–2.

91 Mackillop: Fashioning a 'British' Empire, 226.

92 Germann: Missionar Christian Friedrich Schwartz, 354.

in 1774, there was no Tamil Lutheran in Būdalūr. All Kaḷḷars of Būdalūr were non-Christians. No adult Kaḷḷar stole the golden knob; instead, a few Kaḷḷar-boys took it away. Soon, the Kaḷḷars found the knob, returned it to Schwartz and asked him to punish the boys. Schwartz sent them away without punishment because it was not worth the trouble. Additionally, Schwartz insisted that he did not preach any sermon to anybody. Therefore, Schwartz concluded that Montgomery's allegations were deliberate misrepresentations.

Schwartz was convinced that oppressive taxation was a potent cause of the Kaḷḷars' continued plundering expeditions. They looted European merchants and soldiers. Since 1755, the Company had been sending their soldiers to subdue the Kaḷḷar fighters, who zealously guarded their families and possessions. Apart from killing some of them, the Company remained unsuccessful against them.[93] Hemingway described the Kaḷḷars, *Padaiyāṭci*s and the *Kuṟavar*s as thievish:

> Generalisations are apt to be misleading, but it appears to be commonly believed that the Kallans are responsible for most of the cattle theft. [...] During the Trichinopoly war, Clive's and [Major Stringer] Lawrence's horses were stolen by the Kallan brothers. The Kuravans are given credit for most of the housebreaking, and dacoities are said to be generally committed by Pallans or Valaiyans in the pay of the Kallans or by the Kallans themselves.[94]

Schwartz's gradual and persistent work among the Kaḷḷars in Tanjore, Ramanathapuram and Pāḷaiyamkōṭṭai marked a new beginning for several Kaḷḷars, who embraced the form of Christianity Schwartz had been promoting. Their conversion caused a series of problems.

In April 1792, the tension between the Christian and non-Christian Kaḷḷars became worse. Schwartz shared his worry and fear with Christoph Samuel John in Tirupālāṭuṯai: The non-Christian Kaḷḷars were angry at the Christian Kaḷḷars and took away their lands. They threatened them with death. To avert the danger, John met the *Mūppaṉār*, a poligar and leader of the Kaḷḷars in the area, at a wayside rest house (lit. Ruhehaus) and requested his assistance. The *Mūppaṉār* promised to avert the danger and to restore the rights of the non-Christian Kaḷḷars. The *Mūppaṉār* stayed with Schwartz for the forenoon and heard the good news about the Lord Jesus Christ.[95]

By 11 May 1792, tensions between Christian and non-Christian Kaḷḷars in Tanjore and Ramanathapuram became apparent:[96] Schwartz stated that the Christian Kaḷḷars grew in the knowledge of the Lord Jesus Christ and organised their private and public lives in obedience to his lordship. Gradually, they improved their moral lives. Some Christian Kaḷḷars, who had earlier worked for

---

93 Blackburn 1978, 42: Company's army attacked the Kaḷḷars in 1755. For example, Colonel Heron burned their stronghold at Koyilkudi. However, they could not tame the Kaḷḷar; most of them escaped and went to other places. In 1764, Captain Rumley massacred 3,000 Kaḷḷars in a fort near Melur. However, the Company could not control the activities of the Kaḷḷars effectively.

94 Madras District Gazetteer—Tanjore, 207.

95 AFSt/M 2 E 36 : 1 and NHR 4, 1794, issue 44, 706–707.

96 NHR 4, 1793, issue 43, 679–680.

wealthy, large land-owning non-Christian Kaḷḷars, lost their jobs, possessions, and lands. With the help of the Company officers and Schwartz, they were able to regain their lands. Schwartz addressed the non-Christian Kaḷḷars as friends and relatives, encouraging them to settle their disputes amicably.

Accordingly, the non-Christian Kaḷḷars promised Schwartz they would settle the matter amicably. Unfortunately, after the Christian Kaḷḷars had returned to their native places, the leaders of the non-Christian Kaḷḷars stirred up hatred once again against the Christian Kaḷḷars. Consequently, about two hundred non-Christian Kaḷḷars gathered to attack the Christian Kaḷḷars. Some of the non-Christian Kaḷḷars, who were close relatives of the Christian Kaḷḷars, disagreed with their leaders and tried to help their Christian family members. In the meantime, some of the Christian Kaḷḷars, despite the looming threat, fled to Schwartz, hid in his garden and desperately requested his interference. Not knowing all the causes of the strife, Schwartz responded wisely: as a preacher of Jesus' teachings, he could not tolerate any strife. He repeated that he would suffer significantly if his intervention caused anyone to die. After he and the Christian Kaḷḷars prayed for God's protection, the Christian Kaḷḷars returned to their places.[97] Four months later, on 19 September 1792, Schwartz reported that the unrest among the Kaḷḷars terrified him; it still threatened to become violent. By God's grace, it died down, and the Kaḷḷars resolved their problems peacefully. The Christian-Kaḷḷars, despite the conflict, remained steadfast in their faith and were able to worship God without fear of retribution.[98]

Schwartz continued to work for the welfare of the Kaḷḷar communities. On 4 February 1793, he stated that he had already erected a school for the Kaḷḷar children in Tanjore. He also mentioned that building that school was difficult; he had had to overcome several troubles. However, by February 1793, he managed to educate twenty children in that school.[99] Providing education to the Kaḷḷar children was a beacon of hope in their lives, showing the transformative power of education in uplifting communities.

A year later, on 13 February 1794, Schwartz illustrated his impactful interaction with the Kaḷḷar-community through their leaders: when Archibald Campbell was the Governor of Madras, Ameer Singh's oppressive taxes forced Tanjore's farmers to cease cultivation. A great famine was impending. Ameer Singh was unable to persuade the farmers to start their work. They did not trust him. Finally, he requested Schwartz to intercede with the farmers. Consequently, Schwartz assured them of justice in writing; the Kaḷḷar farmers were among the first to return to cultivate their lands. These Kaḷḷar farmers remembered the honourable deeds that Schwartz had done for them in earlier times. They assured him that they would not let him down. Along with other farmers, they worked hard and cultivated their land. Together, they averted the famine.[100]

---

97 NHR 4, 1793, issue 43, 681.
98 NHR 4, 1793, issue 43, 681.
99 NHR 4, 1794, issue 44, 750.
100 Pearson: Memoirs, Vol. 2, 295–296.

The Company officers had a difficult time dealing with the Kaḷḷars, and they sought Schwartz's intervention. As a result, Schwartz wrote personal letters to the heads of Kaḷḷar communities and requested a meeting. After gathering in Tanjore, Schwartz encouraged them to return the goods they had taken away from European soldiers and others. They returned the goods and promised Schwartz in writing that they would not indulge in stealing the goods of others. In February 1794, Schwartz wrote that for eight months, the Kaḷḷars kept their promise, heeded his advice and cultivated their fields. Some Kaḷḷars told Schwartz that if the ruler of Tanjore imposed exorbitant demands on them, they would have to resort to stealing.[101]

Schwartz reported further that some Kaḷḷars of Tanjore, who had listened to and interacted with him, wanted to get baptised and become Lutherans. Schwartz responded to them cautiously: he would dutifully instruct them in Christian doctrines and ways of life, but thievish habits would prove them "very bad Christians." After receiving their assurances that they would not plunder others and teaching them Lutheran doctrines, he baptised them and asked them to cultivate their field. He went and supervised their work. He could witness how excellently they had grown their lands. Then, he urged them to pay their tax to the king of Tanjore, which they complied with. Schwartz was pleased with this social transformation.[102] He boldly affirmed, "before God and man, that if Christianity, in its plain and undisguised form, were properly promoted, the country would not suffer, but be benefited by it."[103]

The Christian Kaḷḷars, despite their faith, were not immune to challenges. Their non-Christian relatives, fearful of losing more Kaḷḷars to Lutheranism, intimidated them. They used all means to persuade them to renounce Lutheranism and return to their ancestral faith. They threatened the catechists and told them that they would eradicate Christianity among their relatives.[104] Gradually, Schwartz and his catechists persuaded the Christian Kaḷḷars not to retaliate with violence but to maintain "mild and patient conduct" and to return "to their habitations in peace."[105] Some Christian Kaḷḷars chose to live in the same settlement as Lutherans among other *jāti* groups.[106] Others went to live among their non-Christian relatives. In 1802, Gericke noticed that the Kaḷḷars no longer robbed the travellers on the roads from Tiruccirāppaḷḷi to Tanjore. He confirmed that "since the late Mr Swartz had been among them and had formed congregations in these parts, we have heard

---

101 Pearson: Memoirs, Vol. 2, 298.
102 Pearson: Memoirs, Vol. 2, 298–299.
103 Pearson: Memoirs, Vol. 2, 299.
104 Pearson: Memoirs, Vol. 2, 301–302.
105 Pearson: Memoirs, Vol. 2, 302.
106 Germann: Missionar Christian Friedrich Schwartz, 276: During the mid-nineteenth century, a few Anglican missionaries of the Society for the Propagation of the Gospel in Foreign Parts came to work in Tanjore. They viewed caste as a religious institution of detestable hierarchy and tried to get rid of it among Christians. Therefore, they did not appreciate Schwartz's interpretation of caste as a social institution. They did not like Schwartz permitting the Kaḷḷar-Christians to live in the same place but separate from the Vellalar-Christians.

nothing of robberies."[107] The Christian Kaḷḷars, in the face of opposition, chose a path of peace and coexistence, demonstrating their courage and resilience.[108] Their ability to maintain peace in the face of adversity is truly inspiring.

9.5 Creating Work Opportunities

Many inhabitants of Tiruccirāppaḷḷi and Tanjore lost their work during the Anglo-Mysore wars. Widows without the means to earn a livelihood suffered the most. On 20 February 1775, Schwartz wrote about a few healthy widows who belonged to the Tamil Lutheran Church in Tiruccirāppaḷḷi but did not have work to earn their livelihood. He consulted with the local hospital's medical doctor and procured work for them. The process involved identifying the widows in need, negotiating with the hospital for suitable tasks, and securing a place for them to live near the hospital. Accordingly, they would thresh the paddy, separate the rice, and provide it to the hospital daily. To help them live near the hospital, Schwartz met with the local superintendent of Nawab Wallajah and secured a place. Immediately, Schwartz built nine tiny houses for these widows. Each house was nine feet long and nine feet wide. Soon after Schwartz had these homes built, Wallajah did not want the widows to live there. Schwartz wrote directly to Wallajah and explained the situation.[109] Though Wallajah's response to Schwartz is unknown, the fact that Schwartz procured work for the widows was remarkable. They could manage their affairs and lead a dignified life.

In 1791, Schwartz created work opportunities for some widows in Tanjore. Accordingly, they spun cotton and sold it to a Christian weaver. Some women prepared dry rice flakes (*aval*) and sold them, thus earning a living. Some women sold either vegetables or fruits. Schwartz visited these women in the evening and inspected their labour. He believed work was "constantly necessary for them, not only as an occupation but to fix their minds on an object during the hours of solitude [as widows]."[110] His actions profoundly impacted the lives of these widows, and his dedication to their well-being was genuinely beneficial.[111]

---

107 Pearson: Memoirs, Vol. 2, 442.

108 The missionaries of the Leipzig Evangelical Lutheran Mission continued their work among the Kaḷḷars of Būdalūr. Currently, this congregation belongs to the Tamil Evangelical Lutheran Church. Its members fondly and gratefully remember Schwartz's impact on their ancestors.

109 AFSt/M 1 B 65 : 44.

110 Pearson: Memoirs, Vol. 2, 251.

111 AFSt/M 1 C 37a : 34 = NHR 5, 1797, issue 50, 177: Five years later, on 04.04.1796, Schwartz reported about the same widows whom he had helped to find work weaving yarns. A Christian weaver wove clothes for them and charged a small fee. He helped some widows pound the paddy in mortars and sell the husk-less rice for a small gain. Other Christian widows sold fruits. Schwartz met these widows and enquired about their business success and mental well-being. For more details about Schwartz's letter of 04.04.1796, see Memoirs of the Rev. Joseph D[aniel] Jænicke, 130: work was essential to the widows to earn their livelihood and to direct their minds on some valuable things outside of them. Thus, work helped the widows to develop and maintain their physical and emotional health.

Schwartz planned to introduce silk farming in Tanjore to create more work opportunities. He revealed his intention in a letter of 4 February 1793 to Pasche: many people suffered economic and material poverty because they could not find gainful employment.[112] Farming silkworms would provide the people of Tanjore with opportunities to earn a dignified livelihood.[113] Additionally, according to his biographer, Germann, Schwartz assisted the widows of his congregations in weaving cloth and taught young women the art of knitting clothes.[114]

Schwartz was sad that the Company did not hire the Tamil Lutherans for work. They might possess the desired competencies and skills, yet the Company appointed non-Christians. His *Defence of Mission*, drafted in February 1794 and published in 1795, stressed the necessity of gainful employment for Christians with required competencies and expressed it as follows:

> One thing, however, I affirm, before God and man, that if Christianity, in its plain and undisguised form, was properly promoted, the country would not suffer but be benefited by it. If Christians were employed in some important offices, they should, if they misbehaved, be doubly punished; but *to reject them entirely* is not right and discourageth.[115]

Similarly, on 4 February 1794, Schwartz responded to Pastor Uebele, who wanted to know how the Tamil Lutherans could render valuable services to the State and expressed his views as follows:

> I remarked [in my *Defence of Mission*] that it was necessary to employ [Tamil] Christians [in the service of the Company]. Now, they are despised by Europeans. A Brahmin said recently: 'You do your thing only half. After your instruction, you say: Go and work. Alone, what work shall we do? If you could give us jobs that match our talents, you would see that things would be very different. But then you took us out of all [socio-economic and political] connections and cannot place us elsewhere.' This test is too difficult for us, the impotent missionaries. Yes, we must realise that when someone professes the Christian doctrine, he is not only despised by his colleagues but even by Europeans. [it is indeed a] hard test![116].

This passage highlights the discrimination and social isolation faced by the Tamil Lutherans, making it clear that their struggle for employment was not just a matter of finding suitable work but also a battle against societal prejudices and economic

112 NHR 4, 1795, issue 44, 752.

113 Many people in Tanjore, especially the Saurashtrians, adopted Schwartz's idea and produced silk. The silk weavers of Tanjore and Kumbakonam even create great sarees for auspicious occasions. This appears to have marked the beginning of a thriving silk industry in Tanjore; nowadays, the Tanjore Silk Sarees compete with those produced in Kanchipuram.

114 Germann: Missionar Christian Friedrich Schwartz, 361.

115 Claudius Buchanan: An Apology for Promoting Christianity in India, containing two letters addressed to the Honourable East-India Company concerning the idol Juggernaut; and a Memorial presented to the Bengal Government in 1807, in defence of the Christian Missions in India, printed by order of the Hon. The House of Commons, to which are now added Remarks of the letter addressed by the Bengal Government to the Court of Directors in reply to the Memorial with an Appendix containing various official papers, chiefly extracted from the Parliamentary Records relating to the Promulgation of Christianity in India. London 1813, 206.

116 AFSt/M 1 C 35a : 53 and NHR 4, 1795, issue 47, 999.

disparities. On 13 February 1794, Schwartz sent his *Defence of Mission* to the SPCK. As he did not receive Gericke's feedback, he did not include it. In any case, the Company in Madras, Tanjore and Tiruccirāppaḷḷi ignored Schwartz's plea for employing able Christians in their services.[117] The Company was afraid of its non-Christian Indian workers, who did not want Christian co-workers. The non-Christian employees provided essential services, such as revenue collectors, soldiers, and police officers, thereby ensuring the company's survival and prosperity. The Company did not want to offend the sensibilities of its non-Christian service providers.[118] Therefore, Schwartz had to create work opportunities for Tamil Christians.

9.6 Promoting Health Care

All European Company servants needed constant medical care. The eighteenth century necessitated more attention to medical care in Madras because the two Carnatic Wars between the English and the French (1744–1748 and 1749–1754), the Mysore Wars between the English and Hyder Ali (1767–1769 and 1780–1784), and between the English and Tipu Sultan (1790–1792 and 1799) left numerous European soldiers wounded or maimed.[119] Since 1765, more Indian sepoys have worked for the Company, introducing Europeans to Siddha medicine and its

---

117 Sattianaden: Translation of a Sermon in the Malabar or Tamulian Language, composed and preached by Sattianaden on the 26th Day of December 1790, when he received Ordination according to the Rites of the Lutheran Church, in one of the Congregations of the Mission on the Coast of Coromandel connected with The Society for Promoting Christian Knowledge. London: F. and C. Rivington, 1792, here viii: In the preface to the English version of Sattiyanātaṉ's ordination sermon in Tamil (1790), George Gaskin, the secretary of the SPCK remarked the following: the "English in India are too ready to ridicule conversion and despise the converts, but as their prejudices against the Missionaries are wearing out, as their public and private language bears testimony to the pious labours of a Swartz, Gericke and a Polthe [sic! = Pohle], so may we hope, that by degrees they will be brought to receive and employ the converts, who are the work of their hands, to cherish, comfort and promote them."

118 In the name of Queen Victoria, the Company officers favoured those non-Christians who could read, write and speak English and translate texts from Persian and Indic languages into English. Gradually, the British Raj, run by non-Christian Indian elites and financed with Indian money, marginalised Indian Christians and excluded them from any senior appointments. For details, see the Proclamation by the Queen [Victoria] in Council to the Princes, Chiefs and people of India. Allahabad 1858. Available at URL https://www.bl.uk/collection-items/proclamation-by-the-queen-in-council-to-the-princes-chiefs-and-people-of-india (accessed on 20.11.2024).

119 Pratik Chakrabarti: Neither of meate nor drinke, but what the Doctor alloweth; Medicine amidst War and Commerce in Eighteenth-Century Madras. In: Bulletin of the History of Medicine 80, 2006, Issue 1, 1–38, here 2–5: The Company established the first hospital in Madras in 1664. Later, in November 1758, surgeons Robert Turing, James Wilson, and T.S. Hanock requested that Governor George Pigot establish a larger hospital in Madras with separate wards to meet the requirements of various diseases, medical conditions, gender, age, dietary needs, and other curative requirements. As already stated, the defeat of the French in the Battle of Vandavasi on 22 January 1760 (in modern Tiruvaṇṇāmalai District) ensured British military and political dominance in southern India. In 1772, the Company approved the building of a General Hospital in Madras.

practitioners. Each battalion of sepoys had a Siddha practitioner, paid at the level of a *havildar*.[120] Medical doctors of the Company bought "Bazaar Medicine."[121] These ingredients included quicksilver, opium, aloes, cinnamon, cloves, camphor, cumin seeds, fennel seeds, ginger, sesame oil, mustard, and nutmeg.[122] At that time, the Company was desperate to find a cure for smallpox, snake bites, and rabies, and the Company's medical doctors requested Schwartz because he, too, was interested in finding a cure for these fatal ailments.

9.6.1 Seeking a Cure for Snakebites

Albert Calmette (1863–1933) of the Pasteur Institute in Paris developed the antivenom for snakebites in 1895.[123] More than one hundred years earlier, Schwartz tried to find effective means to save people bitten by mad dogs and snakes. For example, on January 16, 1784, he reported to Pasche in London that snake bites were common in Tanjore and described how he had once escaped from a snake hiding among papers on a table. He further narrated that the Siddha doctors' snake pills had saved many lives. He sent a few pills to Pasche and described their use: The person bitten by a snake should dissolve half of the pill in a spoonful of warm water and drink it. He should rub the other half of the pill on the wound. If the person remained restless on the second day, he could take the second pill. During treatment, the person should refrain from eating any meat.[124]

Schwartz narrated another incident on 20 November 1786: On a rainy day, he unknowingly stepped on a snake and ran away.[125] In another letter to Pasche on September 6, 1787, Schwartz described how he had run away from a snake. As was the custom on a rainy morning, he went out to defecate in the open field. As he sat down, he felt something moving under his feet. He quickly realised he was sitting in the middle of a giant snake. He hurriedly jumped to his feet, ran away, and thanked God for protecting him.[126]

---

120 Chakrabarti: Neither of meate nor drinke, 11.

121 Chakrabarti: Neither of meate nor drinke, 16: The Bazaar Medicine, mentioned in the Company's Hospital Records, were "items of trade as much as of treatment." Some medical ingredients derived from plant or animal sources were indigenous. Others were brought from distant countries, such as China (e.g. China-root = smilax, gentian root), and camphor was imported from Java, Sumatra, and Japan.

122 Chakrabarti: Neither of meate nor drinke, 15–18.

123 Barbara J. Hawgood: Doctor Albert Calmette 1863–1933: founder of antivenomous serotherapy of antituberculosis BCG vaccination. In: Toxicon 37:9, 1999, 1241–1258.

124 AFSt/M 1 B 74 : 27.

125 Germann: Missionar Christian Friedrich Schwartz, 376. The snake *kaṭṭuviriyaṉ* (*Odontomus nympha*) has round or square-shaped marks on its body.

126 NHR 4, 1790, issue 39, 1790. AFSt/M 2 A 6 : 3 printed in NHR 3, 1787, issue 32, 869–873: In 1785, Jacob Klein, a Lutheran missionary in Tranquebar, described fifteen types of *viriyans* ('viper,' adder) that lived in the dry and wet areas of Tranquebar. For example, the bite of the *utiriviriyaṉ* ('blood-viper') was fatal, and there was medicine to cure the victim. The victim would bleed internally and externally to death. The *kaḻutaiviriyaṉ* ('ass-viper') was large and

Botanist William Roxburgh (1751–1815),[127] an officer of the Company in Madras, requested Schwartz for information about the Snake Pills of Tanjore. On 6 May 1788 (?), Schwartz recommended to Christoph Samuel John in Tranquebar that he send a description of the snake pills and their preparation to Roxburgh.[128] Schwartz sent John the necessary details to ensure that he had the correct names of the ingredients for making the snake pills. Schwartz suggested that John consult Johann Peter Rottler, another German Lutheran Pietist missionary in Madras, for details on procuring these necessary ingredients. Schwartz expected that Rottler could explain to Roxburgh how the Tamil medical doctors made the snake pills.

Schwartz's note to John names the ingredients that were readily available in local markets (*bazaar*): 1) *veḷḷai pāṣāṇam* ('white arsenic acid'), 2) *ne̱riviṣam* (the plant *Curcuma Zedoaria*) that could be bought in the market, 3) *nērvāḷam* (the plant *Croton tiglium* with purgative qualities and purging seeds), 4) *racam* ('quicksilver'), 5) *miḷaku* (black 'pepper,' i.e. *Piper nigrum*) and 6) *veḷḷai erukkampāl* (the '*milk* of the [white shrub] *Calotropis gigantea*'). John had requested Rottler to respond to Schwartz's request and send his answer directly to Roxburgh. At John's request, Rottler sent Roxburgh a two-and-a-quarter-page report titled *Instructions for Using Pills against Snake Bites*.[129] A paraphrase of this report can read as follows:

> 1) Grind a pill into powder, dissolve it in either warm or cold water, and give the mixture to the person who has been bitten by a *nalla pāmpu* (cobra). 2) Pulverise another pill and apply it to the wound. 3) After fifteen minutes, the patient can tell whether the poison is still working. If the patient is still sick, pulverise two pills, dissolve them in water and ask the sick person to drink it. 4) If the patient becomes dizzy, pulverise half of the pill and apply it to his eyes. Pulverize two pills, mix them in water, and give the mixture to the patient who has been bitten by a viper (*viriya̱n*, 'krait'). Mix half of the pulverised pill with water and apply the paste to the wound. If the poison has not yet started working after half an hour, then give two more

slow as an ass. The *miḷakuviriya̱n* ('pepper-viper') was as small as a pepper. Klein explained how often people died or were cured of snake bites. He also mentioned the *piṭāra̱ns*, who were the professional snake catchers. They understood the diverse types of snakes and their characteristics. Klein referred to snake charmers, who removed the upper and lower fangs of the snakes and entertained the people on the streets. They opined that the upper fangs were less poisonous than the lower fangs, which were considered deadly. They named the upper fangs *kāḷi* (not the Black Goddess, but the name of a female devil) and the lower fangs either *Ema̱n* ('Yama,' the God of Death) or *Ematutā̱n* (the 'messenger of Yama').

127 Chakrabarti: Neither of meate nor drinke, 13 and 75: The botanist William Roxburgh looked after the Company's botanical garden in Samulcotta, i.e. modern Kakinada District, Andhra Pradesh and studied the medicinal plants in southern India. He discovered the curative value of the astringent bark (*Swietenia febrifuga* and *Soymida febrifuga*, also known as *Indian Redwood*). This bark contained medicine to heal dysentery, diarrhoea and several skin infections. Chakrabarti also noted that Roxburgh was excited about his discovery, which could potentially heal Europeans in India and yield higher profits. Medical doctors in Samulcotta and Madras, as well as German Lutheran missionaries in Tranquebar, examined this bark from various scientific perspectives. For additional information about William Roxburgh, see Minakshi Menon (2015).

128 AFSt/M 2 B 1 : 7 contains the date as "6 May," and its year is missing. However, subsequent discussions among British medical doctors on snake pills took place in September and November 1788. Therefore, Schwartz could have written this note on 06.05.1788.

129 AFSt/M 2 B 1 : 6.

pills as explained above. If the patient bleeds from the nose and mouth, give two more pills mixed with the juice from the bark of the *vēlāmaram*. If the patient looks like a dead person, then give him two more pills with the additional water and the white shaft of the shrub *erukkam*.
Sometimes, a sick person does not know whether a snake has bitten them. To rule out this uncertainty, ask the ill person to chew the roots of the plant *āṭutiṉṉāppālai* (the bitter-tasting Indian birthwort, *Aristolochia tagala*). If it tastes bitter, one can be sure that no snake has bitten the person. By contrast, if the person finds the roots sweet, it means a cobra has bitten them. If the taste is sour, a *vaḷḷaṉai*-snake has bitten him. If the taste is tart, a *viriyaṉ* has bitten him. If the person feels suffocated, the snake *mayakkaṭipāmpu* ('bewilderment-causing snake') has bitten him. If his taste is salty, the snake *puṭaiyaṉ* has bitten him. If his taste is like sharp pepper, the snake *irattamaṇṭali* has bitten him. If biting the root causes twitching of the tongue, the snake *kompēṟimūkkaṉ* ('*Dendrelaphis tristis*') has bitten him. The patient must maintain a strict diet: if his purging is severe, he should consume only rice broth for approximately six days. He can eat rice with milk, but without salt. He should drink nothing but warm water. If a person has applied the snake pill to their eyes and cannot recover, they can get some boiled rice wrapped in a cloth and place it gently over their eyes.

Rottler's *Instruction* includes similar treatment for victims bitten by other snakes. In the meantime, in July 1788, Schwartz found Samuel, a Tamil *Vaittiyar* (a 'medical doctor') who had reported healing several persons bitten by snakes.[130] Schwartz informed Strange, a surgeon of the Company near Tanjore, about Samuel and his snake pills. After that, both Schwartz and Strange requested that Governor Archibald Campbell in Madras arrange a discussion between Samuel and the hospital board's medical doctors. Samuel travelled to Madras at Schwartz's request, met the medical doctors, explained the components of his snake pills, and arranged for their further testing. In September 1788, William Duffin, a Company surgeon in Vellore and a Schwartz's friend,[131] encouraged the Medical Board in

130 Ramya Raman, Anantanarayanan Raman and P. Ram Manohar: Tanjore pills used in treating snake bites in the 18th century Madras Presidency. In: Current Science 106, 2014, issue 12, 1759–1763, here 1759: Raman quoted parts of the letter by C.S. John (AFSt/M 2 B 1 : 4) to his mentor Johann Reinhold Forster (1729–1798). Among other things, Foster wanted to know the materials required to produce an antivenom for treating snake bites and rabies. Raman's translation is nearly accurate. I give below a paraphrase of Raman's translation along with information that he has omitted: Samuel, one of Schwartz's servants, cured the persons bitten by either the cobra (*Brillenschlange*) or the dogs with rabies. His healing drew attention, and he became famous. Each of his pills cost half a gold Fano. Each pill is black and as big as a pea. Samuel explained how one should use his pills. He did not reveal either the ingredients or the methods used to make the pills. Finally, the Company's medical doctors in Madras requested that Schwartz persuade Samuel to travel to Madras, disclose the ingredients of his pills to the doctors, and receive a reward. After Samuel disclosed the secrets of his medicine, he received two hundred Star Pagodas as a reward. The newspaper *Madras Courier* published it. Three years later, when missionary C.S. John showed this news about snake pills to other Tamil medical practitioners, they wondered how their secrets could have been given to others. They demanded a lot of money from John because they had been using this medicine for a long time. Now, others knew it.

131 BL MSS. EUR. D.104: Schwartz permitted William Duffin to make a copy of Constantine Beschi's entire *Tamil-Latin Dictionary*. Duffin's copy is housed in the British Library, accompanied by the following remark on its front page: "Vulgaris Tamulica linguae Dictionarium Interpretatione Latina. Presented [to the British Library] by William Duffin Esq, formerly a Surgeon and First Member of the Medical Board on the Madras Establishment – 11 April 1821. Copied from a manuscript furnished by the Revd. C.F. Swartz, Protestant missionary."

Madras to test the snake pills more thoroughly. He had heard about their healing properties, but he urged caution, as they contained poisonous substances such as mercury.

In this context, on 16 September 1788, William Roxburgh presented Rottler's *Instruction* to the Company Board in Madras. Strangely, he did not refer to either Schwartz or Rottler:[132] On receiving this report, Governor Archibald Campbell and his Council ordered the Hospital Board to examine the curative components of the snake pills and the pills for curing rabies. In October 1788, the Medical Board approved and encouraged the use of drugs in cases of snake and mad dog bites. It asked the medical storekeepers to always maintain "a supply of the pills." Then, the Medical Board urged Duffin and others to find competent experts to analyse the chemical ingredients in these Tanjore Pills and publish their findings.[133]

In the meantime, as requested by Schwartz and Strange, Governor Archibald Campbell ordered the "man possessing the secret" to cooperate with James Anderson,[134] the Physician General of the Medical Board in Madras, and his colleague William Duffin.[135] James Anderson and missionary Christoph Samuel John shared common interests in studying plants and identifying their nutritional and medicinal properties. For example, during his three-month journey from Tranquebar to Madras (February to May 1795), John met Anderson, visited his botanical garden in Madras, and became aware of the healing potential of certain plants, including *kīḻvāynelli* (*Phyllanthus niruri*), which can cure jaundice.[136] Anderson's garden had many exotic plants and trees. Notably, he attempted to cultivate the plant *tēṉmaram* (*Theobroma guazuma*) to feed cattle. Anderson showed John his Tibetan and Armenian sheep, which were renowned for producing fine wool. A woollen muffler would cost 50 to 200 Rupees, a fortune then. Anderson maintained cows from Bengal and deer. John felt that Anderson's

---

132 IOR/P/252/27, 2521–2524.

133 Chakrabarti: Neither of meate nor drinke, 19, 21–22: Chakrabarti cites a portion of Duffin's Minute to the Hospital Board dated 17.11.1788: "We do not yet understand many plants' chemical components and healing properties. Notably, we are unsure about consuming one poison to combat another. A poison may be applied externally. We should, however, condemn the poison as a remedy to an illness except in cases where patients have cancer or intermittent fever. With this note, Duffin recommended Samuel's remedy for bites by snakes and rabies dogs to be published in the newspaper *Madras Courier*."

134 Davidson Henry Love: Vestiges of Old Madras, 1640–1800: Traced from the East India Company's Records preserved at Fort St. George and the India Office and from other sources with maps and illustrations. Vol. 3. London 1913, here 551: James Anderson became Physician General in 1786 and died in Madras in 1809.

135 IOR/P/252/27, 2550.

136 AFSt/M 2 E 27 : 12 = NHR 5, 1797, issue 50, 164: John asserted that European doctors, whom he knew, had neglected this plant to treat jaundice. He recommended that the roots of this plant could cure this yellow disease. John thankfully narrated that the juice of this plant saved his life. By interacting with Tamil medical doctors, examining their medicines and studying their medical books, the Lutheran medical missionary Johann Gottfried Klein discovered the healing properties of this plant and wished that more Europeans would know and benefit from it. It is possible that John and Klein would have known the widespread Tamil saying "kāṇum yāvum mañcaḷākavē tōṉṟum kīḻānelli kāṇātavarai" ('one would see everything yellow until they see *kīḻvāynelli*').

main goal was not to help Indians but to assist the British in his "fatherland" in finding and raising sheep that would yield them the best wool. Similarly, Anderson strove hard to establish plantations for silk and cotton in southern India. The Company's Court of Directors in London appreciated his efforts to increase the Company's profits. The Company in Madras gave him 13,397 Star Pagodas (approximately 30,000 German Thaler). John was pleased that Anderson had corresponded with missionaries Rottler and Johann Gottfried Klein (1766–1821), as well as himself.[137]

James Anderson examined the ingredients that the Tamil Siddha medical doctor, Samuel of Tanjore, gave him. Samuel claimed to have received his *Receipt for his Pills* from a mendicant (*Pandaram*), who had taken it from a medical treatise entitled *Chitter Rudum Shaster.*[138] On 18 November 1788, reported to the Company Board in Madras[139] about his assessment of the curative effect of Samuel's pills:

> I [James Anderson] come now to consider the receipt of his [Samoo Vel's] Pills for the bite of serpents, consisting of six articles, viz. Velley Pashanam [*veḷḷai pāṣāṇam*], Velley Navi [*Calotropis procera*?], Neri Visham [*neṟiviṣam*], Milague [*miḷaku*], Ner-Valam [*nērvāḷam*] and Rasam [*pātaracam*, 'quicksilver'].
> The *Velley Pashanam* is ponderous, glossy and white and exposed on live coals or red-hot iron is entirely dissipated in white fumes of the garlic smell from which characters no doubt can exist that it is sublimated arsenic. The noxious qualities of which substance being fully known by many local accounts, it is needless for me to say more than merely to observe the use of it is restrained by Law in Great Britain and the sale limited in a similar manner by the different Governments in this Peninsula. I understand it is brought to this Country from Pegu [i.e. modern Myanmar] and think it is a product of the silver mines of [in the areas of the former Kingdom of] Ava.
> The *Velley Navi* and *Nari Vesham* are exotic dry roots, of which Samoo Vel [Samuel] can give no accounts. Milagu is *Malago Codi* of the *Hortus Malabarines* ['Malabar Garden'] of Class *Diandaia Irigynia* of *Linnaeus* or black pepper. The *Ner Valum* is the kernel of an exotic fruit. The *Rasam* is Quicksilver.
> I must here beg leave to observe that the small quantity of vegetable matter contained in the Pills can have little effect on the arsenic and the quicksilver, none in the way of human digestion that may exist in the stomach a subliming heat in close vessels being necessary for their union.
> Two-thirds of our snakes are not venomous, and if these pills are administered to all that are bitten, three persons must run the risqué of their lives under the idea of saving only by a dose of arsenic. If the part is cut out within a quarter of an hour after the bite of our most venomous snakes, no ill consequence ensues. And where that has been neglected, giddiness, the first morbid symptom, occurred. The life of the patient has been saved by supporting the *vis vitæ* [animating life force] within wine and opium.
> It has been alleged that these Pills have been given with great success in the bite of mad dogs and that those who took the Pills have escaped, while those who have not died. [... one

137 AFSt/M 2 E 27 : 12 = NHR 5, 1797, issue 50, 165–166: Johann Gottfried Klein studied medicine in Halle, received his missionary ordination in Copenhagen in 1791 and landed in Tranquebar in 1792. In 1795, the Danish publisher Horrebowianis printed Klein's 30-page booklet entitled *The Indigenous Sicknesses and Cures of Southern India* (*De morbi venereal curation in India Orientali hesitate specimen inaugural*) in Copenhagen.

138 IOR/P/252/28, 3395. I, the author of this current biography, could not identify this Śaivite-Siddha medical treatise.

139 IOR/P/252/28, 3396–3041.

> illegible word] But such arguments are not conclusive, for it is well known [that] a disposition must exist in the body to receive an infection. Otherwise, none could escape the plague or smallpox when the miasma of these diseases prevails. And likewise, the bite of the same dog may not instill an equal quantity of venom into all whom he wounds.
> When I declare, as I hereby do, that I have been 26 years in the constant and very extensive practice of psychic in India without ever having it in my power to see a person affected with canine madness and am credibly informed the exhibition of the Snake Pill, as it is called, has been attended with such burning pain of the stomach and bowels, violent vomiting, purging and death in some cases as might be expected from the arsenic it contains.
> I hope it will appear [that] I have said enough to limit the internal use of the Thorn Apple and arsenic. To the brute creation for the destruction of dogs that are mad wishing, as I do, to expel,[140] for the sake of Humanity, such noxious drugs from our *Materia Medica*.[141]

Anderson's assessment demonstrated his medical expertise. However, over time, English interest in Tamil medicine increased, leading to the compilation of medical manuals by scholars such as Whitelaw Ainslie and John Forbes Royle. On 27 December 1790, Professor Johann Reinhold Forster in Halle (Saale), Germany, sought information from missionary John about the snakes in Tranquebar, their bites, and the availability of antivenom.[142] In response, on 20 January 1792, John wrote a comprehensive twenty-five-page letter to Foster detailing the Snake Pills' background, ingredients, and success.[143] It is possible that John received relevant information from Samuel, the Tamil Siddha doctor, whom Schwartz had persuaded to share his knowledge about snake bites and their cures with others. Samuel's snake pills garnered significant attention. Other Siddha experts strove to improve antivenom.[144]

9.6.2 Seeking a Cure for Rabies

Again, Schwartz's note to Christoph Samuel John named the necessary ingredients to produce pills against rabies. It is possible that Schwartz received the names of the following five ingredients from Samuel: 1) The plant *matamattai*, also known as the *datura* or the 'thorn-apple,' grows in the gardens.[145] 2) The plant *kōṭakacālai* (lit. "Codaga Saley") likewise grows in the gardens.[146] 3) *Neṟi talai* or *caṭaicci pūṇṭu* (the plant 'old man's cap,' *Achuyarnthis corymbola*), 4) *pulittōl cāmpal* ('ash of the tiger hides'), and 5) *karuppaṭṭi* ('jaggary') gained from palmyra sap or the juice of sugar cane.[147]

140 This strange sentence can be rewritten as follows: "I recommend the destruction of mad dogs, the brute creatures."
141 IOR/P/252/28, 3396–3400.
142 AFSt/M 2 B 1 : 3.
143 AFSt/M 2 B 1 : 4.
144 For details on the contemporary state of Siddha medicine for snake bites, see S. Manonmani, et al.: A Review of beneficial effects of Siddha medicinal herbs on Snake bite. In: International Journal of Current Research in Biology and Medicine 1, 2016, issue 7, 27–25.
145 This plant is called *ūmattam* (*Datura metal, Datura stramonium,* 'Jimson weed or thorn apple').
146 This arsenic plant is called *Justicia procumbens*.
147 AFSt/M 2 B 1 : 7.

On 10 November 1788, James Anderson explained the curative value of these ingredients to the Company Board in Madras. The *matamata*, known in Tamil as *ūmattai*, was described as a "powerfully narcotic."[148] Those who produced *toddy* rubbed the green leaves "on the inside of the still and pots," making the liquor more intoxicating. Those who chose suicide, even for family disagreements, ate *ūmattai* seeds and died within six hours. The second ingredient, *kōṭakacālai*, was a new species of *Justicia* and belonged to the class "Diandria monogynia." The Tamils considered the third ingredient, "Nerri-Talai-Poondoo" (i.e., *kīrippūṇṭu*, the 'Indian snakeroot,' known as *Ophiorhiza mungos*), to be the mongoose medicine. After killing a snake, a mongoose would roll on this plant to neutralise snake poison. Anderson did not comment on the fourth and fifty ingredients. He stated that all plant specimens he had received from the Tamil Siddha doctor Samuel withered. Hence, he was unable to identify them. He opined that of all the named herbs, the pills against the mad dog bite seemed to derive their medical quality only from the *datura* seeds. Therefore, he concluded that these pills were ineffective.[149]

Despite Anderson's pessimistic views, the Tamils persisted in treating one venom's consequences with another. For instance, King Serfoji II, a student of Schwartz, meticulously documented the sources of various poisons, their effects on humans, and their remedies. At his behest, Poet Vēlāyutam of Tanjore verified 342 recipes in May 1828 and inscribed them on palm leaf strips. In 1956, S. Venkataraman transcribed these poems, explained their meaning in prose, and published his work.[150] In more recent times, Professor C.S. Mohanavelu, upon discovering Schwartz's note about pills against rabies, made valiant attempts to persuade medical institutions to recreate and market these pills, despite facing repeated failures.[151] Schwartz's willingness to find curative medicine for people's ailments was praiseworthy.

9.6.3 Seeking a Cure for Smallpox

Available knowledge informs us that on 14 June 1802, the three-year-old daughter of Anna Dusthall, a half-European woman in Bombay (nowadays Mumbai), received the first vaccine against smallpox.[152] In 1805, the queen and two princesses of Mysore were also injected with the vaccine because earlier, the queen

[148] Datura plants are classified according to the colour of their flowers. While the datura plant with white flowers abound in the countryside, other datura plants bear purple and blue flowers.

[149] IOR/P/252/28, 3395–3096.

[150] Carapēntira vaittiya muṟaikaḷ (viṣa rōka cikiccai) [in Tamil: 'Serfoji's Methods of Treatment: Treatments of Poison']. Ed. by. S. Venkatarajan. Tanjore [5]2005.

[151] C.S. Mohanavelu: German Missionaries and Rabies Hydrophobia—Mission History as History of Globalization of Indigenous Tamil Medical Knowledge of 18th century. In: Missionsgeschichte als Geschichte der Globalisierung von Wissen. Ed. by Ulrich van der Heyden and Andreas Feldtkeller. Stuttgart 2012, 213–223.

[152] Chandrakant Lahariya: A brief history of vaccines & vaccination in India. In: Indian Journal of Medical Research 139, 2014, Issue 4, 491–511, here 493–504: On 14.06.1802, a three-

had lost her husband to smallpox. These women removed the common fear of most Indians who believed that the vaccine passed "through bodies of all races, religions, castes and genders" and thus rendered its recipients ritually impure. Additionally, they continued to hold onto their ancient belief that the Goddess *Māriyamman* ('Mother of *Māri*, the Smallpox'), also known as *Sitalā* and *Mahāmāri* (the 'Great Māri'), was responsible for causing smallpox; consequently, people generally tried to appease this angry goddess and used herbal medicine to treat the disease.[153]

These popular narratives overlook earlier attempts to introduce smallpox vaccination in India. For example, in November 1765, the Vestry at St. Mary's Church in Fort St. George[154] supported free inoculation. It urged "the surgeons who attend the Hospital, when the season is most proper, to inoculate such of the Charity children as have not yet had smallpox."[155] This vestry could have alluded to the practice of inoculation in Calcutta. For example, in 1767, Zephaniah Holwell (1711–1798) stated that some Brahmin volunteers in Bengal collected, ground, and protected the bumps of healed persons in dry cloth. They knew that the people of Bengal usually suffered from smallpox from March to May once every seven years. They would reach Bengal between February and March and visit homes to vaccinate unvaccinated inhabitants. Otherwise, they poked the skin with an iron instrument. As soon as some blood appeared, they smeared the bumps on it and advised the vaccinated to abstain "for a month from fish, milk and ghee."[156]

year-old girl, Anna Dusthall, in Bombay, received the smallpox vaccine that had arrived in Bombay in May 1802. A human chain communicated the smallpox vaccine from Bombay to Surat, Pune, Hyderabad and Madras. Observing the benefits of this vaccine, many European countries and others banned variolation. The employees of the Indian Medical Services tried hard to spread the news about smallpox vaccination. However, most Indians were unwilling to accept it because they believed that the Goddess Māriyammaṉ was responsible for it. Additionally, those who practised variolation opposed the introduction of smallpox vaccination. This situation prevailed until the early twentieth century.

153 Aparna Alluri: The Indian queens who modelled for the world's first vaccine. BBC News. 20.09.2020. URL: https://www.bbc.co.uk/news/world-asia-india-53944723 (accessed on 28.10.2024): Smallpox was a prevalent disease in India. Fever and burst pustules caused severe pain and discomfort. The scars on the faces and bodies of the survivors made their lives difficult. Through diverse appeasement rituals, the afflicted attempted to reconcile with the Goddess Māriyammā or Śītalā. Some Indians accepted variolation. Sriram 2021: By 1803, many Hindus rejected the *Gōmāri* ('Cow-Pox') vaccine because they (incorrectly) assumed that the British had killed cows and extracted this vaccine. As a result, the Company had to employ Tamil vaccinators and provide incentives to them, as well as to those who were vaccinated.

154 The vestry members included Governor Robert Palk, General Stringer Lawrence, the wealthy trader Andrew Ross and several Company civil servants. They were aware of the positive impact of vaccination against smallpox in other parts of the world.

155 Penny: The Church in Madras, 349.

156 John Zephaniah Holwell: An Account of the Manner of Inoculating for the Small Pox in the East Indies with some Observations on the Practice and Mode of Treating that Disease in those Parts. London: T. Becket and P.A. de Hondt, 1767, here 14. For a similar report, see The Ancient and Modern Methods of Treating Small-Pox in India. The British Medical Journal 2:1293, 1885, 716–717: In 1885, Dr Pringle reported from the Ganges Plain of the Himalayas about Brahmin vaccinators who did not want their children to be inoculated by non-Brahmins.

Schwartz found Holwell's extraordinary narrative of Brahmin volunteers of Bengal shocking and unreal.[157] He had closely observed the lifestyle of the Brahmins of Tanjore for several years. He knew how they maintained ritual purity by avoiding blood and keeping themselves away from ritually polluting non-Brahmins. The Brahmins whom Schwartz knew did not share their material wealth with the poor of Tanjore. Therefore, after reading Holwell's booklet, Schwartz reported in 1768 that

> [Many] English gentlemen engage Brahmins to keep their books. [...] In every lucrative situation, we find a Brahmin. [...] With the exception of their daily ceremonies and ablutions, they do nothing, living in voluptuousness and corrupting sloth. They possess the best land and give away little or nothing; besides this, the numerous pagan festivals are eminently profitable to them. [... Schwartz asked a wealthy Brahmin] whether they imparted a portion of their great revenues to the poor. [... The wealthy Brahmin responded:] 'No, the people give to *us* and the pagodas [i.e. temples], but *we* contribute nothing.' What is asserted, therefore, in one of Mr. Holwell's books as to the beneficence of the Brahmins is not to be credited.[158]

In the meantime, on 25 April 1786, the Company in Madras designated a few locations for new hospitals, particularly the military barracks, where soldiers required urgent medical attention.[159] On 9 May 1786, they quickly appointed surgeons and their assistants to oversee the health of their soldiers and the people under their rule.[160] One of these surgeons was Nicol Mein, who started his practice in Tiruccirāppaḷḷi. Neils Brimnes, who studied Mein's role in treating smallpox, stated that in 1787, Mein had successfully inoculated "about twenty soldiers" in Tiruccirāppaḷḷi.[161] On receiving this glad news, the Company in Madras authorised him in December to inoculate "all soldiers who had not had the disease." Brimnes noted that Mein had inoculated in early January 1788 the children of European officers and a few sepoys. This caused him to declare optimistically that he did "not despair of being able to introduce the practice among the natives, & especially the Sepoys."

A few European soldiers stationed at St. Thomas Mount near Madras received this inoculation and were spared from smallpox. Consequently, on 22 January 1788, Mein recommended that the Company Board in Madras allow him to inoculate the Tamil people against smallpox.[162] The Tamil Lutherans were not fully ready to receive this vaccination. For example, Schwartz witnessed the ravages of smallpox during the sweltering summer months. In January 1791, he narrated

---

157 In subsequent years, Holwell's booklet created a debate about the history of vaccination against smallpox in India and Britain. For details about this debate, see Harish Naraindas: Preparing for the Pox: A Theory of Smallpox in Bengal and Britain. In: Asian Journal of Social Science, 31, 2003, Issue 2, Special Focus: Asian Development and Welfare in Crisis, pp. 304–339.

158 Pearson: Memoirs, Vol. 1, 193.

159 IOR/P/252/9, 783–785.

160 IOR/P/252/9, 942–948.

161 Niels Brimnes: Variolation, Vaccination and Popular Resistance in Early Colonial South India. In: Medical History 24, 2004, 199–228, here 202.

162 IOR/P/252/23, 85–109.

how the seven- or eight-year-old daughter of Pastor Sattiyanātaṉ died of smallpox. At her funeral, he could not restrain his tears.[163]

However, Schwartz needed five more years to convince the Tamil Lutherans of Tanjore to accept this inoculation. On 7 March 1795, he reported identifying schoolchildren in Tanjore who had not received any vaccination against smallpox. He inoculated them. The Tamil inhabitants watched that not a single inoculated child died. Therefore, they brought their children to Schwartz for immunisation. Schwartz blamed the migration of people due to war[164] and famine as the primary cause of the spread of smallpox among the inhabitants of Tanjore. He stated that smallpox killed unvaccinated people who were between thirty and forty years of age. It ravaged the people of Ramanathapuram once in ten years. When someone became infected with smallpox, the inhabitants of Ramanathapuram carried the sick person into a forest and left them in a specially constructed wooden hut. They also appointed an older woman to nurse them there.[165] Schwartz did not live to witness the use of the smallpox vaccine, which Edward Jenner discovered on May 14, 1796, and publicised in 1798.[166] However, Schwartz's willingness to incorporate modern medical innovations to alleviate human suffering remains noteworthy.[167]

9.7 Mitigating Poverty

In 1658, the Dutch East India Company defeated the Portuguese and captured Nagapattinam, establishing their Dutch Coromandel Government. However, their rule ended with the Fourth Anglo-Dutch War of 1781, forcing them to retreat to the Dutch Settlements of Pulicat (i.e. modern Pazhaverkadu near Chennai) and Nagapattinam. Some Tamils embraced Dutch Reformed Christianity and organised

---

163 Memoirs of the Rev. Joseph D[aniel] Jænicke, 31.

164 Schwartz's assessment of the relationship between the army and smallpox is dependable. Sriram, a historian who examined Madras' medical history, reached an identical conclusion. See V. Sriram: History of Medicine in Madras. 10.09.2021. URL: https://youtu.be/iENqvuz0NOI (accessed 28.10.2024): In India, Syphilis and smallpox spread wherever British soldiers were stationed. Tamils erected temples to appease *Māriyammaṉ* and called them Taṇṭu-Māriyammaṉ-Kōyil ('a temple for Mother Māri/Smallpox in an army camp'). Such temples in Central Chennai are found in Tiruvottiyur, Royapuram, Chintadripet, Egmore and Mylapore.

165 NHR 4, 1796, issue 48, 1120 and its English version in Memoirs of the Rev. Joseph D[aniel] Jænicke, 121–122.

166 Small-Pox Before Jenner. In: The British Medical Journal 1, 1896, issue 1847, 261–1264. Smallpox existed from time immemorial. In Britain, inoculation against smallpox started in various stages, with Princess of Wales in 1722, the Royal College of Physicians in 1754 and the like. See also, Edward Jenner: An Inquiry into the Causes and Effects of the Variolæ Vaccinæ: a Disease Discovered in some of the Western Counties of England, Particularly Gloucestershire and Known by the Name of The Cow Pox. London: Sampson Low, 1798.

167 Hemingway: Madras District Gazetteer—Tanjore, 155: smallpox continued to kill some people in Tanjore. By 1915, only 19% of the people of Tanjore were vaccinated. 3,000 people died of smallpox in 1869 and 1877; in 1878, 9,000 people died in Tanjore alone of smallpox. In 1884, 3,400 lost their lives to smallpox. In 1900, "nearly 3,800 persons died of this disease."

their lives around their church. After the Dutch had left Pulicat in 1781, these Christians lost government protection, work, and trade, leading to severe poverty. Their plight pained Schwartz greatly. He recounted the efforts of his colleague, William Gericke, who, with the help of a few other Europeans, provided relief to the starving:

> When Negapatnam, that rich and populous city, fell into the deepest poverty, by the unavoidable consequences of war, Mr. Gericke behaved like a father to the distressed people of that city. He forgot that he had a family to provide for. Many impoverished families were supported by him; so that when I, a few months ago, preached and administered the Sacrament in that place, I saw many who owed their and their children's lives to his disinterested care. Surely this, my friend, could not be called a disgrace to that place. When the Honourable Society ordered him to attend the Congregation at Madras, all lamented his departure: and at Madras, he is esteemed by the Governor and many other gentlemen to this day.[168]

While visiting these impoverished Christians in Nagapattinam, Schwartz realised that individual humanitarian efforts were insufficient to tackle the systemic issues. Hence, he appealed to the Company leaders for justice to restore the means of sustenance for these Christians. For example, on 24 October 1793, Schwartz requested that Governor Oakley provide financial support to the poor Christian families in Nagapattinam, who had lost all their income. Initially, a few Englishmen raised money to help these families. Later, the wife of the Dutch Governor, Jacob Mossel, purchased a piece of land and donated it to poor families for cultivation. However, before long, the Company captured Nagapattinam. Those Dutch who lived there moved to Pulicat. From there, they controlled and claimed the agricultural produce of this land, which was then annually transported to Pulicat. Hence, Schwartz requested Oakley to grant them an annual subsidy of forty Pagodas to prevent these families from starving. He articulated his plea based on his theological convictions:

> As God is called the Father of the poor, and as he commonly acts mediately, I wish, and I beg, that Government may be blessed instruments of Providence, by taking the calamity of the poor into consideration.[169]

Schwartz prudently sent his letter to Oakley through William Mitchell, the Company Resident in Nagore. On 25 October 1793, Mitchell forwarded Schwartz's letter to Oakley, adding:

> [I] beg leave to observe that, although the English Government have granted most ample endowment to the Malabar Pagodas, they have not substituted any fund to the maintenance of the poor Christians. Many widows and their children received donations in the Dutch time that afforded them a comfortable livelihood, and who must literally have starved, but from the aid of the Revered Mr Gericke, with some other charitable donations, which latter have been decreasing daily.[170]

---

168 Schwartz: Defence of Missions, 7.
169 Taylor: A Memoir of the First Centenary of the Earliest Protestant Mission at Madras, viii.
170 Taylor: A Memoir of the First Centenary of the Earliest Protestant Mission at Madras, ix.

On 2 November 1793, Oakley tentatively granted forty Pagodas for the poor Christian families on urgent humanitarian grounds, awaiting the "pleasure of the Court of Directors". Thanks to Schwartz's intervention, the Christian families in Nagapattinam were spared from famine and starvation.[171] Thus, he equipped these Christian families to ensure their livelihood, strength and vitality. Schwartz's efforts to mitigate poverty would have enabled these Christians to secure resilience, economic stability, social cohesion, improved health, and their sense of human dignity and self-worth.

[171] Taylor: A Memoir of the First Centenary of the Earliest Protestant Mission at Madras, ix.

Chapter 10

Schwartz as an Educator

10.1 Pietist Education

Schwartz's firm commitment to learning, a trait he carried throughout his life, serves as an inspiration. His educational journey, from his native place to the Glaucha Institutions in Halle (Saale), showed his thirst for new knowledge.[1] He focused his attention on studying the Bible, relevant spiritual texts, and various types of vocational training.[2] After arriving in Tranquebar in 1750 and staying there for twelve years, he had opportunities to familiarise himself with the Pietist education in the Tamil and Portuguese schools for girls and boys.[3] These schools fostered biblical scholarship, a study of Pietist devotional literature and gender-specific vocational skills. Schwartz, however, faced significant challenges in convincing non-Christian parents to send their children to the mission schools. His visit to a few Christian and non-Christian families in Tranquebar on July 7, 1754, revealed the deep-seated fear of non-Christian parents that their children might involuntarily adopt Lutheranism. Therefore, they rejected Schwartz's attempts to introduce Pietist education, which aimed to promote both the temporal and eternal happiness of children.[4]

Schwartz emphasised that a good education should foster moral integrity and responsibility. For example, in October 1768, he wrote to the SPCK about his desire to raise morally responsible citizens. He lamented that non-Christian Tamil parents did not educate their daughters. A few boys learned the art of reading, writing and mathematics. The boys read "books in which the fabled epiphanies of their gods, together with all their licentious acts, are delineated." Schwartz worried that such an education encouraged them to imitate their deities, who practiced "lying, impurity, injustice, and revenge." As a result, these children might conclude that these vices were not sinful.[5] By contrast, Schwartz's education instilled in children a sense of moral responsibility and accountability for their thoughts and actions.

---

1 Germann: Missionar Christian Friedrich Schwartz, 47. On 12.10.1754, Schwartz acknowledged his indebtedness to the model of education he had imbibed in Halle (Saale). He viewed schoolchildren as "lambs" and looked forward to a bright teaching career.

2 The vocational training at the Glaucha Institutions included the art of building houses, saddling horses, establishing business networks with friends in key locations, and improving the socio-economic lifestyle of the people around.

3 Germann: Missionar Christian Friedrich Schwartz, 87. On 31.08.1756, Schwartz began overseeing the Portuguese school in Tranquebar.

4 Pearson: Memoirs, Vol. 1, 109.

5 Pearson: Memoirs, Vol. 1, 192.

10.2 Schools in Tiruccirāppaḷḷi and Tanjore

On arriving in Tiruccirāppaḷḷi, Schwartz established a Tamil school for Tamil children[6] and an English-medium school for the children of Europeans. This English-medium school attracted more children. By 1770, approximately sixty children were enrolled in this school. Their teachers were Wheatley and Green.[7] After Green's death, the senior Lutheran missionary in Madras, Johann Philip Fabricius (1711–1791), sent Aldwell, a former helmsman, as a teacher to Tiruccirāppaḷḷi. Missionary Johann Balthasar Kohlhoff (1711–1790), who worked in Tranquebar, sent his eight-year-old son, Johann Caspar Kohlhoff (1762–1844), to study at this English school.[8]

On 22 January 1771, Schwartz reported to Knapp that in Tiruccirāppaḷḷi, forty children were learning English and thirty children were learning Tamil in schools. Each received half a Gulden (i.e. equal to eight Pennies or four Fano) as their monthly allowance. In the morning, they learned to read; they also heard the teachings of the Lord Jesus Christ. In the afternoon, they learned knitting so they could later perform regular work. The financial assistance provided by Schwartz to the schoolchildren was temporary in nature.

Schwartz remained enthusiastic about educating children in his schools and tried to promote them. He requested his friends, who had returned to Britain, to speak with the Company officers in London about the necessity of educating the children in proper schools. For example, he requested that his friend, Major William Stevens, speak with the Court of Directors in London about erecting buildings for churches and schools in southern India. Unexpectedly, as mentioned above (Section 5.2), Stevens died in Pondicherry on 14 October 1778.[9] In a war between the French and the English, a cannonball had pierced through Stevens' leg,[10] and he died on the same night.[11]

On 23 February 1779, Schwartz reported to his trusted friend Pasche in London about his assistance to two or three children in Tanjore, providing them with two

6 Germann: Missionar Christian Friedrich Schwartz, 132.

7 Pearson: Memoirs, Vol. 1, 212, 239–240: Schwartz built a house for Green, a man who promoted "real Christianity." According to his letter of 16.07.1770, Green was already deceased. Schwartz began training George, who was known to Colonel Wood and his family, probably for teaching in his school.

8 Germann: Missionar Christian Friedrich Schwartz, 210.

9 NHR 2, 1780, issue 21, 1119: On 28.10.1778, Pohle remarked that Engineer Stevens, known for his honesty and generosity towards Christians, died in Pondicherry. Many poor people and Tamil Christians bemoaned the death of their benefactor. Just before his death, he wrote a letter to Schwartz, wishing that Schwartz would be a blessing to the English and the French, their enemies in southern India.

10 AFSt/M 1 B 70 : 40: On 23.02.1779, Schwartz informed Pasche that he had lost his good friend, Major Stevens, in Pondicherry. He was willing to speak with the Company's Court of Directors and others about schools that would best help this country. He booked his passage, and his children had already boarded the ship. A painful sickness seized him just a few hours before the boat could leave the harbour and upended all plans. This sickness resulted from the wound caused by a cannonball hitting his leg.

11 Germann: Missionar Christian Friedrich Schwartz, 305.

sets of dresses and an annual bursary. His work was difficult because he had not received any salary for two years from the SPCK. Fortunately, Major Stevens gave Schwartz 50 Royal Dollars against a bill, which the SPCK could transfer to his relatives in England. Schwartz used that money to maintain his work in Tanjore. The financial burden of keeping his ministry in Tanjore, including paying for Pohle in Tiruccirāppaḷḷi, was a constant concern for Schwartz.

At the same time, Schwartz discussed with General Hector Munro the possibility of establishing two schools for Christian children in Tanjore. The English-medium school should educate the children of European soldiers born to Indian mothers, while the Tamil-medium school would train the children of the Tamil Lutherans in Tanjore. General Hector Munro (1726–1805), who had been the commander of the Company's army in Madras since 1778 and visited Tanjore at that time, initiated a fundraising campaign for these schools. However, the Second Anglo-Mysore War thwarted his efforts. In this context, Schwartz utilised the three hundred Pagodas that Hyder Ali had previously given him to complete the school buildings.

In the Autumn of 1780, the English school, for example, educated ten Eurasian children. Wheatley, who had given up his business in Tiruccirāppaḷḷi, joined the school in Tanjore. During the war between Hyder Ali and the Company, the school was unable to function.[12] On 20 January 1782, Schwartz reported that Wheatley had taught fifteen children in the English school. The Tamil school functioned as it had the previous year. A young, unnamed man taught these children the art of reading, writing and mathematics. A young boy was learning well. Schwartz wanted to employ him to serve the local church, but the boy's father took him away and put him to work in the rice business.[13]

Further support for the English and Tamil schools came from an unexpected source. In September 1787, King Ameer Singh donated the village of Āyarpāṭi near Tranquebar to Schwartz and authorised him to collect revenues from there and use that money as he pleased. Schwartz knew that the revenue of this arid village would be negligible; however, he decided to use it to support the Tamil and English schools for Christian children in Tanjore. Thus, these schools became financially independent. Additionally, Schwartz ensured that these two schools remained part of the Tamil Lutheran congregation in Tanjore, allowing them to support one another mutually.[14]

On 1 February 1788, Schwartz reported to Schulze that the English school for Christian children in Tanjore attracted the children of British captains, sergeants, and soldiers.[15] Some Tamil Christian children also attended this school. They followed a pattern of education that deepened their Christian faith and prepared them for gainful employment. At 5 a.m., they got up and woke Schwartz. Each

12 AFSt/M 1 B 70 : 46; NHR 3, 1783, issue 26, 149 and Germann: Missionar Christian Friedrich Schwartz, 315.
13 AFSt/M 1 B 72 : 58.
14 Germann: Missionar Christian Friedrich Schwartz, 345–346.
15 AFSt/M C 29a : 5.

read a saying and its explanation from the Tamil text of the *Golden Treasury for the Children of God* (i.e. *Güldenes Schatzkästlein der Kinder Gottes*) by Carl Heinrich von Bogatzky (1690–1774). Then, Schwartz led all the children to the church for prayer. Around 8 am, the children ate their breakfast. After Kohlhoff's catechetical lesson, the children had classes on reading English texts. Then, they learned to count numbers. A Muslim teacher taught them mathematics from 11 a.m. to 12 noon. After lunch, they rested for some time. Then, at 2 p.m., they returned to school to continue learning about history and geography. Older children learned Tamil from 3 to 4 p.m. Immediately after that, they practice writing English texts. They spent the evenings with Johann Kohlhoff, playing in the open fields. After dinner, they practised spoken English. Then they went to sleep. Seven diligent Christian boys received special training in English.

10.3 English-Medium Provincial Schools

The available literature on English-medium education in India during the British period has neglected its beginnings in southern India, through the agency of the Company Resident John Sulivan, Schwartz, and local rulers.[16] Schwartz watched how fraudulent and greedy European and Indian dubashes and vakkīls cheated the rulers, traders, farmers and negotiating parties in Tanjore. For example, in 1776, Muthu Krishna was the dubash of Governor Pigot. Pigot's opponent, Paul Benfield, had employed Kolidappa Mudali as his dubash. These dubashes negotiated on behalf of their masters. Often, their masters did not fully comprehend everything the dubashes agreed on. They also interacted with the vakkīls of contending parties. For example, Tulāji employed two vakkīls, "Triumbuch Sambajee and Rudragee Punt." Interestingly, most dubashes, vakkīls, and accountants were either Brahmins or members of leading wealth-generating communities, such as the *Mutaliyār*s.

In 1768, Schwartz noted that Brahmin children were "commonly better educated" and "in general clever"; some became priests in temples, while others owned the best farmlands. Some of them worked for the king and acted as "clerks, overseers and accountants." They quickly learned English and Persian and turned their knowledge to their advantage. Europeans and Wallajah employed them as bookkeepers and interpreters. Thus, Brahmins occupied every lucrative position. According to Schwartz, about 100,000 "vigorous young Brahmins" were in Tanjore. They performed "daily ceremonies and ablutions" and lived luxuriously. They possessed the best lands and employed others to cultivate them. They gave away "little or nothing." Additionally, they benefited economically from the

16 Elmer H. Cutts: The Background of Macaulay's Minute. In: The American Historical Review 58, 1953, issue 4, 824–853. John Bowen: The East India Company's Education of its Own Servants. In: Journal of the Royal Asiatic Society, October 1955, 105–123. Parimala V. Rao: Modern education and the revolt of 1857 in India. In: Paedagogia Historia 52, 2016, issue 1–2, 25–42.

number of religious festivals. They remained indifferent or contemptuous towards Christianity because they knew that embracing Christianity would not bring them economic gains, and they would suffer social misery. Schwartz learned that some of the Brahmins were greedy and proud.[17] Often, these Brahmins prevented other Tamils from embracing Christianity.

Despite numerous obstacles, Schwartz persisted in his efforts to introduce a new education system to the Brahmins, aiming to instil a sense of moral living in public places. The Company's struggles in finding morally upright Indian interpreters and legal representatives during the Second Anglo-Mysore War (1780–1784) underscored the importance of direct communication between Company officers and Indian elites. On 11 October 1784, Schwartz shared his discussions with Resident John Sulivan with Pasche: The Governor of Madras had deputed John Sulivan to address the issues of the Maṟavar Prince in Ramanathapuram. Sulivan requested Schwartz to accompany him as his interpreter. Sulivan and Schwartz met the young prince, who appeared inexperienced and stated that he did not seek the Company's help. Despite these challenges, Sulivan and Schwartz extended their stay in Ramanathapuram. On a Sunday, after they had completed their worship, Sulivan proposed establishing an English-medium school in each province of Ramanathapuram and training reliable interpreters. He suggested that the prince could allocate the village's income to support teachers and children at every school. He encouraged Schwartz to provide teachers trained in his school, literally a *seminarium*, meaning a 'nursery'. Despite the discouragement of young English men coming to Tanjore to teach, Schwartz, aware of the dry climate of Ramanathapuram, desired to build the school near a river or lake. Later, Sulivan and Schwartz presented their idea to the ruler of Sivaganga, who approved of their concept. After Sulivan and Schwartz returned to Tanjore, a minister of the young prince in Ramanathapuram wrote a letter to Schwartz stating that he had assigned the revenues of a village for the school. After that, the villagers met Schwartz and pleaded with him to establish a school in their place.[18] By the end of 1784, Schwartz had established the first provincial school in Ramanathapuram[19] and Wheatley had become its teacher.

On 14 January 1785, Schwartz mentioned that Resident John Sulivan would leave Tanjore in five or six weeks and return to England. Sulivan promised to intercede with the Company and the SPCK in London on behalf of the mission and the schools. If he were to come back to Madras, he recommended that the SPCK accept him as its corresponding member.[20] In February 1785, John Sulivan left Tanjore and travelled to London. He promised Schwartz that he would

---

17 Pearson: Memoirs, Vol. 1, 193: Schwartz contradicted John Zephaniah Holwell's (1711–1798) assertions about the religious "beneficence of the Brahmins." Holwell was a surgeon in Calcutta.

18 AFSt/M 1 B 75 : 24.

19 Germann: Missionar Christian Friedrich Schwartz, 322. This is the modern Schwartz Higher Secondary School in Ramanathapuram, where Abdul Kalam (1931–2015), the famous eleventh President of India (2002–2007), studied (1946–1950).

20 AFSt/M 1 B 75 : 25.

intercede with the Company's Court of Directors and the SPCK in London for more provincial schools.[21] After Sulivan's departure, Major Martins oversaw the completion of this school building and helped build a church in Ramanathapuram. However, the teacher's salary at this school remained an issue.

On 23 February 1785, missionary Klein reported on the outcome of Schwartz and Sulivan's discussions with Tulāji. Just before Sulivan's departure, Tulāji agreed to pay a monthly stipend to a teacher at the provincial school in Tanjore and cover all other costs. Sulivan's arrangements for payment to Johann Kohlhoff and the construction of a new school building near the Tamil Lutheran congregation, along with his provision of beams for the building, demonstrated the significant support and collaboration that Schwartz's mission was receiving, reassuring the audience about the success of the schools.

On 24 September 1785, Schwartz wrote to Pasche that he could establish the first provincial school in Ramanathapuram. At the school's inauguration, he spoke about God's reconciliation with humanity through the Lord Jesus Christ. Ten boys joined this school then, and William Wheatley taught them.[22] The prince and his minister sent their sons to this school, a clear indication of the school's positive influence on the local community. Schwartz left Ramanathapuram and travelled to Tuticorin to talk with the Dutch. There, he expounded on Mark 8:36 to his audience.[23] Upon returning to Tanjore on 2 October 1786, he faced difficulty in establishing a provincial school there, as Wallajah opposed it. Additionally, he was unable to find suitable schoolmasters.[24]

After reaching London, John Sulivan proposed the school project to the Company's Court of Directors, who, surprisingly, recognised the school's long-

---

21 AFSt/M 1 C 27 : 5: On 17.07.1786, Schwartz reported to Sorge that John Sulivan had met the SPCK officers and informed them of the schools. The officers at the SPCK requested that he not take any action until they had written to Schwartz and received his response. This response astonished Schwartz because he had repeatedly presented his ideas about the schools to them. Since his best friend Ziegenhagen was no longer in London, Schwartz had no spokesperson for him there.

22 AFSt/M 1 C 27 : 10; Germann: Missionar Christian Friedrich Schwartz, 322–323: On 14.10.1786, Schwartz noted that Wheatley was married in Ramanathapuram and lived with his family there. He received a monthly salary of ten Pagodas as a missionary. However, he complained that he could not support his family with this money. Subsequently, Schwartz raised his salary to fifteen Pagodas. Cotton: List of Inscriptions on Tombs or Monuments in Madras, Vol. 2, 164: "In sure and certain hope of a happy resurrection to eternal life through our Lord Jesus Christ, here reposeth the remains of WILLIAM C. WHEATLEY, who departed this life the 8th January 1810, aged 36 years and 6 months, who with the fewest failings possessed the noblest virtues of the mind. He was a sincere Christian, a true friend, a tender parent, the most indulgent and affectionate of husbands. In testimony of her irreparable loss, this monument is erected as a small tribute to his much-esteemed memory and many amiable qualities by his affectionate and disconsolate widow, Elizabeth Wheatley."

23 AFSt/M 1 C 25 : 23.

24 AFSt/M 1 C 27 : 8. Penny: The Church in Madras, 520: Schwartz's student Kohlhoff superintended the English school in Tanjore. William Wheatley looked after the school in Ramanathapuram. In 1785, Pohle began caring for the school at Sivaganga, located in the modern Pudukkottai District of Tamil Nadu. This Provincial School educated boys from the higher *varṇa*s. For example, the ruler of Ramanathapuram sent his son to the Provincial School in Sivaganga.

term beneficial effects and decided to support it financially. Consequently, on 29 January 1787, John Sulivan sent Schwartz the directors' resolution and conveyed their caution not to convert any of the boys purposefully.[25] On 16 February 1787, the Court of Directors informed the Governor of Madras of their decision to support the provincial schools, which they referred to as "seminaries."[26] For them, the word *seminary* signified the schools as seedbeds to train young Indians who would serve the Company in various capacities.

> 13) The utility and importance of establishing a free and direct communication with the natives, having been sensibly experienced during the late war in India and their acquiring a knowledge of the English language being the most effectual means of accomplishing this desirable object, it is with great pleasure we learn from Mr John Sulivan, our late resident at Tanjore, that he had, seconded in his laudable undertaking by the zealous exertions of the Rev Mr Swartz, prevailed on the Rajah of Tanjore and the Rajahs of the Great and Little Maravar to establish schools for teaching English at Tanjore, Ramanadapurarm and Shivaganga, the capitals of their respective countries. The latter two assigned pagodas three hundred each to support their two seminaries. Sulivan informed us that these works of peace were interrupted by the calamities of war, and the funds assigned for their support necessarily diverted to other purposes. But we hope they will revive with the restoration of tranquillity.
> 14) Highly approving of institutions calculated to establish mutual good faith, to enlighten the minds of the Natives, and to impress them with sentiments of esteem and respect for the British Nation by making them acquainted with the leading features of our Government, so favourable to the rights and happiness of Mankind, we have determined to evince our desire of promoting their success by contributing two hundred and fifty Pagodas [= £100/-] per annum towards the support of each of the schools abovementioned, and of any other school which may be opened for the same purpose, and we accordingly direct you to pay such schools respectively, the annual stipend of the two hundred and fifty Pagodas flattering ourselves that our example will excite the Native Princes in alliance with us to similar ad more extensive benefactions.[27]

On 6 June 1787, John Chamier of the Company's Military Department in Madras forwarded the approval of the Court of Directors to Schwartz:

> Reverend Mr Swartz at Tanjore
> Sir, I am directed by the Honourable President in Council to enclose extracts of a letter lately received from the Honourable Court of Directors and to request [that] you will give every information in your power, respecting the present state of the institutions in question, with your ideas of the measures which should be taken for the effectual execution of the wishes and instructions of the Court of Directors. I am, Sir, your obedient Servant, John Chamier, Jury.[28]

---

25 Bodleian Library: 72290ind-box2, Document 14 dated 29.01.1787: John Sulivan to Schwartz.

26 The Latin noun *seminarium* refers to a seed plot used to raise seedlings that are then transplanted into specially prepared fields to grow, mature, and yield a harvest. Typically, a seminary is a formal institution that trains Christian priests and pastors for mainline Churches.

27 Bodleian Library: 72290ind-box2, Document 15a dated 16.02.1787: The Court of Directors supporting Schwartz's Provincial Schools; Sulivan: Tracts Upon India, 46–48; Germann: Missionar Christian Friedrich Schwartz, 339–341: Simultaneously, the Company officers in London requested the SPCK to appoint able teachers and direct the function of these schools. The SPCK, too, discussed this offer in their meeting on 06.03.1787 and left the entire matter to the discretion of Schwartz, their trusted representative in Tanjore.

28 Bodleian Library: 72290ind-box2, Document 15 dated 06.06.1787: John Chamier to Schwartz about the Provincial Schools.

Instructed by the Company in Madras, the residents of Tanjore, Ramanathapuram, and Sivaganga agreed to pay £100 annually to each provincial school that Schwartz would establish and exclusively train non-Christian children representing the upper *varṇa*s and *jāti*s. These children would learn the English language by engaging with Christian literature in English. At Schwartz's recommendation, the Company in Madras appointed missionaries Pohle and Kohlhoff as the inspectors of these schools and paid each of them a monthly salary of ten Pagodas.[29] According to a surviving copy of a brief syllabus from 1787, students learnt reading, writing, mathematics, English, Tamil, and Persian to interact directly with Company officers without the need for interpreters and translators. Schwartz, Kohlhoff, and an unnamed teacher educated students at the provincial school in Tanjore.[30]

On 1 February 1788, Schwartz reported that the provincial school in Tanjore, which he had started just two months earlier, had ten Brahmin boys who were curious, determined and motivated to acquire the English language for better, more gainful employment with the Company.[31] He noted that the learning abilities and diligence of these boys were incomparably more significant than those of the Christian boys in the other English school. As they aspired for a better future for themselves, they did not waste any time or opportunity. For example, the youngest boy learnt the alphabet within a day and began teaching it to others on the second day. Every day, Schwartz dictated twenty words and translated them into Marathi, as these Brahmin boys were native Marathi speakers. Johann Kohlhoff and Joseph, who was Schwartz's former servant, taught the boys in the room in Schwartz's house. These boys learnt to write English words in Latin script. They did not object to reading Christian books. Schwartz prayed that this school would truly benefit these children and their people in Tanjore. The Company paid for the maintenance of this school. As soon as more peace prevailed in the country, Schwartz wanted to open more similar schools in other places.

On 14 February 1788, Schwartz informed his friend Pasche in London that he had been preparing to establish provincial schools. The Company in Madras ordered £100 for each provincial school. He had already received his monthly salary of twenty Pagodas and twenty Fano. From the £100, he wanted to give ten Pagodas to Johann Kohlhoff and twenty Pagodas to the inspectors. Schwartz

---

29 Germann: Missionar Christian Friedrich Schwartz, 345.

30 Pearson: Memoirs, Vol. 2, 150–151: Schwartz began his day at 6.30 am with a prayer. After prayer, he watched the children having breakfast. Johann Kohlhoff taught them Christian doctrines from eight to nine and read various texts to them from nine to eleven. Then, another teacher gave them a spelling class. Sometimes, Kohlhoff taught mathematics to older children from ten to eleven. The younger children learned to spell and read the Psalms. A Muslim teacher taught them Hindustani from eleven to twelve. In the afternoon, from 2:00 to 3:00, the older children read easy books on history and geography, while the younger children learned to spell and read from 3:00 to 4:00. From four to five, they all wrote copies and practised writing. From 5:00 to 6:00, they exercised under the guidance of Kohlhoff. From seven to eight, they had a joint prayer. From eight to nine, they ate dinner. From nine to ten, they learned to speak English. Everyone related what they had seen, heard, or read before Schwartz.

31 AFSt/M 1 C 29a : 5.

confessed that he did not want to take the salary for personal use. However, he intended to continue working gladly.[32]

Schwartz desired to establish a provincial school in Kumbakonam and Tanjore to benefit the non-Christian children; however, he faced opposition. On 18 March 1789, he mentioned his conscientious discussion with Ameer Singh and stated that the king had permitted the establishment of schools teaching Hindustani, Persian, Marathi, and Tamil. However, he did not want to have an English-medium school. Schwartz reminded him that he had been helping him as a friend. Thus, he indicated his role in nominating him to succeed Tulāji. Therefore, Ameer Singh should not consider him an enemy. He asked Ameer Singh a pertinent question: "Are you afraid some students might become Christians?" Ameer Singh did not answer this question, but mentioned that, at the time, there had been no need for an English-medium school. Schwartz asked, "Should it remain so in the future as well?"[33]

On 12 January 1790, Schwartz wrote that he had already raised three hundred Pagodas from the village's revenue that he had received from King Ameer Singh. This amount was a substantial contribution towards establishing a school in Kumbakonam. He also trained a young man to be a teacher for the school and hoped to build a church there.[34] However, non-Christians in Sivaganga, Kumbakonam, and Tanjore, who understood Ameer Singh's resistance, troubled Schwartz. They wanted to close his provincial schools. The Company officers supervised the building of the provincial school in Tanjore. Schwartz appointed his faithful Joseph to teach in this school.[35] In Kumbakonam, a group of ascetics threatened to commit suicide if Schwartz would not stop building the school. Therefore, Schwartz could not arrange for the school building until July 1790.[36]

The secretary of the Mission Board in Copenhagen also opposed Schwartz's attempts to indirectly familiarise non-Christian children with select concepts of Christianity. Likewise, William Vincent (1739–1815), the principal of Westminster School in London from 1788 to 1792, expressed his displeasure with Schwartz's

---

32 AFSt/M 1 C 29a : 11.

33 NHR 4, 1790, issue 37, 114–115.

34 NHR 4, 1790, issue 37, 118.

35 Germann: Missionar Christian Friedrich Schwartz, 347–348.

36 AFSt/M 2 E 36 : 1 and NHR 4, 1794, issue 44, 705: In April 1792, Christoph Samuel John visited the Provincial School in Kumbakonam. He stated that when this building was built, Schwartz faced much opposition. It stood in a pleasant place near a pond but away from the loud noises of the many nearby temples. It had a small room and a large hall. Pillars stood around this hall; the roof above it cast a shadow over the veranda. A moderate garden was also present. Its soil was fruitful. Many fig trees, orange trees, pomelo trees and other fruit- and flower-bearing trees adorned that garden. Schwartz's courageous servant, Joseph, looked after this school. John wondered why only twelve of the thirty children were present in the school. Joseph responded that the Tamil children had no concept of punctuality. They also represented the Tamil, Telugu and Marathi families. Each family conducted its religious rituals at separate times of the day. After completing these ceremonies, they might come to school or stay away. Some children translated the reading texts from English into Tamil and exclaimed: "Hey! You want to teach us Christianity. We come only to learn the English language." Thus, Joseph found it difficult to conduct the Provision School. For another account of John's visit, see below AFSt/M 2 E 27 : 13 = NHR 5, 1797, issue 50, 149–150.

efforts to establish provincial schools in Tanjore and to teach non-Christian boys the English language through Christian literature. Vincent asked the SPCK to admonish Schwartz that he should not proselytise Indians indirectly. Instead, he urged Schwarz to be honest and courageous about his missionary vocation. When Schwartz learned of Vincent's opinions, he requested that his trusted friend Pasche inform "the worthy Dr. Vincent that, in preaching, we are straightforward, which all people here are aware of."[37]

We are fortunate to have Christoph Samuel John's eyewitness account of this provincial school. During his travel from Tranquebar to Madras (February–May 1795), he stopped by this school and reported the following:

> I entered Schwartz's school and rejoiced over its clean, proportionately built and comfortable structure. The building has a high tiled roof and is thirty-eight feet long and eighteen feet wide. The entire roof rested on bamboo reapers fixed on round pillars all around. Its well-positioned doors and windows regulate airflow. This school building had a small bedroom. The veranda (*tāḻvāram*, 'porch') with a lower roof stood around the school building. It prevented both sunlight and rain from disturbing the occupants. One can walk beneath it and around the school during sunny and rainy days and watch beneficial trees and plants grow. This entire building embodied the simplicity of life. Its economic necessities were manageable. It is beautiful, comfortable and valuable on all sides.[38]

John explained further that the school had a fertile garden near a pond. The pond owner did not want Schwartz to install a traditional well sweep to fetch water (*ēṟṟam*). Pomelo, orange, and lemon trees could not thrive without sufficient water. Strangely, John called the provincial school English National School (i.e. *Englische National-Schule*) because it was an English-medium school that would train interpreters for the Company. During John's visit, the school had twelve young male students, most of whom were already married. An English schoolteacher taught them. They were Maratha Brahmins. They did not attend the school punctually. They placed greater importance on religious ceremonies and family matters. They surrounded John and spoke with him in English. John suggested that, in addition to the Bible and the standard books used in Christian schools, this provincial school could teach select English texts to educate students further and generate more sympathy for Christianity. Thus, the school should promote English education and interreligious understanding and sensitivity.[39] According to John Crane, these schools facilitated interaction between Tamils and English, enabling them to overcome various prejudices. However, their students still maintained bigotries related to their *varṇa*s and *jāti*s. Frykenberg, too, affirmed the positive impact of Schwartz's schools on their students and the people of Tanjore,[40] laying a firm foundation for modern English-medium education in southern India.

---

[37] Germann: Missionar Christian Friedrich Schwartz, 347.

[38] AFSt/M 2 E 27 : 13 = NHR 5, 1797, issue 50, 149–150.

[39] AFSt/M 2 E 27 : 13 = NHR 5, 1797, issue 50, 150.

[40] Robert Eric Frykenberg: Modern Education in South India, 1784–1854. Its Roots and Its Role as a Vehicle of Integration under Company Raj. In: The American Historical Review 91, 1986, issue 1, 37–65, here 41: By "the 1780s schools run by Christian Friedrich Schwartz and his

10.4 Female Asylum in Madras

Schwartz's schools seem to have inspired new schools in Madras. Gericke and Hüttemann intended to establish an English-medium school for European children in Cuddalore in 1772, but they were unable to execute their plan at that time. However, when Gericke stayed in Madras, he took great joy in planning and forming the Female Asylum.[41] This school for girls was founded on the principles of two Company chaplains at St. Mary's Church in Fort St. George. In November 1785, Chaplains Benjamin Millingchamp and Richard Leslie (1748–1804), planned a society to educate the abandoned children of Europeans, expressed their desire to the SPCK, and requested a schoolteacher:

> The Society is informed that the number of these children is very considerable that the fathers being usually soldiers, sailors, &c, neglect these children and abandon them to the care of their mothers, which means they are neither educated as Christians, which is their birthright nor preserved to the community; but that they are mixed with the natives and lost as they grow up. To obviate this, the Society has determined to make a beginning in this work and, however inadequate their endeavours may appear, they doubt not, if an appearance of success can once be shown, but they shall be assisted by contributions both at home and in India for promoting so good a design.[42]

In the meantime, on 20 December 1786, Schwartz informed Pasche that Governor Archibald Campbell had requested his suggestions for a new school in Madras to educate the daughters of Europeans.[43] He also received from the governor the plans for a Female Asylum drafted by his wife, Amelia Campbell. She stated that she conceived of this Female Asylum in the context of the Second Anglo-Mysore War, which had killed many European soldiers. Some of them had families with Indian and European mothers in and around Madras. Their death impoverished these families. Lady Campbell envisioned educating five types of girls. Firstly, orphan girls without access to food would get priority. Particularly, those girls whose fathers had died in the war would be preferred. Semi-orphan girls or girls of destitute parents would be the next category. Legitimate daughters of the Company's European soldiers and officers, who were married to European women and served on the Company's payroll, would form the third category. Legitimate daughters of poor European parents who lived in Madras but did not serve the Company would create the fourth category. Finally, Legitimate daughters of European civilian fathers and Indian mothers who could not afford to educate their

---

associates (John Z. Kiernander, Daniel Joseph Jaenicke, Christian Wilhelm Gericke, John Kasper Kohloff, Philipp Fabricius, among others) were attracting non-Christian students, especially Brahmans and Vellalars, who hoped that the new learning would better qualify them for positions within the rapidly expanding establishments of the Company."

41 Taylor: A Memoir of the First Centenary of the Earliest Protestant Mission at Madras, 54 and 67: According to Gericke's letter of 16.02.1787, Schwartz did not play any part in establishing this school in 1786. Gericke noted that "good men" had long wished for such an institution. Gericke became its secretary and chaplain, receiving his salary from the Company. Schwartz viewed Gericke as "a sincere Christian– a Nathanael in whom there is no guile."

42 AFSt/M 1 C 25 : 44.

43 AFSt/M 1 C 27 : 25.

daughters would form the fifth category. Wealthy parents could contribute more money to the general fund, which would support all girls whose parents could not afford to spend any money on them. Otherwise, educating a single girl would cost around 1,000 Pagodas (or 2,000 Dollars) towards all expenses. All girls would receive free education, board, lodging, a free school uniform, and clothing. They would learn the values of honesty, rationality and practicality, enabling them to build better families. They would have the same female caregivers and schoolteachers. The teachers possessed demonstrated competencies and unblemished character. There would be one teacher for twelve girls. Lady Campbell had already appointed two governesses for the school. Each would receive free food and lodging in a large house, £100 for clothing, and other necessary expenses.[44]

Amelia Campbell sent a copy of her plan to Schwartz and Governor-General Cornwallis and requested their suggestions for improvement. Schwartz forwarded his copy to Pasche, which was published in the *New Halle Reports*: She addressed Schwartz as "My Lord," a typical greeting among the English to a superior man of high standing. She entertained "exceedingly great respect" for Schwartz's character and sought his advice on the school plan "dear to her heart." She intended to uplift impoverished and abandoned European female children and save them from "ruin and misery." She requested Schwartz's "excellent insight and benevolent heart." She stated that her educational plan would integrate spiritual and temporal matters, enabling educated girls to earn their livelihood in a dignified manner, overcome ignorance and vice, and benefit themselves and their societies. She informed Schwartz that, with the help of wealthy donors in Madras, she would later establish a Male Asylum for abandoned European boys and employ competent British teachers to educate them. Thus, she wished that European parents in Madras would not have to send their children to England for studies but educate them in Madras. She invited Schwartz to visit, inaugurate and bless her school for girls. She closed her letter respectfully as your "most devoted servant, Amelia Campbell."[45] Within a month, Amelia Campbell and her associates founded a Female Asylum within Fort St. George in Madras.[46] She had already raised 14,000 Pagodas to support it. Nawab Wallajah and his son provided her 15,000 Pagodas and a spacious building.

---

44 NHR 3, 1788, issue 34, 1166–1169.

45 NHR 3, 1788, issue 34, 1165–1166.

46 Francis S. Muthu: History of Education in Tamil Nadu. Chennai 2020, 63: Francis Muthu stated that this Female Asylum was located within Fort St. George and intended to cater to the needs of about seven hundred children born to European fathers and Indian mothers. In 1787, sixty-two girls joined that school. In the same year, some Company officers started a male asylum at Egmore in Madras. They admitted one hundred boys fathered by Europeans. The Company gave each boy five Rupees. Andrew Bell taught Christianity and morality at the Male Asylum and followed the Tamil system of Veranda Schools. Here, the older students taught the younger students. Bell's teaching method was known as the Madras System of Education. Gradually, this Male Asylum developed into a Military Male Orphan Asylum and functioned in Egmore.

Amelia Campbell's attitude towards Schwarz remained admirable and unchanged. By contrast, Governor Campbell, who initially praised him, grew cold towards him because Schwartz had opposed his attempts to exploit Tanjore and impoverish Ameer Singh.[47] By contrast, Amelia Campbell considered Schwartz's advice to include catechism in the school syllabus. For instance, on 27 April 1788, she informed Schwartz about rehiring a caretaker to look after the increasing number of girls in the Female Asylum. She confessed to Schwartz that this asylum was initially intended for sixty girls. By April 1788, she had ninety girls who received free education, accommodation, clothing and other amenities. She expected that 100 girls would soon be there. Therefore, she wanted to add more buildings to accommodate and teach them. She singled out Anne Bosworth, a young woman Schwartz might have recommended to this asylum. Amelia Campbell stated that this woman was healthy and made progress in reading, writing, needlework, and learned to dress hair and make lace. Amelia Campbell believed this young woman would soon "earn a living in various ways."[48] Her trust in Schwartz and his professional guidance in educating orphan girls was noteworthy. At his recommendation, Gericke taught catechism to these girls and received an annual salary of sixty Pagodas. Later, Amelia Campbell appointed a chaplain for this job.

10.5 Schwartz's School Teachers and Catechists

Schwartz's mediatory and political works required time and energy. As often as he wished, he could not visit the towns and villages for evangelistic work. Therefore, he recruited, trained and employed Tamil Lutheran teachers and catechists for various jobs. By 17 December 1766, thirty children were studying in the English School and ten in the Tamil School in Tiruccirāppaḷḷi. Catechists Dēvanēsaṉ, Iṉṉācimuttu and Jōtināyakkaṉ assisted Schwartz. In Schwartz's estimation, Iṉṉācimuttu was a willing and honest person who, at times, was timid and careless. During evangelistic tours, Iṉṉācimuttu and Dēvanēsaṉ went together. Jōtināyakkaṉ accompanied Schwartz. Schwartz noted that many people appreciated Jōtināyakkaṉ's witness to Christ and did not mind his low *jāti* status. Iṉṉācimuttu read aloud for others either parts of the New Testament or Johann Arndt's *Garden of Paradise*.[49]

By 22 January 1771, Schwartz had employed five catechists. Dēvanēsaṉ ('God-lover') was a calm man. Schwartz appointed Dēvanēsaṉ's son Rāyappaṉ, who had earlier been his servant, as a schoolteacher.[50] Jōtināyakkaṉ ('Lord of Light'), who

---

[47] Germann: Missionar Christian Friedrich Schwartz, 355.

[48] Bodleian Library: 72290ind-box2, Document 20 dated 27.04.1788: Lady Campbell to Schwartz.

[49] AFSt/M 1 B 56 : 20.

[50] AFSt/M 1 B 68 : 42: AFSt/M 1 B 68 : 45 & Germann: Missionar Christian Friedrich Schwartz, 405: On 14.10.1776, Schwartz informed with great sadness that his excellent disciple and the best catechist, Rāyappaṉ, died. The Lord of Harvest called him home. He

was about fifty years old, was especially lively and had a fine way of dealing with all kinds of people. The 30-year-old In̲n̲ācimuttu ('the Pearl') willingly preached the Lord Jesus Christ. Catechist Dēvasagāyam ('God's help') feared God and was capable of teaching school children. Each catechist received a monthly salary of two Pagodas, enough money to sustain their family. Schwartz considered these catechists to be his source of true consolation because each had their own competencies and complemented one another. In October 1770, Schwartz and Jōtināyakkan̲ spent three weeks in Tanjore.[51]

Gradually, Schwartz's work with the Company increased. With his salary, he could pay more catechists. For example, on 12 October 1772, he reported employing eight catechists. He added Ñān̲apirakācam ('Spiritual Light'), Sattiyanātan̲ ('Possessor of the Truth') and Abiṣēkanātan̲ ('Anointed Lord'). Abiṣēkanātan̲ was twenty-two years old, and earlier, he had worked as a teacher in a school for non-Christians. As a catechist, he taught at a Tamil school. These catechists read a chapter from the New Testament every day at 6 a.m. Then they went out for evangelism and returned between 9 and 10 a.m. Schwartz stated that his excellent and able co-workers expanded and continued his missionary work. They could manage problems caused by non-Lutherans, such as the Roman Catholics in Tiruccirāppaḷḷi.[52]

On January 11, 1774, Schwartz informed Freylinghausen that his eight Tamil co-workers were well and safe. Repeated conflicts between the Nawab and the king of Tanjore made their journey into the countryside difficult. However, in 1773, they travelled more than ever before. The Tamil Lutheran congregation in Tiruccirāppaḷḷi had 146 members. Wheatley and Aldwell, the two teachers at the English school, taught thirty children. It was not easy to find teachers for the Tamil school. The catechist who did not go on an evangelistic tour taught the twelve children in the Tamil school. Some of the former students landed good jobs and earned well.

Schwartz knew that one of his eight catechists was perfect, but honest. Schwartz helped them to develop their God-entrusted innate skills. Although they were willing to grow and serve, they flourished under Schwartz's daily supervision and encouragement. He asked them to imitate his faith, ministry and lifestyle. In October 1772, he took some of them to visit the English soldiers at Fort Vallam,

---

had a strong faith in Christ and loved his work. He was gentle even to those who had been harsh to him. His sermons were orderly. His humility and satisfaction endeared Schwartz to him, and Schwartz considered him his brother. AFSt/M 1 B 68 : 46 & Germann: Missionar Christian Friedrich Schwartz, 406: On 03.02.1777, Schwartz bemoaned Rāyappan̲'s death and confessed that one of his chief goals was to prepare appropriate co-workers. Without their help, missionaries would be unable to achieve anything significant. He stated that Rāyappan̲'s sudden, premature death pained him. He could never forget Rāyappan̲'s exemplary nature, teaching and service. He was competent in lecturing. His love for the Gospel and the non-Christians stood out. Schwartz valued his humility and calm behaviour and could not bear his loss; he cried like someone who had lost his brother. He believed that God alone could prepare individuals for His work.

51 AFSt/M 1 B 60 : 23.

52 AFSt/M 1 B 62 : 32.

which the Nawab's armies captured from the king of Tanjore. The English officers there provided him with a small space for prayer. In 1773, he erected a building sixty feet long and thirty feet wide and baptised forty persons. Later, he baptised forty more soldiers. Thus, eighty persons worshipped God in Vallam. Two of Schwartz's catechists lived and cared for them. At that time, the Tamil Lutherans living in the village of "Goinda Kuritschi" (the modern Kuṟicci township under Tiruppaṉantāḷ administration) suffered troubles caused by the Roman Catholics there. Schwartz met them, but he refused to prosecute the Roman Catholic priest. He encouraged the Tamil Lutherans not to retaliate, but to lead a life of forgiveness, reconciliation and understanding.[53]

On 21 January 1775, Schwartz informed Freylinghausen that all his catechists were well and safe. Iṉṉācimuttu disregarded Schwartz's efforts to help him refine his competencies and refused to repent. Hence, Schwartz dismissed him and allowed him to depart.[54] At the same time, Schwartz appointed two additional co-workers, Sāntappan and another unnamed person. Due to his teaching skills, Schwartz appointed Sāntappan as a teacher in the Tamil school; at that time, this school had twenty-two children. Forty children studied in the English School.[55]

On 20 February 1775, Schwartz reported further that the relatives of one of his senior catechists visited him in Tanjore. Even when Tanjore's inhabitants had freedom, they did not want to embrace Christianity. After the Nawab took over Tanjore in 1773 and attempted to impose his Islamic lifestyle, some inhabitants wondered whether they should adopt Christianity. At that time, Schwartz appointed an unnamed young man and tried to train him as a catechist. Schwartz observed that during the Nawab's rule, more inhabitants of Tanjore, such as an aristocratic man and his family, listened to Schwartz more intently than ever.[56] On 23 September 1775, Schwartz noted that the catechists spoke gently with both non-Christians and Roman Catholic Christians. In their interactions, they demonstrated patience and gentleness.[57]

By 28 September 1775, Schwartz was proud of his nine catechists.[58] He considered them God's gift for his comfort and help. Despite the troubles, oppressions, and exploitations by the armies and landlords of the Nawab and the Company, as well as the country's famines, Schwartz and his catechists were grateful to be alive. Schwartz believed that if he had focused his mind and efforts

---

53 AFSt/M 1 B 63 : 28, AFSt/M 1 B 63 : 58: On 15.11.1774, Freylinghausen acknowledged Schwartz's report of 11.01.1774 and praised him for his services in Tiruccirāppaḷḷi and Vallam. He desired an update on permission to build a church in Tanjore. He was glad the Tamil Lutherans of the village "Goinda Kuritschi" did not retaliate, and Schwartz chose not to prosecute the Roman Catholic Priest there.

54 AFSt/M 1 B 66 : 55: On 23.09.1775, Schwartz recalled that Iṉṉācimuttu was sometimes impatient and premature in his conclusions. He sounded harsh. Otherwise, he meant things well.

55 AFSt/M 1 B 65 : 43.

56 AFSt/M 1 B 65 : 44.

57 AFSt/M 1 B 66 : 55.

58 NHR 3, 1790, issue 27, 116–117: They were Ñāṉapirakācam, Ñāṉamuttu, Gabriel, Savarimuttu, Dēvasagāyam, Sattiyanātaṉ, Savarirājaṉ, David and Salomon. Five catechists were Pariahs and the remaining four were Sudras.

solely on troubles, he would have become a melancholy person. Instead, he focused his attention on God's promises that God could turn things for the better. As a Lutheran Pietist missionary, he interpreted the political events in Tirucirāppaḷḷi through the lens of the stories recorded in the books of the Kings and Chronicles of the Hebrew Bible. Accordingly, God punished the people, but they refused to "see the hand that has beaten them." He viewed the English school with forty children and the Tamil school with thirty children as plant nurseries (lit. Pflanzschule), from which trained students could go to other areas for fruitful service.[59] In his report to Freylinghausen on October 9, 1778, Schwartz emphasised the need for closer supervision of his Tamil co-workers. He acknowledged their helpfulness but also their reliance on constant guidance. He believed they would work willingly and kindly with exemplary leadership, correction of mistakes, daily accompaniment, and loving reinforcement.[60]

On 23 February 1779, Schwartz reported to Pasche that the two catechists in Vallam worked well, and he hoped more people would join the Lutheran congregation there. He also deputed a catechist to Tiruppattur, a place approximately forty miles south of Tiruchirappalli. The ministry of this unnamed catechist was successful.[61] On 24 February 1779, he wrote to Freylinghausen about the harsh conditions in which he attempted to erect a church building. The death of Major Stevens, the departure of Wheatley and Aldwell from their teaching positions and the changing socio-political and economic conditions favoured the Company and Wallajah. He appointed Mr Shipmann, an Englishman, to teach in the English school and Abraham, the son of Jōtināyakkaṉ, to teach in the Tamil school. The young Kohlhoff helped in the school for three hours daily.[62] Schwartz saw the potential impact of these students on the mission, which gave him hope for the future.

On 3 February 1780, Schwartz wrote about his five catechists in Tanjore to Pasche:[63] Catechists Sattiyanātaṉ and Samuel worked in Vallam. Both feared God and performed their duties well. The twenty-seven-year-old Sattiyanātaṉ, who had learnt to read in one of Schwartz's schools, was well rooted in biblical knowledge and local culture. He could critically analyse short sayings and long textual passages. He could write well and remained prudent in his financial matters. He was not greedy. He valued the effects of Christ's substitutionary atonement on the cross. His love for the Lord Jesus Christ and his concern for the salvation of non-Christians were exemplary. He disliked the evil deeds of non-Christians and the dishonesty of many Christians. He was industrious in his work and diligent about the reputation of fellow Christians. Schwartz emphasised that even among European missionaries, he could not find a person with better mental and emotional capabilities. (lit. Gemüthsfaßung). Schwartz translated Sattiyanātaṉ's work report and his exposition of Matthew 11:2–3 from Tamil into German.

---

59 AFSt/M 1 B 66 : 57.
60 AFSt/M 1 B 69 : 45.
61 AFSt/M 1 B 70 : 40.
62 AFSt/M 1 B 69 : 46.
63 AFSt/M 1 B 70 : 46.

Eminent non-Christian inhabitants of Vallam respected him. Schwartz liked to have more workers like Sattiyanātaṉ. He knew that more non-Christians and Christians would benefit from interacting with Sattiyanātaṉ.[64] William Taylor noted that Schwartz's translated version of Sattiyanātaṉ's sermon enabled the SPCK to consider ordaining more Tamil Christian leaders for the Tamil church and to continue Christian ministry even without SPCK's assistance.[65] In this sense, Schwartz worked toward establishing an indigenous Tamil Church.

Schwartz continued to give a few glimpses into the personality and work of the remaining catechists:[66] Samuel in Vallam was only a beginner. He followed Sattiyanātaṉ's role model, advice and even chastisement. Hopefully, he would soon become an impactful co-worker. Catechist Savarimuttu worked in Tiruppatūr. Finally, he took his duties seriously and worked conscientiously. His ministry had been successful. Schwartz translated a portion of his diary word-for-word.[67]

Dēvasagāyam of Tanjore was a diligent and hardworking individual. Sometimes, his mind was not honest, but he was willing to correct this thinking and course of action. His family led an everyday Christian life. Catechist Ñāṉapirakācam was a competent person who sincerely feared God. However, he rushed to premature conclusions, which he would later recognise and regret. He was an angry person and sinned in his great anger. Everyone knew it. Therefore, he had to apologise for it in front of everyone after a divine service. Schwartz was deeply sad about this event, and he wrote that his "heart was bleeding" for Ñāṉapirakācam. Catechist Sāntappaṉ was a gifted reader, writer and mathematician. However, his behaviour was not correct. Therefore, Schwartz had to remove him from teaching in a school. He expected that Sāntappaṉ would repent and become a better servant of God.[68]

On 11 October 1784, Schwartz informed Pasche that Johann Caspar Kohlhoff had the competencies to become a school inspector.[69] Since 1783, Schwartz taught Christian Daniel Klein (born in 1768), the eldest son of his colleague Jacob Klein (1721–1790). He also taught Gericke's son. He spent many hours teaching his servant Joseph to spell words and strove to give him a solid education. Schwartz hoped these students would become helpful teachers and ministers in the Lutheran schools and congregations.

---

64 AFSt/M 1 B 71 : 35.

65 Taylor: A Memoir of the First Centenary of the Earliest Protestant Mission at Madras, 69: Around 1792, the SPCK realised they could not support European missionaries working in India for a long time. Therefore, "if we [the SPCK) wish to establish the Gospel in India, we ought to look beyond the casualties of war or the revolutions of empire: we ought in time to give the natives a Church of their own, independent of our support; we ought to have suffragan Bishops in the country, who might ordain Deacons and Priests, and secure a regular succession of truly apostolic Pastors; even if all communications with their parent Church should be annihilated."

66 AFSt/M 1 B 70 : 46.

67 AFSt/M 1 B 71 : 36.

68 AFSt/M 1 B 72 : 57: On 15.02.1781, Schwartz reported to Freylinghausen that he dismissed Sāntappaṉ from service.

69 AFSt/M 1 B 75 : 24.

On 14 October 1784, Schwartz mentioned that his catechists continued their work.[70] He regretted the death of Dēvasagāyam,[71] and they described him as one of the best and most honest catechists. He died peacefully. During his final days, he devoted himself to studying God's Word and prayer. His life ended quickly, as the sudden quenching of a burning light. Schwartz had recently appointed an honest teacher to look after the Tamil school in Tanjore. He elevated his predecessor, namely Ñāṉamuttu, from a teaching role to that of a catechist. Schwartz had to relocate the English school from the fort to another house near his house, close to the Tamil Church, because the children could not walk the mile between the two places in the sizzling summer.

On 14 January 1785, Schwartz stated that his catechists shared his pain with Freylinghausen regarding the condition of the farmers:[72] The five catechists, namely Sattiyanātaṉ, Ñāṉapirakācam, Ñāṉamuttu, Savarimuttu and Dēvasagāyam, were well. He trained Dēvasagāyam to be a catechist for Pāḷaiyamkōṭṭai. David, the teacher in Tanjore, performed his duties well. They went out regularly to meet Christians and non-Christians and wrote their diaries. Schwartz wanted to translate some portions of these diaries if his time permitted. On 12 January 1785, he sent William Wheatley to teach in the provincial school at Ramanathapuram (Section 10.6.7), and the Maṟavar Prince promised to pay him one hundred Gulden or Rupees. The Prince of Sivaganga, also called "the Little Prince," agreed to pay the same amount to teacher David. Schwartz waited to hear how much the king of Tanjore would pay for a provincial school. He knew that the Company might relieve either a soldier or a sergeant to teach in a school. Regrettably, most of the soldiers were addicted to alcohol. Schwartz hesitated to approve their appointment.

On 26 February 1785, Schwartz informed Freylinghausen of the emerging Tamil Lutheran congregation in Pāḷaiyamkōṭṭai:[73] With the help of Europeans, the Tamil Lutherans in Pāḷaiyamkōṭṭai were erecting a church building. Sattiyanātaṉ cared for one hundred members of this congregation. Schwartz felt the financial burden of this congregation. It was four hundred English miles away from Tanjore, and every journey cost a great deal of money. Nevertheless, he did not want to give it up; he wanted to witness its growth and function.

Schwartz's positive opinion about catechists such as Ñāṉapirakācam and Sattiyanātaṉ was noteworthy. He entrusted them with responsibilities that were otherwise reserved for European missionaries. For example, according to his report of 23 December 1788 to Pasche, he deputed Ñāṉapirakācam to represent Gericke in Vellore for a period of five months. He also stated that Sattiyanātaṉ could easily speak about Christian beliefs and practices with fellow non-Christian Tamils.[74]

---

70 AFSt/M 1 B 75 : 23.

71 NHR 3, 1785, issue 29, 557: On 11.03.1784, Schwartz stated that Dēvasagāyam was on his deathbed. A wound caused by a cat bite started this sickness.

72 AFSt/M 1 B 75 : 25.

73 AFSt/M 1 B 75 : 28a.

74 AFSt/M 1 C 30c : 17 and NHR 4, 1790, issue 37, 110–113.

On 5 July 1791, Schwartz described the calling, preparation, and ordination of his beloved catechist Sattiyanātaṉ on 26 December 1790 as the first pastor for the congregation in Pāḷaiyamkōṭṭai. The country pastor, Rayappan, who looked after Pāḷaiyamkōṭṭai, fell ill and did not recover. Hence, Schwartz called Sattiyanātaṉ and other catechists for consultation. Schwartz testified that Sattiyanātaṉ's ability and honesty in answering the ordination questions and his ordination sermon on 1 Timothy 4:16 were impressive. He desired the salvation of his people. He practised what he preached in his house and then in the church. He lost one of his daughters to smallpox. His other seven-year-old daughter, Sāntāyi (meaning 'mother of peace'), could recite the Lord's Prayer by heart.[75]

To illustrate Sattiyanātaṉ's doctrinal fidelity and communication skills, Jänicke recorded the ordination questions, which Schwartz, Jänicke and Kohlhoff gave to Sattiyanātaṉ and his answers: Sattiyanātaṉ believed that the Lord Jesus Christ was fully human and fully divine because he performed miracles, exorcised the devil, fed the hungry and depended on God the Father. Apart from the Lord Jesus Christ, humans could not attain salvation. Jänicke asked Sattiyanātaṉ to comment on the followers of the Lord Jesus Christ, who had recognised him as the source of their salvation and yet sinned. Sattiyanātaṉ explained that God always forgives the repentant sinners. Kohlhoff wanted Sattiyanātaṉ to comment on the relationship between God's general revelation in nature and special revelation in Scripture, the characteristics of a person's spiritual rebirth, and the necessity of doing evangelism. Schwartz, Jänicke, and Kohlhoff were so satisfied that Schwartz ordained Sattiyanātaṉ and delegated him to care for the congregation in Pāḷaiyamkōṭṭai.[76]

Schwartz's admiration for Sattiyanātaṉ remained undiminished. He was aware of his weaknesses but focused on developing his positive characteristics. For example, on receiving a commendatory letter from William Wheatley of Ramanathapuram about Sattiyanātaṉ's preaching and public ministry, on 13 April 1795, Schwartz sent the following reply to Wheatley:

> Your regard for Sattianadan, the country priest, is very pleasing. Be sure none has esteemed him so much as I have done. His preaching is edifying, for his knowledge is competent. But in humility he is deficient, and there to those that are under him over-bearing, which has caused great complaints against him. His indulgence in his children is extravagant, and he has spoilt them. His daughter has been married to a pious catechist. I will not say that she despiseth her husband, but to his mother, brother, and sister, she will not show even common civility by which she has lost their regard. The father observes this, and is grieved, but instead of rebuking the daughter, he follows her example. I have frequently entreated him to show kindness to those people, considering that his son-in-law will not abandon his mother and relations, for his wife's sake. Having a mind to preserve peace betwixt both, I suffer by these animosities.[77]

---

75 AFSt/M 1 C 32a : 11 partly printed in NHR 4, 1792, issue 40, 384–388.

76 AFSt/M 1 C 32 : 35 and NHR 4, 1792, issue 40, 390–396.

77 Taylor: A Memoir of the First Centenary of the Earliest Protestant Mission at Madras, xvi. Every keen observer can detect the importance of esteem and trust in professional workers. This quote highlights the consequences of indulgent parenting, tensions between mothers-in-law and daughters-in-law, the necessity of maintaining peace for the health of marriage and the reputation of stakeholders in public places and functions.

On January 8, 1796, Schwartz mentioned that he had celebrated his seventieth birthday three months prior. Sattiyanātaṉ, who was sick, could not write to the SPCK and needed medicine. His competence was widely recognised among all Christians. Schwartz particularly appreciated his approach to engaging with non-Christians. He stated that he was patient with Sattiyanātaṉ's egoism. Sattiyanātaṉ quickly recognised his mistakes and asked for forgiveness.[78]

On 12 July 1796, Schwartz informed the director of the Glaucha Institutions that he had chosen ten Tamil male students for training as catechists and schoolteachers. He taught them Lutheran theology, history of Christianity, and scriptural exegesis. They, in turn, demonstrated intellectual aptitude and moral convictions. He asked them to accompany the catechists when they visited Christians and conversed with non-Christians. He gave them a small stipend to help them meet their basic needs. Six months later, on January 9, 1797, these boys demonstrated a more profound understanding of biblical theology, based on the Old and New Testaments. They understood the reason for their faith distinctly and convincingly. When they accompanied the catechists, they spoke with both Christians and non-Christians, recording their observations in a journal.[79]

The fellow Catechist Savarirāyaṉ narrates a rare account of the Catechist Aruḷappaṉ: Accordingly, Schwartz identified, trained and baptised Aruḷappaṉ in Tranquebar. His unnamed mother hailed from Madukkūr, in modern-day Tanjore. She brought her two sons, two daughters and a sister's son to Tranquebar. Her other son was Rāyappaṉ. The names Aruḷappaṉ ('Gracious Father' = John) and Rāyappaṉ ('Emperor-Father' or 'Royal Father' = Peter) indicate their Roman Catholic ancestry. They learned Lutheranism from Schwartz and embraced this new form of faith. Schwartz noticed the talented sons. Aruḷappaṉ became a schoolteacher in Tranquebar, and his brother became Schwartz's servant. His ways of training candidates for baptism impressed Schwartz so much that he appointed him as a schoolteacher. Catechist Savarirāyaṉ was a son of Aruḷappaṉ's sister. He praised the faithfulness of his uncle as a catechist in Poṟaiyār near Tranquebar. He expressed unhappiness about his later years, during which Aruḷappaṉ was often ill and could not perform his work effectively. After thirty-two years of service, Aruḷappaṉ died on 6 September 1795.[80]

The foregoing section on Schwartz's teachers and this brief biography of Catechist Aruḷappaṉ demonstrate Schwartz's ability to identify, train, and appoint capable Tamil co-workers to perform delegated tasks. He met them every week, received their work reports and discussed ways to improve their performance with them. He met their needs and ensured their welfare. They carried on his work in and beyond the areas assigned to them.

---

78 AFSt/M 1 C 37a : 2.
79 Memoirs of the Rev. Joseph D[aniel] Jænicke, 135–138.
80 NHR 4, 1797, issue 50, 140–141.

10.6 Schwartz's Students and Friends

10.6.1 Johann Caspar Kohlhoff

Johann Caspar Kohlhoff (1762–1844) was a son of Johann Balthasar Kohlhoff and Pernille Kohlhoff in Tranquebar. When he was eight, Schwartz adopted him in 1770 and took him to Tiruccirāppaḷḷi for education and training. Schwartz often travelled to other places, but he did not forget his protege. For example, on 16 November 1778, he wrote from Tanjore, encouraging Kohlhoff to experience God's love, which he described as "the fountain of our happiness and holiness too." As many prudent non-Christians had done, the person who was unaware of this fountain might outwardly lead a morally upright life. Nevertheless, inwardly, they would never turn to God and give God all glory. They would not permit God to comfort, amend, and reform them. Finally, Schwartz encouraged Kohlhoff to pray for God's love and take comfort in the presence of the Holy Spirit.[81] His trust in Kohlhoff and his paternal love for him knew no bounds. On 23 October 1779, he was overjoyed to receive a letter from Kohlhoff and to know that his mentor, Christian Pohle, had recovered from his sickness. While he was pleased about Kohlhoff's physical well-being, he reminded him to care for the health of his soul by uniting it to "God your Father through the Merit of Jesus. This is the very centre of all our happiness in time." The health of his soul was infinitely more important than anything else. Hence, he advised Kohlhoff to grow more in "grace and knowledge of our Lord Jesus Christ." Finally, Schwartz asked Kohlhoff to greet his friends, Pohle, Mrs. and Mr. Duffin, and send his horse to Tanjore ahead of his arrival there.[82]

Similarly, Schwartz introduced Kohlhoff to his friends and taught him the strategic significance of networking in missionary work. On 29 November 1779, he asked him to send Catechist Siṉṉappaṉ to meet the German army officer, Landsknecht, and to deliver the items he had requested.[83] In the same way, Schwartz was pleased that Kohlhoff had spoken with people from other religious traditions and admonished him: "Sometimes we lose the truth by flattering them; sometimes we lose our temper by attending to their flawed speeches. Both are wrong."[84] Therefore, it was better to state the truths and let them work in the people's hearts and minds.

Again, on 27 July 1780, Schwartz wrote a detailed reply to Kohlhoff's several letters, confessing that although he could not respond to his letters, his affection

81 SPCK D 36, Microfilm frames 4–6.

82 SPCK D 36, Microfilm frames 11–14.

83 SPCK D 36, Microfilm frames 6–7.

84 SPCK D 36, Microfilm frame 15. A testimony of a Muslim illustrates how Schwartz practised what he preached. Lives of Missionaries–Southern India [Ziegenbalg, Schwartz, Jaenicke and Gericke]. London, 1854, 120: "Padre, we always regarded you Europeans as a most irreligious race of men, unacquainted even with the nature of prayer, until you came and told us you had good people among you in Europe. Since you are come here, indeed, we begin to think better of you."

for him had not diminished. His love for him was "hearty and shall be so always by the Grace of God." He encouraged Kohlhoff to persevere despite his problems with the European parents of some schoolchildren. He was unhappy with the arrival of Catechist Sāṉtappaṉ, whose extravagant lifestyle plunged him into debt and who did not "keep his fingers clear from taking even bribes." Schwartz hoped that Sāṉtappaṉ would "turn to God, but his heart is too slippery and worldly. God help and convert him." This was Schwartz's way of advising Kohlhoff to avoid dishonest people like Sāṉtappaṉ. Then, he appreciated Kohlhoff's reading of the Book of Common Prayers in public worship services. He encouraged him to learn both Hindustani and Persian to communicate more effectively with the speakers of these languages. He requested that Kohlhoff air, clean, and safely store his old books. He expressed his happiness about Kohlhoff's efforts to teach Christian doctrines to others: "To instruct a soul in the excellent knowledge of Christ —how great a thing! The world, poor and infatuated, does not value it. But their foolish judgments must not disappoint anyone." He encouraged Kohlhoff to

> read your Bible more and more with [a] hearty prayer to God. I wished you could learn so much Greek as to be able to read your New Testament. Today, our Golden Treasury gives us a passage out of the 23 Psalm. Though I walk through the valley of the shadow of death, I will fear no evil, for Thou art with me—the happiness of the presence of Jesus with [... six unreadable words]. May you and I continually enjoy that inestimable blessing. Amen! [... Let] Jesus be your Wisdom, Righteousness, Sanctification and redemption. Your affectionate friend, C. F. Swartz.[85]

On 7 January 1783, Schwartz taught other significant lessons about maintaining interpersonal relationships. He acknowledged the receipt of Kohlhoff's letter through catechist Ñāṉapirakācam and shared the news of Pohle's stay in Tranquebar, which he termed as "natural." He tried to persuade Pohle to return to Tiruccirāppaḷḷi; however, Pohle preferred to have fellowship with fellow missionaries in Tranquebar more than being alone in Tiruccirāppaḷḷi. Then, Schwartz included these highly instructive lessons:

> I entreat you never to mention anything in your letter which giddy people say of him. It affects him and makes him quite uneasy. I heartily wished he could disregard such trifling speeches. The world is world till the Spirit of Jesus enters into their heart. They will not, and they cannot become better people. Their own nature is like a wilderness where thorns and thistles grow but no wheat or any useful plant. Why should we be disturbed by a few giddy words?
> As you are alone, I entreat you [to] be very careful in your words and actions. The world may try, nay, tempt you. Be you strengthened by the power of God. Be not lazy in prayer and meditation of the word of God. The Greek Christians called it ἀκηδία indolence in divine thing. May the Spirit of Jesus lead you!
> I believe it will not be prosperous for you to visit a house like Mrs Inden's. In the presence of Pohle, it is quite different. It is not as if I doubted her or your intention, but I mean to stop people's mouths, for you know how the English love joking, even that, we ought to avoid as much as possible.

---

85 Bodleian Library: 72290ind-box2, Document 7 dated 27.07.1780: Schwartz's letter to J. C. Kohlhoff.

> Be employed on the Word of God, and the Spirit of Jesus will be with you. Having just preached, I finish this short letter with my best wishes and supplications to the Father of Light to help you plentifully and strengthen and confirm you by his grace. I am truly your friend, Swartz.[86]

In his autobiography dated July 7, 1783, Kohlhoff explained his training with Schwartz from 1770 to 1780: after eight years of learning, he taught English, mathematics, and catechism at the English school there. Apart from briefly visiting his parents in 1780, Kohlhoff stayed with Schwartz until 1781. He helped Schwartz recover from a knee injury caused by the fall of his horse. Kohlhoff read the Book of Common Prayers to the English congregation in Tanjore. Then he returned to Pohle in Tiruccirāppaḷḷi and began learning Greek. He taught in the Tamil and English schools there; on Sundays, he led the worship services for the English congregation.[87]

In another letter, dated 1 August 1783, from Ramanathapuram, on his way to Pāmpaṉ, Schwartz scolded Kohlhoff for not having immediately sent off his letter to Sorge. He asked Kohlhoff to encourage Pastor Rayappaṉ to preach on one Sunday in the city congregation at Tanjore, and on other Sundays, he should visit the village congregations. Likewise, Kohlhoff should instruct the Catechist Ñāṉapirakācam to preach one Sunday in Tiruccirāppaḷḷi and other Sundays in village congregations.[88] Thus, he taught Kohlhoff the administrative skills of delegation and supervision. On 10 August 1783, Schwartz thanked Kohlhoff for sending the letter to Sorge, who had preached at Vallam and baptised two children there. He reported that at Pāmpaṉ, he ministered to Mr. Nevil, his two daughters, and Ms. Paschal. He confessed that he had not seen a better-organised household than Mr. Nevil's, and their desire to commune with the Lord Jesus Christ. Schwartz asked Kohlhoff to arrange for the planting of beans, digging pits and filling them with manure for pumpkins and guava plants. He should send a Brahmin to get local seeds. The children in the provincial school in Ramanathapuram could repeat what he taught them by then. They were still unable to think independently. Hence, Schwartz advised Kohlhoff to ensure that the schoolchildren in Tanjore learned to read, write, and speak well. Finally, he asked him to keep track of receipts for all income, expenses, and outstanding debts. Thus, Schwartz's training encompassed both spiritual and temporal aspects, remaining holistic.[89]

Schwartz appreciated Kohlhoff's dedication to ministry. On 16 February 1784, Schwartz desired to ordain him as his co-worker and successor.[90] A few months

---

86 Bodleian Library: 72290ind-box2, Document 11 dated 07.03.1783: Schwartz's letter to J. C. Kohlhoff.

87 AFSt/M 1 B 74 : 17.

88 SPCK D 36, Microfilm frames 18–20.

89 SPCK D 36, Microfilm frames 21–23.

90 AFSt/M 1 B 74 : 27. The authorities in Halle found it challenging to find suitable missionary candidates for Tranquebar. Even those young missionaries who came to the Tamils proved incompetent and unfit. At the same time, Schwartz grew older, sicker, and increasingly weaker; his ministries in Tiruccirāppaḷḷi, Tanjore, and other places expanded. He wanted to train successors.

later, on 14 October 1784, he reiterated his intention to Freylinghausen: just as Francke's Orphanage had prepared leaders for successive generations and sent them to various parts of Europe, Schwartz wanted his congregations in Tanjore to prepare leaders for various Christian congregations in southern India. For example, the fledgling congregation in Pāḷaiyamkōṭṭai, about four hundred English miles away from Tanjore, urgently needed leaders. Schwartz sent Rāyappaṉ to visit that congregation and paid 20 Pagodas for travel expenses.[91]

On 14 January 1785, Schwartz stated that Kohlhoff preached in the Tamil church on two Fridays of the month and at Sunday worship services. He taught catechism in the English school; every Sunday, he read from the Book of Common Prayer in the English worship services. He led the prayer meetings of the Tamil Christians every Sunday evening. He was learning Greek and improving his interpretive skills. When Schwartz was away, he read the prayers, liturgy and a sermon for the English church. Every day, he spent an hour learning the Persian language. All people appreciated his humility and willingness to learn. Schwartz gave him 20 Pagodas as a monthly allowance, which he received from the Company as a gift. Schwartz planned to appoint Kohlhoff as the inspector of all schools, and thus, he would be eligible to receive a monthly salary from the Company.[92]

On 17 August 1785, Schwartz visited Pāḷaiyamkōṭṭai. He informed Kohlhoff that he had not yet met the Brahmin woman, Clarinda, upon his arrival. Regarding the height of the windows for the Tamil church in Tanjore, Kohlhoff should consult the architect Ripley, who would oversee the project through his brick master.[93] In an undated letter from Pāḷaiyamkōṭṭai, Schwartz encouraged Kohlhoff to read his letters carefully and respond to any queries. For example, he asked Kohlhoff to send him a copy of a Latin Grammar. He found it strange that Kohlhoff could not locate it in his library. Earlier, when he had received it from his father in Tranquebar, he used it seriously. In this context, he recommended Kohlhoff to learn new languages like Latin and German because his young mind was carefree. Hence, he could learn anything with ease. However, he should direct his learning to glorify God by being beneficial to fellow human beings.[94] Otherwise, his learning would be useless. Thus, he helped Kohlhoff to set his priorities right and grow holistically.

On 24 September 1785, Schwartz informed Pasche about his three-week extended stay in Pāḷaiyamkōṭṭai and his joy over Clarinda and her team. They had just finished erecting a church building, where Schwartz daily imparted various aspects of Lutheran Pietist doctrines to the new members. He administered the Eucharist to eighty members. He did not name the things that saddened him, but he stated that, like in all Christian congregations, one could find "wheat and weeds."[95]

---

91 AFSt/M 1 B 75 : 23.
92 AFSt/M 1 B 75 : 25.
93 SPCK D 36, Microfilm frames 24–25.
94 SPCK D 36, Microfilm frames 27–29.
95 AFSt/M 1 C 25 : 23.

In the meantime, in September, the SPCK permitted Schwartz to ordain Kohlhoff as a missionary for Tanjore.[96] On 24 September 1785, he informed Pasche in London and his missionary colleagues in Tranquebar about this permission and requested their blessings.[97] On 23 January 1787, Schwartz ordained Johann Kohlhoff in Tranquebar. It was also the jubilee day of his father, Johann Balthasar Kohlhoff (1711–1790), who had started his missionary work in Tranquebar fifty years earlier in 1736. Schwartz reported that the whole city was celebrating this event. European and Tamil Christians filled the church, and many non-Christians assembled in the churchyard. The ordination service lasted three hours, and everyone was unusually silent, yet they thoroughly enjoyed the event.[98]

On 6 February 1787, Schwartz described the events before and after the ordination:[99] Schwartz and Pohle travelled together to Tranquebar; all missionaries in Tranquebar participated in the preparatory events. Each missionary sent a question; finally, the questions covered the areas of dogmatic theology, casuistic theology (i.e., science and religion), polemics, ethics and morality, exegesis, Church History, and Christian freedom. Just as the Danish Lutheran Rites required, the missionaries led John Caspar Kohlhoff into a school hall, gave him a Bible and their questions and asked him to give his answers in writing. After he had passed the exam, on 23 January 1786, Pohle spoke about Jesus' question to Peter in John 21: "Do you love me?" Pohle stressed the virtues of love, hope and patience. Then, Schwartz went to the altar; Johann Kohlhoff kneeled beside him. His seventy-five-year-old father sat near him. Schwartz spoke about 2 Timothy 2:1: "Be strong, my son, through the grace of Christ Jesus!" He explained the responsibilities of a father. Then he ordained him. This ordination moved the assembled people so emotionally that they shed tears of joy and thanked God. On 24 January 1787, the missionaries in Tranquebar, known as the Danish missionaries, and the missionaries outside of Tranquebar, known as the English missionaries, jointly wrote a letter to the Mission College about Kohlhoff's ordination:

> As the Honourable College de Cursu Evangelii Promovendo, established by His Majesty the King of Denmark at Copenhagen, have given full Power to their Missionaries at Tranquebar to ordain such candidates as they may judge fit for the ministry and as the Honourable Society for Promoting Christian Knowledge at London have declared by the Reverend Mr. Pasche, that they wished that the eldest son of the Reverend Mr Kohlhoff, who has been educated and properly prepared for the ministry by the Reverend Mr. Schwartz, might be ordained to be English Missionary. All the missionaries, Danish as well as English, have examined the abovementioned son of the Reverend Mr. Kohlhoff, viz. Mr. John Caspar Kohlhoff and having found him fit both in respect of knowledge and piety, have accordingly ordained him in the Church of Tranquebar, January 23rd, 1787, in the presence of the Danish Government and clergy. They, therefore, certify by these that the above-mentioned Mr. John Caspar Kohlhoff

---

96 AFSt/M 1 C 25 : 33: On 08.10.1785, Schwartz informed Pasche that the entire committee of the SPCK did not authorise Kohlhoff's ordination. However, one of Schwartz's friends persuaded them to accept Kohlhoff's ordination and him as their missionary.

97 AFSt/M 1 C 25 : 32.

98 AFSt/M 1 C 27 : 27.

99 AFSt/M 1 C 27 : 24.

> has been lawfully ordained and thereby empowered to preach the Word of God publicly, administer the Holy Sacrament and perform all other ministerial functions. They, therefore, entreat everyone to regard him as a minister of the Gospel lawfully ordained. Their fervent wish and prayer to God is that the Reverend Mr John Caspar Kohlhoff may prove a faithful and successful servant of Jesus to the spiritual welfare of many souls.
> Given at Tranquebar, January 24th, 1787, in the presence of the Danish and English Missionaries here assembled.
> Christian Friedrich Schwartz, Christian William Gericke, James Klein, John Frederick Konig, Christopher Samuel John, John Peter Rottler [and] Peder Rubek Hagelund.[100]

If only Schwartz had lived longer, he would have rejoiced in seeing how Kohlhoff influenced the conversion of outstanding Tamil Christian leaders, such as Maharajan Vētamāṇikkam (1762–1827) of Mayilādi (formerly in the Travancore region, now in Kanyakumari District) and David Sundaranantham of Tirunelveli. When they visited Kohlhoff in Tanjore, he received them kindly and taught them the basics of Lutheranism. Consequently, they embraced Lutheranism. Upon their return to their native places, they shared their faith with relatives, friends, and neighbours. Vētamāṇikkam, the first Tamil *Sāmbavar* missionary from Mayilādi, established Lutheranism in his native place. Likewise, David Sundaranantham founded the first Lutheran congregation among the Nadars and established Mudalur ('First Settlement') as the first refuge village in Tirunelveli in 1799. Thus, he provided them with a place free of religious persecution.

Kohlhoff's followers appreciated his ministry dearly. When he passed away in 1844, they mourned and had an epitaph installed in his honour in St. Peter's Church in Tanjore. The epitaph explicitly recognised him as the "Pupil of the Venerable Schwartz and his successor."[101] It ends with the Tamil text of Daniel 12:3, which can be translated as follows: "Those who have been teaching discernment (lit. putti, from Skt. buddhi, 'intellect, discretion') resemble the brightness of the heaven, and those who bring many into righteousness shall always shine like the eternal stars."

Johann Caspar Kohlhoff's grandson, Christian Samuel Kohlhoff, came to Mudalur in 1839. He represented the Society for the Propagation of the Gospel in Foreign Parts. After serving there until 1844, he moved to other places. During this tenure at Mudalur, he established Christianagaram ('Christian City') as another city of refuge. Then, worked in the village of Udangudi and other places. He died in Tranquebar in 1887. Nowadays, these cities of refuge are thriving centres of Christians who send out their missionaries. In a way, the early Protestant Christians of Tirunelveli and Kanyakumari are Schwartz's grandchildren.

100 Bodleian Library: 72290ind-box2, Document 16 dated 24.01.1787: Declaration of John Caspar Kohlhoff's ordination.

101 "Sacred to the memory of the Reverend John Caspar Kohlhoff, Missionary of the Honourable S.P.C.K, who was born in Tranquebar on the 23rd of May 1762 and departed this life at Tanjore on 27th of March 1844. He was the Pupil of the Venerable Schwartz and his successor in this Mission, in which by God's grace he laboured 47 years."

10.6.2 Clarinda

An overview of Schwartz's theological views about marriage and baptism helps us better understand his interactions with Clarinda. Schwartz insisted that marriage embodied the loyalty of the spouses. Unfaithfulness indicated idolatrous relationships that broke the marital covenant.[102] When Schwartz expounded on the sixth commandment of the Decalogue, which prohibits adultery, he explained its visible and invisible forms. The invisible forms of adultery included improper or wicked thoughts (*pollāta niṉaivu*), pondering over promiscuous ideas (*mōka vikāramāṉa iccai*), lustful looks (*mōha pārvai*) and speaking and listening to lewd things (*acutta vārttai*).[103] Schwartz proceeded to describe the moral implications of the tenth commandment of the Decalogue, which prohibits coveting the wife (*peṇcāti*) and female servant (*vēlaikkāri*) of one's neighbour.[104]

Schwartz did not teach baptism (*ñāṉastāṉam*, a 'spiritual bath') as either a ritual of sprinkling water or a ceremony for giving names to the children of Christians or converts. By contrast, he stressed its spiritual contents. According to his teachings to the Tamil people, baptism conferred on the baptised person the spiritual substance (*ñāṉa-p poruḷ*): this substance included not only the sufferings, blood and death of the Lord Jesus Christ but also the salvation (*iraṭcippu*) that he had earned for all human beings. Therefore, the baptised person begins to enjoy a love-induced, intimate relationship (*aṉṉiyōṉṉiyam*) with the Lord Jesus Christ and has the certainty (*uttaravātam*) of forgiveness of sins. God the Father (*pitāvākiya parāparaṉ*) becomes the father of those who have accepted the vicarious sacrifice (*uttiravāta pali*) of the Lord Jesus Christ; he loves them (*cinēkittal*, 'to love as friends') and protects them as his children. The Lord Jesus Christ leads those who have identified themselves with his death and intercedes for them. The Holy Spirit adorns those who have accepted the blood and death of the Lord Jesus Christ with all spiritual blessings. Moreover, the Holy Spirit leads and strengthens them on their spiritual path.[105]

Schwartz responded to Clarinda from his theological perspectives on marriage and baptism. In 1778, some European Christians in Madurai and Pāḷaiyamkōṭṭai requested that Schwartz visit them and conduct their marriages. At that time, he met Clarinda (1746–1806), the founder of the first Lutheran congregation in Tirunelveli. He reported on her and her ministry: during his stay in Pāḷaiyamkōṭṭai, Schwartz prepared a few children for baptism. At that time, a Brahmin widow brought her adopted son for baptism. Schwartz explained her background: after living with an English military officer in Tanjore as his concubine, she sent a messenger to Schwartz to find out whether he would baptise her. Schwartz viewed her concubinage as a sin and refused to baptise her. Later, he discovered that the

---

102 Schwartz: vikkiraka pattik kāraṉukkum, 51: Nobody would appreciate a married woman who simultaneously loves her wedded husband and another man. Likewise, humans cannot worship their true Creator God and idols at the same time.

103 Schwartz: vikkiraka pattik kāraṉukkum, 51.

104 Schwartz: vikkiraka pattik kāraṉukkum, 61.

105 Schwartz: vikkiraka pattik kāraṉukkum, 158–160.

English military officer might have secretly promised to marry her. Schwartz met this officer and admonished him not to keep a concubine. That officer responded to Schwartz that he was always sick with *Podagra* ('gout,' gout of the big toe). The Brahmin widow took care of him well. Hence, he bequeathed to her whatever he possessed.

As Clarinda lived with him, he taught her the English language, biblical stories and Christian doctrines. She decided to embrace the form of Christianity which the officer practised. She wanted to belong to the Tamil Lutheran Church in Tanjore, so she tried to find out whether Schwartz would baptise and take her into the church. After a considerable time, Schwartz met Clarinda in person in Pāḷaiyamkōṭṭai; by that time, her situation had changed drastically. The English military officer died; she had adopted a son, and they lived in Pāḷaiyamkōṭṭai.

Clarinda requested Schwartz a second time for baptism. He taught her various aspects of Lutheran Pietism and listened to what others said about Clarinda. They informed Schwartz that she lived an honourable life and overcame many challenges. Whenever Brahmins tried to persuade her to renounce Christianity, she courageously advised them to give up their image worship. Schwartz baptised her in March 1778; he gave her the baptismal name 'Clarinda' at her request. She eagerly heard God's Word and prayed.[106]

In 1778, Vicuvāci, the Tamil Lutheran catechist of Ramanathapuram, visited Clarinda and assisted her in leading the congregation in Pāḷaiyamkōṭṭai. His report praised her ministry. It stated that Clarinda's former identity as a Brahmin and her determination to embrace Christianity delighted several Tamils. They knew that, in the past, missionaries and catechists had spoken with numerous Brahmins, finding them to be impressive discussion partners; yet, they did not embrace Christianity. They joyfully welcomed the baptisms of Clarinda and her adopted son in March 1778. Vicuvāci admired Clarinda's deep knowledge of God's Word and exemplary Christian life. He remembered how often she had invited him to discuss Christian doctrines with non-Christians and Roman Catholic Christians, especially with the women who had gathered in her house. Some of these women came from distant places. He observed how astonishingly and impactfully Clarinda had been teaching the women.[107]

Clarinda looked after her congregation for eleven years. On 25 June 1799, Pohle solemnised the marriage of an English merchant in the house of Paymaster Light near Pāḷaiyamkōṭṭai. He wanted to meet Clarinda and added a few details about Clarinda's earlier life: she was the widow of a Maratha Brahmin who was employed in the royal service at Tanjore. She also had a royal lineage. People called her "Rasa Clarinda," meaning the "Royal Clarinda." She was known for her honesty as a Christian. She worked for the good of her household and "governed" them well. On 26 June, Pohle met a thirty-year-old non-Christian who desired baptism. This man was a servant of Clarinda. She had instructed him in the Christian faith. Pohle's assistant introduced this non-Christian to some aspects

106 AFSt/M 2 E 17 : 12 and NHR 2, 1780, issue 21, 1095–1096.
107 NHR 2, 1781, issue 22, 1195.

of the Small Catechism. On 29 June 1799, he baptised this man and named him Yōvāṉ (i.e. the Tamil version of John). Clarinda and another Christian man, who possessed several books on Christianity and was well-versed in the faith, were Yōvāṉ's godparents. Pohle noticed Yōvāṉ's desire to know more about Christianity, salvation and baptism. Pohle encouraged him to continue learning from Clarinda, his benefactor. On 30 June 1799, he solemnised Yōvāṉ's marriage in the house of Rasa Clarinda and married him to Mariyammāḷ, Rasa Clarinda's eighteen-year-old adopted daughter. During his eight-day stay in Pāḷaiyamkōṭṭai, Pohle interacted with other Christians, spoke with several Roman Catholics and reached Tiruccirāppaḷḷi on 8 July 1799.[108]

Missionary reports do not talk about Clarinda for the next four years. On 8 March 1784, the missionaries in Tranquebar reported that Rasa Clarinda came to Tanjore to meet Schwartz, who was away on a journey. Two companions accompanied her; they were Roman Catholic Christians who had previously visited Tanjore. Pastor Rayappan did not know what to do with her during Schwartz's absence, so he sent Rasa Clarinda and her companions to Tranquebar. These two companions were aware of a washerman who also practiced medicine. He had read the Tamil New Testament and the *History of Christianity*.[109] He understood the teachings of the Roman Catholic Church of that time and discussed them with his acquaintances. As a result, Roman Catholic Christians in various places became aware of the movement initiated by this washerman. Clarinda's two companions reached Tanjore in the name of Roman Catholic Christians who sought to learn more about the teachings and practices of the Tamil Lutheran Church. They intended to invite a missionary or a Tamil Lutheran Pastor to visit them in Pāḷaiyamkōṭṭai. The missionaries discussed various possibilities and decided to send Catechist Vicuvāci, who was working in Ramanathapuram, to Pāḷaiyamkōṭṭai. Clarinda had no biological children; therefore, she adopted a son, who, immediately after his birth, received an emergency baptism. Schwartz confirmed this baptism. Now, she wanted her son to study under Schwartz. After waiting a month to meet Schwartz, she left Tanjore towards the end of January 1784. As soon as Schwartz returned to Tanjore, he deputed Catechist Ñāṉapirakācam to assist Clarinda in Pāḷaiyamkōṭṭai.[110]

Catechist Vicuvāci's diary for 1784 contains additional information about the visit of Rasa Clarinda and her two Roman Catholic companions: Vicuvāci received them in Tanjore; he observed their sorrow for not being able to meet Schwartz and requested that he, as an able Tamil Lutheran pastor, would engage with the

---

108 NHR 2, 1782, issue 24, 1429, 1432–1433.

109 Christoph Theodosius Walter: Historia Sacra – Rerum in Ecclesia inde ab orbe condito ad nostrum vsque actatem gestarum notitiam exhibens Historia Sacra, [...]. Tranquebar: Typis et sumtibus Missioni Danicæ, 1735. This *Sacred History* presents in seven parts the history of the Church from its origin in the Book of Genesis to 1735. It points out the church's progress, struggles between "the kingdom of light and darkness," governance and discipline, and the origins of ecclesial customs and rituals. Walther wrote it for the benefit of the Tamil Lutheran Church.

110 NHR 3, 1786, issue 31, 757–758.

considerable number of Roman Catholics in Tirunelveli region. The two Roman Catholics wanted to know more about Lutheranism and receive baptism in the Tamil church. Vicuvāci accompanied them to meet the missionaries in Tranquebar; they, in turn, asked Vicuvāci to travel with the visitors to Pāḷaiyamkōṭṭai and gather more information about the Roman Catholics in that region. Vicuvāci stated that the local people referred to Clarinda as a pāppāti (i.e. a Tamil term designating a Brahmin woman). Clarinda requested that Rayappan, the Tamil Lutheran Pastor in Tranquebar, come and work full-time with her. As she could wait no longer, she, her companions, and Vicuvāci returned to Tanjore. On 27 January 1784, they reached Ramanathapuram, and after three days, they began their journey towards Pāḷaiyamkōṭṭai.[111]

Vicuvāci's diary for 1784 states further that Piccaimuttu,[112] the washerman, who was also a medical practitioner, lived in a place called Oṭṭārampaṭṭi. He visited his family members, including his brother-in-law, elder brother, and others, in many villages and explained why he did not follow the teachings and practices of the Roman Catholic Church at that time. Vicuvāci[113] and Piccaimuttu tried to enter the places that belonged to "Wanschimattandan" alias Rama Swami (Vañci Mārttāṇṭaṉ),[114] who ruled Travancore. Customs officers at Fort "Areiwambuli" (Āralvāyamoḻi) stopped them because they realised that Vicuvāci and Piccaimuttu were "Wedakarer" (i.e., Vēdakārer, meaning "people of the Veda," or Christians). Therefore, both men visited other places outside Travancore and returned to the *Pāppāti* Clarinda.[115]

On 22 March 1784, Vicuvāci left Pāḷaiyamkōṭṭai and returned to Ramanathapuram. Schwartz was unhappy with Vicuvāci's lifestyle and professional performance. After eleven years of being patient with him, hoping for improvement, on 13 April 1795, he informed William Wheatley in Ramanathapuram about his disappointment over Vicuvāci and his decision to dismiss him from service: Vicuvāci "belongs to the Tranquebar Mission. The Christians at Ramnad complained before Mr Jänicke that he had neglected them

---

111 NHR 3, 1786, issue 31, 758–775.

112 Germann: Missionar Christian Friedrich Schwartz, 323: Piccaimuttu's name in the Roman Catholic Church was Anthōni Muttu ('the Pearl of St. Anthony'). When people emphasised his medical competency, they called him Antōni Muttu. However, the Lutheran missionaries introduced him as Piccaimuttu ('Muttu as a Gift').

113 Wilhelm Germann: Die Kirche der Thomaschristen – Ein Beitrag zur Geschichte der Orientalischen Kirchen. Gütersloh 1877, 613: When the chaplain Claudius Buchanan left Tanjore in 1806, Johann Caspar Kohlhoff sent with him a Tamil catechist who had been raised by Schwartz and served as a catechist. This catechist lived in Tranquebar for some time and was fluent in Malayalam. He served as Buchanan's interpreter in Travancore. Germann suggested that this catechist belonged to the family of the Tamil medical doctor Piccaimuttu. In 1783, Schwartz sent another catechist, Vicuvāci, to Travancore with a letter for the king. For details on Vicuvāci's travel, see NHR 3, 1786, issue 31, 758–762.

114 Rama Varma I, also known as Dharma Raja, ruled Travancore from 1758 to 1798.

115 NHR 3, 1786, issue 31, 758–75: Clarinda built a House of Prayer at that time. She appointed Mariyacavari as a reader. On 7 March 1784, Catechist Ñāṉapirakācam of Tanjore, deputed by Schwartz, reached Pāḷaiyamkōṭṭai and began working among the people there.

for 3 months, so that they had not seen his face all the while. He has complained of the country priest [Sattiyanātaṉ]. But enough of this. I do not want him."[116]

In this context, Germann opined that the missionaries in Tranquebar did not regard the reliability of Vicuvāci, the medical competency of Piccaimuttu, the reputation of Clarinda, or the genuineness of some Roman Catholics in Tirunelveli, who sought to embrace Lutheranism. These missionaries asked their Tamil pastor to work in Tranquebar and their catechists to serve in the countryside. By contrast, Schwartz trusted his catechists. He valued Clarinda's leadership and sent Catechist Ñāṉapirakācam to assist her in Pāḷaiyamkōṭṭai. His impact on the Christians of Pāḷaiyamkōṭṭai was so remarkable that in July 1784, Schwartz sent Rayappan, the Tamil Lutheran pastor, to Pāḷaiyamkōṭṭai. Rayappan was Ñāṉapirakācam's father-in-law. In November 1784, both men returned to Tanjore. They reported that they had interacted with 51 Christians in Pāḷaiyamkōṭṭai, a group of Tamil Christian sepoys in Srivilliputhur and thirty Christians in Piccaimuttu's native place Oṭṭārampaṭṭi. By that time, Clarinda created "Tereivalli," a place south of Pāḷaiyamkōṭṭai, as a refuge for the Shanar Christians.[117] Twenty-four Christians lived there, and Catechist Mariyacavari was responsible for their spiritual welfare.[118]

One of the converts who belonged to Clarinda's congregation was Dēvasagāyam, the father of the famous poet Vēdanāyagam Sāstiriyār. Dēvasagāyam had joined Clarinda's Lutheran congregation because his Roman Catholic priest did not permit anyone to grow a beard. He opposed this priest, who cut off the beard of his friend. Consequently, the priest excommunicated Dēvasagāyam, who began reading the Tamil New Testament printed in Tranquebar. Catechist Ñāṉapirakācam met him and explained the distinctive Lutheran doctrines and practices to him. When Schwartz came to Pāḷaiyamkōṭṭai, he met Dēvasagāyam and tried to train him as a catechist.[119]

---

116 Taylor: A Memoir of the First Centenary of the Earliest Protestant Mission at Madras, xvi.

117 AFSt/M 1 C 29a : 11: On 07.02.1788, Schwartz wrote about a village near Tiruccirāppaḷḷi as a place of refuge for Christians. Originally, Pohle suggested that if a few Christian families could live together in a town, they could cultivate and earn their livelihood collectively. Schwartz could not support this idea because he feared that non-Christians could attack them quickly and Christians too could develop a ghetto mentality. He suggested integrating the life of Christians with non-Christians. Though he was not for an exclusive place for Christian dwelling, he started a similar place of refuge for the Tamil Lutheran Christians in Tanjore. Thus, non-Christians would have more opportunity to hear God's word. However, he had already established a place of refuge for Christians in Tanjore.

118 Germann: Missionar Christian Friedrich Schwartz, 323–324.

119 Germann: Missionar Christian Friedrich Schwartz, 324–325: After his return to Tanjore by mid-January 1785, Schwartz deputed catechist Sattiyanātaṉ to assist the Christians in Pāḷaiyamkōṭṭai. He also requested the local commander of the Company's army to assist Piccaimuttu and his fellow Christians in worshipping in the same church. These Christians hailed from *vaṇṇār-jāti* ('bleachers', washermen of soiled clothes). Clarinda welcomed them into her congregation. The commander gave beams and other building materials for the church. Clarinda and other Christians invited Schwartz to dedicate the church. Sattiyanātaṉ returned in June and narrated good things about Christians in Pāḷaiyamkōṭṭai. As a result, Schwartz left Tanjore in August 1785, visited Ramanathapuram and Tuticorin and reached Pāḷaiyamkōṭṭai. At that time, this congregation had 150 members, eighty were new communicants.

On 28 January 1785, Schwartz noted that the Tamil Lutheran congregation in Pāḷaiyamkōṭṭai consisted of approximately 150 persons, belonging to around 30 families. Some of them honoured God and led promising lives. Schwartz wanted to have catechists who could teach the whole counsel of God to the new Christians. He observed the short attention spans of those Christians who struggled to concentrate on long sermons. In this report, Schwartz stated that he had brought with him two seventeen-year-old boys from Pāḷaiyamkōṭṭai to train them for church ministry.[120]

On 17 October 1785, Schwartz informed Johann Kohlhoff about his arrival in Pāḷaiyamkōṭṭai the previous day and that he had not yet met Clarinda, the "Brahmin Widow."[121] Clarinda did not appreciate Schwartz's warning to her, and he found her proud and careless in a few matters. At the same time, Schwartz praised her for her hospitality to pastors and catechists, her sacrificial giving to the church and her charitable help to the needy. He praised Piccaimuttu for his evangelistic zeal and dedication to regularly holding prayer meetings in his house. He persuaded Piccaimuttu to allow his seventeen-year-old son to go with him to Tanjore for training. Likewise, he persuaded Dēvasagāyam to send his son Vēdanāyagam to Tanjore. Once, Schwartz heard Vēdanāyagam's prayers and immediately knew he would be a great leader for the Tamil Church. As a poet, Dēvasagāyam, like his son Vēdanāyagam, took pride in his poetic skills. Schwartz admonished him to concentrate on Christ, not merely his lyrical skills.[122]

No information about Clarinda appeared in the *New Halle Reports* for another seven years. On 13 May 1792, Pohle mentioned that Clarinda and her adopted son, Henry Lyttleton, visited Tiruccirāppaḷḷi on their way from Tanjore; they departed from Tiruccirāppaḷḷi on 16 May 1792. Clarinda requested Pohle to pray for her, and Pohle advised her to shun sin and grow further in holiness.[123] On January 14, 1794, Christoph Samuel John lamented that Clarinda had recently passed away.[124] On 1 February 1794, the missionaries in Tranquebar, Johann Friedrich König, Christoph Samuel John, Johann Peter Rottler and August Friedrich Cämmerer, communicated the same message. They mourned Clarinda's death and that of other women leaders in Tranquebar, such as the school principal Aṉpāyi, who passed away in March 1793, and the prayer leader Savariyammai, who recently passed away. The loss of these influential women leaders affected the community, so they appointed the widow Aṉṉamai as the prayer leader.[125]

---

120 AFSt/M 1 C 26 : 1; Germann: Missionar Christian Friedrich Schwartz, 325–326: One of these boys was Vēdanāyagam (Section 10.6.3). The other boy was the son of Piccaimuttu.

121 SPCK D36.

122 Germann: Missionar Christian Friedrich Schwartz, 325–326.

123 NHR 4, 1794, issue 45, 785.

124 NHR 4, 1794, issue 45, 839: John's report also contains the following details: An English officer of the Company met Pohle in Tiruccirāppaḷḷi and urged him to send catechists to Salem and Namakkal. While the Gospel was preached widely in Tiruccirāppaḷḷi and Tanjore areas, the people of Salem and Namakkal had not yet heard it. Consequently, Pohle went to these places. In his absence, Jänicke looked after the Lutherans in Tiruccirāppaḷḷi. After Pohle's return, Jänicke wanted to visit Pāḷaiyamkōṭṭai.

125 NHR 4, 1795, issue 46, 927.

On 12 April 1800, Gericke noted that Schwartz wanted a missionary to visit the congregation in Pāḷaiyamkōṭṭai once a year and stay there for an extended period. On their way, they should see the Lutherans in Madurai and Ramanathapuram, where Schwartz had dedicated church buildings.[126] In 1802, missionaries John, Rottler, and Cämmerer reported that, among all the South Indian congregations Schwartz had initiated, the one in Pāḷaiyamkōṭṭai had the most significant number of members. Jänicke and Sattiyanātaṉ pastored them. They believed that in the future, Pāḷaiyamkōṭṭai would become the centre from which the Gospel of Salvation could reach non-Christians in distant places. The missionaries and Tamil Lutheran pastors observed how the Lutherans of Pāḷaiyamkōṭṭai, as local agents, lived their faith; their lifestyle attracted several non-Christians to embrace Christianity.[127]

On 17 January 1803, Rottler narrated what Gericke had told him about his two-month ministry in Pāḷaiyamkōṭṭai: an unusual revival had taken place in Tirunelveli. It was not about converting ten or twenty people as one might witness in Tiruccirāppaḷḷi, Tanjore, or Tranquebar. Instead, more than 1,000 persons had embraced Christianity.[128] People of entire villages and districts had become Christians and were eager to learn. They dispensed with the images and temples of their earlier worship; instead, they sang praise to the Lord Jesus Christ. After Gericke had left them, Sattiyanātaṉ looked after them.[129]

Successive generations of Christians in Tirunelveli took pride in Clarinda and her legacy. Their opinions about her resemble the views found in the annual reports of the SPCK and local oral traditions. They appreciate her determination and the example she sets for overcoming the stigma attached to widows in India. As a model leader, she gathered members from diverse *jāti* backgrounds to worship in the same church. Thus, she opened a new way for social harmony that was rare in these regions. In 1871, W. T. Satthianadhan, a famous Anglican priest of the Church Missionary Society in Tirunelveli, reminisced about the origins of Protestant Christianity in Tirunelveli and regarded Clarinda as a forerunner.[130]

In 1915, the novelist A. Madavaiah (1872–1925), from Tirunelveli, composed his *Clarinda: A Historical Novel*.[131] It weaves historical information into the

---

126 NHR 5, 1800, issue 56, 799.

127 NHR 5, 1804, issue 60, 1046.

128 These Tirunelveli Christians followed the examples of Clarinda and their first martyr, Siṉṉamuttu Tāvītu Suntarāṉantam.

129 NHR 5, 1804, issue 60, 1804, v.

130 Satthianadhan 1871, 360: "Exactly one hundred years ago, a Native Christian from Trichinopoly, named Schavrimootoo [i.e. Savarimuttu], made his way to Palamcota and employed himself in reading the Scriptures there. Meanwhile, a sergeant in the same place, who had married a native Protestant, undertook to do what he could. He met a young heathen, an accountant, who was willing to be instructed and, after making him learn the five principal articles of the catechism, baptised him." After that, Clarinda "was instrumental in building the first church erected in Tinnevelly. It was from this grain of mustard seed that the stately tree has sprung, which is overshadowing Tinnevelly."

131 The first edition was published by Cambridge University Press in Madras. The Sahitya Academy in Chennai published its third edition in 2005. For its assessment, see Kristen Bergman Waha: Synthesizing Hindu and Christian Ethics in A. Madhaviah's Indian English Novel Clarinda (1915). Victorian Literature and Culture 46, 2018, 237–255.

imaginations of a novelist in a gripping way. Clarinda's original name was Kohila. The English officer with whom she lived was Lyttleton. In 1992, David Packiamuthu, a Christian from Pāḷaiyamkōṭṭai, published a second edition of this novel. He carefully studied available English and Tamil sources on Clarinda. Clarinda's death date differs. As indicated above, the German sources show that Clarinda died in the 1790s. However, Packiamuthu argued that the year of her death was 1806. Otherwise, he captured the essence of Clarinda's contributions and her significance as follows:

> Clarinda (1746–1806) was a historical person. She started the first school in Palayankottai, dug out wells, helped the poor, opened dialogue with catholic Christians and built the first Protestant Church in Tirunelveli. The well to the north of the church, known as Pappathiammal Kinaru ['the well of the Brahmin Woman'], is still in use. [...] Clarinda's activities have been mentioned in missionary dispatches and by some European historians. She was a contemporary of the martyr Chinnamuthu David Sundaranandam, the first Shanar catechist and founder of the first Christian settlement, Mudalur, and Samuel Sawyer, the European merchant who championed the cause of the oppressed Christians and founded the village of Sawyerpuram.[132]

Scholars have used Clarinda's story for various purposes. S. Chinnaiyan understood Clarinda as a woman who accepted European ideas of remarriage, embraced the emancipation introduced by Christianity, and demonstrated the possibility of widows leading respectful lives and making significant contributions to their society. She was willing to overcome caste barriers and serve as a catalyst for social change among the people of Tirunelveli.[133]

In 2006, Eliza Kent presented Clarinda as a "Widow, Concubine, Patroness." She reviewed the facets of Clarinda's life as described by German, English, and Tamil scholars, highlighting her abiding significance for Tirunelveli Christians, women's leadership, and social transformation. She examined the names and backgrounds of the first converts, who belonged to Clarinda's congregation, and how she managed to promote harmony and peace among Christians representing various jāti backgrounds.[134]

---

132 Anantanarayanan Madhaviah: Clarinda—Historical Novel. Tirunelveli ^{2}1992, here 251–262: Madhaviah consulted Orme's History of Hindustan, Ranade's Rise of the Maratha Power, Hemingway's Gazetteer of the Tanjore District, Bishop Caldwell's Tinnevelly Mission, Frank Penny's The History of the Church in Madras, Col. Malleson's Clive and Dupleix (Rulers of India), Sir Charles Wilson's Clive (English Men of Action), Hickey's The Tanjore Principality: The Land of the Tamulians, Narasimmalu's Tamil History of South India, etc.

133 Chinnaiyan: Social History of Thanjavur 1532–1799, 67, 74–75 & 77: The Brahmin widow Kohila married a European military officer and got the name Clarinda. "The advent of Christianity resulted in the emancipation of the widows to some extent." Christian missionaries arranged job opportunities for them (e.g. spinning and weaving). Eighteenth-century Christianity in Tanjore loosened the "policy of rigidity against the remarriage." "The Clarinda episode stands testimony to it." European liberal ideas and Christianity changed the attitudes of Indians towards widowhood, remarriage of widows and their work.

134 Eliza F. Kent: Raja Clarinda—Widow, Concubine, Patroness: Women's Leadership in the Indian Church. In: Halle and the Beginning of Protestant Christianity in India. Vol. II: Communication between India and Europe. Ed. by Andreas Gross et al. Halle 2006, 659–684.

10.6.3 Vēdanāyagam Sāstiriyār

Another influential student of Schwartz was Vēdanāyagam ('Master of the Veda/Bible,' 1774–1864), whom the Tamil Christians still celebrate as the Prince of Tamil Christian lyricists. His biography, written by his second son, Noah Gnanadickam Sāstiriyār (1864–1902), contains several references to Schwartz's impact on him.[135] Vēdanāyagam's Father Aruṇācalam Piḷḷai (b. 1735), a staunch Śaivite and a native of Tirunelveli, met the Tamil Roman Catholic catechist Ñāṉēntira Kaṇiyāṉ, who introduced him to his priest Vētapōtakaṉ (the 'Teacher of the Veda,' i.e. the Bible). Aruṇācalam's conversations with this priest led him to embrace Roman Catholicism and to receive his baptismal name, Dēvasagāyam ('God's Help'). Dēvasagāyam worked as a catechist and composed songs on Christian themes.

On 7 September 1774, Dēvasagāyam and his wife Ñāṉappū ('Spiritual Flower') had a son; they named him Vētapōtakaṉ. Out of reverence to their priest with the same name, they called their son Vēdanāyagam. Dēvasagāyam arranged private tuition for his five-year-old son under a Tamil grammarian. Gradually, Vēdanāyagam came to appreciate the richness of the Tamil language and literature. After the death of his wife Ñāṉappū, Dēvasagāyam asked his parents to look after his son and two daughters. Grandfather Savarirāyaṉ ('Emperor Xavier') did not let Vēdanāyagam continue his studies; instead, he asked him to tend the cows of his village. Dēvasagāyam was unhappy about this arrangement. Therefore, in 1783, he arranged for his son to attend a school in a nearby town. Vēdanāyagam had a vision of the cross that seemed to pass before him. When he narrated this vision to his grandmother, she told him he would become a great man.

Dēvasagāyam's friend Noṇṭi Ñāṉi ('the lame wise man'), who wore a beard, could not follow the instruction of the new Catholic priest. This priest had a beard and did not want any of his congregation members to wear beards. He forcefully cut off Noṇṭi Ñāṉi's beard. This insulting action provoked Dēvasagāyam, who questioned his priest's authority in social and civil matters. Consequently, the new priest excommunicated Dēvasagāyam. Noṇṭi Ñāṉi's role in this incident was that of a friend and fellow believer who faced the same challenges as Dēvasagāyam, highlighting the social and cultural conflicts that arose from the introduction of Christianity in India.

In 1785, Dēvasagāyam heard of *Pāppātti* Clarinda's new building for corporate worship and her assistance to those in need. When Dēvasagāyam approached her for employment, she directed him to Catechist Ñāṉapirakācam. She and Ñāṉapirakācam sent him to Tanjore to study under Schwartz. Dēvasagāyam stayed with Schwartz for four months, got to know the distinctive features of Lutheranism, and returned to Pāḷaiyamkōṭṭai and worked as a Lutheran catechist. During his work, he obtained a copy of the New Testament printed in Tranquebar, copied it onto palm leaves and distributed them freely to others. He also composed many lyrics on the teachings of the New Testament.

---

135 V. Noah Gnanadickam Sastriyar: Life of Vedanayagam Sastriyar. Tanjore 1987.

When Schwartz visited Pāḷaiyamkōṭṭai in October 1785, he observed how earnestly the twelve-year-old Vēdanāyagam prayed. He persuaded Dēvasagāyam to accompany him to Tanjore for training. Vēdanāyagam studied with Schwartz for four years. Schwartz introduced him to the Book of Psalms and demonstrated a life of devotion to God, as well as a commitment to serving the people and evangelising those who had not yet accepted Jesus Christ as their Saviour. In 1789, Schwartz sent him to study under the missionaries Christoph Samuel John, August Friedrich Cämmerer and Johann Peter Rottler in Tranquebar. Vēdanāyagam stayed with them for two years, learning systematic theology, astronomy, mathematics, and storytelling. He tried to understand the German language, but he had limited success. By contrast, he could acquire a working knowledge of English. Schwartz invited him back to Tanjore, sent him as a catechist to work in different congregations around Tanjore, appointed him a schoolteacher and asked him to teach Christian theology and mathematics.

After Schwartz's death, Vēdanāyagam's sphere of activities expanded. Remarkably, he specialised in *Catur*.[136] He staged his dramas in Madras and other places. After watching his drama *Sāstirakkummi* in Tiruccirāppaḷḷi in 1815, Christian Pohle gave him the title Sāstriyār ('theologian, expert, pandit'), a title of profound respect and honour in the Indian cultural context.[137] Vēdanāyagam's admiration for Schwartz was profound. He absorbed his theological, moral, and social teachings and expressed his indebtedness to Schwartz in his Tamil lyrics, poems, dramas, and books. He credited Schwartz with introducing him to music and systematic theology, enabling him to become an expert (*camarttaṉ*) in these disciplines. He considered himself Schwartz's best student of Tanjore, who had become a teacher.[138] As his proud and grateful student, he praised Schwartz as his teacher and himself as his proud and grateful student.[139]

10.6.4 Johann Christian Obeck

Another student of Schwartz was the German Johann Christian Obeck (1731 – ca. 1773), who earlier worked as a teacher in Cuddalore. Schwartz interacted with him in Tanjore. In 1785, Schwartz wrote to Charles Grant (1746–1823) in Calcutta, introducing him as his "old and sincere friend." Schwartz allowed Obeck to live at his house in Tanjore. After Obeck moved to Calcutta to serve Grant, Schwartz expressed his esteem for him. He expected to meet Obeck again "in the world free from sin and grief."[140] Morris, the biographer of Charles Grant, described Obeck's character as follows:

---

136 Catur ('four things') refers to the simultaneous use of drumming, speaking, dancing and singing. It is a form of evangelism.

137 Since that time, he and his male descendants, who receive Protestant episcopal ordination are known as Vēdanāyagam Sāstiriyār.

138 Noah Sāstriyār, 2023, 2: 61st stanza of *Parama Nītippuroṇam*: 'vāttiyār vētanāyakaṉ cōṇāṭṭiṉ | valiya cuvāṭccu aiyaruṭa vaḷamaic cīṭaṉ'.

139 Noah Sāstriyār, 2023, 2: 70th stanza in Part 1 of *Ñāṉa Kummi*: 'tañcai cuvāṭccu aiyar vāḻkavē vēta | nayaka cāstiri vāḻkavē'.

> [Obeck] was a German by birth and had married a Portuguese wife. He was of humble extraction, and his manners were rather uncouth, but he was so excellent, simple, affectionate and such a true-hearted Christian that Grant and his family were much attached to him. He was familiarly called 'the Old Pilgrim.' He was frequently taken into their confidence in matters of importance. He was tolerably skilled in medicine, and in the absence of a resident doctor, he was regarded as the family physician. He appears to have treated Grant most judiciously in a serious dysentery attack.[141]

When Grant faced personal problems, Obeck advised him to meet John Zacharias Kiernander (1711–1799), the only Lutheran Pietist missionary in Calcutta from 1757 to 1799. Kiernander was instrumental in the exchange of letters between Grant and Schwartz.[142] For example, on 20 October 1786, Schwartz asked Pasche in London whether he knew of the Methodists' intention to start a mission station in Bengal and informed him that Thomas Coke (1747–1814) and his friend Barker had contacted three friends in India, namely William Chambers in Calcutta, Kindersley in Madras and Torrians in Vellore.[143] They requested that Schwartz address Coke's plan. Schwartz politely declined because he was unsure how the SPCK would respond to his correspondence with the Methodists in London. He advised his three friends to write to Coke and Barker; without mentioning his name, they should inform them that a faithful Christian would be happy to see the Name of the Lord Jesus preached to the non-Christians. They should not emphasise their denominational distinctives as Methodists. Instead, they should preach Christ as our wisdom, justice, sanctification, and salvation.

Coke had also contacted Charles Grant. After consulting Obeck, whom he esteemed as Schwartz's student, Grant wrote from Malda near Calcutta to Schwartz in November 1785:

> The Methodists have set on foot a scheme and opened a subscription for a Mission to India. Of a letter written to me on this last subject, I enclose you a duplicate, as the communication of it may not be unacceptable to you. I have answered it with the assistance of our friend Mr Obeck, giving such information as we could on the points inquired about, not concealing, but instead explaining difficulties and intentions expressed in the scheme and to suggest the most likely means, under the blessings of God, of rendering them effectual, recommending particularly the obtaining, if possible, of the countenance of the powers ecclesiastical and

140 Pearson: Memoirs, Vol. 2, 91.

141 Henry Morris: The Life of Charles Grant Sometimes Member of Parliament for Inverness-Shire and Director of the East India Company. London 1904, here 72.

142 Morris: The Life of Charles Grant, 98.

143 AFSt/M 1 C 27 : 25. Penelope Susan Elizabeth Carson: Soldiers of Christ: Evangelicals and India, 1784–1833. Diss. phil. London 1988, here 34 and 40: By the mid-1780s, many British evangelicals sought to share the message of Jesus with "Britain's Indian subjects." In 1783, the Methodist leader Thomas Coke shared his missionary desire with Charles Grant. In 1784, Bishop Richard Watson urged the House of Lords to support "the propagation of Christianity in India." In 1786, Bishop Thurlow of Lincoln requested SPG to explore the "great prospects for the evangelisation of India." Charles Grant wanted the Company to finance Christian missions in India, which would be implemented by the Church of England. Grant knew that those Indians who embraced Christianity suffered "a dreadful excommunication in civil life." He believed that if the Company supported Christian missionary activities, Indian Christians would not suffer much.

> civil at home and their influence with the Government here, as also the avoiding as much as may be of all party distinctions in carrying on a work which is equally the duty and the acknowledged duty, of all Christians.[144]

On 25 January 1786, Coke revealed his intention to Grant: he found the works of the Danish and Moravian missionaries admirable but not apostolic enough. He claimed that he and his fellow Methodists, under the guidance of their leader John Wesley, had "gone to the highways and hedges to compel sinners to come in. At the same time, every prudential method consistent with a Scriptural plan should be pursued." Coke also stated that John Wesley proposed that "not fewer than half a dozen missionaries" should go to the Danish missionaries in Tranquebar and learn the local languages. Coke was aware of Grant leading a small group of Christians in Malda and believed that Grant might be "a little leaven to leaven a mighty lump—the little hand rising out of the sea that shall, in time, water the whole land."[145] Grant's biographer, Morris, felt that before July 1786, Grant had urged John Wesley and Dr. Coke to plant a Wesleyan Methodist Mission in Bengal. It was understandable that neither the Anglican bishop of Canterbury nor the Anglican Bishop of London would license the Methodist missionaries to come and work in India. Instead, Grant rejoiced in welcoming David Brown, the Anglican Chaplain in Calcutta. Grant recommended him to William Chambers, who enabled Brown to superintend the Military Orphan Asylum in Calcutta.

On 15 August 1786, Grant wrote to Schwartz about his spiritual struggles; he admired Schwartz for consecrating his life "to the peculiar service of God." Grant supposed that Schwartz might not be able to fully comprehend the struggles and failures of a person who was totally given over to the World. However, he thanked Schwartz for his advice and prayers. Then he related how he enjoyed having fellowship with Schwartz's friends in Calcutta, namely William Chambers and John Obeck, who played a crucial role in planning and executing the missionary enterprise for India. He stated that Chambers, Obeck, and he planned a missionary enterprise for India, and Obeck would contact his friends in England.[146] It was not immediately clear what came of this plan for a mission to Calcutta.

On 31 January 1790, Grant wrote to Schwartz again to inform him of the financial troubles caused by Kiernander's business and his efforts to assist him. He also mentioned how David Brown took care of the affairs of the Mission Church. Grant's letter opened with a heartfelt declaration of his long-standing affection and frequent thoughts of Schwartz. He informed Schwartz of his impending move to London and his subscription to the SPCK, seeking Schwartz's advice on all matters related to missionary undertakings in India. He pledged his commitment, stating, "If I can be of any use in this way after my arrival in England, it is what I wish and propose."[147]

---

144 Morris: The Life of Charles Grant, 98.
145 Morris: The Life of Charles Grant, 99–100.
146 Morris: The Life of Charles Grant, 125.

Grant warmly welcomed Claudius Buchanan, another Anglican chaplain, to Calcutta. On 11 August 1796, Buchanan wrote to Grant from Barrackpore, stating that it was astonishing that the English neglected their Sunday worship services. Instead, they held horse races on Sundays. Even Lord Wellesley was surprised by his habit. People called Obeck the "apostolic Obeck," whose "reverence and esteem" were those of Schwartz.[148] John Obeck, the faithful steward of Grant, died in 1804. By then, William Carey (1761–1834) and his colleagues[149] had founded their Baptist mission in Serampore near Calcutta. Grant kept his promise to Schwartz and attempted to establish a formal missionary enterprise in India. However, his first attempt in 1793 to convince the Company and the British Parliament about the need for missionary work in India failed. Despite this setback, he and his friends continued their work unabatedly. When the British Parliament renewed the Company Charter in 1813, it permitted the establishment of an Anglican Bishopric in Calcutta. Obeck's exemplary life and interactions with the policymakers in Calcutta impressed influential persons like Grant and Chambers. Their respect for Schwartz increased, and they wished that all Protestant missionaries would emulate his service.

10.6.5 Christian David

This section builds on the information about Christian David (1771–1852) found above in Section 6.2.1. Sōmaratna and Napoleon Pathmanathan (2013),[150] Heike Liebau (2017), and Mark Balmforth (2020) have already studied the person, life, and work of Christian David in Tranquebar, Tanjore, Colombo, and Jaffna. Balmforth discussed the contents of David's autobiography and concluded that in 1776, David joined the Tamil Lutheran school in Tranquebar and interacted with missionaries there. Schwartz met him there in 1785; at that time, David was fourteen years old. Schwartz took him to Nagapattinam and introduced him to Joseph Daniel Jänicke (1759–1800), who taught him English and Lutheran theology. David returned to Tranquebar and studied under Christoph Samuel John (1746–1813). By 1787, Schwartz appointed him as his catechist and employed him for three years. During this time, David keenly observed Schwartz's multifaceted work as a missionary, preacher, teacher, diplomat and politician. When English-speaking Europeans learned about David's association with Schwartz, they requested that he narrate his views. Balmforth states that David spoke more about missionary John than Schwartz because he preferred John's

147 Morris: The Life of Charles Grant, 126.

148 Morris: The Life of Charles Grant, 221.

149 William Carey's co-workers included his wife, Dorothea Carey (died in 1807), and companions William Ward (1769–1823), Joshua Marshman (1768–1837), Hannah Marshman, the Bengali Christian Krishna Pal, his Sanskrit teacher Madan Mohan, and others. After Dorothea's death, Carey married Charlotte Emilia, a Danish woman who died on 11.03.1761. Shortly thereafter, he married Grace, who died on 22.07.1835.

150 Jī. Pī. Vī. Sōmaratna and Napoleon Pathmanathan: The Life and Times of Christian David. Colombo 2013.

educational principles to Schwartz's educational methods (Balmforth 2020, 51–52).[151]

As previously discussed, Christian David may have brought a copy of Schwartz's Tamil catechism to Jaffna and utilised it among the Tamil Christians there. He also recalled numerous events that he had witnessed in Schwartz's life. For instance, Thomas Robinson (1790–1873), the archdeacon of Madras, who accompanied Bishop Reginald Heber (1783–1826) during his journey in Sri Lanka in 1825, narrated an incident. On 31 August 1825, Christian David met Bishop Heber. At that time, Heber inquired about Schwartz, "his venerable master, the apostolic Swartz, who was his father's godfather and on whom Christian David waited when a boy." David shared an anecdote about Schwartz, "the good Father." After a long journey, Schwartz and his company sat down to eat their evening meal. He prayed for a long time and thanked God. A hungry boy could not wait and began to taste the food. After Schwartz had ended his prayer, he asked the boy to thank God for the food and then to eat. He reminded the boy to express gratitude for God's protection and care.[152]

10.6.6 Christian Elphinstone

Captain Christian Elphinstone was one of Schwartz's students. He appears to have shared rare details about Schwartz's teaching methods and content with Henry Martyn (1781–1812), the famous but short-lived Evangelical Chaplain of Calcutta. Martyn's diary entry for January 1811 reads as follows:

> Bay of Bengal, January 1811: 'Our captain [Elphinstone] was a pupil of Swartz,' of whom he communicated many interesting particulars. – Swartz, with Kohlhoff and Jaenicke, kept a school for half-caste children, about a mile and a half from Tanjore, but went every night to the Tanjore church to meet about sixty or seventy of the king's regiment, who assembled for devotional purposes; after which he officiated to their wives and children in Portuguese. At the school, Swartz used to read, in the morning, out of the German 'Meditation for every day in the year;' at night, he had family prayer. Jaenicke taught geography, Kohlhoff, writing and arithmetic. They had also mastered Persian and Malabar. At the time when the present Rajah [Serfoji II] was in danger of his life from the usurper of his uncle's throne, Swartz used to sleep in the same room with him. This was sufficient protection, for (said the captain), 'Swartz was considered by the natives to be something more than mortal. The old Rajah [Tulāji], at his death, committed his nephew to Swartz.'[153]

Besides these known individuals, Schwartz also had other students whose names are not yet known. They spread Schwartz's legacy to distant places. Don Wright examined Schwartz's ways of training his Tamil colleagues and came to the following conclusion: Schwartz understood and appreciated his catechists. He

151 Mark Edward Balmforth: A Tamil Pietist in Ceylon: The Educational Experiments of Christian David. In: International Journal of Asian Christianity 3, 2020, issue 1, 44–68, here 51–52.

152 Thomas Robinson: Last Days of Bishop Heber. London 1830, 14–15.

153 John Hall: The Life of Rev. Henry Martyn with some account of Abdool Messeeh, a Hindoo Convert, Revised by the Committee of Publication. Philadelphia 1832, 133–134.

sent them out in pairs for evangelism and to care for converts. He "carefully taught them how to explain the Gospel, planned their work for the day, prayed with them before they went out and met them again in the evening to hear their reports and to mediate and pray one." Whenever he met a promising person, he spared "neither pains nor expense" to train that person for missionary work.[154]

10.6.7 William Wheatley

As mentioned earlier,[155] William Wheatley was not only one of Schwartz's trusted co-workers but also a dear friend who taught in Schwartz's English-medium schools in Tiruccirāppaḷḷi and Ramanathapuram. Their friendship, rooted in shared values and mutual respect, was a significant aspect of their professional relationship. While establishing the English-medium provincial school in Ramanathapuram, Schwartz secured the help of Colonel Martins, the Company's commanding officer there. On 21 December 1784, Schwartz wrote a cordial letter to Martins, requesting that he greet the ruler of Ramanathapuram and, on his behalf, wish the ruler to seek refuge in the Almighty God and accept God's mercy.[156] On 3 January 1785, he wrote again to Martins about Shadi Khan's demand to release a man who had been held as a hostage in exchange for a ransom of 7,000 or 8,000 Pagodas. Schwartz wanted to raise this matter with Resident John Sulivan. Then, he thanked Martins for his support of the school and stated that a "good strong mud wall and thatch is enough: if clean and roomy, and on a good clean, healthy spot, which is free from too much noise," he would be happy. He wished him a blessed New Year and concluded with this suggestion: "May He teach us to do His will. May his Spirit lead us into the way of Righteousness."[157]

Schwartz knew William Wheatley's father, J. Wheatley, in Ramanathapuram. When William informed Schwartz about his father's illness, he wrote a moving letter that demonstrated his deep concern for the welfare of his co-workers and their families. He addressed the father as his good friend, shared with him the frailty of his health, and wished that he and his friend might depart from this life "in peace like good old Simeon." He reiterated his understanding of the Lord Jesus Christ as "our divine surety" in times of need, wisdom, righteousness, justification, the forgiveness of sins, sanctification, strength, redemption, and

> deliverance from all evil–sin, sickness, and death. Though our frail bodies turn to dust, you know the one who will raise us to eternal life. Let us, therefore, take our whole refuge in Jesus, the source of our happiness. To his care, commend your spirit, trusting in his mercy. Spend your last days in fervent prayer and be sure he will kindly hear and deliver you. Come unto me said he, all ye that are heavy laden, and I will give you rest by taking of you the burden, which is too heavy for you. May he comfort, strengthen, and cheer your last moments.

---

154 Wright: Swartz of Thanjavur: Raja Guru, 137.
155 For details on William Wheatley, see Sections 4.5, 4.6, 5.13, 10.3 and 10.5.
156 Taylor: A Memoir of the First Centenary of the Earliest Protestant Mission at Madras, x.
157 Taylor: A Memoir of the First Centenary of the Earliest Protestant Mission at Madras, xi.

> May he introduce you into the house of his Father. Oh! What unspeakable joy will that be to see ourselves free from all troubles [… and] in perfect glory. May the God of all mercy grant you and me that happiness. I am truly, your sincere friend, C. F. Swartz.[158]

While Father Wheatley's response to Schartz's letter remains unknown, the depth of their relationship is evident. Schwartz and William Wheatley shared a warm and trusting bond, one so strong that Wheatley sought Schwartz's theological insights on the nativity of Jesus Christ. Their discussions were not just about religious doctrine, but also about the practical implications of their faith in their daily lives. Consequently, on December 24, 1794, Schwartz sent a letter to Wheatley, which is reproduced verbatim in Appendix 5. This letter is rich in profound theological reflections on the essence, purpose, and implications of Jesus' birth. Schwartz eloquently emphasised Jesus's divine dignity as the holy Son of God, his role in atoning for humanity's sins, and the significance of his humble birth. This humble origin underscored Jesus' humility and self-emptying nature, highlighting God's eternal plan to redeem humanity and guide them toward a meaningful life. The angelic appearances and their message of peace and reconciliation reaffirmed Jesus as the Redeemer. In this letter, Schwartz invoked blessings from the divine-human Son of God for himself and Wheatley.

The remaining letters address Wheatley's routine work, Schwartz's responses to his questions, and spiritual advice. On August 12, 1794, Schwartz responded to the news about Wheatley's mother's illness and death. He advised him to realise the brevity of human life and the need to seek God's forgiveness, peace and hope in Christ.[159] On 26 September 1794, Schwartz recommended being cautious with Mudali, a worker whose marriage had led him astray from spiritual loyalty to Christ. He requested that Wheatley not pull down the church walls but put a thatched roof above them to keep rainwater away. He confessed that due to his age, he felt weak. By knowing that eternity "is now before my eyes," he longed for a "blessed exit."[160] In the meantime, the church's mud walls were crumbling. Colonel Martins was determined to rebuild them. On 28 January 1795, Schwartz expressed happiness over this news and asked Wheatley to inform Martins that he would "cheerfully contribute to it." [161]

Schwartz's letters to Wheatley express deep friendship and professional respect. They reveal Schwartz's unwavering faith and dedication to his mission, as well as his compassionate nature and profound theological insights that would comfort the sick and weak. These letters highlight Jesus' divinity and humility, as well as the universal availability of His forgiveness of sins.

---

158 Taylor: A Memoir of the First Centenary of the Earliest Protestant Mission at Madras, xi–xii.
159 Taylor: A Memoir of the First Centenary of the Earliest Protestant Mission at Madras, xiv.
160 Taylor: A Memoir of the First Centenary of the Earliest Protestant Mission at Madras, xiv.
161 Taylor: A Memoir of the First Centenary of the Earliest Protestant Mission at Madras, xv.

10.6.8 European soldiers and others

Garrison officers in Tiruccirāppaḷḷi encouraged the soldiers to attend Schwartz's worship services. They confessed that "corporal punishment had ceased since the regiment began to relish religious instruction."[162] As discussed in Section 4.6, Schwartz's ministry among the soldiers brought about moral transformation. After the Company had taken Fort Vallam from the Nawab, they stationed their soldiers there. Schwartz visited these soldiers and found that some of them could not read or write. In 1784, he reported that some soldiers participated in worship services and took tracts on spiritual matters with them. Some of them had started learning to read. Schwartz procured "spelling books" for them.[163]

Christian David, the son of Pastor Sattiyanātaṉ, remembered Schwartz's interaction with his father. His recollections helped Hugh Pearson demonstrate Schwartz's work ethic: He derived his principles based on "the soundest principles of reason and Scripture" and was a "lover of order, regularity, and just obedience." During his time, his followers did not require many regulations. They viewed his "presence and his word" as regulations. Christian David explained that Schwartz "gave good advice" to the Tamil pastors, "catechists, schoolmasters, pupils, and converts and composed all their differences with apostolic discretion and love."[164] Thus, Schwartz's followers and successors remembered his contributions to justice, peace and harmony.

Hugh Pearson believed that Schwartz's principal characteristics included "sound judgement, calm and steady energy, great acuteness and sagacity in the discernment of character and the conduct of important affairs, resolution and perseverance in the execution of plans deliberately formed."[165] He also praised Schwartz's linguistic ability, which enabled him to connect with people from diverse backgrounds: in addition to his native German language, he was fluent in Tamil, English, Persian, Hindustani, and Marathi. His "intellectual endowments and attainments" were not focused on "selfish and personal considerations, whether of wealth, fame, or power." His disinterestedness and integrity united friends and foes, as well as contemporaries and successive inquirers. His thoughts, words, and actions embodied virtues such as "simplicity, moderation, self-denial, activity, regularity, patience, kindness, courtesy, and cheerfulness."[166]

Successive generations of his students remembered these virtues and passed them on to their children and grandchildren. In January 1902, the Church Missionary Society established the *Church of England Zenana Mission Training Home* in Madras for English and Eurasian girls. They selected two teachers, one of whom was a Muslim, and the other a Christian descended from one of Schwartz's converts. This young man worked primarily as a clerk in a business

162 An Abstract of the Annual Reports 1814, 254.
163 Pearson: Memoirs, Vol. 2, 33.
164 Pearson: Memoirs, Vol. 2, 427–428.
165 Pearson: Memoirs, Vol. 2, 429.
166 Pearson: Memoirs, Vol. 2, 429–431.

company and volunteered to help his uncle for a few hours before and after his office work. His uncle pastored a large congregation in Tranquebar.[167] Thus, Schwartz's converts kept their Christian faith and volunteered to help others.

10.7 Schwartz's Training of Younger Missionaries

10.7.1 Examples of Failures

On January 31, 1785, Schwartz wrote to Pasche about three younger missionaries who had proven themselves unfit for missionary work among the Tamils. They were unwilling to learn the Tamil language and to engage with the Tamil people. Instead, they believed the Tamils should first adopt European attitudes and ways of life and convert to Christianity. Schwartz described Johann Daniel Mentel (1755–1796) as an uncharacteristically proud and flattering person. On 28 June 1781, he arrived in Tranquebar and attempted to establish a music department within John's school. Shortly after, he disagreed with every other missionary and returned to Germany in 1784. Schwartz felt that even if he had stayed, he would not have been a blessing to anyone. Secondly, Schwartz stated that Johann Christmann Diemer (1745–1792) did not want to work in Tranquebar; he desired to return to Denmark. Thirdly, Schwartz was sad about Johann Wilhelm Gerlach (1738–1791). Shortly after he arrived in Tranquebar, he left and travelled to Calcutta (5 August 1776). Schwartz concluded that these three men were disorderly and untrustworthy.[168]

Additionally, the thirty-year-old Peder Rubek Hagelund (1756–1788) was unwilling to learn the Tamil language from Schwartz. Hagelund was a Dane. He had studied theology in Copenhagen and reached Tranquebar in June 1786. On 12 June 1786, Schwartz stated that Hagelund was unwilling to work with other senior colleagues in the Tamil Lutheran church. His attempts to establish a Danish school in Tranquebar failed. By 2 October 1786, he had lost his desire to be a missionary and sought to join the society of worldly-minded Europeans. Four months later, on 6 February 1787, Schwartz and the missionaries in Tranquebar knew that Hagelund would not serve the mission.[169] Unexpectedly, Hagelund died in September 1788. After his death, the missionaries in Tranquebar discovered copies of letters he had sent to Copenhagen. He genuinely wanted to become a Danish pastor in Tranquebar.[170]

Schwartz had trouble with training Ernest Philipp Heinrich Stegmann (1753–). He was a theologian and Latin teacher. By 10 October 1796, Stegmann wanted to learn Tamil with Schwartz in Tanjore.[171] He knew the missionaries in Tranquebar viewed the seventy-year-old Schwartz as their "teacher, role model and father."

167 M. Ewart: The Church of England Zenana Mission Training Home, Madras. In: India's Women and China's Daughters. London 1903, 64–65, here 64.

168 AFSt/M 1 B 75 : 28a.

169 AFSt/M 1 C 27 : 5.

170 Germann: Missionar Christian Friedrich Schwartz, 332–333.

Stegmann spent two months with Schwartz in Tanjore. By January 9, 1797, Schwartz had become aware of Stegmann's quarrels with his wife and learned of his intentions to divorce her. On 12 March 1797, however, Schwartz said all his efforts to help Stegmann learn the Tamil language were in vain.[172] In the following year, Stegmann returned to Denmark.[173] On 29 September 1798, the missionaries in Tranquebar were informed of Stegmann's desire to become a pastor in Calcutta.[174] In 1799, he returned to Tranquebar as the pastor of the Zion Church. After five years, in 1804, he became a businessperson in Calcutta and worked as a portrait painter. In 1808, he assumed the position of a pastor in Denmark.[175] Missionaries with unsettled minds could not serve the Tamil people. Schwartz's mediatory efforts and examples failed to shape their thinking, living and service.

10.7.2 Examples of Successes

Karl Wilhelm Päzold (1764–1817) was a gifted theologian who studied at the University of Wittenberg, Germany. On 14 August 1793, he joined Gericke at Vepery in Madras. At that time, Schwartz was also in Vepery and immediately began teaching Päzold Tamil. On 29 September 1793, Gericke wrote about how Schwartz asked Päzold to accompany him on his journey from Madras to Tanjore and to learn Tamil. Schwartz paid his expenses, and Gericke's family cared for Päzold's wife in 1794.[176] Päzold's travel diary from 20 September 1793 to 30 April 1794 contains information about Schwartz's missionary dialogues with diverse peoples.[177] Päzold's unpublished report contains his socio-cultural observations (e.g., the oil bath of the Tamils).[178] Päzold wrote about Schwartz's communication skills as follows:

> [Schwartz's] conversations are instructive and encouraging. He knows how to preserve the principal thing in view in them all and to do so in a hearty, cordial and pleasing manner. Without seeming to do it, he suggests the wisest rules of conduct and from the circumstances of place, from the national modes of thought, from their customs and manners, he elicits maxims of great importance to Missionaries towards getting access to the minds of the people.[179]

---

171 AFSt/M 1 C 37b : 36.

172 AFSt/M 1 C 38a : 31 quoted in Germann: Missionar Christian Friedrich Schwartz, 365.

173 NHR 5, 1804, issue 49, Preface.

174 AFSt/M 1 C 38b : 62. AFSt/M 1 C 42b : 24: In 1799, Stegmann became a pastor for the Zion Church in Tranquebar. He remained unsatisfied with this work and became a merchant and portrait painter in Calcutta. On 5 October 1801, Karl Wilhelm Päzold described Stegmann as an "irrational and crazy" man. In 1808, he returned to Denmark and pastored a congregation.

175 NHR 5, 1804, issue 49, iv: On 13.04.1804, Georg Christian Knapp reported that Ernst Philipp Heinrich Stegmann and Fürchtenicht reached Tranquebar in 1795. Due to sickness, Stegmann returned to Europe and later became a pastor of the Zion Church in Tranquebar. Thus, Knapp did not give the correct reason for his return to Germany.

176 AFSt/M 1 C 34c : 41 and NHR 4, 1794, issue 45, 840.

177 AFSt/M 2 E 29 : 2c and NHR 4, 1795, issue 47, 978–995.

178 AFSt/M 1 C 37b : 28.

179 Memoirs of the Rev. Joseph D[aniel] Jænicke, 103–104.

Upon his return to Madras, Päzold oversaw the Tamil Lutheran congregation there, which is now the current St. Mathias Church of the Church of South India. He remained in touch with Schwartz, and on 17 February 1798, he expressed concern about Schwartz's severe illness.[180] By that time, Schwartz was already dead and buried. Päzold, constantly needing more money, accepted a job offer at the College of Fort Williams in Calcutta and taught Tamil to English civil servants (1802). When Gericke died, he returned to Madras and worked with Rottler.

Of all his European colleagues, Schwartz respected Christian Wilhelm Gericke (1743–1803) the most, with whom he worked in Cuddalore (1767–1782), Nagapattinam (1784–1788), and Madras (1788–1803). The Company appointed him as the chaplain to the above-mentioned Female Asylum in Madras. Gericke taught Prince Serfoji when he stayed in Madras, and he was commonly known as the "Second Schwartz." The Company officers in Madras prepared a memorial epitaph for him and placed it on the wall near the main entrance to St. Mary's Church within Fort St. George in Madras.[181]

Gottfried Immanuel Holzberg (1770–1824) reached Tanjore on 2 February 1798, just eleven days before Schwartz's death. After learning Tamil, he served as a missionary of the SPCK in Cuddalore from 1803 to 1813 and again from 1818 to 1824. He heard about Schwartz's fame but did not know him intimately. Christoph Heinrich Horst (1761–1810), whom Pohle ordained in November 1806 for ministry with J.C. Kohlhoff in Tanjore, appears to have been aware of Schwartz. For unstated reasons, he did not permit Schwartz to ordain him.[182] He might have thought that Schwartz had no episcopal authority to ordain others.

August Friedrich Cämmerer (1767–1837), the last missionary of the Danish-Halle Mission, learned Tamil from Schwartz. According to tradition, Schwartz slapped him once for not paying attention to his Tamil lessons. Cämmerer took it in good spirit and learned from Schwartz. When he met him on 1 February 1791 in the provincial school in Kumbakonam, he called him "Papa Schwartz," revered him and prayed for his long life. He enjoyed learning Tamil from Schwartz, whom all missionaries considered a "father."[183] Cämmerer met Schwartz for the last time on January 8, 1798, and documented how, just a month before his death, he had

---

180 AFSt/M 1 C 38a : 75.

181 Julian James Cotton: List of Inscriptions on Tombs or Monuments in Madras Possessing Historical or Archaeological Interest. rev. ed. Vol. 1. Madras 1945, here 76: Cotton stated that Flaxman prepared this simple but powerful marble monument. It shows a Christian minister addressing a non-Christian Indian in the mood of penitence. The minister holds a book with the inscription: "Believe." "Three children of different heights are looking up to the speaker." The inscription beneath this portrayal reads: "Sacred to the memory of the Revd. CHRISTIAN WILLIAM GERICKE. Destined to labour in a peculiar vineyard (that of the conversion of the natives of office) he fulfilled his sacred office with primate simplicity and purity. Worthy associate of the Venerable SWARTZ, like him, he toiled thro' life with sedulous but temperate zeal, to plan in every accessible soil the pure spirit of Christianity. Pagans, uninstructed Christians and especially their children, were the object of his unceasing labours of faith and love. He was called to receive the eternal reward of his patient and unwearied course of usefulness, in the year of our Lord 1803, aged 62 years."

182 AFSt/M 1 C 40a : 46.

183 Germann: Missionar Christian Friedrich Schwartz, 364–365.

gathered around him catechists and approximately sixty schoolchildren, teaching them the spiritual truths that were dear to him; he also sang and prayed with them.[184]

Joseph Daniel Jänicke served in Tanjore with Schwartz from 1788 to 1800. Schwartz was happy with him. Schwartz educated Johann Caspar Kohlhoff in his school in Tirucciräppaḷḷi. In October 1778, Schwartz opined that Kohlhoff had a steady mind and remained trustworthy.[185] With time, Schwartz's health deteriorated. Kohlhoff remarked that Schwartz had been the guide, father, and friend to younger missionaries and to "very many children, widows, and orphans; and whose patience, disinterestedness, and perseverance, we all admire and endeavour to imitate." Kohlhoff affirmed that Schwarz had been their "dear patriarch" and was "a great blessing to the country."[186] Kohlhoff's testimony about Schwartz resonated in the lives and work of several missionaries from Halle (Saale) among the Tamils. His ministry served as an example to inspire later missionaries to serve effectively.[187]

---

184 Germann: Missionar Christian Friedrich Schwartz, 379–380.

185 AFSt/M 1 B 69 : 45.

186 An Abstract of the Annual Reports 1814, 439.

187 For example, see Church Missionary Gleaner, Vol. 4, No. 9, September 1844, 97: The editors of this monthly magazine in London quoted Pastor J.J. Weitbrecht's statement on Schwartz from his book entitled *Missions in Bengal*: "We want more men who are ready to devote their talents and powers to this great and glorious calling; men like Schwartz in the south of India; like Henry Martyn in the north; and like Carey at Serampore, who are ready joyfully to present their talents, wealth and learning, upon the altar of love, as a thank and freewill offering to their Redeemer, saying, 'Here I am; send me, Lord, whither thou wilt'."

Chapter 11

Schwartz and Debates about the Pious Clause in 1793

11.1 The Company and Failed Mission Attempts from 1698 to 1793

Penelope Carson's examination of the intricate relationship between the Company and Christianity from 1698 to 1858 underscores the profound impact of the Pious Clause of 1793 and 1813. In this context, her book names Schwartz in an endnote that refers to Stephen Neill's portrayal of Schwartz.[1] Otherwise, it does not engage with the example of Schwartz, debated in the British Parliament, regarding the inclusion of a Pious Clause in the Company's Charter Act of 1793. Ninety-eight years after the Company's formation, on 5 September 1698, the Company authorised Anglican clergypersons to minister to the spiritual and ecclesiastical needs of the Company's traders and employees overseas. Strangely, the Company proprietors stipulated that every ship weighing 500 tonnes or more should have an Anglican clergy person on board. Likewise, every Company factory should have an Anglican chaplain for the British expatriates there. The clergymen in India were supposed to learn Portuguese and other native languages of the people so that they could "instruct the Gentoos, that shall be the Servants or Slaves of the same Company or their Agent, in the Protestant Religion" (i.e. Anglicanism).[2]

Towards the end of the eighteenth century, the intensity of Anglican representation in the Company territories in India grew. Since the *Regulation Act of 1773*, British laws applied in these territories, and the Company hesitated to formally introduce Anglicanism, which was part of the English legal system at that time, to Indians in their territories. Chaplain William Johnson was one of the Anglican clergymen who attempted to establish an Anglican Cathedral in Calcutta for representational purposes. During his tenure in Calcutta from 1772 to 1788, he married Frances Watt, a wealthy and influential widow. She was associated with Robert Clive, Warren Hastings and Prime Minister Robert Banks Jenkinson (1812–1827). In March 1776, he urged the Company's Court of Directors in London to erect an appropriate building to house the Anglicans in Calcutta.[3] On

---

1 Carson: The East India Company and Religion, 17: "The greatly loved and respected missionary, Christian Schwartz, was appointed chaplain to the Europeans at Trichinopoly in 1767 with a salary of £100 p.a., which he put into the funds of his mission. In 1786, he was granted a salary of £100 p.a. as [an] interpreter at Tanjore, plus 20 pagodas for a palanquin. The Company also supported his schools."

2 Lambeth Palace Library, S.P.G. Papers. Vol. IX., 204r–v: Extract of the Company's Charter dated 5th September 1698.

3 Daniel O'Connor: The Chaplains of the East India Company, 1601–1858. London 2012, here 96–100.

21 August 1784, he requested the Archbishop of Canterbury to advise him about its consecration.[4] On 24 June 1787, according to the directives of the Archbishop of Canterbury, William Johnson consecrated a new church building in Calcutta in the presence of about 500 persons. "Lord Cornwallis, the Judges, Clergy, and principal inhabitants" accompanied Johnson to the altar railings.[5] Eventually, this church became the Anglican Cathedral, also known as St. John Church. Johnson served the British expatriates in Calcutta, but missionary efforts among non-Christian Indians were not his primary focus.

Parallel to this, senior Anglican laypeople in the service of the Company were familiar with the works of the Lutheran missionaries in Tranquebar and Calcutta.[6] Notably, they admired the person and work of Schwartz in Tanjore. They strove to create formal ways for Christian missionaries to serve the Indians living in Company territories in India. Charles Grant was the most influential Anglican layman in this enterprise. He counted on support from William Chambers, the Persian translator for the Company in Calcutta and an ardent follower of Schwarz; George Udney, the famous factor in Calcutta; and others. Chaplain David Brown, an admirer of Schwartz, assisted Grant in this aspect. These men shared their common vision with friends in England, notably William Wilberforce and Charles Simeon, and garnered broader support.

In 1792, Charles Grant composed his famous work entitled *Observations*. When he revised it in 1797, he quoted Schwartz's *Defence of Mission* to support his appeal for recognition from the British Government.[7] He viewed those Indians who lived in the territories governed by the Company as the "Asiatic Subjects of

---

4 Lambeth Palace Library, S.P.G. Papers. Vol. IX. 216r–216v: William Johnson's letter reads as follows: "My Lord, Having resided in Bengal as Chaplain to the East India Company for more than 12 years and, during that time, cherished the Hope of seeing a suitable edifice erected to the Worship of Almighty God, in which hope, I took the liberty in the month of March 1776, to make a representation to the Court of Directors, setting forth the great necessity there was for the immediate erection of a decent Church or Chapel that which has been made use of ever since the Disaster brought on the India Company by Surajah Doulah, in the year 1756, when the former Church was destroyed, being no other, that the Porch of an Old House, incapable of holding a Twentieth Part of the English Settlers, residing at Fort William, a totally improper as to Situation, Decency and Decorum. [...] As the East India Company are restricted from appointing Chaplains to this or any other of their Settlements, but with the Consent of your Lordship or the Bishop of London, I feel a pleasure in acquainting your Lordship, as it is my Duty to do, with this event, and in humbly soliciting your Lordship's Directions, for the consecration of the new Church; which I flatter myself, may be finished within eighteen months from this time." For more information on William Johnson, see O'Connor: The Chaplains of the East India Company, 1601–1858, 96–98.

5 Lambeth Palace Library, S.P.G. Papers. Vol. IX. 219r–219v.

6 William Chambers, Charles Grant, and David Brown were sympathetic towards John Zacharias Kiernander, Calcutta's first Swedish Lutheran missionary, who had deep connections with Tranquebar. The aged Kiernander could not maintain the Bengal Mission, which consisted of the Old Mission Church (i.e., *Beth Tephillah*, 'House of Prayer' or *Lalgirija*, 'the Red Church'), its school and a burial ground. On 31 October 1787, they purchased and protected these properties.

7 Charles Grant: Observations on the State of Society among Asiatic Subjects of Great Britain, particularly with respect to Morals and on Means to improve it, written chiefly in the year 1792. London: n.p., 1797, here 113–116.

Great Britain". He felt that these Indians should benefit from the privileges and responsibilities of the British Government. An essential aspect of British life was the Anglican form of Christianity, which, according to him, possessed "divine authority," "unrivalled excellence and incomparable fitness to promote the happiness of man."[8] He was convinced that Indians, as Asiatic Subjects of Britain, should have an opportunity to engage with "the pure and benign principles" of Anglicanism because they would promote their "true interests."[9] He believed that allowing Anglican clergy to function in the territories of the Company would enable Britain's "Asiatic subjects" to rid themselves of all disorders that destroyed their happiness and prevented their improvement.[10] He was aware of the contributions of Catholics in India, the Lutherans in Tranquebar and other places, and the Dutch Reformed Church in Ceylon (modern Sri Lanka). He was also aware that most Christians in India hailed from Pariah backgrounds.[11]

Grant particularly praised the achievements of the Lutherans in Tranquebar, noting that they had limited funds at their disposal and lacked any "territorial or commercial influence." However, their ministry impacted the lives of both the lowest castes and the highest and most knowledgeable castes, including Brahmins and Pandarams, and some converts became valuable teachers to fellow Indians.[12] In this context, Grant referred to Schwartz's work and its results:

> It is evident that the light of Christianity has not been held out by this [Tranquebar] mission without effect. Such is the force of eminent goodness that the name of *Swartz* in particular, a missionary still living, who has laboured with a spirit truly apostolical for more than thirty years in that country, exposed to its hottest sun and furnished only with the scantiest necessaries of life, is revered all over the peninsula of India, by Hindoos, Mussulmans and Europeans. The Hindoo king of Tanjore, when dying, was solicitous to make him the guardian of his heir and to put the whole management of affairs into his hands, a trust which he declined. The famous Hyder Ali received him as an envoy on the part of the English and offered to take his word as the guarantee of a proposed engagement, when as we have been assured, he would trust no one else, and Colonel Fullarton, who was commander of an English army in that country, though severe in his strictures upon others, has declared publicly, that Mr. *Swartz* singly had retrieved the European character in India. This mission, supported by men of such a stamp, has still had real success in educating the young and converting the adult, not to a new name only, but to a better life and conversation. And if the number of missionaries there were greater, it cannot be doubted that the success would be proportionately increased.[13]

In 1786, Grant, Chambers, and Udney boldly requested the Archbishop of Canterbury to establish a Protestant Mission in Bengal and Bihar to promote Christianity there.[14] As nothing had happened, on 10 September 1787, they requested the Archbishop of Canterbury to establish a Protestant mission in Bengal again. They explained to him the moral depravity and misery of the ordinary

8 Grant: Observations on the State of Society, 82.
9 Grant: Observations on the State of Society, 1.
10 Grant: Observations on the State of Society, 75.
11 Grant: Observations on the State of Society, 85.
12 Grant: Observations on the State of Society, 86.
13 Grant: Observations on the State of Society, 87.
14 Stock: The History of the Church Missionary Society, 58.

people in Bengal and Bihar, which they had observed during their twenty years of living in these regions. They believed that Christian missionary engagement would liberate these Indians to lead a humane life happily. They knew that without the Company's formal protection, these missionaries and Indian Christians would not be able to profess and practice Christianity. Their close relatives and friends would shun and reject them. If the Archbishop of Canterbury could secure "the Royal Favour […] for establishing a Mission in Bengal and Bihar," ensuring "Liberty to the Missionaries, and Safety to the Native Converts,"[15] these men would be willing to find suitable Anglican missionary candidates. They even suggested to the SPCK that Reverend T. Lloyd of King's College, Cambridge, be deputed as a missionary to Calcutta. After a prolonged discussion, the SPCK proposed sending Reverend Abraham Thomas Clarke of Trinity College, Cambridge, to work on their behalf in Calcutta.[16] This proposal yielded no concrete results. Nevertheless, it demonstrated the earnestness of a few Company servants who attempted to establish regular Christian missionary services in India.

On 20 June 1788, four Anglican chaplains in Calcutta, Thomas Blanchard,[17] John Owen, Robert Carr, and David Brown appealed to Governor-General Charles Cornwallis for formal provisions to support missionary work in Bengal. They believed that the Presidencies of Bengal, Madras and Bombay were God's gift to Great Britain. Hence, the Company, the representative of Great Britain in India, should not merely seek to expand its commercial and military activities in India. Instead, it should strive to increase the happiness of Indians by introducing them to British ways of life that were "enlightened and exalted by Science, Liberty and Religion [i.e. Anglicanism]." They believed that the more Indians came to know "the manners and maxims of Englishmen," the more they would shed their prejudices against the English. Cornwallis did not heed this proposal because the Company did not consider Anglicanism an essential part of its operations in India.[18]

On 12 March 1789, Chaplain John Owen (1754–1824), who had family ties to John Wesley, requested that G. Sharpe, a senior Company officer in Calcutta,

---

15 Lambeth Palace Library, S.P.G. Papers. Vol. IX. 217r–218r.

16 An Abstract of the Annual Reports and Correspondence, 278–281.

17 O'Connor: The Chaplains of the East India Company, 77, 98 and 102.

18 Cornwallis aimed to resolve the disputes in Tanjore between Ameer Singh and Serfoji, find solutions for managing lands, and annex the regions governed by rulers such as Tipu Sultan. His Permanent Settlement (enacted on May 1, 1793) secured the loyalty and support of the landed gentry for the continuation and expansion of the Company's rule. He removed the judicial duties from district collectors and assigned them to district judges. The district collectors oversaw tax collection and administered local systems. He placed judges above district collectors and arranged for higher salaries so corruption could not tempt them. Lawyers with fixed wages and fees worked in the district courts. As British laws applied to all people living in the Company's territories, Indians could also complain about British employees to the Company's lawyers and judges. Lawyers and judges considered the local customary practices of Muslims, Śaivites, Vaiṣṇavites, and others regarding marriage, inheritance, funerals, and other matters. Europeans could no longer torture those Indians physically, who could not pay taxes or other revenues. In other words, the Company territories became the overseas territories of Britain.

persuade policymakers in London to permit Christian missionary activities in the Company-administered parts of India. He also referred to his earlier appeal to Cornwallis in June 1788. Owen felt that it was "dishonourable in the highest degree for Christians to rule pagans without seeking to instruct them in the Gospel." He thought that "the belief of the Gospel binds men to diffuse its truths, yet we have not taken the smallest step towards this." Owen referred to Schwartz as a model English missionary: "Mr. Swartz, our missionary on the Coast, affords sufficient evidence of what might be expected in a country where we are Sovereigns & can protect our converts."[19]

Soon, the most influential members of the Clapham Group began supporting the missionary cause in India more intensely.[20] At that time, William Wilberforce, Henry Thornton, and Edward Parry collaborated to abolish slavery in all British territories. Charles Grant, who had returned from Calcutta and settled in London, joined the Clapham Group in 1790. He became the founding director of the Sierra Leone Company, established on March 11, 1792. This company assisted in resettling Afro-Americans from Nova Scotia, Canada, who had aided the British during the American Revolution.

The members of the Clapham Group seized the opportunity when the British Parliament was about to renew the Charter of the Company in 1793. They attempted to persuade the Board of Control and the Court of Directors to include a Pious Clause in the renewed Charter that would legally permit Christian ministers to formally work in the Company's territories and receive financial and other support from the Company. For example, in May 1793, the Board of Control and the Court of Directors met in the India House of the Company. They discussed the possible impacts and implications of permitting Christian missionaries to work in India. They assessed how non-Christian Indians would respond to the introduction of Christian missionaries and how their perceptions might adversely impact the Company's territorial, economic, and political ambitions. Charles Grant, William Wilberforce and their friends highlighted the merits of introducing Christian missionaries to Indians. On 10 May 1793, an observer of these debates pointed out Wilberforce's efforts to include the Pious Clause in the Company's Charter and made the following remark:

> Mr. Wilberforce presents his Compliments to the Archbishop of Canterbury and has the pleasure to acquaint his Grace that the Clauses respecting religious instruction &c. were last night admitted into the India Bill with Mr Dundas's perfect concurrence and with little or no opposition to any part of them from any quarter. It had been found necessary to exchange from the first of them the words 'with the advice of the Archbishop of Canterbury, the Bishop of London for the time being' & some little alterations were made in the second & third which Mr Wilberforce encloses to His Grace in their present state. Palace Yard, May 10, 1793. Mr Wilberforce would have done himself the honor of delivering the Clauses himself, had he not been particularly engaged.[21]

---

19 Lambeth Palace Library, S.P.G. Papers. Vol. IX. 225r–225v.

20 For further details, see Ernest Marshall Howse: Saints in Politics – The 'Clapham Sect' and the Growth of Freedom. London 1953.

21 Lambeth Palace Library: S.P.G. Papers. Vol. IX, 251r – 251v.

Wilberforce was unable to convince the Company's Board of Control and Court of Directors to send Anglican ministers to serve in India. Arthur Mayhew, who had studied the Company's relationship with Christianity, suggested that Wilberforce's ignorance of this relationship led to this failure.[22]

11.2 Montgomery Campbell's Opposition to Schwartz in 1793

In addition to Wilberforce's ignorance about the relationship between the Company and Christian missionaries in southern India, other more dominant causes prevented the inclusion of the Pious Clause into the Company's Charter Act of 1793. By that time, the French Revolution, which began in 1789 and involved rebellions, assassinations, executions, and anticlericalism, profoundly impacted British policymakers. The execution of the French Emperor, Louis XVI, on January 21, 1793, paved the way for the formation of the First French Republic, which, in turn, declared war against Great Britain and the Netherlands.

Secondly, the colossal loss of British territories in North America and the American Declaration of Independence on July 4, 1776, forced British policymakers to re-examine their religious beliefs and practices, as well as their outreach to other peoples. This loss also forced some British policymakers to criticise the education system in American schools. Basu referred to a member of the Company's Court of Directors in London who had confessed that it was indeed their folly that they had allowed the North Americans to establish schools and colleges. Now, they were determined not to repeat the same folly in India. Any Indian who wanted to study had "to come to England for it."[23] Besides, British settlements in North America were characterised as "Protestant, commercial, maritime, and free." Protestants governed these settlements by "English common law," but their representative institutions functioned from London. The Company officers' notion of British overseas territories, as in North America, did not apply to their territories in India because they did not count the cost of their "economic and social oppression and political and territorial expansionism in the mid-eighteenth century."[24] They were careful not to permit any step that might empower Indians to endanger the Company's prospects in India.

---

22 Mayhew: Christianity and the Government of India, 29: According to Mayhew, Wilberforce was ignorant about the life of people in Bengal and Madras Presidencies. "It was ignorance rather than tactlessness which caused his [Wilberforce's] failure in 1793 and the depression that followed. Had he not been preoccupied with his inadequate knowledge of Bengal and ignorant of affairs in south India, he would have realised that the East India Company's bark was far worse than its bite. [… Wilberforce did not know that] for many years, the Directors and their servants in India alike had been establishing the friendliest of relations with Christian missionaries, based on mutual service discreditable to neither side. Though they were not prepared to admit unquestioned any missionary who might desire their license, they had already discovered the potential usefulness of the class as a whole and had not hesitated to express in words and action their gratitude and even sympathy."

23 Baman Das Basu: Education in India under the Rule of the East India Company. Calcutta 1867, 6.

24 Rorabacher: Property, Land, Revenue, and Policy, 230.

Thirdly, senior Company employees like Warren Hastings (1732–1818)[25] and Charles Cornwallis (1738–1805)[26] rejected the proposed Pious Clause. Their political relationships with wealthy Hindu or Muslim powerholders in India led them to believe that the Pious Clause would hurt the Company's neutrality about religious matters. This neutrality translated into vehement opposition to any official support for the spread of Christianity, even in the Company's territories under the control of the British Parliament and Crown.

Fourthly, lesser-ranked Company employees also opposed Christian missionary work in India. For example, as mentioned in section 9.4, Montgomery Campbell, who spent several years in southern India before returning to England, vehemently opposed the Pious Clause. In 1776, he met Schwartz in Tanjore. At that time, Campbell served as Nawab Wallajah's registrar of bonds. Like Wallajah, Campbell opposed Governor Pigot's determination to restore Tulāji to the throne. As Wallajah's representative, he accompanied Pigot to Tanjore and met Schwartz, who served as the interpreter between Pigot and Tulāji. He could not tolerate Schwartz's association with Tulāji.

Archibald Campbell, who became the Governor of Madras in April 1786, appointed Montgomery Campbell as his secretary. When he went to Tanjore to enthrone Ameer Singh in 1787, he asked Montgomery Campbell to accompany him. Montgomery Campbell observed how Schwartz disagreed with the Governor, who had unilaterally and forcefully imposed a treaty on Ameer Singh that would exclusively favour the Company and its army, disadvantaging Tanjore. Additionally, during the debate in the India House in May 1793 about the Pious Clause, Montgomery Campbell would have also recalled how Schwartz had disagreed with him when he failed to persuade Wallajah to repay the loan, which his son-in-law had borrowed from missionary Philipp Fabricius in Madras.[27] He attempted to discredit Schwartz and his services. Therefore, he asserted that some of Schwartz's Kaḷḷar followers were thieves. They had superficially embraced Christianity, but their thievish lifestyle persisted.[28] Campbell's accusation of Schwartz had a profound impact. It strengthened the Company's general aversion to sending Christian ministers to India at its own expense.

On 24 May 1793, the London-based newspaper *Courier* published Montgomery Campbell's accusation as follows.[29]

> In 1793, when the bill depended on the renewal of the Company's charter, certain clauses were proposed in favour of *free schools* and *Christian missionaries*. In the newspaper, called the *Courier*, of Friday evening, May 24, of that year, the following paragraph was inserted:

---

[25] Eugene Stock: Beginnings in India. London 1917, 14. According to the findings of Eugene Stock, Warren Hastings discouraged "all missionary efforts" in India.

[26] Carson: The East India Company and Religion, 36–37. Until 1794, Charles Grant did not know how strongly Cornwallis had rejected the Pious Clause.

[27] Germann: Missionar Christian Friedrich Schwartz, 354.

[28] Germann: Missionar Christian Friedrich Schwartz, 359: Schwartz refuted Montgomery Campbell's accusations as follows: Extract from the Transactions of the Society for Promoting Christian Knowledge for the Year 1795. London: SPCK, 1795, 113–114.

[29] Despite several attempts, I, the author of this biography, was unable to find a copy of the newspaper containing this quote. Hence, I quote Schwartz's version of Campbell's accusation.

Mr. *Montgomerie Campbell* gave his decided vote against the [Pious] Clause and reprobated the idea of converting the *Gentoos* [sic! = Hindus]. It is true, missionaries have made proselytes of the *Paraiars* [Pariahs]; but they were the *lowest order of people* and had even degraded the religion they professed to embrace. *Mr. Swartz*, whose character was held so deservedly high, could not have any reason to boast of the purity of his followers: They were proverbial for their profligacy. An instance occurred to his recollection, perfectly in point: – he had been preaching for many hours to this cast[e] of proselytes on the heinousness of theft and, in the heat of his discourse, taken off his stock, when that and his gold buckle were stolen by one of his virtuous and enlightened congregation. In such a description of natives, did the doctrine of the missionaries operate: men of high cast[e] would spurn at the idea of changing the religion of their ancestors.[30]

11.3 No Pious Clause in 1793

Henry Dundas (1742–1811), the newly appointed but extremely influential President of the Board of Control that oversaw the Company's operations in the United Kingdom and India, observed how most of the Company's Court of Directors and proprietors opposed Wilberforce's request for the Company to officially "promote by all just and prudent means, the interests and happiness of the inhabitants of the British Dominions in India," advance "their useful knowledge" and improve them religiously and morally. The opponents believed that, on the one hand, Wilberforce's proposal would cost the Company immense amounts of money. On the other hand, it would endanger the "peace and good order of the British possessions in India."[31] Dundas, who had requested more time to consider the merits of the Pious Clause, did not endorse it on time. Therefore, without including the Pious Clause, the British Parliament passed the East India Company Act, coded as *33 Geo. III 3 Cap. LII.*[32]

This Charter Act increased the powers of the Governor-General for India (e.g. John Shore). It viewed the territories under the Company's control in India as "British possessions," where British administration and justice should prevail; the senior employees of the Company were indeed functionaries of the British Government. This Act separated the revenue department from judicial control. It empowered the Company officers to grant specific individuals licences for trade in India. It permitted competent Indians to serve as civil servants. It made the Company represent Great Britain in India.

Taylor: A Memoir of the Frist Centenary of the Earliest Protestant Mission at Madras, xxi. William Woodall (1745–1803), who covered the parliamentary debates, appears to have been the reporter of this statement.

30 Schwartz: Defence of Missions in India, 1–2.

31 C. H. Philips. The East India Company 1784–1834. Manchester 1940, 158.

32 A Collection of Charters and Statutes 1817, 288–333; The full title of this *Act 33 GEORGII III. Cap. LII* reads: "An Act for continuing in the East-India Company, for a further Term, the Possession of the British Territories in India, together with their exclusive Trade, under certain Imitations; for establishing further Regulations for the Government of the said Territories and the better Administration of Justice within the same; for appropriating to certain Uses the Revenues and Profits of the said Company; and for making Provision for the good Order and Government of the Towns of Calcutta, Madras and Bombay—[11th June 1793]." .

11.4 Schwartz's Defence of Missions in 1794

Nine months later, Schwartz read the newspaper, *The Courier* and noted Montgomery Campbell's remarks about him and his followers. On 13 February 1794, he composed a response and sent copies to his colleagues in Tranquebar. He requested Gericke in Madras to review his response and forward it to the SPCK. Accordingly, Gericke forwarded it to George Gaskin (1751–1829), the Secretary of the SPCK in London. Immediately, Gaskin requested that William Vincent (1739–1815), the principal of a school at Westminster in London from 1788 to 1792, obtain the opinion of Governor-General Cornwallis on Schwartz. Earlier, Cornwallis had read Schwartz's report about Prince Serfoji. He had also met him in Madras and had great respect for him. Vincent approached Cornwallis through the Bishop of Lichfield and Coventry. On 10 February 1795, Cornwallis replied to this bishop about Schwartz:

> Dear Brother, I have received the letter, which you enclosed to me from Dr. Vincent, requesting, at the desire of the Society for Promoting Christian Knowledge, my testimony of Mr. Schwartz's honesty and integrity. From my knowledge of Mr. Schwartz and what I heard of him whilst in India, I have every reason to believe him to be a man of very respectable character. I am your most affectionate brother, Cornwallis.[33]

The SPCK affirmed Schwartz's integrity as follows:

> As the Society, after forty years of experience, have had constant reason to approve of Mr Swartz's integrity and veracity as a correspondent, his zeal as a promoter of Christian knowledge and his labours as a Missionary, they take this opportunity of acknowledging his faithful services and recommending his letter to the consideration of the public, as containing a just statement of facts relating to the Mission, believing that *Mr Swartz* is incapable of departing from the truth, in the minutest particular.[34]

Schwartz refuted M. Campbell's accusations point by point: firstly, he remembered visiting the village Būdalūr near Tanjore in 1776. At that time, a few Kaḷḷar boys stole his walking stick. Immediately afterwards, their parents brought these boys to Schwartz for punishment. He believed that they imitated their parents' expertise in stealing. Therefore, he chose not to punish them but admonished them not to steal. Schwartz asserted that none of these boys were Christians and that he did not preach to them. He objected to M. Campbell's accusation that all Christian converts were Pariahs; he wished that M. Campbell should have visited the Lutheran congregation in either Tanjore, Tranquebar, or Vepery, as more than two-thirds of these congregations hailed from non-Pariah backgrounds. Schwartz readily accepted that the Lutheran Christians were not perfect humans. Many died with comfort and a well-grounded hope of everlasting life. That some of those who have been instructed and baptised have abused God's servants was well known. "[E]ven the Apostles have experienced this grief."[35]

---

33 Schwartz: Defence of Missions in India, 3.
34 Schwartz: Defence of Missions in India, 2–3.
35 Schwartz: Defence of Missions in India, 6.

Secondly, Schwartz disagreed with M. Campbell's view that a Christian missionary was a "disgrace to any country." Schwartz suggested that the former Governor Macartney of Fort St. George and the former Commander-in-Chief of the Company's armies, Eyre Coote, would not share M. Campbell's flawed assessment. They knew how Gericke cared for many English soldiers during the French capture of Cuddalore; Gericke also protected those in need in Nagapattinam. Before mentioning some examples of his charitable deeds, Schwartz stated his firm conviction in the constructive relationship between the missionaries and the local governments: he hesitated to enumerate his beneficial deeds for the welfare of the local governments; he mentioned them not "as a vain and sinful boasting, but rather as a necessary self-defence. Neither the Missionaries nor any of the Christians have hurt the country's welfare."[36] He fed the soldiers in Tanjore on two occasions when they needed food. When the king of Tanjore and the Company Residents could not convince the farmers of Tanjore to cultivate their lands, Schwartz persuaded them to clear the water channels, plant paddy seedlings and reap a good harvest.

Thirdly, Schwartz pointed out that his Tamil Christian followers were not "profligate." He knew how the European interpreters, known as Madras dubashes, amassed a fortune of two to four lakhs of Pagodas within ten to fifteen years. He asked whether "this extortion" did not amount to a "high degree of profligacy." The Indian dubashes of Europeans were no better. The Company banned three Indian dubashes from Tanjore because "the enormous crimes committed by them filled the country with complaints," and Schwartz did not wish "to enumerate them." He stated further that the "inhabitants dread the conduct of a Madras dubash (like Shiva Rao). These people lend money to the Rajah at an exorbitant interest and could collect their money and interest in an appointed district. "It is needless to mention the consequences."[37]

Schwartz viewed the Indian dubashes as decisive contributors to the sufferings of the ordinary people of Tanjore. Most dubashes hailed from the city of Madras. They determined the welfare, prosperity and ruin of their European employers. They served individual Europeans as translators, mediators, moneylenders and account keepers. They worked in European households as trusted stewards, managers and accountants. European companies and Nawab Wallajah employed them as interpreters, guides, mediators, secretaries, moneylenders, investors, assessors, and managers of cash, as well as keepers of financial accounts and many other secrets.[38] The dubashes enriched their European employers abundantly and simultaneously exploited their fellow Indians ruthlessly and remorselessly. Schwartz could not tolerate their abuses.

Fourthly, Schwartz rejected the assertion that the "inhabitants of the country would suffer by Missionaries" and stated that if "the missionaries are sincere

---

36 Schwartz: Defence of Missions in India, 7.

37 Schwartz: Defence of Missions in India, 12.

38 Susan Neild-Basu: The Dubashes of Madras. In: Modern Asian Studies 18, 1984, issue 1, 1–31, here 4.

Christians, it is impossible that the inhabitants should suffer any damage by them: if they are not what they profess to be, they ought to be dismissed." He persuaded the farmers in Tanjore to cultivate their fields as a missionary. The rich harvest prevented famine and benefited the people of Tanjore. He paved the way for establishing a court of justice in Tanjore; he advised the revenue collectors of the Company in Tanjore to invest five hundred Pagodas in cleaning the water channels in the western parts of the Kingdom of Tanjore. Schwartz and his catechists supervised this work and persuaded the farmers to plant paddy on time. Finally, the western parts of Tanjore "rejoiced in getting 100,000 kalams more than before. The inhabitants confessed that instead of one kalam, they reaped four." Schwartz categorically asserted that "No inhabitant has suffered by Christians: none has complained of it. On the contrary, one of the richest inhabitants said to me: 'Sir, if you send a person to us, send one who has learned all your ten commandments.'"[39]

Fifthly, Schwartz recounted his engagement with the Kaḷḷars and how he persuaded them to give up their thievery. Earlier, the Company sent its armies to suppress the Kaḷḷar raiders, but their attempts failed. By contrast, the Kaḷḷars listened to Schwartz and informed him in writing that they would no longer engage in theft. They cultivated their lands and paid their taxes. They appreciated the dignity of work and learned to lead a worthy life. Some embraced Christianity, and Schwartz baptised them.[40]

Sixthly, Schwartz felt that the Company should not discriminate against anyone based on religion. He insisted that the Company employ a Christian with the required competencies. He agreed that if "Christians were employed in some important offices, they should, if they misbehaved, be doubly punished; but *to reject them entirely* is not right and discourageth."[41] After he had asked his missionary friends in Tranquebar and Madras to review the draft of his response, he confessed to Pastor Uebele in London on 4 February 1794 that he had forgotten to include this vital information about the great difficulty and severe hardships that Tamil Lutherans faced in finding suitable jobs and honestly earning their livelihood.[42] He could not tolerate how contemptuously some Europeans treated the Tamil Lutherans and refused to employ them for a salary. To illustrate his point, he quoted a statement which a Brahmin told him:

---

39 Schwartz: Defence of Missions in India, 12. Buchanan 1805, 66–67: Buchanan quoted this passage: "On one occasion, when the natives doubted the purpose and good faith of the English, they applied to Mr. Swartz: 'Sir, if you send a person to us, send a person who has learned all your Ten Commandments'."

40 Schwartz: Defence of Missions in India, 13.

41 Schwartz: Defence of Missions in India, 13–14.

42 NHR, 4, 1795, issue 47, 999, paraphrased in Memoirs of the Rev. Joseph D[aniel] Jænicke, 117: "You [Uebele] request me to write something to prove that the Mission in the East Indies has been advantageous to the STATE. I have drawn up some remarks in connection with the Mission, on a Paragraph which I met with in the Courier. [...] It is necessary that the Christians should be able to obtain situations [i.e. jobs with the Company. ...] This is an appeal that bears with but too much force on us unfriended Missionaries. Yea, *we are constrained to admit the fact that if anyone confesses the Christian doctrines he is not only despised by his own connections* [i.e. relatives, friends, neighbours and other Tamils], *but by Europeans also. This is a hard trial.*" See also the next footnote below.

> You perform only half of your duty. After teaching us, you say to us: 'Go and work! Where should we go and work? Could you secure jobs that are suitable for our talents? Then, you will see how things become different (and better). You take us away from all our relationships and cannot place us into new ones.' This reality is hard for missionaries. A Tamil person who wishes to embrace Christianity is treated contemptuously not only by their relatives but also by Europeans. This is a severe test.[43]

Seventhly, Schwartz described a healthy relationship between Christian missionary activity and the country's welfare. He affirmed, "before God and man, that if Christianity, in its plain and undisguised form, was properly promoted, the country would not suffer, but be benefited by it."[44] This relationship stemmed from his Lutheran theological conviction that God's reign consisted of two arms: the Church and the State. While humans were engaged separately in the affairs of the Church or the State, they complemented each other.

Eighthly, Schwartz emphasised the importance of Christian missionary engagement among non-Christians. Its legitimacy lay in God and the Redeemer Jesus Christ, who "has commanded his Apostles to preach the Gospel to all nations." Schwartz knew that humans might abuse "the knowledge of God, of his divine perfections and his mercy to mankind [...], but there is no other method of reclaiming mankind than by instructing them well. To hope that the heathens will live a good life, without the knowledge of God, is a *chimaera*."[45]

Finally, Schwartz concluded his *Defence of Mission* by stating that he was then at "the brink of eternity" and did not "repent of having spent forty-three years in the service of my Divine Master." He was confident that God would "remove some of the great obstacles to the propagation of the Gospel." He wished that a reformation should "take place among the Europeans;" he believed that this reformation would indeed "be the greatest blessing to the country."[46]

11.5 Montgomery Campbell's Apology to Schwartz in 1796

Charles Grant gave Montgomery Campbell a copy of Schwartz's *Defence of Missions* (1795) and encouraged him to write to Schwartz. On January 10, 1796, Montgomery Campbell wrote a detailed response to Schwartz; a copy of this letter has survived.[47] This response presents Grant as a "worthy friend" of M. Campbell; the *Courier* article makes Campbell "extremely censurable," but Campbell assures Schwartz that he spoke on an entirely different topic. He "never scoffed at Christianity," "the Sacred Religion," in which he "was educated." This letter claims he "never treated the beautiful Doctrines of Christ with levity or indifference." On the contrary, it speaks of Campbell as "a devout and true

---

43 NHR 4, 1795, issue 47, 999.
44 Schwartz: Defence of Missions in India, 14.
45 Schwartz: Defence of Missions in India, 14.
46 Schwartz: Defence of Missions in India, 14.
47 Montgomery Campbell's letter to Schwartz marked 32 = digital images 308 to 412 = Montgomery Campbell's letter to Schwartz from London on 10 Jan 1796.

Christian." He felt sorry that Schwartz, a person of "Distinguished Piety," questioned his convictions. He recollected how Schwartz had earlier esteemed him and requested that he not allow the debate, "which has been alluded to," to diminish his reasonable opinion. Campbell stated further that the reporter had concocted the story in the *Courier* newspaper:

> The accounts of speeches in the News Paper are never given with any degree of accuracy. Words were put into my mouth, which I never uttered, and sentiments never entered my imagination. The fact is that I said but little on the subject, which was in debate, and the little was to represent the difficulty which attended the conversion of Gentoos to Christianity, which, on political grounds only, I thought dangerous to take up as a National Undertaking and it was under that apprehension only that I recommended deliberation before the measure was adopted.

Campbell accepted that he had already read the report in the newspaper and "did not think it worthwhile to contradict the Newspaper Representation." However, Charles Grant informed the Anglican Bishop of London about it. Immediately, the Bishop requested that Campbell meet him and assure himself of Campbell's intention to assist any friend who would propagate Christianity in India. He promised the Bishop that he would never propose any measure that could be prejudicial to the genuine interest of the Country or the East India Company.

Campbell confessed further that regarding the "story of the *Collaries*" (i.e. Kaḷḷars), he "was misled or misinformed." He mentioned that he was "very sincerely concerned" to have given Schwartz an uneasy feeling and requested that he excuse him if he had "unintentionally erred." Campbell's sincere apology is evident in his request for forgiveness, showing his genuine regret. Campbell requested that his friend, Captain Allen Grant, hand-deliver this letter to Schwartz and explain some circumstances more fully that he could not write about. He conveyed to Schwartz the greetings of his "old friend Lady Campbell," the wife of the former Governor Archibald Campbell. Although she enjoyed good health, her spirits were "very different from" what Schwartz had known her to be. She often spoke of Schwartz "with sentiments of pure esteem and regard." Montgomery Campbell concluded his letter by stating that he was Schwartz's "most faithful and obedient servant." The tone and structure of this letter reveal Montgomery Campbell's earlier determination not to support any provision that would permit Christian missionaries into India. After he had spoken with Charles Grant and the Bishop of London, he changed his opinion because he wanted to please them in London rather than to please Schwartz in distant India.

On 11 July 1796, Resident Alexander Macleod congratulated Schwartz on the publication of his *Defence of the Mission*. He expressed his happiness: "My dear Sir, I have read with great pleasure your Letter to the Society on the misrepresentation in the Papers regarding the Mission and wish with all my heart such productions were more generally circulated in India."[48] Thus, those who knew Schwartz's ambassadorial work for peace, justice and social harmony endorsed his efforts.

---

48 Bodleian Library: 72290ind-box2, Document 30: Alexander Macleod to Schwartz on 11.07.1796 about the *Defence of Mission*.

Chapter 12

Schwartz and the Pious Clause of 1813

12.1 Growing Impact of Schwartz's 'Defence of Mission'

As discussed in Section 11.4, Schwartz's *Defence of Mission* was a document of significant influence, with his missionary colleagues in Madras and Tranquebar endorsing its content. Notably, Governor-General Cornwallis also lent his support to the document. From its creation in February 1793 to the Pious Clause of 1813, this document exerted significant influence over English-speaking mission-minded Christians in the United Kingdom and the United States, as well as among German-speaking populations. Within a year, it had two English editions.[1] The Mission Archives of the Francke Foundations house a German version of Schwartz's *Defence of Mission*. The editorial notes on this sixteen-page manuscript underscore the challenges faced by the German translator in accurately conveying the meaning of the English text in German. The printed version, however, presents a fluid, polished text.[2] Within two years of its existence, this inspirational and visionary text had reached most mission-minded readers in Britain and Germany. Its enduring impact would be felt for generations, as it would become foundational for several mission agencies, shaping the future of missionary work.

In a foreword, the editor, Johann Ludwig Schulze (1734–1799), provided some background information on this text that German readers might not be familiar with: The British Nation was noble and generous in supporting Lutheran missionary work in India. Yet, there too, like in Germany, were critics, such as Montgomery Campbell, who questioned the truthfulness and benefits of Schwartz's ministry and whose critical comments were published in a public newspaper. When Schwartz read it, he felt obliged to defend the honour and integrity of the missionary services that he was rendering to South Indians. Additionally, many British men in Britain and India were aware of Schwartz and his ministries. He wanted to help them better understand the significance of his ambassadorial services in response to Montgomery Campbell's accusations.[3]

Robert Grant, the son of the celebrated Charles Grant, attributed his father's enthusiasm for the missionary cause to Schwartz's influence on him. For example,

---

1 Christian Friedrich Schwartz: Defence of Mission. In: Account of the Society for Promoting Christian Knowledge. London: SPCK, 1795, 114–123; Christian Friedrich Schwartz: Defence of Missions in India by the late Venerable Mr. Swartz, published by the Society for Promoting Christian Knowledge in their Report for 1795. London: H. Brayer, 1796.

2 AFSt/M 1 C 35a : 65; NHR 4, 1797, issue 51, 285–294.

3 NHR 4, 1797, issue 51, 284.

after laying the foundation for the Hindu Medical College in Bombay (now Mumbai) in 1843, Robert Grant made the following impressive statement: "Charles Grant had been awakened to a deep sense of serious and internal piety in India about the year 1778." The sudden death of his daughters disturbed him. At that time, Johann Christian Obeck (1731–ca. 1773), a student of Schwartz, and John Zacharias Kiernander (1711–1799), the first Lutheran missionary in Calcutta and a friend of Schwartz, as well as William Chambers, a member of the Bengal Civil Service, introduced him to Schwartz. Subsequently, Grant exhibited, till the end of his life, both in India and in Britain, "the genuine fruits of real Christianity."[4]

In 1797, Charles Grant revised his work, entitled *Observations on the State of Society among the Asiatic Subjects of Great Britain*, which he had initially composed in 1792 in preparation for the Pious Clause in 1793. Although his first attempt failed, he did not abandon his plan to send Christian ministers to serve in schools and mission centres in India. As already discussed in Section 11.1, in 1797, he revised his work, quoting Schwartz's Defence of Mission, and presented it to the Company's Court of Directors.[5] He wanted to extend the same legal, ecclesiastical benefits to Indians in Company territories, which the British in Britain had been enjoying. His letter to the Court of Directors, dated 16 August 1797, reminded them of their obligation to spread the message of Christianity in India:

> The duty therefore of the Company, as part of a Christian community, its peculiar, superadded obligations, its enlarged means, and its continual dependence upon the divine favour, all call upon it to honor God, by diffusing the knowledge of that revelation which he has vouchsafed to mankind.[6]

The American Tract Society in New York published Schwartz's *Defence of Mission* in 1800. Its editor added the following note: When the British Parliament considered the proposals "in favor of Free Schools and Christian Missionaries" in

---

4 Church Missionary Gleaner 3:7, 1843, 73. On pages 74 and 75, Robert Grant gave additional information about his father: His intuitive mind, sound and impartial business policies, plans, and practices had influenced the Councils of the Indian Government unparalleled. Charles Grant joined "the small but mighty band of Christian statesmen, Mr. [William] Wilberforce, Mr. H[enry]. Thornton, Mr. [Thomas] Babington and a few others. He ultimately won almost every cause of humanity and piety in which he was engaged." Robert Grant elaborated that Charles Grant was influential in starting great institutions such as the British and Foreign Bible Society, the Church Missionary Society for Africa, and the East and the Jews' Conversion Society. Robert Grant recollected that we "are reaping now, in the revived sense of Religion [i.e. Christianity] diffused over our Church and Nation, the harvest of which he and others sowed the seeds. [...] In one view, India owes a debt to this eminent person which can scarcely be too highly estimated." With the help of Charles Simeon, the Chaplain at King's College in Cambridge, Grant selected able chaplains like David Brown and determined their salaries and pensions.

5 Grant: Observations on the State of Society among Asiatic Subjects of Great Britain, 1797, here 113–116.

6 Grant: Observations on the State of Society among Asiatic Subjects of Great Britain, 1797, ii.

1793, Montgomery Campbell opposed the proposals and stated that Schwartz's Tamil followers "were proverbial for their profligacy" and "men of high caste would spurn at the idea of changing the religion of their ancestors."[7] Then, the editor published Schwartz's *Defence of Mission*.[8]

Fred Schneider, who had studied William Wilberforce's role in shaping the British public opinion on the abolition of the slave trade in 1807, highlighted his unwavering advocacy for the missionary cause. Wilberforce organised dinner parties for clergy and stirred them up to work towards obtaining parliamentary permission "for gospel light to pass into India."[9]

On 15 June 1813, the House of Commons of the British Parliament ordered Charles Grant's 234-page *Observations* to be printed for a wider distribution. An appendix in this book reproduces Schwartz's *Defence of Mission*.[10] Grant pleaded for improving the morals of Indians, whom he and his friends had been observing during their time in India. He wanted Christian ministers to play a decisive role in improving the morals, as he understood them.

Claudius Buchanan (1766–1815), who had previously worked as an Evangelical Chaplain in Calcutta, visited King Serfoji II and missionary J. C. Kohlhoff and other Christian leaders in Tanjore, and heard their testimony of Schwartz, was firmly determined to promote Anglican missionary work in the Company's territories in India. For this purpose, he published *Memoir of the Expediency of an Ecclesiastical Establishment for British India*,[11] *The Star in the East*,[12] *Christian Researches in Asia*, *Apology for Promoting Christianity in India*,[13] and *Colonial Ecclesiastical Establishment*.[14] These works frequently refer to the exemplary work of Schwartz. His *Apology* contains extracts from Chaplain Richard Kerr's sermon about Schwartz at St. Mary's Church in Fort St. George,

---

7 The Life of C.F. Swartz: Missionary at Trichinopoly and Tanjore in India, 51.

8 The Life of C.F. Swartz: Missionary at Trichinopoly and Tanjore in India, 52–65.

9 Fred D. Schneider: Parliament, the East India Company and the Calcutta Bishopric. In: Journal of Church and State 16, 1974, issue 1, 51–71, here 61–62.

10 Grant: Observations on the State of Society among Asiatic Subjects of Great Britain, 1813, 225–234.

11 Claudius Buchanan: Memoir on the Expediency of an Ecclesiastical Establishment for British India, both as a Means of Perpetuating the Christian Religion among our own Countrymen and as a Foundation for the Ultimate Civilisation of the Natives. London 1805.

12 Claudius Buchanan: Star in the East—A Sermon preached in the Parish Church of St. James, Bristol, on Sunday, February 26, 1809, for the Benefit of the Society for Missions to Africa and the East. Boston [8]1809.

13 Claudius Buchanan: An Apology for Promoting Christianity in India, containing two letters addressed to the Honourable East-India Company concerning the idol Juggernaut; and a Memorial presented to the Bengal Government in 1807, in defence of the Christian Missions in India, printed by order of the Hon. The House of Commons, to which are now added Remarks of the letter addressed by the Bengal Government to the Court of Directors in reply to the Memorial with an Appendix containing various official papers, chiefly extracted from the Parliamentary Records relating to the Promulgation of Christianity in India. London 1813.

14 Claudius Buchanan: Colonial Ecclesiastical Establishment—Being a Brief View of the State of the Colonies of Great Britain and of her Asiatic Empire in respect to Religious Instruction prefaced by some considerations on the National Duty of affording it, to which is added a Sketch of an Ecclesiastical Establishment for British India, humbly submitted to the consideration of the Imperial Parliament. London [2]1813.

the letter of the Company's Court of Directors about Schwartz's marble monument in be installed in St. Mary's Church, a transcript of the text on this monument, and Schwartz's *Defence of Mission*.[15] Grant and Buchanan used the *Defence of Mission* as the best example in securing the British Government's permission to send Anglican ministers to serve in the Company's territories in India legally. These ministers should emulate Schwartz's lifestyle.

To convince the British Parliament and the Company to permit Protestant Christian workers into the territories of the Company in India, Hugh Pearson (1777–1856) published Schwartz's biography in six parts in 1813.[16] Pearson presented Schwartz as "the Christian Apostle to the East in these latter days."[17] At that time, the Company's territories were under the rule of the British King and Parliament. Therefore, the Company servants followed British laws and established branches of British civil and judicial institutions. Buchanan knew of these attempts; he insisted that the Church of England was an integral part of British society. Therefore, the Church of England should establish an Anglican Church in Bengal. Thus, Wilberforce, Grant and Buchanan significantly shaped public awareness of an ecclesiastical establishment and Christian missionary service in India.

Schwartz's *Defence of Mission* continued to exert its influence beyond 1813. SPCK's annual report for 1814 printed it.[18] The *Remains of the Rev. C. F. Schwartz* reproduced it in 1826.[19] Pearson's magisterial *Memoirs* on Schwartz quoted it.[20] In 1835, the journal *Boston Recorder* published it.[21] These selective references indicate the growing impact of Schwartz's *Defence of Mission* in Western Europe and the United States. Its most significant effect, however, was in Great Britain.

12.2 Growing Missionary Consciousness in Britain

Between 1793 and 1813, British attitudes toward Protestant missionary work in India underwent a significant shift. The British public, who had been exposed to the reports of the Company's atrocities in Bengal, developed a moral crisis. Despite benefiting from India's vast wealth, the news of the Great Bengal Famine (1769–1773), engineered by the Company and resulting in the deaths of more than ten million Indians, saddened them deeply. At that time, the mysterious death of

---

15 Buchanan: An Apology for Promoting Christianity in India, 173–190.

16 Hugh Pearson: The Life of Rev. Christian F. Swartz. In: The Missionary Register for the Year 1813, containing an Abstract of the Proceedings of the principal Missionary and Bible Societies throughout the World. Vol. 1. London ³1816, 193–215, 241–249, 273–282, 305–309, 302–317 and 337–350.

17 Pearson: The Life of Rev. Christian F. Swartz, 193.

18 An Abstract of the Annual Reports and Correspondence of the Society for Promoting Christian Knowledge, 396–411.

19 Remains of the Rev. C. F. Schwartz, 298–316.

20 Pearson: Memoirs, Vol. 2, 287–301.

21 Religious: Swartz, C.F. The Missionary. Boston Recorder. Vol. 20, No. 33, 14 August 1835, 129.

Robert Clive, possibly by suicide, on 22 November 1774, further stirred public distress in Britain. The Company's plundering of Indian wealth created a sense of guilt among many Britons. They believed merely looting India's wealth was unacceptable and felt a moral obligation to assist Indians.

Warren Hastings (1732–1818), Clive's successor in India, was responsible for the Rohilla War (1773–1774) and the Maratha War (1775–1782). These wars depleted the Company's treasury. British policymakers, such as Edmund Burke, stated that Hastings's manners were "repugnant to the Honour and Policy of this British nation."[22] His impeachment in 1782 shamed many influential British citizens. Simultaneously, they read about Hyder Ali's invasion of the Carnatic in the 1780s and the scandalous debts of Nawab Wallajah to numerous British creditors. Some of these concerned British citizens wanted to help Indians enhance their welfare.

At the same time, the Continental Blockade (1806–1814), under Napoleon Bonaparte's (1769–1821) control, limited the import and sale of British goods in continental Europe.[23] Simultaneously, British traders from the Glasgow East India Association (1812–1813) and the Liverpool East India Association (1812–1813) challenged the Company's trade monopoly in Asia and sought to trade directly with Asian countries. This competition further weakened the Company's position.[24] Company officers looked for ways to expand their markets.

During this period, British evangelical leaders like Charles Grant and William Wilberforce expressed their fervent desire for cross-cultural missionary involvement. Their efforts to introduce the English language, European knowledge, and "Christian Revelation" to Indians, despite the Company's resistance, underscored the British Government's obligation to provide more tangible humanitarian services and address moral evils and social disorder among Indians.[25]

Thomas Beck (c. 1755–1844), a dissenting pastor at St. Paul's Church in Deptford, Kent, composed a poem in 1795. This poem summarised the rising British evangelical consciousness for overseas missions and appealed to British Christians for united action. It encouraged the prospective missionaries to imitate the Lord Jesus Christ, who came into this world as a pilgrim, lived a fuller life, and renounced "wealth, pleasure, honor, comfort, and ease."[26] It describes Christian missionary experiences among diverse peoples and refers to well-known missionaries:

---

22 Carson: The East India Company and Religion, 21.

23 For more information about this blockade, see Revisiting Napoleon's Continental System–Local, Regional and European Experiences. Ed. by Katherine B. Aaslestad and Johan Joor. Basingstoke 2014.

24 For details about these lobbying efforts, see Yukishia Kumagai: Breaking into the Monopoly–Provincial Merchants and Manufactures' Campaigns for Access to the Asian Market, 1790–1833. Leiden 2012.

25 Carson: The East India Company and Religion, 36–37.

26 Thomas Beck: The Missionary: A Poem to which are subjoined Hints on the Propagation of the Gospel at Home and Abroad Respectfully Inscribed to the New Missionary Societies. London: W. Button, Paternoster-Row, 1795, 6.

> Where Christ is preach'd with simple zeal for God,
> And honest aim to save the souls of Men,
> My heart anticipates a glorious harvest.
> ELLIOT! MAYHEW! BRAINARD! ZIEGENBALG!
> PLUTSCHALL! [sic! = Plütschau] And other valued names on earth
> Unsung and barbarous to the classic muse,
> [...]
> 'Tis thus the messenger of JESUS now
> Goes forth and throws around the precious seed,
> Oft steep'd in tears and then with earnest cries,
> And trembling heart implores the showers of grace,
> But in the harvest of the world – O with
> What joy shall he return, bearing the sheaves
> Immortal to the garner of the skies![27]

This poem also lamented the "great variety of absurd and contradictory opinions" among the Episcopalians, Methodists, Baptists, Independents, and Presbyterians, who were unable to unite in promoting the gospel "either by educating students, supporting ministers, sending out missionaries, erecting chapels, or distributing religious books."[28] Then, it highlights five benefits of a united mission: firstly, it would reveal the absence of true Christianity in the East Indies, or South Seas, and in Europe itself.[29] Secondly, it would help missionary societies distribute their personnel and resources more evenly. Thirdly, it would prevent conflicts among missionaries by discouraging "Oppositions abroad and separations at home."[30] Fourthly, it would strengthen cooperation in educational and other philanthropic fields, as well as in translating the Bible into the people's living languages.[31] Fifthly, when leaders of various denominations meet in a congress, they would find, to their mutual surprise, "that their differences were less than they supposed – that they had a common interest – and that they all meant the same thing."[32] This unity and shared purpose among the missionaries would have been a powerful motivator.

Thomas Beck's poem *On Foreign Missions* contains ten teachings: first, Christ's Great Commission remained valid and should have been introduced to the 400 million people of the world by 1795.[33] Secondly, the same Lord Jesus who had commanded his disciples to go into all the world would remain with the missionaries and grant them "the same power and grace that converted heathen sinners formerly."[34] Thirdly, success in united missionary work among non-Christians, as reported by the missionaries of the Jesuits and Baptists, would encourage Europeans to become more fervent in overseas missionary activities.[35]

---

27 Beck: The Missionary: A Poem, 11–13.
28 Beck: The Missionary: A Poem, 17–18.
29 Beck: The Missionary: A Poem, 18.
30 Beck: The Missionary: A Poem, 19.
31 Beck: The Missionary: A Poem, 20.
32 Beck: The Missionary: A Poem, 23.
33 Beck: The Missionary: A Poem, 23–26.
34 Beck: The Missionary: A Poem, 24.
35 Beck: The Missionary: A Poem, 24–28: Beck referred to these examples: in 1706, the Lutheran missionaries in Tranquebar began preaching the Gospel to Indians. By 1795, they

Fourthly, committed, unmarried men would be better suited for missionary work than married men. However, some married missionaries would also be required in certain circumstances. All missionaries should remember that they "are likely to be esteemed more for their usefulness than for polite, elegant or literary accomplishments."[36] Beck referred to Reverend Melville Horne's desire to employ an "equal number of pious lay-brethren should be employed in every mission, as schoolmasters, transcribers, exhorters, and to assist in all the emergencies of the mission, to which missionaries themselves may not be able to give attention."[37] Leaders should discern the right kind of missionaries for specific people groups. For example, a missionary more suitable to the inhabitants of African descent in the West Indies might be "ill-qualified to go in the same capacity among the Hindus in the East."[38]

Sixthly, the missionaries should uphold their love for God and people. Seventhly, each place should have enough missionaries according to its circumstances and needs. For example, Jesus employed seventy people in a small area of Judea. Likewise, missionaries should

> Begin with Christ crucified; make him the subject of their first sermon. Those two grand points, the necessity of our Redeemer and his sufficiency, ought to be continual themes for a missionary of Jesus. It was by this method that the world was evangelized at first. This has been the plan of all successful missionaries and every other premise nothing but disgrace and disappointment.[39]

Eighthly, missionary work involves sacrifice. No amount of money can reward it. Only those who feel called will persevere. With their selflessness and dedication, such missionaries will be the apostles, helping thousands turn away from their former "ways of darkness" and follow the Lord Jesus Christ.

Ninthly, financial support to missionaries in distant parts of the world might not be feasible. Therefore, they should generate their own money by farming or similar gainful employment. No missionary work should function as a profit-making business. Medical centres and other charitable institutions would be necessary to save people's souls and physical bodies. All people needed a holistic Gospel. The home churches could raise funds for their missionaries overseas.

Finally, Beck referred to Isaac Kimber's writing about the British past and how the inhabitants of Britain turned from polytheism to worshipping the one God of

---

had shared the Gospel with more than "18,000 Gentoos." The missionaries of the Dutch Reformed Church in Ceylon (modern Sri Lanka), John Eliott and David Brainard, among the indigenous tribes of North America, the support of the Presbyterian Society in Scotland for Propagating the Christian Knowledge among the "American Indians," missionary works among the Greenlanders, the Tartars, the Koikoi in southern Africa (lit. the Hottentots), the blessed works of the African-American Baptist minister George Liele among the Jamaicans and the reports of other missionaries encouraged European Christians to support overseas missionary works.

36 Beck: The Missionary: A Poem, 27–28.
37 Beck: The Missionary: A Poem, 28.
38 Beck: The Missionary: A Poem, 28.
39 Beck: The Missionary: A Poem, 30.

the Bible.[40] They wandered without wearing clothes but with an iron ring around their neck. On the southern coast, they covered themselves with animal hides. They tattooed their bodies with images of flowers and animals and even practised human sacrifice.[41] The Gospel of the Lord Jesus Christ reached Britain and transformed the British.[42] The earliest evangelists in Britain faced the same kinds of "difficulties, hardships and dangers" that modern missionaries faced.[43] Therefore, Beck stressed gratitude as the most compelling reason for engaging in foreign missions. He concluded his book with this most impressive statement: "We are therefore called upon to *do unto others*, not merely as we *would* that they should do unto us, but as others actually *have done* unto us." Not only piety, compassion, and benevolence call for our exertion, but also gratitude, equity, and justice.[44]

In the meantime, the works of the Baptist William Carey and his friends in Serampore, not far from Calcutta, and Carey's professorship at Fort William College, which trained British diplomats for India, bore tangible fruits. Carey's students, such as James Mackintosh (1765–1832), who became the Advocate General of the Company's Bombay Presidency, and Thomas Metcalfe, who became the Governor-General's representative to the Mughal Court in Delhi, were sympathetic to Christian missionary work. British Christians read the works of evangelical chaplains in Calcutta, such as David Brown, Claudius Buchanan, Thomas Trubody Thomason, Daniel Corrie (later Bishop of Madras), and Henry Martyn. Gradually, more British evangelical Christians began to support missionary activities in the Company's territories.[45]

In 1808, John William Cunningham (1780–1861), an evangelical pastor of the Church of England influenced by the Clapham Group, wondered how the Company could govern fifty million Indians without ever introducing them to the knowledge and practice of Christianity. In this regard, the Company had been failing to fulfil its moral obligation. It represented the British Nation in India and did not include the "Religion of Christ" freely practised there. While expanding its territories, the Company disrupted India's internal peace among the inhabitants of towns and villages. Additionally, the British benefited from India's money, goods, and territories. As subjects of British territories, Indians were entitled to all the claims and privileges of the British, including their right to have branches of the Church of England established and maintained among them.[46]

By 1810, some evangelical Christians in England, within the Church of England and with commercial connections to India, had developed their

---

40 Isaac Kimber: The History of England from Earliest Accounts to the Accession of his present Majesty King George II. London: Thomas Cox, 1755.
41 Beck: The Missionary: A Poem, 34–35.
42 Beck: The Missionary: A Poem, 35–36.
43 Beck: The Missionary: A Poem, 36.
44 Beck: The Missionary: A Poem, 36.
45 Mayhew: Christianity and the Government of India, 69 and 77.
46 John William Cunningham: Christianity in India–An Essay on the Duty, Means, and Consequences of Introducing the Christian Religion among the Native Inhabitants of the British Domains in the East. London 1808, i and 1–8.

understanding of mission from the past non-Christian histories of Britons. For example, as discussed in Section 7.10.3, Thomas Thompson, a merchant, reassured the Company in London that it should permit Christian missionaries into their territories. Non-Christian Indians, who were open to religious conversations, welcomed the Christian missionaries. They were eager to test the merits of the Christian faith; if they did not like them, they would leave Christians' religious beliefs and practices without disturbance. Thompson recollected how the British people once worshipped images and sacrificed their children as sacrifices to various deities. Now, they heard and appropriated Christian teachings and chose Christianity as their way of life. Thompson asserted that the British "are a highly favoured nation; our light has come, and the glory of the Lord has risen upon us. It is, therefore, our indispensable duty to communicate the light of the glorious Gospel of Christ to nations." Thompson concluded his passionate support for the Pious Clause of 1813: "May God send Christian preachers throughout the world, and take the Heathen for His inheritance, and the uttermost parts of the earth for His possession!"[47]

12.3 Growing Challenges Posed by the Vellore Mutiny

Eight years after Beck's impressive poem appeared, on 10 July 1806, in response to specific directives from Governor William Bentinck of Madras and his Commander-in-Chief John Cradock, the Vellore Mutiny broke out. Bentinck and Cradock ordered the sepoys to refrain from wearing religious or caste symbols on their uniforms, to shave off their beards, and to wear iron hats with leather cockades.[48] Interpreting these changes as the Company's attempts to Christianise them, a notion they vehemently opposed, the infuriated sepoys mutinied.

However, in 2021, Jennifer Howes presented a more compelling and insightful cause for the Vellore Mutiny than previous assumptions, shedding new light on this historical event.[49] After capturing Tipu Sultan's palace in Seringapatam, the British army gathered 601 women from there and placed them under house arrest. On 30 June 1799, they crowned the five-year-old Krishnaraja Wodeyar III as the legitimate ruler of Mysore. This installation angered the women in Tipu's Palace. In 1802, the British deported these women and Tipu Sultan's sons to Vellore, where they had built *Haider Mahal* and *Tipu Mahal* to accommodate them. Soon, these women received female servants; some of them adopted children. Some reconnected with other Muslim political leaders in Tirucciräppaḷḷi. Some of these

---

47 Thompson: The Gods of the East Indies, 23–24.

48 Manikumar: 1806 revolt at Vellore Fort: the leather cockade offended the sensibilities of the Muslim sepoys who hated pig's skin. Sepoys from upper *varṇa* hated to do anything with an object made of cowhide or pig's skin. They believed that touching or nearing an object made of animal skin would incur ritual pollution. The affected persons must perform the prescribed ritual ceremonies and eliminate the fatalist consequences of Karma.

49 Jennifer Howes: Tipu Sultan's female entourage under East India Company rule. In: Journal of the Royal Asiatic Society Series 3, Vol. 31, 2021, issue 4, 855–874.

political leaders were protesters in the lineage of the deposed Nawab Chanda Sahib. Gradually, the Company had to maintain, at their cost, 790 persons. Increasingly, it became difficult for the Company to readily have the necessary cash on hand for these women and their relatives. Hence, on 28 February 1806, Governor William Cavendish Bentinck reduced their allowances "by one-third and one-half." The women felt offended and began to hate the Company in Vellore. As they could not obtain the money they desperately needed, they rebelled against the Company.[50]

The Indian sepoys in Vellore did not want Governor William Bentinck's approach to alter their dress and personal appearance. Finally, on 3 December 1806, Bentinck assured the sepoys that the Company would continue to respect their religions and customs. He advised them not to trust "the idle rumours which are circulated by enemies of their happiness, who endeavour with the basest designs to weaken the confidence of the troops in the British Government."[51]

Claudius Buchanan, who had visited Vellore immediately after the Mutiny, wrote on 7 November 1807 to Governor-General Minto in Calcutta that "the insurrection at Vellore had no connection with the Christian Religion, directly or indirectly, immediately or remotely, is a truth that is capable of demonstration."[52] On 7 February 1809, Governor Bentinck explained the causes and consequences of the Vellore Mutiny to the Court of Directors in London. He affirmed that the mutiny did not originate in any "misguided workings of religious zeal."[53] But there was distrust between the British soldiers and Indian sepoys.[54] Information about this revolt did not dampen the rising need for Protestant missionaries to India.

---

50 For example, Document 4729 of the EIC's Court of Directors, dated December 1807, is entitled "Applications of the Ladies of the Families of Hyder Ally and Tippoo Sultan for the grant of certain Indulgences" (IOR/F/4/218, 1–43). Accordingly, each of the two widows of Meer Khan, namely "Madzah Khatoor and Peash Begum," would receive one hundred Rupees each month. Immediately, other widows competed to get more money from the EIC. "Fatima Khamum, the first legal wife of Hyder Ally Khan and head Lady of both the Mahals," wanted a monthly allowance of two hundred Rupees. On 28.03.1806, the EIC in Vellore listed twelve women from the household of Hyder Ali and Tipu Sultan who received pensions, stipends, provisions and marriage expenses. For example, the EIC helped Sarem Bibie, Tipu Sultan's adopted daughter, get married. She continued to receive "yearly clothes, a monthly sum of 15 Rupees." Likewise, the EIC treated Kareem Bibie, Tipu Sultan's other adopted daughter.

51 Papers Relating to East India Affairs (Resident Europeans – Police – MISSIONAIRES – Weavers and Investments), Ordered by The House of Commons, to be printed 14 April 1813, 86.

52 Buchanan: An Apology for Promoting Christianity in India, 64.

53 William Cavendish Bentinck: Memorial Addressed to the Honourable Court of Directors, containing an Account of the Mutiny at Vellore. London 1810, 28.

54 Thompson: The Gods of the East Indies, 16–17. "Dr. [Christoph Samuel] John says that the sanguinary catastrophe at Vellore did not originate from any dread which prevailed among the Hindoos or native soldiers of being compelled to embrace Christianity, but from an apprehension of being forced to change their local customs and to accept of European forms against their caste."

55 David Kling: The New Divinity and the Origins of the American Board of Commissioners of Foreign Missions. In: Church History 72, 2003, issue 4, 791–819: The Society for Propagating the Gospel Among the Indians and Others in North America (1787) was an indigenous missionary organisation initiated and organised by US Americans in

12.4 Growing Missionary Consciousness in New England

The missionary consciousness also spread among the American Protestant Christians in New England, who founded various missionary agencies.[55] Notably, the formation of the American Board of Commissioners for Foreign Missions (ABCFM) in 1810 marked a turning point. In 1812, they sent out five missionaries who served in India and Myanmar (formerly known as Burma). Their stories encouraged Protestant Christians in America and Britain.[56] Notably, informed Christians in Britain did not like how the Company officers in Calcutta treated the American missionaries, refusing to permit them to serve in the British territories. When the British Parliament revised and renewed the Company Charter Act in 1813, influential British Christian leaders attempted to persuade the British Parliament to legally permit Christian missionaries to serve the "Asiatic subjects" of Britain, specifically Indians residing in the territories under the Company's rule in India. This service should aim to increase the interests and happiness of Indians.

12.5 Growing Parliamentary Scrutiny of Mission

On 21 May 1813, the Company's Court of Directors in London published the transcripts of interviews with various senior Company officers who had spent considerable time in India. The interviewers examined petitions for and against renewing the Company Charter of 1813. Among them, the petition about the Pious

Massachusetts to reach the Native American communities with the Gospel of the Lord Jesus Christ. On May 26, 1802, the Baptists in Massachusetts established their Massachusetts Baptist Missionary Society to strengthen the Baptist congregations in New England. They studied the conditions of non-Christians and nominal Christians within the United States. In 1806, Samuel Mills and four friends attended the Haystack Prayer Meeting at Williams College in western Massachusetts, where they discussed William Carey's *Inquiry into the Obligation of Christians to Use Means for the Conversion of the Heathen* and dedicated themselves to working toward a missionary revival. Two years later, in 1808, Samuel Mills formed the Society of Brethren and began collecting information about existing missionary movements and the need for new ones. The members of this society requested the General Association of Congregational Ministers of Massachusetts to send missionaries. Consequently, this Association established the American Board of Commissioners for Foreign Missions (ABCFM) in Boston in 1810.

56 Kling: The New Divinity, 792: In 1812, "five ABCFM missionaries – Adoniram Judson, Jr., Samuel Nott, Samuel Newell, Luther Rice and Gordon Hall, accompanied by three wives – Ann Hasseltine Judson, Rosanne Peck Nott and Harriet Atwood Newell – set sail for India." Judson and his wife arrived in Calcutta on 17.06.1812 and stayed with William Carey. There, they renounced their faith in the congregational church and embraced Baptist church polity. The Company did not permit them to remain near Calcutta because they viewed them not only as dissenters but also as unwanted citizens of an enemy country. On 06.06.1812, the United States began waging a war against the British, which lasted until February 1815. In July 1713, Judson and his wife relocated to Rangoon (now Yangon) in Myanmar (formerly Burma). Gordon Hall, Samuel Knott and Luther Rice began their work in Bombay (modern Mumbai). The Company's Governor of Bombay, a leader of the British and Foreign Bible Society, permitted them to stay and minister there.

Clause attracted the sharpest and most consistent resistance. Warren Hastings, John Shore (i.e. Lord Teignmouth), William Cowper and Thomas Graham answered questions about Schwartz and his ministry.

12.5.1 Warren Hastings about Schwartz

Following the *Regulating Act of 1773*, Warren Hastings became the first Governor-General of the Company in Calcutta and remained in that position until 1785. Twenty-five years later, he recollected his tenure in India and reflected on Schwartz in his interview on 30 March 1813. Stephen Rumbold Lushington (1776–1868) chaired the panel that interviewed him on five issues about institutionalising Christianity in India. The panellists asked Hastings to comment on "any persons employed themselves in converting the natives to the Christian religion."[57] Hastings responded that he had known about Schwartz, "the worthy gentleman" in the Carnatic, Kiernander in Calcutta and an old Catholic priest in Dacca. Secondly, the panellists wanted to know whether the Company had employed these clergy persons. Hastings replied that the Company did not appoint any of them. Nevertheless, he stated that Schwartz "could be considered as a subject of the Company: he visited and occasionally resided, I believe, in every part of the peninsula and was everywhere respected."[58] Hastings affirmed that Kiernander resided exclusively in Calcutta and was unaware of the Catholic priest's exact whereabouts.

Thirdly, the panellists desired to know the practical impact of unlicensed and unrestrained Christian missionaries converting non-Christians to Christianity. Hastings gave a twofold answer: if Christian missionaries effected the conversion of non-Christians on their own without any formal attachment to the Company, he would have ignored them. By contrast, if they had irritated the minds of the non-Christians and caused trouble, he would have restrained them. Fourthly, the panellists asked Hastings to give his opinion on the consequences of licensed persons, who "would be more dangerous to the interests of the East India Company in India than the indiscriminate resort of all Europeans to India."[59] Hastings replied that he would oppose any parliamentary legislation that would promote the religious conversion of Indians. Should Company employees or others engage in religious conversion and draw the attention of the Company, the Company should use the most efficient means in its power to keep them under control.

Fifthly, the panellists asked for his thoughts on officially permitting a Church Establishment for India.[60] He responded that this question was intricate and

57 Minutes of Evidence taken before the Honourable House of Commons, in a committee of the whole House, to whom it was referred to consider the affairs of the East-India Company. London 1813, 8.

58 Minutes of Evidence taken before the Honourable House of Commons, 9.

59 Minutes of Evidence taken before the Honourable House of Commons, 9.

60 Minutes of Evidence taken before the Honourable House of Commons, 11.

delicate. The Company should not intend to force its religion upon the consciences of the people of India living in its territories.[61] He regretted that Christianity had spread among Indians in the Bengal, Bombay, and Madras Presidencies, and it "unhappily impressed itself with peculiar force upon the minds of our Native Infantry, the men on whom we must depend in the last resort for our protection against any disturbances that might be the effect of such surmises."[62] He conceded that much "would depend upon the temper, conduct and demeanour of the person elevated to that sacred office."[63] He concluded that spreading Christianity in India would be "one of the great hazards."[64] Thus, Hastings opposed any attempts by Christian missionaries to evangelise Indians. His enthusiasm for Sanskrit literature, particularly the Bhagavad Gita, led him to establish the Asiatic Society in 1784 under the leadership of another Sanskrit enthusiast, William Jones, and to sponsor the publication of their journal, *Asiatic Researches*. Besides recovering, preserving and popularising Sanskrit literature, Hastings was more concerned with ensuring the economic and military prospects of the Company than with allowing Christian missionary activity in India.

12.5.2 John Shore about Schwartz

John Shore (1751–1834, First Baron Teignmouth) served as Governor-General of India from 1793 to 1798 and resided in Calcutta. Of his thirty years of Company Service from 1768 to 1798, he spent twenty-four years in India. During this tenure, he familiarised himself with the attitudes, characters and lifestyle of the Bengalese. In 1808, he expressed his opinion on permitting Christian missionaries to work in India, noting that Christianity had been present in India for a long time, yet most Indians remained indifferent. According to him, Christian missionaries should focus only on preaching God's Word and administering sacraments; they should not critique local religious beliefs and practices.[65]

On 30 March 1813, Randel Jackson, a member of the parliamentary interview panel, questioned him about institutionalising Anglican Christianity in India. Firstly, Jackson wanted to know if institutionalising Anglicanism in India would jeopardise "the security of the British Empire in India."[66] Jackson enquired whether public preaching, attacking the beliefs and rituals of non-Christian Indians and inviting them to embrace Christianity would have any adverse effect on the Company. Shore affirmed his knowledge about the missionaries of the Royal Danish-Halle Mission in Tranquebar and recommended that all Christian preachers be sensitive to people's cultures and religions. As prudent individuals, they should

---

61 Minutes of Evidence taken before the Honourable House of Commons, 11.
62 Minutes of Evidence taken before the Honourable House of Commons, 11.
63 Minutes of Evidence taken before the Honourable House of Commons, 11.
64 Minutes of Evidence taken before the Honourable House of Commons, 11.
65 John Shore: Considerations on the Practicability, Policy and Obligations of Communicating to the Natives of India the Knowledge of Christianity. London 1808.
66 Minutes of Evidence taken before the Honourable House of Commons, 20–21.

not pose any danger or offend others. Then, Shore boldly stated that the character of a missionary cannot and should not offend the people of India.

The interviewer asked Shore whether preaching the Gospel would have a profound impact on the public. Shore declared that Christians would not threaten the public. He recalled reading Ziegenbalg's conversation with the Tamil people in 1717. The Tamil people interacted with the missionaries because they knew they preached a true religion to them. Shore confessed that he could not recall any harmful consequences resulting from the conferences between the Danish missionaries and the natives on the Malabar coast.[67]

Secondly, the interviewer asked Shore to comment on the possible consequences of "an indiscrete zeal to change the national religions in India to be greater or less than in most other countries, from the peculiar habits and feelings" of Indians. Shore readily admitted the dangerous outcome of indiscriminate preaching. Then he emphatically affirmed that he had "proof that a judicious and prudent zeal may be exercised effectually and to the conversion of the natives." The interviewer next inquired whether sending an Anglican bishop to India would strengthen the widespread perception that the Company was imposing Christianity on Indians. Shore replied that Indians would view that action "with perfect indifference." After exploring the presence of different Christian denominations in India, the interviewer asked Shore to name some notable examples of Danish missionaries in India. Without hesitation, Shore responded that he admired Schwartz and Gericke, the two men who "possessed the esteem of the natives in the greatest degree," and he also respected the Danish missionaries.[68] Immediately, the interviewer wanted to know whether these two men rendered "any material services to the British Government" from "the influence which he possessed with the natives." Shore responded briefly: "Swartz, I believe, was, to a very considerable degree." The interviewer sought to determine whether embracing Christianity afforded converts a distinct set of moral values that diverged from those of the Hindus. Shore answered that his limited knowledge would not help him make informed comparisons.

After covering several themes, the interviewer linked the plan to establish an Anglican Episcopacy in India with the ministry of Schwartz.[69] Shore stressed that the proposed creation of Anglican Episcopacy in India would not lead Indians to believe that the Company secretly tried to introduce Christianity to Indians and, hence, they would resist it. Shore indicated that bishops were not new to India; the Orthodox Church in the Malabar Coast and the Roman Catholic Christians had their bishops. He reiterated his observation that these bishops did not

---

67 Minutes of Evidence taken before the Honourable House of Commons, 20: Shore referred to a selection of Ziegenbalg's conversations with the Tamil people, which J. Thomas Philipps translated into English and published as follows: Philipps, J. Thomas (transl.): Thirty Four Conferences between the Danish Missionaries and the Malabarian Bramans (or Heathen Priests) in the East Indies, concerning the Truth of the Christian Religion together with some Letters written by the Heathens to the said Missionaries., London: H. Clements in St. Paul's Church Yard, 1717.

68 Minutes of Evidence taken before the Honourable House of Commons, 31.

69 Minutes of Evidence taken before the Honourable House of Commons, 34–35.

embarrass non-Christians, and he seldom heard of them. In this context, the interviewer asked Shore to comment on the "missionary Schwartz in India."[70] Shore responded that Schwartz resided in southern India, professed Christianity and taught it publicly; after his death, "the Rajah of Tanjore has granted a spot of ground for building a church within his dominions, for the use of native Christians, out of respect to the memory of Swartz."[71] Shore stated that he "never heard of any dissatisfaction of any kind expressed at the conduct of Mr Swartz."[72] He affirmed that the Rajah of Tanjore esteemed Schwartz, and the people held Schwartz "in the greatest credit."[73] The interviewer prompted Shore to comment on Schwartz's impact on the local people, who trusted him more readily than they trusted the Company. Shore replied that his informants had apprised him of how the local people "took the word of Swartz"[74] when they refused to trust the word of their king, Shore felt that if he had known of this interview three days beforehand, he could have answered in a more informed manner.

12.5.3 William Cowper about Schwartz

On 31 March 1813, Stephen Rumbold Lushington chaired the interview panel of the Company that questioned William Cowper, who had resided in the Bengal Presidency for over thirty years. He served as President of the Board of Revenue from 1786 to 1791. He was a member of the Company's Council in Bengal for ten years. He served the Company in other official capacities for the rest of the time. The interviewers quizzed Cowper about his knowledge of Schwartz.[75] They wanted to know whether he had heard of the "very eminent missionary" Schwartz in India. Cowper responded: "I have: a most respectable person, universally respected and beloved; he was at Madras, but I had no personal acquaintance with him, nor ever saw him."[76] Immediately, the interviewers asked him about the services that Schwartz had rendered to the English government. Cowper replied that he spent only a few days in Madras, but he knew of Schwartz's relationship with the king of Tanjore and "that all ranks of people respected him; that he was a great favourite and had a very profound influence over the rajah of that country."[77] At the same time, Cowper confessed that he was unaware of Schwartz's missionary work. The interviewers probed further to determine whether Cowper was aware that the king of Tanjore had made Schwartz the guardian of his adopted son. Cowper confessed to having difficulty recollecting the details of this adoption in 1787. However, he was aware of a proposal that had come to the attention of the Governor General in Bengal, as Cowper belonged

---

70 Minutes of Evidence taken before the Honourable House of Commons, 34.
71 Minutes of Evidence taken before the Honourable House of Commons, 34.
72 Minutes of Evidence taken before the Honourable House of Commons, 34.
73 Minutes of Evidence taken before the Honourable House of Commons, 34.
74 Minutes of Evidence taken before the Honourable House of Commons, 35.
75 Minutes of Evidence taken before the Honourable House of Commons, 58–59.
76 Minutes of Evidence taken before the Honourable House of Commons, 59.
77 Minutes of Evidence taken before the Honourable House of Commons, 59.

to the Council that had examined it. He requested the interviewers to consult the Company's records from Madras or Bengal. When the interviewers asked him to comment on the monument that the king of Tanjore had requested from "Mr. Swartz's friends in England," Cowper confessed his ignorance. The interviewers asked Cowper whether he knew that the "congregations of Christians, to whom Mr. Swartz and Mr. Gericke constantly preached in Tanjore, amounted to some thousands of persons." Cowper stated that he had no idea about these Christians and had never heard of Gericke.

12.5.4 Thomas Graham about Schwartz

On 2 April 1813, Stephen Rumbold Lushington chaired the interview panel of the Company that questioned Thomas Graham (1752–1819), who lived in Calcutta from 1769 to 1808 and served in the council eight months each under Governor Generals Charles Cornwallis (1786–1793) and Richard C. Wellesley (1798–1805). When asked about his knowledge of Schwartz, Graham affirmed that he not only had heard of him but had also seen him in person. However, he was unaware of the ancestral religions from which some Tamils had adopted Lutheran Christianity. The interviewers wanted to know whether Schwartz's works had ever caused "any revolution, or insurrection, or popular commotion." Graham's response was brief but poignant. He stated that Schwartz was a man of great discretion, interacting only with those who were willing to engage with him.[78] Thus, Schwartz remained an envoy for peace and social harmony.

12.6 Contents of the Pious Clause of 1813

The Board of Control in the British Parliament and the Court of Directors in London considered the opinions expressed by individuals such as Charles Grant, William Wilberforce, Claudius Buchanan and Hugh Pearson. They also studied the works of various Protestant missionary agencies, including the SPCK in England, the Society in Scotland for the Propagation of Christian Knowledge, the Baptist Missionary Society, and the General Assembly of the Church of Scotland. Pearson asserted that Buchanan's writings and focused interventions for Christian causes in India left a lasting impression on the public mind. His treatise *Colonial Ecclesiastical Establishment* stressed the British responsibility to permit Anglican ministers to settle in the Indian territories under the Company's control.[79] By June 12, 1813, the British Parliament had received 837 petitions requesting the inclusion of the Pious Clause in the renewed Charter Act.[80] Some of these petitions pointed to the graphic reports of the Baptist missionaries Carey and William Ward of Serampore about female infanticide and

78 Minutes of Evidence taken before the Honourable House of Commons, 84.
79 Pearson: Memoirs, Vol. 2, 458–459.
80 The Missionary Register for the Year 1813, 1816, 235.

the horrid practice of *satī*,[81] i.e. the burning of the widows alive on the funeral pyre of their deceased husbands.

Some parliamentarians regarded Schwartz's life and work as an example of a model missionary. They knew that the renewed charter would place the Company's territories in India under the direct rule of the British monarch. Consequently, British rules should be applicable more fully in these territories. British rules exist in their direct or indirect association with the Church of England. Therefore, the Church of England should maintain a physical presence in India. As a result, on 16 June 1813, Robert Stewart (1769–1822), the leader of the House of Commons since 1812, tabled the following two proposals of the evangelical leaders:

> [12th Resolution:] Resolved, That is the opinion of this Committee that it is expedient that the Church Establishment in the British Territories in the East Indies should be placed under the superintendence of a Bishop and three Archdeacons; and that adequate provision should be made, from the Territorial Revenues of India, for their maintenance.[82]
> [13th Resolution:] Resolved, That it is the opinion of this Committee that it is the duty of this country to promote the interest and happiness of the native inhabitants of the British Domains in India and that such measures ought to be adopted as may tend to the introduction among them of useful knowledge and of religious and moral improvement:- That, in the furtherance of the above objects, sufficient facilities should be afforded, by law, to the persons desirous of going to and residing in India for the purpose of accomplishing those benevolent designs: Provided always, That the authority of the local Governments, respecting the intercourse of Europeans with the interior of the country, be preserved and that the principles of the British Government, on which the natives of India have hitherto relied for the free exercise of their religion, be inviolably maintained.[83]

The opponents of the Pious Clause resisted these two proposals so vehemently that the British Parliamentarians could not reach an amicable agreement. Robert Stewart resumed the debate on 22nd June 1813 and outlined how the current improved proposals differed from those presented to the House of Commons in 1793: at that time, the House of Commons.

> Laid down the duty of communicating moral and religious information to the Natives of India, but did not sufficiently provide a controlling power, which ought to exist as far as was necessary for the security of India, by protecting the Hindoos in the perfect exercise of their religious ordinances.[84]

However, the Pious Clause faced significant opposition from those Company officers who had lived in India for a long time, having appointed and protected Hindu and Muslim subordinates in various positions, yet remained unfamiliar with the Christian missionaries' transformative services, contributions, and achievements. Former Company employees, such as Francis Baring, Colonel Sweny Toone, Thomas Twinging, and the former Governor-General Warren

---

81 The Sanskrit word *satī* means "the true woman." However, it refers to the virtuous wife who remained loyal to her husband in and beyond this world. She demonstrated her loyalty by burning herself alive on the funeral pyre of her dead husband.

82 The Missionary Register for the Year 1813, 1816, 236.

83 The Missionary Register for the Year 1813, 1816, 237 and Pearson: Memoirs, Vol. 1, 109.

84 The Missionary Register for the Year 1813, 1816, 237.

Hastings, were among the leading opponents. They even misquoted the Vellore Mutiny of 1806 as an outcome of Christian missionary activity. In this context, Henry Dundas collected all available evidence about the Vellore Mutiny and concluded that Christian missionaries did not play any role in that uprising. Despite this, the opponents continued to resist the proposals. In this context, Charles Grant became the elected chairperson of the Company's Court of Directors. His friend Parry became the deputy chairperson. Seven fellow members of the Court of Directors opposed Grant and Parry; gradually, Grant and Parry quietened their fear about promoting Anglican Episcopacy in India.[85]

Grant believed Britain was morally obliged "to correct, to raise, to sweeten the social state" of Indians in their territories in India. He also believed that Christian missionaries would impart to Indians a boon far more valuable than all the advantages Britain had derived from them. He opined that Anglican Episcopacy would enable all inhabitants of the Company territories in India to work toward "liberal justice," and this justice would carry them.

[To] greater heights of prosperity than the precautions of selfish policy. Future events are inscrutable to the keenest speculation, but the path of duty is open; the time present is ours. By planting our language, our knowledge, our opinions and our religion in our Asiatic territories, we shall put a great work beyond the reach of contingencies; we shall probably have wedded the inhabitants of those territories to this country [Britain]; but at any rate, we shall have done an act of strict duty to them and of lasting service to mankind.[86]

Eugene Stock (1836–1928), the well-known historian of the Church Missionary Society, stressed the change of approach: Wilberforce and his team did not propose any official "Government Mission"; they highlighted the duty of the British "to promote the interests and happiness of the Indian peoples" and to introduce "useful knowledge and religious and moral improvement." They also requested "sufficient facilities," afforded by law, "to persons desirous of going to and remaining in India" and "to accomplish those benevolent designs." In other words, the British Parliament, recognising the limitations of the British State, permitted the Anglican Church to perform these works.[87]

Finally, the debate continued till early morning. By that time, several members had grown tired and weary.[88] They appreciated Wilberforce's proposal.

---

85 C. H. Philips: The East India Company 1784–1834. Manchester 1940, 161. Vellore. In: The Saturday Review of Politics, Literature, Science and Art 4:100, 1857, 273–274, here 274: After the Great Mutiny of 1857, British opinions about Christian missionary activities in India changed. Most policymakers believed that British administrators should not compel anyone to embrace Christianity. They "should carefully avoid furnishing grounds of suspicion" of religious interference.

86 Henry Morris: Charles Grant and the Part he took in the Formation of the Church Missionary Society. In: Church Missionary Intelligencer 1901, 337–353, here 352–353.

87 Stock: Beginnings in India, 19.

88 Ian Copland: Christianity as an Arm of Empire: The Ambiguous Case of India under the Company, c. 1813–1858. In: The Historical Journal 49, 2006, issue 4, 1025–1054, here 1031–1032: "Thanks to some clever strategizing by the Evangelical parliamentary lobby led by William Wilberforce, the crucial vote in the House of Commons on his 'pious clauses' did

Accordingly, he stated that introducing the Anglican form of Christianity to India and enhancing humanity were interdependent. He believed that Anglicanism would refine and ennoble the lives of Indians. He also insisted that humanity was more interested in the urgent question of introducing the Anglican form of Christianity to India than in abolishing the African Slave Trade. Immediately, Robert Thornton, Henry Thornton, William Smith, and Stephen Rumbold Lushington, all belonging to the Clapham Group, supported Wilberforce's proposal. Their resolution won by "a majority of 53, the number of it being 89 and that against it 36."[89] At that time, the House of Lords recommended this resolution for royal acceptance.

A month later, on 21 July 1813, King George III accepted the renewed Charter Act (53 Geo. III, c. 55).[90] Articles VI and XXXIII of this Act permitted all British citizens, with permission from either the Company's Court of Directors or the Parliamentary Board of Control, to trade in the Company's territories in India from April 10, 1814, onward.[91] Article XLV authorised the Bishop of London "for the Time being, to have and exercise [...] such Visitorial Power and Jurisdiction over all such Persons, Matters and Things, belonging or relating to the said College [for the Civil Service in Calcutta]."[92]

Articles XLIX–LIV contain the Pious Clause, which affirms that, until that time, no official measure was taken to maintain and support a "Church Establishment in the British Territories in the East Indies and other Parts within the Limits of the said Company's character." Henceforth, the King could appoint a bishop "for the Whole of the said British Territories in the East Indies and Parts aforesaid" and archdeacons for Madras and Bombay. This Article also fixed the annual salary of the Bishop of Calcutta as £5,000 and of each Archdeacon as £2,000. The Revenue Department of the Company in India should pay these salaries.[93] Article L prohibited the Bishop and the Archdeacons from accepting other favours besides their salary. Article LI required the Bishop and the Archdeacons to function only within the geographical territories in India, which

---

not take place until 3 a.m., by which time most opponents of the measure had left. But it seems to have made a positive impression on certain senior officials in India. [...] In the meantime, the passage of the Charter Bill, complete with Wilberforce's amendments, opened the gate to the evangelizing of the subcontinent. As well, the legislation provided for the dispatch of a bishop of the Church of England to Calcutta to oversee the spiritual needs of the expatriate English population, an initiative that, in time, helped to bridge the divide between the mainly Evangelical missionary movement and the Anglican establishment."

89 The Missionary Register for the Year 1813, 1816, 238.

90 A Collection of Charters and Statutes relating to The East India Company 1817, 1130–1165. The title of this charter reads as follows: an "Act for continuing in the East India Company, for a further Term, the possession of the British Territories in India, together with certain exclusive Privileges; for establishing further Regulations for the Government of the said Territories and the better Administration of Justice within the same; and for regulating the Trade to and from the Places within the Limits of the said Company's Charter [21st July 1813]."

91 A Collection of Charters and Statutes relating to The East India Company 1817, 1132 & 1139.

92 A Collection of Charters and Statutes relating to The East India Company 1817, 1142.

93 A Collection of Charters and Statutes relating to The East India Company 1817, 1142–1143.

the King would assign to them. Article LII empowered the Bishop by the King's "Letters Patent under the Great Seal of the said United Kingdom" to exercise

> Episcopal Functions, within the East Indies and the aforementioned parts, as His Majesty shall deem necessary for administering holy Ceremonies and the Superintendence and Good Governance of the Ministers of the Church Establishment within the East Indies and the aforementioned parts, notwithstanding any Law, Charter, or other Matter or Thing to the contrary.[94]

Articles LIII and LIV required the Letters of Patent for the bishopric and archdeaconry. They should have the signatures of the King, the President of the Board of Commissioners for the Affairs of India, and the Exchequer Chancellor.[95] Article LIV promised that when the bishop returned to Britain, he would receive £1,500 as his annual pension, and each returning archdeacon would receive £500 as their annual pension.

12.7 Consequences of the Pious Clause of 1813

Missionary records demonstrate that opponents of the Pious Clause resisted its inclusion: "An ineffectual opposition was made to them in the House of Commons, but none in the House of Lords." The supporters of the Pious Clause believed that the Anglican bishops in India should look to the "apostolic and venerable" Swartz and Gericke as their role models.[96] These statements demonstrate Schwartz's impact on introducing the Pious Clause in 1813 and the practical roles of future church functionaries and missionaries in India.

In 1814, the Church Missionary Society (CMS) sent Benjamin Bailey (1791–1871) to work in Kottayam. He translated the Bible into Malayalam. Then, he established the first mechanised press for Malayalam publications in 1821. In 1815, Carl Theophilus Ewald Rhenius and his two colleagues, Bernard Schmid and G.T. Bärenbruck, founded a CMS centre in Madras. Rhenius devoted his time to revising the Tamil Bible and went on missionary journeys to Kanchipuram. In 1816, Rhenius moved to Tirunelveli and established numerous village congregations, which the Protestant Christians of Tirunelveli still consider him to be the "Apostle to Tirunelveli."

In 1816, Thomas Norton settled in Alleppey and gained significant influence over the Syrian clergy, who had left the celibate priesthood to marry. Mar Dionysius, the Metropolitan of the Syrian Christians, received Norton "as sent of

---

94 A Collection of Charters and Statutes relating to The East India Company 1817, 1143.

95 A Collection of Charters and Statutes relating to The East India Company 1817, 1143.

96 The Missionary Register for the Year 1813, 1816, 269. The first Anglican bishop to Calcutta was Thoman F. Middleton. On 8 May 1814, the Archbishop of Canterbury and the bishops of the Anglican dioceses of Lincoln and Salisbury ordained him. A month later, on 8 June 1714, he sailed on board the ship *Warren Hastings* from Portsmouth and reached Calcutta on 28 November 1714.

the Lord [...] to be their Deliverer and Protector."[97] Norton enjoyed the support of Colonel John Munro, the Company Resident and Diwan of Travancore (1810–1819) and Queen Gowri Parvati Bayi of Travancore (1815–1829).[98] In 1817, Henry Backer developed a CMS centre in Cochin. In 1818, another CMS missionary, Joseph Fenn, joined Bailey; soon, CMS missionaries began to work in the major cities of southern India.

In 1814, the American Baptists founded their American Baptist Missionary Union. The branches of the British and Foreign Bible Society came up in Germany and the Netherlands in the same year. Likewise, Pope Pius VII revived and revitalised the Society of Jesus in 1814, empowering the Jesuits to engage in evangelistic work. The following year, after Napoleon's defeat in 1815, Swiss Protestant Christians founded their Basel Evangelical Missionary Society in Basel.[99]

Soon, the Tamil Lutheran congregations in southern India faced unexpected administrative difficulties. On 25 June 1825, the SPCK unilaterally decided to hand over its congregations in Madras, Tanjore, Tiruccirāppaḷḷi, Pāḷaiyamkōṭṭai, Ramanathapuram, Cuddalore, and Calcutta to the Society for the Propagation of the Gospel in Foreign Parts (SPG).[100] Thus, the SPG began to administer the congregations established by Schwartz. They introduced Anglican rites to the Tamil Lutheran congregations, but the Tamil Lutherans were unhappy. Realising this unpleasant situation, Bishops Reginald Heber (1823–1826), Thomas James (1827–1828)[101] and John Turner (1829–1831) allowed Tamil Lutheran congregations to follow their customary Lutheran rites at least temporarily.

---

97 The Missionary Register for the Year 1819 containing the Principal Transactions of the various Institutions for Propagating the Gospel with the Proceedings, at large, of the Church Missionary Society. London 1819, 32–35.

98 For a detailed analysis of the history of Christianity in Travancore, see Christian Masillamoni Agur: Church History of Travancore. New Delhi ²1990 (¹1903).

99 Only in 1834, after the renewed Charter of the EIC in 1833, could the authorities of the Basel Mission depute their missionaries to serve in India. In 1834, they sent Samuel Hebich, John Lehnar and Christoph Grener to Mangalore in modern-day Karnataka. These missionaries worked toward alleviating the people's material poverty. Four years later, in 1838, Hermann Gundert and his wife reached Mangalore; later, they moved to Thalasseri in modern-day Kerala. Gundert translated the Bible into Malayalam and compiled a Malayalam-English Dictionary as well.

100 Germann: Missionar Christian Friedrich Schwartz, 338: Earlier, the SPG could not work in India because its mandate limited its work to British "plantations and colonies." After Schwartz had ordained his student Johann Caspar Kohlhoff on 23.01.1787 and his catechist Sattiyanātaṉ in 1790 according to the Lutheran rite, the SPCK longed to have Anglican bishops in India who would ordain pastors and deacons. Schwartz knew well that his ordination rights did not correspond with the episcopal rites of the Church of England, and the SPCK would work toward establishing an Anglican Order in India. On 06.02.1787, he intended to carefully write a report on Kohlhoff's ordination and send it through his friend Pasche to the SPCK. Schwartz assumed the non-Episcopal ordination might offend the SPCK and requested Pasche's mediation. During Schwartz's lifetime, the SPCK did nothing to support the ordination of Tamil Christian leaders.

101 Edward James: Brief Memoirs of the late Right Reverend John Thomas James, D.D. Lord Bishop of Calcutta, particularly during his residence in India, gathered from his letters and papers. London 1830.

The British Baptist missionaries in Serampore, upriver from Calcutta, introduced humanistic ideas into the mainstream life of the people of Bengal. This included equality of all people at birth and in real-life situations. Everyone could freely choose to have or change their religious opinions and loyalties. Likewise, every person can learn to read spiritual texts and interpret them from the vantage point of their own life. People of diverse *jāti*-backgrounds could worship God together under the same roof. The Baptist missionaries opposed the practice of *satī*, female infanticide, the ritual killing of children dedicated to various deities, child marriage, and other immoral practices done in the name of image worship and so forth. Soon, Indian reformers like Raja Ram Mohan Roy (1772–1833) engaged in dialogue with Baptist missionaries in Serampore, and together, they worked towards revitalising the Bengal Presidency.

In the meantime, mission-minded Protestant Christians founded new missionary societies in Europe and North America, creating networks of sponsors and readers of mission reports across nations and denominations.[102] Some of their mission magazines reproduced Hugh Pearson's essay entitled *Life of Rev. Christian F. Swartz.*[103] After the Pious Clause was introduced into the subsequent renewal of the Company's Charter Act in 1833, most European and North American Protestant missionaries worked in the geographical areas under the Company Raj. The Company, however, did not have a uniform policy to support the missionaries. A few individual officers of the Company were sympathetic towards Protestant missionaries in southern India.

By contrast, Protestant missionaries in the Bengal Presidency experienced the Company's opposition. In addition to their other philanthropic activities, the Protestant missionaries played a significant role in establishing and maintaining schools, hospitals, sanatoria for leprosy patients and tuberculosis patients, vocational training centres, and other philanthropic institutions. Their influence on education and public schooling in India highlights the Christian legacy.

---

102 Some of these societies were, for example, the Wesleyan Methodist Missionary Society (1818), London Jews Society (1820), Danish Missionary Society (1821), Paris Evangelical Missionary Society (1822), Berlin Israel Mission (1822), Berlin Missionary Society (1824), Bombay Missionary Union (1825), Glasgow City Mission (1826), Rhanish Missionary Society (1828), American Baptist Home Missionary Society (1832), London City Mission (1832) and the like.

103 Pearson: The Life of Rev. Christian F. Swartz. The Life of Rev. Christian F. Swartz. In: The Panoplist and Missionary Magazine 10, 1813, 289–298. This essay reproduced Schwartz's *Defence of Mission* (290–297) and stressed the "Utility of Missions to the Heathen, as Exemplified in the Life and Conduct of the Late Rev. Mr. Swartz." The Life of the Eminent Missionary Swartz. In: The Methodist Magazine 37, 1814, 433–443, 451–492, 531–540 and a concluding part in Vol. 38, January 1815. I could not get hold of this 38th volume. The Life of the Rev. C. F. Swartz—Missionary to the East Indies. In: The Methodist Magazine for the Year of the Lord 2, 1819, 49–57, 89–97, 126–34, 167–174, 207–215 and 251–257. The Life of the Eminent Missionary Swartz. In: Episcopal Magazine 1, 1820, 37–43, 69–72, 101–110 and 133–144. Ecclesiastical Memoir of the Four First Decades of the Reign of George the Third. In: The Christian Guardian and Church of England Magazine 13, 1821, issue 3, 83–87, here 83 and 84. The Rev. C.F. Schwartz [based on Schwartz's biography published in the London Christian Guardian]. In: Philadelphia Recorder, 1830, 92. Swartz, the Missionary. In: Boston Recorder, 1835, 129.

Christian leaders of these institutions did not request that the Company provide financial support. Instead, they focused on uplifting the downtrodden sections of the people. These missionaries did not seek financial aid from the Company. Instead, their services enabled the Company to save all the funds they would have spent on beneficial institutions that empowered Indians to lead a quality life.

While both the Company officers and the Christian missionaries were Christians, they represented different nations and denominations. Their goals were starkly different. The missionaries, striving to uplift the downtrodden peoples of Indian societies, found themselves at odds with the Company's plans to exploit these people as harshly as possible. Interestingly, most non-Christian Indians viewed the missionaries as the Company's agents, accusing them of imposing Christianity on them.[104] Authors like Baman Das Basu equated the Company with Christianity and falsely claimed that the Company's rule of India constituted the "Christian Period of Indian History."[105]

A closer examination of the Company Raj during Schwartz's time reveals that most Company employees were Indians and "Hindus." Therefore, according to Professor Robert Eric Frykenberg, the Company gradually evolved into a Hindu Raj. As mentioned in Section 1.2.2, from the inception of the Company's headquarters in Fort St. George in 1639, Company officers depended on the goodwill of the Vaiṣṇavites associated with the Sri Venkateswara Temple in Tirupati.[106] The Company's gold coins, minted at Fort St. George in Madras between 1740 and 1807 and known as the Star Pagodas ('temples'), had the imprints of one or more Vaiṣṇavite deities. If the Company had taken Christianity seriously, it would have had a cross symbol on its official coins. By contrast, they obeyed the dictates of their Indian benefactors. The Company employed Indian dubashes, who mostly worshipped Vaiṣṇavite and Śaivite deities. These dubashes functioned as the "door hinges." They determined the direction of the company's transactions and their success and failures in relation to fellow Indians.[107] From the mid-eighteenth century, most of the Vaiṣṇavite and Śaivite gentry voluntarily adopted the English language. Influential members of these religious communities held high positions in the Company, including roles such as writers, accountants, translators, supervisors, and tax collectors. By 1817, the Company in Madras had brought all the temples in the Madras Presidency under its care, control, and maintenance. In November 1839, the Tamil and Telugu gentry of Madras sent their Education Petition, signed by over 70,000 persons, to Governor John Elphinstone. Frykenberg cites the following portion of this petition:

---

104 Schneider: Parliament, the East India Company and the Calcutta Bishopric, 71.

105 Basu: Rise of the Christian Power in India, 7 and 9: To "understand the Christian period of Indian history, it is necessary to study the conquest of Mexico and Peru by the Spaniards and that of Ireland by the English. There are curious parallels in the modes of administration of those lands and India by Christian conquerors."

106 Frykenberg: The myth of English as a 'colonist' imposition upon India, 306.

107 Two of the most famous Madras dubashes were Ananda Ranga Pillai, a native of Perambur in Madras. He was the dubash of the French East India Company in Pondicherry under the leadership of J. F. Dupleix. His multi-volume *Private Diaries* give valuable insights into the life of the East India Companies on the Coast of Coromandel from 1736 to 1761. Another

> My Lord, *we are the people* of this country, inheriting this land for thousands of generations. From our industry, its wealth is supplied. By our arms, it is defended from foreign foes. By our loyal obedience to the established Government [i.e. the Company], peace and safety are maintained. If diffusion of Education is among the highest benefits and duties of a Government, we, the people, petition for our share.[108]

These attempts to secure an English educational system for Indians did not have any place for Christianity. Indians, who had acquired English in India even with the help of the Christians, equated Christianity with the religion of the Europeans in the Company and understood themselves as "Hindu" custodians of the Company. These Indians suspected the loyalty of Indian Christians. By contrast, this biography of Schwartz demonstrates that Christians in India participated constructively in the nation's public life, serving both Indians and India as salt and light.

well-known dubash was Pachiyappa Mudaliar, a native of Kanchipuram. During his time in Tanjore, he amassed so much wealth that he could not manage it. Finally, one of his well-wishers saved the Pachiyppa Trust. Nowadays, the Pachiyappa College in Chennai bears his name. Most of these dubashes were Brahmins, Cettiyars, Pillais and Mudaliyars. For additional information on dubashes, see Neild-Basu: The Dubashes of Madras.

108 Frykenberg: The myth of English as a 'colonist' imposition upon India, 310.

Chapter 13

Conclusion

This biography aimed to examine diverse facets of Schwartz that made him an ambassadorial nobleman (*cāṉṟōṉ*), as defined by the Tamil criteria in Section 0.1. Additionally, the 240th couplet of Tirukkuṟaḷ defines reputation (*pukaḻ*) as a characteristic of a *cāṉṟōṉ*:[1] Accordingly, the *cāṉṟōṉ* had no record of *vacai* ('flaw') including crime or moral reproach (*kuṟṟam*), blame or ridicule (*paḻi*), and contempt or insult (*nitai*). By contrast, the life of a *cāṉṟōṉ* demonstrated *icai* ('harmony' as in orchestral music). Schwartz, as an ambassador of faith for peace, justice, and social harmony, led a life of harmony (*icai*) without any moral reproach (*vacai*).

Schwartz translated his Lutheran Pietist theology into reformative and restorative actions. He loved every person as being created in God's image with innate dignity, worth and eternal significance. By upholding the ideals of peace, justice, and social harmony, he opposed existential threats to ordinary people of Tanjore, which came from the kings of Tanjore, the Nawab of Arcot, and the Company's diplomats, merchants, renters, and dubashes. His ability to communicate effectively in Tamil, Portuguese, Persian, Marathi, and English, without the need for interpreters, further solidified his ambassadorial work among diverse people groups. His lifestyle and accomplishments demonstrate that he had transcended the expectations outlined in the job descriptions he received from the king of Denmark, G. A. Francke, and the SPCK.

Schwartz's letters, reports, and diaries were not simply a means of communication. Still, they open new windows to glimpse into the socio-cultural and political life of his time in southern India. He wrote about the same individuals, events, and other occurrences in his life to various recipients, tailoring his narratives to the intensity of his formal or informal relationships with them. His letters to trusted friends (e.g. Ziegenhagen in London and Sorge in Germany) contain more personal details than his formal writings to the Directors of the Glaucha Institutions and the Secretaries of the SPCK in London and the Mission College in Copenhagen. He kept his reports on political activities brief and succinct. His shaking hands and poor eyesight prevented him from composing more extended reports. Although he died in 1798, Christians in Tranquebar, Tiruccirāppaḷḷi, Tanjore, Ramanathapuram and Pāḷaiyamkōṭṭai still remember him gratefully. Members of the CSI Christ Church, St. John's Vestry, Anglo-Indian Higher Secondary School, and Bishop Heber College in Tiruccirāppaḷḷi, the CSI Christ Church, St. Peter's School, and the Royal House in Tanjore, the Schwartz

1 vacaiyoḻiya vāḻvārē vāḻvār icaiyoḻiya
vāḻvārē vāḻā tavar. — Tirukkuṟaḷ, 240.

Higher Secondary School in Ramanathapuram, and the Clarinda Church in Pāḷaiyamkōṭṭai commemorate his memory. The marble monuments dedicated to Schwartz still grace St. Mary's Church in Fort St. George in Chennai, the CSI Christ Church in Tanjore, and the CSI St. Peter's Church in Tanjore. The Thanjavur Maharaja Serfoji's Saraswathi Mahal Library in Tanjore acknowledge their indebtedness to Schwartz. The legacy of Schwartz's followers, such as Rasa Clarinda (1746–1806) and his students, including Vēdanāyagam Sāstiriyār (1774–1864), remains alive and vibrant. The members of the Royal Household in Tanjore remember Schwartz as their *Rājaguru* ('royal teacher') because he advised King Tulāji, recommended his successor Ameer Singh and trained Prince Serfoji. They fondly recall how he, as an ambassador of faith, envisioned and created a just, harmonious, and humane society where people of different religious traditions could coexist and flourish.[2]

Secondly, this biography situates Schwartz within the context of his socio-cultural and political life. His writings reflect the spirit of his time. For instance, his unpublished Tamil catechism and his eighteen published dialogues in Tamil reveal his profound Lutheran Pietist theology. His letters and reports, written in both German and English, illustrate his efforts to translate his theological convictions into the socio-religious and political life of the people of Tanjore. They offer a distinct perspective on the conflicts between the Tanjore rulers and the Company officers. He opposed abusive leaders, whether European or Indian, and sided with the ordinary people, especially the farmers. When the Company officers mistreated the rulers of Tanjore, Schwartz intervened and upheld their dignity. He aimed to create a society where people of all faiths could live in harmony and peace, while simultaneously enjoying justice and fair treatment, all in the name of Jesus Christ. By laying the foundation for a court of justice in Tanjore, Schwartz elevated the quality of life for ordinary people by promoting and improving farming practices, wages and taxes. Schwartz introduced smallpox vaccinations and received training. Schwartz remained interested in various sicknesses associated with snake bites and rabies.

Thirdly, Schwartz selected, trained and employed a few Tamil Lutherans as catechists, schoolteachers and pastors. These Tamil co-workers served as a bridge between Schwartz and the Tamil community. They taught the significance of delegated authority, work and accountability via regular written reports. He emphasised the importance of managing time, resources, and potential conflicts. He advised them on creating and maintaining professional networks across vast geographical locations. He strongly emphasised personal visits to homes and Lutheran congregations, where Christians from diverse *varṇa* and *jāti* communities gathered for worship, fellowship, and mutual encouragement, fostering a sense of community and fellowship. He trained them to serve within their Lutheran congregations and in public places. He assisted his catechists,

---

2 Irācu: palturaip paṇipurinta svārṭs pātiriyār, 215: Schwartz was indeed an envoy of peace (*camātāṉat turar*). He participated in the governance of Tanjore. He became the cause for the development of art (*kalai*), education (*kalvi*) and literature (*ilakkiyam*).

schoolteachers, pastors, and trainees in reading, interpreting, and communicating his catechism, dialogues, and sermons. One of his students, who became the most influential catechist, was Vēdanāyagam Sāstiriyār, who wove Schwartz's teachings on God, creation, fellow human beings, sin and salvation into his Tamil lyrics, poems and dramas. Tamil congregations of all theological and ecclesial persuasions sing his lyrics today. Schwartz's trustworthy behaviour in public spaces, his diplomatic engagements with Hindu and Muslim rulers, his interactions with policymakers of the Company in Madras and Calcutta, and his pastoral care for Christians at the grassroots level influenced generations of Christians and non-Christians in and outside Tamil India.

Fourthly, while available biographies on Schwartz highlight his diplomatic journey to Hyder Ali from June 5 to August 24, 1779, they do not contain the confidential report he submitted to Governor Rumbold. I was unable to identify it despite thorough searches in the archival records of India, Germany, and the United Kingdom. As an ordained clergy member, he likely used the "confessional seal." This biography, however, has analysed Hyder Ali's mistreatment of Rumbold's new ambassador, George Gray (January 1780), as opposed to the respectful welcome accorded to Schwartz. Additionally, this biography has studied Schwartz's diplomatic missions to the Wadiyars of Mysore (1782), Tipu Sultan from 15 December 1783 to 26 Jan 1784, Tanjore farmers (1783) and emigrants (1786), the administrators of Tranquebar at various times and to his fellow missionaries in Tranquebar and Madras, who had multiple problems. These diplomatic missions promoted justice, reconciliation and harmony for the people.

Fifthly, Schwartz's role as Serfoji's guardian and educator is well-known. For the first time, however, this biography has examined what Serfoji studied from missionaries Schwartz, Gericke, and John and how he later applied these insights. It has also expanded Schwartz's renown as *Rajaguru*, a title previously associated with his guardianship over Serfoji. However, this biography has pointed out his relationship with Ameer Singh, Tanjore's interim ruler (1787–1798). He opposed Ameer Singh's misgovernance and the Company's exploitations and tried to mitigate the consequences of these systemic evils on ordinary people. Additionally, this biography has explored (Section 8.2.1) Schwartz's voluntary role as the Company's Resident of Tanjore from January 1791 to the end of 1792. Notably, he did not accept the Company's annual salary of a Resident, namely 7,000 Star Pagodas (i.e., £3,000). During that period, he mediated between the Company and Ameer Singh, working towards achieving greater justice for ordinary people. From this experience, he later advised Serfoji (Section 8.3.8) about the basic principles of a just government. Thus, this biography has placed the role of Schwartz as the *Rajaguru* in a broader context.

Sixthly, although some aspects of Schwartz's role as a social transformer were previously known, this biography has broadened our understanding of his social engagement. It highlights his consistent efforts to establish a court of justice in Tanjore for the welfare of the ordinary people. He upheld the dignity of the kings of Tanjore, protecting them from the Company administrators, who sought to shame them publicly. On the other hand, he was unable to resolve the issues related to caste distinctions among the Tamil Lutherans. He probably viewed caste as *adiaphora* ('indifferent things', neither commanded nor forbidden in the Bible) that did not belong to the essential Lutheran doctrine of justification by faith alone. Schwartz helped the Kaḷḷars of Tanjore to give up thievery and, instead, earn their livelihood respectfully through farming and paying taxes. He created job opportunities for needy individuals and introduced smallpox vaccination.

Seventhly, this biography has further explored Schwartz's contribution to public education. Adhering to the Pietist model of education, which he had learned at Francke's Glaucha Institutions in Halle (Saale), he established schools for girls and boys in Tiruccirāppaḷḷi, Tanjore, and Ramanathapuram. The impact of his educational efforts on his students, friends, and colleagues, such as Johann Caspar Kohlhoff, Clarinda, Vēdanāyagam Sāstiriyār, Johann Christian Obeck, Captain Elphinstone, Christian David, William Wheatley, and several European soldiers, is noteworthy. This biography has critically assessed Schwartz's efforts in educating and orienting younger missionaries to Tamil. He succeeded in some instances, and in others he failed. Moreover, this biography highlights the origin and function of English-medium education at the Provincial Schools under Schwartz's tutelage. He persuaded the local rulers and the Company in Madras to meet the running costs of these schools. He sought support for these schools through correspondence from the Company's Court of Directors in London. He envisioned these schools fostering better understanding between Christians and non-Christians in India. However, these schools inadvertently empowered a few Indian elites to communicate with the Company officers in English, reducing their dependence on dubashes.[3] Future studies could investigate whether these Provincial Schools foreshadowed the Company's financial efforts to support local schools.[4] In 1813, the Company set apart one lakh Rupees to support English-medium schools. Macaulay's *Minute on Indian Education* in 1835 and Charles

---

3 Frykenberg: The myth of English as a 'colonist' imposition upon India, 307–310: Schwartz's English-medium schools attracted the sons of "Brahman and Vellalar gentry." These educated men, especially the "Desastha Brahmans," found lucrative jobs in the "upper echelons of the Company's growing bureaucracy." Gradually, the demand for English-medium education increased. For example, the Maratha Brahmin Vennelacunty Soob Row of Ongole pressed the Company in Madras to open more English-medium schools. He read Shakespeare and Milton and became, in 1820, the Secretary of the Madras School Book Society. Soob Row noted that hundreds of schools along Mount Road in Madras taught English. The competition was so intense that English tutors lowered their fees. These English-educated Indians viewed the Company's rule as "both in fact and in law, a 'Hindu Raj'" because by 1817, the Regulation VII of the EIC in Madras "made itself responsible for the care, maintenance and protection of all regular places of worship and for all regular institutions connected therewith."

4 Frykenberg: Modern Education in South India, 1784–1854, 41: the training which the students in Schwartz's schools "received, especially their command of English, became so valuable that the Company began to give these schools annual grants of 250 Pagodas and offered a similar subsidy to any other school that could serve the same function. The schools run by Schwartz had been patronized by the rajahs of Tanjore, Ramnad and Shivaganga for some time. [...] Nor did these schools disappear when Schwartz died in 1799 [sic! = 1798]. Thomas Fisher's *Memoirs*, published in 1827, indicate that a sum of 4,620 rupees a year was still being paid to them."

Wood's *Education Dispatch* of 1854 expanded the scope of modern education, which has had a profound impact on all Indians.[5]

Eighthly, this biography has examined the widespread and profound influence of Schwartz's *Defence of Mission* (1794) on the newly formed Protestant mission societies in the United Kingdom and the United States. This influential work called for further study to fully understand its impact.[6] During the British Parliament's review of the Company's Charter Act of 1813, the Company's prominent civil servants, including Warren Hastings, John Shore, William Cowper and Thomas Graham, were cross-examined about their views on Schwartz and his ministry. Still, further research is needed to comprehend the lasting effects of Schwartz's work on renewing the Company's Charter Act of 1833. At that time, Hugh Pearson was composing his two-volume biography of Schwartz. He likely shared his findings with the influential policymakers who participated in the debate for expanding the scope of the Pious Clause in the Company's Charter Act of 1833. As discussed in Section 12.7, the SPCK transferred Schwartz's congregations and institutions to the Society for the Propagation of the Gospel in Foreign Parts (SPG) in 1825. On 11 December 1833, SPG and the Church Missionary Society (CMS) agreed on a memorandum to exchange their mission stations in Tanjore and Tirunelveli.[7] Johann Caspar Kohlhoff, Schwartz's student and successor in Tanjore, became an SPG missionary and used Anglican liturgy. When Hugh Pearson published his two-volume biography of Schwartz in 1834, he dedicated it to Daniel Wilson, the Anglican Bishop of Calcutta since 1832. He concluded his preface with the following words of hope:

> May the sacred cause to which Swartz was so eminently and so consistently devoted triumph over the ignorance, superstition, guilt and misery which oppress the fairest portions of the earth in which real Christianity is unknown until that divine and saving truth universally prevail, not only in India but throughout the world![8]

Remarkably, the SPG missionaries had a significant influence on Bishop's College in Calcutta, which Bishop Thomas Middleton founded on 15 December 1820. William Hodge Mill, the first principal of Bishop's College, seems to have been familiar with Schwartz's life and work. Bishop Daniel Wilson had taken Schwartz's armchair, made of oak, from Tanjore to Calcutta and deposited it in the archives of Bishop's College.[9] Somehow, the SPG missionaries sent Schwartz's

---

5 For further details, see Frykenberg: Modern Education in South India, 1784–1854.

6 Schwartz's *Defence of Mission* (1795) was printed several times. Representative examples include The Life of C.F. Swartz: Missionary at Trichinopoly and Tanjore in India, 52–65; Grant: Observations on the State of Society, 113–116; Buchanan: An Apology for Promoting Christianity in India, 198–208; An Abstract of the Annual Reports, 396–411; Remains of the Rev. C. F. Schwartz, 298–316; Pearson: Memoirs, Vol. 2, 287–301 and C. F. Swartz: The Missionary, 129.

7 Bodleian Library: 72290ind-box7, Document 45: The document is entitled *Memorandum in reference to a proposed exchange of Missionary Stations between the Society for the Propagation of the Gospel and the Church Missionary Society. Dec. 11/33.*

8 Pearson: Memoirs, Vol. 1, xxi.

9 On 11.05.2020, Rev. Dr. Isaac Devadoss, Professor of History of Christianity at Bishop's

Bible to Bishop's College. Now, this chair and the Bible symbolise Schwartz's presence and missionary ideals for those who are trained at Bishop's College.[10] Nowadays, the Tamil Lutherans do not supervise those congregations and institutions that trace their origin to Schwartz. The bishops and councils of the Trichy-Tanjore Diocese, Madurai-Ramnad Diocese and Tirunelveli Diocese of the Church of South India manage them. The transition of the Tamil Lutheran congregations and institutions into SPG and CMS institutions requires further research. The *India General Papers*, from 1773 to 1900, stored in seven boxes at the Bodleian Library in Oxford, England, contain manuscripts detailing the reasons, processes, and consequences of this transfer. Nowadays, interested researchers can access digital copies of these manuscripts.

Ninthly, this biography has examined Schwartz's human side, which his contemporaries and biographers have largely overlooked. For instance, as discussed in Section 5.15, Hugh Pearson remarked that Schwartz's "infirmities" were "known only to himself and God." His contemporaries recorded no misdeeds, and Pearson considered Schwarz's life "exemplary and blameless."[11] In contrast, this biography identifies five areas that reflect Schwartz's limitations: he perceived the caste system (*varṇa* and *jāti*) as an example of *adiaphora*, i.e. a traditional social institution that embodied a person's identity, status and dignity, but not vital for that person's justification by faith. Hence, he allowed his followers to maintain caste distinctions. He insisted that at the gate of heaven (*cuvarkkam*), the *tōṭṭi*, the menial street sweeper and the *toṇṭaimāṉ*, the ruler of Ramanathapuram, would receive the same welcome.[12] However, no record exists of him strongly opposing untouchability within the caste system. Secondly, as mentioned in Section 4.3, Schwartz's unhealthy attitude towards the Jesuits is not admirable. He opposed their indigenised appearance (e.g. wearing a saffron cassock and eating vegetarian food). He did not count them as fellow Christians, reflecting the theological position of the Halle Pietists towards Roman Catholics in Germany at that time. Thirdly, as referred to in Section 4.5, Schwartz's harmful attitude towards the Moravian missionaries in Poṟaiyār, three kilometres from Tranquebar, was unhelpful. Without his support to live and work there peacefully, many of them sailed for the Andaman and Nicobar Islands, where they succumbed to mysterious sicknesses and died. Fourthly, as discussed in Sections 5.8 and 8.4, Schwartz's failure to examine the competency and trustworthiness of the twelve Maratha Brahmin Pandits who first endorsed Ameer Singh and accepted having received bribes remains unexplained. Fifthly, as discussed in Section 7.10.1, Schwartz's engagements with Philip Fabricius, who had lost the money entrusted to him by others, would not have happened without Schwartz's knowledge because some of his close friends, such as Colonel Wood and his wife, gave their money to

College, emailed me an image of this armchair. I am grateful to Professor Devadoss for this photo.

10 On 21.01.2025, Professor Richard Fox Young sent me an email with information about this Bible. I am grateful to Professor Young for this information.

11 Pearson: Memoirs, Vol. 2, 434.

12 Germann: Missionar Christian Friedrich Schwartz, 273.

Fabricius for safekeeping or further investment. The Woods would not have done this without Schwartz's knowledge and possible consent. Despite these limitations, Schwartz's life and work epitomised integrity, simplicity and responsibility to God and his fellow human beings.

Tenthly, this biography has demonstrated the partnership between Company officers and Indian elites in running the local government of Tanjore for their private benefit. Arthur Mayhew's *Christianity and the Government of India* has a section on Schwartz and his ministry.[13] It illustrates how Schwartz bridged the sacred and secular realms, promoting peace and social harmony. In this regard, Frykenberg's essay, *Christian Missions and the Raj*, is significant.[14] It discusses the negotiated partnership between the Company officers and Indian elites, which enabled their mutual survival and growth. While most Company officers in London and Madras belonged to the Church of England, they did not seek to introduce their form of Christianity to non-Christian Indians in their territories. However, they recognised Schwartz's contributions, erecting a monument in St. Mary's Church in Fort St. George. This biography has provided new details of Schwartz's mediatory works, which earned him respect and recognition.[15]

Eleventhly, Schwartz's relentless efforts towards peace, justice, and social harmony in Tanjore enabled people of diverse religious backgrounds to coexist and live in peace. At the 200th anniversary of Schwartz's death in 1998, Bhonsle Chattrapathy, the Senior Prince at the Palace of Tanjore, stated how Serfoji's "thoughts, words and deeds always revealed his [Schwartz's] merciful and kind heart." Schwartz imparted administrative skills to Serfoji and explained the importance of harmonious coexistence. The secret to this success was Schwartz's insistence on treating everyone equally. In this context, Bhonsle Chattrapathy described Schwarz's enduring impact in Tanjore:

> This [i.e. treating all people alike] resulted in the highest order of communal harmony. People of all faiths co-existed peacefully in the days of Serfoji, showing mutual regard and kindness to each other. There was neither enmity nor hatred among them. Even today, the town of Thanjavur can boast of showing a rare tolerance, leading to harmony and peace among people of various religions. King Serfoji trod along the path shown by Schwartz, which the people follow.[16]

Twelfthly, this biography has, for the first time since Schwartz died in 1798, assembled primary materials that open new avenues for further research. His role as a missionary and founder of schools and churches remains an underexplored area. Similarly, his travel reports and meetings with local leaders and Company officers in various towns and villages are replete with sociocultural details that can shed new light on the history of these places. Digital copies of documents related to Schwartz, initially prepared by Johann Caspar Kohlhoff, are now

---

[13] Mayhew: Christianity and the Government of India, 29–49.

[14] Frykenberg: Christian Missions and the Raj.

[15] To understand nineteenth-century relationships, see Hilary M. Carey: God's Empire—Religion and Colonialism in the British World, c. 1801–1908. Cambridge 2011.

[16] Bhonsle Chattrapathy: The King [Serfoji] and the Clergy Man [Schwartz], 117.

available online via British Online Archives. These documents include letters and reports from missionaries like Christian Pohle, Joseph Daniel Jänicke, and several Company officers, registers for baptisms and marriages in Trichy from 1751 to 1847, records of caste issues, and documents detailing the process of the Society for Propagation of the Gospel in Foreign Parts taking over the Lutheran congregations, and the like. The availability of these English documents, along with their German counterparts, offers new research opportunities. Additionally, researchers will find Schwartz's Tamil Catechism and Dialogues interesting on many fronts. They showcase Schwartz's German Lutheran Pietist theology, which he had masterfully translated into the socio-cultural thoughts and idioms of the Tamil people. New studies of these documents will significantly expand and enrich our understanding of Christian contributions to South Indian history, culture, religion, modern education, healthcare, and the overall enhancement of human life for all inhabitants.

Finally, this biography has contended that Schwartz was not an instrument of the Company Raj in either Madras or Tanjore. The allegation, which the civil servant made in my presence in 2008, as detailed in the Preface of this biography, lacks documentary evidence and remains unreliable and biased (discussed in Section 5.12).[17] This biography has illustrated how Kings of Tanjore, namely Tulāji (Section 4.11), Ameer Singh (Sections 5.8.4 and 5.12), and Serfoji II (Sections 8.5 and 8.7) sought, funded and relied on the Company's assistance and protection, ultimately ceding their independence and territories despite being fully aware of the Company's exploitation through its alliance with their adversary, Wallajah. Schwartz, as an ambassador of faith, stood out as a solitary advocate for peace, justice and social harmony, opposing the Company's exploitative practices and championing the welfare of all inhabitants. He formed alliances with those Company officers who wanted to help ordinary Indians live well. In some cases, he did not hesitate to listen to those Company officers who desired the end of the Company Raj in India.[18]

Schwartz viewed his vocation as a mission for peace with God and fellow human beings, promoting justice and social harmony for the flourishing of all

---

17 Ian Copland: Christianity as an Arm of Empire: The Ambiguous Case of India under the Company, c. 1813–1858. In: The Historical Journal 49, 2006, issue 4, 1025–1054: since the introduction of the Pious Claus in 1813 and its extension in 1833, there was some official connection between the British state and Anglicanism in India. While church buildings came into existence in military cantonment areas, Protestant Christianity did not make any noteworthy inroads into villages.

18 AFSt/M 1 B 75 : 27 = NHR 3, 1785, issue 29, 567: On 20.02.1784, Schwartz narrated his acquaintance with Colonel William Fullarton and recorded, with an affirmative tone, his words as follows: "Colonel Fullarton said with great emotion: 'It is now eight months since I saw you. I have not seen anything I could like all these eight months. As for fencing [i.e. military fighting between the armies of EIC and Tipu Sultan], yes! Some people observed their duties. However, otherwise, what belongs to the country's welfare and contributes to it, I have not noticed any effort on the part of anyone. I wish with all my heart that the English may be driven out of the country. With this wish, I have the best of the country's well-being in mind. Yes, it would also be good for the English and their credibility if they were driven out of the country where they do not want to do any good.'"

inhabitants among whom he lived and worked for forty-eight years (1750–1798). Four years before his death, he reflected on his life and work as an ambassador of faith, serving the people of India for their benefit. What he wrote in the *Defence of Mission* in 1794 summarised his life and work remarkably:

> If the Missionaries are sincere Christians, it is impossible that the inhabitants should suffer any damage by them. [...] One thing, however, I affirm, before God and man, that if Christianity, in its plain and undisguised form, was properly promoted, the country would not suffer, but be benefited by it. [...] The glorious God and our blessed Redeemer has commanded his Apostles to preach the Gospel to all nations. The knowledge of God, of his divine perfections and of his mercy to mankind, may be abused; but there is no other method of reclaiming mankind, than by instructing them well. [...] I am now at the brink of eternity, but to this moment, I declare that I do not repent of having spent forty-three years in the service of my Divine Master.[19]

---

19 Schwartz: Defence of Mission, 1795, 9 and 14–15; Pearson: Memoirs, Vol. 2, 300; Grant: Observations on the State of Society, 115–116.

Appendix

Appendix 1: The Company's Governors and Presidents in Council in Madras

Name	In office	Governor / President
George Pigot	14 Jan 1755	Resigned in 1763
Rev. Robert Palk	14 Nov 1763	Resigned in 1767
Charles Bourchier	25 Jan 1767	Resigned in 1770
Josias Du Pré	31 Jan 1770	Resigned in 1773
Alexander Wynch	01 Feb 1773	Superseded in 1775
George Pigot	10 Dec 1775	Died in captivity in 1777
George Stratton	24 Aug 1776	Usurper and suspended in 1777
John Whitehill	31 Aug 1777	Interim governor
Thomas Rumbold	08 Feb 1778	Resigned in 1780 and was dismissed later
John Whitehill	06 Apr 1780	Interim governor, suspended in 1780
Charles Smith	08 Nov 1780	Interim governor
George Macartney	22 Jun 1781	Resigned in 1785
Alexander Davidson	08 Jun 1785	Interim governor
Archibald Campbell	06 Apr 1786	Governor and Commander-in-Chief
John Holland	06 Feb 1789	Interim governor and resigned in 1790
Edward John Holland	13 Feb 1790	Interim governor
General William Medows	20 Feb 1790	Governor, Commander-in-Chief
John Turing	17 May 1790	Interim president in Medows' absence
Charles Oakley	15 Oct 1790	Interim president in Medows' absence
General William Medows	21 Apr 1792	Resigned in August 1792
Charles Oakley	01 Aug 1792	Resigned in 1794
Robert Hobart	07 Sep 1794	Recalled in 1798
General George Harris	21 Feb 1798	Interim governor
Edward Clive	31 Aug 1798	President and governor

Appendix 2: Answers of the Twelve Pandits

On 5 April 1787, Schwartz gave Governor Campbell two sets of the pandits' answers. The first set, found in Campbell's diary,[1] contains more information than the second summary.[2]

a) Longer Version

Query 1: Did the late Rajah of Tanjore consider Ameer Singh as his brother and give him apartments as such in the palace?

Dada's answer	He has treated him in such a manner.
Biyenrow Kist	He has considered or treated him in such a manner.
Paulel Asary	He has given him proper apartments.
Appa Sastry	He has considered him his brother, procured him a marriage and given him a proper apartment in the palace.
Rama Asary	The Rajah has esteemed Amer Sing as his brother and gave him a proper place in the palace.
Narasinga Asary	He has treated him as his brother.
Sallia Nidy Asary	He has treated him as [a] brother.
Aiyen Asary	He has given him a proper apartment & treatment.
Sey Asary	He has esteemed him and given him a wife, but we do not know what place he has assigned him.
Madava Asary	He has given him a proper place; this I know.
Vija Asary	He has done so.
Bhapana	He has treated him as his brother.

Query 2: Did the late Rajah of Tanjore publicly declare Ameer Sing his illegitimate brother, or had he ever publicly assigned the reasons that led him to form such an opinion?

Dada	He has never declared such a thing.
Biyenrow Kist	He has never declared or published such a thing.
Paulel Asary	He has never done it.
Appa Sastry	He has looked upon him more than he has looked upon himself.
Rama Sastry	He has never said such a thing.
Narasinga Asary	He has never made such a difference.
Sallia Nidy Asary	He has never done so.
Aiyen Asary	He has never dishonoured or distressed him.

1 IOR/P/252/16, 35–40.
2 IOR/H/571, 193.

Sey Asary	He has published no such thing. We never heard of it in the palace.
Madava Asary	There is no confusion or doubt in it.
Vija Asary	I do not know any such a thing.
Bhapana	Such a bad rumour is not [sic!]. No doubt he has treated him as a brother.

Query 3: Whether by the Gentoo Laws late Rajah of Tanjore had a legal right to adopt a distant relation to the prejudice of a brother then living?

Dada	This is not to be found in the Shaster.
Biyenrow Kist	It is not so in the Shaster.
Paulel Asary	This is not in the Darma-Shaster.
Appa Sastry	No, that is not Darma Shaster.
Rama Sastry	It is not Darma Shaster.
Narasinga Asary	As there is a brother, it is improper to adopt a distant relation.
Sallia Nidy Asary	It is not agreeable to the Shaster.
Aiyen Asary	As there is a brother, it is improper to adopt a child.
Sey Asary	It is contrary to the law.
Madava Asary	This is not found in the Shaster.
Vija Asary	This is not according to the Shaster.
Bhapana	It is not agreeable to Darma Shaster.

Query 4: Whether the Pandits and Chief People of Tanjore consider the adoption, notwithstanding the rights of the brother to the succession, to be agreeable to the principles and opinions and confirmable to the laws and religion of the parties?

Dada	It appears to be improper.
Biyenrow Kist	It appears to be improper.
Paulel Asary	It is improper.
Appa Sastry	It is improper.
Rama Sastry	As there is no brother, the adoption is improper.
Narasinga Asary	The adoption is not proper.
Sallia Nidy Asary	It is improper.
Aiyen Asary	The adoption is improper.
Sey Asary	It is improper.
Madava Asary	It is not agreeable to the laws.
Vija Asary	It is improper.
Bhapana	It appears to be improper.

Query 5: Whether the adoption of Serfogee is in any respect defective in terms or contrary to the religious principles of the Chief People of Tanjore

Dada	Both contrary & defective.
Biyenrow Kist	Contrary & defective.
Paulel Asary	The adoption is defective.
Appa Sastry	It is defective.
Rama Sastry	It is defective.
Narasinga Asary	It is defective.
Sallia Nidy Asary	Defective.
Aiyen Asary	The adoption is defective.
Sey Asary	A little defective.
Madava Asary	Defective.
Vija Asary	Defective.
Bhapana	Contrary and defective.

Query 6: Whether in the general opinion of the principal people of Tanjore, the natural right of Ameer Sing to the succession was greater or lesser than those of the adopted?

Dada	Amer Sing's rights are greater.
Biyenrow Kist	The brother of the late Rajah has greater rights.
Paulel Asary	It is right that Amer Sing should be on the throne. He has a better right.
Appa Sastry	Amer Sing has a better right.
Rama Sastry	Amer Sing's right is more or better.
Narasinga Asary	The brother's right to the throne is greater.
Sallie Nidy Asary	The better, proper right, Amer Sing, has.
Aiyen Asary	It is proper and right that Amer Sing should sit on the throne.
Sey Asary	Amer Sing has a better right.
Madava Asary	Amer Sing has more right [than Serfoji].
Vija Asary	The brother's right is greater.
Bhapana	The brother has a better right.

b) Shorter Version

The shorter version of the same queries and answers provides the following overview.[3]

Query	Question	Answers in Schwartz's translation
1	Did the Raja Tuljajee treat Ameer Sing as a brother and give him apartments as such in the palace?	Answered in the affirmative. Two of the pandits said that Tuljajee procured him a marriage.
2	Whether Tuljajee had ever publicly declared Ameer Sing to be his illegitimate brother or had publicly assigned the reasons which led him to form such an opinion.	Answered in the negative unanimously.
3	Whether by the Gentoo Laws Tuljajee had a legal right to adopt a distant relation, to the prejudice of a brother then living.	Answered in the negative unanimously. It would not be found in the Shaster. It was contrary to Law.
4	Whether the Pandits and Chief people of Tanjore considered the adoption, notwithstanding the rights of the brother to the succession, to be agreeable to the principles and opinions and conformable to the Laws and religion of the parties.	3 Pandits: It appears to be improper. 8 [Pandits]: It is improper. 1 [Pandit]: It is not agreeable to the Law.
5	Whether the adoption of Serfoji was in any way respect defective in forms, or contrary to the religious principles of the chief people of Tanjore.	3 Pandits: Contrary and defective. 8 [Pandits] Defective. 1 [Pandit]: A little defective.
6	Whether in the opinion of the principal people of Tanjore, the natural right of Ameer Sing to the succession were greater or less than those of Serfoji.	Answered unanimously in favour of Ameer Sing.

3 IOR/H/571, 193.

Appendix 3: Summary of Schwartz's eighteen Tamil dialogues

Christian Friedrich Schwartz: vikkiraka pattik kāraṉukkum kiṟisatavaṉukkum uṇaṭāṉa camapāṣaṉai ('Dialogue between an image worshipper and a Christian'). Tranquebar: Mission Press, ^{2}1790 (^{1}1777).

Dialogue	Pages	Theme
1	3–28	Non-Christians heard Tamil Lutherans preaching the Gospel and came voluntarily to the missionaries to gain a better understanding of Christianity. This dialogue comprises fifty-six questions posed by non-Christians and answers provided by Christians. At the beginning, the Christian summarises the contents of all dialogues: We believe in the omnipotent God who has created heaven and earth. We gratefully and humbly worship him as the Supreme God *Parāparaṉ*. We desire that all peoples (lit. *cātiyār* from Skt. jāti, i.e., birth-related people groups) should know and lovingly believe (lit. pakti from Skt. *bhakti*, 'ardent devotion') in this God. They should belong to this God because this one God has created all things and remains the source of all good things and blessings (*pākkiyam*). It is a blessing to believe in this God.[4] The *true Veda* (lit. *Satya Veda*, 'the Bible') contains God's accurate word and teaches how to attain salvation (lit. *karaiyērutal*, 'to get ashore' from the ocean of birth and rebirth). In six days, God created everything, including the sun, moon and everything from an ant to an elephant. God created the first man out of the soil. He also made the state of marriage. Therefore, marriage offers a holy way of life.
2	28–34	Fourteen questions and answers about the two trees in the Garden of Eden: God endowed the first humans with all faculties and placed the trees of life and death there. He wanted them to discern things, voluntarily obey his commands and lead a holy life.
3	34–47	Thirty-two questions and answers about the fall of the first humans; they lied to each other and God; thus, they sinned and lost God's likeness (lit. *tēvacāyal*) in them. After that, all humans, including children, are born sinners. They could not fully enjoy the bliss (*iṉpam*, 'blissful exuberance').

4 Schwartz: vikkiraka pattik kāraṉukkum, 3.

4	47–63	Thirty-two questions about the Ten Commandments: God condemns image worship because it darkens the human mind. All theological beliefs must find their moral expressions in real-life situations. For example, for Christians, *satī* is a murder. Those who die and those who allow it are murderers.[5]
5	63–74	Twenty-eight questions about the nature, person and identity of the Lord Jesus, who can grant forgiveness of sins. Performing various religious rituals does not grant forgiveness of sins. Faith in the Triune God alone would secure forgiveness of sins.
6	74–86	Twenty-six questions about Jesus's characteristics to secure God's forgiveness for humans: Jesus remained sinless. The four Gospels are records of Jesus' life and work for thirty years from his birth to resurrection.
7	86–94	Eighteen questions about Jesus' method of securing God's forgiveness of humans: he suffered and died a substitutionary death. He was buried, but on the third day, by raising him back to life, God vindicated Jesus' work.
8	95–103	There were sixteen questions about the transformed lives of the disciples who had received the Holy Spirit. They invited Jews and non-Jews to trust in the risen Lord Jesus. Some believed in him, while others rejected him.
9	103–111	Sixteen questions about trusting and following the Lord Jesus Christ: True asceticism consists of repentance and dependence on the God whom the Lord Jesus has revealed. Self-righteous acts and dependence on the merits of Christian saints are incompatible with Christ's teachings. Trusting and following the Lord Jesus during both good and challenging times is necessary for a life of worth.
10	111–124	Ten questions about the moral life of Christians: They follow the Ten Commandments and the Great Commission, which involves loving God and one's neighbours; they endure suffering. They love all persons equally and annul caste distinctions.

5 Schwartz: vikkiraka pattik kāraṉukkum, 57.

11	124–130	There are fifteen questions about the sufferings of Christians and how prayers, specifically the Lord's Prayer, can provide them with comfort. Christians should not be like those patients who take medicine but do not follow the dietary restrictions (*pattiyam*) and thus destroy the healing power of that medicine.
12	131–147	Twenty-eight questions about the seven petitions mentioned in the Lord's Prayer.
13	147–167	Thirty-seven questions about the power of the Holy Spirit and the sacraments of baptism and Eucharist. The Holy Spirit enlightens our hearts and minds by teaching us God's word enabling us to keep the Ten Commandments and cultivate other spiritual principles. The non-Christian wondered why, in this context, the Lutheran missionaries' ministry seemed limited and even unsuccessful. The Christian responded as follows.[6] The Tamil people have not yet grasped the importance of following Jesus Christ. Medicine can be offered. It will remain useless if the sick refuse to take it. Likewise, the seed not sown into good ground will not germinate and bear fruit. The Lord Jesus instituted the two sacraments of Baptism and the Eucharist to help Christians lead a worthy life.
14	167–176	Sixteen questions on the blessings of following the Lord Jesus Christ: God forgives our sins and helps us escape wrath on the day of judgement. God accepts us as God's children and protects our souls and bodies. There is no reincarnation of the soul. There is only one life here; everyone will face God's judgement.
15	176–186	Eight questions about the Bible: It reveals God's attributes and human characteristics. God cannot do evil things. The Bible portrays the Lord Jesus Christ as our guarantor (*piṇaiyāḷi*), who pays off our debts. We should worship God in spirit and truth and lead a holy life. Our lives should demonstrate God's grace.
16	186–191	Three questions about the prophecy (*muṉṉaṟi vākkiyam*, 'the statements known in advance') and its historical fulfilment as the second proof of Christianity's divine

6 Schwartz: vikkiraka pattik kāraṉukkum, 156.

		origin: when the first humans sinned, God promised to send a saviour. He foretold his manner of birth, life, death and resurrection. Lord Jesus Christ fulfilled these prophecies. His extraordinary teachings on God and humanity reiterate the divine origin of the Christian faith.
17	192–201	Thirteen questions about the place of Jews in the history of salvation: God chose Abraham, the father of all the Jewish people. Some Jews adopted the Christian faith, while others rejected it.
18	201–216	Sixteen questions about God sending humans, not angels, to preach God's Word as the third proof of Christianity's divine origin. He filled these humans with spiritual light and knowledge and equipped them for the holy work. He performed miracles; his resurrection is the greatest of them all. Then, he chose servants and sent them to different people. Therefore, it would be good if you, the Tamil people, would carefully consider these things. This book ends with a prayer of self-dedication to God's worship and service.

Appendix 4: Montgomery Campbell's Letter of 10 January 1796

India General Papers, 1773–1779, Box 2: Document 32: Montgomery Campbell's letter to Schwartz.

Charles Grant gave Montgomery Campbell a printed version of Schwartz's *Defence of Missions*. Consequently, Campbell feared the consequences of his speech in parliament, its publication in the newspaper and Schwartz's response. On 10 January 1796, wrote the following letter to Schwartz:

London, Warpole Street, 10th Jan 1796

Dear Sir,

I am induced to trouble you with a letter in consequence of my worthy friend Mr. Charles Grant having communicated to me the purport of a letter that you had written to the Society for Propagating the Christian Knowledge.

You have therein remarked upon a speech given in my name in one of the Public News Papers and I delivered that speech in the form and language that you have read. I would consider myself highly censurable. However, I can assure you with satisfaction that the speech I delivered was significantly different from what you have read: I never scoffed at the Sacred Religion in which I was educated. I never treated the beautiful Doctrines of Christ with levity or indifference. On the contrary I have from my earliest years sought for the opportunity of proving myself a devout and true Christian and this I have never been ostentatious in my devotion; I have not been less sincere: Judge them Sir what must be [a] concern to have my principles called in question by a person of your Distinguished Piety! If I had the good fortune to be in your company I trust I should soon satisfy you that my tenets are fine pure and undefiled and not undeserving in any respect of that approbation which righteous and enlightened men are ever ready to bestow upon those who worship God with a pure and upright heart: I can safely take upon me to assure you that I feel myself entitled to come under the description I have given; I was strictly and regularly instructed in our Common Faith. I have not deviated from it; it is my pride and my comfort, and I never shall sever from it. These assurances I am induced to make to you from an earnest and anxious desire to preserve as much as possible the share that I flatter myself I formerly enjoyed of your esteem. I can truly take upon myself to say that the part I took in the debate, which has been alluded to, ought not to have diminished your good opinion of me!
The accounts of speeches in the newspaper are never given with any degree of accuracy. Words were put into my mouth which I never uttered and sentiments which never entered my imagination. The fact is that I said but little on the subject

which was in debate and the little was to represent the difficulty which attended the conversion of Gentoos to Christianity, which on political grounds only, I thought dangerous to take up as a National Undertaking. It was under that apprehension only that I recommended deliberation before the measure was adopted.
Yet it unfortunately happened that gentleman who followed into in the debate took up some of the argument to which you naturally object and his words were put in the paper as part of my speech, which I was someone [?] of when I saw the News Paper, but trusting to the correctness of what I had said myself in the hearing of many people, I did not think it worthwhile to contradict the News Paper [backside of the second page] Representation.
Mr. Charles Grant having represented these facts to the Bishop of London, his Lordship desired to see me and to converse with me, when I had the good fortune to satisfy him as to the insincere and purity of my intention on the occasion alluded to and I assured his Lordship as I now beg leave to assure you that whenever opportunities shall offer, by which I can in any way serve or assist the Friend and Propagators of our Religion in India, they may rely on my most cordial exertions in their behalf because I am confident they will never propose any measure which can be prejudicial to the true interest of the Country or the East India Company.

If in mentioning the story of the Colleries I was misled or misinformed I am very sincerely concerned, I would not for any consideration have given you an uneasy feeling and I am persuaded the liberality if your mind will excuse me if I have unintentionally erred. [sheet 3].
I have requested of my friend Captain Allen Grant to deliver this letter to you; he will explain some circumstances to you still more fully than I can detail them in a letter. Permit me to recommend that gentleman to your friendly acquaintance. He is a worthy good man!

Your old friend Lady Campbell enjoys good health tho' her spirits are every different from what you knew them. She often speaks of you with sentiments of pure esteem and regard.

Adieu, Dear Sir and believe me with the highest consideration,

Your most faithful and most obedient servant

A. Montgomery Campbell

[To]
The Revd. Mr. Swartz

Appendix 5:
Schwartz's Christmas Reflection

Taylor: A Memoir of the First Centenary of the Earliest Protestant Mission at Madras, xii–xiii

TANJORE, December 24, 1794

To W. WHEATLEY,

SIR,

Your agreeable letter I have received. I wrote you a letter a few days ago. You wish to have some thoughts on the birth of Christ. To gratify your Christian desire, I will mention some of the most interesting points.

First, we are to consider the divine dignity of the excellent child who was born for our comfort. Surely, he was not a mere man, but the Son of God in the most eminent sense. So (to that degree) God loved the world as to give his only begotten Son. His human dignity was pure and holy without any, even the least contamination.

St. Luke calls him the first-born, not of Mary, but *of the whole* world. The firstborn of any family of the people of God was to be the head, the Priest and Saviour of the family. But as he was unable to be the Saviour of the family, he was redeemed by a sacrifice. By which God declared that mankind should be redeemed and saved by a sacrifice. The whole law concerning the FIRST born concerned principally Christ.

The divine person assumed our nature. One might have thought that considering his divine dignity, he would appear in the most magnificent manner. But we find just the contrary. All circumstances attending his birth, were low, nay, lowest of all. He was born poor and in the greatest ignominy, finding no house in Bethlehem (though the whole country was his, as it is likewise called Immanuel's country). He was born as a pilgrim on a journey in the nighttime, though he was the light of the world; without any provision; the poor mother though when very weak, was obliged to do all (having no help) and even to put him in a Manger. How low, how humiliating was all this. But this happened not to him my accident, but by the holy and wise counsel and decree of God.

Why was this poverty and ignominy appointed by God? Answer, because he was the Mediator and Surety of the World, or of all sinful mankind, who by sinning and rebelling against God, lost the image of God, and, consequently the Paternal Providence and favor of God. The Redeemer came as a Surety, bearing their punishment from the very beginning of His life. His early sufferings were the genuine signs and marks of his being the faithful Redeemer.

But that these humiliating circumstances might not be a scandal or offence to us, that we might not think that all this happened by mere accident. God glorified Christ by undeniable proofs. An Angel, a Prince of Heaven, was sent from heaven

to announce the birth of Jesus. He spoke nothing but what he was ordered to speak. "I bring you," he said to the Shepherds, "glad tidings that shall be to you, and to all the people." For unto you is born the Saviour, who was promised on that every day when man fell into Sin and calamity. Be not offended at his low circumstances. You will find the Baby lying in a Manger. This is the very sign of his being your Surety, for by this, he begins to pay off your debt, which he has taken upon himself.
As soon as the Angel had finished this Annunciation, the host of heaven descending praised God for his mercy to mankind and for his Truth in fulfilling his Promise concerning a Redeemer.
Nay, they joyfully proclaimed the great and glorious benefits which should be procured and purchased by the Redeemer. Then sang:
Glory to God in the heighest – that is – now is the blessed time come, when the Glory of God shall be manifested. The glory of his holiness. Justice by all the Sufferings of Jesus, by which mankind shall clearly see that God halteth sin, and punisheth iniquity, (that all the World may fear God and repent of their sins), but as these sufferings properly were our merit, but laid by God upon Jesus our Mediator and Sacrifice, so God declared by this his mercy to mankind, that all might believe in Jesus, seek and find pardon, and be restored to happiness.
Peace on Earth. Now shall peace and reconciliation be established so that mankind who were fallen and obnoxious to the wrath of God may be received into the favor of God.
And good will in (towards) mankind. Now mankind may again rejoice in God and say, Oh! My Father. All their doubts and dissidence are hereby removed.
Remember me to Mrs. Nevil and explain to her and her children the contents of this letter, as likewise to your consort: the birth of Jesus must *humble* and *comfort* us. God bless you all. So wishes, your friend, C.F. Swartz.

Appendix 6: Schwartz's Monuments

In St. Mary's Church, Fort St. George in Chennai

SACRED TO THE MEMORY
of the REVEREND FREDERICK CHRISTIAN SWARTZ,
Whose life was one continued effort to imitate the example of his BLESSED MASTER.
Employed as a Protestant Missionary from the GOVERNMENT of DENMARK,
And in the same character by the Society in ENGLAND for the Promotion of Christian Knowledge,
He, during a period of FIFTY YEARS, went about doing Good;
Manifesting, in respect to himself, the most entire abstraction from temporal views,
But embracing every opportunity of promoting both the temporal and eternal Welfare of others.
In him RELIGION appeared not with a gloomy Aspect or forbidding mien,
But with a graceful Form and placid Dignity.
Among the many fruits of his indefatigable Labours was the erection of the CHURCH at TANJORE.
The Savings from a small Salary were, for many years, devoted to the pious work,
And the Remainder of the Expense supplied by Individuals, at his solicitation.
The Christian Seminaries at RAMNADPORAM and in The TINNEVELLY province were established by him.
Beloved and honoured by EUROPEANS,
He was, if possible, held in still deeper Reverence by the Natives of this country, of every degree and every sect;
And their unbounded Confidence in his Integrity and Truth
Was, on many occasions rendered highly beneficial to the Public Service
The POOR and the INJURED
Looked up to him as an unfailing friend and advocate;
The GREAT and POWERFUL
Concurred in yielding him the highest homage ever paid in this Quarter of the Globe to EUROPEAN Virtue.
The late HYDER ALLY CAWN
In the midst of a bloody and vindictive war with the CARNATIC,
Sent orders to his Officers 'to Permit the venerable FATHER SWARTZ to pass unmolested and shew him Respect and Kindness,
For he is a Holy Man and means no harm to my Government'.
The late TULJAJI, RAJAH of TANJORE,
When on his Death-bed Desired to entrust to his protective Care
His adopted Son SERFOJI, the PRESENT RAJAH

With the administration of all affairs of his Country,
On a Spot of Ground granted to him by the same Prince, 2 Miles east of TANJORE,
He built a House for his Residence and made it an ORPHAN ASYLUM.
Here the last 20 years of his life were spent in the Education and religious Instruction of Children,
Particularly those of indigent parents - whom he gratuitously maintained and instructed;
And here, on the 13th of February, 1798,
Surrounded by his Infant Flock and in the presence of several of his disconsolate Brethren,
Entreating them to continue to make RELIGION the first object of their care,
And imploring with his last breath the Divine Blessing on their Labours,
He closed his truly Christian Career, in the 72nd year of his Age.
THE EAST-INDIA COMPANY,
Anxious to perpetuate the memory of such transcendent worth,
And gratefully sensible of the Public Benefits which resulted from its Influence,
Caused this Monument to be erected, Ann[o] Dom[ini]. 1807.

In Christ Church, Tanjore

To the memory of the
REVEREND CHRISTIAN FREDERICK SCHWARTZ,
Born at Sonnenburg of Neumark, in the kingdom of Prussia,
the 26th of October 1726,
and died at Tanjore, the 13th of February 1798,
in the 72nd year of his age.
Devoted from his early manhood to the office of
Missionary in the East,
the similarity of his situation to that of
the first preachers of the Gospel
produced in him a peculiar resemblance to
the simple sanctity of the
Apostolic character.
His natural vivacity won the affection,
as his unspotted probity and purity of life
alike commanded the
reverence of the
Christian, Mahomedan and Hindu.
For sovereign princes, Hindu and Mahomedan,
selected this humble Pastor
as the medium of political negociation [sic! = negotiation] with
the British Government:
and the very marble that there records his virtues

was raised by
the liberal affection and esteem of the
Raja of Tanjore,
Maha Raja Serfojee.

In St. Peter's Church, Tanjore

Sacred to the memory of
The Rev.d Christian Fred[erick] Swartz, Missionary to the
Hon.ble Society for Promoting Christian Knowledge in London, who departed
this life on
The 13th of February 1798
Aged 71 years and 4 months.

Firm was thou, humble and wise,
Honest, pure, free from disguise,
Father of orphans, the widows' support,
Comfort in sorrow of every sort,
To the benighted dispenser of light,
Doing and pointing to, that which is right,
Blessing to Princes, to People, to me;
May I, my Father, be worthy of Thee,
Wishes and prayeth thy
Sarabojee.

Glossary

adalat	The Company's law courts in the territories of its influence, which were previously under the rule of a *nawab* or a nizam (a ruler). *Adalat diwani* in Bengal and other places decided civil matters. *Nizamat adalat* decided criminal court
agraharam	*Akkirakāram* from Skt. *agrahāra*, i.e., a village or a street where Brahmins alone reside; in the text, this noun refers to land donated by a royal person to another person of royal status
amildar, amuldar	*Amiltār* or *amaltār* from Urdu *amaldār* (an official 'revenue collector'), also an officer in the economic, political, or military administration of a region appointed by a nawab
āṭutiṉṉāppālai	The Indian birthwort, *Aristolochia tagala*
bahadur	An honorific title for an exceptionally qualified and able person
batta	*Pattā*, from Urdu: *bhatta*, 'an allowance' in addition to wages for one's subsistence, usually on a daily, monthly or annual basis
cakkaram, chuckrams	*Cakkaram* ('circle'): a unit of money
camarttaṉ	The one who is strong, competent and skilful; an expert
cārai pāmbu	A rat snake (*Ptyas mucosus*)
cāti	Skt. *jāti*, i.e. a birth-based blood-related group, lineage, family, tribe, clan, race, attributes and traditions about this group
cātipētam	Skt. *jātibhēda*, i.e. birth-based caste differences
Catram, Cattiram	Either Telugu *satramu* or Kannada *satra*, a wayside rest house where weary travellers could receive cost-free food, water and rest
cāvaṭi	From the Marathi noun *sāvaṭī* or Telugu *cāvaḍi*, it refers to the public building in a village where disputes are settled, such as an office or a booth. See *Catram*

cēvakan̲	A servant
choultry	See *catram* and *cāvaṭi*
cīmai	An administrative territory of the Kingdom of Tanjore. Otherwise, *cīmai* can mean boundary, a country or countries in the west of India (e.g. England)
circar	*Carkkār* from either Urdu *sarcār* or Persian *sarkār*. This noun refers either to the government itself or to the land that the government owns and controls
cītamaṇṭali	A type of viper, the krait
coolie	*Kūli* ('wage'), i.e. a (menial) waged worker without any contract or rights
cowl, cowle	*Kavul* from Urdu *qaul* = a written document such as a lease agreement, a grant, assurance for safe conduct, amnesty and the like
cuṅkam	Duty on goods, customs, and toll
cutcherry, cutchery (kacheri)	*Kaccēri* = an office for public transactions that serves as a place for local administration involving record keeping, revenue collection, a police office or a lower court
cuthwals	*Kottavāl* from Urdu *kotwāl* ('a chief of a place'), e.g., a police officer of a town or a city, a superintendent of a marketplace
cuvarkkam	Skt. *svarga* refers to the celestial world of gods, the world of Indra, the 'entrance door to heaven'
cuvarkkavācal	The 'entrance to *svarga*,' also the terrestrial door of the Viṣṇu-temple that opens for ten days during the middle of the Tamil month of Mārkaḻi for devotees to move in and out
danam	*Tan̲am* ('wealth'); see *fano*
devadasi	*Tēvatāci* from Skt. *devadāsī* (a female 'servant of God'), an unmarried and unmarriable female servant of a god, who serves a deity in a temple or a human patron. Her profession requires her to read, memorise, sing and dance
dewal	A *diwan*
diwan	*Tivān̲* is derived from Urdu *dīwān*, which refers to a chief of state or the chief administrator of civil justice on behalf of a ruler, or a chief collector of revenues. In

	1765, the Company became the Diwan of Bengal. The Company engaged with Diwan Bahadur (*tivāṉ pakatūr*), a title of honour, for select distinguished persons
dubash	*Tupāci* from Skt. *tupāṣi* ('a man of two languages') or *tupāṣi* from Urdu *dobhāshiya* (derived from Skt. *dvibhāṣin*, i.e. an interpreter, an Indian agent, envoy, mediator or broker who worked for a commission in a European company or a European
Fano	*Paṇam* (in Tamil: 'money'), a silver coin. In 1793, 22½ Fanam was equal to one Star Pagoda. Otherwise, sixteen or eighteen *Paṇam* equalled one Star Pagoda; later, twelve *Paṇam* equalled one Rupee of the Company
Farman	A written order from the Mughal emperor or his court, attested with their official seal
Hindoo	A Hindu
inam	*Iṉām* from Urdu *inām* (a 'gift'), i.e. a landholding free of tax and rent
irattaviriyaṇ	A type of viper, the krait
jagir, jaghir	*Jākīr*, from Persian *jāgīr* ('tenure of land/estate/domain for service'), refers to a land grant where an empowered person (jāgīrdār) can collect revenues either as a reward or as a salary. The Mughal territories not assigned to anyone were known as *khalifa*; the revenue of a *khalifa* was paid into the Mughal treasury
jamadar	*Camataṉ* (an 'associate'), i.e. a leader of a village or a region
jumma	A Mughal system of taxing agricultural produce before it was harvested. Tax on actual harvested produce was known as *hasil*
kalam	*Kaḷam* ('a locality, a region')
kalam	*Kalam* is a dry grain measure; one *kalam* equalled to 96 *paṭi* or twelve *marakkāl*s. Eight *nāḻi* or *paṭi* equalled one *marakkāl*
kaṇakkuppiḷḷai	An accountant, a record keeper
kañji	*Kañci* from Telugu, i.e., the broth made from boiled rice, which most Tamils drink. See *sōru*
kār nel	Paddy is harvested during the rainy season

kas	*Kācu* (in Tamil). A small gold coin or a silver coin. This is the root word for 'cash'
kāvalkārar	'Protectors,' who administered smaller administrative units of Tanjore under Ameer Singh. They collected revenues, examined offenders and reported directly to Ameer Singh
killadar	*Killētār* from Urdu *qiladār* (a 'commander of a fort')
kirāmam	A village
kist, quist	*Kisti* is derived from Arabic and Urdu, *qisṭ*, meaning a collection of fixed revenue in regular instalments, known to the Tamil people as *cistuvacūl*. See *peshkush*
kompē̱rimūkka̱n	The snake *Dendrelaphis tristis*
kudiyā̱navarkaḷ	Agricultural families, villagers
lac, lakh	100,000
maṇiyakkāra̱n	Village administrator and tax collector
Ma̱ravar	Name of a jāti, who specialised as war heroes, the inhabitants of an arid land such as Ramanathapuram
māhān	*Mākāṇam* from Urdu *mākāṇ* (a 'district, province')
Matasree	Skt. *mātāstrī* ('respected mother'), used as a title for a woman who has given birth to children
mayakkaṭipāmpu	A snake whose bite causes confusion and delirium
miḷaku	Black pepper (*Piper nigrum*)
mirācutār mirasdar	Hereditary landowners in Tanjore
mujumutār	*Mucumutār* from Urdu: *majmūadār*, 'district accountant' or a taluk accountant next to the *tehsildar*
mu̱ṉna̱ri vākkiyam	A statement known beforehand, a prophecy
music	*Mu̱nicīppu* from Arabic *munsif*. This term refers to a presiding officer of a subordinate court
musnud	Arabic *mas̱nat* ('throne')
nabob	A contemptuous designation for a Company employee who returned from India to the United Kingdom with an enormous fortune for extravagant living
nalla pāmbu	Cobra (*Cobra capella*, *Coluber naja* and *Naja tripudians*)

nawab — *Navāpu* or *napāpu* from Urdu *nawāb* = a deputy, a vice-regent, or a provincial governor under the Mughal Emperor; a title accorded to a Muslim gentleman recognising his distinguished services

ne̱rivișam — The plant *Curcuma zedoaria* is also known as white turmeric. Its Tamil names are *pūlāṅkiḻaṅgu* and *kaccōram*

nērvāḷam — The plant *Croton tiglium*

olla — *Ōlai* ('a stripe of palm leaf' or a palm leaf)

pagoda — Probably from Persian *putkada* ('a temple for image worship') or Sanskrit *Bhagavatī* ('the glorious goddess'). The adjective *bhagavat* means illustrious, prosperous, glorious, divine and adorable. The gold coins, known as the Star Pagodas and especially the Swami Pagodas, feature the image of a goddess or Viṣṇu on one side. According to www.royalmint.com, one gold Star Pagoda is worth £575.00 (as of August 2024). Otherwise, a *pagoda* refers to a Buddhist temple, especially its steeple

palankeen — *Palau = a palanquin,* a litter, i.e. a covered carriage on poles, carried by four men on their shoulders

Panam — See *Fano*

pandit — *Paṇṭitaṉ* ('an erudite person'), typically during Schwartz's time, a learned Brahmin scholar whom Europeans consulted for legal matters enshrined in Sanskrit writings

parāparaṉ — God, who is the highest and Supreme Being (in heaven), also known as *parāparavastu* (the 'Divine Substance') or *paramporuḷ* (the supreme 'Being, Substance, Signification, Meaning, Quality')

pāṣāṇam — Arsenic acid, see *veḷḷai pāṣāṇam*

patakakkārar — Leader of a *patakam*

patakam — An administrative unit of Tanjore under Ameer Singh. Each *patakam* consisted of several villages

patakkatār — An officer in charge of a *patakam*

paṭṭaikāraṉ — A belt-wearing guard

pattiyam — Prescribed diet for patients who take medicine or undergo a treatment

peon	Arabic *piyūṉ* ('a servant'), an attendee at an office
pergunah	*Pargana* = a sub-division of the revenue district under the Mughals
peshkush	*Pēṣkisti* from Urdu *pēṣkist* ('land tax, revenue, rent, tribute,' which the landowner pays to the government); a zamindar used to pay *peckish*. See *kist*
pilly	A type of tax on paddy used in Tanjore
piṇaiyāḷi	One who stands as a guarantor
poligar	*Pāḷaiyakkāraṉ* (a 'protector of a *pāḷaiyam*,' i.e. a region and an army), a chief of warriors
Progiden	*purōkitaṉ* (Skt. purōhita) = a family priest
puddukkam	See *patakam*
puḷḷipārkkiṟatu	Assessment of agricultural produce and its tax
puṟakkuṭi	Also: *parakuṭi*; Non-residential tentative farmers for specific agricultural
quist	See *kist*
racam	*Pātaracam* ('quicksilver')
rajya	*Rājyam* (Skt. *rājya*, 'kingdom')
ryot, ryots, ryotts, raiyat	*Rayat* from Urdu *raiyat* ('farmers, cultivators, tenants'); in Tamil: *kuṭiyāṉavaṉ* (the 'resident' cultivator)
Saheb, Sahib, Sāhibā	Persian *sāhib* (a 'companion'), used in Marathi as Sir. The feminine noun means 'Madam'
Sankranti	*Caṅkarānti* or *caṅkirānti* from Skt. *saṅkrānti*, i.e. the first day of the month, especially the ninth Tamil month *tai* (January–February)
Sarakhela	See *sirkeel*
sarkel	See *sirkeel*
saruvamaniam	*Carvamāṉiyam* from Skt. *Sarvamānya*, i.e. a rent-free and tax-free land
sāsanam	*Cācaṉam* from Skt. *śāsana*, i.e. a government order, edit, written document
satī	*Cati* from Skt. *satī* ('a true woman, wife'), i.e. the self-immolation of a widow on the funeral pyre of her deceased husband
Sattam	*Cattam* ('sound, noise')

sepoy	*Cipāy* or *cippāy* from Urdu *sipāhī* (an 'Indian infantry soldier') in the Company army as opposed to a foreign or a European soldier
shaster	*Cāstiram* (Skt. *śāstra*, a religious or scientific 'treatise'), code of conduct
shawl	*Cālvai* from *Urdu shāl* = a long, fine cloth worn over the shoulder as an upper garment. The Cashmere shawl was, and still is, famous
sibbendies	Plural form of *cippanti* from Urdu *sibandī* ('clerk, servant')
sirkeel	*Carkkīl* from Urdhu *sarkhail*, i.e. a commander of forces, a government minister administering a region, especially the most senior officer in the government of Marathas (e.g. a prime minister)
sīrmai	*Cīmai* ('western country'), a Tamil noun for Europe, especially for England
sonnud	A Hindi noun, *sunnud,* from Arabic *sanad*, i.e. a written deed of office, grants, privileges and rights, by those who oversaw the government
sōru	*Cō<u>r</u>u* ('boiled rice), the stable food of the Tamils. See *kanji*
soubahdar	See *Subaidar*
subah	*Cupai* from Urdu *subā* ('a district, a province') under the Mughal rule, later adopted by the kings of Tanjore
Subaidar, subedar	*Cupaiyatār* or *cupētār*, from Urdu *subādār*, i.e., an Indian military officer equivalent to a captain, also the chief revenue officer of a Subah
tadigal	Plural form of the Tamil noun of *taṭi* from Kannada *daḍi* ('a wooden staff, rod, cane or club')
tankhah	Persian: *tank was* ('payment, salary')
Tasealdary	Office or duties of a *Tehsildar*
Tehsildar	*Tāciltār* from Urdu *tāḥsīldār*: a revenue officer overseeing a *tahsil,* i.e. a specific revenue administrative territory
tendam	*Teṇṭam* ('punishment, penalty in cash or kind, tax')
tēr	a tall temple car for procession, decorated with ornamental hangings

tēr tiruviḻā	A festival in which devotees pull a temple car along designated streets with an image of their deity on it
tīrvai	Tax paid at customs houses or toll booths
toddy	Palm wine, known in Tamil as *kaḷḷu*
toṇṭaimāṉ	A ruler of *Toṇṭaimaṇṭalam* (i.e., modern Pudukkottai), also a common alternative name for jāti groups such as Kaḷḷar, Maṟavar, and others in the Tanjore and Ramanathapuram regions
tōraṇam	Skt *tōraṇa*, i.e. festoons decorated with leaves, flowers and colourful paper stripes and hanging from hooks and crossbeams
tōṭṭi	A menial servant of a village, like the one who burns the corpses, a despised sweeper of streets
uḷkuṭi	Permanent residential farmers working for a *mirācutār*
vakeel, vakkīl	*Vakkīl* from Urdu *wakil*, a high officer next only to the chief executive, an authorised legal representative or an attorney or a pleader
vaḷḷaṉai	A type of viper, the krait
varṇa	*Varuṇam* ('colour'), especially the *caturvaruṇam*, the four-fold castes in Sanskrit, namely the Brahmins, Kṣatriyas, Vaiśyas and Sūdras
vaṭṭa maṇiyakkāraṉ	An overseer of circles, territories
vēlāmaram	A tree. People used the juice of its bark as an antivenom
veḷḷai erukkampāl	The white sap of the plant *Calotropis gigantea*
veḷḷai pāṣāṇam	The white arsenic acid
vely	*Veḷi*, i.e. a unit of land
viriyaṉ	A viper, the krait
zamindar	*Jamīṉtār*, from Urdu *zamīndār* (an indigenous, permanent 'landholder' with special rights), i.e., rural elites who collected taxes for the Mughal state and, under the Company, became owners of extensive lands
zilla	*Jillā* from Arabic *zilā*, namely an administrative unit that included several subdivisions known as *tālukā* or *tāluk*s
zilladar	The chief administrator of a *zilla*

Bibliography

1 Primary Sources: Archival Manuscripts

1.1 The Danish-Halle Mission Archives (AFSt/M)

1 B 38 : 24	G. A. Francke to M. Bosse, J. C. Wiedebrock, J. B. Kohloff, D. Zeglin, O. Maderup, J. Klein, J. Z. Kiernander and J. C. Breithaupt on 20 May 1749
1 B 40 : 20	Schwartz to Inspector Sommer, circa Dec 1750
1 B 40 : 21	Schwartz to G. A. Francke on 8 Oct 1750
1 B 40 : 22	Schwartz to G. A. Francke on 9 Jan 1751
1 B 41 : 6	J. C. Wiedebrock, J. B. Kohlhoff, D. Zeglin, O. Maderup, J. Klein, Schwartz and D. Poltzenhagen to G. A. Francke on 27 Sep 1751
1 B 41 : 19	Schwartz to G. A. Francke on 16 Oct 1752
1 B 41 : 30	G. A. Francke to Schwartz on 21 Feb 1753
1 B 42 : 15	Schwartz to G. A. Francke on 23 Oct 1752
1 B 42 : 34	G. A. Francke to Schwartz on 23 Mar 1754
1 B 43 : 16	Schwartz to G. A. Francke on 08 Oct 1753
1 B 43 : 17	Schwartz to G. A. Francke on 04 Jan 1754
1 B 43 : 19	Schwartz to A. v. Struensee on 08 Oct 1753
1 B 43 : 31	Schwartz to G. A. Francke on 28 Aug 1753
1 B 43 : 32	G. A. Francke to Schwartz in Nov 1754
1 B 44 : 11	Schwartz to G. A. Francke on 12 Oct 1754
1 B 47 : 15	Schwartz to G. A. Francke on 04 Oct 1756
1 B 47 : 21	Schwartz to G. A. Francke on 29 Dec 1757
1 B 47 : 56	G. A. Francke to Schwartz in March 1759
1 B 48 : 19	Schwartz to G. A. Francke on 10 Jan 1760
1 B 49 : 7	J. C. Wiedebrock, J. B. Kohlhoff, D. Zeglin, O. Maderup, J. Klein, Schwartz and D. Poltzenhagen to Francke on 8 Jan 1760
1 B 49 : 16	Schwartz to G. A. Francke on 30 May 1759
1 B 49 : 18	Schwartz to G. A. Francke on 15 Jun 1759
1 B 49 : 19	Schwartz to G. A. Francke on 10 Jan 1760
1 B 49 : 20	Schwartz to G. A. Francke on 12 Jan 1760
1 B 50 : 9	Schwartz and J. B. Kohlhoff to G. A. Francke on 17 Feb 1761
1 B 50 : 12	Schwartz to G. A. Francke on 16 Oct 1760
1 B 50 : 25	Schwartz and others to Francke on 12 Jan 1760
1 B 50 : 28	Schwartz to G. A. Francke on 23 Oct 1760

1 B 50 : 35	G. A. Francke to Schwartz on 1 Dec 1760
1 B 51 : 14	Schwartz to G. A. Francke on 2 Sep 1761
1 B 51 : 15	Schwartz to G. A. Francke on 14 Jan 1762
1 B 52 : 13	Schwartz to G. A. Francke on 8 Feb 1762
1 B 52 : 15	Schwartz to G. A. Francke on 17 Jan 1763
1 B 52 : 33	G. A. Francke to Schwartz on 1 Dec 1762
1 B 53 : 17	Schwartz to G. A. Francke on 13 Oct 1763
1 B 53 : 18	Schwartz to G. A. Francke on 3 Mar 1764
1 B 53 : 19	Schwartz to J. F. Sorge on 3 Mar 1764
1 B 54 : 22	Schwartz to G. A. Francke on 12 Oct 1764
1 B 54 : 23	Schwartz to G. A. Francke on 17 Jan 1765
1 B 54 : 24	Schwartz to G. A. Francke on 3 Mar 1765
1 B 54 : 53	Schwartz to G. A. Francke on 19 Jan 1756
1 B 54 : 54	G. A. Francke to Schwartz on 16 Oct 1765
1 B 54 : 55	G. A. Francke to Schwartz on 3 Jan 1766
1 B 55 : 30	G. A. Francke to Schwartz on 16 Nov 1767
1 B 56 : 16	Schwartz to G. A. Francke on 15 Jan 1766
1 B 56 : 17	Schwartz to G. A. Francke on 14 Mar 1766
1 B 56 : 18	Schwartz to G. A. Francke on 10 Jul 1766
1 B 56 : 20	Schwartz to G. A. Francke on 17 Dec 1766
1 B 57 : 14	Schwartz to G. A. Francke on 24 Oct 1767
1 B 57 : 15	Schwartz to G. A. Francke on 20 Jan 1768
1 B 57 : 16	Schwartz to G. A. Francke on 30 Mar 1768
1 B 57 : 17	Schwartz to F. W. Pasche on 24 Oct 1767
1 B 58 : 37	Schwartz to G. A. Francke on 30 April 1769
1 B 58 : 39	J. C. Breithaupt and J. B. Fabricius to Schwartz on 20 May 1769
1 B 58 : 40	Schwartz to G. A. Francke on 6 Oct 1768
1 B 58 : 41	Schwartz to G. A. Francke on 22 Oct 1768
1 B 58 : 45	Schwartz to the SPCK on 21 Mar 1770
1 B 58 : 57	G. A. Francke to Schwartz on 28 Oct 1768
1 B 59 : 28	Schwartz to Francke on 13 Jan 1770
1 B 59 : 31	Schwartz to F. W. Pasche on 16 Jan 1770
1 B 60 : 23	Schwartz to J. G. Knapp on 22 Jan 1771
1 B 61 : 40	Schwartz to J. G. Knapp on 14 Oct 1771
1 B 61 : 41	Schwartz to J. G. Knapp on 18 Feb 1772
1 B 62 : 32	Schwartz to F. M. F. M. Ziegenhagen on 12 Oct 1772
1 B 62 : 33	Schwartz to G. A. Freylinghausen on 12 Oct 1772
1 B 63 : 28	Schwartz to G. A. Freylinghausen on 11 Jan 1774
1 B 63 : 58	G. A. Freylinghausen to Schwartz on 15 Nov 1774
1 B 65 : 42	Schwartz to G. A. Freylinghausen on 22 Sep 1774
1 B 65 : 43	Schwartz to G. A. Freylinghausen on 21 Jan 1775
1 B 65 : 44	Schwartz to F. W. Pasche on 20 Feb 1775
1 B 66 : 54	Schwartz to F. W. Pasche on 8 Sep 1775
1 B 66 : 55	Schwartz to F. M. F. M. Ziegenhagen on 23 Sep 1775

1 B 66 : 57	Schwartz to G. A. Freylinghausen on 28 Sep 1775
1 B 66 : 58	Schwartz to F. M. F. M. Ziegenhagen on 18 Jan 1776
1 B 66 : 59	Schwartz to F. W. Pasche on 18 Jan 1776
1 B 66 : 60	Schwartz to G. A. Freylinghausen on 26 Jan 1776
1 B 67 : 71	Schwartz to G. A. Freylinghausen on 25 Sep 1777
1 B 67 : 73	Schwartz to F. W. Pasche on 17 Feb 1778
1 B 67 : 74	C. Pohle to G.A. Freylinghausen on 19 Sep 1778
1 B 67 : 99	G. A. Freylinghausen to Schwartz on 17 Nov 1778
1 B 68 : 42	Schwartz to G. A. Freylinghausen on 14 Oct 1776
1 B 68 : 43	Schwartz to F. W. Pasche on 11 Oct 1776
1 B 68 : 45	Schwartz to F. W. Pasche on 21 Jan 1777
1 B 68 : 46	Schwartz to G. A. Freylinghausen on 3 Feb 1777
1 B 69 : 45	Schwartz to G. A. Freylinghausen on 9 Oct 1778
1 B 69 : 46	Schwartz to G. A. Freylinghausen on 24 Feb 1779
1 B 69 : 47	Schwartz to G. A. Freylinghausen on 9 Oct 1778
1 B 69 : 107	G. A. Freylinghausen to Schwartz in Feb 1780
1 B 69 : 108	Schwartz to G. A. Freylinghausen in Feb 1780
1 B 70 : 40	Schwartz to F. W. Pasche on 23 Feb 1779
1 B 70 : 42	Pohle to Halle on 27 Sep 1779
1 B 70 : 43	Schwartz to G. A. Freylinghausen on 13 Oct 1779
1 B 70 : 45	Schwartz to G. A. Freylinghausen on 14 Mar 1780
1 B 71 : 30	Schwartz to J. F. Sorge in 1780
1 B 71 : 32	Schwartz to G. A. Freylinghausen on 10 Oct 1780
1 B 71 : 35	Diary of Sattiyanātaṉ in Vallam
1 B 71 : 36	Diary of Savarimuthu in Tiruppathur
1 B 72 : 10	Impact of Hyder Ali's war and its effects on Tranquebar, 1781
1 B 72 : 47	J. P. Fabricius and J. C. Breithaupt to G. A. Freylinghausen on 20 May 1781
1 B 72 : 52	Schwartz to F. W. Pasche on 15 Feb 1781
1 B 72 : 57	Schwartz to G. A. Freylinghausen on 15 Feb 1781
1 B 72 : 58	Schwartz to G. A. Freylinghausen on 20 Jan 1782
1 B 74 : 17	J.C. Kohlhoff to Freylinghausen on 7 Jul 1783
1 B 74 : 27	Schwartz to G. A. Freylinghausen on 16 Feb 1784
1 B 74 : 31	Schwartz's journey to Hyder Ali (1779). See also 2 E 17 : 13
1 B 75 : 23	Schwartz to G. A. Freylinghausen on 14 Oct 1784
1 B 75 : 24	Schwartz to F. W. Pasche on 11 Oct 1784
1 B 75 : 25	Schwartz to G. A. Freylinghausen on 14 Jan 1785
1 B 75 : 26	Njanapragasam's diary of his travel to Pāḷaiyamkōṭṭai
1 B 75 : 27	Schwartz to G. A. Freylinghausen on 20 Feb 1784
1 B 75 : 28	Schwartz to F. W. Pasche on 31 Jan 1785
1 B 75 : 28a	Schwartz to F. W. Pasche on 26 Feb 1785
1 B 75 : 29	C. Pohle to G. A. Freylinghausen on 12 October 1784
1 B 75 : 32	F. W. Pasche to G. A. Freylinghausen on 5 Sep 1786

1 C 25 : 23	Schwartz to F. W. Pasche on 24 Sep 1785
1 C 25 : 32	Schwartz to J. L. Schulze on 8 Oct 1785
1 C 25 : 33	Schwartz to F. W. Pasche on 8 Oct 1785
1 C 26 : 1	Schwartz to F. W. Pasche on 28 Jan 1785
1 C 26 : 3	Schwartz to F. W. Pasche on 15 Oct 1785
1 C 26 : 8	Schwartz to J. L. Schulze on 17 Jan 1786
1 C 26 : 9	Schwartz to S. A. Fabricius on 17 Jan 1786
1 C 27 : 4	J. Klein to G. A. Freylinghausen on 27 Jan 1786
1 C 27 : 5	Schwartz to J. F. Sorge on 17 Jul 1786
1 C 27 : 8	Schwartz to F. W. Pasche on 2 Oct 1786
1 C 27 : 24	Schwartz to J. L. Schulze on 6 Feb 1787
1 C 27 : 25	Schwartz to F. W. Pasche on 20 Oct 1786
1 C 27 : 26	Schwartz to F. W. Pasche on 8 Jan 1787
1 C 27 : 27	C. W. Gericke to F. W. Pasche on 14 February 1787
1 C 28 : 70	Schwartz to F. W. Pasche on 6 Sep 1787
1 C 28 : 72	Schwartz to F. W. Pasche on 24 September 1787
1 C 29a : 5	Schwartz to J. L. Schulze on 1 Feb 1788
1 C 29a : 11	Schwartz to F. W. Pasche on 7 and 14 Feb 1788
1 C 29b : 6a	Schwartz to an unnamed recipient on 30 Jan 1787
1 C 29b : 6b	Schwartz to an unnamed recipient on 7 Mar 1787
1 C 29b : 6c	Schwartz to an unnamed recipient on 2 Mar 1787
1 C 29b : 6d	Schwartz to an unnamed recipient on 4 Feb 1787
1 C 29b : 6e	Schwartz to an unnamed recipient on 21 Mar 1787
1 C 29b : 7	Schwartz to J. Klein on 29 May 1787
1 C 29b : 7a	Schwartz to J. Klein, circa May 1787
1 C 29b : 7b	Schwartz to J. Klein on 29 May 1787
1 C 29b : 24	C. S. John to C. H. Wadum on 30 Mar 1787
1 C 29b : 29	J. Klein, J. F. König, John, J. P. Rottler, P. R. Hagelund to J. L. Schulze on 8 Oct 1787
1 C 30c : 7	J. Klein, J. F. König, C. S. John and J. P. Rottler to J. L. Schulze on 29 Sep 1788
1 C 30c : 17	Schwartz to Pasche on 23 Dec 1788
1 C 30c : 22	J. Klein, J. F. König, C. S. John and J. P. Rottler to J. L. Schulze on 19 Jan 1789
1 C 32b : 66	Schwartz to F. W. Pasche on 16 Sep 1791
1 C 35a : 53	Schwartz to J. C. C. Uebele on 4 Feb 1794
1 C 35a : 65	Schwarzt's Defence of Mission in German dated 13 Feb 1794
1 C 37a : 1	Schwartz to J. C. C. Uebele on 5 Jan 1796
1 C 37a : 2	Schwartz to J. C. C. Uebele on 8 Jan 1796
1 C 37a : 4	Schwartz to J. C. C. Uebele on 8 Jan 1796
1 C 39b : 36	Schwartz to J. L. Schulze on 29 Aug 1798
1 C 41 : 88	K. W. Päzold to G. C. Knapp on 12 Apr 1800
1 C 41 : 89	C. W. Gericke to G. C. Knapp on 12 Apr 1800
1 C 42a : 22	C. W. Gericke to G. C. Knapp on 28 Feb 1801

1 C 42a : 54a	J. G. Knapp to C. W. Gericke on 14 Jan 1801
1 C 42a : 54b	J. G. Knapp to K. W. Päzold on 4 Jan 1801
1 C 42b : 24	K. W. Päzold to J. G. Knapp on 5 Oct 1801
1 C 43a : 54	K. W. Päzold to J. G. Knapp on 27 Mar 1802
1 C 43b : 26a	J. G. Knapp to K. W. Päzold on 4 Jul 1802
1 C 44a : 40b	J. G. Knapp to C. W. Gericke on 3 Apr 1803
1 C 45 : 95	C. S. John to J. C. C. Uebele, circa 1804
1 C 46 : 21	J. T. Strubell to J. G. Knapp on 27 Nov 1805
1 K 5 : 18	J. F. Backe (to J. G. Knapp?), circa 1800
1 K 5 : 19a	K. W. Päzold (to J. G. Knapp?) on 10 Oct 1801
1 K 10 : 26	G.A. Francke's 26 Instructions to Schwartz, D. Poltzenhagen and G. H. C. Hüttemann on 3 Oct 1749
1 K 10 : 48	Schwartz to G. A. Francke on 16 Dec 1749
1 K 10 : 55	Schwartz to G. A. Francke on 29 Dec 1749
1 K 10 : 59	Schwartz to G. A. Francke on 10 Jan 1750
1 K 10 : 71	Schwartz's autobiography until Dec 1749
2 A 6 :3	J. Klein to J. L. Schulze on 13 Oct 1785
2 B 1 : 3	J. R. Forster to C. S. John on 27 Dec 1790
2 B 1 : 4	C. S. John to J. R. Forster on 20 Jan 1792
2 B 1 : 6	J.P. Rottler (?) about pills against snakebites, circa 1788–1792
2 B 1 : 7	Schwartz to C. S. John 6 May (1788?)
2 B 9 : 14	Poem "Die aufgeklärte Zeit" by an unknown author, 1792
2 D 36 : 1	J. C. Wiedebrock, J. B. Kohlhoff, D. Zeglin, O. Maderup, J. Klein, Schwartz, P. Dame to Frederik V, King of Denmark on 7 Jan 1760
2 E 17 : 12	Schwartz's Diary of 1778
2 E 17 : 13	Schwartz's journey to Hyder Ali (1779). See also 1 B 74 : 31
2 E 27 : 13	C. S. John's travel diary from Feb to May 1795

1.2 Manuscripts in the British Library in London (BL)

ADD 13612	Papers relative to the Country Powers and the Northern Circars 1774–1784
ADD 13663	Journal of the Operations of the Siege of Seringapatam with the Bombay Army on the North Side of the Cauvery in 1799
ADD 13690	Letters and Papers Relative to Tanjore 1797–1798
ADD 29140	Warren Hasting's Papers: General Correspondence. Vol. IX. Jan.–May 1778
ADD 29147	Warren Hasting's Papers: General Correspondence. Vol. XVI. Jan.–Feb 1781

ADD 29153	Warren Hasting's Papers: General Correspondence. Vol. XXII. Feb–Mar 1782
ADD 35381	Hardwicke Papers: Vol. XXXIII. Correspondence of the 2nd and 3rd Lord Hardwicke. 1783–Feb 1784
ADD 38400	Liverpool Papers. Vol. CCXI. East India Papers. 28 Jul 1776–31 Dec 1777
ADD 38403	Liverpool Papers. Vol. CCXIV. East India Papers Mar–Dec 1779
ADD 38404	Liverpool Papers. Vol. CCXI. East India Papers. 1780
ADD 41622	John Coxe Hippisley Papers presented by Lady Horner
ADD 57313	Papers of Col. Mark Wilks
ADD 57939	Correspondence of Montague John Guest
EAP971/2/3/1	Christian Friedrich Schwartz: *ki̱risattamāṉa upatecattin viḷakkam* (in Tamil: A Description of the Teaching of Christian Religion'): Catechetical Instructions, or An Explanation of Christian Doctrine written by Swartz [1777]: Copied from the MS in possession of Rev. G.H. Apthorp and rec[ive]d by him from Rev. Brotherton, Tanjore, March 1, 1841. URL: https://eap.bl.uk/archive-file/EAP971-2-3-1 (accessed on 05.10.2024)
IOR/E/4/871	Madras Despatches, 10 Sep 1783 – 8 Jul 1785
IOR/E/4/872	Madras Despatches, 13 Sep 1785 – 21 Jul 1786
IOR/E/4/875	Madras Despatches,10 Dec 1788 – 19 Aug 1789
IOR/E/4/876	Madras Despatches, 02 Dec 1789 – 18 Aug 1790
IOR/F/4/42	Board's Collections, 1798–1799
IOR/F/4/48	Board's Collections, 1799–1800
IOR/F/4/80	Board's Collections, 1768–1799
IOR/F/4/136	Board's Collections, 1802–1803
IOR/F/4/218	Board's Collections, 1807–1808
IOR/H/115	Home Miscellaneous, East India Series, 23, 1773–1774
IOR/H/285A	Home Miscellaneous, On the Nawab of Arcot and Tanjore (1780–1798)
IOR/H/457	Home Miscellaneous, Wellesley Papers No. 1 (1799–1800)
IOR/H/571	Home Miscellaneous, On Kurnool, Coorg and Tanjore (1784–1795)
IOR/P/252/10	Madras Military Consultations, 4 Jul – 26 Oct 1786
IOR/P/252/15	Madras Military Consultations, from Jan 1787
IOR/P/252/16	Madras Military Consultations, 1 Apr – 20 Oct 1787
IOR/P/252/23	Madras Military Consultations, 1 Jan 1788 – 29 Feb 1788
IOR/P/252/26	Madras Military Consultations, 16 Jul 1788 – 12 Sep 1788
IOR/P/252/27	Madras Military Consultations, 13 Sept – 21 Oct 1788
IOR/P/252/28	Madras Military Consultations, 21 Oct – 2 Dec 1788
IOR/P/252/37	Madras Military Consultations, 9 Sep – 1 Dec 1789
IOR/P/252/42	Madras Military Consultations, 1 Jan – 9 Feb 1790
IOR/P/252/45	Madras Military Consultations, 1 May – 8 Jun 1790

IOR/P/252/57	Madras Military Consultations, 1 – 28 Jan 1791
IOR/P/252/60	Madras Military Consultations, 8 Apr – 3 May 1791
IOR/P/253/03	Madras Military Consultations, 6 Nov – 7 Dec 1792
IOR/P/253/10	Madras Military Consultations, 1 Jan – 4 Feb 1793
IOR/P/253/11	Madras Military Consultations, 5 Feb – 12 Mar 1793
IOR/P/253/12	Madras Military Consultations, 14 Mar – 16 Apr 1793
IOR/P/253/57	Madras Political & Military Consultations, 1 Jan – 2 Feb 1796
IOR/P/253/58	Madras Political & Military Consultations, 3 Feb 1796 – 11 Mar 1796
IOR/P/253/64	Madras Political & Military Consultations, 13 Aug – 13 Sep 1796
IOR/P/253/65	Madras Political & Military Consultations, 14 Sep – 11 Oct 1796
IOR/P/254/20	Madras Military Consultations, 29 Jun – 17 Jul 1798
IOR/P/316/89	Madras Proceedings, 1790
IOR/T 663	Extract of a letter from a Gentleman at Fort St. George, 10 Oct 1776
MSS Eur D 788	Letters 1781–91 of Sir Thomas Rumbold (1736–1791)
MSS Eur D 1208	East India Papers, 1752–1778
MSS Eur Orms 33	Extract from the Diary and Proceedings of the Select Committee at Fort St. George

1.3 Manuscripts in the Lambeth Palace Library in London

Note: All folios are in the manuscript book *S.P.G. Papers. Vol. IX.*

204r–204v	Extract of the Company's Charter dated 5 Sep 1698
216r–216v	Chaplain William Johnson's letter of 21 Aug 1784 to the Archbishop of Canterbury
217r–218r	William Chambers, Charles Grant and George Udny with Chaplain David Brown's letter to the Archbishop of Canterbury on 10 Sep 1787 about establishing an Anglican mission to Bengal and Bihar
219r–219v	Chaplain William Johnson's letter of 10 Sep 1787 to the Archbishop of Canterbury
220r–223r	Thomas Blanchard, John Owen, David Brown, Robert Carr's letter of 5 Aug 1789 to Governor General Charles Cornwallis in Calcutta
225r–225r	John Owen's letter of 12 Mar 1789 to G Sharpe in Calcutta
251r–251v	About the Pious Claus of 1793

1.4 Manuscripts in the Tamil Nadu Archives in Chennai (T)

Vol. 3450 A	Tanjore Records
Vol. 4448	Tanjore Records
Vol. 4452	Tanjore Records
Vol. 3449 A	Tanjore Records
Vol. 3449 B	Tanjore Records

1.5 Manuscripts in the Bodleian Library, Oxford

72290ind-box1-2: Register of baptisms and marriages at Trichinopoly, 1751–1847: C/IND/GEN/Box 1/2. Baptisms conducted between 1751 and 1847 and marriages solemnised between 1751 and 1791 by Swartz, Kohlhoff, D. Rosen, Schreyvogel, W. Hickey and T.C. Simpson of the Danish Halle Mission. URL: https://microform.digital/boa/collections/28/volumes/138/cindgen-ca-1770-1844 (accessed 07.01.2022).

72290ind-box1: India General Papers: C/IND/GEN/Box 1/3:Swartz's notes on divinity lectures at Halle (1749). URL: https://microform.digital/boa/collections/28/volumes/138/cindgen-ca-1770-1844 (accessed 07.02.2022)

72290ind-box2: India General Papers 1773–1797: C/IND/GEN/Box 2. URL: https://microform.digital/boa/documents/2168/india-general-papers-1773-1797 (accessed 10.02.2022)

Document Number	Date	Description
1	No date	Schwartz's sermon on Luke 16:16–24
5	26.03.1778	Alexander Davidson's letter to Schwartz
7	27.07.1780	Schwartz's letter to Kohlhoff
8	18.10.1782	A copy of the Introduction to Rana Treaty
11	07.03.1783	Schwartz's letter to Kohlhoff
12	No date	Schwartz to Alexander Campbell about Tulāji's dignity and the welfare of Tanjore inhabitants
14	29.01.1787	John Sulivan to Schwartz about the Provincial Schools
15	06.06.1787	John Chamier to Schwartz about the Provincial Schools
15a	16.02.1787	The Court of Directors supporting Schwartz's Provincial Schools
16	24.01.1787	Declaration of John Caspar Kohlhoff's ordination by Danish and English missionaries

17	03.02.1787	Schwartz to the mother of John Hudleston about her son
18	01.02.1802	The mother of John Hudleston to her son, reminding him to think of Schwartz
19	13.02.1802	John Hudleston to J. C. Kohlhoff about his memories of Schwartz
20	27.04.1788	Amelia Campbell to Schwartz about the Asylum (Orphanage) for girls
21	19.09.1788	William Petrie to Schwartz about his professional behaviour with Ameer Singh
22	16.11.1788	William Petrie to Schwartz about Tanjore lands mortgaged to the Danes in Tranquebar
23	18.11.1790	Charles Oakley to Schwartz about his mediatory role with Ameer Sing
24	23.02.1791	W.C. Jackson to Schwartz about Ameer Singh mortgaging villages to the Danes in Tranquebar
25	16.031791	Charles Oakley's private letter to Schwartz about his mediatory role with King Ameer Singh
26	09.05.1793	Cornwallis to Schwartz about contacting pundits in Bengal and Banares regarding Serfoji
27	19.11.1793	Mrs Chambers, the sister-in-law of Sir Robert Chambers, to Schwartz about her late husband's conversion
28	19.09.1794	Charles Oakley to Schwartz about Serfoji as the prospective heir
29	25.01.1796	Hobart to Schwartz about Serfoji's return to Tanjore
30	11.07.1796	Alexander Macleod to Schwartz about *Defence of Mission*
32	10.01.1796	Montgomery Campbell's Letter to Schwartz
31	1794–1796	Information about natural and illegitimate children baptised by Jänicke in Pāḷaiyamkōṭṭai and Ramanathapuram. Frank Penny prepared this list in 1905
32	10.01.1796	Montgomery Campbell's Letter to Schwartz

72290ind-box3: India General Papers, 1800–1815: C/IND/GEN/Box 3
Correspondence and other items relating chiefly to South India, including an autograph copy of a sermon on Luke 13.7–9, preached by Henry Martyn

at Dinapore on 11 January 1807. URL: https://microform.digital/ boa/ collections/23/volumes/138/cindgen-ca-1770-1844 (accessed 12.02.2022)

Document Number	Date	Description
42	04.01.1809	Buchanan's letter from Bristol to missionaries Kohlhoff and Horst in Tanjore

72290ind-box7: India General Papers, 1800–1815: C/IND/GEN/Box 7. Includes a list of questions sent by G.T. Spencer, Bishop of Madras to C.S. Kohlhoff, asking for information on his late father, John Caspar Kohlhoff, with Kohlhoff's responses. URL: https://microform.digital/boa/collections/28/volumes/138/cindgen-ca-1770-1844 (accessed 14.02.2022)

Document Number	Date	Description
45	11.12.1833	Memorandum in reference to a proposed exchange of Missionary Stations between the Society for the Propagation of the Gospel and the Church Missionary Society Dec. 11/33.

2 Primary Sources: Printed Materials

A Bill for Inflicting certain Pain and Penalties on Sir Thomas Rumbold, Baronet, and Peter Perring, Esquire, for certain Breaches of Public Trust, and High Crimes and Misdemeanours, committed by them whilst they respectively held the Offices of Governor and President, Counsellors and Members of the Select Committee, of the Settlement of Fort Saint George, on the Coast of Coromandel, in the East Indies. London 1782.

A Collection of Charters and Statutes, relating to The East India Company with an Appendix. London 1817.

An Abstract of the Annual Reports and Correspondence of the Society for Promoting Christian Knowledge from the Commencement of its Connexion with the East India Missions, A.D. 1709, to the Present Day together with the Charges Delivered to the Missionaries at Different Periods on their Departure for their several Missions. London 1814.

An Act for the better Regulation and Management of the Affairs of the East-India Company and of the British Possessions in India; and for establishing a Court of Judicature for the more speedy and effectual Trial of Persons accused of Offence committed in the East Indies, in: Collection of Charters and Statutes, relating to the East India Company. London 1817.

An Enquiry into the Policy of Making Conquests for the Mahometans in India by the British Arms, in Answer to a Pamphlet intituled "Considerations on the Conquest of Tanjore." London: J. Dodsley, [2]1779.

An Impartial View of the Origin and Progress of the Present Disputes in the East-India Company, Relative to Mahomed-Ally-Khan, Nabob of Arcot and Tulja-gee, Raja of Tanjore to which are annexed Observations on Mahomed-Ally-Khan's Letter to the Court of Directors. London: T. Cadell, 1778.

Art. IV (A review of Pearson: Memoirs of the Life and Correspondence of the Reverend Christian Frederick Swartz). Ed. by Edward Smedly et al. In: The British Critic and Quarterly Theological Review and Ecclesiastical Record 15, 1834, issue 30, 363–392.

Thomas Beck: The Missionary: A Poem to which are subjoined Hints on the Propagation of the Gospel at Home and Abroad Respectfully Inscribed to the New Missionary Societies. London: W. Button, Paternoster-Row, 1795.

Andrew Bell: An Experiment in Education made at the Male Asylum of Madras suggesting a System by which a School or Family may teach itself under the Superintendence of a Master or Parent. London: Cadell and Davies, 1797.

Andrew Bell: The Madras School or Elements of Tuition comprising the Analysis of an Experiment in Education made at the Male Asylum, Madras. London [4]1808.

William Cavendish Bentinck: Memorial Addressed to the Honourable Court of Directors, containing an Account of the Mutiny at Vellore. London 1810.

Claudius Buchanan: Memoir on the Expediency of an Ecclesiastical Establishment for British India, both as a Means of Perpetuating the Christian Religion among our own Countrymen and as a Foundation for the Ultimate Civilisation of the Natives. London 1805.

Claudius Buchanan: Star in the East—A Sermon preached in the Parish Church of St. James, Briston, on Sunday, February 26, 1809, for the Benefit of the Society for Missions to Africa and the East. Boston [8]1809.

Claudius Buchanan: Christian Researches in Asia with Notices of the Translation of the Scriptures into the Oriental Languages. London [4]1811.

Claudius Buchanan: Colonial Ecclesiastical Establishment—Being a Brief View of the State of the Colonies of Great Britain and of her Asiatic Empire in respect to Religious Instruction prefaced by some considerations on the National Duty of affording it, to which is added a Sketch of an Ecclesiastical Establishment for British India, humbly submitted to the consideration of the Imperial Parliament. London [2]1813.

Claudius Buchanan: An Apology for Promoting Christianity in India, containing two letters addressed to the Honourable East-India Company concerning the idol Juggernaut; and a Memorial presented to the Bengal Government in 1807, in defence of the Christian Missions in India, printed by order of the Hon. The House of Commons, to which are now added Remarks of the letter addressed by the Bengal Government to the Court of Directors in reply to the Memorial with an Appendix containing various official papers, chiefly extracted from the Parliamentary Records relating to the Promulgation of Christianity in India. London 1813.

William Carey: An Inquiry into the Obligation of Christians to Use Means for the Conversion of the Heathen, in which the Religious State of the Different Nations of the World, the Success of Former Undertakings and the Practicability of Future Undertakings, Are Considered. Leicester: Ann Ireland, 1792.

Copies of Treaties concluded by Sir Archibald Campbell, Governor in Council of Fort Saint George, with the Nabob of Arcot and Rajah of Tanjore; together with Extracts of Letters to the Court of Directors, on Subject of those Treaties and also Extracts from Copies of Correspondence between the Governments of Bengal and Fort Saint George and the Nabob of Arcot, relative to the Government of Madras having assumed the Management of the Revenues of the Carnatic, Ordered to be printed 6 May 1791. London: n.p. n.d.

Julian James Cotton: List of Inscriptions on Tombs or Monuments in Madras Possessing Historical or Archaeological Interest, rev. ed. Vol. 1. Madras 1945 and Vol. 2. Madras 1946 (^{1}1905).

William Fullarton: A View of the English Interests in India and an Account of the military operations in the Southern Parts of the Peninsula during the Campaigns of 1782, 1783 and 1784 in two letters addressed to the Right Honourable the Earl of ***** and to Lord Macartney and the Select Committee of Fort St. George. London: T. Cadell, 1787.

Wilhelm Germann: Johann Philipp Fabricius–Seine fünfzigjährige Wirksamkeit im Tamulenlande und das Missionsleben des achtzehnten Jahrhunderts daheim und draußen nach handschriftlichen Quellen dargestellt. Erlangen 1865.

Wilhelm Germann: Ziegenbalg und Plütschau—Die Gründungsjahre der Trankebarschen Mission—Ein Beitrag zur Geschichte des Pietismus nach handschriftlichen Quellen und ältesten Drucken. Two Vols. Erlangen 1868.

Wilhelm Germann: Missionar Christian Friedrich Schwartz: Sein Leben und Wirken aus Briefen des Halleschen Missionsarchivs. Erlangen 1870.

C.B. Gohdes: Schwartz—The Apostle to India. Columbus/Ohio 1923.

Charles Grant: Observations on the State of Society among Asiatic Subjects of Great Britain, particularly with respect to Morals and on Means to improve it, written chiefly in the year 1792. London: n.p. 1797.

Charles Grant: Observations on the State of Society among Asiatic Subjects of Great Britain in 1792. London: The House of Commons, 1813.

George Gray's embassy to Hyder Ali, 1780. In: Notes on Indian History. 16.01.2018. URL: https://www.notesonindianhistory.com/2018/01/george-grays-embassy-to-hyder-ali-1780.html (accessed on 20.11.2024).

Hermann Gundert: Arbeiter in der Tamil-Mission: 6. Chr. F. Schwartz. In: Evangelisches Missions-Magazin 12, 1868, 225–242.

Nathaniel Brassey Halhed: A Code of Gentoo Laws, or Ordinations of the Pandits, from a Persian Translation, made from the Original written in the Shanscrit [sic = Sanskrit] Language. London: n.p. 1776.

John Hall: The Life of Rev. Henry Martyn with some account of Abdool Messeeh, a Hindoo Convert, Revised by the Committee of Publication. Philadelphia 1832.

Halle Reports: Der Königl. Dänischen Missionarien aus Ost-Indien eingesandter Ausführlichen Berichten, Von dem Werck ihres Amts unter den Heyden, angerichteten Schulen und Gemeinen, ereigneten Hindernissen und schweren Umständen; Beschaffenheit des Malabarischen Heydenthums, gepflogenen brieflichen Correspondentz und mündlichen Unterredungen mit selbigen Heyden [... 'Detailed Reports from East India sent in by the Royal Danish Missionaries of the work of their ministry among the heathen, the schools and congregations which they had established, the obstacles and the difficult circumstances that they encountered, the nature of the Tamil Society, their customary letter correspondence and oral dialogues with the Tamils']. Vols. I–IX. Halle: Waisenhaus, 1710–1772.

John Zephaniah Holwell: An Account of the Manner of Inoculating for the Small Pox in the East Indies with some Observations on the Practice and Mode of Treating that Disease in those Parts. London: T. Becket and P. A. de Hondt, 1767.

Instruction for the English Missionaries. In: Halle and the Beginning of Protestant Christianity in India. Vol. III: Communication between India and Europe. Ed. by Andreas Gross et al. Halle 2006, 1391–1400.

Christoph Samuel John: On Indian Civilization. In: Halle and the Beginning of Protestant Christianity in India. Vol. III: Communication between India and Europe. Ed. by Andreas Gross et al. Halle 2006, 1467–1491.

JR: Reflections on the Conversion of the Natives of India to Christianity. In: The New Monthly Magazine and Universal Register 2, August 1814, issue 7, 27–33.

Letter from Mahommed Ali Chan, Nabob of Arcot, to the Court of Directors, to which is annexed a State of Facts relative to Tanjore with an Appendix of Original Papers. London: T. Cadell, 1777.

James Barton Longacre: The Life of Christian F. Swartz: An Early Missionary in India. Philadelphia 1830.

Madras District Gazetteer—Tanjore, rpt. Ed. by F. R. Hemingway. Madras 1915.

Memorial on behalf of the King of Tanjore presented to Lord North. N.p. n.p. n.d.

Memoirs of the Rev. Joseph D[aniel] Jænicke, a Fellow Labourer of Schwartz at Tanjore, Interspersed with many original letters and notices of Schwartz. London 1833.

Minutes of Evidence taken before the Honourable House of Commons, in a committee of the whole House, to whom it was referred to consider the affairs of the East-India Company. London 1813.

New Halle Reports: Neuere Geschichte der evangelischen Missionsanstalten zu Bekehrung der Heiden in Ost-Indien aus den eigenhändigen Aufsätzen und Briefen der Missionarien ('Recent History of the evangelical missionary institutions for the conversion of Gentiles in East India from the missionaries' own essays and letters'). Vols. I–VIII. Halle: Waisenhaus, 1776–1847.

Johann Lucas Niekamp: Kurzgefaßte Missions=Geschichte oder Historischer Auszug der Evangelischen Missions=Berichte aus Ost=Indien. Halle: Waisenhaus, 1740.

Anders Nørgaard: The Mission Instruction. In: Halle and the Beginning of Protestant Christianity in India. Vol. III: Communication between India and Europe. Ed. by Andreas Gross et al. Halle 2006, 1277–1280.

Papers Relating to East India Affairs (Resident Europeans–Police–MISSIONARIES–Weavers, and Investments). Ordered by the House of Commons, to be printed 14 April 1813. London 1813.

Henry Pattullo: An Essay upon the Cultivation of the Lands and Improvements of the Revenues of Bengal in London. London: T. Becket and P.A. De Hondt in the Strand, 1772.

Hugh Pearson: The Life of Rev. Christian F. Swartz. In: The Missionary Register for the Year 1813 containing an Abstract of the Proceedings of the principal Missionary and Bible Societies throughout the World. Vol. 1. London ^{3}1816, 193–215, 241–249, 273–282, 305–309, 3012–317 and 337–350.

Hugh Pearson: Memoirs of the Life and Correspondence of the Reverend Christian Frederick Swartz. Two Volumes. London 1834.

Hugh Pearson: Memoirs of the Life and Correspondence of Swartz, to which prefixed, a Sketch of the History of Christianity in India. First American Edition. New York, Boston and Philadelphia 1835.

Processional scene with Amar Singh, ruler of Thanjavur (Tanjore) and Serfoji (ca. 1797). Victoria and Albert Museum. URL: https://collections.vam.ac.uk/item/O17560/processional-scene-with-amar-singh-painting-unknown/ (accessed 29.01.2025).

Bapu Rao: Bhonsle Vamsa Charitra Being the Marathi Historical Inscription in the Big Temple Tanjore on The History of the Maratta Rajas of Tanjore (dated 13 December 1803), Thanjavur 2009.

Remains of the Rev. C.F. Schwartz consisting of his Letters and Journals. London 1826.

Royal Appointments and Instructions to the First Missionaries [Ziegenbalg and Plütschau]. In: Halle and the Beginning of Protestant Christianity in India. Vol. III: Communication between India and Europe. Ed. by Andreas Gross et al. Halle 2006, 1337–1339.

Sattianaden: Translation of a Sermon in the Malabar or Tamulian Language, composed and preached by Sattianaden on the 26th Day of December 1790, when he received Ordination according to the Rites of the Lutheran Church, in one of the Congregations of the Mission on the Coast of Coromandel connected with The Society for Promoting Christian Knowledge. London: F. and C. Rivington, 1792.

W.T. Satthianadhan: Notes of a Tour through Travancore and Tinnevelly. In: Intelligencer, December 1871, 360–377.

Christian Friedrich Schwartz: kiṟisattamāṉa upatecattin viḷakkam (in Tamil: 'A Description of the Teaching of Christian Religion'): Catechetical Instructions, or An Explanation of Christian Doctrine written by Swartz: Copied from the MS in possession of Rev. G.H. Apthorp and rec[ive]d by him from Rev. Brotherton, Tanjore, March 1. 1841, 1777. URL: https://eap.bl.uk/archive-file/EAP971-2-3-1 (accessed on 05.10.2024).

Christian Friedrich Schwartz: vikkiraka pattik kāraṉukkum kiṟisatavaṉukkum uṇaṭāṉa camapāṣaṉai ('Dialogue between an image worshipper and a Christian'). Tranquebar: Mission Press, ^{2}1790 (^{1}1777).

Christian Friedrich Schwartz: Defence of Missions. In: Account of the Society for Promoting Christian Knowledge. London: SPCK, 1795, 114–123.

Christian Friedrich Schwartz: Defence of Missions in India by the late Venerable Mr. Swartz, published by the Society for Promoting Christian Knowledge in their Report for 1795. London: H. Brayer, 1796.

Serfoji: Kumārasambhavachampū [in Sanskrit] by Śrī Śarabhoji Mahārāja of Tanjore. Ed. by T. K. Balasubramanya Aiyar. Srirangam 1939.

Serfoji: Devendra Kuravanji [in Marathi] by Serfoji Raja. Ed. by T. L. Thyagaraja Jatawallabhar. Kumbakonam 1950.

Serfoji: Sarapēntira Vaittiya Ratṉāvaḷi (Tamil: 'A Collection of Medical Treatments by King Serfoji'). Transl. and Ed. by A. Krishnasamy Madikrow. Tanjore ^{8}2008.

Philip Jacob Spener: Speners Katechismuserklärung. Bielefeld 1984.

Elisabeth Strandberg: A Tanjore Marāṭhī letter in Moḍī script to Chr. F. Schwartz. In: Acta Orientalis 41, 1980, 17–25.

Elisabeth Strandberg: The Moḍī Documents from Tanjore in Danish Collections. Edited, Translated and Analysed. Wiesbaden 1983.

John Sulivan: Tracts Upon India written in the years 1779, 1780 and 1788 with subsequent observations. London: W. Bulmer and Co., 1795.

Mark Taylor: Historical Sketches of the South of India in an attempt to trace the History of Mysoor from the origin of the Hindu Government of that State to the extinction of the Mohammedan Dynasty in 1799. Vol. 1. Madras: Higginbotham and Co., ²1869.

William Taylor: A Memoir of the First Centenary of the Earliest Protestant Mission at Madras. Madras 1847.

The History and Management of the East-India Company, from its Origin in 1600 to the Present Times. Volume the first containing the Affairs of the Carnatic, in which the Rights of the Nabob are explained, and the Injustice of the Company proved. The whole [is] compiled from authentic records. London: T. Cadell, 1782.

The Missionary Register for the Year 1813 containing an Abstract of the Proceedings of the Principal Missionary and Bible Societies throughout the World. Vol. 1. London ³1816.

The Missionary Register for the Year 1819 containing the Principal Transactions of the various Institutions for Propagating the Gospel with the Proceedings, at large, of the Church Missionary Society. London 1819.

Philipps, J. Thomas (transl.): Thirty Four Conferences between the Danish Missionaries and the Malabarian Bramans (or Heathen Priests) in the East Indies, concerning the Truth of the Christian Religion together with some Letters written by the Heathens to the said Missionaries. London: H. Clements in St. Paul's Church Yard, 1717.

Treaty concluded by Sir Archibald Campbell with the Nabob of Arcot in February 1787; the Approbation transmitted by the Court of Directors of that Treaty; and the several Papers relative to it and to the Assumption of the Government and Revenues of The Carnatic, in the Year 1790, which were presented to the House of Commons in the last Session of Parliament. London: n.p. 16 March 1792.

Christoph Theodosius Walter: Historia Sacra – Rerum in Ecclesia inde ab orbe condito ad nostrum vsque actatem gestarum notitiam exhibens Historia Sacra, […]. Tranquebar: Typis et sumtibus Missioni Danicæ, 1735.

B. Ziegenbalg: caruvēcuraṉuṭaiya vētattilē uṇṭāṉa aḻutta mettaiyākiya kuṟippiṭam ('Catechism containing the summary of the teachings in God's Veda,' the Bible). AFSt/P TAM 37, Palm Leaves 80–90.

3 Secondary Sources

August Hermann Francke Study Centre – Archive and Library. URLs: https://www.francke-halle.de/en/science/archives-and-library and https://archiv.francke-halle.de/start.fau?prj=ifaust8_afst (accessed on 06.01.2025).

Christian Masillamoni Agur: Church History of Travancore. New Delhi ²1990 (¹1903).

Anglo Mysore Wars: Second Anglo Mysore War—Treaty of Mangalore. In: Notes on Indian History, 13.05.2016. URL: https://www.notesonindianhistory.com/2016/05/anglo-mysore-wars-second-anglo-mysore.html (accessed on 29.10.2024).

Aparna Alluri: The Indian queens who modelled for the world's first vaccine. BBC News. 20 September 2020. URL: https://www.bbc.co.uk/news/world-asia-india-53944723 (accessed on 28.10.2024).

Mark Edward Balmforth: A Tamil Pietist in Ceylon: The Educational Experiments of Christian David. In: International Journal of Asian Christianity 3, 2020, issue 1, 44–68.

Baman Das Basu: Education in India under the Rule of the East India Company. Calcutta 1867.

Baman Das Basu: Rise of the Christian Power in India. Calcutta ²1931 (¹1923).

Susan Neild-Basu: The Dubashes of Madras. In: Modern Asian Studies 18, 1984, issue 1, 1–31.

C. A. Bayly: Indian Society and the Making of the British Empire, 6th rpt. (1988). Cambridge 2006.

Michael Bergunder: Christian Friedrich Schwartz (1726–1798) in German Mission Literature. In: Christian Friedrich Schwartz: His Contributions to South India. Ed. by Daniel Jeyaraj. Madras 1999, 36–57.

Tulajendra Rajah P Bhonsle: Raja Serfoji II with a Short History of Thanjavur Mahrattas. Tanjore ²1999.

Pratap Sinh Serfoji Raje Bhosle: Contributions of Thanjavur Maratha Kings. Chennai: Notion Press, ²2017 (¹2015).

Stuart H. Blackburn: The Kallars: A Tamil 'criminal tribe' reconsidered. In: South Asia: Journal of South Asian Studies 1, 1978, issue 1, 38–51.

Christian Gottlieb Blumhardt: Christian Friedrich Schwartz: der deutsche Missionar in Südindien nach dem Englischen des Hugh Pearson. Basel 1846.

Raja Senior S. Babai Rajah Bhonsle Chattrapathy: The King [Serfoji] and the Clergy Man [Schwartz]. In: Christian Friedrich Schwartz: His Contributions to South India. Ed. by Daniel Jeyaraj. Chennai 1999, 117–118.

John Bowen: The East India Company's Education of its Own Servants. In: Journal of the Royal Asiatic Society, October 1955, 105–123.

Henry Bower: Caṅkai Poruntiya Cuvāccu Aiyyar Carittiram ('History of the Venerable Reverend Schwartz'). Madras 1839.

Niels Brimnes: Variolation, Vaccination and Popular Resistance in Early Colonial South India. In: Medical History 24, 2004, 199–228.

G. J. Bryant: The Emergence of British Power in India, 1600–1784: A Grand Strategic Interpretation, Woodbridge 2013.

Anne Buddle, Pauline Rohatgi and Iain Gordon Brown: The Tiger and the Thistle—Tipu Sultan and the Scots in India 1760–1800. Edinburgh 1999.

Carapēntira vaittiya mu̱raikaḷ (viṣa rōka cikiccai) [in Tamil: 'Serfoji's Methods of Treatment: Treatments of Poison']. Ed. by S. Venkatarajan. Tanjore [5]2005.

Hilary M. Carey: God's Empire—Religion and Colonialism in the British World, c. 1801–1908. Cambridge 2011.

John Carne: Lives of the Eminent Missionaries. Vol. 1. London 1833.

Penelope Susan Elizabeth Carson: Soldiers of Christ: Evangelicals and India, 1784–1833. Diss. phil. London 1988.

Penelope Carson: The East India Company and Religion, 1698–1858. Woodbridge 2012.

Mu. Catācivam (ed.): Māmaṉṉar Cracapōci—Āyvukkōvai Tokuti 3 ('The Great King Serfoji—Collection of Research Essays'). Tanjore 1990.

Ī. Ē. Cellatturai: "Tañcai Marāttiya Maṉṉarkaḷum Kiṟistavarkaḷum [Tamil: 'The Marathi Kings of Tanjore and Christians]," Māmaṉṉar Carapōji. Ed. by Catācivam. Tañcāvūrar 1990, 23–40.

Pratik Chakrabarti: Neither of meate nor drinke, but what the Doctor alloweth; Medicine amidst War and Commerce in Eighteenth-Century Madras. In: Bulletin of the History of Medicine 80, 2006, issue 1, 1–38.

S. Chinnaiyan: Social History of Thanjavur 1532–1799. Diss. Phil. Trichy 1999.

S. Chinnaiyan: Tax Structures in Tanjore Kingdom under the Nayaks and Marathas (A.D. 1532–1799). In: Proceedings of the Indian History Congress 66, 2005–2006, 456–459.

Christian Friedrich Schwartz: His Contributions to South India. Ed. by Daniel Jeyaraj. Chennai: 1999.

Church Missionary Gleaner 3, 1843, issue 7, 73–75.

Ian Copland: Christianity as an Arm of Empire: The Ambiguous Case of India under the Company, c. 1813–1858. In: The Historical Journal 49, 2006, issue 4, 1025–1054.

John William Cunningham: Christianity in India—An Essay on the Duty, Means, and Consequences of Introducing the Christian Religion among the Native Inhabitants of the British Domains in the East. London 1808.

Elmer H. Cutts: The Background of Macaulay's Minute. The American Historical Review, 58, 1953, issue 4, 824–853.

William Dalrymple and Anita Anand: Koh-I-Noor—The History of the World's Most Infamous Diamond. London 2017.

A. P. Dasgupta: The Central Authority in British India 1774–1784. A Study of the Relations of the Supreme Council with the Madras Government under the Regulating Act of 1773. Calcutta 1931.

Dyron B. Daughrity: A Worldly Christian: The Life and Times of Stephen Neill. Cambridge 2021.

Henry Dodwell: The Nabobs of Madras. London 1926.

Ecclesiastical Memoir of the Four First Decades of the Reign of George the Third. In: The Christian Guardian and Church of England Magazine 13, 1821, issue 3, 83–87.

I. Elangovan: Colonial Acquisitions and Socio-Economic Trends in Madras, 1765–1827. Diss. phil. Madurai 2012.

Ainslie Thomas Embree: British East India Company Raj. In: Encyclopedia of India. Vol. 1. Detroit 2006, 176–183.

William Enfield: The Speaker or Miscellaneous Pieces selected from the best English Writers and disposed under proper heads with a view to facilitate the Improvement of Youth in Reading and Speaking, to which is prefixed an Essay on Elocution. London: Joseph Johnson, 1774.

M. Ewart: The Church of England Zenana Mission Training Home, Madras. In: India's Women and China's Daughters. London 1903, 64–65.

Ole Feldbæk: India Trade under the Danish Flag 1772–1808: European Enterprise and Anglo-Indian Remittance and Trade. Copenhagen 1969.

Johannes Ferdinand Fenger: Den Trankebarske Missions-Historie. Kjøbenhavn 1843.

Johannes Ferdinand Fenger: Geschichte der Trankebarschen Mission. Transl. Emil Francke. Grimma 1845.

Johannes Ferdinand Fenger: History of the Tranquebar Mission. Transl. Emil Francke. Tranquebar 1863.

Duncan B. Forrester: Caste and Christianity: Attitudes and Policies on Caste of Anglo-Saxon Protestant Missions in India. London 2018.

Wilhelm Fries: August Hermann Franckes Grosser Aufsatz. Halle (Saale) 1894.

Robert Eric Frykenberg: Modern Education in South India, 1784–1854. Its Roots and Its Role as a Vehicle of Integration under Company Raj. In: The American Historical Review 91, 1986, issue 1, 37–65.

Robert Eric Frykenberg: Legacy of Christian Friedrich Schwartz. In: International Bulletin of Missionary Research 23, 1999, issue 3, 130–135.

Robert Eric Frykenberg: Christian Missions and the Raj. In: Missions and Empire. Ed. by Norman Etherington. Oxford 2005, 107–131.

Robert Frykenberg: India to 1858. In: The Oxford History of British Empire. Vol. V: Historiography. Oxford 2007, 194–213.

Robert Eric Frykenberg: Christianity in India—From Beginnings to the Present. New York 2008.

Robert Eric Frykenberg: The myth of English as a 'colonist' imposition upon India: a reappraisal with special reference to South India. In: Journal of the Royal Asiatic Society 120, 2011, issue 2, 305–315.

Wilhelm Germann: Die Kirche der Thomaschristen – Ein Beitrag zur Geschichte der Orientalischen Kirchen. Gütersloh 1877.

Noah V. Gnanadickam Sastriyar: Life of Vedanayagam Sastriar. Tanjore 1987.

E. W. Grinfield: Sketches of the Danish Mission on the Coast of Coromandel. London, 1831.

Jürgen Gröschl: Directors of the Francke Foundations. In: Halle and the Beginning of Protestant Christianity in India. Vol. III: Communication between India and Europe. Ed. by Andreas Gross et al. Halle 2006, 1551–1556.

Jürgen Gröschl: Lutheran Chaplains in London. In: Halle and the Beginning of Protestant Christianity in India. Vol. III: Communication between India and Europe. Ed. by Andreas Gross et al. Halle 2006 1557–1559.

A.C.L. Grove-Rasmussen: Christian Friedrich Schwartz: Anledning af Hundredårsdagen for hans Død (Danish: 'Christian Friedrich Schwartz: On the Occasion of his first Death Anniversary'). Copenhagen 1898.

J.D. Gurney: The Debts of the Nawab of Arcot 1763–1776. Diss. phil. Oxford 1968.

Julius Hardeland: Der Königspriester von Tandschâur: Lebensbild des Gesegnetesten unter den alten halleschen Missionaren. Leipzig 1901.

Barbara J. Hawgood: Doctor Albert Calmette 1863–1933: founder of antivenomous serotherapy of antituberculosis BCG vaccination. In: Toxicon 37, 1999, issue 9, 1241–1258.

Conjeevaram Hayavadana Rao: History of Mysore 1399–1799. Vol. 3: 1766–1799. Bangalore 1946.

Reginald Heber: Narrative of a Journey through the Upper Provinces of India from Calcutta to Bombay, 1824–1825 (with Notes upon Ceylon). An Account of a Journey to Madras and the Southern Provinces, 1826 and Letters Written in India in Three Volumes. Vol. 3. London ^{4}1829 (^{1}1828).

Reginald Heber: The Life of Reginald Heber. Vol. 2. London 1830.

William Hickey: The Tanjore Maratha Principality in Southern India: The Land of the Cholas; the Eden of the South. Madras ^{2}1874.

J.J. Higginbotham: Men Whom India Has Known—Biographies of Eminent Indian Characters. Madras ^{2}1874.

Samuel Charles Hill: Yusuf Khan—The Rebel Commandant. London 1914.

Jeetendra Hirschfeld: Seraglios of the Tanjore Mahārājahs: Sword Wives of the Kalyāṇa Mahāl and Vijayā Maṅgala Vilāsam Mahāl. In: Sathir Dance Art. 2 May 2009. URL: https://sathirdance.wordpress.com/2009/05/02/seraglios-of-the-tanjore-maharajahs-sword-wives-of-the-kalya%E1%B9%87a-mahal-and-vijaya-ma%E1%B9%85gala-vilasam-mahal/ (accessed on 20.11.2024).

James Hough: The History of Christianity in India from the Commencement of the Christian Era. Vol. III. London 1845, 549–569.

George Howells and A.C. Underwood: The Story of Serampore and its College. Serampore 1918.

Jennifer Howes: "Tipu Sultan's female entourage under East India Company rule." In: Journal of the Royal Asiatic Society Series 3, Vol. 31, 2021, issue 4, 855–874.

Courtenay Ilbert: The Government of India Being a Digest of the Statue Law relating thereto with Historical Introduction and Illustrative Documents. Oxford 1898.

Gottlieb Werner Luetkehoelter: Adiaphora. Consensus 12, 1986, issue 1, 117–135.

James Hough: The History of Christianity in India from the Commencement of the Christian Era. Vol. 4. London 1845.

Ernest Marshall Howse: Saints in Politics – The 'Clapham Sect' and the Growth of Freedom. London 1953.

Ce. Irācu: palturaip paṇipurinta svārṭs pātiriyār (Tamil: 'Reverend Schwartz, who served in different fields'). In: Christian Friedrich Schwartz: His Contributions to South India. N.p. 1999, 215–221.

Edward James: Brief Memoirs of the late Right Reverend John Thomas James, D.D. Lord Bishop of Calcutta, Particularly During his Residence in India Gathered from his Letters and Papers. London 1830.

Roget Jeffery and Duncan Money: India in Edinburgh: 1750s to the Present. In: India in Edinburgh. 1750s to the Present. Ed. by Roger Jeffery. London 2019, 1–21.

Edward Jenner: An Inquiry into the Causes and Effects of the Variolæ Vaccinæ: a Disease Discovered in some of the Western Counties of England, Particularly Gloucestershire and Known by the Name of The Cow Pox. London: Sampson Low, 1798.

Daniel Jeyaraj: Luther's Works in Tamil. In: Lutheran Quarterly 37, 2023, issue 2, 159–171.

Peter Joseph du Plat: Brief vom 29. Mārz 1784. In: A Great War in South India: German Accounts of the Anglo-Mysore Wars, 1766–1799. Ed. by Ravi Ahuja and Martin Christof-Füchsle. Berlin 2020, 345–356.

M. Justus: Schwartz: A Missionary in Politics 1750–1798. In: Indian Church History Review 27, 1992, issue 1, 36–49.

John William Kaye: The Administration of the East India Company. A History of Indian Progress. London ²1853.

Kenneth A. R. Kennedy: The Legacy of Sir William Jones: Natural History, Anthropology, Archaeology. In: Bulletin of the Deccan College Post-Graduate and Research Institute 54 & 55, 1994–1995, 23–33.

Eliza F. Kent: Raja Clarinda—Widow, Concubine, Patroness: Women's Leadership in the Indian Church. In: Halle and the Beginning of Protestant Christianity in India. Vol. II: Communication between India and Europe. Ed. by Andreas Gross et al. Halle 2006, 659–684.

Isaac Kimber: The History of England from Earliest Accounts to the Accession of his present Majesty King George II. London: Thomas Cox, 1755.

David Kling: The New Divinity and the Origins of the American Board of Commissioners of Foreign Missions. In: Church History 72, 2003, issue 4, 791–819.

Elizabeth Kolsky: Colonial Justice in British India—White Violence and the Rule of Law. New Delhi 2009.

Xavier Koodapuzha: Christianity in India. Kottayam 1998.

R. Krishnamurthi: The Hindu Religious Institutions: State and Society in the Thanjavur Region, AD 1532–1855. Diss. phil. Trichy 2000.

Yukishia Kumagai: Breaking into the Monopoly–Provincial Merchants and Manufactures' Campaigns for Access to the Asian Market, 1790–1833. Leiden 2012.

Chandrakant Lahariya: A brief history of vaccines & vaccination in India. In: Indian Journal of Medical Research 139, 2014, issue 4, 491–511.

G.H. Lamb: Memoir of Christian Friedrick Schwartz. Madras 1948.

Charles Lawson: Memoirs of Madras. London 1905.

Arno Lehmann: Es begann in Tranquebar: Die Geschichte der ersten evangelischen Kirche in Indien. Berlin 1955.

Charles Leslie: A Short and Easy Method with the Deists, wherein the Certainty of the Christian Religion is demonstrated by infallible Proof from Four Rules, which are incompatible to any Imposture that ever yet has been, and that can possibly be. London: George Strahan, ⁹1745 (¹1694).

Heike Liebau: Christoph Samuel John's Essay on Education Policy. In: Halle and the Beginning of Protestant Christianity in India. Vol. III: Communication between India and Europe. Ed. by Andreas Gross et al. Halle 2006, 1323–1332.

Heike Liebau: Cultural Encounters in India – The Local Co-Workers of Tranquebar Mission, 18th to 19th Centuries. Transl. Rekha V. Rajan. London 2017.

Life of Christian F. Swartz: Missionary at Travancore [sic! = Tanjore], A.D. 1750–1798. London 1855.

Life of the Eminent Missionary Swartz. In: The Methodist Magazine 37, 1814, 241–250.

Life of Swartz. In: The Sunday at Home—A Family Magazine for Sabbath Reading 1860, 629–632, 644–648, 662–662 and 677–680.

Hans Lilje: Der Königspriester: eine indische Novelle. Tübingen 1946.

Lives of Missionaries—Southern India [Ziegenbalg, Schwartz, Jaenicke and Gericke]. London 1854.

Henry Davidson Love: Vestiges of Old Madras 1640–1800 traced from the East India Company's records preserved at Fort St. George and the India Office and from other sources with maps and illustrations. Vol. 1. London 1913. Vol. 3. London 1913.

Andrew Mackillop: Fashioning a 'British' Empire: Sir Archibald Campbell of Inverell & Madras, 1785–91. In: Military Governors and Imperial Frontiers c. 1600–1800: A study of Scotland and Empires. Ed. by Andrew MacKillop and Steve Murdoch. Leiden 2003, 205–231.

Hugh MacLeod: Introduction. The Decline of Christendom in Western Europe, 1750–2000. Ed. by Hugh MacLeod and Werner Ustorf. Cambridge 2003, 1–26.

Anantanarayanan Madhaviah: Clarinda—Historical Novel. Tirunelveli ²1992.

K. Manamalar: Administration and Social Life under the Mahrathas of Thanjavur. Diss. phil. Trichy 1995.

K.A. Manikumar: 1806 revolt at Vellore Fort. In: Frontline, 30 July 2021. URL: https://frontline.thehindu.com/the-nation/spark-from-vellore-1806-fort-mutiny-1857-revolt/article35257752.ece (accessed on 28.10.2024).

S. Manonmani et al.: A Review of beneficial effects of Siddha medicinal herbs on Snake bite. In: International Journal of Current Research in Biology and Medicine 1, 2016, issue 7, 27–25.

A.T. Markose: Judicial Control of Administrative Action in India – A Study in Methods. Madras 1956.

Arthur Mayhew: Christianity and the Government of India. London 1929.

James William McClendon: Biography as Theology: How Life Stories Can Remake Today's Theology. Nashville 1974.

Minakshi Menon: Medicine, Money and the Making of the East India Company State: William Roxburgh in Madras, c. 1790. In: Histories of Medicine and Healing in the Indian Ocean World. Ed. by Anna Winterbottom and Facil Tesfaye. Vol. 1. London 2015, 151–178.

B.B. Misra.: The Central Administration of the East India Company, 1773–1834. Bombay 1959.

C.S. Mohanavelu: German Missionaries and Rabies Hydrophobia. Mission History as History of Globalization of Indigenous Tamil Medical Knowledge of 18th century. In: Missionsgeschichte als Geschichte der Globalisierung von Wissen. Ed. by Ulrich van der Heyden and Andreas Feldtkeller. Stuttgart 2012, 213–223.

Henry Morris: Charles Grant and the Part he took in the Formation of the Church Missionary Society. In: Church Missionary Intelligencer 1901, 337–353.

Henry Morris: The Life of Charles Grant Sometimes Member of Parliament for Inverness-Shire and Director of the East India Company. London 1904.

Innes Munro: A Narrative of the Military Operations on the Coromandel Coast: Against the Combined Forces of the French, Dutch and Hyder Ally Cawn, From the Year 1780 to the Peace in 1784. London: T. Bensley, 1789.

Francis S. Muthu: History of Education in Tamil Nadu. Chennai 2020.

Harish Naraindas: Preparing for the Pox: A Theory of Smallpox in Bengal and Britain. In: Asian Journal of Social Science 31, issue 2: Special Focus: Asian Development and Welfare in Crisis 2003, 304–339.

Stephen Neill: A History of Christianity in India (1707–1858). Vol. 2. Cambridge 1985.

Stephen Neill: God's Apprentice: The Autobiography of Bishop Stephen Neill. Ed. by Eleanor M. Jackson. London 1991.

Anders Nørgaard: Secretaries of the Mission Board in Copenhagen 1714–1868. In: Halle and the Beginning of Protestant Christianity in India. Vol. III: Communication between India and Europe. Ed. by Andreas Gross et al. Halle 2006, 1565–1567.

Pramod K. Nayar: The British Raj–Keywords. London 2017.

V. Noah Gnanadickam Sastriyar: Life of Vedanayagam Sastriyar. Tanjore 1987.

Sāstiriyār Noah: Vētanāyakam cāstiriyāriṉ paṭaippil tantai Schwartz (in Tamil: 'Father Schwartz in the works of Vēdanāyagam Sāstiriyār'). An unpublished essay in commemoration of Schwartz's 225th death anniversary. I am grateful to Judah Vincent, who emailed me a copy of this essay on 16 September 2023.

Daniel O'Connor: Secretaries of the Society for Promoting Christian Knowledge (SPCK) […]. In: Halle and the Beginning of Protestant Christianity in India. Vol. III: Communication between India and Europe. Ed. by Andreas Gross et al. Halle 2006, 1561–1564.

Daniel O'Connor: The Chaplains of the East India Company, 1601–1858. London 2012.

Rosalind O'Hanlon: Letters Home—Banaras pandits and the Maratha regions in early modern India. In: Modern Asian Studies 44, 2010, issue 2, 201–240.

Jesse Page: Schwartz of Tanjore. London 1921.

Papers Relating to East India Affairs (Resident Europeans – Police – MISSIONAIRES – Weavers and Investments), Ordered by The House of Commons, to be printed 14 April 1813, 86. N.p: n.p. n.d.

Julius Pauli: Roberto dei Nobili und Christian Friedrich Schwartz: zwei Missionare in Ostindien. Nürnberg 1870.

Frank Penny: The Church in Madras being the History of the Ecclesiastical and Missionary action of the East India Company in the Presidency of Madras in the Seventeenth and Eighteenth Centuries with illustrations. Vol. 1. London 1904.

India Viswanathan Peterson: The Cabinet of King Serfoji of Tanjore: A European Collection in early nineteenth-century India. In: Journal of Historical Collections 11, 1999, issue 1, 71–93.

Indira Viswanathan Peterson: Multilingual Dramas at the Tanjavur Maratha Court and Literary Cultures in Early Modern South India. In: The Medieval History Journal 14, 2011, issue 2, 285–321.

Indira Viswanathan Peterson: Tanjore, Tranquebar and Halle: European Science and German Missionary Education in the Lives of Two Indian Intellectuals in the Early Nineteenth Century. In: Christians and Missionaries in India: Cross-Cultural Communications since 1500. Ed. by R. E. Frykenberg. Grand Rapids 2003, 93–126.

P. Perumal: The Sanskrit Manuscripts in Tamilnadu. In: Aspects of Manuscript Culture in South India. Ed. by Saraju Rath. Leiden 2012, 157–172.

C. H. Philips. The East India Company 1784–1834. Manchester 1940.

Jim Phillips: A Successor to the Moguls: The Nawab of the Carnatic and the East India Company, 1763–1785. In: The International History Review 7, 1985, issue 3, 364–389.

Philochristos: Respecting the late Mr. Swartz. In: The Christian Observer 1, 1802, issue 6, 349–350.

Otto Podczeck: August Hermann Franckes Schrift über eine Reform des Erziehungs- und Bildungswesens als Ausgangspunkt einer geistlichen und sozialen Neuordnung der Evangelischen Kirche des 18. Jahrhunderts: Der Grosse Aufsatz mit einer quellenkundlichen Einführung. Berlin 1962.

Savithri Preetha Nair: Raja Serfoji II: Science, Medicine and Enlightenment in Tanjore. London 2012.

Savithri Preetha Nair: Diseases of the Eye: Medical Pluralism at the Tanjore Court in the Early Nineteenth Century. In: Social History of Medicine 25, 2012, issue 2, 573–588.

Charles C. Prinsep: Record of Services of the Honourable East India Company's Civil Servants in the Madras Presidency from 1741 to 1858. London 1885.

Proclamation by the Queen [Victoria] in Council to the Princes, Chiefs and people of India. Allahabad 1858. URL https://www.bl.uk/collection-items/

proclamation-by-the-queen-in-council-to-the-princes-chiefs-and-people-of-india (accessed on 20.11.2024).

V.S. Radhika: Development of Sadir in the court of Raja Serfoji-II (1798–1832) of Tanjore. Diss. phil. Hyderabad 2011.

V. Raghavan: The Sarva-Deva-Vilāsa edited with Critical Introduction and Notes, rpt. (1957). Madras 1958 ([1]1957).

K. Rajayyan: British Annexation of the Carnatic, 1801. In: Proceedings of the Indian History Congress 32, Part 2, 1970, 54–62.

Anantanarayanan Raman: Samuel Cnoll in Tranquebar and establishment of the first pharmacy – Laboratorium Chymicum in India in 1732. In: Current Science 11,2017, issue 3, 368–369.

Ramya Raman, Anantanarayanan Raman and P. Ram Manohar: Tanjore pills used in treating snake bites in the 18th century Madras Presidency. In: Current Science 106, 2014, issue 12, 1759–1763.

Vijaya Ramaswamy: Historical Dictionary of the Tamils. Lanham, MD [2]2017 ([1]2006).

Chidambaram Srinivasachari Ramanujam: British Relations with Tanjore (1748–1799). Dr. phil. London 1968.

Parimala V. Rao: Modern education and the revolt of 1857 in India. Paedagogia Historia, 52, 2016, issue 1–2, 25–42.

Simon Rastén: The Tranquebar tribute: Contested perceptions during the reign of Rajah Serfoji II of Tanjore. In: Review of Development and Change 14, 2009, issue 1 and 2, 41–60.

Revisiting Napoleon's Continental System–Local, Regional and European Experiences. Ed. by Katherine B. Aaslestad and Johan Joor. Basingstoke 2014.

Julius Richter: A History of Missions in India. Transl. Sydney H. Moore. New York 1908.

Brian Roberts: Biographical research. Buckingham 2002.

J. Albert Rorabacher: Property, Land, Revenue and Policy: The East India Company, c. 1757–1825. London 2016.

M. Ruthnaswamy: Some Influences that Made the British Administrative System in India. London 1939.

S. Santha Praburaj: An Analysis of Schwartz materials in the Tamil Nadu Archives. In: Christian Friedrich Schwartz: His Contributions to South India. Ed. by Daniel Jeyaraj. Chennai 1999, 105–116.

P. Richter: Christian Friedrich Schwartz. In: Geschichte und Bilder aus der Mission 16 (Der Ostindischen Missions-Nachrichten – Neue Folge. Ed. by W. Fries), 1898, 1–15.

Thomas Robinson: Last Days of Bishop Heber. London 1830.

K. Sasikala: Tipu Sultan's Invasions in Tamilnadu 1782–1799: A Study. Diss. phil. Annamalai 2015. URL: http://hdl.handle.net/10603/181671 (accessed on 10.10.2024).

Karl Christian Gottlieb Schmidt: Kurzgefaßte Lebensbeschreibungen der merkwürdigsten evangelischen Missionare. Vol. 1. Leipzig 1836, 71–101.

Fred D. Schneider: Parliament, the East India Company and the Calcutta Bishopric. In: Journal of Church and State 16, 1974, issue 1, 51–71.

Selections from the Letters, Despatches and Other State Papers Preserved in the Bombay Secretariat—Home Series. Ed. by George W. Forrest. Vol. II. Bombay 1887.

Radhika Seshan: From Folk Culture to Court Culture: The 'Kuravanji' in the Tanjore Court. In: Proceedings of the Indian History Congress 65, 2004, 331–334.

Graham Shaw: The Tanjore 'Aesop' in the Context of Early Marathi Printing. In: The Library 5, 1978, issue 3, 207–214.

John Shore: Considerations on the Practicability, Policy and Obligations of Communicating to the Natives of India the Knowledge of Christianity. London 1808.

Elin Silen: Christian Friederich Schwartz. Stockholm 1924.

Christina Smylitopoulos: Portrait of a Nabob: Graphic Satire, Portraiture and the Anglo-Indian in the Late Eighteenth Century. In: Canadian Art Review, 37, 2012, issue 1, 10–25.

Jī. Pī. Vī. Sōmaratna and Napoleon Pathmanathan: The Life and Times of Christian David. Colombo 2013.

Small-Pox Before Jenner. In: The British Medical Journal 1, 1896, issue1847, 261–1264.

V. Sriram: History of Medicine in Madras. URL: https://youtu.be/iENqvuz0NOI (accessed on 28.10.2024).

C. S. Srinivasachari: Vignettes from the History of Wallajah Dynasty of the Carnatic, 1744–1855 – Part I & II – Lectures delivered under the auspices of the Osmania University. Hyderabad 1947.

Armin Stein: Christian Friedrich Schwartz: der Apostel Indiens – Ein Lebensbild. Halle (Saale) 1894.

Armin Stein: Christian Friedrich Schwartz: De Apostel von Indië: Een Levensbeeld uit de vorgie eeuw [Dutch: 'Christian Friedrich Schwartz: The Apostle to the Indies—A Portrayal of a Life in the last century'). Gravenhage (i.e. The Hague) 1894.

Eugene Stock: The History of the Church Missionary Society: Its Environment, Its Men and Its Work. Vol. 1. London 1899.

Eugene Stock: Beginnings in India. London 1917.

K. R. Subramanian: The Maratha Rajas of Tanjore. Madras 1928.

J. T. Sunderland: India in Bondage: Her Right to Freedom. New York 1929.

P. Suresh Kumar: The Carnatic Wars and Tanjore Politics 1736–1764. Diss. phil. Tirunelveli 2012. URL: http://hdl.handle.net/10603/133782 (accessed on 20.11.2024).

C. F. Swartz: The Missionary. In: Boston Recorder 20, 14 August 1835, issue 33, 129.

Tamil Lexicon. Vols. I–VI and a Supplementary Volume. Madras 1982.

The Ancient and Modern Methods of Treating Small-Pox in India. The British Medical Journal 2:1293, 1885, 716–717.

The Hibernian Magazine or Compendium of Entertaining Knowledge, January 1771–April 1785, October 1777.

The History of Parliament: British Political, Social & Local History. URL: https://www.historyofparliamentonline.org/ (accessed on 06.01.2025).

The Life of C. F. Swartz—Missionary at Trichinopoly and Tanjore in India. New York 1800.

The Life of Rev. Christian F. Swartz. In: The Panoplist and Missionary Magazine 10, 1813, 289–298.

The Life of the Eminent Missionary Swartz. In: Episcopal Magazine 1, 1820, 37–43, 69–72, 101–110 and 133–144.

The Life of the Eminent Missionary Swartz. In: The Methodist Magazine 37, 1814, 433–443, 451–492, 531–540 and a concluding part in Vol. 38, January 1815. I could not get hold of this 38th volume.

The Life of the Rev. C.F. Swartz—Missionary to the East Indies. In: The Methodist Magazine for the Year of the Lord 2, 1819, 49–57, 89–97, 126–34, 167–174, 207–215 and 251–257.

The Rev. C.F. Schwartz [based on Schwartz's biography published in the *London Christian Guardian*]. In: Philadelphia Recorder, 1830, 92.

The Writings and Speeches of Edmund Burke. Ed. by Peter J. Marshall. Vol. 5: India: Madras and Bengal. Oxford 1981.

Schwartz (From the Gallery of Portraits). In: Littell's Living Age. N.p. July 1844.

Swartz, the Missionary. In: Boston Recorder, 1835, 129.

Thomas Thompson: The Gods of the East Indies: Or, an Account of the Religion of the Hindoos, with a Short Vindication of the Attempts to Propagate Christianity in India. London 1810.

Ruth A. Tucker: Biography as Missiology: Mining the Lives of Missionaries for Cross-Cultural Effectiveness. In: Missiology: An International Review 27, 1999, issue 4, 429–439.

James M. Vaughan: The Politics of Empire at the Accession of George III: The East India Company and the Crisis and Transformation of Britain's Imperial State. New Haven 2019.

Vellore. In: The Saturday Review of Politics, Literature, Science and Art, 4:100, 1857, 273–274.

Vita del Rev. C.F. Swartz: Missionario nelle Indie Orientali, etc. (Italian: 'Life of Rev. C.F. Swartz: Missionary in East India'). Malta 1825.

Gotthilf Heinrich von Schubert: Christian Friedrich Schwartz. Erlangen 1860.

Gotthilf Heinrich von Schubert: Christian Friedrich Schwartz, der Sendbote des Evangeliums in Indien—Aus dem zweiten Bande der vermischten Schriften besonders abgedruckt. Erlangen 1860.

Vaṇakkam. Ed. by S. Rajamanickam. Tuticorin 1963.

Kristen Bergman Waha: Synthesizing Hindu and Christian Ethics in A. Madhaviah's Indian English Novel Clarinda (1915). Victorian Literature and Culture 46, 2018, 237–255.

Ruf Walther: Christian Friedrich Schwartz: der Königspriester von Tanjore. Stuttgart 1957.

Arthur Westcott: Our Oldest Indian Mission: A Brief History of the Vepery (Madras) Mission. Madras 1897.

Mark Wilks: Report on the Interior Administration, Resources and Expenditure of the Government of Mysoor under the system prescribed by the Orders of the Governor General in Council dated 4th September 1799. Fort William (Calcutta) 1805.

Don Wright: Swartz of Thanjavur: Raja Guru? In: Indian Church History Review 15, 1981, issue 2, 123–144.

Don Wright: Swartz of Thanjavur: A missionary in politics. In: Journal of South Asian Studies 1981, 94–105.

Index of Names

A

Abbestée, Peter Hermann 225–226, 229–230, 232–233, 321
Abdul Kalam 365
Abiṣēkanātaṉ 374
Abraham (son of Jōtināyakkaṉ) 376
Aiyen Asary (Ayena Chari) 114, 288, 458–460
Aldwell (teacher in Tiruccirāppaḷḷi) 362, 374, 376
Allan, Alexander 299, 301
Ambāji Jaggarnat Pandit 125
Ambrose (Tamil pastor) 36
Ameer Singh (Amar Singh) / Ramasamy (Rama Swamy, Ramaswamy), Raja of Thanjavur 5, 14–15, 19, 26, 89, 93, 96–101, 103–104, 106–107, 109–137, 145–146, 148, 158, 170, 178, 198, 223–233, 253–264, 272, 274–275, 277, 281–282, 285–293, 296–307, 317, 319–324, 327, 332–335, 344, 363, 369, 373, 412, 415, 448–449, 452, 454, 458, 460–461
Ananda Ranga Pillai 445
Anderson, James 297, 352–355
Anewerdee Cawn Behauder 127
Aṉṉamai 392
Anne, Queen of England, Scotland, and Ireland, Queen of Great Britain and Ireland 53
Annojee Panth 267
Aṉpāyi 392
Anwaruddin Khan, Nawab of the Carnatic (Arcot) 55
Appa Sastry (Appa Chari) 114, 288, 458–460
Appaneh Gady 307
Apthorp, George Henry 164
Arndt, Johann 373
Arulappan 211, 380
Arunachalam 247, 306
Asoph Dowlah 127
Aston, Henry Hervey 299–300
Atwood Newell, Harriet 433

B

Baba (Diwan) 89–90, 92, 98–99, 105, 107, 125, 232, 257, 322, 324, 333–334
Babajee Bhonsle 94, 289
Babington, Thomas, 424
Backe, Johann Friedrich, 31–33, 171
Backer, Henry 443
Bagavati 296
Bailey, Benjamin 442–443
Baillie, William 209, 211
Baird, David 218–219, 296
Baldaeus, Philipp, 48
Bärenbruck, Georg T. 442
Baring, Francis 439
Baumgarten, Siegund Jakob 32
Baupanā (Baupanah) 108–109, 131, 333
Bāvanna Pandit (Bava) 119, 231, 318–319
Beck, Thomas 427–431
Becker, Wilhelm David 174, 243
Bell, Andrew 246, 270–271, 372
Benfield, Paul 25, 56, 67–68, 71, 73–76, 189, 210, 364
Bentinck, William Cavendish 431–432

Berg, Johann Wilhelm 45–46, 52–53, 59, 62–63
Berkeley, George 248
Bhapana (Bapina) 114, 253, 265, 288, 458–460
Bhavana Jetro 266
Bhavānī Bāi 306–307, 315
Bie, Ole 174, 232
Bijenrow Krist (Biying Rao, Biyenrow Kist) 114, 288, 458–460
Bille, Gerhard Sievers 234
Binny, Charles 127
Blackburn, William 120, 148, 203, 306–307, 309
Blake, William Herbert 84
Blanchard, Thomas 412
Blood, James 271
Bogatzky, Carl Heinrich von 364
Bonaparte (Buonaparte), Napoleon, Emperor of the French 218, 427
Bosworth, Anne 373
Bourchier, James 56
Brainard, David 428–429
Braithwaite, John 269, 278, 292, 311
Breithaupt, Johann Christian 19, 63, 143, 176, 209, 239
Brochmann, Anna Christiana 48
Brochmann, Johann Burchard 48
Brotherton, Thomas 162, 164–165
Brown, David 97, 174, 398, 410, 412, 424, 430
Buchan, George 149
Buchanan, Claudius 149, 154, 175–176, 181, 185, 191, 390, 399, 425–426, 430, 432, 438
Burghall, George 75–76, 201
Burke, Edmund 210, 427
Butler, John 296, 301

C

Call, James 56
Call, John 56
Calmette, Albert 349
Cämmerer, August Friedrich 143, 159, 295, 313, 326, 392–393, 396, 406
Campbell, Alexander Montgomery 15, 117, 127, 342, 414–418, 420–421, 423, 425, 466
Campbell, Amelia 271, 371–373, 421, 467
Campbell, Archibald 89–90, 92–99, 102–105, 109, 112–117, 119–121, 123–128, 131, 198, 221, 224, 228, 230–231, 236, 253–255, 258, 285, 287–289, 291, 297, 319–321, 323, 329–330, 333, 342, 344, 351–352, 371, 373, 415, 421, 458
Campbell, Charles 58
Campe, Theodor Rudolf 30
Cāntappā 108
Carey, Charlotte Emilia 399
Carey, Dorothea 399
Carey, Grace 399
Carey, William 174, 399, 407, 430, 433, 438
Caroline Mathilde of Great Britain, Queen consort of Denmark and Norway 227
Carr, Robert 412
Casamajor, James Henry 97, 99, 121, 127
Cawn, Mohamed Lassier 105
Chambers, Robert 144–145, 319, 324
Chambers, William 144–145, 172, 174, 188, 235, 324, 397–399, 410–411, 424
Chamier, John 90, 104, 120, 123–124, 127, 253, 328, 367
Chana Saheb 296
Chanda Sahib 18, 58, 432
Charlotte Amalie, Princess of Denmark and Norway 35

Charlotte of Mecklenburg-Strelitz, Queen consort of Great Britain and Ireland 55
Chinna Marudhu 208
Chintaman Row Putwardan 309
Christian Krishna Pal 399
Christian VI, King of Denmark and Norway 227
Christian VII, King of Denmark and Norway 35, 200, 227, 447
Ciṉṉaiyā Mudali (Ciṉṉappā Mutali, Chenniah Moodely, Chinnia) 296, 323, 333–334
Clarinda / Kohila 180, 187, 326, 384, 387–395, 448, 450
Clarke, Abraham Thomas 412
Classe, Samuel 159
Clive, Edward 307
Clive, Robert 45, 173, 190, 199, 210, 319, 343, 409, 427
Cnoll, Samuel 44, 52
Cobb, James 149
Coke, Thomas 397–398
Colitapa Moodally 74
Congreve, Charles Walter 165
Coote, Eyre 55, 86, 199, 202, 209, 418
Cornwallis, Charles 12, 27, 102, 112–113, 132, 190, 198, 218, 255, 263–264, 272, 275, 285–287, 289–291, 372, 410, 412–413, 415, 417, 423, 438
Corrie, Daniel 430
Cowper, William 434, 437–438, 451
Cradock, John 431
Cunningham, John William 430

D

Dada Rao (Dada Row) 113, 255, 264, 266, 268, 275–276, 284, 288, 319, 458–460
Damarla Vengadappa 11
Dame, Peter 46, 51
Dattajee (Dettajee) 264–268, 272, 274–277, 284, 292–293, 295–297, 299, 305
David, Christian / Chinnamuthu David Sundarānantham (Sundaranandam) 157, 164, 180, 337, 378, 386, 394, 399–400, 403
Davidson, Alexander 79, 99, 121, 127, 198
Davidson, Elizabeth 79
Davidson, Lydia 79
Davidson, Margaret 79
Davidson, Mary 79
Day, Francis 11
De Marchis, Francoise 247
De Souza, Bento 174, 230, 291
Dēvanēsan 64, 373
Dēvasagāyam 374–375, 377–378, 391–392, 395–396
Devaynes, William 23
Diago (Tamil pastor) 36, 45, 224
Diemer, Johann Christmann 174, 241, 404
Dost Ali Khan, Nawab of the Carnatic (Arcot) 17
Draupadī Bāi Sāhibā (Dropada Bhaie) 97, 111, 254–255, 257–258, 260, 263–268, 272, 295, 297, 304
Du Pré, Josias 68
Duffin, Elizabeth 381
Duffin, William 188, 351–352, 381
Dundas, Henry 117, 342, 413, 416, 440
Dupleix, Joseph François 445
Dusthall, Anna 355–356

E

Eck, Lubbert Jan van 47
Egerton, Henry 38
Elers, George 300
Elphinstone, Christian 400, 445, 450
Enfield, William 270
Evans, Elisabeth 48, 247

F

Fabricius, Johann Philipp 19, 37, 51, 62–64, 154–155, 165, 173–174, 176, 192, 203, 209, 234, 236, 238–241, 243, 248–249, 340, 342, 362, 371, 415, 452–453
Fabricius, Sebastian Andreas 31, 37
Fallowfield, Earnest William 131–132, 134, 254, 257–258, 324–325
Fatima Khamum 432
Faulkner, William, 271
Fenn, Joseph 443
Finckenhagen, Johann 33, 49, 168
Fitzgerald, Thomas 75
Flaxman, John 149, 406
Fletcher, Robert 71
Floyer, Charles 18
Forster, Johann Reinhold 354
Francke, August Hermann 3, 29, 31, 169, 184
Francke, Gotthilf August 4, 30, 32–33, 36–38, 41–46, 49, 52–53, 56–57, 59–63, 156, 166, 168, 174, 200, 447
Francke, Johanna Sophia Anastasia 29
Frederick (Friedrich) IV, King of Denmark and Norway 34–35, 227
Frederick (Friedrich) V, King of Denmark and Norway 4, 35, 227
Frederick (Friedrich) VI, King of Denmark and Norway 227
Frederick (Friedrich), Hereditary Prince of Denmark and Norway 227
Frederick William (Friedrich Wilhelm) II, King of Prussia 205
Frenzel, Johann Gottfried 174
Freylinghausen, Auguste Sophie 29
Freylinghausen, Gottlieb Anastasius 63, 77, 80, 84, 87, 165, 169, 174–175, 204, 207–208, 234, 238–240, 242–244, 248–249, 339–340, 374–378, 384
Freylinghausen, Johann Anastasius 29, 32
Friskin, John 271
Fullarton, William 145
Fürchtenicht, Lambert Christian 405

G

Gabriel (catechist) 339, 375
Gadiasalam 267
Ganapathy Subbiah 131, 333
Garrow, Edward 236
Gaskin, George 348, 417
George III, King of Great Britain and Ireland 5, 25–26, 55, 66, 72–73, 209, 227, 441
George of Denmark, Consort of the Queen of Britain 53
Gericke, Christian Wilhelm 48, 138–144, 147, 154–155, 176, 182–184, 189, 192, 218, 236, 239, 244, 247–249, 264, 266–279, 282–284, 292–293, 295–298, 302–303, 345, 348, 359, 371, 373, 377–378, 381, 386, 393, 405–406, 417–418, 436, 438, 442, 449
Gerlach, Johann Wilhelm 79, 174, 243, 250–251, 404
Goethe, Johann Wolfgang von 29
Govinder Row Gady 306–307
Gowri Parvati Bayi, Maharani Regent of Travancore 443
Graham, Thomas 434, 438, 451
Grant, Allen 421, 467
Grant, Charles 174, 341–342, 396–399, 410–411, 413, 415, 420–421, 423–427, 438, 440, 466–467
Grant, Robert 423–424
Gray, George 207, 449
Gründler, Johann Ernest 48
Grundt, Michael 30
Gude, Jacob 168, 243–244

Guldberg, Christiana Sophia 243
Gunavathy 131
Gunna Pilly Soubiah 253

H

Hagelund, Peder Rubek 225, 245, 386, 404
Hagemeister, Lubert Johann 238
Halhed, Nathaniel Brassey 114–115, 290, 325
Haliburton, David 264
Hall, Gordon 433
Halle, Johanna Catherina 48
Hamilcar Barca 218
Hamshaw, John 181
Hancock, Charles 271
Hannibal 218
Hanock, Tysoe Saul 348
Harland, Robert 66
Harris, George 298–299, 301
Hasseltine Judson, Ann 433
Hastings, Warren 25, 27, 190, 200–202, 409, 415, 427, 434–435, 439–440, 451
Haubroe, Lawrence Peter 83
Heber, Reginald 151–153, 188–189, 194, 400, 443, 447
Hee Wadum, Christen 168, 244
Helm (Rector in Sonnenburg) 30
Heron, Alexander 343
Hersleb, Peter 4, 34
Hindenburg, Johann Heinrich Bernhardt 32
Hippisley, John Coxe 25, 89, 93–95, 97, 99, 101, 105–106, 109–110, 119, 124, 212–213, 224, 329
Hobart, Robert 136, 267, 269, 273–274, 292–294, 296–299, 304–305, 334
Hodge Mill, William 451
Høegh-Guldberg, Ove 227
Holland, John 97, 146, 322
Holstein, Johann Ludwig von 33
Holwell, John Zephaniah 356–357, 365
Holzberg, Gottfried Immanuel 138–140, 174, 182–183, 406
Horne, Melville 256, 429
Horst, Christina Magdalena 185
Horst, Christoph Heinrich 185, 406
Hudleston, John 89–91, 93–101, 103, 111, 148–149, 151, 188, 213–214, 328–331
Hudleston, William 101
Hüttemann, Andreas 247
Hüttemann, Anna Sophia 247
Hüttemann, Carl 247
Hüttemann, Christian Friedrich 247
Hüttemann, Elisabeth *see* Evans, Elisabeth
Hüttemann, Ernst Georg Friedrich 247
Hüttemann, Georg Heinrich Conrad 33–34, 37, 41, 46, 48, 51, 57, 138, 173–174, 243, 247, 248–250, 371
Hüttemann, Georg Heinrich Conrad, Jr. 247
Hüttemann, Gracy Dorothea 247
Hüttemann, Johann Heinrich 247
Hüttemann, Samuel 247
Hyder Ali, Sultan of Mysore 4–5, 12, 14, 23–24, 60, 64–66, 68–69, 84, 86, 88, 126, 145, 148, 151, 174–175, 177, 185–186, 189–190, 197, 199–214, 219, 228, 234–235, 256, 318, 327, 348, 363, 411, 427, 432, 449

I

In̲n̲ācimuttu 14, 60, 62, 373–375

J

Jackson, Randel 435
Jackson, William Collins 232–233, 257–260, 262–263, 286, 328
James, John Thomas 188–189, 443

Jänicke, Joseph Daniel 124, 139, 141–142, 144, 155, 157, 176, 183, 187, 295, 299–302, 371, 379, 390, 392–393, 399–400, 407, 454
Jenkinson, Robert Banks 409
Jenner, Edward 187, 358
John, Christoph Samuel 79–80, 128–129, 137–139, 143, 146, 164, 183–184, 187, 209, 225, 229, 242–247, 261, 279, 282–283, 311, 313, 336–337, 343, 350–354, 369–370, 392–393, 396, 399, 432, 449
Johnson, Francis 271
Johnson, William 409–410
Jones, William 435
Joseph (Schwartz's servant) 85, 143, 368–369, 377
Jōtināyakkaṉ 14, 54, 62, 173, 373–374, 376
Judson, Adoniram, Jr. 433
Juliane Marie of Brunswick-Wolfenbüttel, Queen consort of Denmark and Norway 35, 227

K

Kanagasabai Pillai 75
Kant, Immanuel 169
Kareem Bibie 432
Kenrich, Robert 271
Kerr, Richard Hall 149, 151, 425
Kiernander, Ann 173–174
Kiernander, Johann (John) Zacharias 38, 46, 173–174, 187, 225, 248, 250, 371, 397–398, 410, 424, 434
Kiernander, Robert 174
Kindersley, Nathaniel Edward 397
Klein, Christian Daniel 377
Klein, Jacob 49, 52–53, 56, 119, 122, 124, 225, 228–229, 234, 240, 242–243, 245, 349–350, 366, 377, 386
Klein, Johann Gottfried 352–353
Knapp, Georg Christian 31, 169, 171, 182–184, 188, 405
Knapp, Johann Georg 30, 32, 62, 66, 168, 362
Knospe, Christian Friedrich 30–31, 33, 143
Knospe, Maria Sophia *see* Schwartz, Maria Sophia
Kohlhoff, Anna Regina 49
Kohlhoff, Christian Daniel 185
Kohlhoff, Christian Samuel 386
Kohlhoff, Daniel Friedrich 185
Kohlhoff, Dorothea Elisabeth 185
Kohlhoff, Elias Eobanus 85, 185
Kohlhoff, Johann (John) Caspar 32, 80, 83, 85, 139, 143–144, 146, 148, 151–152, 155, 158, 164, 175–176, 181–188, 194, 217, 241, 295, 302, 314, 362, 364, 366, 368, 376–377, 379, 381–386, 390, 392, 400, 406–407, 425, 443, 450–451, 453
Kohlhoff, Johann Balthasar 21, 49, 51–52, 148, 185, 242–245, 362, 381, 383, 385
Kohlhoff, John Schwartz Adolphus Arthur 176
Kohlhoff, Pernille *see* Thors, Pernille
Kolidappa Mudali 364
König, Johann Friedrich (John Frederick) 225, 243, 386, 392
Krahe, Atilia Elisabeth 48
Krishna Rao 213
Krishnacharya Purnaiah 213
Krishnaji Pandit 126
Krishnaraja Wadiyar II, Maharaja of Mysore 199–200, 212
Krishnaraja Wadiyar III / Mummadi Krishnaraja Wadiyar (Wodeyar), Maharaja of Mysore 199, 213, 431
Krüger, Johann Gottlob 32

L

Lakshmi Ammani Rao, Maharani of Mysore 199, 212–213
Lalla Sahib 211
Landon, James 236
Lawrence, Stringer 45, 343, 356
Leslie, Charles 165
Leslie, Richard 371
Liele, George 429
Lindsay, John 55, 205
Lloyd, T. 412
Louis XV, King of France 18
Louis XVI, King of France 283, 414
Lushington, Stephen Rumbold 434, 437–438, 441
Luther, Martin 183
Lütkens, Franz Julius 34
Lygaard, Oluf 48
Lyttleton, Henry 326, 387–388, 394
Lyttleton, Henry, Jr. 387, 388–389, 392

M

Macartney, George 26–27, 85–87, 170, 198–199, 212–215, 418
Machiavelli, Niccolò 134, 326
Mackenzie, Colin 100
Mackintosh, James 430
MacLeod, Alexander 104, 303
Macpherson, John 127
Madan Mohan 399
Madava Asary (Madava Chari) 114, 288, 458–460
Maderup, Oluf 242
Madhav Rao I 200
Madzah Khatoor 432
Mahadie Row 265
Majendie, Andrew 56
Manapa 319
Māppillai Tevar 208
Mar Dionysius 442
Mariyacavari 390–391
Mariyammāḷ 389
Marshman, Hannah 399
Marshman, Joshua 399
Martini, Dorothea Louisa *see* Schwartz, Dorothea Louisa
Martini, Gottlieb Friedrich Ludwig 30
Martins (Martinz), Manuel 141, 176, 366, 401–402
Martyn, Henry 400, 407, 430
Maunsell, Robert 97, 230
Maya Bāi Sāhibā 303–304
Meadows, William 132
Meer Khan 432
Mein, Nicol 357
Mentel, Johann Daniel 243, 404
Metcalfe, Thomas 430
Middleton, Thomas Fanshawe 164, 187–189, 442, 451
Millingchamp, Benjamin 371
Mills, Samuel 433
Mīnāṭci 264
Minto, Gilbert Elliott Murray-Kynynmound 149, 432
Mir Sadiq 218
Mitchell, William 359
Mohana Bāi Sāhibā (Mohana Bhaie Saheb) 135, 183, 190, 254–258, 260–268, 272, 279, 285, 288-289, 292, 295–296, 297, 303–306
Mohana Chatrapati Maharani Bāi Sāhibā 315
Mootiamoopeh 107
Mossel, Jacob 359
Muhammad (Mohammad) Ali Khan Wallajah, Nawab of the Carnatic (Arcot) 12, 18–22, 24–25, 45, 54–61, 64–77, 80, 82–85, 88, 90–91, 93, 98, 102, 105, 107, 109–111, 117–118, 121, 125–128, 135, 141, 145, 172, 176, 178, 195, 199–203, 206, 208, 210–211, 219–220, 228, 234–236, 238–239, 266, 318–319, 327, 330–331, 342, 346,

364, 366, 372, 376, 415, 418, 427, 454
Muhammad Lassier Cawn 105
Muhammad Panah 235
Muhammad Yusuf Khan 57
Müller, Friedrich Max 341
Munro, Hector 25, 75, 82–85, 202, 208–211, 363
Munro, John 443
Murari Row 200
Muthu Krishna 364
Mutturāmaliṅgam 65

N
Nadir Shah, Shah of Iran 60
Nagappa Chetty 135
Ñāṉamuttu 339, 375, 378
Ñāṉapirakācam 54, 64, 173, 336, 339, 374–375, 377–378, 382–383, 389–391, 395
Ñāṉappū 395
Ñāṉēntira Kaṇiyāṉ 395
Narain Pillay 74
Narasinga Asary (Narasingha Chari) 114, 288, 458–460
Narasiṅga Rao (Row) 65
Nebuchadnezzar II, King of Babylon 281
Newell, Samuel 433
Newman, Henry 37
Niekamp, Johann Lucas 39–40
Niemeyer, August Hermann 29, 169
Niemeyer, Johann Konrad Philipp 29, 33, 37
Nobili, Roberto de 192
Noṇṭi Ñāṉi 395
North, Frederick 24, 73
Norton, Thomas 442–443
Nott, Samuel 433

O
Oakley, Charles 132–135, 176, 256, 259–260, 262, 272–275, 285–286, 288, 291, 304, 307, 359–360
Oakley, Helena 269
Obeck, Johann Christian 396–399, 424, 450
Obuch, Anna 46, 48
Obuch, Anna Dorothea 51
Omdit ul Mulk 127
Owen, John 182, 412–413

P
Pachiyappa Mudaliar 446
Paḻaṉiyappā 108
Palk, Robert 19, 59, 356
Pap, Anna Sophie 49, 51
Parry, Edward 413, 440
Pārvatī Bāi 306
Pasche, Friedrich Wilhelm 62–63, 69–70, 76–77, 81–82, 85–88, 92, 124, 138, 158, 169–170, 172–174, 197–198, 218–220, 222, 224, 239–242, 248–249, 329, 340, 347, 349, 362, 365–366, 368, 370–372, 376–378, 384–385, 397, 404, 443
Paulel Asary (Pattala Chari) 114, 288, 458–459, 460
Päzold, Karl Wilhelm 159, 183–185, 405–406
Pearson, Hugh Nicholas 153, 176, 181, 187–189, 191, 403, 426, 438, 451
Peash Begum 432
Peck Nott, Rosanne 433
Periya Marudhu 208
Perumāḷ Nāyakkar 223
Petrie, William 76, 131, 145–146, 229–231, 321–322, 333
Philipp (Tamil Pastor) 211
Piccaimuttu / Antōni Muttu 390–392
Pigot, George 19, 21, 68, 70–71, 74, 76, 83, 85, 93, 102, 111–112, 189, 201–202, 210, 330, 348, 364, 415
Pillay, Daniel 122, 124, 211, 225, 229, 320–321, 325

Piragasam 337
Pitt, William, the Elder 25
Pitt, William, the Younger 25
Pius VII, Pope 443
Plütschau, Heinrich 34–35, 192, 428
Pocock, George 200
Pohle, Christian 79–80, 83, 107, 138–139, 142, 147, 170, 173, 183–185, 187, 217, 240–244, 339–340, 348, 362–363, 366, 368, 381–383, 385, 388–389, 391–392, 396, 406, 454
Poltzenhagen, David 33–34, 37, 43, 173, 247
Pratap Singh (Pratāpasimha, Pratab Sing), Raja of Thanjavur 17–18, 21, 45, 52–56, 64, 73, 85, 93, 106–107, 109–111, 125, 253, 317
Preston, Achilles 53–59
Pybus, John 56

R
Raghunatha Rao (Row) 65, 68
Rājanāyakkaṉ 36
Rajesh Bāi Sāhibā 135, 183, 190, 254–258, 262–268, 272, 279, 285, 288–289, 292, 295–297
Ram Mohan Roy 444
Ram, George Andrew 131–132, 134, 146, 223, 253–255, 257–259, 296, 322, 324–325, 332–334, 351
Rama Sastry (Rama Asary, Rama Shastri, Ramasastri) Prabhune 114, 288, 290, 458–460
Ramaiah 106
Ramaswamy *see* Amar Singh
Raout Row Nerwall 307
Rätzel, Benjamin Friedrich 234, 238
Raumer, Karl Georg von 31
Rauschen Chan 215–217
Rāyappaṉ 64, 81, 138, 337, 373–374, 379–380, 383–384, 389–391
Read, Alexander 91
Redhead (secretary of Thomas Rumbold) 74
Rennell, James 22
Rhenius, Carl Theophilus Ewald 442
Rice, Luther 433
Ringeltaube, Wilhelm Tobias 174
Robinson, Thomas 400
Ross, Andrew 270, 356
Ross, William 278, 331–332
Rottler, John (Johann) Peter 79, 83, 154, 185, 225, 243, 313, 350, 352–353, 386, 392–393, 396, 406
Roxburgh, William 350, 352
Rüdel, Abraham Johann 31
Rudragee Punt 331, 364
Rulfsen, Lorenz Friedrich 243
Rumbold, Thomas 5, 56, 71, 74–75, 84, 177, 189, 200–204, 206–210, 212, 219, 449
Rumbold, William 210

S
Sadasivarow Maitra 268
Sadlier, Anthony 213–214
Sahaji Bhonsle 94
Sallia Nidy Asary (Satta Nidi Achari) 114, 288, 458–460
Salomon (catechist) 375
Salzmann, Maria Dorothea 48
Sambabar of the Carnatic 127
Sambajee Baroh 264
Sambhaji Trimbak 305
Samuel (catechist) 376–377
Samuel (Tamil medical doctor) 139, 351–355
Sāntappaṉ 173, 375, 377, 382
Sarem Bibie 432
Sattiyanātaṉ (Sattianadan) 14, 44, 81, 187, 240–241, 249, 348, 358, 374–380, 391, 393, 403, 443
Savarimuttu 375, 377–378, 393

Savarirājaṉ (Savarirāyaṉ) 375, 380, 395
Savariyammai 392
Sāvitrī Bāi 306
Schmid, Bernard 442
Schultze, Benjamin 30, 32, 48, 157, 161, 184, 248
Schulze, Johann Ludwig 124, 130, 140, 158, 169, 182, 224, 227, 240, 245, 248, 302, 320–321, 327, 363, 423
Schwartz, Anna Katharina Elisabeth 31
Schwartz, Carl Ludwig 30–31, 143, 157, 171
Schwartz, Dorothea Louisa 30, 143
Schwartz, Georg 30, 33–34, 43, 156
Schwartz, Georg Wilhelm 31, 33
Schwartz, Johann Gottlieb 31
Schwartz, Margarethe (Maria) 30, 34, 156, 192
Schwartz, Maria Sophia 30, 33, 143
Sembuga Pandiden 319
Serfoji II (Serfogee, Serfojee, Sherfogee), Raja of Thanjavur 3, 5–7, 14–15, 19–20, 31, 93–98, 101, 106–107, 111–116, 135, 137, 140–141, 148–149, 151, 156, 168, 178–180, 183–184, 186, 190–191, 194, 225, 233, 253–269, 271–315, 323, 325, 355, 400, 406, 412, 417, 425, 448–449, 453–454, 460–461
Sey Asary (Jeyachari) 114, 288, 458–460
Shadi Khan 401
Shah Alam II, Mughal Emperor 54
Shankar Rao (Row) 296, 333–334
Shaw, Herman 218
Shiva Rao (Shiva Row, Shevarow) 94–95, 97–98, 102–104, 108–109, 111, 131, 134, 136, 253, 255, 289, 291, 296, 317, 322–324, 332–334, 418
Shivaji I, Chhatrapati of the Marathas 94
Shore, John 297, 299, 301, 305, 416, 434–437, 451
Simeon, Charles 410, 424
Siṉṉamuttu Tāvītu Suntarāṉantam 393
Siṉṉappaṉ 381
Sippa Salar 127
Sivarāya 225, 229
Smith, Charles 84
Smith, George 68
Smith, Joseph 65–66, 200
Smith, Nathaneal 23
Smith, William 441
Sonnenburg, Karl von 30
Sophie Magdalene of Brandenburg-Kulmbach, Queen consort of Denmark and Norway 35
Sorge, Christian Ehrhard 171
Sorge, Johann Friedrich 31, 57, 82, 84, 157, 175, 205, 221, 226, 366, 383, 447
Soubajee (Soobajee) 93
Soubhagyavati Avu Bāi Chatrapati Maharani Sāhibā 315
Soubhagyavati Muktambal Bāi Sāhibā 314
Spencer, George John Trever 84, 176
Spener, Philipp Jacob 163
Sperschneider, Johann Georg Philipp 188
Stables, John 127
Staunton, George Leonard 213–214
Stegmann, Ernest Philipp Heinrich 404–405
Steinkopf, Carl Friedrich Adolf 188, 191
Stevens, George 271
Stevens, William 79, 82–83, 91, 145, 362–363, 376
Stewart, Robert 439

Strange, James Charles Stuart 261
Strange, Thomas 261
Stratton, George 71, 331
Sträußler, Anna Louise 30
Strobel, Friedrich Albrecht 52
Strubell, Johann Tobias 184
Struensee, Adam 33
Struensee, Johann Friedrich 227
Stuart, James 89, 94–95, 97–102, 110–111, 119, 131
Stuart, John 117, 287, 329–330
Subba Rao 134
Subbarao Bhavana 266
Suburau Gopal Rao 223
Sulivan, John 25, 85, 178, 188, 212–213, 233, 303, 328, 341, 364–367, 401
Sullivan, Laurence 23
Sulochanā Bāi Sāhibā (Sulochana Bhaie Saheb) 254–258, 260–261, 267, 304
Sumbhajee Pandit 126

T

Taylor, James 56
Taylor, Richard 271
Thomasius, Christian 29, 169
Thomason, Thomas Trubody 430
Thompson, Thomas 247, 431
Thornton, Henry 413, 424, 441
Thornton, Robert 441
Thors, Pernille 49, 185, 381
Thurlow, Thomas 397
Tipu Sultan, Sultan of Mysore 24, 27, 86–87, 93, 145, 190, 199, 213–215, 217–219, 250, 275, 278, 327, 348, 412, 431–432, 449, 454
Tiruciluvai 249
Tirumala Rao 212
Tondaman Mudaly 57
Toone, Sweny 439
Topping, Michael 278–279
Torin, Benjamin 148, 298–302, 307–308
Totobey Mohilik 306
Trimbach Sumbhajee (Triumbuch Sambajee) 125, 331
Trimbuck Rao 66
Tukkoji, Raja of Thanjavur 106
Tulāji II / Sri Ram Pradap Tulāji (Thuljaji, Tuljajee), Raja of Thanjavur 5, 18–20, 24–27, 53, 62–77, 82–116, 118–119, 121, 124–126, 131, 133, 137, 148, 151, 165–166, 176–178, 197–199, 201–202, 207–208, 210, 219–222, 231–233, 235, 253–265, 268, 272, 285–288, 293, 296–300, 304, 306, 317–319, 322–323, 326–333, 364, 366, 369, 400, 415, 448, 454, 458–459, 461
Turner, John Matthias 188–189, 443
Turow, Friedrich Joachim 32
Twinging, Thomas 439

U

Udaiyāt Tēvar 65, 233
Uebele (Ubele), Johann (John) Christian Christoph 138, 160, 169–170, 182, 184, 263, 347, 419
Umdat ul-Umara, Nawab of the Carnatic (Arcot) 65–66, 172
Unmeer ul Hind 127
Uraiyur 172
Ursin, Christian Friedrich 168

V

Vēdanāyagam Sāstiriyār / Vētapōtakan̲ 151, 179–180, 194, 391–392, 395–396, 448–450
Vēlāyutam 355
Vencana 110–111
Vengadachala Pillay 296
Vēṅkan̲ Periya Udaiyā-t Tēvar, King of Sivaganga 233

Venkatachalam 261
Venkoji Bhonsle / Ekoji, Raja of Thanjavur 93–94
Vētamāṇikkam (Vēdamānickam) 180, 386
Victoria, Queen of the United Kingdom 178, 348
Vicuvāci (Wisuwasi) 388–391
Vija Asary 114, 458–460
Vincent, William 369–370, 417

W

Wallajah *see* Muhammad Ali Khan Wallajah
Walther, Christoph Theodosius 48
Ward, William 399, 438
Watson, Richard 397
Watt, Frances 409
Webb, William 236
Wellesley, Richard Colley 12, 232, 399, 438
Weston, Charles 174
Wheatley, Elizabeth 366
Wheatley, J. (father of William Wheatley) 401
Wheatley, William 59–60, 142, 176, 300, 362–363, 365–366, 374, 376, 378–379, 390, 401–402, 450, 468
Whitehill, John 74, 84, 202
Wiedebrock, Johann Christian 38
Wiger, Margaretha Wilhelmina 49, 185
Wilberforce, William 341–342, 410, 413–414, 416, 424–427, 438, 440–441
Wilmot-Horton, Robert John 152
Wilson, Daniel 165, 188–189, 451
Wilson, James 348
Winslow, Miron 152
Wolff, Christian 29, 169
Wood (Wife of John Wood) 172, 234–240, 362, 452–453
Wood, Basil 237
Wood, John 57, 59–60, 63, 145, 155, 171, 234–237, 362, 452–453
Wood, John, Jr. 171, 234–237
Workman-McNaughton, Francis 325
Worm, Andreas 48
Wynch, Alexander 67–68, 71

Y

Yowan 389

Z

Zeglin, Daniel 43, 45–46, 48, 51, 242–243
Ziegenbalg, Barholomäus Leberecht 46, 48
Ziegenbalg, Bartholomäus 9, 34–35, 46, 48, 162, 192, 248, 381, 428
Ziegenhagen, Friedrich Michael 36–38, 44, 62, 67, 165, 169, 366, 447
Zupher Jung 127

Index of Places

A
Adoni 209
Alleppey 442
Ambapoor 255
Amsterdam 37, 247
Āṉantamaṅkalam 223
Angamaly 218
Āralvāyamoḻi 390
Arcot 55, 128, 200, 208, 209, 210
Ariyalūr Udaiyārpālayam 125
Āyarpāṭi 124, 224, 363

B
Barrackpore 399
Basel 191–192, 443
Berlin 31, 143, 444
Bombay (today: Mumbai) 24, 26, 28, 178, 200, 209, 215, 355–356, 412, 416, 424, 430, 433, 435, 441, 444
Bremen 45
Būdalūr 342–343, 346, 417

C
Calahasty (today: Srikalahasti) 266
Calcutta (today: Kolkata) 13, 15, 19, 24, 27, 46, 55, 57, 102, 112, 144–145, 164, 173–175, 178, 182, 184–185, 187–188, 201, 209, 225, 235, 241, 248, 250–251, 270–271, 286, 288, 297, 299, 305, 307, 319, 324, 334, 356, 365, 396–400, 404–406, 409–410, 412–413, 416, 424–425, 430, 432–435, 438, 441–444, 449, 451
Calicut (today: Kozhikode) 204, 207, 227–228
Cambridge 393, 412, 424
Cauvery Puram 200
Chandra Nagar 55
Chengalpattu 21, 54, 56
Chennai passim
Chinsura (today: Hugli-Chunchura) 174
Christianagaram 386
Cittūr (Chittoor) 54, 213
Cochin (today: Kochi) 162, 245, 443
Coimbatore 145, 212, 215–217
Colombo 46–47, 51, 399
Copenhagen XVI, 4, 6, 12, 33–35, 48–49, 61, 168–169, 191, 225, 227, 234, 240, 243–244, 250, 353, 369, 385, 404, 447
Cuddalore 14, 21, 36, 38, 46, 48, 51, 57, 63, 79, 138, 173, 182, 185, 199–200, 247–248, 250, 262–263, 278, 292, 371, 396, 406, 418, 443

D
Dacca (today: Dhaka) 434
Deal 38
Delhi 18, 54, 60, 72, 312, 430
Deptford 427
Devakottai 200
Dharapuram 215
Dindigul 13, 215–216

E
Erukkañcēri 223

F
Fort St. David 199
Fort St. George 3, 5, 7, 19–20, 27, 55–56, 71, 87, 93, 100–101, 107, 131, 135, 145–146, 149–150, 202, 206, 208–209, 214, 232–233, 259, 269–270, 286, 294, 299, 301, 356, 371–372, 406, 418, 425, 445, 448, 453, 470
Fort Vallam (Wallam) 65–66, 374, 403
Fort William 24, 184, 290, 406, 410, 430
Friedrichsnagar (today: Serampore) *see* Serampore

G
Gingee 94, 269
Glaucha 3–4, 29–32, 36, 39, 45, 84, 140, 143, 161, 168–169, 171, 181–182, 188, 234, 240, 245, 250, 302, 310, 361, 380, 447, 450
Goinda Kuritschi (today: Kuṟicci) 375

H
Halle (Saale) XV–XVIII, 3–4, 6, 8, 12, 15, 29–34, 36–37, 39, 48, 63, 124, 130, 137, 157–158, 161, 165–166, 168–169, 171, 173–174, 176, 182, 184, 190, 192–194, 206–207, 227, 245, 310, 327, 339, 354, 361, 383, 407, 450, 452
Hamburg 33–34, 45, 52
Hannover 37
Hohenziatz 30
Hull (Kingston upon Hull) 247
Hyderabad 54, 200, 218, 356

J
Jaffna 46–48, 51, 162, 164–165, 399–400
Jakarta 246

K
Kanchipuram 19, 208–211, 364, 266, 272, 314, 347, 442, 446
Kandy 47, 312
Kanyakumari 179–180, 228, 386
Karaikal 18, 46, 55, 64, 89, 99, 211, 221, 269
Karur 200
Kōlār 213
Kolhapur 290
Könnern 37
Kottayam 442
Koyilkudi 343
Kumbakonam 2, 17, 19, 65, 107–108, 121–122, 129, 138, 193, 222–224, 258, 292, 296, 318, 326–327, 347, 369, 406
Kurumudi 206
Küstrin (today: Kostrzyn nad Odrą) 30–31

L
London XVI, XVIII, 1, 4–6, 11–12, 21–27, 34, 36–38, 63, 65, 69–74, 83–84, 86–87, 101, 108, 112, 122, 127–128, 130, 132, 136–138, 149, 151–152, 159–160, 165, 168–170, 172–174, 182, 187–188, 190, 197–198, 201–202, 207, 209–210, 224, 246, 255, 261, 263, 270–271, 297, 299, 309, 319, 327, 341, 342, 349, 353, 362, 365–369, 385, 397–398, 407, 409–410, 413–415, 417, 419, 421, 431–433, 438, 441, 447, 450, 453, 466–467, 472
Lübeck 45
Lucknow 202

M
Madras (today: Chennai) *see* Chennai
Madukkūr 380

Madurai 54, 57–59, 61, 64, 73, 80, 142, 177, 183, 189, 208, 387, 393, 452
Magdeburg 30, 33
Mahé 55, 202, 204
Malda 397–398
Maṇappāṟai 217
Mangalore 213–215, 217, 443
Mannār 47
Mannārgudi 120, 129, 256
Masulipatnam 79
Māyāpuram 256, 296
Mayilādi (Myladi) 180, 386
Melur 343
Minden 37
Mudalur 386, 394
Mysore (today: Mysuru) 1, 6, 10, 14, 68, 85, 88, 199–200, 205, 208, 212–214, 217–218, 220–221, 278, 346, 348, 355, 363, 365, 371, 431, 449

N

Nagapattinam (Negapatnam, Nagapatnam) 47–48, 68, 75, 98, 125, 211, 221, 246–247, 336, 358–360, 399, 406, 418
Nagari 17
Nagore 74, 89, 99, 131, 172, 211, 292, 359
Namakkal 235, 392
Nāmakkal 325, 392
Nellore 54, 269
New York 185, 189, 191, 312, 424

O

Orathanadu 315
Oṭṭārampaṭṭi 390f.
Oxford XVIII, 12, 176, 187, 341, 452

P

Pāḷaiyamkōṭṭai 2, 7, 13, 88, 138, 142–144, 154, 157, 183, 186–187, 241, 302, 343, 378–379, 384, 387–396, 443, 447–448
Palani 341
Pāmpaṉ 383
Papanasam 107, 135, 258
Philadelphia 189, 191
Plassey 1, 21, 45, 173, 199, 318
Point Pedro 48
Pondicherry 21, 44, 51, 55, 64, 82–83, 99, 199–200, 202, 208, 269, 278, 292, 362, 445
Poona (today: Pune) XVIII, 120, 196, 290, 312, 356
Poonamallee 56, 202
Poṟaiyār 41, 44, 59, 124, 211, 380, 452
Portsmouth 442
Pribrow (Priebrow), (today: Przyborów) 143
Pudukkottai 65, 311, 366
Pulicat (today: Pazhaverkau) 358–359
Pune *see* Poona

R

Ramanathapuram 2, 7, 15, 18, 54, 58, 65, 88, 125, 141–142, 144, 155, 157, 176, 178–179, 183, 208, 234, 241, 337, 341, 343, 358, 365–366, 368, 378–379, 383, 388–391, 393, 401, 443, 447–448, 450, 452
Rameswaram 3, 14, 19
Rangoon (today: Yangon) 433
Rottenburg 33
Rotterdam 37

S

Sadayangal 224
Sadras 51, 278
Salem 392
Samulcotta 350
Satara 68, 290

Sathyamangalam 217
Sattiyamaṅkalam 214
Serampore 46, 174, 225, 227–228, 232, 399, 407, 430, 438, 444
Seringapatam 4, 6, 186, 192, 203–204, 206–207, 209, 212–215, 217–219, 278, 431
Shiyāli 256
Sīrkāḻi 44–45, 228, 318
Sithāmangalam 256
Sivaganga 15, 65, 233–234, 365–366, 368–369, 378
Sonnenburg (today: Słońsk) 29–30, 32–34, 161, 193, 471
Sri Rangam 21, 62, 70, 125, 200, 208
Surat 356

T

Tanjore (today: Thanjavur) passim
Thirupuvanam 17
Tillaiyāṭi 224
Tiruccirāppaḷḷi 2, 4, 6, 13–14, 44–45, 51–54, 56–63, 65, 68, 70, 79–81, 83, 99, 125, 138, 144, 147, 151, 154–155, 157, 161, 171–173, 178, 180–181, 183–187, 189–191, 193–194, 203, 208, 215, 217, 234–235, 238, 240–242, 244, 269, 271, 328, 340, 345–346, 348, 357, 362–363, 373–376, 381–383, 389, 391–393, 396, 401, 403, 407, 443, 447, 450
Tirukkaṭaiyūr 211
Tirumullaivācal (Thirumullaivasal) 17, 211
Tirunellur 126
Tirunelveli (historically also: Tinnevelly) 9, 13, 54, 165, 176, 178–179, 386–387, 390–391, 393–395, 442, 451–452, 470
Tirupālāduthurai 61
Tirupati 11, 264, 266, 445
Tiruppattūr 376
Tiruvaiyāru 121, 295–296, 315
Tiruvārūr 45, 314, 319
Tiruvidaimaruthur (Thiruvidaimarudur) 264, 336
Tiruviṭaikkāṭu 211
Tlangadu 90
Tranquebar (today: Tharangambadi) XVI, 2, 4–7, 13–14, 17, 21, 27, 29–30, 32–36, 38–42, 44–46, 48–49, 51–52, 55–57, 60–63, 68, 79–80, 95, 101, 122, 124–126, 129–130, 139, 146, 161–162, 164, 166, 168–169, 173, 177, 180, 182–185, 187, 190–191, 193–194, 198, 200, 209–211, 223–234, 238, 240–248, 250, 283, 292, 308, 311, 313–314, 320–321, 325, 327, 336–337, 339, 349–350, 352–354, 361–363, 370, 380–386, 389–393, 395–396, 398–399, 404–405, 410–411, 417, 419, 423, 435, 447, 449, 452, 462
Tripasore 209
Triplicane 56
Trivady 303–304
Tuticorin (today: Thoothukudi) 88, 165, 242, 366, 391

U

Udangudi 386

V

Vadamadurai 215, 217
Vallam 70, 122, 157, 178, 242, 249, 375–377, 383
Vandavasi 21, 199, 348
Varanasi 314
Velankulam 19
Vellore 94, 210, 269, 351, 378, 397, 431–432, 440
Vepery 83, 154, 164–165, 176, 239, 247, 268, 271, 288, 405, 417

W
Warrington 270
Wernigerode 37, 173, 240

Y
Yāṉaikkōvil 211
Yānam 55